D0478141

INFORMATION TECHNOLOGY and SOCIETY

Other titles in Computer Information
Systems from Wadsworth:

Business Systems Analysis and Design,
William Davis

Database System: Design, Implementation, and Management,
Peter Rob and Carlos Coronel

MS/PC DOS: Concepts, Exercises, and Applications,
Mary Auvil, Joyce Arntson, and Barbara Stockler

Multimedia Presentation Technology,
Fred Hofstetter

Networks in Action: Business Choices
and Telecommunications Decisions,
Peter G. W. Keen and Michael Cummins

The Software Tool Kit Series, Tim Duffy

DOS 6.0
DOS 5.0
DOS 3.3
Windows 3.1
WordPerfect 5.1
WordPerfect 6.0 for DOS
WordPerfect for Windows
Lotus 1-2-3 (Release 2.2)
Lotus 1-2-3 (Release 2.3)
Lotus 1-2-3 (Release 2.4)
Lotus 1-2-3 (Release 3.4)
Quattro Pro 4.0
dBase III Plus
dBase IV
Paradox 3.5

The Windows Workshop, James E. Shuman

Windows 3.1
WordPerfect 6.0 for Windows
Lotus for Windows
Lotus 1-2-3 for Windows-R
Excel 4.0 for Windows
Quattro Pro for Windows
Paradox for Windows
Access 1.1 for Windows

Information Technology and Society

Kenneth C. Laudon
New York University

Carol Guercio Traver
Azimuth Corporation

Jane Price Laudon
Azimuth Corporation

Wadsworth Publishing Company
A Division of Wadsworth, Inc.
Belmont, California

Business Editor: **Kathy Shields**

Development Editor: **Alan Venable**

Editorial Assistant: **Tamara Huggins**

Production Editor: **Angela Mann**

Cover and Interior Designer: **Cloyce Wall**

Print Buyer: **Karen Hunt**

Art Editor: **Nancy Spellman**

Permissions Editor: **Marion Hansen**

Copy Editor: **Robert Fiske**

Photo Researcher: **Photosynthesis**

Technical Illustrator: **Illustrious, Inc**.

Cover Illustration: **Valerie Sinclair**

Signing Representative: **Connie Jirovsky**

Compositor: **TSI Graphics**

Printer: **Arcata, Hawkins**

International Thomson Publishing
The Trademark ITP is used under license

©1994 by Wadsworth, Inc. All rights reserved. No part of this book may be reproduced, stored in a retrieval system, or transcribed, in any form or by any means, without the prior written permission of the
publisher, Wadsworth Publishing Company, Belmont, California 94002.

Printed in the United States of America
  3 4 5 6 7 8 9 10—98 97 96 95

Library of Congress Cataloging in Publication Data

Laudon, Kenneth C.,
    Information technology and society/Kenneth C. Laudon, Carol Guercio Traver, Jane Price Laudon.
        p.   cm.
    Includes bibliographical references and index.
    ISBN 0-534-19512-1
    1. Information technology—Social aspects. 2. Computers and civilization. I. Traver, Carol Guercio.
    II. Laudon, Jane Price. III. Title.
    T58.5.L38 1994
    004—dc20   93-32754

CONTENTS

PART ONE
Information Technology and Society

2 Information Technology and Systems: Yesterday, Today, and Tomorrow   35

PART TWO

Information
Technologies

4   Storage Technologies   109

PART THREE

Creating Solutions with Information Technologies

PART FOUR
Applications Software

13   Management Support and Knowledge Work Systems   455

Artificial Intelligence and Knowledge-Based Systems   483

15 **Ethical and Social Issues in
the Information Age   513**

Take a close look at the cover of this book. You'll see a number of different elements—a telephone keypad, a newspaper, an artist's palette, an envelope, a gear from a machine, a dollar bill, a grand piano, part of an integrated circuit, cables, the sun—all wrapped together into a single sphere. What do all these different objects have in common? More important, what are they doing on the cover of a book about information technology?

We chose this cover because we felt that it graphically represented an important theme of our book. The objects shown symbolize things that make up our everyday world—business and the pursuit of the dollar, art and culture, science and the search for knowledge, communications. Today, all of these things are affected by information technology. Our ability to conduct business, to communicate with one another, to discover and create, to work—in short, our whole way of living and our society—is becoming increasingly intertwined with information technology. We cannot expect to live successfully in the 21st century, now just right around the corner, without a basic understanding of this technology.

Our Goals

Our book has three primary goals: to introduce students to the world of information technology in a way that will capture their interest, excite them and provoke them to think; to help prepare students to succeed in the new digital world of the 21st century; and to strengthen students' basic skills.

The book is particularly well suited for the liberal arts, business or other nontechnical undergraduate student seeking to learn about the world of information technology, as well as a first introduction to that world for the student who hopes to go on and major in information systems or computer science.

Broad Information Technology Perspective

Our first and most important aim is to illustrate the effect of information technology on the world around us—on society, culture, careers, and every-

day lives. We provide a broad introduction to the vast array of information technologies used today, as well as a survey of the global, ethical, political, cultural, social, and environmental issues raised by information technology. These issues are dealt with throughout the book, not just in a single chapter. Although an understanding of the technological underpinnings of information systems is important, we believe that it is not enough. Technology cannot and should not be separated from a consideration of the issues raised by the uses of that technology.

To keep students interested and encourage them to think while reading, we intersperse stories throughout the text that illustrate the uses of information technology in the real world (with numerous examples drawn from the domestic and international business arena as well as many other organizations like colleges, governments, hospitals, and other private groups) and raise thought-provoking issues for students to consider as they are reading. Students learn much faster when they play an activist role and this book encourages them to do so by engaging them, asking them to think, react, and come up with new ideas and solutions.

Preparing for the Year 2000

Our second goal is to build student skills and understanding so they can succeed in the new digital world. Today, business, law, engineering, science, art, journalism, academics, as well as a whole host of other professions and occupations all require a basic understanding of, as well as the ability to work with, information technology. By the year 2000 information technology skills will be even more in demand. Regardless of a student's major in college, or intended occupation in the future, information technology will play an important role. Understanding how information technologies work and how to use them will be vital for success. The book covers all the necessary material for a solid technical foundation, yet does not overwhelm students with too much, or unnecessary, detail. After completing the book, students will be familiar with a wide variety of information technologies, how they work and how they are used. In addition, throughout, the book covers current state-of-the-art technology, as well as technology that is just around the corner and will be affecting lives by the year 2000.

Basic Personal Skills

Our third goal is to bolster basic skills in reading, writing, information gathering, and presentation. Students need more than just an understanding of information technology, more than just computer literacy, to succeed in the 1990s. We have aimed to create not just a "computer book," but a book that will reinforce what students are learning in their other classes as well. We think basic skills are so essential that we have included a number of features and exercises that will help students strengthen those skills.

In addition to basic skills, students also need to learn how to think critically and creatively, and work with others. Increasingly, businesses are emphasizing problem-solving, critical-thinking skills, and teamwork. To be competitive, students will need to know how to analyze situations, define problems and objectives, and come up with solutions. We place a great deal of emphasis on critical thinking—we ask students not only to analyze the causes of a situation, find connections, and consider problems from multiple perspectives but also challenge them to come up with new solutions. Throughout we encourage them to brainstorm and work in small groups in addition to working on their own.

Unique Features

This book has a number of unique features that will help students learn more effectively.

Opening Vignette and Diagram

Each chapter begins with an opening vignette about a real-world organization or individual that has solved a problem using the information technology that is the subject of the chapter, or that previews some of the issues that will be discussed in the chapter. The stories show how information technology can be used, for example, to control air pollution, create new virtual realities, or resurrect a failing business. The vignettes are designed to spark the student's interest about what follows. Those vignettes that focus on the use of information technology to solve problems are accompa-

nied by a diagram that breaks the process down for the student. The diagram helps the student identify the problem that needs to be solved, the technologies chosen to solve the problem, how those technologies work together to create an information system, and how the information system created in fact solves the particular problem. This diagram provides students with a conceptual framework that they can use to analyze other problems that might be solved using information technology.

Integrative Framework

The chapters in this book are integrated around four major themes: knowledge, careers, organizations, and society. In each chapter, boxed stories related to the material being discussed in the chapter highlight how specific kinds of information technologies are adding to our stock of knowledge, and helping us to discover new things that may help make our life better in the future; how jobs and careers are changing as a result of information technology; how information technology is changing organizations and the way work is organized, products and services are produced and who produces them; and how our entire society is changing as a result of information technology. This framework helps students tie materials together and look for recurring issues when confronted with new material. In each instance, the boxed material relates to a real-world organization, individual, or event.

Dilemmas and Controversies Feature

The pervasiveness of information technology in our society raises important issues about the proper use of that technology. Rapid technological change has created many gray areas where laws and standards of ethical conduct are not yet fully developed. A boxed "Dilemmas and Controversies" feature included in many of the chapters explores a specific ethical dilemma or controversy related to the material in the chapter and challenges the students to think about the choices. In addition, ethical issues are explored in depth in the concluding chapter.

Critical Thinking Questions

We have already noted the importance that we place on critical thinking. In addition to challenging students to think critically and creatively while reading the text of each chapter, we have also included "Critical Thinking Questions" at the end of each Knowledge, Careers, Organizations, and Society box, and in each Dilemmas and Controversies feature. The types of questions posed vary: some ask students to relate material from the chapter to the story in the box, others ask students to reflect on issues raised by the story, while still others require students to apply what they have learned to a new and different situation. In each instance, though, the questions require the students to think about and respond to what they have read. In addition, they can be used as a starting point for class discussion.

Problem-Solving and Skill-Building Exercises

At the end of each chapter, there are three exercises designed to give students an opportunity to hone their own problem-solving capabilities and to develop their basic skills in research, writing, and oral presentation as well as other communication skills. Many of the problems require working with other classmates as a team, in small groups; others can be the subject of class discussion.

Skill Development Boxes

At the end of many of the chapters there are Skill Development boxes contributed by well-known and successful individuals who most students will recognize—people like Bill Cosby, George Plimpton, Malcolm Forbes, Tony Randall, Walter Cronkite, Jane Bryant Quinn. These materials take a look at essential skills like reading, writing, making a presentation, writing a business letter or resume, improving your vocabulary, and the like, give students some tips for improving these skills, and explain how the information technologies discussed in the chapter can also help.

Personal Technology Boxes

In addition to learning about how information technology affects the world around them, students also need to know how to deal with information technology on a personal level: namely, how to go about putting together their own information system. We address this need with "Personal Technology" boxes at the end of selected chapters. These features answer some basic questions and give students some useful guidelines that they can follow when purchasing computer hardware and software.

Overview of the Book

The book is divided into five parts. Part One provides an introduction to the world of information technologies and society. In Chapter 1, we sketch the primary types of information technology in use today, use a real-world example to show how information technologies are combined to create an information system, and illustrate the major impact areas—knowledge, careers, organizations, and society. Chapter 2 contains a brief history of information technology and systems (from the first writing systems to today's supercomputers), looks at how information systems are being used today and then describes how some emerging technologies (wireless computing, multimedia systems, and inexpensive supercomputers) may change the way we live and work in the near future.

Part Two focuses on understanding the building blocks that make up information systems: CPUs, storage technologies, input and output technologies, communication technologies, and operating systems and systems software. Chapter 3 explains how a computer processes information and explores the different components that make up a system unit. Chapter 4 details how digital information is stored. Chapter 5 explores the different ways information can be entered into an information system and displayed. Chapter 6 focuses on the world of telecommunications. Chapter 7 examines the important role that operating systems and systems software play. We believe students need a strong foundation in how the technology works to fully understand and be able to deal with the societal issues raised by the technology. Although the primary focus of Part Two is technology itself and how it works, these chapters also address the societal issues raised by the different forms of technology being discussed in the chapter.

In Part Three, we show the student how to use the knowledge about information technology that he or she has gained in the previous sections to analyze and design solutions. Chapter 8 walks the student through the design of a real-world information system developed by The Progressive Corporation, a large insurance company headquartered in Mayfield Heights, Ohio. Chapter 9 gives the student a taste of the programming development process needed to implement the Progressive information system and a tour of the different programming languages available for use in the programming process. The purpose of these chapters is not to make students systems analysts or programmers, but to show them how professional problem solvers and critical thinkers use information technology to invent new products and services, and sometimes re-engineer entire organizations.

Part Four surveys contemporary applications software available for personal computers. Chapter 10 reviews the most common packages: word processing, spreadsheet, and database management software. Chapter 11 broadens the picture considerably and showcases some of the newest leading edge software applications, as well as most, if not all, of the standard applications that students are likely to encounter in school, on the job or at home.

Part Five provides an overview of how information systems and technologies can be used (as well as abused) in business and society. Chapter 12 describes the basic applications of technology used by business organizations (and describes basic business concepts as well). Chapter 13 extends on the basics and discusses some of the more sophisticated applications for managers and other information workers like engineers, lawyers, and doctors. Chapter 14 reviews the latest advances in artificial intelligence and knowledge-based systems. Finally, Chapter 15 takes an in-depth look at the ethical and social issues raised by information technology, enlarging upon previous discussions of those issues.

Throughout, the book focuses not only on the technology being examined, but on the far-reaching impacts of the technology on our society and everyday lives.

Chapter Elements

Each chapter contains the following elements:

▶ A detailed outline at the beginning of each chapter provides an overview of the chapter to come, followed by a list of chapter objectives

▶ An opening vignette, accompanied in most instances by a diagram that provides a conceptual framework for students

▶ Knowledge, Careers, Organizations, Society, stories within each chapter

▶ Dilemmas and Controversies boxes in six chapters

▶ A summary that identifies the key ideas of each chapter

▶ Key terms boldfaced within the text, and listed at the end of the chapter for students to review

▶ For those chapters for which there is material in the Interactive Supplement software, an icon for that material

▶ A set of review questions that tests students' mastery of the concepts discussed in the chapter

▶ Problem-Solving and Skill-Building exercises

▶ A Skill Development box or Personal Technology box at the end of the chapter

▶ Notes to material referenced in the chapter

Instructional Support Materials

Wadsworth Publishing offers a number of additional resources in conjunction with the text.

Interactive Edition

The Interactive Edition (available for both Windows and Macintosh) is a special edition of this text that gives students hands-on experience with interactive technology, and extends the learning experience of the textbook with new material.

The Interactive Edition is composed of three diskettes that contain ten interactive chapters, which parallel the sequence of the book chapters. The Interactive Edition chapters use animations, color photos, sound, and text to extend and reinforce concepts in the textbook. Using the latest in object-oriented technology, the Interactive Edition includes built-in, self-paced quizzes that can be printed out and handed in to the instructor.

Annotated Instructor's Edition

The *Annotated Instructor's Edition* contains lecture hints, class discussion questions, small group activities, and student project ideas written by Sandra Stalker of North Shore Community College, Beverly, Massachusetts.

Instructor's Manual, Test Item Booklet, Computerized Test Bank, and Transparencies

Written by Brenda Killingsworth of East Carolina University, the Instructor's Manual contains learning objective previews, detailed lecture outlines, techniques to introduce new topics and to apply critical thinking and problem-solving skills, information science brainteasers, and information technology notes. The test item booklet contains over 2,000 true/false, multiple choice, short answer, and critical thinking questions. Every item in the test item booklet has been computerized and will be available for both IBM-PC or compatibles and Macintosh. Also included in the package are approximately 50 transparency acetates and masters, some of which will be available in digitized form.

Software Support Materials

Wadsworth will provide adopters of this text with a series of short software manuals that provide a brief tutorial to specific software packages, operating systems, and programming languages, all free of charge. The manuals cover the basics of using the particular kind of software. There are manuals available for the following kinds of software:

▶ DOS Versions 5.0 and 6.0
▶ Windows Version 3.1
▶ WordPerfect Versions 5.1 and 6.0
▶ Microsoft Word Versions 5.5 and 6.0
▶ Lotus 1-2-3 Versions 2.3 and 2.4
▶ dBASE Versions III Plus and IV
▶ Paradox Versions 3.5 and 4.0
▶ Microsoft Access
▶ Microsoft Works Version 3.0
▶ QuickBasic
▶ Pascal

Acknowledgments

There were many hands, hearts, and minds involved in the creation of this book. Many academic colleagues from around the country reviewed the manuscript and participated in focus group sessions to help define the book. We sincerely thank the following persons for their help:

Verl A. Anderson, Eastern Oregon State College; James L. Bode, Manatee Community College; David V. Bourque, Middlesex County College; C. T. Cadenhead, Richland College; Jerry M. Chin, Southwest Missouri State University; Mark Ciampa, Volunteer State Community College; Sasa Dekleva, DePaul University; Keith Hallmark, Calhoun Community College; Albert L. Harris, Appalachian State University; B. Loerine Helft, Baruch College of the City University of New York; Lister W. Horn, Pensacola Junior College; James J. Johnson, University of Tennessee at Martin; Carroll L. Kreider, Elizabethtown College; Victor Lafrenz, Mohawk Valley Community College; Rajiv Malkan, Lamar University at Orange; Merry McDonald, Northwest Missouri State University; John Melrose, University of Wisconsin - Eau Claire; Anthony J. Nowakowski, Buffalo State College;

Pauline Pike, County College of Morris; Leonard Presby, William Paterson State College of New Jersey; Louis Pryor, Garland Community College; Mary E. Rasley, Lehigh County Community College; Sharon Underwood, Livingston University; and Diane Walz, University of Texas at San Antonio.

We would also like to give a special thanks to the reviewers who made special contributions to the development of the text at the very early stages in focus groups, review sessions, and/or through continuing comments on the emerging manuscript: Lynda Armbruster, Rancho Santiago College; Curtis R. Bring, Moorhead State University; Bruce W. Brown, Salt Lake Community College; William R. Cornette, Southwest Missouri State University; Robert A. Fleck, Columbus College; Brenda L. Killingsworth, East Carolina University; George Novotny, Ferris State University; John W. Petro, Western Michigan University; Carol E. Pollard, The University of Calgary; Harold Smith, Brigham Young University; Sandra M. Stalker, North Shore Community College; and Suzanne Tomlinson, Iowa State University.

In addition, we would like to thank all those at Wadsworth who have worked so hard to make sure that this book is the best that it can be. We owe a debt of special thanks to them for their great effort and the high-quality result. Alan Venable, our development editor, kept us on our intellectual toes and helped us make the text more interactive, activist, and inviting. Kathy Shields, our acquisitions editor, helped make sure we achieved the goals of the project. Cloyce Wall, the book's designer, developed an exquisite design and a perfect cover. And Angela Mann, our production editor, kept all the details together under an extremely tight production schedule. Thanks also to Nancy Spellman, our art editor, and Marion Hansen, our permissions editor, for their hard work.

Closer to home, we would like to thank Russell Polo for his review and comments on various chapters.

Finally, last but not least, very special thanks to Frank Ruggirello, without whom this book would not have been.

Kenneth C. Laudon
Carol Guercio Traver
Jane Price Laudon

From image scanners to fax machines, from virtual reality to high definition television, everywhere you look information technologies have created exciting and far reaching changes in our society and culture. Becoming computer literate is not enough to live and work in the 1990s and beyond. You'll also need to know how information technologies are changing the world around you and how they're being used to get things done. *Information Technology and Society* will help you do this. Our focus is not only on the computer but on the many other emerging information technologies and how they impact four major areas: the acquisition and communication of new knowledge, high-growth careers, organizational behavior, and society.

Research on learning shows that the larger part *you* play in your own education, the more you'll learn and the faster you'll learn it. So our aim is to get you actively involved in learning.

To do this, we've included numerous hands-on activities and skill development exercises to challenge you to solve the types of problems you'll be faced with in your future careers. In addition, we've worked hard to come up with thought-provoking questions to encourage you to think critically about ethical dilemmas, social issues, and career opportunities.

And we've included lots of examples—more than 300 of them—drawn from business, education, government, and health care to give you a current, real world view of the many issues, controversies, and problems created by information technology as well as the successes.

Information technologies will give you powerful new ways to visualize, understand, control, and create new opportunities. The following pages show you how our book will help you learn about and use these new technologies now and in the future.

K N O W L E D G E
Using Information Technology to See the Unseen

Imagine if you could peer back into the past. Think about all the things you could see that no longer exist, that have become hidden, or that have changed with the passage of time. For a historian or archaeologist, this would be a dream come true. Today, with the help of information technology, these dreams are no longer so impossible.

The Great Sphinx in Egypt is the last of the Seven Wonders of the Ancient World. Built over 4,000 years ago, in 2500 B.C., the Sphinx looked very different before sand, water, wind, air pollution, and other hazards combined to erode away many of its distinctive features. Mark Lehner, a specialist in Egyptian archaeology at the University of Chicago, spent four years climbing around the Sphinx with a measuring tape and special camera. From this data, [he created] contour maps and other drawing[s of how the] Sphinx looks today. Though usef[ul, these maps] didn't have the visual impact tha[t he wanted.] They also couldn't solve the ridd[le of its ap]pearance.

How did they do it? Thomas Jaggers, director of computer-aided design at Jerde Partnership, first used a software package called Autocad, running on an IBM-compatible personal computer. He traced over Lehner's drawings with a stylus attached to an electronic drawing board called a digitizer, which converted the drawings into digital form. The digitizer merged the various drawings, each of which had been done from a different perspective, into one multidimensional model. Next, Jaggers and his team used a different software product called Quicksurf (originally designed to map the ocean floor) to create a realistic-looking surface for the model.

Knowledge Boxes
These boxes help you understand how information technology is extending our vision, creativity, and knowledge. This understanding will help you anticipate change and make better decisions about your life.

O R G A N I Z A T I O N S
Where's My Seat—Airline Reservations at Aeroflot

Air travel today has become so commonplace that it's easy to take some things for granted, like the ability to pick up the telephone, reserve a plane ticket, and then actually have a seat on a plane waiting for you when you get to the airport.

How would you like it if, instead, once you had bought your ticket, you had to stand in a line at the airport for the next available seat on the next available airplane, with no assurance that either might become available anytime soon or even that day. That's what passengers who have to fly on Aeroflot, Russia's national airline, face. The reason: right now, unlike airlines in America, Aeroflot has no way to track the number of airline seats that it has sold. Aeroflot tickets merely entitle a passenger to service on a first-come, first-served basis. In 1990, Aeroflot reportedly could not seat 30 percent of its ticketed passengers. Some ended up spending days at the airport before ever getting on an airplane.

Do you react to this situation by saying to yourself, "I'm sure glad I don't have to put up with that"? If you do, your ex-

pectations about the services a business organization like an airline should provide to you as a consumer have been influenced by computers. In this case, it would be almost impossible for airlines to serve you in the manner to which you've become accustomed without a computerized system that

▶ *Information technologies have changed, and continue to change, the way business gets done. The explosion of knowledge and information that we have de-*

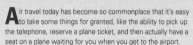

Class Discuss
How many students have ATM cards, use faxes, or use e-mail?

Organizations Boxes
How are information technologies changing the kinds of goods and services produced, the expectations we have about organizational behavior, the kinds of work done within organizations, and even the shape of the organizations themselves? Organizations boxes shed light on these thought-provoking issues.

C A R E E R S
Unanticipated Skills

What kind of career do you hope to begin when you finally finish school? Maybe you want to go into the arts, or some kind of service industry like banking or insurance, or start your own business. If your goal involves something other than becoming a computer professional, you may be wondering whether you really need to learn about the technologies described in this book. Well, read on. The following are just a few examples of how information technologies are changing the way organizations and businesses operate, as well as the jobs of people who work in them.

Take, for example, Kim Perlman, the head trainer at Touchstone Farm, a horse farm in Garrison, New York (see photo). Kim never anticipated that he'd have much use for a computer in his line of work—training horses and riders, running a horse farm, organizing horse shows. But after he purchased an Apple laptop computer to use at home, he began to think of all sorts of interesting possibilities. For instance, whenever the farm holds a horse show, Kim has to design the fences that the horses will jump. He also has to decide how to arrange those fences into different jumping courses. He used to do both of these jobs by hand, drawing them on paper. If he

tinker, trying out different designs and moving the fences around until he finds the perfect combinations.

Or how about tailors at Albert Andrews Ltd., a Boston suit maker. They now take suit measurements with a computerized tape measure hooked to a laptop computer. The process takes about 20 minutes. Because the system is portable, a customer can be measured not only at the store but also in an office or at home. The measurements are then sent via modem to the company's manufacturing plant in Cleveland, Ohio, where they are used to create a custom pattern, from which the suit can be cut and assembled. In four weeks, a custom suit is delivered that is accurate to within 1/1,000th of an inch! As a result, unlike suits measured in the traditional way, these suits require few alterations. Time and money are saved for the customer as well as the manufacturer. Because of the success of this system, Albert Andrews Ltd. is planning a nationwide expansion.

Finally consider Calvin Hunt, Daniel Bonitzky, and other members of the production crew for the Alvin Ailey American Dance Theatre. In the past, theater productions were accomplished manually using pads of paper and pencils. But during a

Careers Boxes
Virtually all of the fast-growth job categories in the United States projected for the year 2005 will require some minimal computer and computer-related skills. These boxes highlight some of the new jobs and careers created by the emergence of information technologies and point out the various skills you'll need to become more marketable in these fast-growth areas.

SOCIETY
Digital Giants

The world is totally going digital." So says Bill Gates, the chairman of Microsoft Corporation, one of the world's largest producers of software. Many companies are jumping on the bandwagon, hoping to use digital technologies to get into new markets. Today, the boundaries between computer companies, entertainment companies, consumer electronics companies, cable companies, telephone companies, and other types of utility companies are becoming increasingly blurred. Reflect on the following:

Time Warner is one of the largest entertainment companies in the country. Among other activities, it operates the nation's second largest cable television system, as well as Warner Brothers, a producer of movies and TV shows, and the cable television channel Home Box Office. US West is one of seven Bell Telephone regional operating companies, serving over 25 million customers in 14 Western states. US West recently announced that it plans to invest $2.5 billion in Time Warner to help it build the country's most advanced cable network, one with hundreds of channels and a vast library of entertainment and information services that subscribers can call up on demand.

Microsoft, which dominates the personal computer software market, Intel, the world's largest manufacturer of microprocessors, and General Instrument, a cable technology, have formed a generation of interactive cable T technology.

Sony Corp., one of Japan's large men and camcorders, owns Col electronic books. It is now work Bell regional operating company less phone system.

GTE Corp., the local phone com

Information technolog

has started providing cable TV, home shopping and bill paying, movies on demand, and videophone as well as regular telephone service to certain of its customers in a test run.

The Glasgow Electric Board, Glasgow, Kentucky's electric utility company, recently put in a digital electronic monitoring system to help customers save electricity. The system has an added advantage: it can also deliver audio and video images. So now the electric company is in the cable-TV business, and it would like to get into the telephone business as well!

Sources: Based on FabriKart, Geraldine, "US West Will Buy into Time Warner," New York Times, May 17, 1993; Markoff, John, "Battles Loom for Control of TV's Portal to Cable," New York Times, April 3, 1993; Zachary, G. Pascal, "Blurred Borders: Industries Find Growth of Digital Electronics Brings in Competitors" and "Coming Digital Age May Transform Your Living Room in Many Ways," Wall Street Journal, February 18, 1992.

Critical Thinking Questions

1 What kinds of social, economic, or political impacts do you think this increasing convergence of previously unrelated, distinct industries might have? It's probably easy for you to think of advantages that might result, such as the creation of new products and services (or the delivery of old products and services in a new, less expensive manner). Discuss some other advantages that you could foresee.

2 The disadvantages might not be so evident to you at first

DILEMMAS AND CONTROVERSIES
Rethinking the Photograph

Have you ever heard the phrase "a picture doesn't lie"? Photographs have long had a special authority as a record of reality. A photograph is usually perceived as an objective record of the physical world. The medium's claim to truthfulness is founded on the negative, the physical manifestation of the image. Negatives cannot be altered easily without the changes being obvious.

Consider then the effect of technologies like Photo CD and digital cameras (cameras that record scenes directly onto disk), which allow images to be converted into a series of digits that can then be translated into tonal values and printed. Any of the digits can be changed at will to alter the image. Photographs can be blended with others, colors changed, elements within the picture rearranged, all with remarkable ease. While it was always possible to alter traditional photographs through cropping, retouching, and other methods, what's different now is that these and even more significant changes can be made instantly and with little effort.

Many are excited by the prospects this new technology offers. Weston J. Naef, curator of photography at the J. Paul Getty Museum in Malibu, California, compares it to the effect the Leica (a compact camera that made it possible for photographers to capture street scenes) had in 1927: "It changed the way we see the world." Some foresee a blurring of the boundaries between photography and art. David Hockney, a well-known painter and photographer, feels that in the future photography will take on some of the characteristics of draw-

ing, with the photographer working on a photograph the way a draftsman might work on a drawing.

But others are concerned these systems have the disturbing potential to erode photography's function in society by undercutting the photograph's status as a picture of reality. They feel that digital technology is transforming photography so fundamentally that its basic function and character are changing beyond recognition. As Peter Campus, an artist whose computer-manipulated photographs have appeared in a number of exhibitions says, "I tell my students this is not photography. It's something else, although at this point it's still not clear just what."

Source: Based on Hagen, Charles, "Reinventing the Photograph," New York Times, January 31, 1993.

Critical Thinking Questions

1 In the future, you may no longer be able assume a photograph is an accurate depiction of a reality that in fact existed at some given point in time. What impact do you think this will have on the use of photographs to convey information?

2 Consider the ethical dimensions of digitally altered photographs. Under what circumstances should photographers be required to disclose changes made to a photograph?

3 In the future, what factors might you need to consider in assessing the meaning and believability of a photograph?

WORM (Write-Once, Read-Many)

WORM devices allow users to record data on optical disks themselves, but once the data has been written onto the disk, it cannot be erased. As you saw

Society Boxes

Satellite broadcasts, e-mail, and facsimile transmissions are just a few of the ways that information technology is changing the way we communicate within the United States and around the globe. These boxed vignettes give examples of how the new technologies are transforming some of our basic institutions.

Dilemmas and Controversies Boxes

These boxes encourage you to think critically about ethical issues (for example, software piracy and wire tapping) raised by information technologies. These issues are also highlighted in a separate chapter and in discussions throughout the text.

Skill Development Boxes

Focusing on a particular skill—such as reading, writing a business letter, or giving a presentation—these boxes provide tips on how information technology can help you develop and refine these skills even further.

SKILL DEVELOPMENT

How Bill Cosby Learned to Cope with Too Much Information

How would you like to read this textbook in half the time and learn twice as much as you normally do? It's possible with speed-reading. In the future, as knowledge and information become more important in our society, and as information technologies bring you more and more of it, you'll soon find yourself overwhelmed. Unless, that is, you do something about it. One thing you can do is learn how to read faster (and better). Bill Cosby tells you how.

How to Read Faster

By Bill Cosby

When I was a kid in Philadelphia, comic book ever published. (The than there are now.)

1. Preview—If It's Long and Hard

Previewing is especially useful for getting a general idea of heavy reading like long magazine or newspaper articles, business reports, and nonfiction books.

PERSONAL TECHNOLOGY

Storage Options for your Microcomputer

Once you've decided on the basic type of microcomputer that you'd like to buy (see the Personal Technology box at the end of Chapter 3), there are still some other important decisions that you need to make. Chief among these is the question of secondary storage. In this section, we'll discuss your options and make some recommendations about what kind and how much storage you need.

First, you definitely need a floppy disk drive. If you can only afford a system unit that has one drive, choose the 3 1/2 size. However, if you can afford it, it is very convenient to have a system unit that has a floppy drive for both floppy disk sizes.

The next question is whether you need a hard disk drive. Here too the answer is almost certainly yes. Luckily, the prices of hard disk drives have been dropping while their storage capacities have been increasing. Only a few years ago, a 20MB hard drive was standard, but now you can purchase an 80MB to 120MB drive for approximately the same price. In considering which hard drive to choose, remember that you can never have enough secondary storage, and go for the largest hard

standards which provides enhanced audio performance.

Another type of CD-ROM drive is Phillips/Sony's CD-I. Unlike a standard CD-ROM drive, which operates as a peripheral device, CD-I operates as a complete system, with an integrated computer, and comes equipped to play on a TV. CD-I is superior to regular CD-ROM drives in its ability to integrate audio, video, text, and graphics, but is being marketed primarily as a home entertainment system. Also, a CD-I drive doesn't read regular CD-ROM disks—only those set up to work with CD-I. Right now, a standard CD-ROM drive is probably still your best all-purpose choice.

Once you've gotten past these basic decisions concerning floppy disk, hard disk, and CD-ROM drives, there are several ancillary issues to consider. Your computer system is very vul-

Personal Technology Boxes

These practical vignettes describe some aspect of personal computing and provide useful guidelines for evaluating and purchasing your own computer equipment and software.

Problem-Solving and Skill-Building Exercises

1 Identify an information system that you come into contact with in your day-to-day life. Prepare a poster using the framework laid out in Figure 1.3 on page 13 to describe the problem the information system was designed to address; the sensing, communication, analyzing, and display technologies used in the system; and how the system enables people who use it to organize or control some aspect of life.

2 Talk with someone you know about his or her career or job. Find out what role information technology plays in the person's job and whether technology has changed, or is changing, the skills needed to do the job or the kind of activities that make up the job. Prepare a 5-minute oral presentation about your findings.

3 Alone, or with a group of two or three others, think about some of the ways that computers have been portrayed in popular media like movies and television. What kinds of images come to mind? Are they positive or negative? Put together a short (1–2 pages) report on your thoughts and discussions.

Skill-Building Exercises

In addition to understanding how information technologies can be used, good communication is the key to success in your future careers. These end-of-chapter activities give you the chance to develop writing, speaking, and research skills individually and in groups.

Interactive Text Version

If your instructor selected the interactive version of this text, you'll find a set of disks in the back of your book. You'll be able to experience the power of information technologies first hand through exercises and simulations on these disks. (For example, one activity asks you to manipulate on-screen objects to build a local area network.) The disks also include self-paced quizzes you can take on the computer to test your understanding. How will you know when to use them?

Just look for the icons at the end of Chapters 2, 3, 4, 5, 6, 8, 9, 12, 13, and 14.

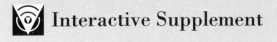

Interactive Supplement

Kenneth C. Laudon is Professor of Information Systems at New York University's Stern School of Business. He holds a B.A. in economics and philosophy from Stanford University and a Ph.D. from Columbia University. He has authored nine books dealing with information systems, organizations, and society and numerous articles about the organizational, social, and management impacts of information systems. He is currently the Director of Stern School's Virtual Multimedia Project.

Carol Guercio Traver is general counsel to Azimuth Corporation, a developer of software-based learning materials and commercial software packages. She received a B.A. from Vassar College and a J.D. from Yale Law School. In addition to her work with Azimuth, she is currently working on a comprehensive review of the legal literature relating to information technology and privacy for the Department of Energy's Human Genome Project. Her special interests include the impact of information technology on ethics, privacy, and the law.

Jane Price Laudon is a management consultant in the information systems area and the author of six books. Her special interests include systems analysis and design, data management, software evaluation, information systems auditing, and teaching business professionals how to design and use information systems. Jane received her B.A. from Barnard College, her M.A. from Harvard University, and her Ph.D. from Columbia University. She has taught at Columbia University and the New York University's Stern School of Business. She maintains a lifelong interest in Oriental languages and civilizations.

ONE

Information Technology and Society

Chapter 1
Information Technology, Society, and You

Chapter 2
Information Technology and Systems: Yesterday, Today, and Tomorrow

Gemstone Mine
Melvin Prueitt, Los Alamos National Laboratories

Chapter 1 contains:

Cleaning the Air with Information Technology

After completing this chapter, you will:

▶ Know the major kinds of information technology being used today.

▶ Understand how information technology is used to create an information system and how an information system works.

▶ Be more aware of the impact that information technology has, and can
   have, on your life.

Information Technology, Society, and You

Cleaning the Air with Information Technology

ave you ever watched an unfamiliar television program because you heard it had received high ratings? Seen the cashier at your local mall wave a wand over some black lines on a product you've purchased? If you have, you've come into contact with the same kind of information technologies that the South Coast Air Quality Management District will be using to help clean up air pollution in Southern California.

Southern California is well known for its smog. In the past, regulators there tried to improve air quality by telling companies exactly what equipment they had to use in order to reduce pollution. Regulators also required companies to keep detailed paperwork to show they were operating as required. Although this approach works, it can result in high costs to businesses and reduce innovation. Recently, Southern California air-quality authorities, armed with new information on smog formation generated by computer simulations at Carnegie-Mellon University, decided to try something different (see photo).

The South Coast Air Quality Management District's new system will allow companies to operate in whatever manner and with whatever equipment they choose, so long as they meet required reductions in emissions. However, as William J. Fray, assistant deputy executive officer for the district, explains, in order to make sure companies are complying with the plan, regulators will now need to know exactly how much pollution each company creates.

The diagram on the next page illustrates the regulators' new approach. Sensing devices in smokestacks are the key. The sensors will continuously measure emissions, much like the way the Nielsen rating company measures television programs watched by certain households. The sensors are hooked to a personal computer at the site of the smokestack. This computer will send the data collected by the sensors directly to the district's central computer for analysis.

Some forms of pollution do not enter the air from one particular point like a smokestack. Gases given off by paints, other coatings, or solvents will be measured by using bar code scanners, like the type used at your local mall, to track the number of paint cans a company uses as each can is opened. The information collected by the scanners will be transferred to an on-site computer and then sent over phone lines to the district's central computers, where the raw data on the number of cans used can be processed into an estimate of pollution.

Sources: Based on Stevenson, Richard W., "Monitoring Pollution at Its Source," *New York Times,* April 8, 1992; Markoff, John, "A Fresh Eye on the Environment: The Supercomputer Assesses Change," *New York Times,* January 31, 1991

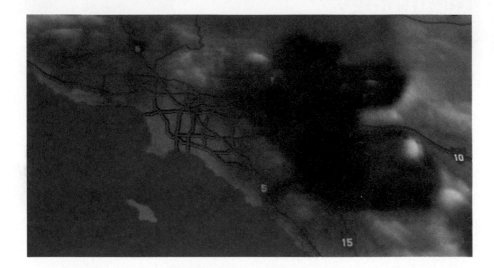

A computer-generated simulation of smog over southern California.

Source: National Center for Atmospheric Research.

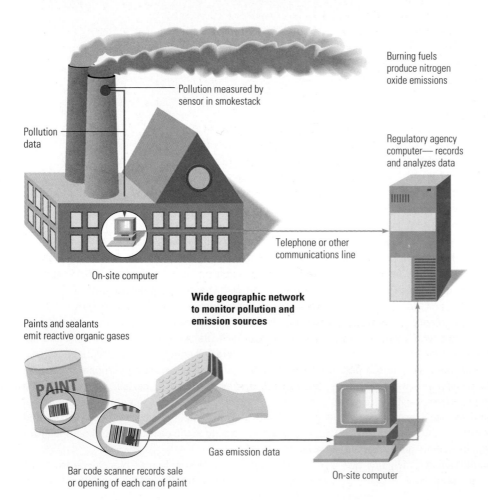

Burning fuels produce nitrogen oxide emissions

Pollution measured by sensor in smokestack

Pollution data

Regulatory agency computer— records and analyzes data

Telephone or other communications line

On-site computer

Wide geographic network to monitor pollution and emission sources

Paints and sealants emit reactive organic gases

PAINT

Gas emission data

Bar code scanner records sale or opening of each can of paint

On-site computer

Regulators in Southern California plan to use a computer network to monitor major sources of pollution to measure emissions. The data will be transmitted to a central computer for record keeping and analysis.

Smokestack Pollution

Factories that burn fuels typically produce nitrogen oxides.

The pollution would be measured directly through sensors in the smokestack linked to a personal computer at the site.

The information would then be sent directly to the regulatory agency computer.

Solvent Pollution

Solvents such as paint and sealants emit reactive organic gases.

The pollution would be measured indirectly by requiring companies to scan each can of paint, for example, that they open.

The information would then be sent through the phone lines to the regulatory agency computer.

I n Southern California and throughout the world, people are using a wide variety of *information technologies* to understand problems and create solutions. Today, these new technologies—from sensing devices in smokestacks to product scanners, telephone networks, fax machines, and computers of all kinds—are permitting us to reshape our lives, jobs, businesses, and entire societies. Even global political and economic affairs are subject to the influence of information technologies.

No matter what you do with your life, you will need to be able to understand and use information technology. Information technologies are used to create and keep track of documents in most offices, control production in factories, design new products, repair automobiles and other complex equipment, and market products around the world.

In short, information technologies are a part of your future. Your effectiveness as a businessperson, employee, artist, or entrepreneur (and your future income) will depend on your ability to understand and work with information technologies. This book will help you develop the understanding that you need to succeed.

1.1 Information Technologies and Civilization

The tools and techniques for gathering and using information are at the core of civilization. Information technologies range from physical devices like paper, pencils, books, newspapers, cameras, tape recorders, and computers to more symbolic tools like written languages, mathematical symbols, chemical models, and tables of natural elements. Without these tools and techniques, we would not be able to visualize our environment, understand it, and creatively control it.

From the invention of writing, around 5,000 years ago, to the present day, the most powerful, far-reaching, and transforming information technologies have been the printed word, the newspaper, and the book, all based on the printing press and movable type. The modern world as we know it depends on the printed word. Invented in the 15th century, the movable type press created the potential for widespread literacy and therefore self-governance, democracy, and popular culture.

Today, we are in the middle of a similar transformation: **digital information technologies** (technologies that use electronics to transform information into a digital, binary—0s and 1s—format) are extending and in some cases replacing the printed word technologies of the last 500 years. Now, the accumulated wisdom of 5,000 years of civilization, as stored in the 100 million items (including books, journals, and technical reports) in the United States Library of Congress, can be put on a few hundred compact optical storage discs called CD-ROMs.

If print technology made our current world possible, what will the new digital information technologies do to our perceptions and knowledge of the world, careers, organizations, and society?

How Information Technologies Help Us

The information technologies of today and tomorrow include not just computers but a whole host of other technologies. Working together, these technologies help us *see and visualize* the world around us and *communicate* that information to a wide variety of computing devices that then help us *analyze and understand* the information. With this information and understanding, we can begin to *create* solutions to problems and *control* our lives, our environment, our jobs, and even entire societies and global economies (see Figure 1.1).

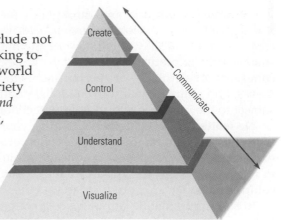

Figure 1.1
How Information Technologies Help Us
Information technologies have a profound impact on our lives because of their potential for changing how we see the world. By extending our vision, information technologies create the foundation for understanding. With understanding, we can begin to control our environment and start to create solutions—new services, products, and even changes to human behavior.

The Four Basic Types of Information Technologies

The different kinds of information technologies available today can be categorized into four basic types: sensing, communication, analyzing, and display.

Sensing Technologies   Devices that help us gather information from the environment and translate that information into a form that can be understood by a computer fall within the category of **sensing technologies.** In the opening vignette, *sensors* are placed in smokestacks to gather precise data (information) on the flow of polluting chemicals, and *bar code scanners* are used to gather data about a company's use of paints and solvents. This data can then be used to help determine the amount and timing of pollution caused by organic gases emitted from paint and solvent cans.

Here are some more examples of the newest sensing technologies and how they are being used:

▶ *Image scanners.* California's Department of Motor Vehicles is now using image scanners to digitize (translate into a series of 0s and 1s) color photographs, fingerprints, and signatures of the 20 million licensed drivers in that state (see photo). The digitized images can be stored on a computer in electronic form, making them much more accessible than paper or microfilm records. The new licenses are also a lot harder to fake, and should help reduce the number of false IDs being created.[1]

California uses image scanners to store a driver's photograph, fingerprint, and signature on a computer.

Source: Courtesy of California Department of Motor Vehicles, Program and Policy Administration.

▶ *Sensors.* The wings of new Boeing 777s feature ice sensors. The sensors, only 7 inches long, 3 inches wide, and weighing less than 1 pound, use an ultrasonic vibrating probe to check for ice. Data collected by the probe is sent to a microprocessor (a tiny computer on a silicon chip) in a cannister holding the probe. If the microprocessor determines that too much ice is building up, it sends a signal that automatically activates the plane's de-icing system. The signal is also sent to the cockpit to let the pilots know the de-icing system has been turned on.[2]

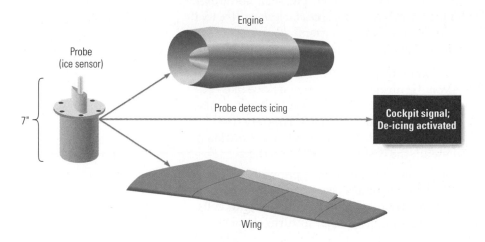

Ice sensors located on wings may prevent tragic accidents caused by icing. *Source:* Rosemount, Inc.

▶ *Digital gloves.* Digital gloves or suits, goggle headsets, and motion-sensing devices can be used with a computer to create a computer-generated, three-dimensional virtual reality that you can interact with through sight, sound, and touch (see photo). The digital glove or suit and motion-sensing devices track your movements. This information is then sent by fiber-optic cable to a computer. The headset (described more fully under "Display Technologies") displays visual and audio images that are appropriately modified as information about your movements is recorded by the sensors and processed by the computer.[3]

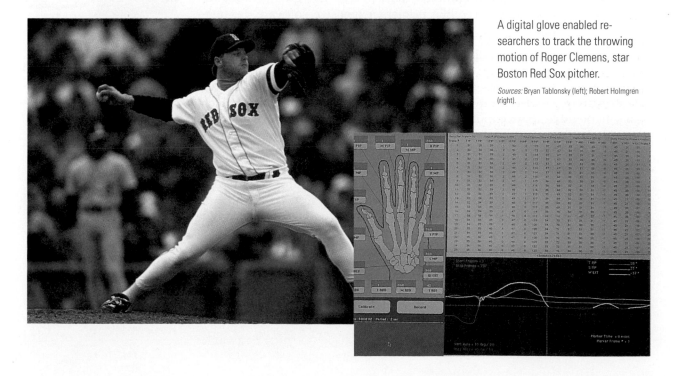

A digital glove enabled researchers to track the throwing motion of Roger Clemens, star Boston Red Sox pitcher.

Sources: Bryan Tablonsky (left); Robert Holmgren (right).

Other more traditional types of sensing technologies include computer keyboards, which translate typed information into a form that can be used by a computer and computer mice, which translate hand movements into commands a computer can follow.

Communication Technologies   Technologies that tie together and communicate information between sensing, analyzing, and display technologies are **communication technologies.** In the opening vignette, smokestack sensors communicate via *communication cables* with an on-site personal computer that gathers the information and then sends it over a *special telephone line* to a central computer at pollution control agency headquarters.

Some examples of contemporary communication technologies include:

▶ *Fax (facsimile) machines.* A few years ago, the only way to send a document from New York to London was via airmail or a courier service like Federal Express or DHL. Today, there are about 30 million installed fax machines in the world, some of which sell for as little as $300. They are used by individuals and businesses to transmit copies of documents over ordinary telephone lines in minutes at one-tenth the cost of overnight carriers.

▶ *Cellular telephones.* Cellular phones are wireless mobile phones that transmit and receive computer-controlled radio signals (see photo). Transmitting stations are placed strategically throughout a region, dividing it into cells. Mobile cellular units transmit to these stations, which in turn, connect the user to the regular phone system. As the user moves (in a car, for instance) from one cell area to another, computers in the cell station hand off the transmission to stations in adjoining cells.

▶ *Local area networks.* About one-third of the 55 million microcomputers (small desktop computers, also often called personal computers) used in organizations today are tied together into local area networks (LANs). These networks make it possible for groups of people to work on shared problems—most work in organizations is accomplished by groups of people. LANs use communication technologies to link desktop microcomputers into a computer network. With a LAN, you can send memos, letters, and documents in electronic form to other users. In addition, groups of microcomputers can share resources like printers, expensive software, fax machines, and storage devices.

Other forms of communication technologies include the ordinary telephone system (which can be used to carry signals from one computer to another), computer networks that use satellites to transfer data across the country, and special communications equipment such as modems (which make it possible for computers to use ordinary voice telephone lines to transmit data).

Analyzing Technologies   Computer hardware (the physical equipment) and software (the programs or instructions that tell the computer what to do) come within the category of **analyzing technologies.** Computers take in information from sensing and communicating devices and then *store* and *process* the information. In the opening vignette, *personal computers* and the regulatory agency's large *central computers* analyze the information coming from smokestack sensors and bar code scanners.

Computers are often categorized by size: small (microcomputers), medium (workstations and minicomputers), and large (mainframes and supercomputers). Generally, the larger the computer, the faster and more powerful it will be.

Cellular telephones help people who need to stay in frequent contact with others. For instance, cellular phones help salespeople keep track of customers, customer orders, and administrative messages no matter where they are. Portable computers can also be used with cellular phones to receive and send information.

Source: Courtesy of Motorola, Inc.

a.

b.

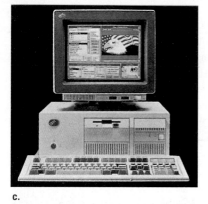
c.

d.

Microcomputers (also called **personal computers** or PCs) are based on a single tiny silicon chip called a microprocessor, which contains all the essential elements of a computer. Microcomputers themselves come in a range of sizes. The most common (and most powerful) are *desktop* units like Apple's Macintosh, IBM's PS/2, and other IBM-compatible PCs (sometimes called *clones*). Right now, though, the fastest selling are lightweight (6 pounds or less) *laptop* and *notebook* portable computers that can be carried from place to place. Most recently, handheld or *palmtop* computers weighing less than 1.5 pounds have hit the market. These tiny machines can perform many useful functions, such as storing your calendar and address list, and doing limited word processing.

One size up in the computer world are **workstations.** Faster, more powerful, and more expensive than microcomputers, workstations are used by engineers, architects, scientists, commercial artists, and others who need computers for speedy number-crunching and graphics. **Minicomputers** generally have more speed and power than workstations, but less than mainframes. They are most likely to be used by small businesses or divisions of larger companies. They are too expensive for individuals to own, but far cheaper than mainframes. Minicomputers can handle several hundred simultaneous users and can run multiple programs concurrently.

Mainframe computers are still the standard for large businesses and government agencies although computer networks composed of smaller computers are threatening to surpass them. Right now, though, mainframes still play a critical role for banks, airlines, insurance companies, and any organization with thousands of customers. The "back office" functions of these organizations—clearing checks, taking reservations, processing claims, tracking sales, and so on—require the speed and power that only a mainframe can provide. **Supercomputers**, the largest and most powerful comput-

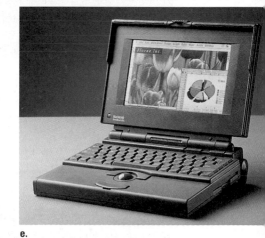
e.

Different types of computers: **(a)** IBM mainframe; **(b)** Hewlett Packard minicomputer; **(c)** IBM personal computer; **(d)** Cray supercomputer; **(e)** Apple PowerBook laptop computer.

Source: Courtesy of IBM; Courtesy of Hewlett Packard Company; Courtesy of IBM; Courtesy of Martin Marietta Corporation; Courtesy of Apple Computer, Inc.

ers, used to be so expensive that only government agencies could own them. They began as tools used to design nuclear weapons, rockets, and other military devices, which required an enormous number of calculations. Today, they are much less expensive and are used by businesses and universities for various commercial and scientific applications.

Let's look at some examples of how people are using computers to analyze problems and design solutions:

▶ *Designing the 80,000-mile tire.* Engineers at Groupe Michelin S.A., a French-based firm that is the largest tire manufacturer in the world, use a *supercomputer* at their research center in Greenville, South Carolina, to create and test hundreds of tires before building actual prototypes and doing road testing (see photos). The engineers discovered that ordinary tires wear out early because they strike the road with an oval pattern. The new supercomputer-designed tires strike the road in a square pattern, which distributes the stress more evenly. Before the use of supercomputers to design and test tires, engineers would build prototypes, hire drivers to drive them for two months or more, and then change the design as needed. Developing a tire could take several years. Now, with the help of a supercomputer, the company can go from prototype to finished tire within a matter of weeks.[4]

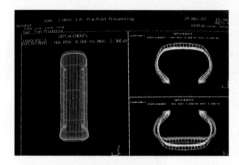 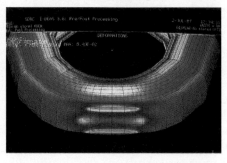

Michelin has used a supercomputer to design a tire that distributes stress more evenly. The tire leaves a wider, squarer "footprint" on the road.

Source: Courtesy of Michelin North America.

▶ *Learning about global warming.* Oceanographers at Oregon State University are using IBM RISC System/6000 *workstations* and software to analyze vast data sets derived from satellite and ground-based observations of the ocean and the atmosphere (see photo). They plan to use what they learn to try to predict future global environmental conditions.

Researchers at Oregon State University's College of Oceanography use workstations and software to create simulations of oceanographic and atmospheric conditions.

Source: Courtesy of Precision Visuals, Inc.

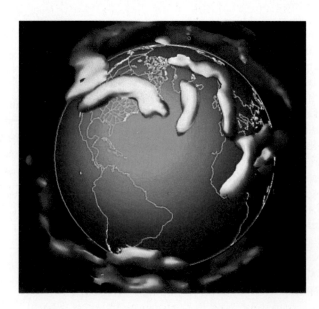

▶ *Redesigning your living space.* Using a $49 program called Floorplan and an ordinary *personal computer,* people planning changes to their houses or apartments can draw up professional quality plans (see photo). The program automatically calculates square footage and aligns and draws walls, circles, and polygons; and it can rotate, magnify, copy, and invert objects. A library of common fixtures is included—including the kitchen sink.

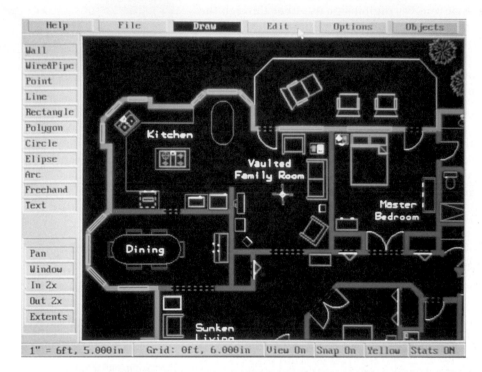

Redesigning your house with a personal computer.

Source: Courtesy of Computer Easy International, Inc.

Display Technologies   Devices and related software that make processed data available to human users, either through sight or sound, make up our last category of information technologies. **Display technologies** form the interface, or connection, between sensing, communication, and analyzing technologies and the human user. They are incredibly important, even critical, to the operation of information technologies. No matter what has been sensed, measured, analyzed, and communicated, unless it can be displayed properly a great deal of information is lost. In the opening vignette, computer *display screens* and *printers* help managers of the pollution control district understand and visualize precisely how much pollution is entering the air.

The following are some examples of new display technologies:

▶ *Color liquid crystal display (LCD) screens.* Everyone prefers a color screen to a black and white one. A color screen is simply more interesting to look at, and the color variations can be used to highlight screen elements. Until recently, color screens required a heavy and power-hungry tube like the one in your television set, making color screens for portable computers impossible. Today, however, laptop computers with color displays (see photo) are available for $2,000, and the price will likely continue to drop.

▶ *Virtual reality display devices.* These devices create images that are so close to reality that you perceive yourself as "being inside" the image. The visual images are displayed on a screen mounted inside a helmet that you wear on your head. If you turn your head to the left, the visual display generated by the computer shifts images to the right, giving you the sensation that you are actually turning to the left. Virtual reality devices are being used in such diverse settings as teaching young surgeons how to perform neurosurgery to

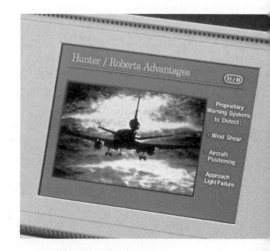

The color display screen used by a Toshiba laptop computer.

Source: Courtesy of the Computer Systems Division of Toshiba America Information Systems, Inc.

entertaining future space pilots with virtual reality games. Commercial applications of this technology are just now being developed, but as costs decrease, and the technology components become less cumbersome, it is likely to become more widespread.

▶ *High-definition television (HDTV).* By the year 2009, you will no longer be watching television as you know it today. Instead, you will be watching a high-definition television set that receives digital signals either through the air or over a cable. The Federal Communications Commission (the federal agency that regulates television in the United States) is expected to decide on an HDTV standard in early 1994, and the transition will begin then. Your TV will in effect become a very large computer display screen that can be connected directly to your computer.

▶ *Computers that talk.* Microsoft Corporation now offers Windows Sound System, a combination of hardware and software that enables a personal computer to talk and make other sounds. With this system, if you are working with a spreadsheet, the computer can read out the numbers to you aloud. It can even read aloud voice messages that have been attached to electronic documents—what Microsoft calls "audible notes."

Other types of common display technologies include high-resolution monochrome and color computer display screens, and a wide variety of printers.

Figure 1.2 summarizes these sensing, communication, analyzing, and display technologies.

Virtual realities are computer-generated electronic images that create the impression that you are participating in a "real world."
Source: Courtesy of AutoDesk, Inc.

Sensing	Communication	Analyzing	Display
Image scanners	LANs and other computer networks	Microcomputers	LCDs
Digital sensors	Cellular phones	Workstations	HDTV
Virtual reality digital gloves	Fax machines	Minicomputers	Virtual reality display
Bar code scanners	Modems	Mainframes	Voice output
Keyboards	Telephone networks	Supercomputers	High-resolution monitors
Mice		Software	Printers

Figure 1.2 Summary: Sensing, Communication, Analyzing, and Display Technologies

A Conceptual Framework: Information Technology and Problem Solving

Though these technologies are interesting in and of themselves, the ways we can use them are even more important. These information technologies are a key ingredient in modern problem solving. Information technology helps us understand problems better, design solutions, and ultimately create the kind of society we want. Figure 1.3 gives you a conceptual framework that you can use when thinking about the role that information technologies play.

To help you learn how to use this framework, we will apply it to the opening vignette that appears at the beginning of each chapter. Let's look again at the opening vignette in this chapter. The first step is to identify the problem. Here the problem was air pollution—specifically, that there was no economical system for accurately measuring specific sources and amounts of pollution. There was never enough precise data to truly understand where pollution came from and how much each source contributed. As a result,

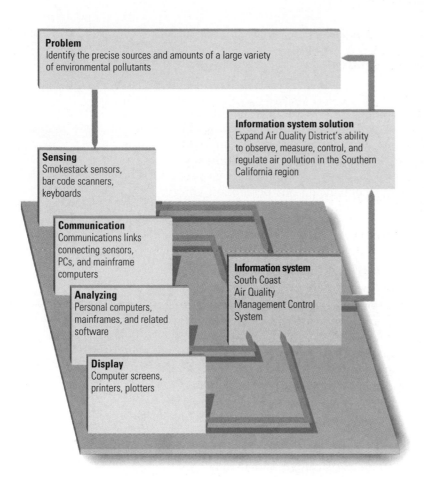

Figure 1.3
A Conceptual Framework

Source: Azimuth Corporation, 1993.

policymakers were forced to take a "shotgun" regulatory approach that required all factories—whether or not they contributed to pollution—to install regulated equipment that met certain pollution standards. This was very costly. Now, think about the information technologies that can be used to solve this problem. Let's review what the South Coast Air Quality Management District used:

1   Smokestack sensors and bar code scanners (sensing technologies)

2   Communications links (cables and radio transmitters) between sensors and personal computers and special dedicated telephone lines linking personal computers to central mainframe computers (communication technologies)

3   Personal computers, mainframe computers, and related software to analyze information coming in from smokestack sensors and bar code scanners (analyzing technologies)

4   Computer screens and printers to display processed data (information) about pollution (display technologies)

Working together, these technologies created an information system that provided regulators with the kind of information they needed to design a solution: a new model of pollution control. Called "regulation by performance," this method is fairer, less expensive, and allows each source of pollution to be controlled on the basis of its actual performance.

Here, then, lies a major part of our story: new information technologies are radically changing our knowledge base and hence the ways in which we structure our lives, careers, organizations, and society.

1.2 How Information Technologies Work Together

As we have discussed, information technologies take on new significance when they work together in a system. Just as a human being is composed of many different parts working together, an information system is composed of different information technologies working together. An **information system** is a set of interrelated components that sense, communicate, analyze, and display information for the purpose of enhancing our perception, understanding, control, and creative ability.

The Information System Concept

A modern information system takes in data from the environment using sensing and communication technologies (input), analyzes this information using computer hardware and software (process), and finally displays the product as useful information (output). You can then use this information to act on the environment surrounding you (feedback).

Let's elaborate on these concepts one at a time. **Input** is the raw data from the world around us. It could be anything: employee names, pictures and sounds, weather patterns, traffic information. It means little to us in raw form—we generally perceive raw data as just a stream of events, one after the other. We use sensing devices to gather input and to translate it into a form that can be understood by a computer.

Processing entails converting this raw data into a useful form. How? Computers first store data and then manipulate, rearrange, and analyze this data according to a set of instructions called a **program** or **software.** The program contains detailed instructions written by a programmer telling the computer precisely how to process the information and how to display it.

The information in a computer would be useless without some way of letting the user know the result of processing. **Output** entails displaying this information to users—usually on computer screens but also on television screens, printers, or even through loudspeakers.

Users of information systems typically have a goal in mind, some problem that they would like to solve. **Feedback** involves using the information that is output as a basis for acting on the data that was input.

Hand-held bar code scanners help Walgreens track inventory.

Source: Courtesy of Walgreen's.

Example: Walgreens' Information System

Let's take a practical example of an information system built by Walgreens, Inc., to illustrate these concepts (see Figure 1.4). Walgreens is America's largest drug store chain with 1,678 stores in 29 states. Walgreens has had 17 years of record sales and earnings, and its goal is to add 1,300 new stores by the year 2000. Walgreens has invested heavily in information technologies to achieve this record.

Walgreens was among the first to install microcomputers in all its stores and to link them via a satellite to the company's central computer in Des Plaines, Illinois. At first, the stores' microcomputers were used to enter orders for the local pharmacies and to control inventory at the central warehouse. This helped Walgreens provide better customer service (by making sure items were in stock at the store) and kept costs down (by not storing too much inventory). Then Walgreens added bar code scanners to the store microcomputers. This meant that when a customer bought a drug, it was automatically recorded back at central headquarters. Reordering by the local pharmacy became automatic: the central computer tracked what was sold and automatically shipped replacements. Electronic links for billing information were also built. Such links allow customers to have their insurance companies pay for drugs automatically without filling in complex reimbursement forms. That added to customer service and reduced costs for Walgreens—their pharmacists did not have to fill in forms either. Another benefit: if you are a Walgreens customer, you can count on any local Walgreens, wherever you go, to refill your prescription because your records are stored on their central computer.

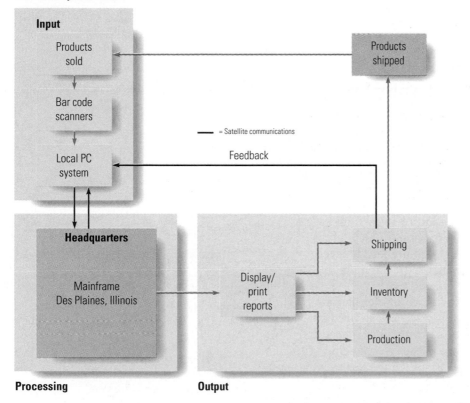

1,678 local pharmacies

Processing   **Output**

Figure 1.4
Walgreens' Information System
This is a schematic overview of a typical business information system cycle. Raw data is input to the system from 1,678 stores using bar code scanners and personal computers connected via satellite to the company's central computer. There the information is stored and processed. Output from the system includes automatic shipping of replacement drugs, sales and management reports, communications to third-party insurers, and reports to customers about their prescriptions. Managers use this output to develop marketing strategies, control costs, and identify problem stores where sales are weaker than expected. As these strategies are implemented, managers watch the output carefully to see if the intended results are achieved.

Source: Based on Henkoff, Ronald, "A High-Tech Rx for Profits," *Fortune,* March 23, 1992.

The Computer as Universal Machine

As you can see from the Walgreens example, the computer plays a central role in the modern information system: it controls the sensing, communication, and display devices. In addition, it performs the processing and storage of raw data and transforms it into useful information through the use of software programs. It is this ability to "be programmed" at will by human beings that makes the computer a *"universal machine"*—one that can perform any task that the user can clearly describe. In the Walgreens example, microcomputers in each store take in information using a software program and then communicate that information to the central computer using a different software program.

Think about this concept of a universal machine. Most of the machines we come into contact with are *hard-wired,* or designed to do a limited number of tasks—a tape player plays a music program, a car transports us down highways, a drill press makes holes in steel and wood, an eggbeater mixes eggs. Computers used to be like this, as you will learn in Chapter 2. But since the 1940s, computers have had the capability of using different programs to perform different tasks. For instance, a personal computer can work as a word processor and later run a game program, a spreadsheet program, or a graphics drawing tool. As long as you describe precisely what you want the computer to do (this is what programming is all about), the computer and its related devices will be able to do it.

Although today's general-purpose computers indeed are universal machines, they still lack the power of human beings. You might consider for a moment some of the ways in which human beings are more powerful than even the most powerful computers. What can humans do that computers cannot?

1.3 How Does Information Technology Affect Your Life?

If you plan to live and work in the 1990s, you will need to know something about how information technologies work. Exactly how much you need to know depends on the kind of job you would like to have. As we show you later, virtually all the fast-growing job categories in the United States projected for the year 2005 will require some minimal computer and related skills. Some jobs will require more skills than others: generally, the higher the level of job in terms of responsibility and pay, the more information technology skills will be required.

But you will need more than just computer literacy to succeed in the 1990s. Knowing what key to hit on a computer keyboard is not enough. You will also need to know how information technologies are changing the world around you so that you can anticipate these changes and adjust your life. For instance, if you want to have a successful career, you should know something about the new jobs and careers created by the emergence of new information technologies. You should also know something about how information technologies are changing business organizations so you can avoid ending up in a dead-end career or a vanishing job.

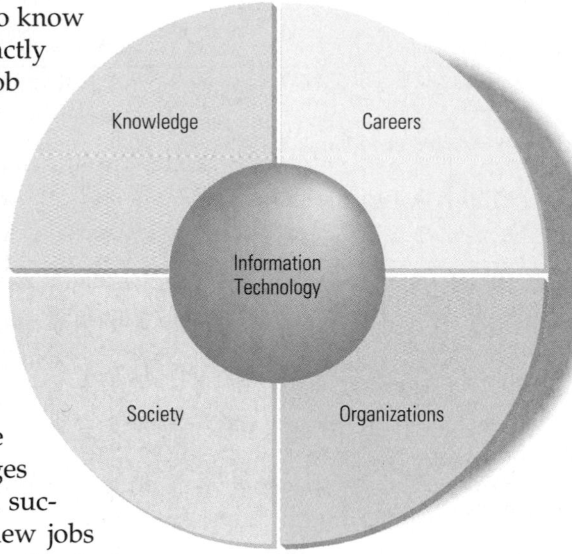

In addition to careers and jobs, you need to know how information technologies can be used to get things done. You may want to organize a Boy or Girl Scout troop for your children to participate in or a charity drive for your place of worship. You may want to set up your own small business or organize a political campaign to elect new members to the local board of education. How can information technology be helpful?

Knowledge is power. Knowledge about the new information technologies will empower you to take greater control of your life, anticipate change, and succeed in a rapidly changing environment. We will focus on four major areas of technological impact: *knowledge, careers, organizations,* and *society* (see Figure 1.5). In each chapter, we will address these four issues and show you how information technology makes a difference. Here we describe each of these areas and give brief examples.

Figure 1.5
Knowledge, Careers, Organizations, Society
Information technologies directly affect our knowledge base, careers and related job skills, organizations, and the society at large.

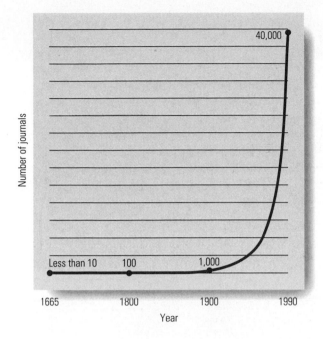

Figure 1.6
The Growth of Scientific Knowledge
Knowledge is growing exponentially, making it difficult for people to stay informed. Two measures of knowledge are the number of scientific journals and the number of articles in those journals. Both have been growing at a compound rate of about 3 percent per year since the first journal, *The Philosophical Transactions of the Royal Society of London*, was published in 1665.

Knowledge and Understanding: The Knowledge Explosion

Information technologies are extending our vision of the world, permitting us to see and understand new areas of physical and social life. As the microscope made it possible for us to see bacteria, and as the telescope made it possible to discover new star systems and galaxies, so too do information technologies extend our ability to see, to measure, to calculate. Increasing your knowledge about information technology will help you anticipate new and upcoming technological breakthroughs in science and technology, which you can use to make better decisions about careers, places of work and living, and lifestyles.

We live in the middle of a *knowledge explosion* that is propelled by new information technologies that help us see the unseen and understand the unimaginable. Just keeping track of all this new knowledge requires new kinds of information services. Consider the following:

▶ The first editions of the *Encyclopedia Britannica* [1745–1785] were written by one or two people. The 1989 edition required 12,500 specialists.[5]

▶ Over the last century, major American university libraries doubled in size every 16 years.[6]

▶ In this century, the number of scientific journals has grown exponentially, estimated conservatively to be at a rate of about 3 percent per year and doubling every 15 to 25 years[7] (see Figure 1.6).

Information technologies are both a cause of, and a solution to the problems of, the knowledge explosion. On the one hand, information technology is rapidly expanding our vision and creativity in new fields. On the other hand, information systems are making it easier for us to store, access, display, and communicate new knowledge. The story "Using Information Technology to See the Unseen" provides one example of how information technology is extending our ability to see things. Other examples throughout the book show you how information technology not only extends our knowledge but also permits us to control the vast amount of new information and knowledge.

Imagine if you could peer back into the past. Think about all the things you could see that no longer exist, that have become hidden, or that have changed with the passage of time. For a historian or archaeologist, this would be a dream come true. Today, with the help of information technology, these dreams are no longer so impossible.

The Great Sphinx in Egypt is the last of the Seven Wonders of the Ancient World. Built over 4,000 years ago, in 2500 B.C., the Sphinx looked very different before sand, water, wind, air pollution, and other hazards combined to erode away many of its distinctive features. Mark Lehner, a specialist in Egyptian archaeology at the University of Chicago, spent four years climbing around the Sphinx with a measuring tape and special camera. From this data, Lehner created hand-drawn contour maps and other drawings documenting how the Sphinx looks today. Though useful, the maps and drawings didn't have the visual impact that a 3-D model would have. They also couldn't solve the riddle of the Sphinx's original appearance.

Enter information technology. Using the same kind of personal computer that you can purchase at your local computer store and mostly "off the shelf," prepackaged software, Jerde Partnership Inc., an architectural design firm in Los Angeles, took Lehner's drawings and transformed them not only into an accurate 3-D model of the Sphinx as it currently exists but also a photo-realistic rendering of the Sphinx as it probably looked 3,000 years ago (see photos).

How did they do it? Thomas Jaggers, director of computer-aided design at Jerde Partnership, first used a software package called Autocad, running on an IBM-compatible personal computer. He traced over Lehner's drawings with a stylus attached to an electronic drawing board called a digitizer, which converted the drawings into digital form. The digitizer merged the various drawings, each of which had been done from a different perspective, into one multidimensional model. Next, Jaggers and his team used a different software product called Quicksurf (originally designed to map the ocean floor) to create a realistic-looking surface for the model.

A digitizer, used together with Autocad software on a personal computer, produced this 3-D image of the way the Sphinx looks today.

Careers: What Kinds of Jobs Will There Be?

The knowledge explosion is rippling through society, creating more demand for high skill levels among employees and extended retraining during an adult's life. This trend will continue and even accelerate in the next decade, changing the kinds of work being done, the kinds of jobs available, and the kinds of skills required to find lifetime employment. One thing is certain: information technology skills—and related skills of reading, writing, public speaking, and mathematics—play a larger part than ever before in work of all kinds. Consider the job projections by the U.S. Department of Labor shown in Figure 1.7.

As you look over these fast-growth careers, ask yourself how information technologies may be used in them. At first glance, it may be hard to imagine how some fast-growth occupations—for example, food counter workers—might make use of information technology. But more and more restaurants now use computerized order entry to the kitchen or use information technology in other ways to serve food. Food is also increasingly delivered to restaurants using computerized order entry and inventory controls. As the story "Unanticipated Skills" indicates, many jobs today use computers and information technology in ways not dreamed of just a few years ago.

Once this model had been created, it was a short step to modifying it to look as Lehner envisioned the Sphinx had once looked. The face of Pharaoh Khafre, who commissioned the Sphinx, was digitized and overlaid over the Sphinx's missing face. A beard and a statue of another Pharaoh between the Sphinx's paws were also added. Color and texture were the final elements. By using another software package, Jaggers was able to create a computerized image with highlights and shadows that easily passed for an actual photograph.

The work done by Lehner, Jaggers, and their helpers has the potential to add to our knowledge base in several ways.

They have created a detailed record of the Sphinx as it exists today, which will be valuable for future researchers. The model can also be used to simulate what the Sphinx might look like in 50 or 100 years, using data on air pollution and other environmental hazards collected with sensors placed around the Sphinx (like the smokestack sensors you learned about in "Cleaning the Air with Information Technology"). The information provided by this kind of simulation may help save the Sphinx before it erodes away.

Sources: Based on Rifkin, Glenn, "Rebuilding the Sphinx with PCs," *New York Times,* September 25, 1991; Booker, Ellis, "Rebuilding the Sphinx in Electronic Form," *Computerworld,* August 19, 1991.

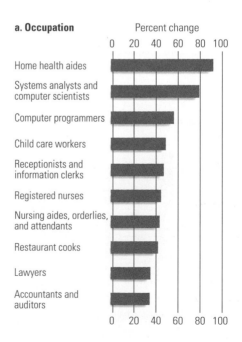

A computerized image of the way Lehner believes the Sphinx once looked.

Source: Courtesy of the Jerde Partnership, Inc. and Dr. Mark Lehner for Giza Plateau Mapping Project.

Critical Thinking Questions

1 How do the information technologies described in this story help us perceive and better understand the world around us?

2 Drawing on your knowledge of history or art, what are some other things you might be able to recreate, restore, or uncover using the information technologies described here?

3 The information technologies discussed in this story, which help scientists see the unseen, could be very useful to more than just archaeologists. What are some other areas to which these technologies could be applied?

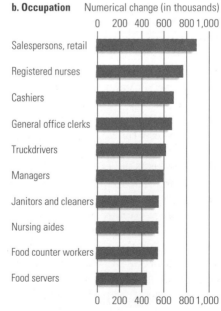

a. Occupation — Percent change

Occupation	
Home health aides	
Systems analysts and computer scientists	
Computer programmers	
Child care workers	
Receptionists and information clerks	
Registered nurses	
Nursing aides, orderlies, and attendants	
Restaurant cooks	
Lawyers	
Accountants and auditors	

b. Occupation — Numerical change (in thousands)

Occupation	
Salespersons, retail	
Registered nurses	
Cashiers	
General office clerks	
Truckdrivers	
Managers	
Janitors and cleaners	
Nursing aides	
Food counter workers	
Food servers	

Figure 1.7
The Fastest Growing Occupations to 2005
(a) shows the ten occupations that should experience the greatest job growth, on a percentage basis, to 2005. **(b)** shows the ten occupations expected to grow the most in terms of absolute number of new positions. Most of these occupations will require significant information technology skills, supported by reading, writing, math, and presentation skills.

Source: Silvestri, George, and Lukasiewicz, John, "Occupational Employment Projections: Outlook 1990–2005," *Monthly Labor Review,* November 1991, Bureau of Labor Statistics, U.S. Department of Labor.

Unanticipated Skills

What kind of career do you hope to begin when you finally finish school? Maybe you want to go into the arts, or some kind of service industry like banking or insurance, or start your own business. If your goal involves something other than becoming a computer professional, you may be wondering whether you really need to learn about the technologies described in this book. Well, read on. The following are just a few examples of how information technologies are changing the way organizations and businesses operate, as well as the jobs of people who work in them.

Take, for example, Kim Perlman, the head trainer at Touchstone Farm, a horse farm in Garrison, New York (see photo). Kim never anticipated that he'd have much use for a computer in his line of work—training horses and riders, running a horse farm, organizing horse shows. But after he purchased an Apple laptop computer to use at home, he began to think of all sorts of interesting possibilities. For instance, whenever the farm holds a horse show, Kim has to design the fences that the horses will jump. He also has to decide how to arrange those fences into different jumping courses. He used to do both of these jobs by hand, drawing them on paper. If he wasn't satisfied with the way they came out, he'd have to redraw them. Kim then discovered that he could use MacDraw, a drawing program, to create designs for different fences and draw different jumping courses. It's now a lot easier for him to tinker, trying out different designs and moving the fences around until he finds the perfect combinations.

Or how about tailors at Albert Andrews Ltd., a Boston suit maker. They now take suit measurements with a computerized tape measure hooked to a laptop computer. The process takes about 20 minutes. Because the system is portable, a customer can be measured not only at the store but also in an office or at home. The measurements are then sent via modem to the company's manufacturing plant in Cleveland, Ohio, where they are used to create a custom pattern, from which the suit can be cut and assembled. In four weeks, a custom suit is delivered that is accurate to within 1/1,000th of an inch! As a result, unlike suits measured in the traditional way, these suits require few alterations. Time and money are saved for the customer as well as the manufacturer. Because of the success of this system, Albert Andrews Ltd. is planning a nationwide expansion.

Finally consider Calvin Hunt, Daniel Bonitzky, and other members of the production crew for the Alvin Ailey American Dance Theatre. In the past, theater productions were accomplished manually using pads of paper and pencils. But during a recent world tour, the Alvin Ailey Company used PCs to keep track of itineraries, revise lighting requirements for each ballet as new theaters were visited, and help crew members keep in touch with one another. The computers were particularly use-

But take note: it isn't just information technology skills that will be required of you in the future. You will also need more years of schooling, specifically, more language, math, and general problem-solving skills, to participate in the "high growth" sector of the job market (see Figure 1.8). We hope to help you attain these more general skills as well as specific knowledge about information technology.

Figure 1.8

Occupations of the Future Will Require More Education

(a) In the year 2005, all occupations will require more years in school. **(b)** The number of low-skill jobs will decline markedly. **(c)** Fast-growing occupations will, in particular, require more language, math, and reasoning skills—many of which you will learn through the use of a variety of information technologies.

Sources: Based on data from *Workforce 2000: Work and Workers for the Twenty First Century,* Hudson Institute, Indianapolis: June 1987; Sylvestri, George, and Lukasiewicz, John, "Occupational Employment Projections, Outlook 1990–2005," *Monthly Labor Review,* November 1991; Bureau of Labor Statistics, U.S. Department of Labor.

a. Years of Education Required

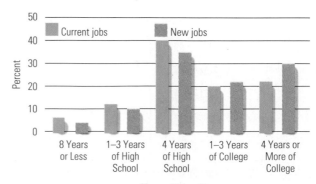

ling stage lights. In the past, a manual list of which light to turn on or dim was required for each theater. Now using a system called a computerized lightboard, the lighting cues for each theater and each of 26 different ballets are stored on the laptop computer. No manual lists are required. The system has tripled the production crew's efficiency: whereas it used to take 8 hours to set up the ballet, it now takes only 5 hours.

Each of these examples illustrates how important information technologies have become to the performance of jobs and the development of careers. Most of the people described here never dreamed when they were in college that computers and information technology would play such a central role in their lives.

Sources: Based on Hildebrand, Carol, "PCs Fit Suit Maker Perfectly," *Computerworld*, December 2, 1992; Fitzgerald, Michael, "Dance Troupe Crew Works Some PC Magic," *Computerworld*, April 28, 1992.

Kim Perlman, head trainer at Touchstone Farm, uses a laptop computer to design fences and courses.

ful for adjusting the lighting cues for each of the ballet theaters where they performed. Theaters have manual lightboards composed of hundreds of numbered switches control-

Critical Thinking Questions

1 Come up with one or two other examples of people using information technology in jobs that you wouldn't expect to require its use.

2 What kind of skills do you think you will need to succeed in the 1990s? How do you plan to develop those skills?

Organizations: How Will We Work?

One consequence of the knowledge explosion and changes in skills is the gradual transformation of organizational life in the United States. Information technology is changing the kinds of services and goods produced, the expectations we have about organizational behavior, the kinds of work we do within organizations, and even the shape of the organizations themselves. Let's look at each of these impacts in a little more detail.

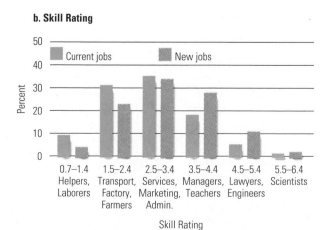

b. Skill Rating

c. Language, Math, and Reading Skills

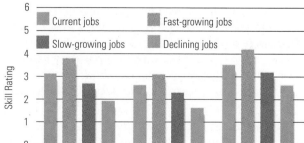

Air travel today has become so commonplace that it's easy to take some things for granted, like the ability to pick up the telephone, reserve a plane ticket, and then actually have a seat on a plane waiting for you when you get to the airport.

How would you like it if, instead, once you had bought your ticket, you had to stand in a line at the airport for the next available seat on the next available airplane, with no assurance that either might become available anytime soon or even that day. That's what passengers who have to fly on Aeroflot, Russia's national airline, face. The reason: right now, unlike airlines in America, Aeroflot has no way to track the number of airline seats that it has sold. Aeroflot tickets merely entitle a passenger to service on a first-come, first-served basis. In 1990, Aeroflot reportedly could not seat 30 percent of its ticketed passengers. Some ended up spending days at the airport before ever getting on an airplane.

Do you react to this situation by saying to yourself, "I'm sure glad I don't have to put up with that"? If you do, your ex-

Computerized airline reservations systems make it easy to make airline reservations in the United States.

Source: Courtesy of American Airlines.

▶ *Information technologies have changed, and continue to change, the way business gets done.* The explosion of knowledge and information that we have described translates into real-world products and services undreamed of a decade ago. Consider some of the products and services that did not exist before the 1980s: automated teller machines (ATMs), compact disks (CDs), overnight delivery services, fax machines, palmtop and laptop computers, caller ID, voice mail, and hundreds of other products. New products and services make it easy to forget what the world would be like without them. Take, for example, the airline reservation system in the United States. The story "Where's My Seat—Airline Reservations at Aeroflot" above helps you visualize what it might be like without the computerized reservation systems used today by all major U.S. airlines.

Clearly, few Americans would tolerate waiting for days at the airport just to get an airline seat. New information technologies change our *cultural expectations* of acceptable organizational performance. Today, for instance, we tend to expect much more of an instantaneous response from service organizations than would ever have been possible in years past.

▶ *"Brain power" is becoming more important than brawn.* Most of the new products and services produced by organizations are based on information technology and new kinds of knowledge. More and more workers in organizations are recruited because of what they can contribute with their minds rather than with their bodies. Information workers, people who create or use knowledge and information to solve business problems, are becoming the typical employees.

▶ *Organizations are becoming flatter and less hierarchical.* People are working together in groups rather than individually. Information workers usually need far less supervision than factory workers because they have know-how—they know what to do and when to do it. They need information, not orders from above or close supervision.

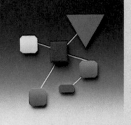

pectations about the services a business organization like an airline should provide to you as a consumer have been influenced by computers. In this case, it would be almost impossible for airlines to serve you in the manner to which you've become accustomed without a computerized system that enables them to handle reservations, track passengers, and issue tickets and boarding passes.

Today, with the downfall of communism, these kinds of consumer expectations are being recognized as important by organizations that once paid little attention to them. Now, Aeroflot plans to purchase the same kind of computerized reservation system that American Airlines uses in the United States. Called Sabre, this system is expected to drastically improve the services that Aeroflot can provide to its customers, and most important, help make sure that passengers get a seat.

Source: Based on Rifkin, Glenn, "I.B.M. and American Airlines in Aeroflot Deal," *New York Times,* April 23, 1992.

Critical Thinking Questions

1 Think about some of the transactions you may have with other types of business organizations, like stores, banks, and so on. What expectations do you have about those transactions? How do you think computers may have affected those expectations?

2 Compare purchasing an airline ticket to registering for your classes and paying your bursar's bills. How are the two alike or different? Which do you think is easier for you to do and why?

3. What training do you think an airline reservation or travel agent would be required to have today? How might this training differ from what was required before airlines adopted computerized reservation systems?

Society and Culture: How Will We Live Together?

The knowledge, career, and organizational changes we've described add up to a transformation of American society and, even, global life. Information technologies are changing our communities, our nation, and global relations among nations. A number of new ethical, political, social, and cultural issues are raised by these technologies.

Information technology changes our society by affecting our economy, culture, social relations, and global relations. Information technology tends to have its first impacts in the economic sphere by changing what we produce and how we produce it. These changes reverberate and filter through the culture, changing our values of what is appropriate behavior and what is inappropriate behavior or forcing us to exercise and strengthen our traditional values.

Social relations—the relationships between groups in a society—are also affected by information technology. Some groups, for instance, will be able to use the new information technologies to their advantage, whereas less fortunate groups may be unable to do so. This typically happens with any new technology or resource. We need to think about how information technology can be developed so as to preserve traditional American values such as equal opportunity.

Changes wrought by information technology do not stop at our national borders. On the contrary, these technologies put us in instant touch with other cultures around the globe. The spread of democratic values to the former Soviet bloc of nations in the 1990s was surely due in part to the influence of global information technologies like satellite broadcasts, E-mail, facsimile transmission, and others. These technologies helped spread democratic values and culture to countries that previously were behind the iron curtain.

a. The Four Sectors of the U.S. Labor Force 1860–1990

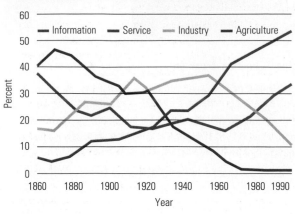

b. Services as Share of Production

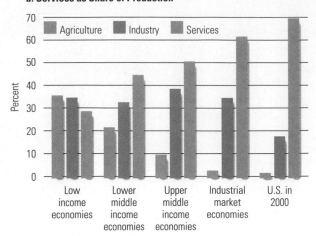

Some specific social impacts to be aware of now are:

▶ *Globalization.* A growing percentage of the American economy—and other economies in Europe, Africa, and Asia—depend on imports and exports (see Figure 1.9). In 1992, about 25 percent of the U.S. gross national product (total economic activity) depended on international trade, including both imports and exports of goods and services of all kinds. Information technology plays an important role in globalization by providing the communication power to conduct trade and manage businesses on a global scale.

▶ *Transformation of the economy toward information and knowledge-based services.* One consequence of the knowledge and information explosion, and the changing nature of careers and organizations, is that more and more of our economy involves using information and knowledge to produce services rather than to manufacture goods. In the 19th century, most people worked on farms. By the beginning of the 20th century, a large part of the labor force had shifted from farms to factories. Now, at the end of the 20th century, the majority of people work in offices, in an information or service industry. In fact, today, services make up a whopping 75 percent of the American gross national product and nearly 70 percent of the labor force (see Figure 1.10).

Percent of GNP

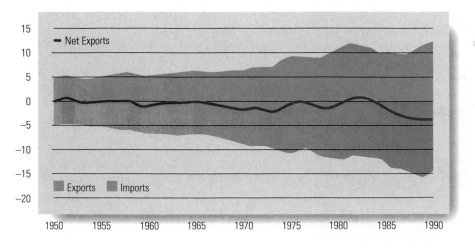

Figure 1.9
The Growing Importance of Global Trade

Exports account for about 10–12 percent of the U.S. GNP, while imports total about 15 percent.

Source: Office of Technology Assessment, Technology and the American Economic Transition, 1990.

c. The Nine Largest Service Industries

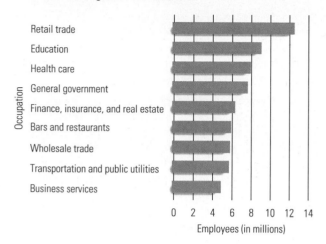

Figure 1.10
The Transformation of the American Economy
(a) The American economy is going through a transformation from manufacturing to information and knowledge-based services. Information workers (people like insurance agents, bankers, managers, and teachers, who create or process information at work) and service workers (people like bus drivers, waiters, and cooks, who provide noninformation services to the public) together are the dominant force in the American economy and will likely continue to be for a number of years. **(b)** The transformation toward an information and service-based economy is worldwide, affecting all advanced industrial market societies. **(c)** This graph gives you an idea of the largest service and information sector industries in the United States.

Sources: Based on data from *Workforce 2000: Work and Workers for the Twenty First Century*, Hudson Institute, Indianapolis: June 1987; *Historical Statistics of the United States, Colonial Times to 1970*, U.S. Department of Commerce; *Statistical Abstract of the United States, 1991*. U.S. Department of Commerce; U.S. Bureau of Labor Statistics, *Employment and Earnings*, January 1987.

Information technology plays an important role in the transformation to an information and service-based economy. Information technologies make factory workers much more productive and, as a result, reduce the need for as many factory workers. Second, the growing power of information technology makes possible new services of great economic value. Credit cards, overnight package delivery, and worldwide reservation systems are examples of new services based on information technologies.

▶ *Extension of markets, shrinking of organizations.* More and more people are going into business for themselves, working for other small businesses, or working for pared-down, formerly large organizations. Today, 53 percent of the labor force works in organizations with fewer than 100 people.

Small businesses and organizations are where most people work, and this trend is growing. More small businesses are being formed today than ten years ago, and this is where most new jobs are being created (see Figure 1.11).

a. Rate of New Business Formation

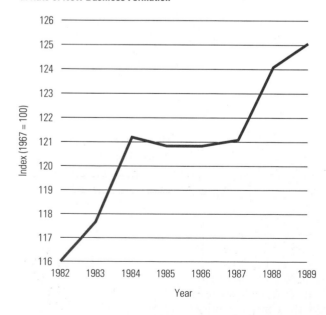

b. Company Size

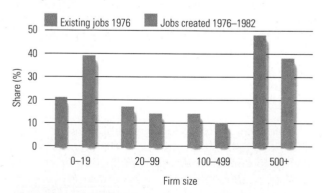

Figure 1.11
Small Businesses Are Growing Rapidly and Creating Many New Jobs
(a) The rate of new business formation in the United States is up substantially in the last decade, and most of these new businesses have fewer than 100 employees. **(b)** Most of the new jobs are being created in these small businesses.

Sources: Statistical Abstract of the United States, 1991. United States Department of Commerce; U.S. Small Business Administration.

"The world is totally going digital." So says Bill Gates, the chairman of Microsoft Corporation, one of the world's largest producers of software. Many companies are jumping on the bandwagon, hoping to use digital technologies to get into new markets. Today, the boundaries between computer companies, entertainment companies, consumer electronics companies, cable companies, telephone companies, and other types of utility companies are becoming increasingly blurred. Reflect on the following:

Time Warner is one of the largest entertainment companies in the country. Among other activities, it operates the nation's second largest cable television system, as well as Warner Brothers, a producer of movies and TV shows, and the cable television channel Home Box Office. US West is one of seven Bell Telephone regional operating companies, serving over 25 million customers in 14 Western states. US West recently announced that it plans to invest $2.5 billion in Time Warner to help it build the country's most advanced cable network, one with hundreds of channels and a vast library of entertainment and information services that subscribers can call up on demand.

Microsoft, which dominates the personal computer software market, Intel, the world's largest manufacturer of microprocessors, and General Instrument, a leading provider of fiber-optic cable technology, have formed an alliance to create a new generation of interactive cable TV converters based on digital technology.

Sony Corp., one of Japan's largest corporations, makes Walkmen and camcorders, owns Columbia Pictures, and publishes electronic books. It is now working with BellSouth, another Bell regional operating company, to create a new type of wireless phone system.

GTE Corp., the local phone company in Cerritos, California, has started providing cable TV, home shopping and bill paying, movies on demand, and videophone as well as regular telephone service to certain of its customers in a test run.

The Glasgow Electric Board, Glasgow, Kentucky's electric utility company, recently put in a digital electronic monitoring system to help customers save electricity. The system has an added advantage: it can also deliver audio and video images. So now the electric company is in the cable-TV business, and it would like to get into the telephone business as well!

Sources: Based on Fabrikant, Geraldine, "US West Will Buy into Time Warner," *New York Times,* May 17, 1993; Markoff, John, "Battles Loom for Control of TV's Portal to Cable," *New York Times,* April 3, 1993; Zachary, G. Pascal, "Blurred Borders: Industries Find Growth of Digital Electronics Brings in Competitors" and "Coming Digital Age May Transform Your Living Room in Many Ways," *Wall Street Journal,* February 18, 1992.

Critical Thinking Questions

1   What kinds of social, economic, or political impacts do you think this increasing convergence of previously unrelated, distinct industries might have? It's probably easy for you to think of advantages that might result, such as the creation of new products and services (or the delivery of old products and services in a new, less expensive manner). Discuss some other advantages that you could foresee.

2   The disadvantages might not be so evident to you at first. Remember, though, that throughout its recent history, America has had a highly diversified economy and society with millions of small, local business establishments. Information technologies make it possible for very large corporations to become even larger and more powerful. For instance, what if a single company provided you with all home communications—not only telephone service but also cable, television, video, and audio music? And what if this company was not American but German, French, or Japanese? What impact might this have on life as we know it today?

Information technology probably has a lot to do with the growing importance of small organizations. With computers so inexpensive, and with the ability to connect powerful microcomputers to national and international communication networks, it becomes possible for even small businesses to reach very large markets, even international markets. You don't have to be General Motors anymore to reach an international marketplace. All you need is a product and a fax machine. If you know the right people to contact (if you have the right information), you can start a business or extend an existing business.

Consider the case of a small haberdasher (hat maker), the Bee Hat Company in St. Louis, Missouri, maker of Davy Crockett hats as well as zany party hats and fur-lined baseball caps. Founded in 1926, the company never

a.

b.

considered exporting. Then a couple of years ago, company vice president Stewart Dahlberg discovered the United States and Foreign Commercial Service, an export arm of the Commerce Department. The Commercial Service keeps an extensive list of export contacts, listing agents, and distributors country by country, with phone numbers included. Using a fax machine and international telephone calls, Bee Hat now sells $300,000 in hats each year to countries as diverse as Bermuda and Israel. Many other small business firms—today's leading exporters—exploit new information technologies and cheap international communications to expand their export business.[8]

But although small organizations are growing, and people are relying less on large organizations for jobs, there are some disturbing tendencies of the Information Age. Many of the remaining large organizations are joining together to jointly exploit digital technologies, raising the possibility that they may become even more powerful despite shrinking work forces. The story "Digital Giants" opposite explores this possibility.

(a) Art museums are using information technology to preserve priceless works of art in electronic form. **(b)** Information technology is revolutionizing the process by which maps are created.

Sources: Robert Frerck/Tony Stone Worldwide; Andy Sacks/Tony Stone Worldwide.

1.4   How This Book Works

To finish up this chapter, we'd like to tell you a bit about the way this book is designed and the authors' views on key issues. This will make the book easier for you to use and learn from.

An Activist Student Role

This book seeks to involve you as much as possible in the learning process by encouraging you to think, speak out, and act. Virtually all educational research has shown that the larger a part you play in your own education, the more you learn and the faster you learn it. We implement this basic philosophy by frequently asking you questions about material you just read, asking you to think critically. *Critical thinking* means to analyze a topic from different perspectives, to seek out causes or potential consequences of issues and events, and to apply what you have learned to new, possibly unrelated or previously undiscussed areas or issues.

To encourage your own critical thinking, we try to engage in it ourselves through our writing. We present you with many issues, controversies, and problems created by information technology—as well as the successes. We try to be honest: information technology is not the solution to all the world's problems but does offer hope, and challenges us all to think about how to use it properly.

Our View of Information Technology

We believe information technology is a long-standing tool of civilization given incredible new strength and power by digital technology. We believe information technology involves everyone from anthropologists to zoologists, from businesspeople to rock groups, and from religious clerics to state bureaucrats. We believe information technology will play an exciting role in creating civilization throughout the next century.

We do not believe that information technology is just the job of computer scientists and technicians to worry about. Instead, we think information technology presents us all with powerful new ways to visualize, understand, control, and create whole new worlds. It also presents us with new responsibilities: it's our job to find worthwhile uses for this technology, as well as to try to prevent its harmful uses and consequences.

To help you focus on these issues, each chapter contains boxed vignettes that illustrate the impact of the information technology being discussed on four different areas: knowledge, careers, organizations, and society.

Developing Your Skill Set and Portfolio

Each chapter also includes elements designed to help you develop your *skill set:* the collection of important skills you will need to succeed in jobs, careers, and business.

First, throughout the text and in the exercises, we emphasize *critical thinking* and *problem solving,* two skills that are crucial for success.

Second, at the end of each chapter, you will find Problem-Solving and Skill-Building Exercises. In these exercises, you will be given a chance to develop your research, writing, or speaking skills in connection with topics related to the chapter. In many of the exercises, you will be encouraged to develop group-work skills such as leading a discussion, making a group presentation, or persuading others to accept your point of view. These exercises have been designed to give you the opportunity to develop a *portfolio* of your work that you can use to demonstrate the skills you have acquired.

Finally, in addition to these exercises, you will find either a Skill Development box or a Personal Technology box at the end of each chapter. Skill Development boxes focus on some particular skill—like reading, writing a business letter, or giving a presentation—and give you some tips on how to do it better. Personal Technology boxes describe some aspect of personal computing and help you learn how to make the right choices when purchasing computer equipment and software.

Summary

Information Technologies and Civilization

▶ Information technologies help us better perceive the world around us. They help us better communicate, analyze, and understand information. With understanding, we can create, control, and organize our lives and society.

▶ Digital information technologies transform information into binary form (zeros and ones), process that information, and then display results for human users.

▶ Sensing technologies help us see, visualize, and gather information from the environment. Examples of sensing technologies include image scanners, bar code readers, sensors, and keyboards.

▶ Communication technologies tie together sensing, analyzing, and display technologies. Computer networks, modems, fax machines, and telephone lines that transmit digital signals are all examples of communication technologies.

▶ Analyzing technologies include computers (both the hardware and software), which take in information from sensing and communication devices and then store, arrange, and process information. Microcomputers, workstations, minicomputers, mainframes, and supercomputers are some of the types of analyzing technologies that exist today.

▶ Display technologies form the interface between sensing, communication, and analyzing technologies and the human user. Examples of display technologies include high-resolution color monitors, liquid crystal display screens, high-definition television, and printers.

How Information Technologies Work Together

▶ Information technologies work together in an information system. An information system is a set of interrelated components that sense, communicate, analyze, and display information.

▶ An information system works by taking in raw data from the environment (input), analyzing this raw data into useful form (processing), and then displaying it to users (output). Users then use the information as a basis for acting on the environment (feedback).

▶ The computer plays a central role in an information system. It is a universal machine because it can be programmed to perform any task that can be clearly described.

How Does Information Technology Affect Your Life?

▶ Information technologies influence our lives by expanding our knowledge base, by affecting the kinds of job skills we need and the kinds of careers that are available, and by transforming organizations of all kinds. By changing our knowledge, careers, and organizations, information technology has created wide-ranging changes in our society and culture.

Key Terms

digital information technologies

sensing technologies

communication technologies

analyzing technologies

microcomputers (personal computers)

workstations

minicomputers

mainframe computers

supercomputers

display technologies

information system

input

processing

program (software)

output

feedback

Review Questions

1 What are some of the ways that information technology can be used to change our lives?

2 List the four basic types of digital information technology. Give examples of each type.

3 Define input, processing, and output. How do these concepts relate to the four types of information technology?

4 Draw a diagram that applies the conceptual framework illustrated in Figure 1.3 on page 13 to the Walgreens' information system described on pages 14–15.

5 Why is the computer a universal machine?

6 What are the primary characteristics that distinguish microcomputers, workstations, minicomputers, mainframe computers, and supercomputers from one another?

7 How has information technology contributed to the knowledge explosion?

8 What kinds of skills will be important in order to find a good job in the next five to ten years?

9 How have organizations changed as a result of information technology?

10 What are some of the impacts that information technology has had on our society in the last 20 years?

11 Read Bill Cosby's article at the end of this chapter. What kind of strategy would you use so as to read the next chapter more quickly and with greater comprehension?

Problem-Solving and Skill-Building Exercises

1   Identify an information system that you come into contact with in your day-to-day life. Prepare a poster using the framework laid out in Figure 1.3 on page 13 to describe the problem the information system was designed to address; the sensing, communication, analyzing, and display technologies used in the system; and how the system enables people who use it to organize or control some aspect of life.

2   Talk with someone you know about his or her career or job. Find out what role information technology plays in the person's job and whether technology has changed, or is changing, the skills needed to do the job or the kind of activities that make up the job. Prepare a 5-minute oral presentation about your findings.

3   Alone, or with a group of two or three others, think about some of the ways that computers have been portrayed in popular media like movies and television. What kinds of images come to mind? Are they positive or negative? Put together a short (1–2 pages) report on your thoughts and discussions.

*How Bill Cosby Learned to
Cope with Too Much Information*

How would you like to read this textbook in half the time and learn twice as much as you normally do? It's possible with speed-reading. In the future, as knowledge and information become more important in our society, and as information technologies bring you more and more of it, you'll soon find yourself overwhelmed. Unless, that is, you do something about it. One thing you can do is learn how to read faster (and better). Bill Cosby tells you how.

How to Read Faster

By Bill Cosby

When I was a kid in Philadelphia, I must have read every comic book ever published. (There were fewer of them then than there are now.)

I zipped through all of them in a couple of days, then reread the good ones until the next issues arrived.

Yes indeed, when I was a kid, the reading game was a snap.

But as I got older, my eyeballs must have slowed down or something! I mean, comic books started to pile up faster than my brother Russell and I could read them!

It wasn't until much later, when I was getting my doctorate, I realized it wasn't my eyeballs that were to blame. Thank goodness. They're still moving as well as ever.

The problem is, there's too much to read these days, and too little time to read every word of it.

Now, mind you, I still read comic books. In addition to contracts, novels, and newspapers. Screenplays, tax returns and correspondence. Even textbooks about how people read. And which techniques help people read more in less time.

I'll let you in on a little secret. There are hundreds of techniques you could learn to help you read faster. But *I* know of 3 that are especially good.

And if I can learn them, so can you—and you can put them to use *immediately*.

They are commonsense, practical ways to get the meaning from printed words quickly and efficiently. So you'll have time to enjoy your comic books, have a good laugh with Mark Twain or a good cry with *War and Peace*. Ready?

Okay. The first two ways can help you get through tons of reading material—fast—*without reading every word*.

They'll give you the *overall meaning* of what you're reading. And let you cut out an awful lot of *unnecessary* reading.

1. Preview—If It's Long and Hard

Previewing is especially useful for getting a general idea of heavy reading like long magazine or newspaper articles, business reports, and nonfiction books.

It can give you as much as half the comprehension in as little as one tenth the time. For example, you should be able to preview eight or ten 100-page reports in an hour. After previewing, you'll be able to decide which reports (or which *parts* of which reports) are worth a closer look.

Here's how to preview: Read the entire first two paragraphs of whatever you've chosen. Next read only the *first sentence* of each successive paragraph. Then read the entire last two paragraphs.

Previewing doesn't give you all the details. But it does keep you from spending time on things you don't really want—or need—to read.

Notice that previewing gives you a quick, overall view of *long, unfamiliar* material. For short, light reading, there's a better technique.

2. Skim—If It's Short and Simple

Skimming is a good way to get a general idea of light reading—like popular magazines or the sports and entertainment sections of the paper.

You should be able to skim a weekly popular magazine or the second section of your daily paper in less than *half* the time it takes you to read it now.

Skimming is also a great way to review material you've read before.

Here's how to skim: Think of your eyes as magnets. Force them to move fast. Sweep them across each and every line of type. Pick up *only a few key words in each line*.

Everybody skims differently.

You and I may not pick up exactly the same words when we skim the same piece, but we'll both get a pretty similar idea of what it's all about.

To show you how it works, I circled the words I picked out when I skimmed the following story. Try it. It shouldn't take you more than 10 seconds.

My brother Russell thinks monsters live in our bedroom closet at night. But I told him he is crazy.

"Go and check then," he said.

I didn't want to. Russell said I was chicken.

"Am not," I said.

"Are so," he said.

So I told him the monsters were going to eat him at midnight. He started to cry. My Dad came in and told the monsters to beat it. Then he told us to go to sleep.

"If I hear any more about monsters," he said, "I'll spank you."

We went to sleep fast. And you know something? They never did come back.

Skimming can give you a very good *idea* of this story in about half the words—and in *less* than half the time it'd take to read every word.

So far, you've seen that previewing and skimming can give you a *general idea* about content—fast. But neither technique can promise more than 50 percent comprehension, because you aren't reading all the words. (Nobody gets something for nothing in the reading game.)

To *read faster and understand most*—if not all—of what you read, you need to know a third technique.

3. Cluster—To Increase Speed *and* Comprehension

Most of us learned to read by looking at each word in a sentence—*one at a time*.

Like this:

My—brother—Russell—thinks—monsters . . .

You probably still read this way sometimes, especially when the words are difficult. Or when the words have an extra-special meaning—as in a poem, a Shakespearean play, or a contract. And that's O.K.

But word-by-word reading is a rotten way to read faster. It actually *cuts down* on your speed.

Clustering trains you to look at *groups* of words instead of one at a time—to increase your speed enormously. For most

of us, clustering is a *totally different way of seeing what we read.*

Here's how to cluster: Train your eyes to see *all* the words in clusters of up to 3 or 4 words at a glance.

Here's how I'd cluster the story we just skimmed:

My brother Russell thinks monsters live in our bedroom closet at night. But I told him he is crazy.

"Go and check then," he said.

I didn't want to. Russell said I was chicken.

"Am not," I said.

"Are so," he said.

So I told him the monsters were going to eat him at midnight. He started to cry. My Dad came in and told the monsters to beat it. Then he told us to go to sleep.

"If I hear any more about monsters," he said, "I'll spank you."

We went to sleep fast. And you know something? They never did come back.

Learning to read clusters is not something your eyes do naturally. It takes constant practice.

Here's how to go about it: Pick something light to read. Read it as fast as you can. Concentrate on seeing 3 to 4 words at once rather than one word at a time. Then reread the piece at your normal speed to see what you missed the first time.

Try a second piece. First cluster, then reread to see what you missed in this one.

When you can read in clusters without missing much the first time, your speed has increased. Practice 15 minutes every day and you might pick up the technique in a week or so. (But don't be disappointed if it takes longer. Clustering *everything* takes time and practice.)

So now you have 3 ways to help you read faster. *Preview* to cut down on unnecessary heavy reading. *Skim* to get a quick, general idea of light reading. And *cluster* to increase your speed *and* comprehension.

With enough practice, you'll be able to handle *more* reading at school or work—and at home—*in less time*. You should even have enough time to read your favorite comic books—and *War and Peace!*

Source: Reprinted by permission of International Paper Company.

Notes

1   **Booker, Ellis,** "New Calif. License Speeds Law," *Computerworld,* March 9, 1992.

2   **Cuff, Daniel F.** "An Automatic Remedy," *New York Times,* March 1, 1992.

3   **Newquist, Harvey P.,** "Virtual Reality's Commercial Reality," *Computerworld,* March 30, 1992.

4   **Hicks, Jonathan P.,** "Computer Tests Pump More Miles into Tires," *New York Times,* April 1, 1992; **Jacobs, Ed,** "Black Art," *Popular Mechanics,* February 1993.

5   **Bell, Daniel,** *The Coming of Post Industrial Society.* New York: Basic Books, 1973, p. 174.

6   **Rider, Fremont,** *The Scholar and the Future of the Research Library,* New York, 1944.

7   **Price, Derek,** *Science Since Babylon.* New Haven: Yale University Press, 1961.

8   **Lohr, Steve,** "A Hat Company Profits in Many Markets Abroad," *New York Times,* May 5, 1992.

Chapter 2 contains:

Keeping Nabisco in Cookies

After completing this chapter, you will:

▶ Be able to place information technology and systems in historical context and recognize what they derive from the past.

▶ Understand how three basic forms of information systems (transaction processing systems, management information systems, and knowledge work systems) are used by organizations.

▶ Be aware of some emerging technologies that may change the way you work and live by the year 2000.

Information Technology and Systems: Yesterday, Today, and Tomorrow

Keeping Nabisco in Cookies

Nabisco Biscuit Company is the world's largest cookie maker with more than $2.7 billion in sales in 1992. That's a lot of cookies and biscuits for the 3,000-person sales force to sell in the United States and Canada. Altogether, the sales force puts in over 5 million hours each year and is the lifeblood of the company: no cookie sales, no company. Anything Nabisco can do to help the sales force has a direct impact on the company's sales and profits. Realizing this, Nabisco executives got MAD and created VAST. The three-year effort to build the systems cost about $3 million, but so far MAD and VAST have resulted in around $50 million in additional sales.

MAD is the Merchandising Activities Database system. Here's how MAD works. Salespersons are armed with handheld computers into which they input store-by-store information on Nabisco product sales, prices, and the impact of weekly promotions. This information is sent electronically using phone lines to Nabisco's mainframe computer in East Hanover, New Jersey. There, the data is organized and processed by product type—for instance, oatmeal cookies. Later, this database can be accessed by sales personnel and store buyers using VAST (Value Added Selling Techniques) to help decide how to effectively use shelf space in a given store or how to combat a competitor.

For instance, suppose a competitor offers a store $100 "up-front money" to put in a big display and promotion for its cookies. A salesperson for Nabisco using a personal computer can look up a VAST application like "Combating Up-Front Money." Based on the MAD database on previous sales of Nabisco cookies, the sales rep can show the store owner that putting in a Nabisco promotion will make more money, generate a sales chart to support the claim, and suggest other tactics to use in the situation.

Prior to MAD and VAST, sales representatives spent hours poring over computer printouts looking for data to support their sales efforts. Now, in a few

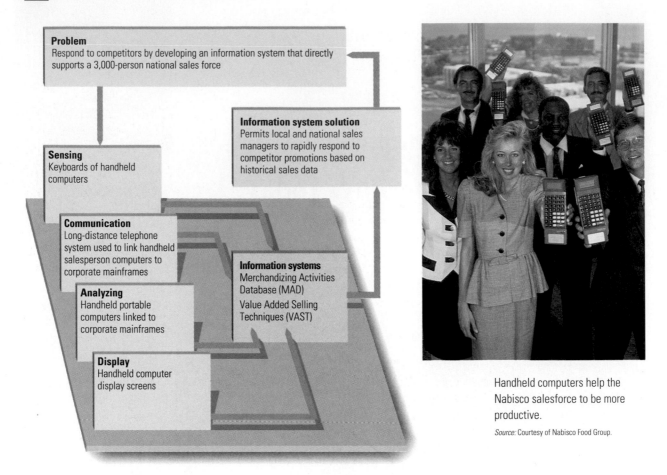

Problem
Respond to competitors by developing an information system that directly supports a 3,000-person national sales force

Information system solution
Permits local and national sales managers to rapidly respond to competitor promotions based on historical sales data

Sensing
Keyboards of handheld computers

Communication
Long-distance telephone system used to link handheld salesperson computers to corporate mainframes

Information systems
Merchandizing Activities Database (MAD)

Value Added Selling Techniques (VAST)

Analyzing
Handheld portable computers linked to corporate mainframes

Display
Handheld computer display screens

Handheld computers help the Nabisco salesforce to be more productive.

Source: Courtesy of Nabisco Food Group.

minutes they plug their handheld computers into a telephone, and VAST walks the sales rep through the process of creating an effective sales presentation in a competitive situation based on specific products at a specific store.

Source: Based on Horwitt, Elisabeth, "High Tech Keeps Nabisco No. 1," *Computerworld,* March 2, 1992.

In Chapter 1, you learned about the four basic types of information technologies and how they combine to create an information system. As you can see from the diagram above, the information system described in the Nabisco story contains all the elements of a generic information system: handheld computers input information, the telephone system connects these small computers to a large mainframe, and the resulting information is organized and stored for later use and display.

The features illustrated by the Nabisco information system are fundamental not only to today's information systems but also to information systems employed by humankind since the beginning of recorded history. People have always used information systems to help manage information, conduct business, communicate with others, and understand the world around them. The tools may become more and more sophisticated as time marches on, but the fundamental concepts remain the same.

In this chapter, we describe how information technologies and systems have evolved. With this historical background, we then take you on a tour of contemporary information systems—the basic kinds of systems needed to run an advanced industrial society like ours. We conclude by talking about the future: some new types of information technologies and systems that may change the way we run businesses (and even our lives) before the turn of the century.

2.1 The History of Information Technology and Systems

The year is 1500 B.C. You are scrambling along a steep mountain trail in the French Alps and come upon a rock drawing of a mountain goat and a man riding a horse. In the drawing, the mountain goat is upright, but the man and horse are upside down. What does it mean?[1]

The rock drawing is an early example of our use of available tools to live in and understand the world around us. Today's information technology and information systems have a long heritage, going back to the earliest days. You will be able to better understand the role and impact that information technology has on our lives if you can look at it within a historical context. As you learn more about different forms of information technology, you will be able to recognize the many common elements that new technologies have with discoveries that preceded them.

The history of information technologies and systems falls into four basic periods, each characterized by a principal technology used to solve the input, processing, output, and communication problems of the time. The four periods are premechanical, mechanical, electromechanical, and electronic. (The time line in Figure 2.1 will help orient you.)

Three themes pervade this history: (1) many cultures contributed to the techniques we employ today; (2) the use of information technologies and systems is, and has always been, driven by a desire to solve problems; and (3) input, process, and output have been the fundamental components of information systems since the beginning of time.

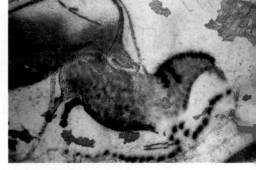

Rock drawing.
Source: Superstock.

The Premechanical Age: 3000 B.C.–1450 A.D.

How to physically represent concepts like language and numbers, and how to store and display information so that it would remain precise, unambiguous, and permanent—these were the key issues facing humans during the premechanical age. The solutions: writing and numbering systems, aided by the technologies of the day—tools like paper, pens, and the abacus.

Writing and Alphabets   The ability to write seems so natural, so intuitive that it's hard to realize there was a time when humans did not know how to do it. But in fact, the first humans communicated only through speaking and picture drawings. They had no real way to store knowledge. Instead, they had to rely primarily on individual and collective memory. It was only about 5,000 years ago, around 3000 B.C., that Sumerians in Mesopotamia (today, southern Iraq) devised a writing system. The system,

Figure 2.1
Information Technology and Systems Time Line

The Premechanical Age:
3000 B.C.–1450 A.D.   The First Writing Systems and Alphabets   The First Numbering Systems; Abacuses

3000 B.C.	1000 B.C.

Early Tools: Clay, Stylus, Papyrus, Reeds

called cuneiform, used signs corresponding to spoken sounds, instead of pictures, to express words. The Sumerians used this new system to help build the world's first cities, where people lived in organized society for the first time. From this first information system—writing—came civilization as we know it today.

Around 2000 B.C., the Phoenicians further simplified writing. They forever severed the relationship between pictures and words by creating symbols that expressed single syllables and consonants (the first true alphabet). The Greeks later adopted the Phoenician alphabet and added vowels; the Romans gave the letters Latin names to create the alphabet we use today.

Paper and Pens For the Sumerians, input technology consisted of a penlike device called a stylus that could scratch marks in wet clay. (In fact, in most languages, the word *write* derives from words meaning to scratch or carve.) Some 4,500 years ago (around 2600 B.C.), the Egyptians discovered that they could write on the papyrus plant. They used hollow reeds or rushes to hold the first "ink," pulverized carbon or ash mixed with lamp oil and gelatin from boiled donkey skin. Other societies wrote on bark, leaves, or leather. The Chinese developed techniques for making paper from rags, on which modern-day papermaking is based, around 100 A.D.

Books and Libraries: Permanent Storage Devices The urge to organize information into a more usable form, and to store information permanently, led to the creation of books and libraries almost as soon as writing techniques were perfected. Religious leaders in Mesopotamia kept the earliest "books"—collections of rectangular clay tablets, inscribed with cuneiform and packaged in labeled containers—in their personal "libraries." The Egyptians kept scrolls—sheets of papyrus wrapped around a shaft of wood.

Books did not become easier to use until thousands of years later (around 600 B.C.), when the Greeks began to fold sheets of papyrus vertically into leaves and bind them together. The dictionary—an important advance in processing information through the creation of sorted lists of words—made its first appearance about the same time, as did the encyclopedia. The Greeks are also credited with developing the first truly public libraries around 500 B.C.

The First Numbering Systems And what about numbers? Although early peoples could keep track of quantities with physical objects (carved notches on sticks or bones, piles of stones), the development of numbers that could be easily added, subtracted, multiplied, or divided did not come quickly. Early cultures each had their own methods. The Egyptians, who along with the Arabs developed the first systematic trading routes

A Mesopotamian "book."

Source: Robert Frerck/Odyssey Productions.

The Phoenician alphabet.

throughout the Mediterranean, struggled with a system that depicted the numbers 1–9 as vertical lines, the number 10 as a U or circle, the number 100 as a coiled rope, and the number 1,000 as a lotus blossom. Despite the difficulties this entailed, the Egyptians used this numbering system to keep records and accounts not totally dissimilar to today's accounting spreadsheets or worksheets.

The first numbering systems similar to those in use today were not invented until between 100 and 200 A.D. by Hindus in India who created a nine-digit numbering system. It took 700 years—until around 875 A.D.—to develop the concept of zero. Arab traders who had commercial dealings with the Hindus adopted their numbering system. It was through the Arab traders that today's numbering system—nine digits plus a zero—made its way to Europe sometime in the 12th century.

The First Calculators   As symbolic numbering lumbered forward—the Greek and Roman system of representing numbers with letters like I, V, and X was not much easier to work with than the Egyptian system—the existence of a counting tool called the *abacus* made life easier for traders, merchants, and others. The abacus, one of the very first information processors, permitted people to "store" numbers temporarily and to perform calculations using beads strung on wires. It continued to be an important tool throughout the Middle Ages.

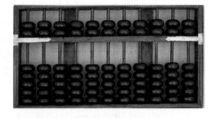

An abacus.

Source: Courtesy of IBM.

The Mechanical Age: 1450–1840

Writing, paper, pen, books, and numbering systems were the basic building blocks that humans used to begin to better understand the world around them. They allowed ideas to be recorded and communicated. But owing to the time and cost involved in creating a book by hand, books were generally available only in limited quantities to a limited number of people. Libraries were for the truly rich, the churches, or governments. The dissemination of ideas beyond that group could take many, many years. For civilization to progress, information needed to become more accessible to a broader group of people. Inventors in the mechanical age tackled this problem by using the techniques and tools available to them—precision engineering of metals, cogs, and wheels and mechanical power transmission—to begin to create machines that could do some of the work that humans used to have to do themselves.

The First Information Explosion   The limitations of the earlier age were decisively overcome by a man named Johann Gutenberg in Mainz, Germany, who invented the movable metal-type printing press in 1450. Until then, books were either written out by hand or printed with wood blocks (each

An excerpt from a Gutenberg bible.

Source: North Wind Picture Archives.

Papermaking in Europe	**The Mechanical Age: 1450–1840**	Gutenberg's Movable Metal-Type Printing Press
1100	1450	1500

page was carved in wood over several weeks and then pressed). Unfortunately, the wood blocks would last only a hundred or so impressions before they needed to be recarved. With movable type, pages could be composed in minutes rather than weeks. Metal type also was far more durable than wood, permitting tens of thousands of copies to be printed in a single run.

The printing press made written information much more accessible to the general public by reducing the time and cost that it took to reproduce written material. It became possible, for instance, to explain the "new" Arabic numbering system and the use of tools like the abacus to the common people. Moreover, as the new technology made books and other forms of writing more available, innovations in ways of presenting and spreading information sprang up: pamphlets, flyers, newspapers, journals, magazines, and so on. The development of book indexes (alphabetically sorted lists of topics and names) and the more widespread use of page numbers also made information retrieval a much easier task. These new techniques of organizing information would become valuable later in the development of files and databases.

The "information explosion" that resulted from the invention of the printing press helped empower people who previously did not have access to information and ultimately helped create new, more democratic forms of government based on an educated, literate citizenry.

Johannes Gutenberg examining a proof.
Source: North Wind Picture Archives.

Math by Machine   Around the same time that mechanical printing-press technology was beginning to have an impact on the dissemination of information, people were also turning their attention to using technology to help powerful organizations deal with numbers more easily. The first general-purpose "computers" were actually people. Sitting in government tax offices, working in libraries, and assisting early scientists, these people were reasonably well paid, but their jobs were tedious and error prone. One "computer" was given the assignment of computing the mathematical formula pi to 500 places, a task that was completed in three years. A second check of the data found an error early in the series of calculations, and it all had to be recalculated. Such difficulties in calculating numbers by using available technology (abacus, pen, and paper) were slowing scientists and mathematicians in their pursuit of greater knowledge.

A Pascaline.
Source: Courtesy of IBM.

Slide Rules, the Pascaline, and Leibniz's Machine   In the early 1600s, William Oughtred, an English clergyman, invented the *slide rule,* a device that allowed the user to multiply and divide by sliding two pieces of precisely machined and scribed wood against each other. The slide rule is an early example of an *analog computer*—an instrument that measures instead of counts. The slide rule proved so useful that it remained a mainstay of scientists for hundreds of years, until the 1950s. Blaise Pascal, later to become a famous French mathematician, built one of the first mechanical computing machines as a teenager, around 1642. The son of a French tax collector, Pascal built the machine to help his father avoid the drudgery of long series of computations. The machine, called a *Pascaline*, used a series of wheels and cogs to add and subtract numbers. Gottfried von Leibniz, an important German mathematician and philosopher (he independently invented calculus at the same time as Newton), was able to improve on Pascal's machine in the 1670s by adding components that made multiplication and division easier.

Babbage's Engines   Around 150 years later, mathematicians were still struggling with the difficulties of accurate computation. It had become even more important as science and math became more complex. By the early 1800s, everything from astronomy and geography to pure mathematics relied on long mathematical tables, produced by hand by humans. Invariably, the tables contained mistakes. An eccentric English mathematician named Charles Babbage, frustrated by those mistakes, set his mind to creating a machine that could both calculate numbers and print the results. In the 1820s, he was able to produce a small working model, which he called the **Difference Engine** (the name was based on a method of solving mathematical equations called the method of differences). Made of toothed wheels and shafts turned by a hand crank, the machine could do computations and create charts showing the squares and cubes of numbers.

The Difference Engine.
Source: Courtesy of IBM.

Babbage had plans for an even more complex Difference Engine that could work out complicated equations. He was never able to actually build that machine because of difficulty obtaining funding, but he did create and leave behind detailed plans. (In 1991, the London Museum of Science assembled a later version of this machine, using Babbage's plans and methods of manufacturing available during his time. The machine weighs 3 tons, is 7 feet high, 11 feet long and 1-1/2 feet deep, and has 4,000 parts. It works exactly as Babbage had envisioned.)

Even more impressive is another machine that Babbage began to dream about during the 1830s while working on the Difference Engine. He called this new idea the **Analytical Engine.** Some parts of its design have proved to be remarkably similar to modern-day computers. For instance, the Analytical Engine was to have a part, called the store, which would hold the numbers that had been inputted and the quantities that resulted after they had been manipulated. It was also to have a part, called the mill, where the numbers were actually manipulated. As you will see in Chapter 3, these concepts are very similar to a modern-day computer's memory and central processing unit. Even more remarkably similar, Babbage planned to use punch

Babbage's Engines: The Difference Engine and the Analytical Engine

cards to direct the operations performed by the machine. He had developed this idea from seeing the results that a French weaver named Joseph Jacquard had achieved using punched cards to automatically control the patterns that would be weaved into cloth by a loom. These ideas presaged the development of the stored program concept and general-purpose computing nature of modern-day computers.

An unusual friend aided Babbage in his efforts—the young daughter of the poet Lord Byron. Seventeen when she first met Babbage, Augusta Ada Byron understood mathematics exceptionally well for a young woman of that era. She helped Babbage design the instructions that would be given to the machine on punch cards (for which she has been called the "first programmer") and to describe, analyze, and publicize his ideas. Babbage eventually was forced to abandon his hopes of building the Analytical Engine, once again because of a failure to find funding. He died in 1871 a forgotten man, and almost all who followed him were unaware of the machines he had envisioned. It was not until the mid-1950s that researchers rediscovered Babbage's inventions, largely as a result of the correspondence and records left behind by Ada.

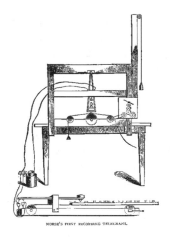

Jacquard's loom.

Source: North Wind Picture Archives.

The Electromechanical Age: 1840–1940

As the demands of industrial society became more complex, the need for powerful technologies to support sophisticated information systems grew. The discovery of ways to harness electricity was the key advance made during this period. Knowledge and information could now be converted into electrical impulses.

The Beginnings of Telecommunications   At the same time that Babbage was working on his "Engines," discoveries were being made that would pave the way for revolutionary changes in how people could communicate with one another. The printing press had represented a major advance, but it still required the physical delivery of a tangible object—a book or newspaper, for instance—for information to be transmitted. The oral transmission of information was likewise limited to people within hearing distance. The discovery of a reliable method of creating and storing electricity (with a voltaic battery) at the end of the 18th century made possible a whole new method of communicating information. The *telegraph*, the first major invention to use electricity for communication purposes, made it possible to transmit information over great distances with great speed. The usefulness of this invention was further enhanced by the development of *Morse code* in 1835 by Samuel Morse, an American from Poughkeepsie, New York. Morse devised a system that broke down information (in this case, the alphabet) into bits (dots and dashes) that could then be transformed into

MORSE'S FIRST RECORDING TELEGRAPH.

Morse's first recording telegraph.

Source: Bettmann Archives.

The Electromechanical Age:
1840–1940   The Beginnings of Telecommunications: Electricity Harnessed; Telegraph and Telephone Invented

1840   1880

electrical impulses and transmitted over a wire (just as today's digital technologies break down information into zeros and ones). The next major developments in communications occurred around the end of the 19th century with the invention of the *telephone* by Alexander Graham Bell in 1876, followed by the discovery that electrical waves travel through space and can produce an effect far from the point they originated at, which led to the invention of the *radio* by Marconi in 1894. These technologies form the basis for modern-day telecommunications systems.

Electromechanical Computing   The technologies behind electricity and mechanical computing machines were first combined in the late 1880s by Herman Hollerith, a young man with a degree in mining engineering who worked in the Census Office in Washington, D.C. The desire to keep track of population has existed since the time of the Egyptians. The United States had been taking a census every ten years since 1790, but census officials were becoming overwhelmed by the task of manually tabulating census results as the population of America reached over 50 million people in 1880. Hollerith picked up on an idea expressed by one of his superiors that perhaps punched cards could somehow be used to record information and then counted using a machine. By 1890, Hollerith had perfected a machine that could automatically sort census cards into a number of categories using electrical sensing devices to "read" the punched holes in each card. In this way, it was possible to count the millions of census cards and categorize the population into relevant groups. It was extremely successful, and the company that he founded to manufacture and sell it eventually became International Business Machines Corporation (IBM), a leader in punch card machines (and later, electronic computers).

During the early years of the 20th century, scientists, the military, and large business firms continued to clamor for help with calculations and paperwork. Researchers focused on electromechanical computing as a possible answer. The technology reached its height in the late 1930s and early 1940s when Howard Aiken, a Ph.D. student at Harvard University, decided to try to combine Hollerith's punched card technology with Babbage's dreams of a general-purpose, "programmable" computing machine. With funding from IBM, Aiken built a machine known as the Automatic Sequence Controlled Calculator (ASCC), or more simply, the **Mark I.** It used paper tape to supply instructions (programs) to the machine for manipulating data (input on paper punched cards), counters to store numbers, and electromechanical relays to help register results. The machine was 51 feet long, 8 feet high, and contained 750,000 parts, 500 miles of wire, and 3 million electrical connections. It certainly worked but was obsolete even before it was finished in 1944. The electromechanical age was about to end and a new era, based on electronic components, about to begin.

a.

b.

(a) Hollerith's machine.
(b) Detail of Hollerith's punched cards.

Source: Courtesy of IBM.

Electromechanical Computing: Hollerith's Machine and the Mark I

The Electronic Age: 1940–Present

During the last 50 years, a key problem has been the need for faster, more powerful, and more reliable technologies to help us keep up with the fast-paced and quickly changing world around us. The main advances in this period have revolved around the discovery that electronic, digital technologies could fulfill that need.

First Tries   There is disagreement over who built the first **electronic digital computer.** Electronic components, unlike the electromechanical relay switches used in the Mark I, do not move—they simply change from one state to another, depending, for instance, on whether electric current is running through them. In the early 1940s, scientists around the world began to realize that electronic vacuum tubes, like the type used to create early radios, could be used to replace electromechanical parts. In the United States, in 1939, John Atanasoff and Clifford Berry at Iowa State University created a small, working prototype using 300 vacuum tubes. In Germany, in 1942, Konrad Zuse, who had built an electromechanical, programmable computer called the Z3 in 1941 (even before Aiken built the Mark I) proposed redesigning it using 2,000 vacuum tubes. The proposal was turned down because of Hitler's embargo on anything but short-term research projects. In England, in 1943, Alan Turing, a brilliant mathematician (in 1936, the 24-year-old Turing had written what was to become a seminal paper in computer science, in which he envisioned an automatic computing machine with many of the same characteristics that were later developed), helped build a machine called Colossus. Designed to break German codes, Colossus used 1,800 vacuum tubes to count, compare, and perform simple arithmetic. Although a special-purpose machine, Colossus represented a breakthrough in showing that vacuum tubes could be used for high-speed data processing.

Colossus.

Eckert and Mauchly   Back in the United States, a physicist, John Mauchly, and an electrical engineer, J. Presper Eckert, at the Moore School of Electrical Engineering at the University of Pennsylvania, had made a proposal in August 1942 for a high-speed, general-purpose computer using vacuum tubes. The U.S. Army, desperate for help in calculating firing tables, awarded them a contract to build the computer in 1943. The Electronic Numerical Integrator and Calculator **(ENIAC)** took two years to assemble and was finally unveiled to the press in early 1946. Too late to help with the war, the machine nonetheless performed admirably: it could add, subtract, multiply, and divide in milliseconds and calculate the trajectory of an artillery round in about 20 seconds. To accomplish this, the machine em-

The Electronic Numerical Integrator and Computer (ENIAC).

Source: Hagley Museum and Library.

The Electronic Age:
1940–Present   First Tries: Atanasoff/Berry prototype; Z3; Colossus

Eckert and Mauchly develop ENIAC

ployed over 17,000 vacuum tubes. It weighed 30 tons and was 100 feet long, 10 feet high, and 3 feet deep.

One problem with the ENIAC was that it had no means of storing program instructions in its memory; instead, the instructions were a function of the way its electrical circuits were wired. To change the instructions, the machine would literally have to be rewired. Mauchly and Eckert realized this, and at the same time they were finishing ENIAC, they were already at work designing a new and improved machine called the Electronic Discreet Variable Computer **(EDVAC).** They planned to store instructions internally using mercury-filled vacuum tubes enhanced with quartz crystals. Around the same time, a prominent mathematician, John von Neumann, who was also involved in the Manhattan Project to build an atomic bomb, became interested in computers and joined the team as a consultant. Von Neumann produced an influential report in June 1945 synthesizing and expanding on Eckert and Mauchly's ideas, which resulted in von Neumann's being credited as the originator of the **stored program concept.** Not many realized that Eckert and Mauchly had been talking about the idea for some time or that back in 1936 Alan Turing had included the concept of an internal memory in his visionary paper. Von Neumann's paper was still enormously important for its crystallization of the key components and concepts governing the creation of general-purpose electronic computers.

Ironically, Eckert and Mauchly did not even manage to build the world's first stored program computer. They left the Moore School over a dispute about who owned the patent rights to the machines and went into business for themselves. In 1949, two years before EDVAC was finished by the team remaining at the Moore School, Maurice Wilkes, a British scientist at Cambridge University, took that prize when he built **EDSAC** (Electronic Delay Storage Automatic Calculator). Eckert and Mauchly ran out of money before they could finish a computer they called **UNIVAC** (Universal Automatic Computer), which they hoped would be the world's first general-purpose computer for commercial use. They had to sell their company to Remington Rand, and although UNIVAC was a gigantic technical success when released in 1951, Eckert and Mauchly had once again been beaten to the punch by Great Britain: a machine called LEO (Lyons Electronic Office) went into action a few months before UNIVAC, and claimed the honor of being the world's first commercial computer.

The Four Generations of Digital Computing   The recent history (the last 50 years or so) of information technology has traditionally been broken down into four or five distinct stages or *computer generations,* each marked by the technology used to create the main **logic element** (the electronic component used to store and process information) used in computers during the period.

The Electronic Discreet Variable Computer (EDVAC).

Source: Courtesy of University of Pennsylvania Archives.

UNIVAC programmers.

Source: Hagley Museum and Library.

EDSAC, EDVAC, LEO, UNIVAC

The First Generation (1951–1958) The first generation of computers used **vacuum tubes** as their main logic element. Although vacuum tubes represented a great advance over electromechanical technology, they were not particularly reliable, used a lot of electricity, and produced a lot of heat. In addition, their large size and the fact that so many had to be used to achieve even relatively meager memory and processing capacity meant that the machines that contained them had to be huge. Other hallmarks of first-generation machines include the use of *punched cards* to input and externally store data, rotating *magnetic drums* for internal storage of data, and programs written in *machine language* (instructions written as a string of 0s and 1s) or *assembly language* (a language that allows the programmer to write instructions in a kind of shorthand that is "translated" by another program called a compiler into machine language). First-generation computers were used primarily for scientific, engineering, and large-scale commercial applications like payroll and billing. Telecommunications of that era were conducted by telephone and teletype at a very slow rate.

Vacuum tubes.

Source: Courtesy of IBM.

The Second Generation (1959–1963) The disadvantages of vacuum tubes led scientists to search for an alternative to take their place. In the late 1940s, researchers at AT&T's Bell Laboratories discovered that a class of crystalline mineral materials called **semiconductors** could provide the answer. From this material, a device called a **transistor** could be fashioned. (Transistors were originally made with a rare mineral called germanium and were initially much more expensive than vacuum tubes. It was not until 1954 that a transistor using silicon, the main ingredient of ordinary sand, and next to oxygen the most abundant chemical element in the world, was perfected. Once it was, the cost of transistors dropped drastically.) Transistors performed the same functions as tubes but took much less space, were more reliable, did not use as much energy or produce as much heat, and were faster and more powerful. However, like the tubes they replaced, transistors still had to be hand-wired and soldered together to form circuits.

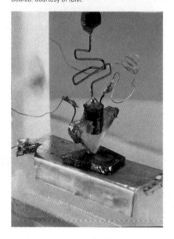

A transistor.

Source: Courtesy of AT&T Archives.

At the same time, advances were also occurring in other areas. *Magnetic cores* (very small donut-shaped magnets that could be polarized in one of two directions to represent data) strung on wire within the computer became the primary internal storage technology, gradually replacing the more slowly accessed magnetic drums of the first generation. *Magnetic tape and disks* began to replace punched cards as external storage devices, also providing faster access speeds and the ability to compress more data into less space. Digital telecommunications between computers were also developed during this period. *High-level programming languages* (program instructions that could be written with simple words and mathematical expressions), like FORTRAN (Formula Translator) and COBOL (Common Business Oriented Language) were developed, making computers more accessible to scientists

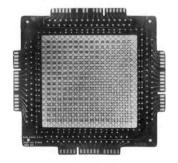

A magnetic core.

Source: Hagley Museum and Library.

First Generation: Vaccum Tubes   Second Generation: Transistors

1951   1958   1959   1963

and businesses. It is estimated that the number of computers in the United States during this time grew from around 2,500 to around 18,000.

The Third Generation (1964–1979)   In the mid-1960s, the next major transition in computer technology occurred. Individual transistors were replaced by **integrated circuits**—thousands of tiny transistors etched on a small silicon chip. The chips saved space, did away with the need to hand-wire and solder the transistors into circuits, and most important, were even more reliable and faster than transistors. (You will learn more about chips in Chapter 3.) Magnetic core memories began to give way to a new form, *metal oxide semiconductor (MOS) memory*, which like integrated circuits, used silicon-backed chips. The increased memory capacity and processing power made possible the development of *operating systems*—special programs that help the various elements of the computer work together to process information. (You will learn more about operating systems in Chapter 7.) The faster chips also made development of minicomputers and later, even smaller microcomputers, possible. Programming languages like BASIC were developed, making programming even easier to do, and the number and variety of languages began to rapidly increase. The first telecommunications satellite was launched, ushering in a new era of communication by microwaves, and telecommunications using coaxial cables continued to improve.

First integrated circuit.
Source: Courtesy of Texas Instruments, Inc.

The Fourth Generation (1979–Present)   The hallmarks of fourth-generation computers are **large-scale integrated circuits** and **very-large-scale integrated circuits** (**LSICs** and **VLSICs**), containing hundreds of thousands to over a million transistors on a single tiny chip, and **microprocessors.** Microprocessors contain memory, logic, and control circuits (an entire CPU) all on a single chip, and together with VLSICs helped fuel a continuing trend toward *microminiaturization*. During this time, semiconductor memories increased memory size and speed at ever-decreasing prices. *Personal computers,* like the Apple Macintosh and IBM PC, were introduced and quickly became popular for both business and personal use. *Fourth-generation-language software* products, such as dBASE, Lotus 1-2-3, and WordPerfect, that allowed persons without any technical background to use a computer also found a ready market.[2]

From this brief history of information technologies and systems, you can see a progression in which the predominant technologies of civilization were applied to very practical problems of writing, calculating, and recording information. Not only have information systems been with us throughout history, but they can also be used, as the story "Rediscovering Columbus by Exploring a New World" illustrates, to help us discover our history.

A microprocessor.
Source: Courtesy of Intel Corporation.

Third Generation: Integrated Circuits

Fourth Generation: LSICs and VLSICs

| 1964 | 1979 | Present |

What do you think about Christopher Columbus? Was he a courageous explorer, a heroic discoverer of America? Or was he a greedy exploiter of the world that he "found," without any thought for the Native Americans who already lived here?

The 500th anniversary of the voyage of the Niña, Pinta, and Santa Maria across the Atlantic in October 1492 has rekindled interest and controversy about Columbus. Today, new information systems are helping illuminate the issues for both serious scholars and schoolchildren.

Ten years ago, if a researcher wanted to look at original documents or artwork relating to Columbus's exploration of America, he or she probably would have had to journey to Seville, Spain, where the Spanish government has kept its archives since 1785. Now though, through the use of an imaging system like the one you will read about later in this chapter, nine million pages of handwritten documents and artwork such as letters and maps have been optically scanned and transferred onto 450 optical storage disks.

Source: North Wind Picture Archive.

2.2 Information Technology and Systems Today

As they have throughout history, information technology and systems today continue to play a vital role in businesses, government, and other organizations. Indeed, in America, organizations without computers are now generally the exception. Because information systems are so closely tied to organizations, you should know something about organizations—what they do, how they do it, and what they look like in a formal sense.

How Organizations Work

Organizations are entities built to accomplish goals through the creation of products or services. The goals may be profits, more converts to a religious group, or military conquest. The products and services can vary from automobiles to psychological counseling. By coordinating and planning the work of many people through teamwork, organizations can accomplish much more than the same number of people working alone. As you have seen, from the beginning of history, organizations have relied on information technologies and systems of one sort or another—from writing and hand calculation of accounts to computers and electronic accounting.

The optical disks are in Spain, but today's explorers don't have to cross the ocean to get to them. Instead, they merely have to travel to the Huntington Library in San Marino, California. There, the library's network of IBM PS/2 personal computers can be connected via satellite to an IBM Application System/400 computer in Seville, which then provides access to the material on the optical disks. Users can search for documents they want in a variety of ways. Once they've found what they are looking for, it can be viewed either on a high-resolution display screen or printed out on a laser printer.

Multimedia systems that can integrate written text, sound, and moving images have also been tapped as an exciting new resource that can be harnessed for educational purposes. A multimedia product called "Columbus: Encounter, Discovery and Beyond" enables students to look through Columbus's diaries, see and hear what native American culture was like in 1492, watch an interview with a 14th-generation granddaughter, and link different ideas (like "Columbus" and "religion") to discover how they are connected. It contains 2,600 text articles, 5 hours of video images, 1,800 still images, 200 maps, a 20,000-word dictionary, and 7 hours of digital-based audio (both narration and music). Students can explore text, video, and graphics (all often accompanied by sound) with the click of a mouse.

Sources: Based on Daly, James, "Old World Meets New in Optical Storage Project," *Computerworld,* April 6, 1992; Stewart, Doug, "'Totally Awesome'—Multimedia," *Think,* No. 2, 1992.

Critical Thinking Questions

1 Why do you think that the information systems described here might make it easier to learn about a subject? How do they differ from merely picking up a book and reading?

2 Identify the forms of sensing, communication, analyzing, and display technologies used by the Huntington Library system, and then describe the system's input, process, and output.

3 Pick a favorite person or subject from history. If you were asked to develop a multimedia product about that person or subject, what kinds of things might you include?

Organizations build information systems for two primary reasons: (1) to manage and control the internal groups and forces used to create products and services and (2) to manage and control external groups and forces. An external group or force can be anything from customers who buy the products, to government regulators who want monthly reports, to irate citizens protesting pollution at a factory.

Business organizations have four internal functions they must manage and control (see Figure 2.2). They usually have a production group that produces the products or services, a sales and marketing group that sells the product, a human resources group that recruits and trains workers, and a finance and accounting group that seeks out funds to pay for all these activities and keeps track of the accounts. Even government organizations often have a sales and marketing group to encourage citizens to use government services. Surrounding the organization is an environment (usually supportive but sometimes hostile) of customers, competitors, government officials, and the public.

Figure 2.2

Activities in an Organization

Business organizations perform four functions: production, sales, human resources, and finance. Organizations reside in an environment composed of government regulators, customers, competitors, and other interested parties.

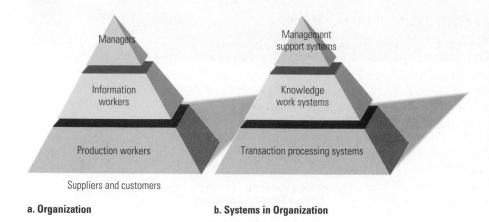

Figure 2.3
Organizations and Information Systems
(a) Organizations are hierarchical and arranged in three tiers: management, information workers, and production workers.
(b) Each level in an organization has specific kinds of information systems.

Most organizations are hierarchical: they are arranged in an ascending order of power, pay, and privilege (see Figure 2.3a). From the top down, the three major levels in an organization are management, information workers, and production workers.

The management group is a small cadre of people whose job is to control existing operations and plan for the future. Just below this level is a complex group called information workers. Most members of this level are clerical workers who process information—they write letters, keep track of customers, produce lists, and plan meetings. However, a substantial and growing proportion of this group are professional and technical workers: college-educated engineers, technicians, doctors, lawyers, and some managers who create new information and knowledge for the organization based on their special expertise. This new information and knowledge is then used to create new products and services.

The last level in the organization is the production group, which actually produces the product or service. They could be factory workers, clerks at an airline reservation office, or claims-processing workers at an insurance company.

Types of Information Systems in Organizations

With this background in organizations, it is much easier to understand the kinds of information systems you will find in today's organizations. For each level in the organization, and for each functional area, you will find a unique class of information system: for instance, **management support systems (MSS)** serve management's need to control and plan the organization; **knowledge work systems (KWS)** serve the needs of clerical and professional workers to process and create information and knowledge; and **transaction processing systems (TPS)** serve the needs of production workers who must deal with thousands, sometimes millions, of transactions with customers and suppliers (see Figure 2.3b).

From what we have said so far, you can see that most organizations do not have just one information system but instead often have several. In fact, large organizations can have hundreds of information systems. Generally, most organizations do not have just one big computer; instead, they have information stored in several and sometimes hundreds, or even thousands, of computers.

We examine information systems used in the business world in much greater depth in Part Five of this book, but let's take a first look now at some examples of the three basic kinds of systems.

Transaction Processing Systems: The Internal Revenue Service

Many organizations have to keep track of thousands or even millions of transactions per day. What are transactions? Every time you deposit or withdraw money from a bank, every time you sign up for a college course, and every time you receive a paycheck, a transaction has occurred. **Transactions** are all those recorded events that surround the production, distribution, sale, and transportation of goods and services. Transactions are the basis of organizations, and the information systems that keep track of transactions are the most fundamental. Without transaction processing systems (TPS), an organization would have a very difficult time functioning.

There are two kinds of TPS. The Internal Revenue Service system we describe in this section is a **batch processing system:** taxpayers submit tax forms, they are collected into a batch, and then processed in a batch sometime later. The other kind of TPS is **on-line transaction processing.** An airline reservation system, for instance, must process the request for an airline seat immediately. On-line systems are typical of reservation systems, banking systems, stock trading systems, and other systems where an instant response is needed.

The Internal Revenue Service (IRS) is the U.S. federal tax agency; it collects taxes from 130 million individuals and 70 million business and other institutions. These 200 million tax return transactions each year add up to a staggering 1.7 billion pages of paper. In addition to this paper blizzard, the IRS takes in 170 million tax payments amounting to $1 trillion dollars. Needless to say, the IRS has enormous transaction management problems. It developed a number of manual and automated TPS in the 1960s and 1970s to cope with these problems, but now these systems are outdated and being replaced.

The IRS Today   Here's how the IRS's current TPS works:

Step 1: Most taxpayers fill in their returns by hand and then file their returns by mail. Four million returns are also filed electronically.

Step 2: The returns are opened and sorted alphabetically by last name.

Step 3: The returns are read manually and edited for errors, incorrect forms, and legibility.

Step 4: Information from each return is input into a database kept on a mainframe computer. This database contains files: a master taxpayer file containing basic identifying information like name and address, an account file containing information on the taxpayer's account, and several others.

Step 5: The computer performs some of its own error checking, and detected errors are printed out and corrected manually and then re-entered.

Step 6: The returns are sorted electronically by TAX ID account number. Each taxpayer's account is updated with the latest information, and this is then stored on the mainframe computer database.

Step 7: Some returns are selected for auditing on a random basis, and some returns are selected because of suspicious errors.

Step 8: Paper returns are filed in cabinets.

Step 9: Tax refunds or notices, bills, and correspondence are posted.

Step 10: Using the latest information, IRS tax agents retrieve information from the mainframe database through remote terminals and desktop PCs to answer taxpayer questions and check the files for fraudulent returns.

Step 11: Some information is summarized and reports generated for managers or transferred electronically to management information systems.

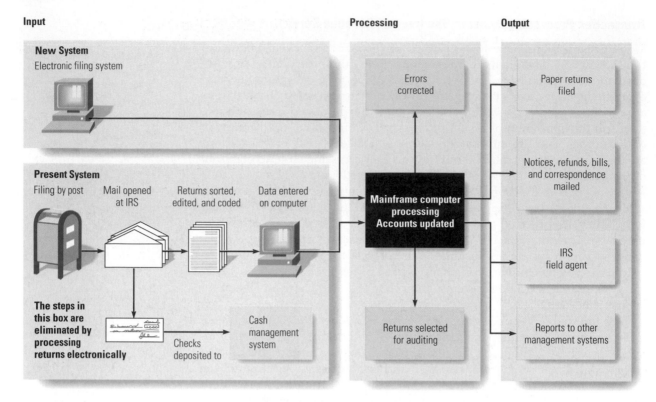

Input   **Processing**   **Output**

Figure 2.4

The New Electronic Filing System and Present IRS System Compared

The existing IRS system mixes manual and computerized procedures. The numerous steps result in a greater possibility of errors occurring along the way. The new electronic filing system will require certain taxpayers to submit tax returns in electronic form. Using a modem attached to a personal computer, these taxpayers will send their tax information directly to the IRS computers, eliminating manual input and sorting.

Source: Adapted from *Tax System Modernization: Input Processing Initiative,* General Accounting Office, December 1990.

These steps are illustrated in Figure 2.4.

In addition to the familiar types of information technologies used to create the information system, and the familiar input, output, and process logic of information systems, the IRS TPS introduces you to a new concept: a computer **database** and **files.** You will learn more about how data is organized into files and databases in Chapter 4, but we give you the basics here. The IRS database consists of several interconnected files (see Figure 2.5). Each file contains a collection of **records,** which identify a person, place, or thing. Each record is composed of a number of **fields,** which are used to record information about that person, place, or thing.

As you can see, the basic idea of a database is to maintain lists of people, places, and things. A great part of business, government, and other organizational work involves maintaining lists: lists of customers, clients, prospects, cases, parishioners, and so forth. Once information is captured by a database, it can be manipulated, processed, and reused for a variety of purposes. For instance, once you have a list of customers within a database, you can have the list arranged in alphabetical order to help you call them on the telephone. Later, you might want the list organized by ZIP code so that you can send them letters efficiently. A database can do these tasks automatically and very quickly.

The IRS Tomorrow   Now 30 years old, the IRS's existing transaction processing system is barely adequate for the job: it is slow, labor intensive, error prone, and very expensive to operate. The IRS is spending $8 billion over the next 10 years to bring the system up to date. Two major systems being built or planned are the Electronic Filing System and the Document Processing System. The new Electronic Filing System will require businesses, and strongly encourage individuals, to submit their returns in electronic form so that the current labor-intensive data entry tasks can be eliminated (see Figure 2.4). This means tax filers will be required to have a computer of some sort or have their tax preparer use a computer to generate the tax return.

The planned Document Processing System will handle all returns that are not electronically filed. The Document Processing System is an *imaging system:* it will use image scanners to digitize incoming forms and convert them to computer images that can be stored electronically (see Figure 2.6). This will reduce the number of paper records, allow electronic forms to be fed directly into the mainframe computer, and permit IRS tax agents to retrieve taxpayer records on-screen in seconds rather than going to a filing cabinet.

Many other large organizations that have huge transaction processing loads are also looking to information technology as one element of a solution. Perhaps one of America's largest transaction processors is the postal system. As the story "Moving the Mail with People and Machines" illustrates, information technology will likely pay a large role in keeping the postal system inexpensive and highly efficient.

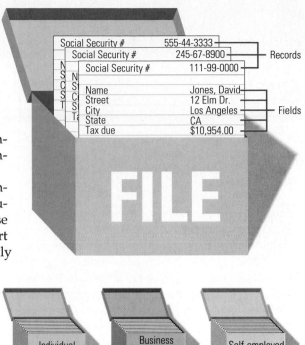

Figure 2.5
The IRS Database
The IRS keeps track of all its transactions through the use of a number of interconnected files called a database.

Management Support Systems: Au Bon Pain

There are many different kinds of management support systems (MSS), but they all share a common focus: they are designed to help managers monitor organizational performance, control the organization by making changes, and plan for the future. A good example is the MSS built by Au Bon Pain.

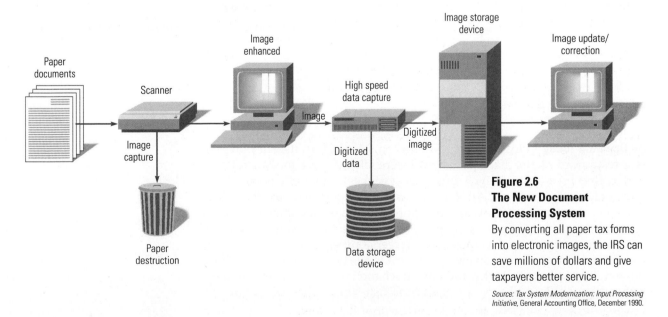

Figure 2.6
The New Document Processing System
By converting all paper tax forms into electronic images, the IRS can save millions of dollars and give taxpayers better service.

Source: Tax System Modernization: Input Processing Initiative, General Accounting Office, December 1990.

Moving the Mail with People and Machines

Seeing what has been received in the mail is an important moment in the average person's day, yet we rarely give much thought to how the mail manages to reach us. Considering that a whopping 555 million pieces of mail travel through the United States Postal Service *each day*, it's amazing that the mail makes it to its intended destination as quickly and as often as it does.

An organization like the U.S. Postal Service would have a difficult time without the help of information technology. Right now, the Postal Service makes use of a digital sensing device called a multi-line optical character reader. The reader can "scan," or read, typewritten or machine-printed words on envelopes at a rate of 13 pieces of mail per second. The machine then prints a bar-coded version of the ZIP code on the envelope. The envelope is then sent along to a bar-code sorter, which can read the bar code and sort the mail accordingly. (Here's an interesting side note. If you're wondering why you're seeing fewer red or other dark-colored greeting card envelopes at Christmas time or Valentine's Day, it's because

the Postal Service has asked card manufacturers to phase them out. The readers and sorting machines have a tough time picking up ZIP codes and bar codes against dark backgrounds.)

The Postal Service would like to automate its mail sorting system even further. The present system can handle typewritten or machine-printed envelopes but spits out handwritten addresses. Unlike humans, who are able to read and understand handwriting in an infinite number of styles because they are able to recognize the fundamental components that make up a letter or number, the computers hooked to the optical scanners can still only understand exact replicas of what they have been programmed to recognize. Researchers are hoping to use concepts like "neural networks," derived from work on artificial intelligence (see Chapter 14), to come up with a workable system.

The handwritten envelopes are currently funneled to a postal worker who codes the letters using a special keyboard-operated sorting machine. The Postal Service would like to

A new system for moving the mail.

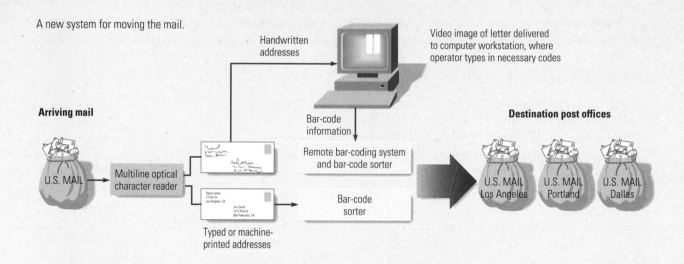

Au Bon Pain Today   Headquartered in Boston, Massachusetts, Au Bon Pain is a restaurant chain that specializes in French cafeteria foods: croissant and coffee breakfasts, french bread sandwiches, and light meals. With gross sales of $68 million, Au Bon Pain is a relatively small fast-food firm, with 85 cafeterias and 22 franchised stores. Its small size imposes special constraints when it comes to information systems: they must be inexpensive but just as powerful as those of its larger competitors.

For restaurant chain managers, the most important questions are who is buying what, when, and why, and how much money do we make from these transactions? Why sell a lot of plain tuna fish sandwiches when you can

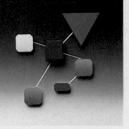

work to the sorting machine, which can then print the information on the letter (see Illustration). This system has already been tried successfully on an experimental basis in a few post offices.

Why does further automation of its mail sorting system matter to the Postal Service? For starters, consider that it costs around $3 to machine-sort 1,000 letters; when postal workers must do it, it costs around $40. The Postal Service also has plans to eliminate at least 50,000 jobs by 1995. Using the remote-computer network system just described removes the need for workers to be physically close to the mail; instead, the jobs can be consolidated among fewer, centrally located workers. Ultimately, much of the work performed by present-day keyboard operators would be done by the automated handwriting-recognition system. The Postal Service hopes that these innovations will help stem the losses that it has been incurring during the past several years.

Source: Based on Stiz, Gary; "Zip Code Breakers," *Scientific American*, February, 1993; Race, Tim, "Moving Scribbled Mail Along," *New York Times*, May 27, 1992.

Critical Thinking Questions

1 This story illustrates how the use of information technology by an organization may benefit some (here, the general public) while perhaps harming others (workers who might lose their jobs). If you were the head of the Postal Service, what would you say to support this decision? If you were the leader of the American Postal Worker's Union, how would you argue against it?

2 What other kinds of businesses could use handwriting-recognition technology? Think of two or three examples, and explain why you think the technology would be a valuable addition to the businesses' present information systems.

3 Compare the IRS's systems (old and new) with the Postal Service's systems. What elements do they have in common? How do they differ?

A bar-code mail sorting machine can sort 35,000 pieces of bar-coded mail per hour.

Source: Courtesy of Martin Marietta Corporation.

further automate this step by replacing the physical channeling of letters with a still video image of the letter delivered via a computer network to an operator sitting at a personal computer. The person can then read the address and input the relevant code, which can then be transferred back via the net-

make much more money selling a fancy French croissant? With this knowledge, managers can focus the organization's efforts. Originally, Au Bon Pain relied on its store managers to fill out lengthy end-of-the-day reports on how many items sold and at what price. These reports were mailed to headquarters, where the data was input into a minicomputer, which in turn spilled out reams of paper reports. A month or so after the sale was made, headquarters might have some idea of what sold and how much money they made. The store manager might get the reports even later. In today's competitive environment, this is not good enough.

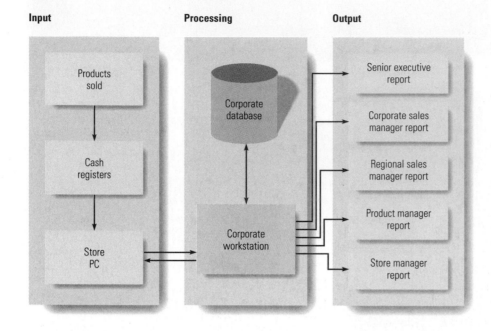

Figure 2.7
Au Bon Pain's MSS System
Au Bon Pain's information system records information on individual purchases in each store. The information eventually arrives at corporate headquarters where it is analyzed and distributed to managers at various levels of the company.

To get really up-to-date information, Au Bon Pain created its Retail Operations Management System (see Figure 2.7). Now sales managers at headquarters know that last week about 22,000 customers visited Au Bon Pain in Harvard Square, 5,500 of them before 11 A.M. This breakfast crowd paid $1.86 on average, about 22 percent of that for croissants. The store managers also have access to this information within a week of sales. How can managers at all levels of the company know all this so fast? Here's how:

Step 1: A customer buys some food—you can't have a business without a sale!

Step 2: Cash registers in each restaurant feed information on sales of over 300 items to a personal computer in the restaurant. The PC contains a database that stores this transaction information (each sale from coffee to extra cheese) and stores other information in related files (the inventory of cheese and coffee).

Step 3: At the end of each day, a PC at headquarters uses a modem to call each of the 75 restaurants and transfer the information on sales to headquarters.

Step 4: At the end of each day, the local restaurant PCs print out reports for the local store manager on sales of each item.

Step 5: At headquarters, the information is stored in a database until the end of the week, and then on Friday, a series of management reports are printed.

Step 6: The reports are distributed to PCs at headquarters and displayed in spreadsheet format (a spreadsheet is an accountant's way of presenting accounting information in columns and rows) using a software program called Lotus 1-2-3.

Step 7: Reports on comparative store performance are distributed electronically to each store manager showing last week's results of all restaurants in the region. Figure 2.8 shows you some of the reports produced by An Bon Pain's MSS.

Figure 2.8
Reports Produced by Au Bon Pain's MSS
Au Bon Pain's MSS can put out a variety of reports
(a) The Retail Operating Report shows detailed breakfast, lunch, and dinner sales for all stores during various accounting periods and compares actual sales to last year's results.
(b) The Executive Summary shows the overall sales and costs at all stores.
(c) The Product Mix Report shows the detailed sales of various items both for this year and the previous year.
(d) The R & D Test Products Report shows the sales results for new products being tested.

a.

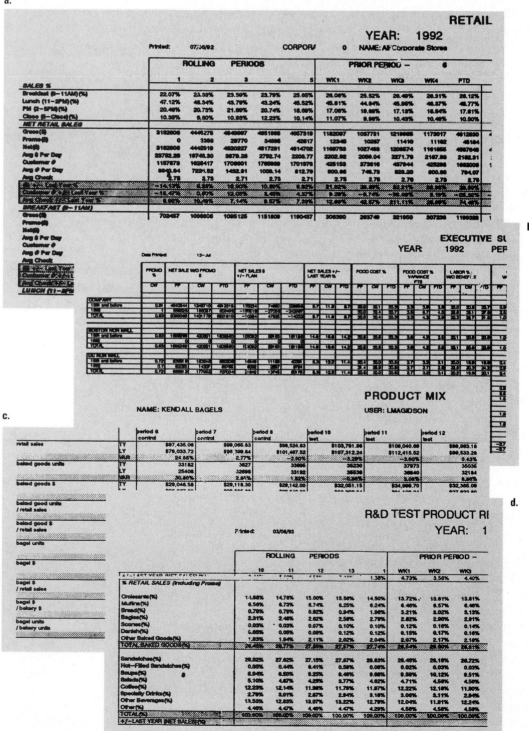

In this small corporate system, there are all the familiar technologies that we described in Chapter 1—sensing, communication, analyzing, and display. As in the IRS case, the role of a database is very important. Storing, sorting, selecting, updating, retrieving, and posting (displaying) information—all typical capabilities of a database—play a very important role in management. Indeed, management is impossible without systems to do this work in a timely fashion. Au Bon Pain needs to be able to respond to marketing challenges from McDonald's and Burger King. So it needs information on its own sales quickly.

Au Bon Pain Tomorrow   Au Bon Pain is planning a number of enhancements to its system for the 1990s. It would like to give managers more flexible access to the information stored in the MSS and more powerful tools to analyze relationships in the information. For instance, what impact do coffee sales have on pastry sales? If the price of a cup of coffee is dropped 10 percent, does this induce more customers to walk in and increase sales of breakfast rolls?

Further, there is no reason store managers must wait to the next week to obtain management reports on the prior week's results. It is possible to change the entire reporting system to a daily basis. For instance, Tuesday morning, managers at all levels could look at Monday's results.

To achieve these changes, Au Bon Pain is building a more powerful headquarters network to share more information among managers and increasing the power of software at each manager's desk so that they can analyze and display the information. Of course, managers at all levels will have to have more training to achieve these objectives.

Knowledge Work Systems: Young and Rubicam

Knowledge work systems (KWS) are used by information workers to help deal with problems requiring knowledge or technical expertise. They are used by engineers for computer-aided design, by scientists doing scientific research, by graphic artists creating computer art, and by clerical workers putting out letters and brochures. KWS can also be used to increase the productivity of information workers in an office.

Word processing programs, databases, and spreadsheets are the most common computer applications today in all organizations. They also form an important component of many knowledge work systems. But there is more to organizational life than memos, lists, and numbers. How about messages, drawings, and notes, for example? (One of the most successful products of the 1980s was 3M Corporation's Post-it Note Pads—the little yellow notepads with stickum on the back. Walk into any administrator's or secretary's office today, and you will likely find a large number of yellow Post-it notes on desktops, walls, and bulletin boards.) What about mail and correspondence, or telephone calls to customers? Or how about sending messages to people you are working with on a project? Offices are filled with telephone messages, letters, and notes that can be extremely useful for groups of people who work together in organizations.

Until recently, there was very little information technology support for groups of people working together in an organization. Most PCs stood alone on isolated desktops, helping individuals, but not directly supporting groups of people working together. But a new kind of knowledge work system that uses software called *groupware* is starting to address this problem. Let's look at one example of how it is being used.

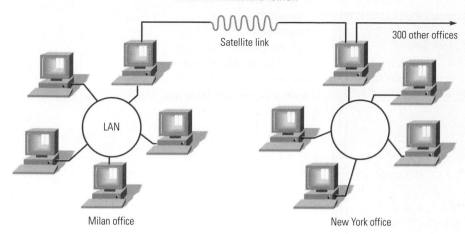

Figure 2.9
Young and Rubicam's
Knowledge Work System

Young and Rubicam is one of the world's largest advertising agencies. A privately held corporation with approximately $7.5 million in revenues and 12,000 employees (half of whom work overseas), Young and Rubicam has 300 offices in 60 countries worldwide.

Despite its size, Young and Rubicam's primary business is based on very personal relationships. Business clients work closely with small teams of Y & R professional account representatives, graphic artists, and media analysts who provide public relations, advertising, market research, and promotional services. Much of the business involves creating graphics: pictures, drawings, and line art. Just keeping track of clients around the globe is very difficult: a client might be working with a Y & R group in the Milan office for Italian sales and with a group in New York handling U.S. sales, and neither Y & R group might know about the other or be able to communicate easily. But using a new product called Lotus Notes from Lotus Development Corporation, Y & R has been able to solve some of these problems. Here's how it works:

Step 1: A copy of Lotus Notes is installed on desktop PCs in all Y & R offices. Every user of Notes is greeted by the same *graphical user interface,* which allows users to interact with Notes using a mouse to click on pictures or symbols (*icons*) that appear on the screen (Figure 2.10).

Step 2: An account agent in Milan is working with a group in the New York office on a sales report for the United Enterprises account. The agent in Milan uses a computer mouse to choose the Discussion icon. There, she can review the comments of all Y & R people working on the United Enterprises account.

Step 3: She wants to respond to comment 4, so she clicks on the mail icon, writes a response, and sends it to all members of the workgroup in both Milan and New York. She includes a pie chart of Regional Sales for United Enterprises.

Step 4: The message is sent to New York in a few minutes via Notes' electronic mail facility, and the use of a global communications network (a communications network that uses telephone lines or satellites to connect computers located around the world) (see Figure 2.9).

a.

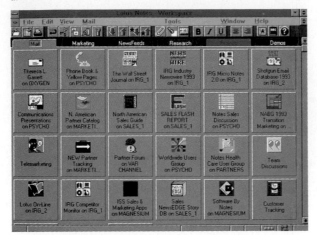

Figure 2.10
Lotus Notes
Lotus Notes helps different Y&R teams to work together to service clients. Here you see the opening screen and an incoming customer document screen.
Source: Courtesy of Lotus Development Corporation.

b.

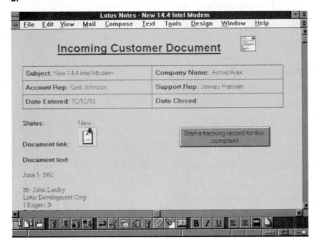

Step 5: The agent in Milan also wants to know who is handling United Enterprises in London. By clicking on the Client Tracking icon, she can find the contact in the London office handling the client.

Step 6: In New York, a Y & R account representative working on the United Enterprises account signs onto his computer in the morning. (New York is six hours behind Milan.) He reads the message from Milan and responds.

Step 7: Headquarters in New York can create a new database on clients, and replicate the database in all 300 offices worldwide where local employees fill in information on local clients. This information can be automatically posted back to New York whenever requested. (Other built-in functions of Lotus Notes include a document library, a status report feature that allows project team members to stay up to date, and a newswire template to disseminate news throughout the organization.)

With the power of information technologies growing rapidly, organizations are learning that it may not be necessary for everyone to be in the office when working and that many employees can work productively at home or on the road. In fact, as the story "Working at Home" discusses, millions of people already do a substantial amount of work at home using information technology.

Working at Home

Are you the kind of person who might do better outside an office environment? Perhaps you have obligations that require you to stay at or near home for all or part of the day, but you would still like to keep working for your present employer. Or maybe you are an entrepreneur at heart, and want to run your own show, but you don't have much money and need to start small.

If you recognize yourself in any of the above (and even if you don't) you might want to consider working from your home. More and more people are doing it: according to a recent survey, more than 39 million people in the labor force did all or part of their paid work at home in 1992. Some are running their own businesses, whereas others are on a company payroll. No matter what the type of work, information technology—a computer equipped with a modem, a fax machine, and a telephone hooked to an answering machine—is becoming essential. In fact, over half of those who did work at home in 1992 had a personal computer to help them.

Let's look at one couple that decided to use information technology to conduct a very sophisticated form of business—commodities trading—from their home in the rolling New Jersey countryside.

Michael Berger and Polly Siegal used to commute 50 miles each way to their brokerage firm in New York City. They felt there had to be a better way and decided to strike out on their own. They now have seven personal computers hooked to four display monitors. Most people who have satellite dishes use them to get television signals, but Michael and Polly use the dish on their roof to gain access to information on the Dow Jones Industrial average, current bond prices, changing commodities indexes, and other financial information. Michael has created a software program that incorporates the various principles that he has used over the years in making trading decisions and automates them. For instance, when the program detects a pricing trend that indicates that a certain commodity should be purchased or sold, it causes the computer to make an audible beep to alert them. The program also allows them to keep track of how much money they are making or losing at any time during the day. With the help of information technology, they are doing as well at home as they were when they worked at the Wall Street brokerage house.

Even if the work you do at home is a lot less complicated than commodities trading, you still need information technology to stay competitive and get the work done in the most efficient manner possible. Businesses as distinct as bookkeeping, pet-sitting, custom crafts, and almost anything else you can think of will all benefit from the advantages that information technology can provide.

Sources: Based on Lewis, Peter H., "More Home Workers and More Machines in Their Offices," *New York Times,* May 24, 1992; Race, Tim, "Going It Alone, Bit by Bit," *New York Times Magazine,* December 2, 1990; 1992 Telecommuting Survey, LINK Resources Corporation.

Critical Thinking Questions

1　Discuss how advances in information technology over the last 50 years made the choice by Michael and Polly to work from home possible.

2　What are some of the drawbacks that might be associated with working at home? How might the disadvantages that you identify be alleviated?

3　Do you agree or disagree with the following statement: "The computer, as an extension of our brain, has become as indispensable to operating a business as the telephone, as an extension of our voice." Give at least two real-world examples to support your position.

2.3　Information Technology and Systems: A Taste of the Future

We have taken a broad historical perspective in this chapter, beginning with the first writing systems circa 3000 B.C. up to present-day knowledge work systems. But where is this leading? Where will we be in the future? What new technologies are coming along, and what kinds of changes will they produce?

We've chosen three emerging technologies—wireless mobile computing, multimedia computing, and inexpensive supercomputers—that have the potential to change the way we live, work, learn, shop, and relax. These technologies are being developed today and require no further technological breakthroughs to achieve success. They are technologies that will have widespread applications, affecting a broad spectrum of individuals, businesses, and society. After looking at each of these technologies, we finish up with some speculation about the changes they may hold in store for us.

Wireless Mobile Computing

By the year 2000, a new generation of portable digital devices that combines computing and two-way communications capabilities will be transforming life as we know it today. You will not only be able to make and receive telephone calls while on the go but also send and receive electronic mail and facsimiles, work on databases and spreadsheets, receive stock quotes, as well as send any work you do back to the computer in your office. No longer will you have to worry about missing that crucial business message: it will find you no matter where you are. And when you're finished working, you may be able to use the device to read a book, play a computer game, or listen to music off a miniature CD.

Making all this possible are small wireless personal communicators (also called personal digital assistants or even just wireless widgets) that will use new radio and satellite digital communications networks to transmit and receive data from computers anywhere in the world.

Today, a number of precursors are starting to show up on the market. The Federal Communications Commission has already set aside a part of the radio spectrum for wireless data transmissions. AT&T plans to take advantage of this with the EO Personal Communicator. Developed for AT&T by EO Inc., a Silicon Valley think tank, the 2.2-pound device looks like a thin tablet. It contains a powerful new AT&T microprocessor called Hobbit and allows users to input data using a pen. The basic unit can be equipped with a cellular modem for the exchange of electronic mail and faxes and a cellular telephone module (see photo). Apple Computer Corporation also has a personal digital assistant on the market. Called the Newton Message Pad, it weighs less than a pound and can fit into a pocket (see photo). Newton contains roughly as

You can use Apple's Newton Message Pad to store handwritten notes as well as send and receive faxes.

Source: Courtesy of Apple Computer, Inc.

The EO Personal Communicator combines fax, E-mail, cellular telephone, and personal computing capabilities.

Source: Courtesy of AT&T Archives.

much power as a small PC and can perform such functions as recording handwritten notes, faxing documents, and storing telephone numbers. Eventually, it will also be able to send and receive data over wireless networks. And Skytel Corporation offers SkyWord: a wireless paging and message system that allows travelers anywhere in the continental United States to send and receive electronic messages up to 80 letters long (see photo).

By the year 2000, analysts expect a $3.5 trillion industry combining computing, communications, and entertainment with handheld, wireless devices. Although expensive now, costs are expected to drop radically as the technology becomes more advanced. This means that by the year 2000 people will no longer need to remain tied to their desks or offices to take advantage of information technology and information systems. This new generation of information technology will allow our lives to be more mobile than ever, freeing people to work when and where they choose.

Skytel's SkyWord wireless paging and messaging system allows you to send and receive E-mail anywhere in the U.S. Actual size of the unit is about 4 inches.

Source: Courtesy of Skytel.

Multimedia Computing

Multimedia computing combines video, text, and sound with the ability of computers to store, retrieve, and process information. (You will learn how in Chapter 5.) Today's computers require extensive and expensive add-on equipment to create rudimentary multimedia systems. But by the year 2000, all computers, regardless of size, will have built-in capabilities that allow them to marry text, numbers, and graphics with music, full-motion and still-frame video (snapshots), animation, and voice messages. Couple multimedia with techniques that allow the user to interact with the material presented, and you have a technology that can be as mesmerizing as television, yet, at the same time, pushes the user to become intellectually engaged.

How will multimedia technology affect information systems? Right now, it is being used mostly for educational and training purposes. Interactive multimedia means that textbooks could be presented on a series of CD-ROM optical storage disks. Get ready for textbooks that contain videos, color pictures, recordings of authors and other professors, or people being interviewed in addition to regular text. You will be able to check how well you have learned by calling up on-screen quizzes. If you come across a concept that interests you, you will be able to browse on-screen for related topics. Publishers expect multimedia to revolutionize the market by the year 2000, if not sooner.

In the business world, Lotus Development Corp. now offers Multimedia Smarthelp, which allows users to call up videos to learn how to use Lotus 1-2-3. Organizations like hospitals use multimedia products to help train their doctors and nurses to do new procedures. And Diane St. Martin, president of CDT Micrographics in Exeter, New Hampshire, has created a multimedia papermill factory simulation. The interactive application gives trainees a chance to run their own plant without risking on-the-job disaster. Today's multimedia products can also create powerful presentations that mix slides with moving pictures, music, and narration.[4]

By the year 2000, multimedia will have become a general-purpose business tool. When multimedia technology is coupled with the new powerful emerging digital communications networks, desktop-to-desktop videoconferencing and file sharing become feasible and will radically change the way people across organizations meet and interact with one another. Right now, AT&T Bell Laboratories is developing Rapport, a multimedia conference system that integrates telephones, video, and computers.

a.   b.

Figure 2.11

Multimedia Computing

(a) In 1992, Apple computers were the first to come equipped with software (called QuickTime) and some of the hardware needed to play multimedia disks containing text, graphics, video, and sound. Microsoft Corporation and other leading computer companies are currently developing multimedia standards so that future PCs will also be able to play and even author multimedia presentations. **(b)** IBM spent $5 million to create the multimedia program on Columbus and the discovery of the New World that you read about earlier in this chapter.

Source: Courtesy of Radius; Courtesy of IBM's Multimedia Publishing Studio.

Figure 2.11 gives you some idea of the kinds of multimedia devices and applications that are or soon will be available.

Inexpensive Supercomputers

By the year 2000, if history is any guide, the cost-effectiveness of computers will have increased a thousand times over 1993's capabilities. Three million transistors could be put on a single 1/4-inch "super" chip. This would exceed the computing power of several supercomputers today. Supercomputers today cost about $20 million. But by the year 2000, these super chips could cost less than $100, and a complete supercomputer around $2,500, or about the same as a mid-priced personal computer today. Of course, the personal computer of today will cost less than $100 and fit in your shirt pocket or purse, and you will buy it at Kmart or a supermarket. These may sound like fantastic predictions, but in fact they are modest projections based on the historical rate of increasing power and the declining cost of computer chips.

What would ordinary citizens possibly do with the power of a supercomputer? The same was said of illiterate people and books in the 15th century. For one thing, inexpensive supercomputing power will make computers with voice and handwriting recognition capabilities available to the common person. As a result, computers will be far easier to use and much more accessible to the ordinary individual. Imagine having a computer that you can use as your personal assistant, as in, "Pay the bills," "Call the doctor and tell her I will be late," or "Give me a list from the local library dealing with computers in education."

And how will the availability of inexpensive supercomputers affect business information systems? One effect will be to make product design and redesign much easier: instead of taking years, companies can use supercomputing power to bring new products to market within months. Another effect will be to vastly increase the size of the customer databases that businesses can keep. This would allow businesses to conduct global direct marketing campaigns reaching millions of people around the world. Finally, with supercomputing power, the management of a business may be able to make better use of available information. Today, much of the data that businesses can generate is not useful for management because the computers at management's disposal do not have the speed and power needed to properly analyze the data. With a supercomputer, managers will have a tool that will allow them to uncover trends, make better decisions, and "micro-manage" the operations of the business.

Life in the Year 2000

The continuing revolution in information technologies and systems will have an enormous impact on our individual lives, organizations, and society as a whole. The three trends discussed in this chapter show you how information technology is causing the lines between computers, communications, entertainment, and publishing to become much less distinct. Education, small business, publishing, and entertainment as we know them today will all be affected. Even the role of something as familiar as the public library may change, as indicated in the story "The New Public Library."

With so much communication and computing power available, many changes become possible. For instance, college education might be transformed. With the electronic delivery of information, college human resource costs would fall because far fewer professors would be needed. Instead, master teaching professors could store their lectures on a multimedia CD-ROM and distribute them to colleges who would replay them for students. Colleges might also require less real estate as they focus more on the electronic delivery of knowledge. Lower tuitions might be the result.

Not only the delivery of education but also the delivery of information to the general public may be transformed. Electronic newspapers could be personalized according to each individual's tastes, supplemented with multimedia video clips, and then sent to personal communicators over wireless networks.

What about everyday business transactions? These might become more oriented toward at-home ordering as opposed to face-to-face transactions: why "go" to the store when everything you need can be displayed on your television set and then ordered from home? The concept of "local business" may become less relevant in a global marketplace where customers can communicate around the world to obtain the best prices and the best quality.

New information technologies are making the development of specialized electronic newspapers possible.

Source: Courtesy of CPC Communications, Inc.

Shelves of books, racks of newspapers and magazines, wooden cabinets filled with yellow catalog cards: these are fond and familiar sights to many. You may have taken it for granted, but the public library is an important backbone of American society. By serving as an egalitarian and free source of information, education, and culture, libraries have helped generations of Americans improve their economic and social position.

If you haven't been to your local library in a while, take some time to go and look around. Chances are, you might find some things you don't recognize. New information technology and systems are starting to make inroads into the way things are done at the library.

For starters, the card catalog may have disappeared, as it has at the White Plains Public Library in White Plains, New York. Instead, patrons access a database of book titles, subjects, and authors via computer. Some books themselves have been replaced by CD-ROM disks or a computer that has access to one or more of the many electronic reference databases that are now available. And though electronic books displayed on devices like Sony's Data Diskman haven't yet become widespread, it's quite possible that printed books will become obsolete not too far in the future. Consider also that in the future, with new communication technologies in place, people might be able to "go to the library" by using their television to browse the shelves of their local library.

What's your reaction? Do you like what you see happening at libraries around you and the prospects for a "paper-less," even "bookless," future? Perhaps you now find it easier to do research and are happy to have access to materials you might not have otherwise had. But before you make up your mind that these developments are all overwhelmingly positive, you might want to reflect on some of the following issues.

Right now, it doesn't cost you anything to find a book on a shelf and pick it up and read it. The library's not out to make a profit, but the providers of electronic reference databases certainly are, and access to their services isn't free. Who should pay? One approach that seems to be fair would be to charge the user of the services, on the theory that those who benefit from a service should pay for it. But think some more. Doesn't that help create two classes of people: the information rich, who can afford to pay for access to information, and the information poor, who cannot. How does this mesh with a public library's mission to be a "free university of the people"?

Now, expand the concept beyond the individual to whole communities. As we have said, knowledge is power, and new technology can help empower people by making information more accessible to them. However, what happens if that technology is available in affluent communities but not in others because residents cannot afford it? What effect do you think this might have on the class distinctions that still exist in our society today?

Source: Based on Alberts, Nuna, "Bionic Libraries," *Citizen Register,* April 12, 1992.

Personal communicators, multimedia computers, and inexpensive supercomputers each will play a role in increasing our ability to communicate, access new ideas, "see" and interact with different peoples in different parts of the globe, and express ourselves. Each has the ability to radically change life as we know it today.

In the next chapter, we take a closer look at the engine of information systems, the *central processing unit* (CPU). Almost all future advances in information technology depend at least in part on a steady increase in the power of the CPU and a steady decline in its price.

Summary

The History of Information Technology and Systems

▶ Information technology and systems include all the different means, methods, and tools that humans have used throughout history to help manage information, conduct business, communicate with others, and better understand the world.

▶ Input, process, and output have been fundamental concepts behind information systems since the beginning of recorded history.

▶ Writing, alphabets, paper and pen, the first books and libraries, early numbering systems, and tools like the abacus are all ways that humans in the premechanical age (3000 B.C.–1450 A.D.) tried to solve problems involving the representation, storage, and display of information.

▶ During the mechanical age (1450–1840), people began to use technology to build machines like the printing press and mechanical calculators to help improve access to information and increase the accuracy of available information.

▶ The electromechanical age (1840–1940) increased the need for more advanced technology to support more sophisticated information systems. Technologies that resulted from the harnessing of electricity (telegraphs, telephones, and electromechanical computing machines) helped meet this need.

▶ The last 50 years have focused on the use of electronic digital technology to create ever faster, more powerful, and more reliable technologies to help deal with the demands of our fast-paced world.

▶ The recent history of information technology is usually broken down into four generations, each distinguished by the main logic element used in computers. First-generation computers used vacuum tubes; second-generation computers replaced tubes with transistors; third-generation computers were made with integrated circuits (chips); and fourth-generation computers use LSI and VLSI circuits.

Information Technology and Systems Today

▶ A primary function of information systems is to help organizations accomplish their goals. Information systems help organizations manage and control the internal groups and forces used to create products and services and external forces like customers, citizens, and government regulators.

▶ Production, sales, human resources, and finance are the four basic internal functions of an organization. Organizations are usually arranged in three levels: management, information workers, and production workers. Each functional area and each level in an organization often has its own unique information systems.

▶ Transaction processing systems help workers manage transactions—the recorded events that surround the production, distribution, sale, and transportation of goods and services. TPS may either be a batch processing system (transactions handled in batches instead of immediately) or an on-line processing system (each transaction recorded at the time it occurs rather than later).

- All management support systems (MSS) share a common focus: they are designed to help managers monitor organizational performance, control the organization, and plan for the future.

- Knowledge work systems (KWS) help information workers solve questions requiring knowledge and technical expertise. Groupware is a kind of software used to help groups work together in an organization.

Information Technology and Systems: A Taste of the Future

- Wireless mobile computing, multimedia computing, and inexpensive supercomputers are three emerging technologies that will be affecting information systems, individual life, organizational life, and society by the year 2000.

Key Terms

Difference Engine
Analytical Engine
Mark I
electronic digital computer
ENIAC
EDVAC
stored program concept
EDSAC
UNIVAC
logic element
vacuum tubes
semiconductors
transistors
integrated circuits
large-scale integrated circuit
    (LSIC)

very-large-scale integrated circuits
    (VLSICs)
microprocessors
organizations
management support systems
    (MSS)
knowledge work systems (KWS)
transaction processing systems
    (TPS)
transactions
batch processing system
on-line transaction processing
database
files
records
fields

 Interactive Supplement

Review Questions

1 What were the key advances in the development of information technology and systems in the premechanical, mechanical, electromechanical, and electronic ages?

2 Pick one of the components of an information system (input, storage, communications, processing, or output) and trace the evolution of the various technologies used to accomplish that function through the four periods. What elements do later forms of the technology have in common with earlier forms?

3 Besides the differences in logic elements, what are the other characteristics that distinguish the four different generations of information technology?

4 What are the major functions and levels of an organization? How do the information systems used in an organization relate to those functions and levels?

5 What are some of the ways that data can be manipulated by the TPS used by the IRS?

6 How will the new systems planned by the IRS improve its transaction processing capabilities?

7 Why do managers need management support systems? Use the Au Bon Pain story to illustrate your reasons.

8 What elements do TPS, MSS, and KWS have in common?

9 In what category of system is the Postal Service's mail sorting system?

10 Describe the three emerging technologies that are likely to impact the way we do business and our everyday lives by the year 2000.

Problem-Solving and Skill-Building Exercises

1   Many different companies, such as IBM, Digital Equipment Corporation, Wang, Hewlett-Packard, Apple Computer Corporation, Microsoft Corporation, and Lotus Development Corporation, have made important contributions to the advancement of information technology. Pick one of these companies (or another company of your own choosing) and prepare a short written report (no more than 5 pages) tracing the company's history and the contribution it made to the progress of information technology.

2   Interview a local businessperson or administrator of some other type of organization (such as a school, community group, or club) and identify a transaction processing, management support, or knowledge work system he or she uses to conduct business or the organization's activities. Make a short oral presentation (no more than 5 minutes) or write a report (3–5 pages) that describes the system and suggests how information technology might be used to make the organization more efficient.

3   Choose an area of everyday life, such as education, law enforcement, banking, politics, transportation, or the environment. Then, with a group of other students, brainstorm to consider how this area of life might change by the year 2000 if the technological predictions made in this chapter come true. Create a list of possible changes, and present the results to your class for further discussion.

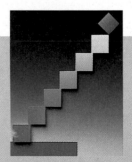

SKILL DEVELOPMENT

Becoming a Better Writer

In many of the exercises in this book, we ask you to write. Writing is one of the most important skills that you will need to develop if you want to succeed in life. The following article, "How to Write Clearly" by Edward T. Thompson, editor-in-chief of Reader's Digest, will give you some pointers on how to improve your writing skills.

Information technology can also help you become a better writer. Word processing programs make correcting and revising your work a snap. Many word processing programs also include a spelling checker, grammar checker, on-line dictionary, and thesaurus. The spelling checker identifies possible misspellings and offers corrections, and the grammar checker points out possible errors of grammar. The on-line dictionary helps you make sure you're using the right word, and the thesaurus provides you with alternatives if you find that you're using the same word too frequently. These aids help take a lot of the mechanical effort out of writing so that you can focus on what's important: what you have to say and how you say it.

How to Write Clearly

By Edward T. Thompson
Editor-in-Chief, Reader's Digest

If you are afraid to write, don't be.

If you think you've got to string together big fancy words and high-flying phrases, forget it.

To write well, unless you aspire to be a professional poet or novelist, you only need to get your ideas across simply and clearly.

It's not easy. But it *is* easier than you might imagine.

There are only three basic requirements:

First, you must *want* to write clearly. And I believe you really do, if you've stayed this far with me.

Second, you must be willing to *work hard.* Thinking means work—and that's what it takes to do anything well.

Third, you must know and follow some *basic guidelines.*

If, while you're writing for clarity, some lovely, dramatic or inspired phrases or sentences come to you, fine. Put them in.

But then with cold, objective eyes and mind ask yourself: "Do they detract from clarity?" If they do, grit your teeth and cut the frills.

Follow Some Basic Guidelines

I can't give you a complete list of "dos and don'ts" for every writing problem you'll ever face.

But I can give you some fundamental guidelines that cover the most common problems.

1 Outline What You Want to Say.

I know that sounds grade-schoolish. But you can't write clearly until, *before you start,* you know where you will stop.

Ironically, that's even a problem in writing an outline (i.e., knowing the ending before you begin).
So try this method:

▶ On 3" × 5" cards, write—one point to a card—all the points you need to make.

▶ Divide the cards into piles—one pile for each group of points *closely related* to each other. (If you were describing an automobile, you'd put all the points about mileage in one pile, all the points about safety in another, and so on.)

▶ Arrange your piles of points in a sequence. Which are most important and should be given first or saved for last? Which must you present before others in order to make the others understandable?

▶ Now, *within* each pile, do the same thing—arrange the *points* in logical, understandable order.

There you have your outline, needing only an introduction and conclusion.

This is a practical way to outline. It's also flexible. You can add, delete or change the location of points easily.

2 Start Where Your Readers Are.

How much do they know about the subject? Don't write to a level higher than your readers' knowledge of it.

CAUTION: Forget that old—and wrong—advice about writing to a 12-year-old mentality. That's insulting. But do remember that your prime purpose is to *explain* something, not prove that you're smarter than your readers.

3 Avoid Jargon.

Don't use words, expressions, phrases known only to people with specific knowledge or interests.

Example: A scientist, using scientific jargon, wrote, "The biota exhibited a one hundred percent mortality response." He could have written: "All the fish died."

4 Use Familiar Combinations of Words.

A speech writer for President Franklin D. Roosevelt wrote, "We are endeavoring to construct a more inclusive society." F.D.R. changed it to, "We're going to make a country in which no one is left out."

CAUTION: By familiar combinations of words, I do *not* mean incorrect grammar. *That* can be *un*clear. Example: John's father says he can't go out Friday. (Who can't go out? John or his father?)

5 Use "First-Degree" Words.

These words immediately bring an image to your mind. Other words must be "translated" through the first-degree word before you see the image. Those are second/third-degree words.

First-degree words	Second/third-degree words
face	visage, countenance
stay	abide, remain, reside
book	volume, tome, publication

First degree words are usually the most precise words, too.

6 Stick to the Point.

Your outline—which was more work in the beginning—now saves you work. Because now you can ask about any sentence you write: "Does it relate to a point in the outline? If it doesn't, should I add it to the outline? If not, I'm getting off the track." Then, full steam ahead—on the main line.

7 Be as Brief as Possible.

Whatever you write, shortening—*condensing*—almost always makes it tighter, straighter, easier to read and understand.

Condensing, as *Reader's Digest* does it, is in large part artistry. But it involves techniques that anyone can learn and use.

▶ *Present your points in logical ABC order:* Here again, your outline should save you work because, if you did it right, your points already stand in logical ABC order—A makes B understandable, B makes C understandable and so on. To write in a straight line is to say something clearly in the fewest possible words.

▶ *Don't waste words telling people what they already know:* Notice how we edited this: "Have you ever wondered how banks rate you as a credit risk? ~~You know, of course, that it's some combination of facts about your income, your job, and so on. But actually,~~ Many banks have a scoring system. . . ."

▶ *Cut out excess evidence and unnecessary anecdotes:* Usually, one fact or example (at most, two) will support a point. More just belabor it. And while writing about something may remind you of a good story, ask yourself: Does it *really help* to tell the story, or does it slow me down?"

(Many people think *Reader's Digest* articles are filled with anecdotes. Actually, we use them sparingly and usually for one of two reasons: either the subject is so dry it needs some "humanity" to give it life; or the subject is so hard to grasp, it needs anecdotes to help readers understand. If the subject is both lively and easy to grasp, we move right along.)

▶ *Look for the most common word wasters:* windy phrases.

Windy phrases	Cut to . . .
at the present time	now
in the event of	if
in the majority of instances	usually

▶ *Look for passive verbs you can make active;* Invariably, this produces a shorter sentence. "The cherry tree *was* chopped down by George Washington." (Passive verb and nine words.) "George Washington *chopped* down the cherry tree." (Active verb and seven words.)

▶ *Look for positive/negative sections from which you can cut the negative:* See how we did it here: "The answer ~~does not rest with carelessness or incompetence. It lies largely in~~ is having enough people to do the job."

▶ Finally, to write more clearly by saying it in fewer words: when you've finished, stop.

Source: Reprinted by permission of International Paper Company.

Notes

1 The rock drawing is intended to convey the following: Keep going at your own risk! A mountain goat can climb this trail, but a man on horseback is likely to come tumbling down.

2 **Boorstein, Daniel J.,** *The Discoverers: A History of Man's Search to Know His World and Himself,* New York: Random House, 1983; **Shurkin, Joel,** *Engines of the Mind: A History of the Computer,* New York: W.W. Norton, 1984; **Weiser, Mark,** "The Computer for the 21st Century," *Scientific American,* September 1991, p. 94.

3 **Johnson, Maryfran,** "At Au Bon Pain, Accent Is on Client/Server," *Computerworld,* March 23, 1992.

4 **Semich, J. William,** "Multimedia Tools for Development Pros," *Datamation,* August 15, 1992.

two

Information Technologies

Vortex
Melvin Prueitt, Los Alamos
National Laboratories

Chapter 3 contains:

After completing this chapter, you will:

▶ Understand the importance of the CPU in a computer system and what each of its components does.

▶ Know how a computer understands words, numbers, and pictures, and how data and instructions are stored and retrieved.

▶ Understand how a computer processes data.

▶ Recognize different types of microprocessors and memory chips.

▶ Know the important parts of your computer's system unit and the role that each part plays.

▶ Be aware of recent trends affecting how computers are constructed and used.

The Central Processing Unit:
The Analyzing Engine

Training Computers to
Recognize What They See

Once you have learned to read, if you know a word, you are able to recognize it wherever you see it—in a book, a magazine, or a newspaper. Computers can do that, too; they can easily search through huge databases and recognize whenever a certain word occurs. But what if you met someone on a sunny afternoon? Chances are, you would still be able to recognize that person on a cloudy evening. You can do something that a computer still has a lot of difficulty doing—recognizing and retrieving images from a database filled with them.

Some of the most exciting forms of new information technologies, like multimedia, are based on the ability of a computer to process visual images. Methods have been developed that allow computers to process both still and moving pictures in much the same way that they process written information—by "digitizing" them into a series of zeros and ones. Now, researchers at MIT's Media Laboratory and elsewhere are working on techniques that will enable a computer to sort and retrieve those visual images as

easily as they can currently manipulate text and numbers. So far, Edward Adelson of MIT and his colleagues have had some success in teaching a computer to recognize "things" like chairs and other discrete objects but less success with what they call "stuff"—sky, water, and other images that might have texture and color but are not sharply defined. Nonetheless, they feel great advances are just around the corner (see photo).

Such new technology promises to be useful in a wide range of applications, such as video consumer catalogs, video-editing systems, satellite data gathering, and video-conferencing. However, as often happens, this new technology harbors certain perils. For example, once your picture has been entered into an image database, computers might be able to recognize and identify you as you enter a department store or bank, without your knowledge or permission.

Source: Based on Markoff, John, "Training Computers to Note Images," *New York Times*, April 15, 1992.

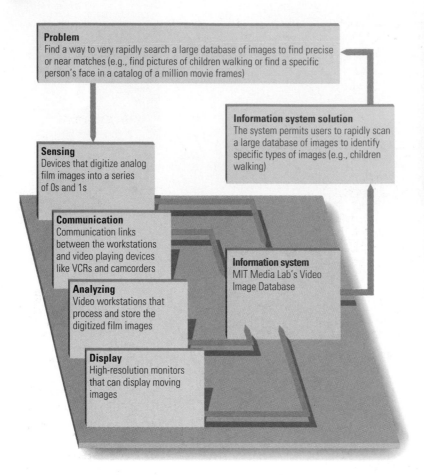

Problem
Find a way to very rapidly search a large database of images to find precise or near matches (e.g., find pictures of children walking or find a specific person's face in a catalog of a million movie frames)

Information system solution
The system permits users to rapidly scan a large database of images to identify specific types of images (e.g., children walking)

Sensing
Devices that digitize analog film images into a series of 0s and 1s

Communication
Communication links between the workstations and video playing devices like VCRs and camcorders

Information system
MIT Media Lab's Video Image Database

Analyzing
Video workstations that process and store the digitized film images

Display
High-resolution monitors that can display moving images

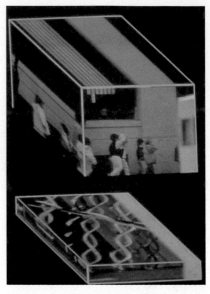

The three-dimensional box at the top shows a digitized image of children walking. When a slice is cut through the box (shown at bottom of screen), the movement of the children is revealed by certain characteristic patterns (here, the helix-shaped lines). The computer can be trained to recognize such patterns and identify them.

Source: Ted Adelson, Mid-Level Vision, Copyright MIT Media Lab, 1992.

To many people, the kinds of things described in the opening vignette sound almost magical. How can a computer understand words and numbers, let alone pictures? How can a machine remember and retrieve data, whatever its form? In this chapter, you'll start to discover how it is done.

3.1 The Central Processing Unit: Center of the Computer Universe

In the first two chapters, you learned about digital information technologies that sense, communicate, analyze, and display, and how they can be combined into an information system. As you have seen, at the heart of those systems is the computer, and the engine that drives the computer, that actually enables the computer to manipulate data, is the **central processing unit (CPU)** (see Figure 3.1). In this chapter, you'll learn what a CPU does in a computer, how it does it, and how the CPU works together with other components in the **system unit** (the container—usually a metal box—that holds the CPU, primary storage, and other devices). Then you'll learn about some new developments in technology that may revolutionize the way computers are constructed and how they process information.

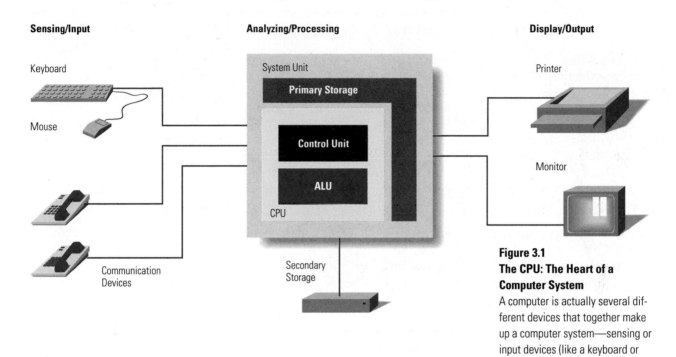

Figure 3.1
The CPU: The Heart of a Computer System
A computer is actually several different devices that together make up a computer system—sensing or input devices (like a keyboard or mouse), communication devices (like a modem), secondary storage devices (like hard disk drives or floppy disks), display devices (like a printer or monitor), and at the center of it all, the system unit containing the CPU and primary storage.

An Overview of the CPU and Primary Storage

The CPU has two important functions in a computer. First, it processes data through the manipulation of numbers, letters, and symbols. Second, it controls the other parts of a **computer system.** The type of CPU contained in the computer determines how much and how quickly data can be processed.

The CPU consists of two basic elements: an arithmetic/logic unit (ALU) and a control unit. Closely connected and integrally related to the CPU is primary storage, which stores program instructions and data. Figure 3.2 illustrates the relationship between the CPU and primary storage. CPUs and primary storage are made from silicon semiconductor chips on which a million or more tiny transistors have been etched. As you learned in Chapter 2, today's semiconductor chips can contain so many transistors that microcomputers and workstations rely on a single chip (a microprocessor) to house the entire CPU. We explore the world of processor and memory chips in more depth in Section 3.2.

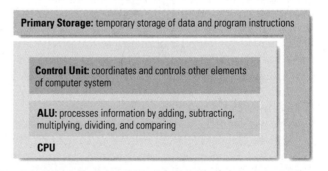

Figure 3.2
The CPU and Primary Storage

The Arithmetic/Logic Unit (ALU)   The **ALU** is the part of the CPU that manipulates and processes data. All forms of processing performed by a computer are based on one of two basic types of operations: arithmetical operations (for example, the addition, subtraction, multiplication, and division of numbers) or logical operations (for instance, the comparison of two numbers to see whether one is greater than, less than, or equal to another). Because all data coming into the CPU has been transformed into digital form, the ALU can perform logical operations on letters and words, as well as on numbers. The ability of a computer to perform comparisons allows it to take alternative courses of action depending on what state of facts it finds (for example, if X is greater than Y, do Z; if it is less than or equal to Y, do something else). This is one of the reasons that computers have become so useful as multipurpose machines.

The Control Unit The **control unit** is the part of the CPU that coordinates and controls the other elements of the computer system. For instance, the control unit directs each of the other components of the system to perform certain tasks at certain times, based on the instructions contained in the program that is in place at the time.

Primary Storage Primary storage is so closely related to the functioning of the CPU that some actually consider it to be a part of the CPU. **Primary storage** (also called **primary memory, main memory,** or just **memory**) stores, or holds in memory:

1 The operating system programs that manage the operation of the computer (see Chapter 7).
2 The program that is being used at the time.
3 The data that is being used by the program.

Primary storage holds data and programs before processing, between processing steps, and after processing has finished prior to releasing data as output.

Within primary storage, there are different storage locations for different types of data and program instructions. Data coming in from an input device is stored in the input area; data going out to a display device is stored in the output area. Program storage holds processing instructions; working storage holds intermediate processing results. These storage areas don't have actual built-in physical locations within primary storage; instead, their location within primary storage changes depending on which program is being used.

Whatever data or instructions are being held in primary storage, they can always be found by the computer because they have been assigned a specific **address,** much like your own specific unique street address or mailbox. However, unlike the storage capacity of mailboxes, which can vary depending on their size, the storage capacity of each address in primary storage is usually fixed; for instance, in many computers, an address can store only one character (like a letter or numeral) of data. When new data is stored at an address location, it erases and replaces the previous contents at that address. Obviously, then, space for many different storage locations, or addresses, is needed in primary storage to hold the data and program instructions required in even simple processing functions.

The basic unit of measurement of the storage capacity of primary storage is the **byte.** Each address in primary storage usually can hold one byte. There are around 1,000 bytes (actually 1,024) in one **kilobyte (KB or K),** around 1 million bytes in one **megabyte (MB or meg),** around 1 billion bytes in one **gigabyte (GB or gig),** and around 1 trillion bytes in one **terabyte (TB).** As you'll learn in Section 3.2, today's semiconductor memory chips have the capacity to hold hundreds of thousands of bytes.

Registers The ALU and the control unit both contain parts called **registers.** These function as temporary storage locations and staging areas for program instructions and data that need to be transferred from primary storage to the CPU before processing begins. There are different types of registers. The **instruction register** holds the part of the program instruction that tells the ALU what it is supposed to do next. The **address register** holds the part of the program instruction that tells the ALU the address of the data that is to be processed next. The **storage register** stores data transferred from primary storage. And the **accumulator** temporarily stores the results of processing.

How the Computer Represents and Stores Information:
Transforming Data into Digital Form

One of the things that people find most amazing about a computer is its seeming ability to understand information that is fed to it via a keyboard, mouse, or other input device. We now start to unravel these mysteries. You may be surprised to learn that it's really not all that complicated—in fact, it turns out to be based on a concept that is as simple as counting from zero to one.

First, think back to what you learned in Chapter 2 about how humans learned to express and symbolize information. As you saw there, our present-day alphabet and decimal numbering system evolved over time. Even though those systems became the predominant way of expressing information, scientists and mathematicians continued to look for other ways. One of those ways was a **binary** system. Binary means having only two possible states. A binary system uses just two symbols to represent all information. The symbols could be anything from a dot and a dash (like Morse code) to a zero and a one (digits used in a binary numbering system).

During the 1930s, researchers involved in the development of computers realized that electrical circuits created with vacuum tubes (and later, with transistors) could be used to represent information expressed in binary form. This was so because electrical circuits can exist in either one of two states: current is either flowing or not flowing, a circuit is either closed or open, on or off (see Figure 3.3). In addition, researchers discovered that information expressed in binary form could also be stored using the same principles—electrical circuits could be opened or closed to represent zeros and ones and would remain that way until changed at a later time.

A closed circuit allows current to flow and represents a 1.

An open circuit does not allow current to flow and represents a 0.

Figure 3.3
Electrical Circuits Can
Represent Binary 0s and 1s

So, the first step in the digitizing process is to reduce the information, be it a number, letter, symbol, picture, or sound, into a sequence of **bits** (short for *binary digits*), each of which is either a zero or a one. But which binary digits mean which numbers, letters, and symbols? In the case of numbers, binary numbering has its own internal rules governing how a number is expressed. Just as we know that the concept of twenty-three ones should be expressed as 23 in our decimal numbering system, mathematicians and computer scientists know that in binary form, the concept of twenty-three ones should be expressed as 10111. Figure 3.4 shows you the basic concepts of decimal and binary numbering systems.

a. Decimal System

In a decimal numbering system, each place in a number is some exponential value of 10. For instance, in the decimal number 721, the 1 is in the "ones" place, or 10 to the zero power (10^0); the 2 is in the "tens" place, or 10 to the first power (10^1); and the 7 is in the "hundreds" place, or 10 to the power of two (10^2).

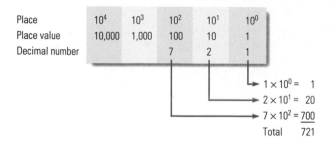

b. Binary System

In a binary numbering system, each place in a number is some exponential value of 2. For instance, in the binary number 101, the 1 on the right is the "ones" place, or 2 to the zero power (2^0). The 0 in the middle position (the "twos" place) means that there are no 2s. A 1 in this position would mean there was one 2 ($2^1 = 2$). The 1 on the left (the "fours" place) means that there is one 4 ($2^2 = 4$). The binary number 101 equals the decimal system number 5.

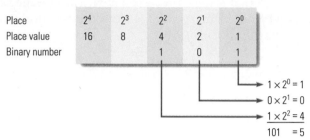

But no such internal rules were in place to govern the use of binary form to represent the alphabet or other symbols. Instead, the scientists involved in creating computers developed **binary codes.**

There are two common types of computer binary codes: **EBCDIC** (pronounced *eb-si-dik,* and short for Extended Binary Coded Decimal Interchange Code) and **ASCII** (pronounced *as-kee,* and short for American Stan-

Figure 3.4
Basic Concepts of Decimal and Binary Numbering Systems

Figure 3.5
Representation of Characters in EBCDIC and ASCII-8

Character	EBCDIC	ASCII-8	Character	EBCDIC	ASCII-8
A	1100 0001	1010 0001	S	1110 0010	1011 0011
B	1100 0010	1010 0010	T	1110 0011	1011 0100
C	1100 0011	1010 0011	U	1110 0100	1011 0101
D	1100 0100	1010 0100	V	1110 0101	1011 0110
E	1100 0101	1010 0101	W	1110 0110	1011 0111
F	1100 0110	1010 0110	X	1110 0111	1011 1000
G	1100 0111	1010 0111	Y	1110 1000	1011 1001
H	1100 1000	1010 1000	Z	1110 1001	1011 1010
I	1100 1001	1010 1001	0	1111 0000	0101 0000
J	1101 0001	1010 1010	1	1111 0001	0101 0001
K	1101 0010	1010 1011	2	1111 0010	0101 0010
L	1101 0011	1010 1100	3	1111 0011	0101 0011
M	1101 0100	1010 1101	4	1111 0100	0101 0100
N	1101 0101	1010 1110	5	1111 0101	0101 0101
O	1101 0110	1010 1111	6	1111 0110	0101 0110
P	1101 0111	1011 0000	7	1111 0111	0101 0111
Q	1101 1000	1011 0001	8	1111 1000	0101 1000
R	1101 1001	1011 0010	9	1111 1001	0101 1001

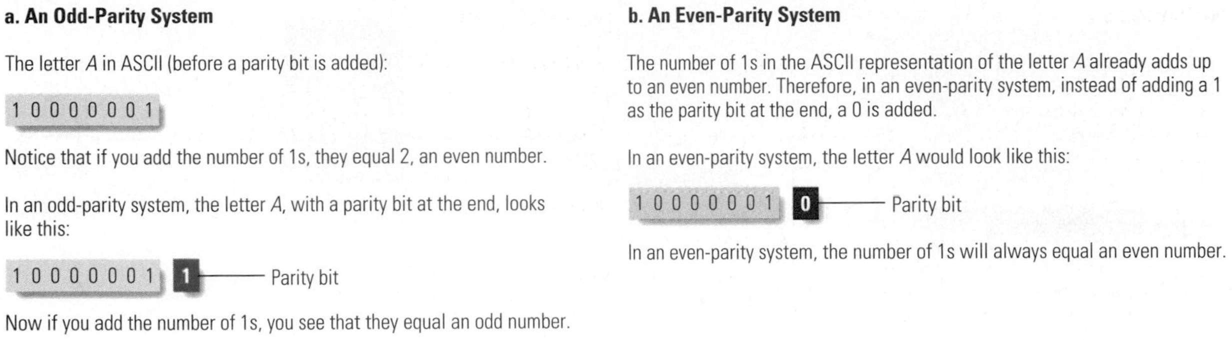

a. An Odd-Parity System

The letter *A* in ASCII (before a parity bit is added):

1 0 0 0 0 0 0 1

Notice that if you add the number of 1s, they equal 2, an even number.

In an odd-parity system, the letter *A*, with a parity bit at the end, looks like this:

1 0 0 0 0 0 0 1   **1** ———— Parity bit

Now if you add the number of 1s, you see that they equal an odd number.

b. An Even-Parity System

The number of 1s in the ASCII representation of the letter *A* already adds up to an even number. Therefore, in an even-parity system, instead of adding a 1 as the parity bit at the end, a 0 is added.

In an even-parity system, the letter *A* would look like this:

1 0 0 0 0 0 0 1   **0** ———— Parity bit

In an even-parity system, the number of 1s will always equal an even number.

Figure 3.6
Odd- and Even-Parity Systems

dard Code for Information Interchange). EBCDIC was developed by IBM and is used primarily in IBM and other mainframe computers. ASCII was developed by the American National Standards Institute (ANSI) to provide a standard code that could be used by many different manufacturers. Both represent numbers, letters, and symbols as strings of bits (zeros or ones). EBCDIC uses an 8-bit version that can represent up to 256 items—more than enough for numbers from 0 to 9, uppercase and lowercase letters, and a variety of other symbols. ASCII originally used a 7-bit code, but a later version that is now more commonly used (called ASCII-8) uses 8 bits. Figure 3.5 shows how EBCDIC and ASCII represent letters, numbers, and symbols.

All EBCDIC and ASCII characters also contain an additional bit position for a **parity,** or **check, bit,** which helps the CPU make sure that the characters being transmitted have not been garbled or partly lost because of some electrical disturbance or other reason. The manufacturer of the computer decides whether the system will be an odd-parity or an even-parity system. In an odd-parity system, the computer expects all the bits within a string that are 1s to add up to an odd number. The parity bit will automatically be whatever number (either 0 or 1) is required to make this occur (see Figure 3.6a). If a CPU with an odd-parity system receives a character whose bits add up to an even number, it knows immediately that something is wrong. In an even-parity system, the bits are expected to add up to an even number (see Figure 3.6b).

Let's now look at what happens when you start to input data by, for instance, typing your name on your keyboard. As you strike each key, the letter represented by that key is converted into a byte, a series of 8 bits of zeros and ones. The byte is represented within the computer by a combination of transistors, some of which are closed, or on (in this state—represented by a 1—they are able to conduct) and some of which are open, or off (in this state—represented by a 0—they are not able to conduct). Each bit is stored within one transistor, so eight transistors are needed to store one 8-bit byte. Each byte making up the letters in your name is then stored in primary storage, where it is assigned an address. Later, when your name is needed in response to whatever processing is being done, the bytes will be transferred to the CPU, processed, and then sent back into primary storage. From there, the bytes making up your name will be sent to whatever output device is being used, where they will be reconverted from binary into alphabetic letters.

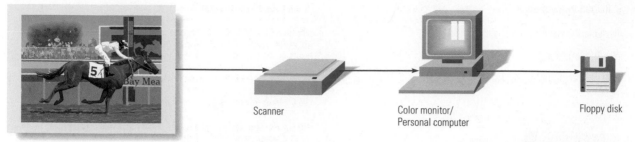

Color photograph   Scanner   Color monitor/ Personal computer   Floppy disk

A computer handles pictures in much the same way. Processing of an image begins with a piece of hardware called a *scanner* and related software, which creates a grid of cells, or *bitmap,* overlaying the picture and assigns a code, expressed in 0s and 1s, to the light or color in each cell (also called a *pixel)* of the grid. The computer can then store this information just like any other number (see Figure 3.7).

How the CPU Processes Data

Let's now explore how a machine is able to carry out procedures like addition, subtraction, and comparisons. Just as the concepts behind binary numbering are the key to the computer's ability to represent and store data, they also form the key to the computer's ability to process information. In the 1840s, a brilliant mathematician named George Boole used the concepts of binary systems to create a type of algebra (now called Boolean algebra) that included a form of mathematical operation called a logic gate. Logic gates are binary—that is, they handle only information that represents one of two states, like true or false, yes or no (see Figure 3.8).

Using Boole's principles, logic gates can be used to add, subtract, multiply, divide, and compare symbols or numbers. From there, it was a short jump for computer researchers to realize that just as circuits in transistors could be used to represent and store data in binary form, they also could be used to create logic gates. When the circuits are laid out using Boole's system of logic, they could express logic and test the truth of propositions (by making comparisons) as well as carry out complex calculations. Figure 3.9 shows circuits laid out as logic gates that can add.

Just as the representation of data begins with digitizing it into binary digits, so too, the processing of information begins with breaking down each instruction contained in a program into binary-based **machine language in-**

Figure 3.7
How Computers Process Images
A photograph can be placed in a scanner and translated into a series of 0s and 1s by breaking it down into a grid called a bitmap. Each cell of the bitmap is given a code expressed in 0s and 1s to indicate its color. This information is then fed into a personal computer that translates the 0s and 1s into an image, and displays the proper colors and image on a screen for the user to examine. The user can, in turn, print out the photograph (recreating the original photo completely) or store the image as a series of 0s and 1s on a floppy disk.

Source: Photograph used by permission of Illustrious, Inc.

Figure 3.8
Computer Building Blocks: Logic Gates

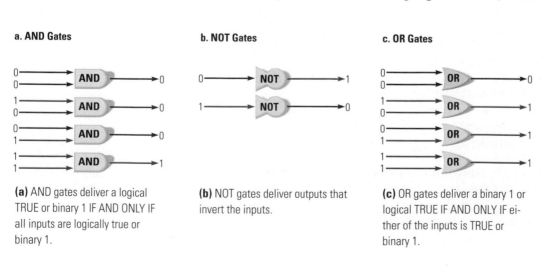

a. AND Gates

b. NOT Gates

c. OR Gates

(a) AND gates deliver a logical TRUE or binary 1 IF AND ONLY IF all inputs are logically true or binary 1.

(b) NOT gates deliver outputs that invert the inputs.

(c) OR gates deliver a binary 1 or logical TRUE IF AND ONLY IF either of the inputs is TRUE or binary 1.

a. This is how a gate adds a binary 1 and 0 in the "ones" place. If you feed a 1 and a 0 to the gate, it puts out a 1, which is the correct result of adding a binary 1 and 0.

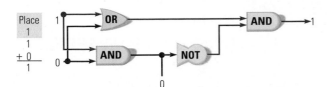

b. Addition with a carryover is a little more difficult, for instance, adding 1 plus 1. If you feed the gate a 1 and 1, it will put a 0 in the ones place and put a carryover of 1 in the twos place. This produces the correct result for adding 1 and 1 in binary.

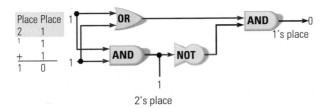

Figure 3.9

Logic Gates: Circuits That Can Add

Circuits arranged to form logic gates can perform simple addition. Figures a and b show precisely the same circuit; they differ only in terms of what we are asking the circuit to do.

a. Most machine language instructions have three basic parts: (1) an operation code, which signals what operation is to be performed; (2) a section that indicates the number of characters to be processed; and (3) a part that specifies where the data is located in primary storage. This instruction tells an IBM System 370 computer to multiply one number by another and to replace the first number with the product. The instruction would be entered into the computer as an uninterrupted stream of 1s and 0s. Here, it is separated into bytes to make it easier for you to see the different parts of the instruction.

b. To avoid having to work with long streams of 0s and 1s, shorthand codes substitute for binary digits. Figure 3.10b shows the instruction represented in a more modern format, called assembly language.

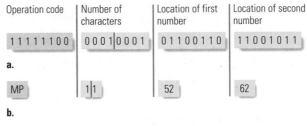

Figure 3.10

Machine Language Instructions

structures. This is done by yet another program, called a *compiler*. Figure 3.10 shows you what a machine language instruction looks like. Each set of instructions corresponds directly to, and can thereby activate, a set of the computer's circuits. These circuits (called the computer's *instruction set*) have been arranged into systems of logic gates, which enable the computer to perform its tasks using the coded pulses of binary language.

As Figure 3.10 illustrates, although the machine language instruction may just look like a long series of zeros and ones, it actually has several different parts. One part of the instruction, called the operation code, is usually stored in the first byte (the first eight zeros and ones) and indicates what operation is to be performed. Another part of the instruction indicates the number of characters to be processed by the instruction. The final part of the instruction specifies the locations, or addresses, in primary storage of the data that will be processed by the instruction. Figure 3.11 lists some basic machine instructions included in an IBM computer's instruction set.

The processing of a single machine-level instruction is called a **machine cycle.** A machine cycle has two parts: the *instruction cycle* (the I-cycle) and the *execution cycle* (the E-cycle). The instruction cycle begins when the control unit in the CPU fetches and decodes an instruction from primary storage. The control unit then places the part of the

Figure 3.11

Some Basic Instructions That Can Be Represented By Circuits

Add	Compare and Swap	Move
Subtract	Branch and Save	Move Character
Multiply	Branch on Condition	Reset
Divide	Load	Store
Compare	Load Register	Store Character

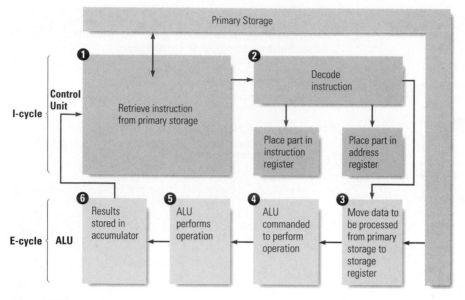

Figure 3.12
The Machine Cycle
Retrieving an instruction from primary storage, decoding it, executing it, and storing the results are the basic steps of a machine cycle. We call the first half of the machine cycle the I-cycle (instruction cycle) and the second half the E-cycle (execution cycle).

instruction that tells the ALU what it is supposed to do in the instruction register and the part of the instruction indicating where the relevant data is located in the address register. Then the execution cycle begins. Data that is to be processed is moved from its location in primary storage into the storage register. The control unit then tells the ALU to perform the operation specified by the instruction in the instruction register. The results of the operation are sent to the accumulator, where they are stored temporarily until they are returned to primary storage. Figure 3.12 illustrates the machine cycle.

Type of Computer	MIPS Rating
Supercomputers	Usually measured by flops
Mainframes	
IBM ES/9000 Model 900	230–240
Minicomputers	
DEC VAX 7000	160
Workstations	
Using a Sparc RISC chip	59
IBM RS/6000	56
Microcomputers	
Using an Intel 80486 chip	54
Using a Motorola 68040 chip	35

Figure 3.13
MIPS Ratings

Note: MIPS are just one measure of a computer's performance and are useful primarily for a ballpark estimate of one type of processing speed.

All the amazing things that most computers do are based on this simple machine cycle. To execute even the most complicated programs, the computer merely repeats the machine cycle over and over and over again, perhaps millions of times per second, until the entire program has been processed. (We describe another form of processing, called parallel processing, that can execute instructions simultaneously instead of sequentially in Section 3.3.) Of course, all this occurs at blindingly fast speeds. Speed in the computer world can be measured in a number of different ways. One way is the number of *instructions per second* that the CPU can process. Today's computers can process millions of instructions per second. This unit of measurement is called **MIPS (millions of instructions per second).** Figure 3.13 lists speeds in MIPS for microcomputers, workstations, minicomputers, and mainframes. Speed, particularly of supercomputers, is also sometimes measured in **flops** (floating point operations per second). A floating point operation is a specialized form of mathematical calculation. Figure 3.14 lists speeds in flops for various types of computers.

Another way to measure computer speed is to look at the time it takes to complete one machine cycle. Cycle times may range from **milliseconds** (1/1,000 of a second) for very slow machines, to **microseconds** (1/1,000,000 of a second) for standard microcomputers, to **nanoseconds** (1/1,000,000,000 of a second) for modern mainframe computers, to **picoseconds** (1/1,000,000,000,000 of a second) for the fastest, experimental devices. Although the difference between microseconds and nanoseconds may seem trivial to you, the story "Heaven on Earth" illustrates how important it is to scientists who need high-speed computers to help them make scientific breakthroughs.

So there it is: incredible as it may seem, all those computer games, computer graphics, spreadsheets, databases, simulations, and the whole array of exciting computer applications, have their origin in a relatively simple concept—the ability of tiny circuits embedded within processing and memory chips to represent, store, and process data (see photo).

Even sophisticated computer-generated special effects such as this one (from the movie *Terminator 2*) are created using the same basic techniques discussed in this chapter.

Source: © 1991, TRI-STAR, courtesy of Industrial Light & Magic.

Type	Rating (in Megaflops)
Supercomputers	
Intel Touchstone Delta	8,600.00
Thinking Machines CM-2	5,200.00
NEC SX-3/12	4,231.00
Cray Y-MP/832	2,144.00
Mainframes	
IBM 3090 Model 1200	1,600.00
Minicomputers	
DEC Vax 8800	1.30
Workstations	
IBM RISC System/6000	62.00
Sun Sparcstation 1-plus	1.60
Microcomputers	
Apple Macintosh IIfx	0.23
IBM PS/2 Model 70	0.15

Figure 3.14
Flops Ratings

Source: Data courtesy of Jack J. Dongarra, University of Tennessee.

Flops are measured in megaflops (millions of floating point operations per second) and gigaflops (billions of floating point operations per second). The megaflops ratings for supercomputers and mainframes could also have been expressed in gigaflops (8,600 megaflops = 8.6 gigaflops).

At the University of Chicago, researchers set themselves an ambitious goal: to examine the surface of the sun without using a telescope. How? By using a computer to create a simulation (a form of model) of the sun's surface. The scientists faced a daunting task, however. Although the mathematical equations describing solar physics are conceptually simple, the solutions, according to Fausto Cateneo, who along with Andrea Malagoli, wrote the sun-modeling program, "are horrendously complex."

Luckily, the team at the University of Chicago had access to a Cray Y-MP supercomputer at NASA's Ames, Iowa, research laboratory to work on these equations. Even still, it took the Cray hundreds of hours to run the program, and the resulting simulation covered only an extremely small portion (1/100,000,000) of the sun's surface. However, the team is not discouraged. "Understanding comes from modeling simple things and making them gradually more complex," says Robert Rosner, professor of astronomy and astrophysics. They have plans to scale up their model, using approximations, until they can represent the sun's surface over several thousand kilometers.

None of what the team has accomplished thus far would have been possible without advances in supercomputer and workstation technology. Those advances have now made it possible to visualize the vast amounts of data generated by the modeling program. The team has been using a Sun Microsystems Sparcstation workstation that uses a microprocessor based on RISC—reduced instruction set computing (more about RISC in Section 3.2). The Cray supercomputer plots hundreds of points in each dimension, compared with tens of points for earlier technology. The Sun workstation displays these points in a three-dimensional, rather than two-dimensional, image—a critical element when studying phenomena like turbulence on the sun (see photo).

At the University of Chicago and elsewhere, computer speed and power are allowing scientists to translate rows of numbers into vivid images and patterns. Most people can absorb visual images much more easily than a column of numbers. Images can sometimes help scientists make unexpected connections, leading to new discoveries.

Source: Based on Brooker, Ellis, "Simulating the Turbulent Sun," *Computerworld*, November 4, 1991.

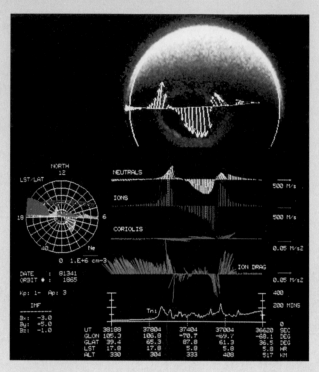

A Cray Y-MP supercomputer helps create simulations of the sun's surface.

Source: National Center for Atmospheric Research..

Critical Thinking Questions

1 In this story, scientists created a *simulation* of the sun's surface using computers, rather than use an instrument like a telescope to observe what they were studying directly. What are some advantages and disadvantages of this approach?

2 We live in a three-dimensional (height, width, and depth) world, but generally represent and express data using only two (for example, in a picture that is flat and does not show depth). Now, using computers, scientists can express raw data as three-dimensional images much more easily. Why do you think this might be useful, and how important do you think this development is?

3 Describe the basic steps a computer goes through to process the data needed to create a simulation.

Unmasking the Electronic Genie: Inside Your Computer's System Unit

You now know about the important functions and characteristics of the CPU and primary storage and how they work together to allow a computer to represent, store, and process information. But what about the actual physical components that make up CPUs and primary storage and the other devices that are part of the system unit in a typical personal computer? After reading the following section, you should be able to decipher and understand all those PC advertisements that use words like motherboard, RAM, card, MIPS, bus, and port.

System Unit Components

A system unit in a typical personal computer generally includes a microprocessor (a single silicon chip containing the CPU and a small amount of special-purpose memory) and one or more memory chips mounted on a main circuit board called the **motherboard** (sometimes called the system board or main board). Figure 3.15a shows a diagram of a system unit and Figure 3.15b identifies the important parts of a motherboard. The motherboard often has sockets or slots that allow specialized processor chips and additional memory to be added. A **system clock** helps regulate the pace of operations. (In some computers, the system clock is a part of the microprocessor rather than on a separate chip.) Add-in boards or cards that perform specialized functions, such as enhanced graphics display, are often plugged into **expansion slots** on the motherboard. The system unit also has ports, where external devices like a printer, mouse, or modem can be connected. The system unit also contains a power supply, circuitry hooking all the components together, and a fan to keep the components from overheating. They also usually contain a floppy disk and hard disk drive (which we discuss in Chapter 4). Let's now look at each of the components a little more closely.

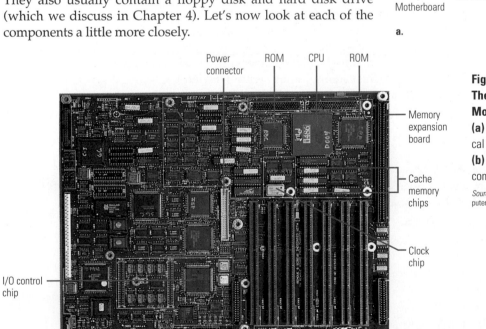

Figure 3.15
The System Unit and the Motherboard

(a) Interior configuration of a typical IBM-compatible computer.
(b) Motherboard of a typical 486 computer.

Source: Reprinted with permission of Compaq Computer Corporation. All rights reserved.

Figure 3.16
Constructing a Chip

Source: Courtesy of IBM; Courtesy of AT&T Archives; Courtesy of IBM; Courtesy of IBM; Courtesy of AT&T Archives; Courtesy of Intel Corporation.

a. A chip consists of millions of electronic pathways, created layer by layer on a wafer of silicon. Making the chip begins with designing a "blueprint" for each layer of the design.

b. A photographic process captures and miniaturizes each blueprint and duplicates it many times onto a glass photomask. A separate photomask is created for each layer of the design.

c. Layer by layer, the tiny designs are photochemically transferred from the photomask and etched onto batches of wafers.

Microprocessor Chips

Microprocessors today are made from silicon crystals sliced wafer-thin (around 4/1,000 of an inch). Layers of conducting and nonconducting material are added to the wafer's surface and then etched away into patterns that form miniaturized transistors and other elements that make up an integrated circuit (see Figure 3.16).

The microprocessor, with its ever-increasing speed and processing power and ever-decreasing prices, has helped revolutionize the way companies do business, as the story "Using Microprocessors to Bring the Customer Closer to the Cows" illustrates.

The major manufacturers of microprocessors today are Intel, IBM, Motorola, and Sun Microsystems. Intel makes the "86" series of chips. These are commonly referred to as 286s, 386s, and 486s and are used primarily in IBM and IBM-compatible personal computers. Intel has introduced several different versions of its 386 and 486 chips, identified by the letters DX, SX, and SL. Figure 3.17 explains the differences among the versions. Intel also makes the new Pentium™ chip that is the successor to the 486.

Once almost a monopoly, Intel recently has been facing competition from companies like Advanced Micro Devices, Chips and Technologies, and Cyrix Inc., which have challenged Intel by producing clones, or copies of Intel's chips. Motorola makes the "68000" family of chips, which are used primarily by Apple personal computers. Sun Microsystems, along with Hewlett-Packard, Digital Equipment Corporation, and IBM, makes RISC chips, an alternative form of microprocessor (still used mainly in workstations).

486DX and **386DX**	32-bit data word length. 32-bit data bus.
486SX	Similar to 486DX but lacks internal math coprocessor. Less expensive than DX version.
386SX	32-bit data word length. 16-bit data bus. Can run software designed for 386DX, but is slower. Less expensive than 386DX version.
SL	A version of SX chip that consumes less electricity than standard SX or DX. Used primarily in portable laptop and palmtop computers.

Figure 3.17

DX, SX, and SL: What's the Difference?

When you purchase a PC or listen to others going through the process, you will be barraged with buzzwords. One confusing area is the designation of Intel and Intel-clone microprocessor chips as DX, SX, or SL versions.

d. Since a single speck of dust can ruin a chip, manufacturers use special "clean rooms" and workers dressed in special suits to lessen the chance of contamination. Manufacturers also use robots to handle the wafer between processing steps.

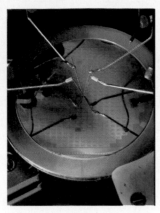

e. Each of the chips on a wafer is tested to make sure that it is not defective.

f. The wafer is "diced" into separate chips.

g. Each chip is then mounted on a frame so that its circuits can be connected by pins to the motherboard.

Not all microprocessors are created equal; some are faster and more powerful than others. Let's now explore how microprocessors differ and what determines their speed and power.

Figure 3.18 lists some of the most common microprocessors in use today, from slowest to fastest. Not surprisingly, the fastest chips are those created

Figure 3.18
Some Common Types of Microprocessors

Name and Date Introduced	Manufacturer	DataWord Length	Bus Width	Clock Speed (MHz)	Systems Using Chip	MIPS*
8088 (1979)	Intel	16	8	4–8	IBM PC and XT	.5
68000 (1979)	Motorola	32	16	8–16	MacintoshPlus Macintosh SE Commodore Amiga	1.6
80286 (1982)	Intel	16	16	8–28	IBM PC/AT IBM PS/2 Model 50/60 Compaq Deskpro 286	1.2-2.66
68020 (1984)	Motorola	32	32	16–33	Macintosh II	5.5
Sparc (1985) (RISC)	Sun Microsystems	32	32	20–25	Sun Sparcstation 1 Sun Sparcstation 300	12.5–20
80386DX (1985)	Intel	32	32	16–33	IBM PS/2s IBM-compatibles	5–11.4
68030 (1987)	Motorola	32	32	16–50	Macintosh IIx series Macintosh SE/30	12
80486DX (1989)	Intel	32	32	25–66	High-end IBM PS/2 models and IBM-compatibles	20–54
68040 (1989)	Motorola	32	32	25–40	Mac Quadras	15–35
RISC 6000 (1990)	IBM	32	32	20–50	IBM RISC/6000 Workstation	30–56
MicroSparc (1992)	Sun Microsystems	32	32	50	Sun Sparcstation LX	59
Pentium (1993)	Intel	32	64	60–66	H-P Net Server Compaq Deskpro 5/60M	100–112
Alpha AXP (1993)	DEC	32	64	150	Digital PC AXP 150	300

*Range indicates MIPs at launch and highest MIPS to date.

Darigold is one of the country's largest dairy cooperatives, with over 2,000 different kinds of milk, cheese, yogurt, and other dairy products. The co-op employs 1,700 people at 30 production facilities serving Washington, Idaho, Oregon, and California.

In the past, the co-op had one large mainframe computer at headquarters and nine minicomputers at the production sites. Orders had to be called in from the field to central headquarters. From there, the orders were dispatched to warehouses to see if the goods were in stock, and then to production sites if more goods needed to be manufactured. It might take 24 hours or more for orders to be received by production.

To make sure customers received what they wanted, Darigold had to make more inventory than it needed and store it in coolers. This created spoilage when the products did not sell and waste when the products sat in coolers without generating any cash. Worse, salespeople had no way of knowing if the products they ordered were in stock or when they would be available. As a result, delivery time to the customer was much longer than it should have been.

Enter the 80386 microprocessor. With the power of a minicomputer in a PC box, at an inexpensive price, corpora-

tions like Darigold could radically reorganize how they served their customers and how they organized their business. First, Darigold bought 200 AT&T 386 PCs for its 30 production and distribution facilities. Then, it tied these PCs together into local area networks at each facility with a powerful PC called a file server. (We describe local area networks and file servers in Chapter 6.)

Now salespeople can call in to find out precisely what is in inventory and to place their orders. The orders are instantly transmitted to distribution and production plants, reducing the order process time by 30 percent. Most important, the customer order actually drives production: much less product is produced and stored in coolers. Products are made only when customers order. This change alone has saved millions of dollars' worth of product, and much less electricity is needed to run the coolers.

In the next few years, Darigold plans to arm its sales force with palmtop or handheld computers. These would eliminate the need for salespeople to call into production facilities and permit the direct transmission of orders from the field to the factory.

Source: Based on "Darigold Sours on Mainframe," *InformationWeek,* May 25, 1992.

most recently. Figure 3.19 illustrates the increasing power of microprocessors over the last 15 years. The three main variables that influence the speed and power of "traditional" chips are clock speed, word length, and bus width. First, we explain each of these terms. Then we look at how RISC chips use a different method to achieve even better performance.

Clock speed refers to the pace set by the system clock included in the system unit. When a computer is turned on, electric current causes the system clock to emit electronic pulses at a constant rate, which are used by the computer to synchronize and control the pace of operations. Clock speeds are measured in **megahertz (MHz)**, with 1 megahertz equaling one million pulses per second. The circuitry of each type of chip is only equipped to handle clock speeds within a certain range. For instance, Intel's 486 microprocessor (see photo) can operate at clock speeds of between 25 and 66 MHz, whereas the 286 can only handle clock speeds of between 8 and 25 MHz. Intel has also developed a technology called "clock-doubling" or "dual speed." This technique lets Intel's newer chips process information internally at twice the speed that it interfaces with other parts of the computer. This allows the rest of the machine to be built with parts that operate at a lower speed and reduces costs. Intel's 486DX/2 chip, introduced in August 1992, is an example of this technology.

A computer **word** is a group of bits that the CPU processes as a unit; **word length** or size refers to the number of bits that make up such a unit. Along with clock speed, the word length that a microprocessor can handle affects the speed at which it can manipulate data. For instance, if the CPU

Critical Thinking Questions

1 As systems like Darigold's spread, what impacts may this have on employees as well as consumers?

2 What kinds of skills do you think future Darigold employees will require to succeed?

3 Given that the power of computers is doubling each year, in a few years Darigold's sales personnel could have portable mainframe computers in their hands. What kinds of knowledge might it be possible for them to obtain with these more powerful computers?

Handheld computers will allow the Darigold salesforce to transmit orders directly to dairy production sights.

Source: Courtesy of Darigold Inc.

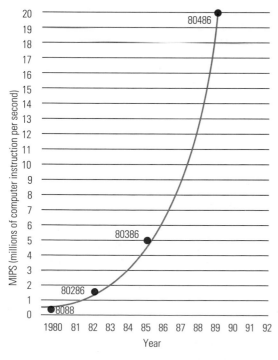

Figure 3.19
The Changing Power of Microprocessors
The power of Intel's "86" series of microprocessors has increased dramatically over the past 15 years. Motorola's 68000 family of microprocessors follows the same pattern.

Intel's 50 MHz, 486 DX microprocessor.

Source: Courtesy of Intel Corporation.

can handle data and instructions only 16 bits (2 bytes) at a time, it will obviously be slower than one that can handle 32 bits (4 bytes) during a single machine cycle. (Think about it this way. Imagine that the only way you could read is one letter at a time—you have to stop to think about what each letter signifies before moving on to the next letter. Pretty slow going. But think how much faster you could read if suddenly you could understand two, four, or even eight letters or whole words at a time.) Right now, the longest computer words that even the most powerful processors can handle are 64 bits long. Experts believe that as the 64-bit chip becomes cheaper to produce and more commonplace, leading-edge applications like virtual reality and artificial intelligence will become easier to develop and run. Right now, most personal computers contain processors that can handle 32-bit words.

The final major factor affecting the speed of traditional microprocessors is the size of their buses, or their bus width. A **bus** is a pathway or connection that the electronic impulses that form bits travel along within the microprocessor and throughout the system unit. Buses connect input devices with primary storage, primary storage with the CPU, and so on.

There are three basic types of buses. An *address bus* carries signals used to locate a given memory address in primary storage. A *data bus* carries data to and from primary storage. A *control bus* carries signals that tell the computer to "read" or "write" data to or from a given memory address, input device, or output device (see Figure 3.20).

The term **bus width** refers to the amount of data that can be transferred through a bus at one time. Early microprocessors had data buses that allowed only 8 bits (1 byte) to be transferred at one time. As a result, for example, four separate cycles would be required to move a piece of data that was 32 bits (4 bytes) long from primary storage to the CPU. The early microprocessors had 20-bit address buses with which to identify locations in memory. More modern chips have data buses and address buses that are 32 bits wide, allowing a 32-bit piece of data to be transferred from RAM and to other devices in one fell swoop. IBM's Micro Channel Architecture (MCA), used in IBM's PS/2 line, the Extended Industry Standard Architecture (EISA), used in many IBM-compatible computers, and Apple's NuBus, used in the most recent Macintoshs, all allow 32-bit transfers. The very newest chips, such as the Pentium, feature 64-bit architecture.

RISC Chips   Clock speed, word length, and bus width play major roles in determining the speed and power of traditional microprocessors. How-

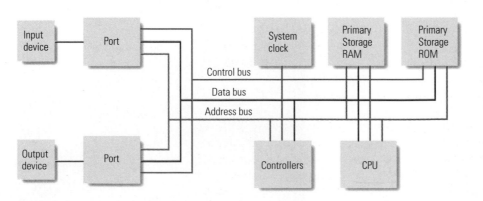

Figure 3.20
Buses

Buses are the pathways upon which electronic signals representing data and instructions travel between different parts of the computer system. The width of the bus affects the speed at which information can be processed.

ever, in recent years, chip designers discovered another way to increase the speed of a chip. As you learned earlier, the instructions that enable a computer to process data are actually physically represented in the circuitry of a microprocessor. There are many such instructions, but only about 20 percent are actually required for about 80 percent of what a computer is usually called on to do. Reducing the number of instructions represented within the circuitry of the chip (**RISC** stands for **reduced instruction set computing**) to only those that are most frequently used increases the speed at which the remaining instructions can be executed. For instance, a RISC chip can execute most of its instructions within one tick of the system clock compared to several ticks for traditional microprocessors. In addition, a feature called pipelining allows instructions to be decoded while another instruction is being executed. Right now, RISC chips are used primarily in the more powerful workstations, but they are beginning to show up in lower-cost and laptop workstations, as well as in systems that combine aspects of both personal computers and workstations (see photo). RISC chips are also expanding from their workstation niche into other roles, such as controlling printers. RISC technology is also behind chips that are being touted by some as the "foundation for advanced 21st-century computing."

The Sparcbook 1 notebook is powered by a 25 MHz RISC chip.

Source: Courtesy of Tadpole Technologies, Inc.

On the other hand, some question whether RISC technology is, in fact, the wave of the future. So far, software manufacturers have been reluctant to design new versions of software for RISC-based personal computers because they feel such machines will not be popular enough to support the cost required to develop the software. And RISC chips are not without their own complications. Many experts still believe that advances in the architecture of traditional microprocessors, including importing some features of RISC technology, will allow them to keep pace for all but the most demanding applications.

Low-Voltage Microprocessors   Another way that some microprocessors can be categorized is by the amount of electrical power (voltage) they require. Low-voltage CPUs are most important for portable computers that rely primarily on batteries for a power supply. Low-power versions of the 386 and 486 chips that run with only 3.3 volts compared to a normal 5 volts have already been introduced by Intel and Intel-clone manufacturers. Advances in low-voltage chip design are expected to help fuel the trend toward portable "nomadic computing," but other parts of a portable system, like the hard drive and screen, continue to be power hogs.

Coprocessors   In some system units, specialized processor chips called **coprocessors** are added to enhance the computer's performance. These chips perform a specific task and can do so at the same time that the CPU is working on something else. A numeric (math) coprocessor increases the speed of arithmetical calculations. A graphics coprocessor enhances the ability of the CPU to process the calculations needed to create graphics displays. Recently developed communications coprocessors help computers use communications networks. Further, multimedia technology is beginning to spawn new coprocessors that compress video images, process speech, and create the audio equivalent of 3-D sound. The story "Traders of Tomorrow Will Need Numbers at Their Fingertips" illustrates how the availability of specialized processor chips is transforming one occupation.

Memory Chips

As we mentioned, primary storage in today's computers is, like a microprocessor, constructed from a silicon chip containing thousands of transistors embedded on its surface. As you learned in Chapter 2, this form of computer memory is often called semiconductor memory. The chips are often mounted on a small circuit board (one type is called a SIMM, or Single In-Line Memory Module) and then plugged into the motherboard. Memory chips are less complicated, slower, and therefore less expensive to produce than microprocessors. Over the years, the storage capacity of memory chips has been doubling every three to four years, and the cost of memory chips has been decreasing (see Figure 3.21).

Memory chips can vary, both in storage capacity and in the speed at which they can be addressed (that is, the speed at which they can send data to the CPU). Today, an individual memory chip in desktop computers can store over 4 megabits (4 million bits). In 1992, IBM introduced a 16-megabit chip, which is able to store the equivalent of about 1,600 pages of double-spaced typewritten text. This type of chip is expected to be in more common use by 1995.

Memory chip speeds are measured in nanoseconds (ns), and the lower the number of nanoseconds, the faster the chip. Memory chip speed for chips used in newer desktop computers range from 60 ns to 80 ns.

The system unit usually will contain several different types of memory chips, each serving a different purpose.

RAM (random access memory) is the name for the chips that are used in primary storage. There are two types of RAM chips: DRAM, or dynamic random access memory, which are used to make up the majority of primary storage, and a more complex type called SRAM, or static random access memory, which are used for specialized functions within primary storage. RAM is called by that name because any location on the chip can be randomly selected to store data and instructions, which can then be directly accessed and retrieved. As you know, the function of primary storage (and therefore RAM) is the short-term storage of data and program instructions: data and instructions are held at particular addresses within RAM until they are replaced with new data and instructions. The representation of data and instructions within a RAM chip depends on the flow of electric current. If the current is turned off or disrupted by a power surge, a brownout, or electrical

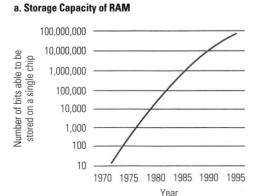

a. Storage Capacity of RAM

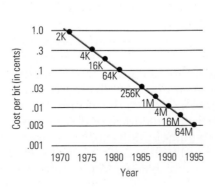

b. Declining Cost of RAM

Figure 3.21

Storage Capacity and Price of Memory Chips

(a) The storage capacity of RAM chips has been doubling every three or four years. **(b)** The cost of RAM has been declining as storage capacity has increased.

Source: Ryan, Bob, "Farewell to Chips," *BYTE,* January 1990. Used by permission of McGraw-Hill, Inc.

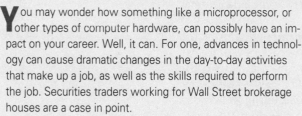
You may wonder how something like a microprocessor, or other types of computer hardware, can possibly have an impact on your career. Well, it can. For one, advances in technology can cause dramatic changes in the day-to-day activities that make up a job, as well as the skills required to perform the job. Securities traders working for Wall Street brokerage houses are a case in point.

In the past, traders were able to get away with relying primarily on gut instinct, word of mouth, and "street smarts." Some traders had nothing more than a high school diploma. But today, making money on Wall Street has become much more mathematically and technologically complex. As workstations powered by RISC chips and math coprocessors have made more and more computing power available at ever-decreasing prices, the ability to use mathematical models in making trading decisions has become increasingly important. As a result, companies like UBS Securities Inc., Bankers Trust Co., and Credit Suisse Financial Products are now looking for traders who can work with numbers, apply them to trading scenarios, and exploit computers as a trading tool. Gut-instinct trading is becoming a much smaller part of the money-making process as advanced math skills push to the forefront. "A seat-o'-the-pants trader can't cut it when juggling multidimensional risk," says Remy Goldstein, managing director of equity products at UBS Securities. Although traders don't need to be programmers, they often work closely with researchers to define and test trading models. What they do need to know is what's behind the math used to trade and how to be able to use their computers to get the results they want. A trader won't be able to compete in tomorrow's marketplace without this ability. And the driving force that has created the need for traders with these new skills is a tiny piece of hardware called the microprocessor.

Source: Based on "Trader of the Future," *Wall Street Computer Review*, Vol. 9, No. 4.

Trading stocks and bonds on Wall Street is fast becoming a computer-intensive occupation.

Source: Tony Stone Worldwide.

Critical Thinking Questions

1 Can you think of some other occupations whose skill requirements might change as a result of the increasing availability of fast and powerful microcomputers?

2 This story describes traders relying more and more on computer-generated models rather than other methods, like street smarts. Do you think this is a positive development? Do you see any potential problems that could result if traders begin to rely exclusively on models?

"noise" generated by lightning, solar flares, or nearby machines, the contents of the chips at the time the disruption occurs will be lost. For this reason, RAM memory is said to be **volatile.**

The amount of manufacturer-installed RAM memory in current desktop microcomputer systems can range anywhere from 256K to 16MB, depending on the cost of the system. As we noted, in most systems, additional RAM can be added directly onto the motherboard or through the use of add-in boards, allowing some microcomputers to possess upward of 64MB of RAM. This development has blurred attempts to classify micro, mini, and mainframe computers by amounts of RAM as microcomputers increasingly encroach on levels of RAM previously possessed only by larger machines.

In addition to utilizing RAM chips as primary storage, most current desktop computer systems today also use a small amount (anywhere from

16K to 256K) of high-speed RAM memory, usually composed of SRAM chips, between the CPU and primary storage. Called **high-speed buffer,** or **cache** (pronounced *cash*), memory, these chips hold the most frequently used instructions and data. These data and instructions can then be retrieved more quickly than if they were located in the more slowly accessed primary storage.

ROM (read-only memory) chips are used for the permanent storage of certain instructions, most frequently parts of the computer's operating system software that check the computer hardware when you turn your computer on and that provide the interface between the CPU and the rest of the motherboard and peripheral devices. (The software located in the ROM chip is often called the system's BIOS, or Basic Input Output System.) Instructions stored in ROM chips cannot be written over or altered and are not lost when electric current is disrupted or turned off, so unlike RAM, ROM is considered nonvolatile. Permanent instructions embedded in ROM chips are sometimes called **firmware,** because it has some characteristics of software and some characteristics of hardware.

Another form of ROM is called **PROM (programmable read-only memory).** PROM chips are just like ROM chips, except that initially the chip is blank—the instructions they contain are specified and added by the purchaser with the use of a special machine. Once the instructions have been added, the chip is the same as a ROM chip, that is, its contents cannot be altered or erased. **EPROM (erasable programmable read-only memory)** chips function the same as PROM chips, except that instructions on the chip can be erased with the use of a special machine using ultraviolet light and new data and instructions inserted in their place. A further variation, the **EEPROM (electrically erasable programmable read-only memory)** chip, can be reprogrammed using special electrical pulses without having to be removed from the computer.

The leading manufacturers of memory chips include NEC, Toshiba, Hitachi, Samsung, Fujitsu, Motorola, Texas Instruments, Phillips, and IBM.

Add-In Boards, Cards, and Controllers

Most newer personal computers can be enhanced and customized by the addition of **add-in boards,** cardlike pieces of equipment that plug into expansion slots on the motherboard. Add-in boards allow you to upgrade and enhance the power and functionality of your computer without going to the expense of replacing the entire unit. The terms *board* and *card* are often used interchangeably in advertisements and popular literature. Some common types of boards include:

▶ Accelerator (or turbo) boards that give the CPU greater processing speed.

▶ Memory expansion boards (or SIMMs) that allow additional RAM chips to be added to the system.

▶ Coprocessor boards on which a math or graphics coprocessor is mounted.

▶ Display adapter boards that act as a translator, converting the CPU's commands so that different types of display devices can be used.

A memory expansion board can be plugged into the motherboard to increase a system's primary storage capacity.

Source: Frederik D. Bodin/Offshoot.

▶ Graphics adapter boards that enable the computer to take advantage of enhanced resolution abilities of advanced monitors (sometimes, display and graphics adapter functions are combined in one board).

▶ Local bus cards that allow signals from peripheral devices to travel directly to the CPU rather than going through the system's regular bus system.

Different forms of **controllers,** which also often come on boards or cards, will usually be included on the motherboard as well, and these, too, can often be replaced with upgraded versions. Controllers are boards that enable the CPU to interface with the system's different peripheral devices. A floppy/hard disk controller card allows the CPU to work with different types of hard and floppy disk drives, and a video/graphics controller helps coordinate the transmission of video data among the CPU, RAM, and display devices.

Ports

The last component of the system unit that we discuss are the **ports.** Ports come through the outside of the system unit's case and are sockets with small pinholes that allow other devices, like a monitor, printer, modem, or mouse, to be plugged into and communicate with the computer system (see Figure 3.22a). Each pin that plugs into a port pinhole has a different function—some carry current, some carry data, and some carry control instructions for the printer or other devices. Ports can be either parallel or serial, the difference between the two relating to the way data is transmitted (see Figure 3.22b). Most systems use parallel ports to connect printers, whereas serial ports are used for communication devices like modems. If the system unit does not have enough ports for all the devices that are to be connected, it may be possible to purchase an add-in board that contains an additional port. However, each computer system has a limit to the number of devices it can support.

a. The System Unit: The Back of the Box

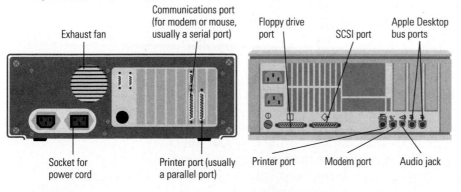

IBM-compatible

Apple Macintosh

b. Parallel Versus Serial Ports

Figure 3.22
Ports
(a) Ports allow input/output and communication devices to be connected to and communicate with other parts of the computer system. **(b)** Parallel ports transmit all 8 bits in a byte at one time. Serial ports transmit a single stream of bits, one bit after the other. (Think of it as data traveling on an eight-lane highway compared to a single-lane road.)

3.3   The Future of the Analyzing Engine

You now know about the way today's computers work. You should also know a little bit about what's around the corner—developments that may change the way computers process information and advances that may make some of the technology you've just read about obsolete. This section should help you get a jump on what's going to be happening in the near future so that you'll be able to anticipate change rather than be surprised by it.

Chips on the Way

As we noted in Chapter 2, continued advances in the speed and power of microprocessors and the storage capacity of memory chips will be critical to the success of many of the new digital technologies, like multimedia, virtual reality, inexpensive supercomputers, and others. Here's what's new or on the way right now.

Alpha Leads the Parade   In early 1992, Digital Equipment Corporation (DEC) announced the Alpha AXP, a 64-bit microprocessor using advanced RISC architecture (see photo). The chip operates at 150 MHz and has the potential to reach 300 MIPS. (In comparison, Sun Microsystem's RISC chip, the MicroSparc, operates at 50 MHz and can process only 59 MIPS, while Intel's fastest chip, the Pentium, has a clock speed of up to 66 MHz and can process 112 MIPS.) A single Alpha chip has roughly the same peak performance as a Cray-1 system, a small supercomputer, according to John Rollwagen, Cray Research Inc.'s chief executive officer. DEC intends to make its chip available to others in the hopes of becoming the RISC-industry standard, much like Intel has for traditional microprocessors. DEC has already placed Alpha chips in its VAX line of mainframe, midrange, and workstation models and recently introduced its first desktop PC powered by the Alpha chip.

Digital's 64-bit Alpha chip.

Source: Courtesy of Digital Equipment Corporation.

    DEC faces a number of obstacles in its drive to make Alpha an industry-wide standard. It has a number of competitors, such as Sun Microsystems, Hewlett-Packard, Silicon Graphics, and Mips Computer Systems. These companies all plan to introduce their own next-generation RISC chips, with performance levels approaching, though not surpassing, that of the Alpha. An alliance created by IBM, Apple, and Motorola has also recently joined the fray, with the Power PC, a powerful new RISC chip that will be finding its way into Apple computers during 1994.

Intel's New Generation   In March 1993, Intel introduced the Pentium, the fifth generation of its "86" chip. Although right now the Pentium is still too expensive to replace its predecessors (it is being used initially in file servers priced between $5,000 and $10,000), it will eventually trickle down to the mass market PC. The Pentium packs over 3 million transistors into a 2.16-inch square of silicon and operates at 66 MHz. It can process up to 112 MIPs and features a 64-bit data bus width. Intel also has another new generation of chips under development. Code-named P-6, they are expected to become available sometime in 1995. Intel engineers have purportedly designed many RISC technologies into the P-6, and it is believed that the P-6 will boost performance significantly from the Pentium.

Super Memories   IBM and Siemens have jointly developed an experimental version of a DRAM chip that can store 64 megabits and hope to have it ready for mass production by 1995. And IBM, Siemens, and Toshiba have announced a $1 billion joint venture to develop and produce a chip a mere .25 microns wide that will be able to store 256 megabits, or the equivalent of around 25,000 double-spaced pages of type, by the late 1990s.

Flash Memory   One of the most exciting new products in the chip arena is a chip that has been dubbed "flash memory." Unlike conventional RAM, flash memory chips can store data even when power is turned off, but data can also be erased by the user and new data inserted in its place. Their technology is very similar to the EEPROM chips you read about earlier in this chapter. Manufacturers hope to use flash memory chips to replace hard disk drives as a means for permanently storing data. Right now, flash memory chips are starting to be used in notebook and palmtop computers because, though they are still more expensive than a comparable capacity hard disk drive, they are smaller, faster, more rugged, and use less power. With joint ventures between IBM and Toshiba and between Advanced Micro Devices and Fujitsu now competing with Intel in the market, chip prices are expected to decrease, and the market is expected to grow from $130 million in sales in 1991 to around $1.5 billion by 1995.

Many American companies like IBM and others are entering into joint ventures with Japanese companies. The story, "Japanese Chip Makers— Should We Fight or Join Them?" discusses some of the issues surrounding this development.

Beyond the Present Limits

Let's now take a minute to look at some technologies that, though still in the experimental stage, may be influencing our lives in five to ten years.

Smaller Is Faster   The traditional method for increasing the speed and power of chips has been to decrease the distance that electrical current must travel between transistors by making transistors smaller and smaller. This allows them to be packed closer and closer together. The width of the lines forming transistors has shrunk to less than 1 micron (transistors on Digital's Alpha chip are only .75 microns wide), and the number of transistors on microprocessors and memory chips have reached into the millions. Nonetheless, scientists continue to search for ways to make even smaller transistors. For instance, in spring 1992, IBM announced that its scientists had built the world's smallest transistor to date, so small that its active area is just 1/75,000 of the diameter of a human hair (or .00133 microns wide). Transistors of this size would eventually enable RAM chips to hold up to 4 billion bits of data, compared to the 64 million bits held by chips currently being produced. On an even smaller scale, other scientists at IBM have demonstrated an ultra-tiny electrical switch that relies on the motion of a single atom as its critical moving element. These scientists are investigating a new field, called *nanoelectronics,* in which chips and other electronic devices would be assembled one atom or molecule at a time in order to bypass the physical limits of current silicon technology. Commercially practical devices based on nanoelectronics are probably still far off, but one researcher, Joseph Demuth, a senior manager at IBM's Watson Research

S O C I E T Y

Japanese Chip Makers—Should We Fight or Join Them?

The specter of Japanese domination of the world's computer industry has loomed on the horizon for a number of years. In the late 1980s, many experts predicted that Japanese companies would soon monopolize the semiconductor industry, particularly the manufacture and sale of semiconductor memories, and that U.S. companies' supply of these critical components of computer systems would become totally dependent on Japan. Between 1980 and 1990, the U.S. semiconductor industry's world market share fell from 60 to 35 percent, and during the same period, Japan's doubled to more than 50 percent. In the last half of the 1980s, American employment in the semiconductor industry dropped by 27,000 jobs, or about 10 percent.

The federal government, concerned that American producers of semiconductors were in danger of extinction, contributed over a half-billion dollars to an industry consortium called Sematech to help rebuild America's sputtering chip industry. At the same time, politicians pressured Japan to open its own markets to chips made in America. Trade agreements signed with Japan in 1986 and 1991 had as their goal increasing U.S. companies' share of the Japanese market from around 8.5 percent in 1985 to 20 percent by the end of 1992. And in 1988, Congress formed the National Advisory Committee on Semiconductors to come up with a comprehensive strategy for the industry. These efforts have since borne some fruit: the American share of the worldwide market has increased to around 40 percent, and its share of the Japanese market to around 14.5 percent.

But rather than continuing to focus on "America First," U.S. companies now appear to be increasingly abandoning nationalistic strategies. They, instead, are entering into joint ventures and other alliances with their Japanese and other global competitors. In 1992 alone, Advanced Micro Devices and Fujitsu entered into a $700 million joint venture to develop, build, and market a form of chip called a flash memory; IBM, Siemens, and Toshiba formed a $1 billion joint venture to design memory chips that can hold 256 megabits; and Sharp agreed to make flash memory chips for Intel, among others. The alliances result in part from the huge costs involved in developing and producing new generations of advanced chips.

Sources: Based on Ferguson, Charles H., "Computers and the Coming of the U.S. Keiretsu," *Harvard Business Review,* July–August 1990; Pollack, Andrew, "U.S. Chip Makers Stem the Tide in Trade Battles with the Japanese," *New York Times,* April 9, 1992; Markoff, John, "Rethinking the National Chip Policy," *New York Times,* July 14, 1992.

Critical Thinking Questions

1 Are U.S. companies being short-sighted and leaving themselves open to future ambush when they agree to share technological developments with companies from foreign countries? Even if such alliances are good business strategy for a company, should the U.S. government be concerned? What if the result is to move even more jobs outside the United States?

2 If the United States develops a national industrial strategy, and spends tax dollars helping hi-tech companies develop new chips, should this information be shared with foreign corporations? Can sharing of tax-paid research be avoided in the current climate when globalization appears to be the leading trend?

Center in Yorktown, New York, says he would not be surprised to see products using the technology as early as the year 2000.

New Materials   Other researchers are looking at alternative materials from which chips and transistors could be constructed. One candidate is *gallium arsenide,* which allows electrical pulses to be transmitted, and switches to be turned off and on, at much faster speeds than silicon now allows. Chips made from gallium arsenide also require less power and therefore generate less heat than silicon chips. As a result, they can operate at higher temperatures. However, they are still more difficult to handle and expensive to use. For example, in 1992, Cray Computer Corporation, a maker of supercomputers, had to abandon plans to build a commercial version of a high-speed supercomputer based on gallium arsenide chips because it could not find any customers willing to risk $30 million (the cost of the machine) on unproven technology.

Another avenue hopes to take advantage of the phenomenon of *superconductivity*—a property of certain metals that allows current to flow without creating any electrical resistance when the metals are cooled to extremely low temperatures. When conventional integrated circuits are packed closely together, they generate heat, and when heat builds, electrical resistance increases, slowing the flow of current or, even worse, melting the circuit. Interest in a form of experimental circuit called a *Josephson junction*, which uses superconductor technology, has increased as research breakthroughs indicate that superconductivity may be achievable at much warmer temperatures than previously believed.

Another exciting possibility is Carbon-60 molecules, called *bucky balls* for their resemblance to geodesic domes created by Buckminster Fuller. A material that looks like black soot until you see it under a microscope, bucky balls were once thought to exist only in space as interstellar dust, but in 1990, researchers discovered that they could be mass-produced in a laboratory (see photo). Bucky balls can be arranged in layers only 1/1,000 of a micron thick, a thousand times smaller than the thinnest silicon materials used in integrated circuits. Early experiments indicate that bucky balls could be used as a component for superconducting circuits and, since they seem to react to light, for optical applications.

A fourth avenue of research has focused on possible biological components. For instance, Professor Robert Birge, the director of the Center for Molecular Electronics at Syracuse University, has been experimenting with creating computer memories from a protein derived from a bacterium called *Halobacterium halobium*, which lives in salt marshes. When a light is shone on the bacterium, a protein called bacteriorhodopsin releases a small electrical charge that allows it to turn on and off like a light switch and to store digitized data. The speed at which the transition is made must be measured on a picosecond time scale compared to the nanosecond time scale used for today's semiconductors.

Finally, IBM, AT&T, General Electric, and Honeywell have recently formed a consortium to step up research on *optoelectronics*—a technology that would create chips that use light waves traveling over fiber-optic filaments instead of electrical pulses traveling through copper wire to transmit binary signals.

Although it is impossible to predict which, if any, of these experimental technologies will be the next wave of the future, one thing's for sure: by the year 2000, existing technologies will almost certainly have been transformed beyond what we can probably contemplate today.

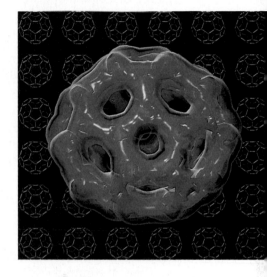

Bucky balls may make superconducting circuits easier to construct.

Source: J. Bernhole et al., North Carolina State U/Science Photo Library. Photo Researchers, Inc.

New Forms of Processing

In addition to striving for even higher levels of microminiaturization and searching for new materials, researchers are focusing on alternative methods of processing information.

The Virtues of Parallelism   Earlier in this chapter, you read a description of how conventional computers process data: during a machine cycle, the CPU performs instructions one step at a time, in sequential order, until the entire program is finished. This method is called **sequential,** or **serial, processing** and has been the way computers have processed data since the days of John von Neumann, who was instrumental in creating the original architecture (or design) for the modern-day computer. (In fact, scientists sometimes refer to computers as "von Neumann machines" for this reason.) However, many experts now believe that a different design, called **parallel processing,** will provide a more efficient, faster, and less expensive method. Parallel processing divides up a problem; parcels it out to be worked on simultaneously by dozens, hundreds, or even thousands of CPUs; and then brings all the finished pieces of work together at the end. Computers that use hundreds or thousands of CPUs are called **massively, or highly, parallel computers** (see Figure 3.23).

The technology behind parallel processing started to develop steam in the early 1980s, as scientists at Cray Research Company looked for ways to make their supercomputers faster. For a number of years, parallel processing was used primarily in supercomputers for military and scientific applications, but now it is poised to invade the commercial market. Oracle Systems, for example, which makes database software used for airline reservations and banking transactions, has introduced a version specifically designed to run on parallel computers. Companies such as Dow Jones, American Express, Prudential Securities, and even the Slovakian state savings bank, Slovenska Statna Sporitelna, have purchased systems based on parallel processing.

David Gelenter, a computer scientist at Yale University, has created software that could make the technology available to even smaller companies. Using this software (called Piranha Linda), any company with a dozen or so workstations hooked together in a local area network could use the workstations' idle time to work on problems with supercomputerlike efficiency. For instance, the idle time of brokers' workstations in one Wall Street brokerage is harnessed to run large computational projects involving mathematical models of financial market behavior. The firm gains the power of a supercomputer at a fraction of the cost while providing its brokers with workstations. Technology like Piranha Linda does concern some who believe it could infringe on the rights of computer users: what if you don't want to share?

Neural Networks   Another new form of processing, called a neural network, or simply a neural net, mimics, to a certain extent, the human brain in that it enables a computer to "learn" through observation and repetition. Researchers originally developed neural networks with software programs running on conventional computers, but they have recently been successful in creating a chip that embodies this new form of processing. Instead of processing instructions and data in a traditional, sequential order, the switches of neural network chips, which form a highly interconnected grid (like a neuron in the brain), operate and process in parallel. In doing so, it is able to detect patterns and learn from them. This exotic technology is still in its infancy, but commercial applications are beginning to be developed and marketed. You will learn more about neural networks in Chapter 14.

Figure 3.23
Parallel Processing

Computers that use parallel processing have multiple CPUs that work on different parts of a problem simultaneously and then bring all the parts together to obtain the result.

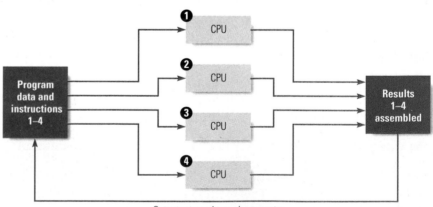

Output returned to main computer

Summary

The Central Processing Unit: Center of the Computer Universe

▶ The central processing unit (CPU) processes data and controls the other parts of the computer system. It consists of two primary parts: the arithmetic/logic unit (ALU) and the control unit.

▶ The CPU works closely with primary storage, which stores program instructions and data needed for processing. Every character stored in primary storage is assigned an address that identifies where it is located within primary storage.

▶ Addresses usually have a fixed storage capacity and can hold 1 byte, which is sufficient to store a single character (a letter or number). Total storage capacity of primary storage may range from kilobytes (thousands of bytes) to megabytes (millions of bytes) to gigabytes (billions of bytes).

▶ The ALU and control unit contain registers that function as temporary storage locations and staging areas for program instructions and data that need to be transferred to the CPU from primary storage before processing begins. There are several different types of registers, each with a specific function.

▶ Binary systems need just two symbols to represent all information. A binary numbering system uses zeros and ones (also called binary digits or bits). Electrical circuits can represent and store information expressed in binary form because they themselves exist in one of two states.

▶ EBCDIC and ASCII are two common types of computer binary codes. Each uses a string of bits to represent numbers, letters, and symbols. Both codes also include an additional bit, called a parity, or check, bit, that helps ensure that the CPU correctly understands which character is being transmitted.

▶ Logic gates, a form of mathematical operation used in Boolean algebra, are binary and can be used to add, subtract, multiply, divide, and compare symbols or numbers. Just as circuits can be used to represent and store data, they can also be used to create logic gates. Logic gates enable the CPU to perform arithmetical and logical operations.

▶ Machine language instructions correspond to, and can thereby activate, a set of the computer's circuits. The processing of a single machine language instruction is called a machine cycle. A machine cycle has two parts: the instruction cycle and the execution cycle. The machine cycle is repeated over and over until the entire program has been processed.

▶ Computer speed can be measured in MIPs (millions of instructions per second), flops (floating point operations per second), or the time it takes to complete one machine cycle. Cycle times can vary from milliseconds (thousandths of a second), to microseconds (millionths of a second), to nanoseconds (billionths of a second), to picoseconds (trillionths of a second).

Unmasking the Electronic Genie: Inside Your Computer's System Unit

▶ Some of the important components found within the system unit of a typical personal computer include the CPU, specialized processor chips, a system clock, various add-in boards, and memory chips all mounted on a motherboard.

- Microprocessors are made from silicon semiconductor chips containing up to millions of transistors. The three main elements that affect the speed and power of a microprocessor are clock speed, word length, and bus width. Current traditional microprocessors have clock speeds of up to 66 MHz, handle word lengths up to 64 bits, and have bus widths of 16 to 64 bits. A different form of microprocessor uses RISC technology to enhance performance.

- Primary storage is also made from silicon semiconductor chips. There are several types of memory chips. Random access memory (RAM) chips are the primary component of primary storage. Read-only memory (ROM) chips are used for permanent storage of certain instructions. Other forms of memory chips include the PROM, EPROM, and EEPROM.

- Coprocessors are specialized processor chips that can be added to enhance a computer's performance. Add-in boards also allow a computer user to upgrade performance without replacing the entire computer. Controllers are boards that enable the CPU to interface with different peripheral devices.

- Parallel and serial ports allow printers, monitors, modems, mice, and other input/output devices to be connected and to communicate with other parts of the computer system.

The Future of the Analyzing Engine

- Some advances in technology that may impact processing performance and storage capacity in the near future include Digital's RISC-based Alpha chips, Intel's next-generation P-6 chip, the 64-megabit memory chip, and flash memory. Researchers are also focusing on creating even smaller transistors, on alternatives to silicon, and on new forms of processing like parallel processing and neural networks.

Key Terms

central processing unit (CPU)	EBCDIC
system unit	ASCII
computer system	parity, or check, bit
arithmetic/logic unit (ALU)	machine language instructions
control unit	machine cycle
primary storage	MIPS (millions of instructions per second)
address	
byte	flops (floating point operations per second)
kilobyte (KB or K)	
megabyte (MB or meg)	milliseconds
gigabyte (GB or gig)	microseconds
terabyte (TB)	nanoseconds
registers	picoseconds
instruction register	motherboard
address register	system clock
storage register	expansion slots
accumulator	clock speed
binary	megahertz (MHz)
bits	word
binary codes	word length

bus
bus width
RISC (reduced instruction set computing)
coprocessors
RAM (random access memory)
volatile
high-speed buffer, or cache
ROM (read-only memory)
firmware
PROM (programmable read-only memory)

EPROM (erasable programmable read-only memory)
EEPROM (electrically erasable programmable read-only memory)
add-in boards
controllers
ports
sequential, or serial, processing
parallel processing
massively, or highly, parallel computers

 Interactive Supplement

Review Questions

1 Describe the functions of the ALU, control unit, and registers.

2 What role does primary storage play in processing?

3 Explain why the binary system is so important to the representation, storage, and processing of information in modern-day computers.

4 What are binary codes, and why were they necessary? How are EBCDIC and ASCII similar, and in what ways are they different?

5 What is a parity bit, and why is it used? (Include a discussion of odd- and even-parity systems in your response.)

6 What are logic gates, and what role do they play in the processing of information by a computer?

7 List the steps the CPU takes in executing a single program instruction.

8 Name and describe three different ways that computer speed can be measured.

9 Identify the major components within a typical system unit and their respective functions.

10 Name the primary factors that affect the speed and processing power of a microprocessor, and explain the role that each plays in determining processing speed.

11 How do RISC chips differ from traditional microprocessors?

12 Define the following terms: RAM, DRAM, SRAM, ROM, PROM, EPROM, and EEPROM.

13 Why are coprocessors and add-in boards used? Name and describe the functions of at least two types of coprocessors and four types of add-in boards.

14 How do a parallel port and serial port differ?

15 Discuss the potential impact of flash memory.

16 What new materials and forms of processing are researchers hoping to use to create faster computers?

Problem-Solving and Skill-Building Exercises

1 Get together with a group of three other students, and assign each student to play the role of one of the logic gates in Figure 3.9. Use arms to represent the input channel and voice to represent the output channel. Talk your way through the addition of a 1 and a 0, and then a 1 and a 1.

2 A manufacturer of semiconductor chips would like to construct a plant in your area. Your local government is conducting public hearings on whether to approve the project. Prepare a short oral presentation (no more than 5 minutes) or report (no more than 3 pages) for the hearing focusing on (a) the environmental hazards associated with chip manufacture, (b) the jobs that would be created, or (c) some other relevant topic of your choice. After listening to the presentations of your classmates or reading their reports, take a vote on whether the project should be approved.

3 You have been given $1,500 to purchase a microcomputer. Pick two that you might consider purchasing, and make a checklist for each that identifies their system unit components, such as the type of microprocessor (including clock speed, word length, and bus width), amount of RAM, and number and type of ports. (Don't worry about peripheral devices like monitors, hard disk drives, or printers.) Which of the two machines would you choose and why? (*Note:* Good sources of information include advertisements in recent issues of computer magazines such as *PC Week*, *PC Magazine*, *BYTE*, or *MacWorld*, or sales literature from your local computer store.)

PERSONAL TECHNOLOGY

Buying Your First Microcomputer

Buying your first personal computer is always confusing. After reading this chapter, you should at least be able to better understand PC advertisements and salespersons' lingo. Though that's certainly a start, it doesn't really answer the question, "What computer should I buy?" There are three basic issues to consider: how much money you have (and are willing to part with), what you want to do with the computer, and the time dimension of the investment you are about to make.

The tradeoffs you should think about before deciding on a purchase are summarized in Figure 3.24. One place to begin your decision process is to ask, "How much money am I able to spend?" Sometimes this will answer the problem all by itself. Right now, if you have only $500 or so to spend, you will only be able to buy a relatively slow machine that does not have much RAM memory (usually only 640K to 1 megabyte), like a small Apple Macintosh or one of the IBM PC compatibles called XTs or ATs.

A second factor to consider is what you want to do with your computer. Simple word processing and spreadsheets (electronic accounting tools) can be done entirely adequately on an XT or AT machine or small Macintosh, with a black-and-white monitor.

But if you want to do graphics, complex spreadsheeting, long-document word processing, or if you want to run graphical interface programs like Windows, you will need a machine using a 386- or 486SX series microprocessor or an Apple Macintosh LC or II, with at least 2 (and preferably 4) megabytes of RAM. Right now, these cost from $1,000 to $1,500 although prices have been dropping rapidly due to increased competition.

A third factor to consider is the time value of your purchase: how long do you want this investment to last and be useful? How quickly do you need this computing power? The price of computers is dropping by half every two years, and their power is doubling every two years. (For instance, a computer with a 386DX microprocessor cost approximately $4,800 in 1990, but only around $2,400 in 1992. And you could buy a computer with a 486SX microprocessor in 1992 for the same price you would have paid for a computer with a 386SX microprocessor in 1990.) No matter what you buy today, it will be quickly outdated in five years for sure. What to do?

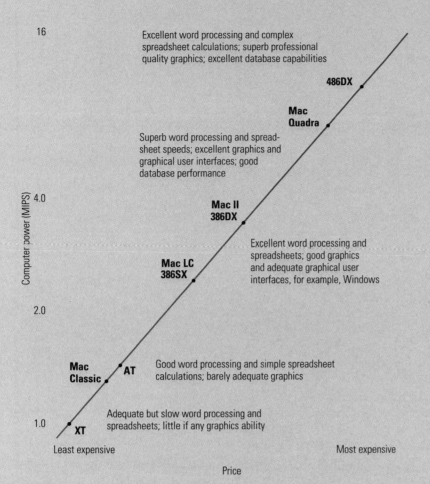

16

Excellent word processing and complex spreadsheet calculations; superb professional quality graphics; excellent database capabilities

486DX

Figure 3.24
This figure illustrates the power and price tradeoffs that you need to consider when purchasing a microcomputer.

Mac Quadra

Superb word processing and spreadsheet speeds; excellent graphics and graphical user interfaces; good database performance

4.0

Mac II 386DX

Excellent word processing and spreadsheets; good graphics and adequate graphical user interfaces, for example, Windows

Mac LC 386SX

2.0

Mac Classic • **AT**

Good word processing and simple spreadsheet calculations; barely adequate graphics

Adequate but slow word processing and spreadsheets; little if any graphics ability

1.0 • XT

Least expensive   Most expensive

Computer power (MIPS)

Price

You can spend a large amount of money now ($1,500 to $2,000 or more) and have a machine that will be capable of running the latest, most powerful software for the next 3 to 5 years. Or you can spend between $500 and $1,000 and buy an adequate machine for now but one that will be obsolete in 3 to 5 years. Machines in the range between these two extremes are probably the best values.

Once you have determined the basic trade-offs you want to make between price, power, and time, it's time to start seriously looking for a machine. Begin your comparison shopping by first checking out magazines, catalogs and local newspaper advertisements. You will find that there are a number of places where you can purchase a computer. Your options include the computer departments of national retail chains such as Walmart, Sears, Caldors and others (best for relatively inexpensive, prepackaged systems), national and local stores specializing in computers (these usually will have the widest selection and the most knowledgeable staff), mail order companies (often a source of good deals, but not necessarily the best choice for a beginner), buying directly from the manufacturer (now becoming increasingly popular) and finally, purchasing a used machine, either from an acquaintance or through a used computer exchange (usually a good value, but often somewhat risky).

Choosing your basic system is only the first step in the process. What about secondary storage options and other peripheral devices like monitors and printers? What communications capabilities will you need? What is the most appropriate operating system for your computer? And what about software? We'll consider these questions in later Personal Technology sections.

If you're shopping for your first computer, a national or local store specializing in computers will likely be your best bet.

Source: Courtesy of CompUSA.

After completing this chapter, you will:

▶ Understand what secondary storage is.

▶ Be familiar with the major types of storage media and devices.

▶ Understand how data is organized within secondary storage.

Storage Technologies

4

WORM a Big Winner for Vegas Bookies

Leroy's Horse and Sports Palace in Las Vegas, Nevada, does not look like the kind of place where you'd find leading-edge information technology. A smoke-filled parlor littered with racing forms and tout sheets contains a long gambling counter and a crowded bar. But look beyond the views that first confront you, and you'll find one of the most modern automated bookie operations in the world.

It's not all that surprising when you think about it. Vegas bookies need to keep track of bets on hundreds of different games and horse races that take place each day throughout the country, and most important, they need to know that the bets cannot be altered or erased after the game's or race's results are known.

In the past, Leroy's used an old-fashioned system—paper and pens. A bettor would merely write down his or her bet on a piece of paper and hand it over to someone at the betting counter. Although this was the way it had been done for centuries by bookies, it was a shaky system that left the door wide open for abuse: bets could easily be changed after a game or race had started.

Enter storage technology. When the Nevada Gaming Commission ruled that all Vegas bookies had to become computerized, Leroy's owner, Vic Salerno, went looking for a system. Not finding any to his liking, he and several partners created one of their own based on Write-Once, Read-Many (WORM) optical storage technology (you will learn more about WORM in Section 4.3). Salerno saw that the unique characteristics of WORM—the ability to record a large amount of data that could not be accidentally or purposefully erased—made it perfect for high-security, long-term data storage and retrieval.

Leroy's WORM system uses an Intel 80386-based personal computer equipped with a Plasmon Data Systems 940MB WORM optical disk and disk drive.

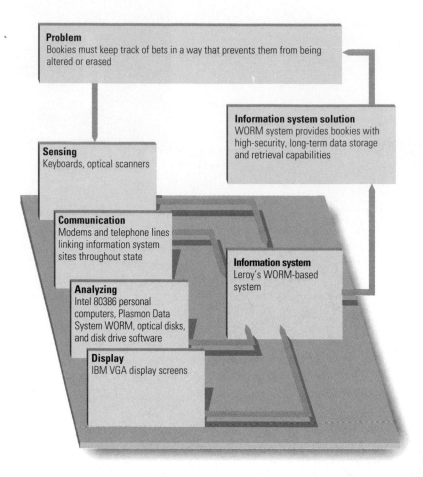

Problem
Bookies must keep track of bets in a way that prevents them from being altered or erased

Information system solution
WORM system provides bookies with high-security, long-term data storage and retrieval capabilities

Sensing
Keyboards, optical scanners

Communication
Modems and telephone lines linking information system sites throughout state

Information system
Leroy's WORM-based system

Analyzing
Intel 80386 personal computers, Plasmon Data System WORM, optical disks, and disk drive software

Display
IBM VGA display screens

Ticket agents record every bet made on the disk. Bettors can also process their own betting slips by using an input device called an optical reader. The reader then generates a ticket automatically. With the system, Salerno can keep tabs on winning bets paid out by his cashiers and display information from any report stored during the past eight months on the system's IBM VGA computer monitors. The system is linked by modem to 18 other sites throughout the state.

WORM has proved a winner for Leroy's in more ways than one: it has been so successful that 65 of the 72 legal bookies in Nevada have purchased it to use as well. As Vic Salerno says, in Nevada, "Betting will never be the same."

Source: Based on Daly, James, "WORM Big Winner for Bookies," *Computerworld,* July 15, 1991.

One of the reasons information systems are so valuable is that they give us the ability to store large quantities of information in a form that can be easily accessed. Storage technology makes this possible. Chapter 3 showed you how primary storage temporarily stores program instructions and data being processed by the CPU. But what about permanent storage? The answer lies with something called **secondary storage**, which stores programs and data while they are not being actively used. It holds much more data and is much less expensive, per kilobyte stored, than primary storage. Unlike primary storage, which is *volatile* (it loses what is stored unless electricity is flowing through it), secondary storage has the advantage of being *nonvolatile* (it does not need electricity to retain data). However, although data can be transferred from secondary storage to the CPU quite rapidly, it is still

Most expensive / fastest

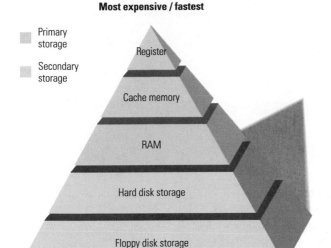

Primary storage

Secondary storage

Register

Cache memory

RAM

Hard disk storage

Floppy disk storage

Least expensive / slowest

Figure 4.1
Memory Pyramid for a Typical Microcomputer
There are two basic forms of computer memory—primary storage and secondary storage. The pyramid illustrates the expense and amount of time required to access data stored in the various types of memory within a typical microcomputer, ranging from the most expensive and fastest at the top to the least expensive and slowest at the bottom. Storage capacities also generally follow a pyramid shape. Registers have the least capacity (less than 1KB), and secondary storage, the most (although hard disks hold more than floppies).

Source: Adapted from Ryan, Bob, "Scaling the Memory Pyramid," *BYTE,* March 1992. Used by permission of McGraw-Hill, Inc.

much slower than primary storage. Figure 4.1 shows you how different types of primary and secondary storage compare in terms of expense and the amount of time required for data transfer.

In this chapter, we first look at **secondary storage media** (such as magnetic tapes and disks), which the data and programs are actually stored on, and **secondary storage devices** (such as disk drives and tape units), which write data and instructions onto storage media, read what is on the media, and then communicate it to the CPU. As you will see, each form has advantages and disadvantages. The physical media and devices used for secondary storage are just half the story, however. Equally important are the various methods of organizing the data that is to be stored. We finish up our examination of secondary storage with a look at those methods and how they are related to the storage medium chosen.

A high-density 1/4-inch tape cartridge manufactured by 3M can hold up to 1.35 gigabytes.

Source: Courtesy of 3M Corporation.

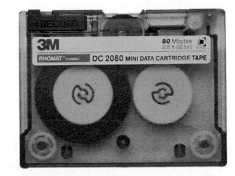

4.1   Magnetic Tape

Once the most common form of secondary storage medium, **magnetic tape** has been bypassed in recent years by magnetic disks. Today, magnetic tape is most frequently used as a low-cost way to store data that does not require immediate access and as a way to back up, or duplicate, data and programs used in large and medium-sized computer systems.

Magnetic tape is created from thin plastic coated with a substance that can be magnetized. Traditional varieties of magnetic tape include one that is 1/2 inch wide and stored on large reels up to 14 inches in diameter (about 3,600 feet of tape) and another which is 1/4 inch wide and stored in cartridge form (typically up to 1,000 feet of tape) (see photos).

Traditional magnetic tape records each byte of data in sequential order in a column separated into nine separate **tracks:** one for each bit of information

A 10 1/2-inch magnetic tape reel can hold 2,400 feet of tape and has a storage capacity of 200MB–250MB.

Source: Chip Henderson/Tony Stone Images.

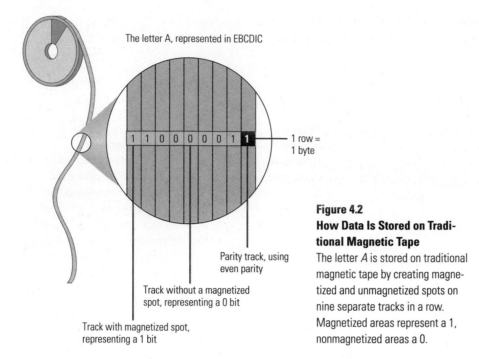

The letter A, represented in EBCDIC

1 row =
1 byte

Parity track, using
even parity

Track without a magnetized
spot, representing a 0 bit

Track with magnetized spot,
representing a 1 bit

Figure 4.2
How Data Is Stored on Tradi-
tional Magnetic Tape
The letter *A* is stored on traditional
magnetic tape by creating magnetized and unmagnetized spots on
nine separate tracks in a row.
Magnetized areas represent a 1,
nonmagnetized areas a 0.

in the byte, plus a parity bit. Magnetized spots represent 1s; nonmagnetized
spots, 0s. Figure 4.2 illustrates how data is stored on a magnetic tape.

A tape's storage capacity (the amount of data that can be stored) is affected by two factors: the length of the tape and the amount of data that can
be physically squeezed onto each inch. Tape densities for traditional tape
range from 1,600 bytes per inch (bpi) for low-density tapes to 6,250 bpi for
high-density tapes. A 10½-inch high-density tape reel can hold up to
200–250 megabytes of data, whereas a tape cartridge containing 1,000 feet of
high-density tape might hold up to 1.35 gigabytes.

Recently, manufacturers, borrowing in part from the technology behind
digital audiotapes (a new form of music tape that uses digital recording
technology to achieve extremely high audio quality), have developed a
slightly different form of magnetic tape. Called *R-DATs*, the tapes are 4 to 8
millimeters wide and have greatly enhanced storage capacities. For instance,
a single R-DAT cartridge containing 90 meters of 4-millimeter tape has a
storage capacity of more than 2 gigabytes. By 1994, manufacturers are expected to introduce 120-meter-length tapes that can hold 4 gigabytes, and
further enhancements are planned to increase storage capacities to 8 gigabytes by 1995.[1] The high densities are achieved by using a method of recording data different from that used by traditional tapes. Instead of laying down
the data in horizontal rows, R-DATs use a technique called *helical-scanning* to
put down the data in diagonal stripes. R-DATs are sometimes called helical
scan tapes for this reason.

The peripheral devices most commonly used with magnetic tapes are
called **tape units.** Reel-to-reel units use two reels: a reel with the tape that is
to be read or written on and a second reel to take up the tape as it unwinds.
The tape passes through a **read/write head,** the part of the device that can
sense or read the magnetic status of the bits and that can write magnetic
spots onto the tape. The magnetic status of the bits is translated into patterns
of electric current when being communicated back and forth from the CPU.

Cartridge tape units are increasingly replacing reel-to-reel units for mainframe and minicomputers and are frequently used for backup on microcomputers. Both reel-to-reel and cartridge tape units suffer from the

same disadvantage, however: they can only access, or retrieve, data on magnetic tape in the same sequential order as it was recorded. To read the tenth record on a tape file, a user must read or skip over the first nine records. As a result, access time (the amount of time required to retrieve data and transfer it to the CPU) can be relatively slow if the data you need is spread throughout the tape. In addition, in systems that store large amounts of data on tape, access time can be further slowed by the need to find the appropriate tape in the **tape library,** as well as the time required to manually mount or load the tape onto the tape unit. However, automated tape library systems that use robot arms to move magnetic cartridge tapes back and forth are now being marketed by Storage Technology, Inc. and IBM for both mainframe and midrange computer systems (see photo).[2]

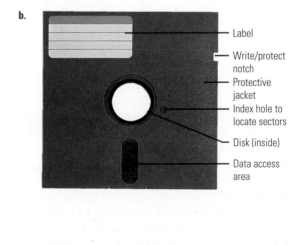

Magnetic tape cartridges can now be handled in a more efficient manner by automated tape libraries that use robots.

Source: Courtesy of IBM.

4.2   Magnetic Disks

The most common secondary storage medium is the **magnetic disk.** Unlike magnetic tape, data stored on magnetic disks can be accessed in any order that the user chooses (called *direct,* or *random, access*) and therefore can be retrieved more quickly. There are two basic types of magnetic disks: floppy disks and hard disks.

Floppy Disks

The secondary storage medium that you are probably most familiar with is the **floppy disk** (sometimes called a **diskette**). Floppy disks are available in two sizes: 5-1/4 inches and 3-1/2 inches. The 5-1/4-inch version contains a thin and flexible (hence the name "floppy") circle of mylar plastic coated with a magnetizable substance and encased in a flexible square jacket. An opening in the jacket exposes the part of the disk's surface that is being read or written on. The 3-1/2-inch version, which is quickly becoming the new

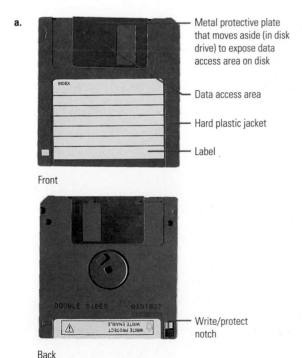

a.

— Metal protective plate that moves aside (in disk drive) to expose data access area on disk

— Data access area

— Hard plastic jacket

— Label

Front

Write/protect notch

Back

b.

— Label

— Write/protect notch

— Protective jacket

— Index hole to locate sectors

— Disk (inside)

— Data access area

Floppy disks come in two sizes: **(a)** 3-1/2" disks and **(b)** 5-1/4" disks.

Source: Fredrik D. Bodin/Offshoot.

standard, is enclosed in a stiff, square plastic cover with a piece of metal that slides open to uncover the surface of the disk (see photos). Floppy disks are one of the most inexpensive storage mediums and the most commonly used for microcomputers.

Like magnetic tape, floppy disks are divided into **tracks**. On floppy disks, tracks take the form of 40 to 80 concentric rings. The disk is further divided into a number of pie-shaped wedges called **sectors.** On a traditional floppy, each track within each sector contains the same amount of information—tracks at the narrow end of the wedge are packed more densely than tracks at the wide end. An alternative method, called constant-density recording, is used by Apple Macintosh computers. This method uses the larger outside tracks to hold more data than the smaller inside tracks. Figure 4.3a illustrates how floppy disks traditionally store data, and Figure 4.3b illustrates constant-density recording.

No matter which method is used, the exact number of tracks and sectors depends on the type of floppy disk, disk drive, and operating system being used. The process of defining a disk's tracks and sectors is called **formatting** and must be done the first time a disk is used.

After a disk has been formatted, data can be recorded on it. As with magnetic tape, data is broken down into bits and represented by magnetized and nonmagnetized spots, but instead of being recorded in rows, it is recorded on a section of track within a given sector. This is called the **sector method.** When data needs to be retrieved, it can be located using an address consisting of a sector number and an individual data record number.

The overall storage capacity of a floppy disk depends on several factors, such as whether the disk can store data on one side *(single-sided disks)* or two sides *(double-sided disks)*, the number of tracks per inch the disk has, and the bits per inch that can be recorded on the disk. Although physically larger than 3-1/2-inch floppy disks, 5-1/4-inch floppy disks actually have smaller

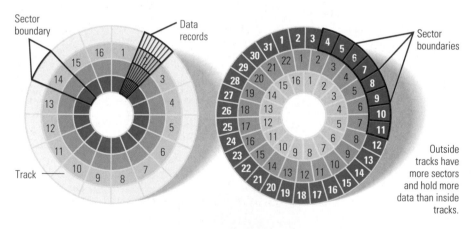

a. Traditional Method   **b. Constant-Density Method**

Figure 4.3
How Floppy Disks Store Data
(a) On a typical floppy disk, the amount of the data recorded on each track is the same, but the density varies because more data needs to be packed into the narrow ends of the sector compared to the wide ends. Outer tracks hold less data than they might otherwise be able to hold. **(b)** An alternative method uses the larger, outside tracks to hold more sectors and data than the smaller, inside tracks. As a result, outer track space is used more efficiently.

Source: Adapted from Kirk, Rod, et al., "More Bits per Inch," *BYTE,* March 1992. Used by permission of McGraw-Hill, Inc.

storage capacities—from 360K for low-density disks to 1.2MB for high-density disks. Right now, high-density (HD) 3-1/2-inch disks store 1.44MB to 2MB and low-density 3-1/2-inch disks store 720K to 1MB.

A number of efforts are underway to produce floppy disks and disk drives that can handle higher densities. The original high-density floppy was the 10MB Bernoulli pioneered by Iomega. The Bernoulli system uses a special drive that allows a 5-1/4-inch floppy disk, spinning at high speed, to float on a cushion of air. The technology uses principles of fluid dynamics to position the drive's read/write head. Iomega has since developed a Bernoulli cartridge containing two floppy disks that together can hold up to 90MB of data.

Another system creates high-density floppies by combining them with optical technology called *flopticals.* A floptical system uses regular 3-1/2-inch floppy disks coupled with a special floptical disk drive that uses a light beam to position the read/write head. The technology enables flopticals to hold up to 21MB.[3]

Japanese manufacturers are also looking at ways of increasing the storage capacities of floppy disks without the need for a special drive. Production of a 4MB floppy has recently begun, while Toshiba has developed the technology to produce very-high-density floppies that would have about 12MB of storage space. Both of these floppies will be able to be used with a regular floppy disk drive.

A regular **floppy disk drive** accepts either a 5-1/4-inch floppy or a 3-1/2-inch floppy, but not both. (Many microcomputers, though not all, come with two floppy disk drives—one for each size disk.) A diskette is inserted into a drive by pushing it through a slot (see photo). Disk drives for 3-1/2-inch disks require nothing further, but those for 5-1/4-inch drives need to be closed, usually by flipping a lever. Once inside the disk drive, the disk spins continuously within its cover at 360 revolutions per minute, and data is read and recorded by a read/write head similar to the one used for magnetic tape. Disk drive controllers (which you learned about in Chapter 3) work with the CPU to govern input to and output from the disk drive.

The speed at which data can be located on a disk and transferred to primary storage is referred to as **disk access time.** Disk access time is affected by several factors, including the time it takes the read/write head to position itself over the proper track (called *access motion* or *seek time*), the time it takes for the disk to rotate so that the read/write head is positioned at the proper sector (called *rotational delay*), and the time needed to read and transfer the data from the disk to primary storage (called the *data transfer rate*). Disk access times for floppy disks range from 175 milliseconds to around 300 milliseconds, which, as you'll see, is much slower than the time required by hard disks. Figure 4.4 shows you typical access times for various types of secondary storage systems.

This system unit features two floppy drives—one for a 5-1/4-inch disk and one for a 3-1/2-inch disk.

Source: Fredrik D. Bodin/Offshoot.

Figure 4.4
Access Time for Different Types of Secondary Storage

Type of Media	Access Time
RAM disks	.05 millisecond
DASD for large computers	1–10 milliseconds
Hard disks for microcomputers	15–20 milliseconds
Floppy disks	175–300 milliseconds
Optical disks	300–500 milliseconds

Hard Disks

One of the most versatile forms of secondary storage media is the **hard disk.** Hard disks are thin but rigid metallic platters that are coated with a substance that allows data to be recorded in magnetic form. Data can be recorded on both sides of the hard disk. Some hard disks are a permanent part of a **hard disk drive** encased within the system unit, and unlike tapes and diskettes, cannot be removed. (Tapes and diskettes are called **removable media** secondary storage systems; hard disks that cannot be removed are **fixed media** secondary storage systems.) A hard disk drive contains one or more hard disks mounted on a spindle, multiple read/write heads attached to *access arms* (sometimes called *actuators*), and various kinds of circuitry. Figure 4.5 illustrates a hard disk drive.

As the disks rotate around the spindle at around 3,600 revolutions per minute (60 revolutions per second), the read/write heads float between 10 and 20 millionths of an inch above the surface of the disk. If the head collides with the disk surface (an occurrence called a *head crash*) as a result of being jarred or contaminated from dust or other particles on the disk, the surface of the disk can be damaged and data lost. This is one of the reasons all the parts of a hard disk drive are normally enclosed within a sealed airtight case. Because hard drives have a number of moving parts, they are also more susceptible to breakdowns, or failures, than most other parts of a computer system. For these reasons, it is very important to back up, or make duplicate copies of, data stored on a hard disk drive on some other storage medium, such as a floppy disk or magnetic tape.

Data is stored on a hard disk in much the same way it is stored on a floppy disk. Like floppy disks, hard disks are organized into concentric tracks, and the sector method is often used to record data on the disk, especially for hard disks used in microcomputers.

Hard disk drives that have several disks, like the systems for large computers, often use the **cylinder method** to record data instead of the sector method. Because the access arms holding the read/write heads in a disk drive all move together, the heads are always over the same track on each of the disks at the same time. The cylinder method takes advantage of this to organize data vertically: track 1 on each of the disks that are part of the drive make up cylinder 1; track 2 on each of the disks that are part of the drive

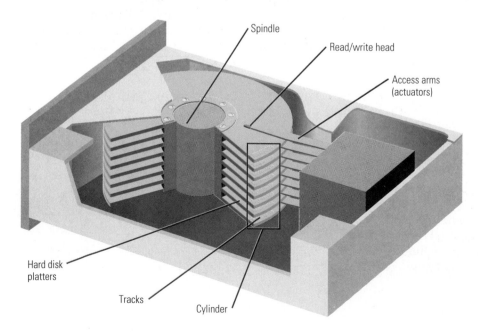

Figure 4.5
Cutaway View of a Hard Disk Drive

make up cylinder 2; and so on. Data recorded using the cylinder method is retrieved by providing the cylinder number, surface number, and individual data record number.

Hard Disk Technology for Large Computers   Hard disks and hard disk drives are the primary storage technology used by mainframe and midrange computers. These types of computers require hard disk drives that have storage capacities ranging into gigabytes, and disk access times of 1 millisecond to 10 milliseconds. When used with mainframe and midrange computers, hard disks and their associated hard disk drives are often referred to as **DASD (Direct Access Storage Devices).** A number of different types of DASD are used by large computer systems. One type employs a **removable-pack hard disk system**—several (from 6 to 20) 10-1/2- to 14-inch hard disks are assembled into an indivisible pack that can be mounted on and removed from a disk unit. Removable-pack systems were more common in the 1980s; in recent years, they have been overshadowed by high-speed, high-capacity **fixed disk drives** in standalone cabinets. IBM's 3390 disk drive is a leading example of this kind of technology. Over 100 high-speed disk drives might be attached to a single mainframe computer at one time, whereas a midrange computer might have 10 to 20 disk drives attached to it.

Recently, several of IBM's competitors have introduced products that will provide a high-performance alternative to fixed disk drives. These devices use a technology called **RAID (Redundant Array of Inexpensive Disks)** and contain over 100 smaller 5-1/4-inch disk drives with a controller chip and specialized software within one large box. Instead of delivering data from the disk drive along a single path as traditional disk drives do, RAIDs can deliver data over multiple parallel paths simultaneously and so have faster response time. Figure 4.6 illustrates the differences between traditional disk drives and RAIDs. RAIDs also promise to be more reliable than standard disk drives because the failure of one drive is much less critical when others are available to take its place. In addition, power consumption and the amount of space required for the device is also reduced.

RAID devices have just begun to infiltrate the market. EMC Corporation has installed a few thousand of its Symmetrix models, and Storage Technology's Iceberg models are not expected out until late 1993. By 1994, though, RAID will probably be a significant factor in the DASD marketplace.

Increases in the amount of data that can be stored by disk drives have played an important role in the growth of many businesses, as illustrated by the story "Dialog Grows Along with Storage Capacity."

Hard Disk Technology for Microcomputers   Microcomputers and small minicomputers frequently use a form of hard disk drive called a **Winchester disk system.** A Winchester disk system is a smaller version of the fixed disk drive systems used for large computers and generally contains several 3-1/2-inch disks (the 5-1/4-inch sizes are becoming obsolete) sealed within a disk unit. Spin rates tend to be faster—4,500 to 5,400 revolutions per minute compared to 3,600 for disk drives used in larger computers. The disk drives may be found either within the system unit or as a detached external unit that has its own power supply.

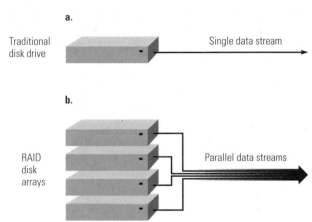

a.

Traditional disk drive   Single data stream

b.

RAID disk arrays   Parallel data streams

Figure 4.6
How RAIDs Work

(a) A traditional disk drive reads and writes data in single file onto a hard disk. (b) RAIDs let data move at more than double the speed (up to 10 million characters per second compared to a maximum of 4.5 million characters per second for traditional drives) by using parallel data streams.

Twenty years ago, Dialog Information Services was a fledgling enterprise with a good idea: to provide libraries, government agencies, and businesses with access via computer to indexes that contained abstracts (short summaries) of newspaper, magazine, and journal articles. Today, Dialog is a multimillion-dollar operation, with 120,000 customers worldwide. Full-text articles have replaced the abstracts. None of this would have been possible without dramatic increases in secondary storage capacities over the years.

Today, Dialog's computer room is dominated by two Hitachi EX 100 mainframes, coupled with Hitachi disk drives providing a total of 1.3 terabytes of storage capacity. IBM-compatible tape drives and tape cartridges are used to back up Dialog's over 400 databases for safekeeping. But although Dialog's storage capacity has grown over the years, the size of its computer room hasn't had to. Terabytes of information can now be kept in the same space as the 270 gigabytes they stored six years ago.

Dialog continues to add 20 to 40 gigabytes of storage per month, with no end in sight. It is also adding image databases, which will further boost its storage requirements. Gordon Schick, vice president of systems and operations, predicts that even Dialog's present extended storage facilities will be strained by future subscriber demands. "It's called instant gratification," says Roger Summit, Dialog's chief executive officer and founder. "People want access to on-line files right away rather than accessing an abstract first and then sending a request for an article." To accommodate customer demand, Schick is looking into new storage options such as RAID systems.

Source: Based on Bozman, Jean, "Storage Keeps Up with Dialog Growth," *Computerworld,* June 17, 1991.

Critical Thinking Questions

1 Why do you think on-line database services like the ones that Dialog offers are so successful? In what ways are they useful to organizations?

2 If Dialog uses 14-inch high-density tape reels that hold 250 megabytes of data, how many would they need to back up the 1.3 terabytes of data stored on its Hitachi hard drives? How many high-density 3 1/2-inch floppy disks would it take?

Hard disks used for desktop microcomputers typically have a storage capacity of anywhere from 40MB to 200MB (up to 330MB for workstations or file servers) and disk access times of around 15–20 milliseconds. Because disks cannot be removed, if they become filled, data must be transferred to some other storage device or deleted. However, most microcomputers have the ability to handle more than one hard disk drive, thereby expanding their potential total storage capacity into the gigabyte range. Another technique to increase storage capacity of a hard disk is **data compression.** This technology uses special software techniques, sometimes combined with an add-in processor board, to compress the size of data files by eliminating strings of redundant characters and replacing them with more compact symbols. Data compression is less expensive than a hardware upgrade and the software-only versions don't require any extra physical space—an important consideration for portables. Data compression programs can increase disk drive capacities by as much as 50 percent, stretching a 20MB hard disk into 40MB or more of storage space.[4] Stac Electronic's Stacker and Add Stor's SuperStor are two of the most popular programs for PCs. Leading programs for the Macintosh include Fifth Generation System's AutoDoubler and Aladdin's Stuffit Deluxe.

Hard disk drives are becoming increasingly popular for portable computers as well as microcomputers. Most laptop and notebook computers

Hewlett-Packard's Kittyhawk disk drive is only 1.3 inches in size.

Source: Courtesy of Hewlett Packard.

still use 3-1/2-inch hard disk drives, but manufacturers are now beginning to offer smaller 2-inch, 1.8-inch, and even 1.3-inch (Hewlett-Packard's Kittyhawk) drives (see photo). These smaller drives consume less power, generate less heat, and are much lighter; in some cases, they are removable as well. Their storage capacity still remains somewhat limited though: the current high capacity for 2-inch drives is around 120MB; for 1.8-inch drives, around 64MB; and for the Kittyhawk disk drive, 20MB.

Hard Disk Technology Expanded Beyond Hard Disk Drives   Hard disk drives are not the only form of storage devices to employ hard disk technology. One innovation has been a **hard card:** an add-in board with a built-in hard disk. The board plugs into an expansion slot in the system unit. A hard card usually takes up less space than a regular hard disk drive. Another device is the removable **disk cartridge,** which contains a hard disk encased within a cartridge. The cartridge is popped into a cartridge drive much like a floppy disk is inserted into a floppy disk drive. Disk cartridges currently offer up to 88MB of storage. Disk cartridges are popular because they combine the storage capability of a hard disk with the portability of a floppy disk. Prices are still more expensive than regular hard disk drives but are beginning to drop.

RAM Disks and Disk Cache   In addition to actually using hard disks, researchers have discovered a way to use RAM memory chips to emulate hard disks. One technique is to create something called a **RAM,** or **virtual, disk** (also called a solid-state disk drive). A RAM disk uses a bank of RAM memory chips coupled with a controller to create a "fake" disk drive that can store entire data files and programs. (Normally, primary storage holds only a limited amount of data or program instructions, and when additional data and instructions are needed, they are fetched from a secondary storage device.) RAM disks provide much faster access time (about .05 millisecond compared to 10–15 milliseconds for regular hard disk drives) but suffer the same disadvantage that primary storage does—their contents are lost if power is turned off or disrupted. RAM disks can be implemented either through software or via an add-in board or disk controller.

Another strategy to improve access time is to establish a **disk cache.** A disk cache enables the computer to anticipate the data and program instructions that will be needed by the user, access the hard disk drive, and then place a duplicate of the information into RAM, where it can be accessed much more quickly. A disk cache is generally more versatile than a RAM disk because it is larger. Disk caches can be implemented either through software (for example, Microsoft includes a disk cache called SmartDrive with both Microsoft Windows 3.1 and DOS 6.0) or through hardware with an add-in board called a cache card or special disk controller.

4.3   Optical Disks

One of the most important new forms of storage media is **optical disks.** Created by the same kind of laser technology as the compact disks (CDs) that have revolutionized the music business, optical disks are poised to have a similar impact on the computer industry. Optical disks can provide tremendous storage capacities at a relatively inexpensive price. As a result, technologies that have large storage requirements, such as imaging systems and multimedia, have benefited tremendously from the availability of optical disks.

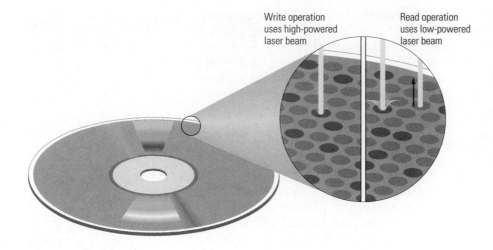

Write operation uses high-powered laser beam

Read operation uses low-powered laser beam

Figure 4.7
Recording and Reading Data on Optical Disks
Data is recorded on CD-ROM and WORM optical disks by using a high-powered laser to burn tiny holes onto the surface of the disk. A low-powered laser is used to read the disk. The smooth areas reflect the light and are interpreted as 1 bits. The tiny holes do not reflect light and represent 0 bits.

Optical disks can be divided into three basic types: those that are prerecorded and cannot be modified (CD-ROMs and videodisks or laserdisks); WORMs, which can be written on once by a user but then cannot be altered; and erasable disks that can be written on, erased, and reused.

On the first two types of optical disks, data is recorded by using a laser device to burn miniscule holes onto the surface of a hard plastic disk. Because the spots are so small, extremely high data density can be achieved. Once the data has been burned onto the disk, it cannot be changed. When a low-power laser light is beamed across the surface, the smooth areas reflect light, which are interpreted as 1 bits. The pitted areas do not reflect light and are interpreted as 0 bits. Figure 4.7 illustrates how data on optical disks is recorded and read.

CD-ROMs and Other Prerecorded Optical Disks

The **CD-ROM (Compact Disk Read-Only Memory)** is probably the most familiar kind of optical disk. CD-ROMs are prerecorded. Many microcomputers now come with an optical drive that can read CD-ROMs although most CD-ROM users still buy drives separately and hook them up to their computers. CD-ROMs are also playable on handheld units like Sony's Data Discman. A single CD-ROM can hold up to 660MB, equal to 330 high-density floppy disks (enough to hold about 300,000 pages of information).[5]

CD-ROM applications cover both the consumer and the business market, and the number of products is growing every year (see Figure 4.8). They are particularly useful for storing large quantities of information so long as the information need not be frequently updated. As a result, they are great for reference materials like encyclopedias, catalogs, and directories. For instance, Ford provides its dealers with CD-ROMs that contain complete parts catalogs for all Ford cars going back to the 1980 model year, as well as technical information for servicing the cars. Large storage capacity also makes CD-ROMs a good choice for storing both sound and images, and therefore they are frequently used for multimedia applications. American Airlines has begun to take advantage of this capability by offering a CD-ROM hotel directory to all travel agencies hooked to its Sabre computer reservation system. The directory, updated quarterly, allows an agent to provide a customer with a wide variety of information as well as pictures of lodgings across the country. Some of the exciting new CD-ROM products now available include:

a. CD-ROM Titles in Print

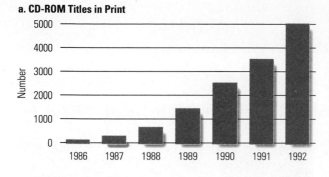

b. CD-ROM Players Installed

Figure 4.8
The Growth of CD-ROMs
CD-ROM titles and CD-ROM players have experienced dramatic growth.

Source: Udell, Jon, "Start the Presses," *BYTE,* February 1993, based on data from InfoTech. Used by permission of McGraw-Hill, Inc. and Infotech.

3M makes several different types of optical disks, including CD-ROMs, videodisks, and erasable disks.

Source: Courtesy of 3M Corporation.

The Oxford English Dictionary: 20 volumes on a single CD-ROM disk

Phonedisc USA: Listing of every residential phone in the United States

Street Atlas U.S.A.: Street-level maps for every square mile of the United States

Patent Images: Every patent issued in the United States during 1991 and 1992

Terrorist Group Profiles: Detailed information, statistics, and chronology of some of today's most dangerous factions

Multimedia Beethoven/The Ninth Symphony: The Vienna Philharmonic plays and the text on screen provides running commentary about the music (see photo)

The Total Baseball CD-ROM: Statistics on over 13,000 players, with trading-card photos and sound clips of famous moments

National Geographic's Encyclopedia of Mammals: Text essays, sound clips, and still and moving images of over 200 animals

As the story "Art on a Disk" illustrates, CD-ROMs and other types of prerecorded optical disks (such as the 12-inch videodisks or laserdisks that can be played on a television set or computer monitor) are creating new ways to learn about traditional topics.

The technology used to create CD-ROMs is now beginning to filter down to the desktop. CD-R (CD-recordable) drives, now available for less than $10,000, let the user write data onto a specially

Microsoft's Multimedia Beethoven on CD-ROM includes everything from an overview of Beethoven's world to an in-depth analysis of each movement of the Ninth Symphony.

Source: Courtesy of Microsoft Corporation.

Art on a Disk

How would you like to be able to see 2,500 of America's greatest artworks without having to travel to a museum? Optical disk storage technology makes it possible with a little help from the National Gallery of Art in Washington, D.C.

Carter Brown, head of the National Gallery, is a firm believer in "harnessing modern technology for the great cause of education in the arts." Over the last year, the Gallery's technology specialists have been photographing and then scanning and digitizing works of art for storage on optical disk. Details of the works can be illuminated by magnifying sections of the images already scanned. When the project's complete, a single thin, iridescent videodisk will hold over 10,000 images (7,500 of them details) of those works, plus captions (see photo).

Optical disks were chosen as the storage medium for their capacity (they can hold up to 54,000 images), their dura-

A videodisk image and detail of Gilbert Stuart's "Skater."

Source: Karen Kasinauski/NYT Pictures.

manufactured disk that can then be read by any standard CD-ROM drive. For instance, until recently, searching for medical periodicals at the National Library of Medicine in Bethesda, Maryland, meant wading through fat notebooks full of printouts. Now a custom CD-ROM produced monthly by the library's staff with a Sony CD-R drive gives researchers electronic access to medical citations.[6]

Another application of CD-R technology is Kodak's Photo CD system, which allows photo labs to transfer conventional 35-mm negatives onto an optical disk that can store up to 100 high-quality color photographs. Instead of dragging out a family photo album or slide projector, you can pop the disk into a Photo CD player or a specially equipped CD-ROM drive and show your snapshots on a television set or computer monitor (see photo). Special software is also available that lets you resize, brighten, distort, or even merge the photos with others. Because the image is digital, it can be taken apart pixel by pixel and then put back together any way you choose. The Dilemmas and Controversies feature "Rethinking the Photograph" focuses on some of the issues surrounding this new technology.

Photos can be stored on CD-ROM disks and displayed on a television screen or computer monitor using Kodak's Photo CD system.

Source: Courtesy of Eastman Kodak.

WORMs

WORM (Write-Once, Read-Many) devices allow users to record data on optical disks themselves, but once the data has been written onto the disk, it cannot be erased. As you saw in the opening vignette, for many organizations, this is an asset rather than a liability. WORM has found enthusiastic acceptance as a relatively low-cost means of storing accounting, quality control, records management, and other information that needs to be retained in unchanged form. The U.S. State Department uses WORMs for

bility, and the "stunning" reproduction of the image they can provide. The accessibility of the images was equally important: using an optical disk, a single frame can be found in an instant.

The National Gallery plans to give away 2,500 copies of the disks to schools throughout the country. According to Linda Downs, head of education at the National Gallery, the disks will probably be used to help students study American history. Students will be able to see Gilbert Stuart's famous painting of George Washington as they study the American Revolution, and George Catlin's paintings of Indian life while studying the conquest of the American West. Additional copies of the disks will be awarded to winners in a competition on innovative ways to use it in the classroom. And even if a school isn't given or doesn't win a free copy of the disk, it can always borrow one. The National Gallery is the only American museum that will lend its disks, videotapes, and slide packages anywhere in the country.

Sources: Based on Molotsky, Irvin, "America's Art Treasures Go to School on Video," *New York Times,* June 6, 1993; Goldberg, Vicki, "American Art to Go, on a Pizza-Size Disk," *New York Times,* March 1, 1992.

Critical Thinking Questions

1 Why couldn't magnetic tape or magnetic disks be used for the purposes described in this story?

2 Do you think videodisk art could replace the need for museums? Why or why not?

3 Your school has been asked to participate in the contest the National Gallery is running on innovative uses of the art videodisk in the classroom. What suggestions do you have?

its Secretariat Tracking and Retrieval System to store over 200,000 new document pages annually.

Digital Paper is an alternative form of write-once, read-many technology. Digital Paper uses a low-power (and, therefore, lower-cost) laser to write data onto an inexpensive reflective plastic film instead of an optical disk. A piece of Digital Paper 2,400 feet long and 1/2-inch wide (equal in size to a 10-1/2-inch magnetic tape reel) can store 600 gigabytes of data and the equivalent of 1,000 CD-ROMs. Although still a relatively new technology, Digital Paper has the potential to someday replace optical disk–based WORMs.

Erasable Optical Disks

In some cases, the inability to erase and reuse an optical disk proves to be a disadvantage. Researchers have developed several methods to create erasable, rewriteable optical disks. **Magneto-optical disks** are probably the most common. With this technology, a high-powered laser beam works with an electromagnet to record data on the disk by heating tiny spots on a layer of magnetic film sandwiched between two layers of clear plastic. The heat causes the atoms in the magnetic film to have a different magnetic direction from the spaces that have not been heated. Spots with a reversed magnetic direction are interpreted by the computer as binary 1s, and those with the original direction as binary 0s. The magnetic polarizations remain permanent until the disk is exposed again to a high-powered laser.

Data is retrieved from a magneto-optical disk by shining a lower-powered polarized laser at the magnetic layer and reading the reflected light. The reflected beam's magnetic polarization is rotated in one direction or another depending on the polarization it encounters on the magnetic film. The drive then interprets rotation in one direction as a 1 bit and rotation in the other direction as a 0 bit.

Have you ever heard the phrase "a picture doesn't lie"? Photographs have long had a special authority as a record of reality. A photograph is usually perceived as an objective record of the physical world. The medium's claim to truthfulness is founded on the negative, the physical manifestation of the image. Negatives cannot be altered easily without the changes being obvious.

Consider then the effect of technologies like Photo CD and digital cameras (cameras that record scenes directly onto disk), which allow images to be converted into a series of digits that can then be translated into tonal values and printed. Any of the digits can be changed at will to alter the image. Photographs can be blended with others, colors changed, elements within the picture rearranged, all with remarkable ease. While it was always possible to alter traditional photographs through cropping, retouching, and other methods, what's different now is that these and even more significant changes can be made instantly and with little effort.

Many are excited by the prospects this new technology offers. Weston J. Naef, curator of photography at the J. Paul Getty Museum in Malibu, California, compares it to the effect the Leica (a compact camera that made it possible for photographers to capture street scenes) had in 1927: "It changed the way we see the world." Some foresee a blurring of the boundaries between photography and art. David Hockney, a well-known painter and photographer, feels that in the future photography will take on some of the characteristics of draw-

ing, with the photographer working on a photograph the way a draftsman might work on a drawing.

But others are concerned these systems have the disturbing potential to erode photography's function in society by undercutting the photograph's status as a picture of reality. They feel that digital technology is transforming photography so fundamentally that its basic function and character are changing beyond recognition. As Peter Campus, an artist whose computer-manipulated photographs have appeared in a number of exhibitions says, "I tell my students this is not photography. It's something else, although at this point it's still not clear just what."

Source: Based on Hagen, Charles, "Reinventing the Photograph," *New York Times,* January 31, 1993.

Critical Thinking Questions

1   In the future, you may no longer be able to assume a photograph is an accurate depiction of a reality that in fact existed at some given point in time. What impact do you think this will have on the use of photographs to convey information?

2   Consider the ethical dimensions of digitally altered photographs. Under what circumstances should photographers be required to disclose changes made to a photograph?

3   In the future, what factors might you need to consider in assessing the meaning and believability of a photograph?

Drawbacks of Optical Disk Technology

Though optical disk technology provides an increasingly popular, low-cost mass storage alternative, it has some disadvantages. Its chief drawbacks are the slow data transfer rate and access time that optical drives provide. And like hard disk drives, optical drives are also susceptible to contamination from circulating air, dirt, and dust.

4.4   Other Forms of Secondary Storage

We finish our discussion of secondary storage media and devices with a quick look at some special-purpose forms.

Bubble Memory

Bubble memory uses bubblelike magnetic areas on a semiconductor chip's surface to represent data. The presence of a "bubble" is interpreted as a binary 1, and the absence as a binary 0. Unlike regular RAM chips, bubble memory is nonvolatile and does not lose its data when power is shut off. It tends to be more expensive than other types of storage. However, because bubble memory is able to maintain data under high temperatures, is resistant to dirt, and is unaffected by vibration, it is frequently used for applications like military equipment, robots, and communications devices, where such qualities can be critical.

Memory Cards and Smart Cards

Measuring about 2 by 3 inches and only several millimeters thick, **memory cards**—sometimes called credit-card memory or Personal Computer Memory Card International Association (PCMCIA) cards—can hold up to 100MB of data using the flash memory chips we described in Chapter 3. Without any moving parts, they are faster, more power-efficient, and much more shock-resistant than hard or floppy disk drives. Their size and other features make them a natural for notebook and palmtop computers though they are still much more expensive than disk drives. PCMCIA cards are also beginning to make their way into desktop systems—IBM's new energy saver PC has slots for up to 4 PCMCIA cards.

Smart cards contain a microprocessor and memory chips on a slim, credit-card-sized card. The memory chips can contain the equivalent of three pages of typewritten information. When placed in a specialized card reader, the data contained on the card can be read and updated. Right now, smart cards that contain the medical histories of consumers are being tested in New York. The card can be scanned by card readers at hospitals, medical offices, and pharmacies, providing accurate patient records and eliminating many paper forms. Smart cards are also being tested as a way to collect tolls electronically: as you pass through a toll booth, a radio signal is sent to an identification number on a smart card mounted on the dashboard. The signal is then reflected to a scanner, which transmits the ID number to a computer and automatically charges a driver's account for the toll. And in France, smart cards called *telecartes* have virtually eliminated coin-operated telephone booths. The cards can be purchased for around $7.50. When inserted into a telephone, the chip automatically deducts the cost of the call from the card until the value of the card is reduced to zero (see photo).[7]

Memory Buttons

A **memory button** is about the size of a dime and looks like a watch battery. Inside its case is a special read/write microchip that can hold up to 512 characters of data. To read the data within the button or write new data, the user simply touches the outside of the case with a penlike probe that is attached to a handheld data terminal. The buttons are relatively inexpensive ($2 to $7 each) and can be attached with adhesive backing to virtually anything. Because the information content of the buttons can be changed, they promise to be particularly useful for keeping track of equipment maintenance as well as more straightforward asset tracking.[8]

Smart cards may eventually make coin-operated telephones obsolete.

Source: Chuck O'Rear/Woodfin Camp and Associates.

Who Knows You?

You probably think that you know who knows you and what they know about you. But guess again. Today, information about your life is being collected and stored in computer databases, and it is being used for purposes over which you have little or no control.

Here's a short look at some of the massive databases now being compiled in the United States. First, three giant credit bureaus—TRW, Equifax, and TransUnion Credit Information—together have over 400 files on 160 million individuals. What do they know about you? For starters, your name and address, age, social security number, balances on your credit cards, mortgages or other personal loans, when you opened those accounts, your payment records and credit limits, any bankruptcies, judgments or liens against you, and who has requested credit information on you within the past two years. In addition, they will know your job title, the name of your spouse, the number of children you have, any previous addresses you've had, your estimated income, and the value of

your home and car. Equifax even collects information on your driving record. Every month, this information is updated with computer records purchased from banks and retailers that you have done business with.

And what do credit bureaus do with this information? They sell it. Most likely, your employers, your landlord, your local utility company, even your school if you're on financial aid, have all checked out a report on you. TRW and TransUnion also identify credit-card holders, mail-order buyers, people who have moved recently, and prospects for financial service companies and other marketers; Equifax's insurance division gives insurers information about your lifestyle and driving record.

The big three credit bureaus are not the only ones collecting and selling data on you and your life. Hundreds of small firms compile and rent specialized lists; act as middlemen to resell information; and perform specialized services like tracking bounced checks, accident victims, or difficult tenants. Fi-

Memory Cubes

Industry experts believe that mass storage systems may be revolutionized within the next decade or so by a technology known as *three-dimensional optical storage media*. Currently under development, these devices look like sugar cubes, and are capable of storing as much as 6.5 terabytes of data (see photos). They are created using transparent polysterene plastic treated with a chemical that reacts to laser light in ways ideal for storing binary data. The cube can be erased selectively with infrared radiation or entirely by applying heat. A number of challenges must still be met, however, before the cubes are ready for commercial use. Right now, for instance, the cubes must be kept at very low temperatures, or they lose their data. When perfected, this technology is expected to hold the greatest benefits for massively parallel computer systems.[9]

Memory cubes are an experimental form of 3-D optical storage media developed by Professor Peter Rentzepis at the University of California, Irvine.

Source: Kerry Klayman/Courtesy of the University of California, Irvine.

nancial institutions; credit-card issuers; insurance companies; magazine publishers; mail-order companies; retail chains and department stores; supermarkets; telephone companies; even federal, state, and local government agencies all compile information about you. They may later sell, rent, or share the data, or they may use it for a purpose unconnected to the one for which it was initially collected. When and if all the data available about you is combined in one place, a crystal-clear picture of who you are will be available to all, for only a small fee. And that's if you're lucky and the data is accurate.

What role has information technology played in these developments? Advances in secondary storage have made it possible to store massive quantities of data and to retrieve them with great speed, something that would be impossible with paper records. Secondary storage media can be much more permanent than paper records, which decay over time, get lost, or are discarded for lack of room. And data on an individual that is stored in a computer database can be matched

with other data on that person with much greater ease than is possible with snippets of data spread across dozens of pieces of paper.

Sources: Based on Simon, Ruth, "Stop Them From Selling Your Financial Secrets," *Money*, March 1992; Lacayo, Richard, "Nowhere to Hide," *Time*, November 11, 1991.

Critical Thinking Questions

1 What are some of the benefits consumers derive from computerized databases that contain personal information about individuals? How do the benefits stack up against the costs to individual privacy outlined in the story?

2 What measures might you suggest to provide greater assurances that personal data is not misused by companies that collect it?

3 Keep track of your actions for two or three days, and make a list of those that would generate data about you that could be stored in a computer database.

As you have seen in reading this chapter, a key trend in secondary storage technologies has been the ever-increasing ability to store more and more data, in smaller spaces, at cheaper cost, and with quicker access time. There are many benefits from this trend; for instance, the ability to store data and then retrieve it quickly helps organizations be more efficient and productive, and it helps provide better customer service. But what happens if the data being stored is not about some product or service but is about *you?* The story "Who Knows You?" offers some insight into computerized databases that contain personal information about you.

4.5 Organizing Data Within Secondary Storage

The way data is organized within storage media affects how quickly and easily it can be accessed and used and, therefore, can be critical to making productive use of an information system. In this section, we review some basic concepts that underlie all types of data organization and then discuss different methods for organizing data.

The Data Hierarchy

Data organization in an information system begins by breaking complex information down into its tiniest component parts and then reorganizing it in a coherent structure, called the **data hierarchy.** The smallest piece of data that computers can handle is the *bit,* a digital 0 or 1. Eight bits grouped together form a *byte*, which represents an individual character—a single letter or number. A *field* is a group of characters that together form a whole word, group of words, or number that conveys a single piece of information, such as a person's name or street address. A *record* is a collection of related fields; in Chapter 2, you read about IRS records that included a person's social security number, name, address, and amount of taxes due. Every record has, as one of its fields, a *key field* that uniquely identifies the record so that it can be retrieved and processed. The key field is usually expressed as some form of identification number. A *file* consists of a collection of related records. Finally, a *database* holds multiple related files. Figure 4.9 illustrates the data hierarchy.

Methods of Organizing Data

The three main ways of organizing data within secondary storage are sequential file organization, indexed-sequential file organization, and random (or direct) file organization. The type of method that must be used is determined in part by the type of storage media chosen.

Sequential File Organization   The only method that can be used with magnetic tape, **sequential file organization** stores records in sequence, one after the other; the records must then be retrieved in the same physical sequence as they were stored. As we discussed, it is not appropriate when fast access to records spread throughout a file or database is required. Just as magnetic tape has been overshadowed by other storage media, sequential file organization has been largely overtaken by other methods though it continues to be used for older batch processing applications that process records all at one time, one after the other.

Indexed-Sequential File Organization   Indexed-sequential file organization uses sequential organization to store records but also creates indexes that list each record by its key field and identifies the physical location, or storage address, of the record. Although records may always be accessed sequentially, the existence of an index also allows individual records to be directly accessed in whatever order the user desires. Magnetic tapes cannot be used for indexed-sequential file organization because they lack the ability to allow for direct access. Though providing for quicker access than sequential organization, indexed-sequential file organization is still slow owing to the time it takes to find records through index searches.

Random, or Direct, File Organization   The third method, **random, or direct, file organization,** uses a mathematical formula called a *hashing*, or *randomizing*, *algorithm* to translate the key field of a record directly into the record's physical location on the storage media without the need for a special index. There are a number of different types of hashing algorithms. One of the simplest types works by dividing the record's key field number by the prime number closest to, but not greater than, the total number of records stored. The re-

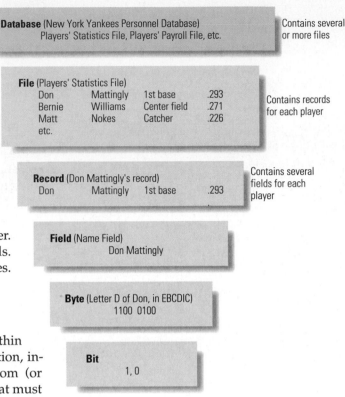

Figure 4.9
The Data Hierarchy
The data in an information system is organized in a hierarchy, beginning with the smallest piece of data that a computer handles—the bit. A byte contains 8 bits plus a parity bit. A field contains a group of bytes that convey a single piece of information (here, a player's name). A record contains a number of related fields (here, name, position, and batting average). A file is composed of a number of related records (here, records on each player for the Yankees). A database holds multiple related files.

Keepers of the Flame

What do Marilyn Cumberland, Al Flournoy, Dean Flannigan, Mike Ewanowski, and Jose Martinez have in common? They have all been entrusted with the care of their companies' most valuable corporate asset—their databases. Cumberland, Flournoy, Flannigan, Ewanowski, and Martinez are database administrators, one of the fastest growing fields in information systems.

What database administrators do can be critical for the smooth operation of an enterprise. As Marilyn Cumberland, a database administrator at COMSAT Corp. in Washington, D.C. says, "We're sort of the engine that runs everything."

Database administrators manage the physical aspects of a database (how data is actually organized and structured physically on storage media) as well as the logical aspects (making different views of the data available to users). They work with systems analysts to create tables and indexes to let users access data, maintain those tables, back up and recover data, monitor storage devices, and troubleshoot. In addition to these tasks, database administrators often are also responsible for ensuring data integrity, testing, and tuning the database's performance, and training users.

Salaries for database administrators usually range from $35,000 to $65,000 per year, in line with the demanding nature of the job. Starting salaries in the neighborhood of $50,000 are not uncommon.

What kinds of people make successful database administrators? According to Al Flournoy, a senior database administrator at M. W. Kellog Co., a Houston-based engineering and construction firm, you need to be "curious, tenacious, and self-assured" in order to keep up with the demands of the job: staying current with new technologies, solving problems as they occur, serving as a jack-of-all-trades, and constantly being on call.

In addition, a successful candidate for a database administration position will generally have three to five years' experience as a programmer or systems analyst, as well as some experience as a data analyst. A bachelor's degree in computer science or information systems is a plus, although not necessarily required. A business degree is also a good start. Courses and curriculums that focus on problem-solving ability, whether in math, philosophy, or some other subject, are also recommended, according to Dean Flannigan, database administrator at Quality Stores, Inc. in North Muskegon, Michigan.

Database administration can also be a springboard into management because, as Mike Ewanowski, a database administrator at the Data Resources Management Group at Emory University explains, it allows you to see the big picture in addition to dealing with a lot of different users. The job offers technical challenges as well as a bird's-eye view into the organization. One person who made the jump was Jose Martinez, a database administrator at the Pacific Maritime Association in San Francisco, California. Martinez leveraged his database experience to become Assistant Director of Information Services.

So if you're interested in a career as an informations systems professional, consider database administration. As more and more organizations realize the strategic value of information, the demand for database administrators will likely continue to mushroom. If you fit the bill, you'll be among the most sought-after information systems workers of tomorrow.

Sources: Based on Goff, Leslie, "Database Administrators: Super Stress Handlers," *Computerworld*, November 16, 1992; King, Julia, "Demand for Database Managers Intensifies," *Computerworld*, September 23, 1991.

Critical Thinking Questions

1   Why is database administration so important to an organization?

2   Create a resume that would qualify you for a job as a database administrator. Cover both the educational background (using actual courses from your own college catalog) and professional experience that you might eventually have.

3   Let's assume you are a database administrator for your college. What kind of databases might you be responsible for? What kind of secondary storage devices might you need to look after? What do you think a typical day might be like?

mainder indicates the disk address for that particular record. Random file organization provides the quickest form of direct access to records and is most frequently used for applications that require on-line processing.

Figures 4.10 through 4.12 compares the different methods of organizing data within secondary storage.

Organizing data into a database and then maintaining that database are critical tasks within an organization. The story "Keepers of the Flame" gives you some insight into what it's like to be a database administrator.

When using the sequential file access method (tape or other storage media), records are stored in sequence as they are created and must be searched and retrieved in the same sequence. (See Figure 4.10.)

Figure 4.10
The Sequential File Access Method

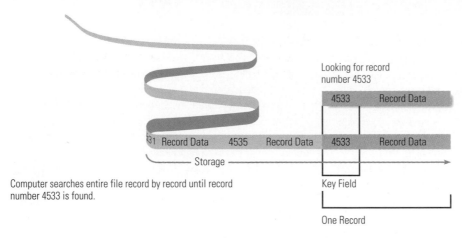

When using the indexed sequential access method (non-tape storage media), records are stored in sequence as they are created. Indexing allows search for individual records by non-sequential means. (See Figure 4.11.)

Figure 4.11
The Indexed Sequential Access Method (ISAM)

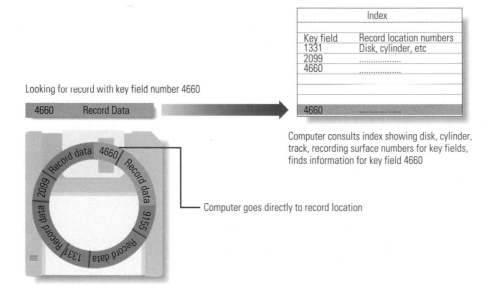

When using the random or direct access method (non-tape storage media), a key field number is assigned to each record. This number is used in conjunction with a hashing formula to determine the address in memory where the record will be stored. Given the key field, the computer can use the formula to locate the record directly wherever it is in storage. (See Figure 4.11.)

Figure 4.12
The Random or Direct Access Method

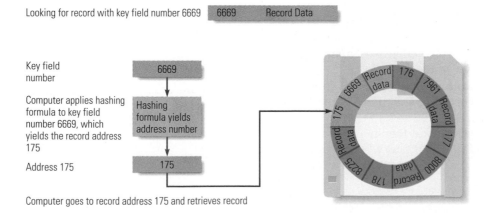

Figure 4.13 summarizes the various secondary storage media and devices discussed in this chapter.

Name of Media/Device	Description
Magnetic Tape/Tape Units	Plastic tape covered with magnetizable substance Comes in reels and cartridges Used primarily for backup Must be accessed sequentially
Magnetic Disks/Disk Drives	
Floppy disks	Thin circle of magnetizable plastic encased in plastic cover Two sizes: 5 1/4 inch and 3 1/2 inch Storage capacities from 360K to 2MB
Flopticals	Combines traditional floppies with optical drive to achieve greater storage capacity
Hard disks	Thin metal platter covered with magnetizable substance Much larger storage capacities than floppies Varieties available for microcomputers to mainframes Variations include hard cards and disk cartridges
RAM disks	RAM memory chips used to emulate hard disk
Optical Disks	
CD-ROMs	Compact disk read-only memory Prerecorded optical disk Cannot be erased Very high storage capacity
WORMs	Write once, read many Can be written on once but then cannot be erased
Magneto-optical disks	Can be written on, erased, and reused
Other Forms of Storage	
Bubble memory	Uses bubblelike magnetic areas on semiconductor chip Unaffected by high temperatures, dirt, vibration
Memory cards	Credit-card-sized cards most often used for portables
Smart cards	Contains microprocessor and memory chips
Memory buttons	Small metal container that has read/write chip holding up to 512 characters
Memory cubes	Experimental form of memory using 3-D optical storage technology

Figure 4.13
Summary of Secondary Storage Media and Devices

Summary

▶ Secondary storage stores data and programs while they are not being actively used. The principal types of secondary storage media are magnetic tape, magnetic disks, and optical disks.

Magnetic Tape

▶ Magnetic tape is used most frequently to store data that does not require immediate access and as a backup for data stored on other media. Data stored on magnetic tape can only be accessed sequentially—in the same physical order as it was stored. The secondary storage device used with magnetic tape is called a tape unit.

Magnetic Disks

▶ Magnetic disks are the most commonly used secondary storage medium and enable the user to have direct access to data stored on the disks. There are two basic types of magnetic disks: floppy disks and hard disks. Floppy disks and floppy disk drives are commonly used for storage on microcomputers. Hard disks and hard disk drives can be used in a wide variety of computers, from portable to mainframe.

▶ The two primary methods of storing data on magnetic disks are the sector method and the cylinder method.

▶ The speed at which data can be located on magnetic disks is referred to as disk access time and is affected by seek time, rotational delay, and the data transfer rate.

▶ RAM disks and disk caches are techniques that use RAM memory chips to emulate hard disks and therefore decrease disk access time.

Optical Disks

▶ Optical disks use laser technology to create tremendous storage capacities at a relatively inexpensive price. Examples of optical disk technology include CD-ROMs, which are prerecorded disks that can only be read from; WORM disks, which can be written on once, but read many times; and magneto-optical disks, which can be erased and reused.

Other Forms of Secondary Storage

▶ Other forms of secondary storage in use today include bubble memories, memory cards, optical cards, and smart cards.

Organizing Data Within Secondary Storage

▶ Data organization in information systems begins with breaking down data into its smallest component parts and then reorganizing it into a coherent structure. The data hierarchy is as follows (in order from smallest to largest): bit, byte, field, record, file, and database.

▶ The different forms of data organization include sequential file organization, indexed-sequential file organization, and random (or direct) file organization.

Key Terms

secondary storage
secondary storage media
secondary storage devices
magnetic tape
tracks
tape units
read/write head
tape library
magnetic disk
floppy disk, or diskette
sectors
formatting
sector method
floppy disk drive
disk access time
hard disk
hard disk drive
removable media
fixed media
cylinder method
DASD (Direct Access Storage Device)
removable-pack hard disk system

fixed disk drive
RAID (Redundant Array of Inexpensive Disks)
Winchester disk system
data compression
hard card
disk cartridge
RAM, or virtual, disk
disk cache
optical disks
CD-ROM (Compact Disk Read-Only Memory)
WORM (Write-Once, Read-Many)
magneto-optical disks
bubble memory
memory cards
smart cards
memory button
data hierarchy
sequential file organization
indexed-sequential file organization
random, or direct, file organization

 Interactive Supplement

Review Questions

1 What is secondary storage, and how does it differ from primary storage?

2 What elements do magnetic tape and magnetic disks have in common? Why have magnetic disks overtaken magnetic tape as the most common form of secondary storage today?

3 Explain the different methods for recording data both on magnetic tape and magnetic disks.

4 Compare the ways tape units, floppy disk drives, and hard disk drives work.

5 What is disk access time, and what are the factors that affect it?

6 Discuss the different DASD devices now available for large computers.

7 What are CD-ROMs and WORMs? How do they differ from magneto-optical disks?

8 Why was WORM such an appropriate choice of secondary storage for Leroy's Horse and Sports Palace?

9 Prepare an example illustrating the data hierarchy.

10 Describe the three main ways of organizing data within secondary storage and their relationship to the secondary storage medium being used.

Problem-Solving and Skill-Building Exercises

1 Prepare a short oral presentation, accompanied by some form of visual aid (a transparency or a poster if your class does not have an overhead projector), describing how a real-world company has used one of the storage technologies discussed here to increase business efficiency or productivity.

2 What kinds of storage technologies might be appropriate for American Airlines' Sabre on-line reservation system, a law firm that is using an image processing system to archive documents, a dentist's office that uses microcomputers to track patient records and billing, and a student with a notebook computer? Write up your recommendations.

3 Do you think reading a book on CD-ROM is any different from reading a printed book? If so, how? Do you think CD-ROMs will eventually replace printed books? Why or why not? If they do, what impact might this have? Engage in a group discussion on these and related issues with other members of your class.

PERSONAL TECHNOLOGY

Storage Options for Your Microcomputer

Once you've decided on the basic type of microcomputer that you'd like to buy (see the Personal Technology box at the end of Chapter 3), there are still some other important decisions that you need to make. Chief among these is the question of secondary storage. In this section, we'll discuss your options and make some recommendations about what kind and how much storage you need.

First, you definitely need a floppy disk drive. If you can only afford a system unit that has one drive, choose the 3 1/2 size. However, if you can afford it, it is very convenient to have a system unit that has a floppy drive for both floppy disk sizes.

The next question is whether you need a hard disk drive. Here, too, the answer is almost certainly yes. Luckily, the prices of hard disk drives have been dropping while their storage capacities have been increasing. Only a few years ago, a 20MB hard drive was standard, but now you can purchase an 80MB to 120MB drive for approximately the same price. In considering which hard drive to choose, remember that you can never have enough secondary storage, and go for the largest hard drive that you can reasonably afford. Even a gigabyte is no longer totally out of range at today's prices. Other considerations include the type of interface (the connection between the disk drive and the system's buses) the drive uses (an IDE or SCSI interface will be your best bet); the data access time and data transfer rate of the drive (the speed and power of 386- and 486-based systems will be wasted without a disk drive that has an access time of less than 20 milliseconds); and the physical size of the drive (smaller is better).

If you want to be equipped to take advantage of the latest information technology, you will also want to consider purchasing a CD-ROM drive. Many manufacturers are starting to bundle CD-ROM drives with their microcomputers. If the system you choose doesn't offer this option, you can purchase a drive to add as a peripheral device. There are a number of different types of CD-ROM drives available. The most basic is a single-speed drive with an average data access time of around 400–450 milliseconds and a data transfer rate of around 150 kilobits per second (Kbps). This type of drive is adequate for access to static information—encyclopedias, technical manuals, reference books, and so on. However, if you're interested in multimedia CD-ROM applications involving sound and animation, it would be worthwhile to invest in a dual-speed drive that will decrease access time to around 280 milliseconds and double the data transfer rate to 300 Kbps. It will also help to have a drive that meets CD-ROM XA (extended architecture) standards, which provide enhanced audio performance.

Another type of CD-ROM drive is Phillips/Sony's CD-I. Unlike a standard CD-ROM drive, which operates as a peripheral device, CD-I operates as a complete system, with an integrated computer, and comes equipped to play on a TV. CD-I is superior to regular CD-ROM drives in its ability to integrate audio, video, text, and graphics, but is being marketed primarily as a home entertainment system. Also, a CD-I drive doesn't read regular CD-ROM disks—only those set up to work with CD-I. Right now, a standard CD-ROM drive is probably still your best all-purpose choice.

Once you've gotten past these basic decisions concerning floppy disk, hard disk, and CD-ROM drives, there are several ancillary issues to consider. Your computer system is very vulnerable to fluctuations in electrical power. You should purchase a surge suppressor (a relatively inexpensive device) to help protect the system from the electrical ups and downs that can affect its operation. An uninterruptable power supply (UPS), although more expensive than a surge suppressor, gives you added insurance: if your electrical power goes out unexpectedly, the UPS will give enough power to run the system for several minutes so that you can save your work to your hard disk.

Finally, once you have your system up and running, it will be easy to take your hard drive, in particular, for granted. But don't be fooled—although your hard drive is likely to become obsolete before it crashes, hard drives have been known to fail suddenly and for no apparent reason. Because a hard drive failure can obliterate all your files in a matter of seconds, you would be wise to do what you can to protect against such a catastrophic occurrence. The answer is to back up your hard drive onto floppy disks (or tape cartridges, if you have a very large hard drive) frequently. Special back-up software can help speed the process. Popular programs include: Norton Backup, Back-It for Windows, and PC Tools for DOS and Windows machines and Fastback and Retrospect for Apple Macintosh machines.

Notes

1 **Fitzgerald, Michael,** "Industry Team Plans 16G-Byte Data Storage Standard for Tape," *Computerworld*, March 30, 1992.

2 **Markoff, John,** "IBM Shows Library for Data Storage," *New York Times*, May 20, 1992.

3 **Ryan, Bob,** "Floppy—But Very Large," *BYTE*, March 1992; **Ga Côté, Raymond**, and **Wszola, Stanley,** "The New Wave of Removable Storage," *BYTE*, October 1992.

4 **Markoff, John,** "Double-Hard-Disk Capacity, Through Software," *New York Times*, February 23, 1992.

5 **Alpert, Mark,** "CD-ROM: The Next PC Revolution," *Fortune*, June 29, 1992.

6 **Udell, Jon,** "Start the Presses," *BYTE*, February 1993.

7 **Betts, Mitch,** "Smart Cards Hit Medical Industry," *Computerworld*, November 25, 1991; **Rifkin, Glenn,** "Electronic Toll-Taking Is Being Put to the Test," *New York Times*, September 9, 1992; **Cohen, Roger,** "The Calling Card," *New York Times*, January 3, 1993.

8 **Betts, Mitch,** "Big Things Come in Small Buttons," *Computerworld*, August 3, 1992.

9 **Wilder, Clinton,** "Storage Coming in Small Packages," *Computerworld*, October 14, 1991; **Stein, Richard,** "Terabyte Memories with the Speed of Light," *BYTE*, March 1992.

Chapter 5 contains:

After completing this chapter, you will:

▶ Understand the role that input and output devices play in an information system.

▶ Know the various types of devices used for input, how they work, and their respective advantages and disadvantages.

▶ Know the primary kinds of output devices in use today and how to distinguish among the different types of display screens, printers, and plotters.

▶ See how input, output, and storage technologies can be combined to produce exciting new kinds of computing, such as multimedia systems.

Input and Output Technologies

Image Becomes Reality

You sneak around a corner, trying to hide from the person that you know is stalking you. Suddenly, a large flying beast (a pterodactyl, no less!) appears from nowhere, swoops down, snatches you up, and starts to carry you through the air. As you stare down at the passing landscape, the beast lets go and suddenly you are falling, falling, falling . . .

What's going on here? Where in the world are you? Well, in fact, you've entered a world that feels very real but doesn't actually exist. This is the world of Dactyl Nightmare, a new "virtual reality" created by Spectrum Holobyte (see photo).

Virtual reality systems use the latest in input and output devices to create simulations so sophisticated that they trick your mind into believing that they are real. You are actually in an amusement arcade, wearing a motion-sensing device tethered to a computer-equipped platform. You are holding a two-button trigger-gun and have a Star Wars–type helmet on your head. The outside world has disappeared—instead, you see only those sights that appear on the helmet's wraparound display screen and hear only those sounds piped into your ears by the helmet's 3-D sound system. The motion sensor conveys your position to an Amiga 3000 microcomputer, which adjusts the scene around you so that it moves when you move. Software that generates three-dimensional images has created the "feels real" scene that surrounds you.

Virtual reality systems are just now beginning to emerge as commercial realities. As the technology behind them continues to advance, you may find that the line between image and reality will become even more blurred.

Source: Based on Rosenblum, Daniel J., "Virtual Reality No Longer a Fantasy," *Computer Shopper,* March 1992.

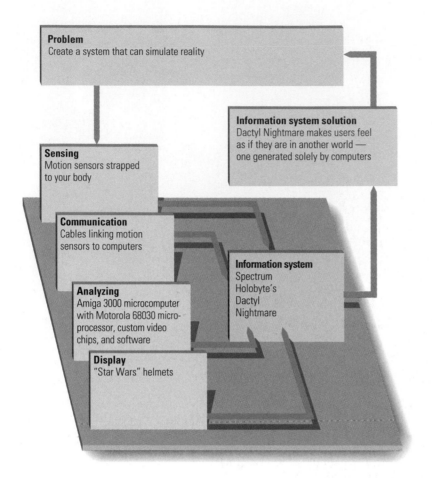

Problem
Create a system that can simulate reality

Information system solution
Dactyl Nightmare makes users feel as if they are in another world — one generated solely by computers

Sensing
Motion sensors strapped to your body

Communication
Cables linking motion sensors to computers

Information system
Spectrum Holobyte's Dactyl Nightmare

Analyzing
Amiga 3000 microcomputer with Motorola 68030 microprocessor, custom video chips, and software

Display
"Star Wars" helmets

Spectrum Holobyte's virtual reality system sends you into the world of Dactyl Nightmare.

Source: Edward Keating/NYT Pictures.

M any of the most exciting developments in information technology, like the virtual reality system just described, have become possible only because of advances in input (sensing) and output (display) devices. This chapter focuses on these important components of the computer system. We'll look at today's technology and highlight some trends that will shape the way we interact with and use computers during the next five to ten years.

5.1 Introduction

As you learned in Chapter 1, there are four basic types of information technologies—sensing, communication, analyzing, and display—that correspond to the input, process, and output functions of an information system. (To refresh your memory, review Figures 1.2 and 1.4, pages 12 and 15.)

Input (sensing) devices gather or take in data from the environment (either directly or with human participation) and translate that data into a form that can be processed by the CPU. Output (display) devices display processed data in a form that can be used and understood by humans.

Einstein's epidermal nerves sense heat, cold, pain, pressure, and vibration.

Einstein's binocular, depth-sensitive vision "sees" electromagnetic radiation patterns within the wavelengths of 400–700 nanometers (billionths of meters). Resolving power declines with age.

Einstein's ears detect frequency, direction, and strength of atmospheric pressure waves (sound): voices, music, oncoming firetruck. Frequency range: 20–20,000 cycles per second (cps), most sensitive at 1,000–4,000 cps. Powers decline with age and damage from overstimulation.

Einstein's vestibular (inner ear) balance organs help him to stand upright and ride a bicycle.

Einstein's voice output ranges from under 100 cps when singing bass to about 1500 cps when singing falsetto soprano. His highest sounds reach about 8,000 cps. He also communicates by gesture, facial expression, and manual use of paper, pencils, keyboards, etc.

Einstein's nose detects thousands of different odors in airborne substances, possibly based on 20 to 30 different types of nerve receptors. His taste buds detect sweet, salty, bitter, and sour tastes in salivary fluid.

Einstein's extremities (hands, arms, feet, and legs) are highly sensitive and flexible tools for gesturing, probing, grasping, and pedaling.

Figure 5.1
Do the Sensing and Displaying Capabilities of Information Technologies Rival Human Biological Functions?

Can computers simulate people? Could we replace Albert Einstein? Compustein might never have Einstein's curiosity, compassion, love of life, or scientific imagination. And no supercomputer presently rivals the computing power, speed, or subtlety of Einstein's—or your—brain. Still, neither your brain nor Einstein's can do mathematical calculations as fast as common microprocessor. And Compustein's "senses" (input devices) and powers of expression (output devices) might one day, in some respect, outperform their human counterparts.

Input and output devices are critical to our ability to use information technology effectively. They are the way that people "connect" and interact with a computer system. If that connection (or *interface*) with the machine is not easy to use and understand, much of the value that a computer can provide may be lost.

As you will see, exciting new input and output devices being developed today seek to make our interactions with computers easier and more productive by establishing a more "human" connection between man and machine. Humans connect to the world through the use of the senses—primarily sight, sound, and touch—and a machine that can either engage our senses or actually possesses these senses itself will be easier for us to use. Today, with the help of new input and output technologies, we are starting to communicate with computers through writing, speech, touch, and other gestures. Computers are now able to "sense" things on their own. And they can communicate to us through displays that capture our eyes, that "speak" to us, figuratively and sometimes literally (see Figure 5.1). Together, these advances may someday help create a seamless interface between people and their computers, one in which it is difficult to tell where man stops and machine begins.

5.2   Input Devices

The word *input* refers both to the information that is to be processed by the computer and to the process of conveying that information to the computer. Input can take a variety of forms. It may be "raw" data, program instructions, sounds, or even images.

In this section, we take a look at some of the different **input devices** that are used to perform this important function. First, we concentrate on devices such as keyboards, mice, trackballs, electronic pens, touch screens, digitizing tablets, and voice recognition systems, all of which rely primarily on people to act as the connection between the information being input and the computer. As we noted, researchers and developers are now creating devices that feel more "natural" and are easier for people to use. Then we'll switch to devices such as scanners, readers, sensors, and other data collectors, all of which aim to eliminate people from the input side of the equation and instead gather input directly from a nonhuman source.

Keyboards

The input device that requires the greatest amount of human participation is the **keyboard.** To input data using a keyboard, you must press appropriate keys on a board. Pressing a key triggers a series of electronic pulses that represent, in binary code, the character on that key. These pulses then travel to primary storage, where the character will be temporarily stored and from primary storage to a display screen. The display screen reconverts the pulses back into a form that a person can understand and displays the character on the screen.

The keyboard itself has its origins in the 19th century, when it was developed for use with the first typewriters. Most keyboards designed for use with computers contain the same key arrangement for letters and numbers as a typewriter, but computer keyboards have additional keys that a typewriter does not have. These include:

1 Function keys, which have different uses depending on the software being used

2 A numeric keypad (a separate set of number keys arranged in the same way as keys on a calculator)

3 Arrow or cursor keys that enable you to move the cursor, a symbol on the screen, up, down, to the left, and to the right

4 Insert, delete, page up, and page down keys that make performing those tasks easier

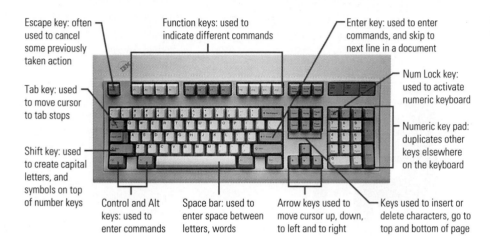

Escape key: often used to cancel some previously taken action

Function keys: used to indicate different commands

Enter key: used to enter commands, and skip to next line in a document

Num Lock key: used to activate numeric keyboard

Tab key: used to move cursor to tab stops

Numeric key pad: duplicates other keys elsewhere on the keyboard

Shift key: used to create capital letters, and symbols on top of number keys

Control and Alt keys: used to enter commands

Space bar: used to enter space between letters, words

Arrow keys used to move cursor up, down, to left and to right

Keys used to insert or delete characters, go to top and bottom of page

Figure 5.2
The Keys on the Keyboard

Figure 5.2 identifies these keys and other important elements of a typical keyboard.

As a result of its familiar origins, the keyboard is probably still the least intimidating input device for someone who has not previously used computers. However, a keyboard can be very time consuming for those who do not know how to type. Keyboards can also pose a threat to your health if you use one for several hours a day, day after day.

Severe and sometimes crippling arm, wrist, and hand injuries can result from the repetitive motions involved with typing on a keyboard. Most experts agree that the design of the typical keyboard forces users to strain muscles from the shoulders to the fingertips. Figure 5.3 gives you some tips to reduce your risk. An increasing number of lawsuits have been filed against manufacturers of keyboards, charging that the injured parties' repetitive stress injuries (RSIs) resulted from defective design and the manufacturer's failure to provide adequate warning. RSIs are fast becoming the leading job-related injury of the 1990s. In 1982, they accounted for about 18 percent of job-related injuries; today, the figure has climbed to 55 percent, according to the Department of Labor.

Although a significant redesign of keyboards is still probably some years away, a few manufacturers have begun work on new designs that are more *ergonomic,* that is, designed to be more comfortable and less physically stressful for people to use. Apple has recently introduced a keyboard hinged in the middle so that the typist can hold his or her wrists in a more natural position. Another type combines the functions of a keyboard into a 5-inch handheld device called a Twiddler (see photo). The Twiddler has 12 finger keys on the front that emulate a 101-key keyboard via chord keying: you press and release one or more keys at a time, with each combination generating a unique command.

The Twiddler.

Source: Courtesy of Hand Key Corporation.

a.

Gently pull thumb down and back until you feel the stretch; hold for 5 seconds

Grasp fingers and gently bend back wrist; hold for 5 seconds

Massage inside and outside of hand with thumb and fingers

Clench fist tightly, then release, fanning out fingers; repeat five times

b.

Posture
Back angled backward a few degrees to widen angle between torso and thighs, increase blood flow, and reduce compression of spine
Arms relaxed and loose at sides; forearms and hands parallel to floor
Thighs at right angle to torso
Knees at right angle to thighs

Chair
Back rest fits curve of lower back
Seat inclines forward slighty to transfer pressure from spine to thighs and feet
Cushion curves downward at front to ease pressure on thighs

Monitor
Top of screen at eye level, center viewed with slight downward gaze

Figure 5.3
How to Avoid Repetitive Stress Injuries
(a) Try some exercises for the hands, wrists, and fingers. **(b)** To avoid injury: (1) Start with a chair that allows you to adjust the height of the seat and the tilt of the back, that supports your lower back, and that can swivel and roll on casters. (2) Your posture is important: Sit with your feet flat on the floor, your thighs at right angles to your torso, your forearms and hands relaxed and parallel to the floor, your head erect, and your eyes looking slightly downward. (3) Try to type with a flat wrist: lift your hand to reach outlying keys rather than stretching your fingers. Try to avoid resting your wrists on the edge of the table; also consider using a padded wrist and palm rest. (4) Take periodic rest breaks.

Source: Jaegerman, Megan, "Choosing the Right Angles for Keyboard Safety," *New York Times*, March 4, 1992. Copyright ©1992 by The New York Times Company. Adapted by permission.

Mice and Trackballs

Another popular form of input device, particularly for microcomputers, is the **mouse.** A mouse is a small, plastic *pointing device* that fits within the palm of your hand. It attaches to the system unit by a thin cable and looks a little like a mouse with a long tail (see photo). Underneath the mouse is a small ball that rolls when you push the mouse along a flat surface. There are also usually one or more buttons on top of the mouse.

You can use a mouse to control the movement of the **cursor** on your display screen. The cursor is a symbol—a line, arrow, or box—that most software uses to indicate where you are on the screen. As you roll the mouse, the computer measures the movement, converts it into a digital value, and then moves the cursor a corresponding amount. Most software also lets you use a mouse to choose program options and commands by moving the cursor to a word or **icon** (a pictorial symbol) on the screen and then pressing a button on top of the mouse.

A mouse allows you to move the cursor around the screen and issue some commands much more rapidly than you can from a keyboard. However, many people find that a mouse can be a little tricky to use: it may take some practice before you are able to easily coordinate your hand movements to move the cursor to where you want on the screen.

Some people prefer to use a **trackball,** which is simply a mouse turned upside down (see photo). A trackball has a ball on the top rather than on the bottom like a mouse. To move the cursor, you place your hand directly on the ball and rotate it in the desired direction. To select program options or

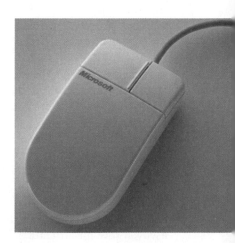

Rolling a mouse along a flat surface moves the cursor on the screen. Pushing one of the buttons on top allows you to select options and give commands.

Source: Courtesy of Microsoft, Inc.

commands, you either press a button or, on some types, push the ball in slightly. In addition to being easier to use, the trackball has the advantage of not requiring as much clear desk surface as a mouse.

A third type of pointing device is the **joystick**. A joystick looks like a small gearshift lever and allows you to move a cursor around the screen. Joysticks are used primarily for computer games but sometimes also for computer-aided design.

Pointing devices have become so important to most computer users that some keyboard manufacturers are now introducing keyboards with track-balls embedded within the board. Portable laptop and notebook computers also often include built-in trackballs or other pointing devices.

A trackball allows you to move the cursor by rolling the ball with your fingertips.

Source: Courtesy of Kensington Microware, Inc.

Pen-Based Systems

Some people have never learned to type and, as a result, shy away from using computers. However, help may be on the way for those who find a pen easier and more natural to use. **Pen-based systems** now making their way into the marketplace could ultimately revolutionize the way people interact with their computers.

Several different types of pen-based systems are beginning to emerge. One type functions like an electronic clipboard and allows the user to make check marks or place letters or numbers in boxes. These are most useful for companies whose employees must fill out simple forms. For instance, Ford Motor Co. uses a device called Scriptwriter to record defects and repairs to newly assembled cars. A paper checklist is placed on top of the sensing surface of the device. As an inspector touches a box on the surface with an electronic stylus or pen, the sensing surface picks up the marks, translates them into bits, and transmits them to an IBM PS/2.[1]

IBM's pen-based Thinkpad computer.

Source: Courtesy of IBM Corporation.

A second form of pen-based system uses notebook computers with an electronic stylus and a touch-sensitive tablet screen. You input data by writing on the screen; software enables the system to recognize and transform your writing into typewritten output. Right now, most systems can recognize only handwriting that the system has been "trained" to recognize, and the writing must be neatly printed, not written in script. IBM's Thinkpad is one example of this type of system (see photo).

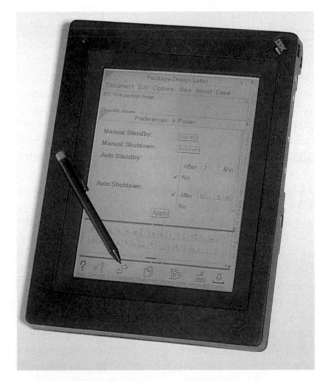

Manufacturers have targeted the "mobile worker" (those who must walk around to do their job, such as field sales representatives or insurance adjusters) as a likely first market. The story "Trading Paper for Pen" illustrates how pen-based computers could change the way companies do business.

In addition to the mobile worker, manufacturers believe notepad computers will be attractive to office workers once the systems have been perfected. Manufacturers are also beginning to develop "penpads" that can be hooked to a regular microcomputer as an alternative input device. For instance, Apple Computer plans to give pen input capabilities to its entire Macintosh line by the end of 1994.

A third pen-based system is the handheld electronic organizer, exemplified by Apple's Newton. Designed to act as a "personal digital assistant," the Newton transforms handwritten notes into typeset documents and automat-

Trading Paper for Pen

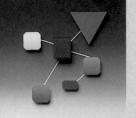

When an accident occurs, an insurance agent is generally not too far behind. To resolve an insurance claim, agents need to both inspect damage and process paperwork. Finding a way for agents to get their jobs done more efficiently can provide a company with a significant competitive edge. State Farm Mutual Automobile Insurance Company thinks pen-based computers may be the key.

For years, State Farm had been looking for ways to automate paperwork for its field force. Data processing vice president Norman Vincent didn't think that laptop personal computers were the answer—he felt they were too unwieldy for the sometimes dangerous and inaccessible accident sites that agents were required to inspect. Agents couldn't carry and use a laptop at the same time since keyboards require two hands. Laptops didn't make filling out claim forms much easier either, and they couldn't accept signatures.

IBM's pen-based notepad computer answered most of Vincent's concerns in a recent pilot program. The computer stored evaluation forms, up-to-date parts and labor price lists, and parts diagrams for a typical car. An insurance agent can use its stylus to fill out forms, call up parts diagrams, and mark parts that need to be replaced. The machine can then calculate the damages and store the results for transmission to State Farm's central computers at the end of the day.

With the help of this new computer, State Farm is thinking of giving its agents the authority to write car owners a check for the damages on the spot. Previously, it took two visits to the car owner and heaps of paperwork to get that far. State Farm's Vincent is impressed: "This is honestly the most exciting technology I've ever seen. I could easily come up with 25,000 people who could use these things at State Farm."

Source: Based on Schlender, Brenton R., "Hot New PCs That Read Your Writing," *Fortune,* February 11, 1991.

Critical Thinking Questions

1 How might a pen-based system be used to increase productivity or provide enhanced customer service in some other businesses that you are familiar with?

2 Why is the computer industry so excited about pen-based systems? Are they really so special, or are they just another example of market hype?

---

ically links whatever you wrote with other databases. For instance, if you write "Call Susan to set up meeting for Tuesday at 9 A.M.," it adds a line to your to-do list along with Susan's phone number; it also adds the meeting to your appointment calendar. Even more impressive, instead of requiring you to use commands based on software languages, the Newton has been programmed to recognize certain gestures. For instance, if you want to delete something you have written, instead of having to write the word *delete*, all you need to do is cross it out. If you write a column of numbers with a plus sign and a line underneath them, Newton automatically knows that you want to add them. With the Newton, the pen isn't merely a substitute for a keyboard or mouse but an entirely different way of telling the machine what you want to do.

Although pen-based computing will probably be an important trend of the 1990s, a number of hurdles need to be overcome before these systems can sweep the marketplace. Handwriting recognition systems still find it hard to deal with sloppy handwriting and variations in the shape of letters, and most systems need to be trained to recognize the writing of the specific user before they become accurate. In addition, even though several operating systems, such as Go Corporation's PenPoint and Microsoft's Windows for Pen Computing, have been introduced, pen-based hardware continues to lag behind. Finally, not much applications software has yet been developed to take advantage of the unique features of pen-based systems: most applications still simply use the pen as a substitute for a mouse. None of these technological challenges appears impossible to overcome, however, and most of the problems identified are likely to disappear within the next several years. When they do, pens may become the input device of choice.

Touch screens are particularly useful when dealing with users who are likely to be unfamiliar with computers.

Source: Mike Abramson 1988.

Touch Screens

A **touch screen** allows you to input data by touching a specified word, number, or location on the surface of a screen with your finger. Sensors on the screen identify the touched location and communicate the choice to the rest of the computer. Touch screens have the advantage of simplicity: nothing is much easier than pointing a finger to what you want. Touch screens are most often used for automatic teller machines, in restaurants, in retail stores, and increasingly, in computer "kiosks" that dispense information and sell services or products (see photo). One example is the 15 Info/California kiosks around San Diego and Sacramento that allow you to order a copy of your birth certificate, apply for a fishing license, get information about job listings, and much more.

Applications using touch screens have increased, but they remain of somewhat limited use. For instance, they are not very useful if large amounts of data need to be input. In addition, the screen's ability to determine what has been touched is not very precise—it needs a fairly large area to figure out where you are pointing.

Digitizing Tablets

Digitizing tablets combine elements of pointing device, pen, and touch screen technology. A digitizing tablet allows you to write, draw, and trace designs on top of a pressure-sensitive tablet with a *puck* (a flat, handheld pointing device with a small glass window with intersecting crosshairs) or electronic stylus.

Digitizing tablets are particularly useful for computer-aided design and graphic artists. For instance, when used in connection with a paint or drawing program, a digitizing tablet and stylus allows you to emulate the range of effects possible with pen, pencil, and charcoal.

Voice Recognition Systems

Speech is probably our most powerful and natural method of communication. Imagine that your computer could understand and respond to your voice commands and automatically record everything that you said to it. Researchers have been working for years to develop devices and software that would enable computers to recognize speech. Now, powerful processors and increased storage capacity are beginning to move voice recognition from the realm of the possible into the world of reality.

A **voice recognition system** begins with a microphone attached to your computer system. Words spoken into a microphone are analyzed by a signal processor and converted into a set of digital numbers, with each number representing an extremely short segment (usually around 1/100 of a second) of the sound. The computer then compares the pattern produced by the sound of the spoken word to a set of stored patterns. When a match occurs, the computer recognizes the word. Figure 5.4 illustrates how a computer deciphers speech. Some systems use neural networks, expert systems software, and fuzzy

Figure 5.4

How a Computer Can "Understand" Speech

1 Digitize the spoken words.

A microphone picks up the speech. A digitizer converts the soundwaves into digital signals by taking tiny samples of the sound thousands of times per second. Digitized sound is a stream of bits that describe numerically the frequencies and intensities of the sound.

2 Analyze the sound and determine its features.

kumpeeooturzkanheeureeoo

The computer analyzes the digitized sound for patterns and changes in frequency, volume, and so on. From this the computer constructs a "phonetic map" (a model) of the sequence of sounds.

3 Compare the analyzed sound to previously stored patterns.

kumpeeooturzkanheeureeoo
　　Come pewters canny are ewe
　　Computers can he are you
　　Computers can hear you

The computer contains stored digitized patterns for individual spoken sounds, syllables, and words. It compares the incoming data against these resident patterns to guess at probable words. It also uses stored information about grammar and syntax to help determine where one word is likely to end and the next word begin.

The ability of computers to recognize a given individual's speech can be greatly improved by giving it sample sounds from that individual to use in the recognition process.

Source: Based on "Coming Soon: The PC with Ears," *New York Times,* August 30, 1992.

This voice recognition system speeds the inventory taking process by allowing inventory counts to be recorded verbally.

Source: Fredrik D. Bodin/Offshoot.

logic (see Chapter 14) to help categorize the sounds into their probable meaning.

Although great strides have been made in the development of voice recognition systems, they are still limited in what they can do. First, most systems today are "speaker dependent"—they need to be trained to recognize the voice of the user by listening to him or her speak and then storing the pattern created by the sound. (Can you think of any circumstances under which this might be a benefit?) People don't pronounce words exactly the same every time they say them, so the system has to be sophisticated enough to deal with those variations. Creating a system that is "speaker independent"—one that can handle a wide range of voices, with varying accents and pronunciation, without first having been exposed to them—is even more difficult. However, an increasing number of systems are beginning to have this capability.

Second, many systems can still process only single, isolated words and have relatively small vocabularies (1,000 words or less). Attention is now being focused, though, on systems that can understand continuous speech (whole sentences spoken without unnatural pauses) and that will have large vocabularies. For instance, Dragon Systems Inc., of Newton, Massachusetts, offers a continuous-recognition dictation system with a 30,000-word vocabulary (which is larger than the average person's). The system runs on a standard microcomputer built around an Intel 40 MHz 486 microprocessor.

Finally, not until voice recognition systems can actually comprehend and respond to everyday language rather than merely convert sounds into characters will they find widespread use. The Defense Advanced Research Projects Agency has a Spoken Language Systems program that provides funding for projects seeking to achieve this goal. Some of the systems now being tested include a military routing system and an air travel system. These systems not only recognize spoken words but also understand the meaning of a question, search a database, and respond with an answer on the screen; for instance, the air travel system can understand and answer a question about available flights on a given date between two airports.

Even though voice recognition system technology may still be in its infancy, researchers have made tremendous strides over the last several years. Verbex Voice Systems in Edison, New Jersey, is now selling a speaker-dependent system for microcomputers for less than $500. The system lets users control Windows software and other applications like spreadsheets and word processing programs. Low-cost, speaker-independent systems with continuous-recognition capabilities and large vocabularies will probably be developed within the next five to ten years. When and if this occurs, voice recognition systems may become the ultimate input device.[2]

Voice recognition systems are one type of audio input system. We discuss audio input further in Section 5.4 on multimedia systems.

Biological Feedback Input Devices

In addition to speaking and writing, humans communicate by gestures and body movement. Many researchers believe that devices that can interpret body language will be the most natural form of input device of all.

Although **biological feedback devices** are still in their infancy, researchers and manufacturers are making rapid progress. Some of the devices developed so far include body suits, cyber gloves, and robotic hands. Body suits and cyber gloves, like VPL's DataGlove, are made of stretchy lycra material that fits tightly on your body or hand. Sensors attached to the fabric detect and measure your body movements and convey them over fiber-optic cables to a computer that uses the data to determine your position. Researchers are also working on cyber gloves equipped with pressure pads to provide tactile feedback. As you grasp a "virtual object" the gloves create the sensation that you are actually holding something in your hand. Right now, body suits and cyber gloves are being used primarily in virtual reality systems and for medical research. For instance, California-based Telepresence Research has created a virtual reality application that allows an aircraft wing designer to use his or her own hand motions to simulate the flow of air across a wing.

Robotic hands (also called exoskeletons) use a lightweight and natural-feeling metallic "skeleton" that you place around your hand. They have a slight advantage over cyber gloves because the sensors, mounted on the metal skeleton, remain more firmly in place than when attached to an elastic fabric (see photo). NASA has been experimenting with a robotic hand to control robotic arms in space. Robotic hands that control robotic arms may also prove useful for oceanographic research, radioactive waste sites, and anywhere else it would be helpful to have human hands, but where a human's actual presence would be impossible or inadvisable.

The ultimate in biological feedback devices may be a computer that can interpret brain waves. A research team at the Wadsworth Center for Laboratories and Research in Albany, New York, has developed a system that allows users, after some training, to move a cursor up and down or side to side by mental action alone. And University of Illinois psychologists have developed a way of allowing people to type, albeit very slowly, by spelling out words in their heads. Both systems are based on having computers analyze electrical signals emitted by the brain as it works.

Michael Ali, a graduate student at Rensselaer Polytechnic Institute, is the primary developer of the first anatomically correct robotic hand. The hand has five fingers and has the same joints and range of motion as a human hand.

Source: David Jennings, NYT Pictures.

Brain-control computers are, as a practical matter, still the stuff of science fiction. But researchers hope that within the next several decades they can use these techniques to develop limited systems that may be able to help the severely disabled.[3]

Reducing Human Involvement: Source Data Automation

We now switch our focus to input devices that try to reduce the level of human participation required to the barest minimum. **Source data automation** technology aims to collect data in a machine-readable form so that the data enters the computer without having to be interpreted or handled directly by humans (by being typed in on a keyboard, for instance). The idea behind these devices is that they will be more accurate, faster, cheaper, and more efficient than traditional input methods. Technologies that we discuss here include magnetic ink character recognition, optical recognition systems, imaging systems, sensors, and other data collection devices.

Magnetic Ink Character Recognition Readers You have undoubtedly been exposed to **magnetic ink character recognition (MICR).** MICR reads the strange-looking numbers printed at the bottom of your personal checks. Figure 5.5 illustrates a check and its identifying magnetic ink characters. MICR characters, which are printed using a special kind of magnetized ink, generate a digital signal that can be interpreted by an MICR reader and relayed directly to a computer. MICR readers are used primarily by the banking

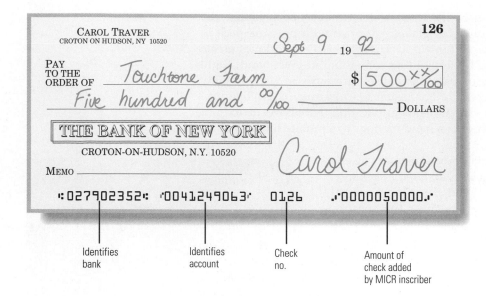

Identifies
bank

Identifies
account

Check
no.

Amount of
check added
by MICR inscriber

Figure 5.5
MICR Characters
MICR characters are printed on the bottom of checks and help banks process them more quickly. All the characters are preprinted except for the amount of the check, which is added by an operator at the bank when the check is presented to be cashed.

industry to sort and process the hundreds of thousands of checks that pass through their offices on any given day. An MICR reader can sort and process over 2,400 checks per minute.

Optical Recognition Systems   Optical recognition systems use a device called an **optical scanner** to translate characters (both printed and handwritten), codes, and marks into a digital form that can be understood by the computer. Although there are a number of different types of scanners, they are all based on the same principle: the scanner reflects light off the character, mark, or code and converts the pattern created by the reflection into a digital format. Optical recognition systems get high scores for their ability to capture and decipher data accurately on the first try.

Recognition of **optical marks** is one of the oldest and simplest forms of optical recognition technology. The optical mark reader scans a form, specifically designed to be used with the reader, for pencil marks that fill in a box or circle. This form of system is used primarily to score tests and tally questionnaire results.

Another kind of optical recognition system is **optical character recognition (OCR)**. Optical characters can be understood by people but are printed using special *fonts* (the typeface, or style of lettering of the characters) that can also be recognized by an optical character reader. Figure 5.6 shows you some typical optical characters.

Figure 5.6
Optical Characters
(a) A common set of optical characters. **(b)** Optical characters are used on billing statements to convey information. Can you pick out the optical characters on this bill?

a.

ABCDEFGHIJKLMN
OPQRSTUVWXYZ
1234567890

A common set of optical characters looks like this.

b.

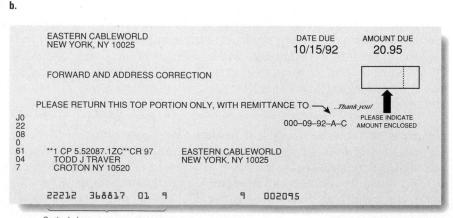

Optical characters on a statement
that you return with your payment

An optical character reader scans the character, converts its shape into digital form, and then compares that form to forms already stored in memory. The reader can recognize the character only if it already knows the font being used. (What type of input technology that you've already learned about does this remind you of?) Some OCR devices can read carefully printed handwritten characters. As you read in Chapter 2, both the Internal Revenue Service and the Postal Service are hoping to use this type of OCR to ease their transaction-processing loads.

Optical character recognition is widely used in industry. In retail stores, wand readers that scan merchandise tags are usually part of **point-of-sale (POS) terminals** that obtain the price of the item from the store's computer system, record the sale when it occurs, and function as a cash register. Utility, insurance, and credit-card companies use OCR devices to read your account number on statements that you return to them when you pay your bills.

Probably the most common form of optical recognition system in use today involves the familiar **optical codes,** called *bar codes,* found on most retail products. Optical codes consist of special shapes that are scanned or read—by handheld wands or guns or devices built into countertops—and then converted into digital form. The bar code records data based on the width of vertical bars and the spaces between them. The code usually conveys information identifying the product and its manufacturer. Like OCR readers used by retail stores, many bar code readers are used in conjunction with a POS system that provides the price of the item and automatically updates the company's sales and inventory records. Many supermarkets are also beginning to offer "check-out" cards that automatically enter your name and purchase into a database kept by the store. In return, you receive automatic discounts on certain brands, points toward future rebates, or free gifts. Many consumers welcome such cards, but others consider them an invasion of privacy. How do you feel about a company being able to monitor your buying habits?

Although the grocery industry is still the most visible and common user, bar codes have spread far beyond the supermarket. Here are just a few interesting examples: Parkland Memorial Hospital in Dallas, Texas, uses bar codes to keep track of patients' blood samples. Northwest Airlines' new automated luggage handling system uses bar code technology to track luggage from check-in to pickup at your destination. A handheld bar code reader even made it into outer space, aboard a recent flight by the space shuttle *Atlantis,* where it was used to collect data on food consumption by astronauts.[4]

Imaging Systems   An **imaging system** allows images of documents, photographs, and drawings to be input, processed, stored, and displayed (see photo). An image scanner transforms the image on paper or film into digital bits in the form of a bitmap, as described in Chapter 3. Once scanned, images are most often stored on optical disks. Some systems may also use new *digital cameras* that take pictures and store them as digital data in the camera's built-in memory. The images can then be transferred to a computer system without any loss in quality. Workstations with high-resolution display screens and laser printers or plotters complete the systems.

An imaging system allows an insurance agent to process claims more quickly by providing all of the relevant data (including a photo of the damaged car) on screen.

Source: Courtesy of Wang.

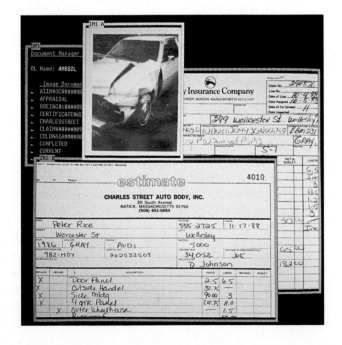

Imaging systems are starting to affect the way people interact with the physical world. Increasingly, instead of actually holding a book or piece of paper in our hand, we merely look at its image on a computer screen. For example, a number of libraries, such as the Library of International Relations in Chicago, Illinois, are beginning to use these systems to preserve their valuable, rare, and old books and other documents in electronic form. When a user requests a book, he or she gets its computerized image.[5]

Imaging systems help deal with the mountains of paper that are generated by businesses and government. Designed to ultimately replace the file cabinet, they improve access to documents, save space, cut paper usage, and contribute to higher productivity. For instance, Goshen Rubber Companies, a company in Goshen, Indiana, that manufactures seals and gaskets, uses imaging to track and process the 600 or so 5–6-page price quotes that it must prepare and send out each month. According to Jim Holsopple, Goshen's manager of data processing, imaging has cut the average time to process a quote nearly in half from 15 to 8 days. Documents that used to have to be passed by hand can now be quickly sent from workstation to workstation.[6]

Sensors and Other Data Collection Devices A **data collection device** collects specific kinds of data directly from the environment and then conveys them to a computer system. In Chapter 1, you read about **sensors** collecting data on air pollution and ice buildup on plane wings. Sensors are being put to an increasing number of other interesting and important uses. NASA has recently tested a system to detect wind shears by using sensors on the nose of a jet to look for sudden changes in wind and rainfall direction. In Florida, General Motors, Avis, and the Automobile Association of America have joined to test "smart cars" that use sensors to navigate. The GM cars are equipped with an on-board computer and video screen that displays a map of the area and your route. As the car moves, sensors in each wheel and a magnetic compass feed the information necessary for the computer to determine the car's location (see photo). Sensors are also being used to help move traffic in a slightly different way, as described in the story "Using Sensors to Speed Traffic."

A "smart car" uses sensors, a compass, and an on-board computer with a video screen to help you find the best route to your destination.

Source: James Wilson/Woodfin Camp and Associates.

Tiny sensors coupled with microprocessors are also beginning to be embedded within certain materials. These "smart materials" are set up to react to certain changes in the environment and to communicate their occurrence. Coming next are materials that not only detect problems but can correct them. One researcher, Professor Mukesh Gandhi at Michigan State University, is working on helicopter rotor blades that automatically stiffen when they are hit by a gust of wind or begin to vibrate too much.[7]

Other forms of data collection devices also collect data at the locations where the data is generated. Most include some form of scanning device. Common applications include keeping track of inventory and production costs, as well as time-keeping systems. Samco Time Recorders Inc., in Carlstadt, New Jersey, offers a data collection system that collects, time-stamps, and stores data on employee attendance. An employee enters data by swiping a plastic badge with a bar code or magnetic strip through the device. (Models using a wand reader or keypad are also available.) Such devices can

Don't you become frustrated when you get stuck in traffic? Don't you wish someone would do something about it? Then check out New York City, where the term *gridlock* was born. The city's transportation department has begun to use a new method to try to alleviate New York's infamous traffic congestion.

New York City has started to install an elaborate and costly system of sensors beneath roadways to monitor congestion, identify trouble spots, and control the flow of traffic. The 1,100 sensors, each 36 square feet, detect cars as they pass over. Information about the speed and volume of traffic is transmitted over 1 million feet of underground cable to a central computer in Queens, New York. Traffic officials will use the data to identify where and why tie-ups are occurring. That information can then be used to adjust traffic lights to move vehicles from congested areas and keep others away (see diagram). The central computer will also feed the data from the sensors to government agencies and companies that provide traffic reports to radio and television stations. By the year 2000, motorists may be able to tap into the system directly from their home or car to help plan their way around the city.

A study of traffic congestion in major metropolitan areas estimated that New York loses $7 billion a year from traffic de-lays, after taking into account the cost of pollution controls, delays in delivering goods to merchants, accidents, and car in-surance. Transportation officials hope that by reducing conges-tion, the new system will help reduce pollution and boost the city's economy.

Source: Based on Levy, Clifford, "Complex System to Monitor New York Traffic Congestion," *New York Times,* August 29, 1992.

Critical Thinking Questions

1 The computer system described in the story will cost New York City approximately $45 million. Some have criticized the city for spending so much money on a computer system when its roads continue to deteriorate and less and less money is being spent on mass transit. What do you think?

2 What are some other ways that computers and input/out-put technologies might be used to help solve traffic and travel problems?

3 Besides sensors, what other types of input devices do you imagine are being, or could be, used in the computer sys-tem described here?

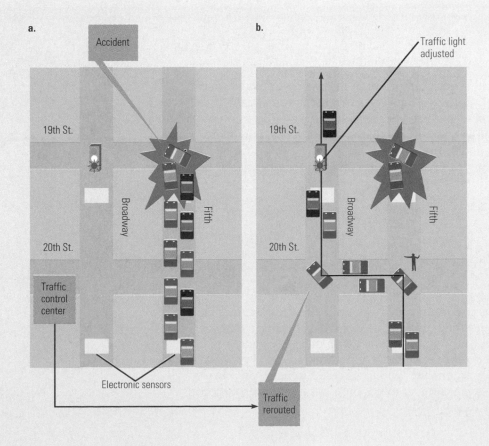

a. Accident
19th St.
Broadway
Fifth
20th St.
Traffic control center
Electronic sensors
Traffic rerouted

b. Traffic light adjusted
19th St.
Broadway
Fifth
20th St.

(a) An accident occurs at the inter-section of 5th Avenue and 19th Street, creating congestion. Sensors underneath the street detect that traffic has slowed, and alert the traffic control center in Queens. **(b)** The control center uses the information from the sensors to adjust traffic lights in the area of the accident. Longer green lights on Broadway will speed traffic away from the accident.

Source: "Transportation: Speeding Up the Flow of Traffic," *New York Times,* August 29, 1992. Copyright © 1992 by The New York Times Company. Adapted by permission.

Name of Device	Description
Keyboard	Most common input device; requires typing skills; includes special keys
Mouse/trackball/joystick	Popular pointing devices for microcomputers; moves cursor; indicates commands; easier to use than keyboard
Pen-based system	Recognizes handwriting; most use electronic stylus and touch-sensitive screen
Touch screen	Input by touching screen
Digitizing tablet	Pressure-sensitive tablet with puck or stylus allows user to write, draw, or trace designs
Voice recognition systems	Allow user to enter data and commands using voice
Biological feedback devices	Interpret body language; mostly used in virtual reality systems
Source data automation devices:	
MICR reader	Used by banks; reads magnetic ink characters on checks
Optical mark reader	Reads specially marked forms; mostly used for tests and questionnaires
OCR scanner	Reads specially printed characters; used in variety of industries
Optical code scanner	Reads bar and other special codes; widespread use in retail industry
Imaging system	Allows images to be input, processed, stored, and displayed
Sensors and data collection devices	Collect data directly from environment

Figure 5.7
Summary of Input Devices

also restrict employees from clocking in or out at the wrong time and lock out unauthorized personnel. Collected data is transferred automatically to a microcomputer, where it can be analyzed to see how much overtime an employee has worked, whether he or she is entitled to vacation pay, how many absences he or she has had, and so on.

Figure 5.7 summarizes the features of various input devices described in this section.

5.3   Output Devices

Whereas input devices let us communicate to a computer, **output devices** let computers communicate to us: they display processed data in a form that we can understand and use. Output devices interact with our visual and auditory senses. We may be able to appreciate how important increased processing speed or storage capacity is, or that a mouse is easier to use than a keyboard, but it is the crystal-clear color graphics on a super-high-resolution computer screen that makes us say "Wow."

Display Screens

You may sometimes hear people refer to the **display screen** attached to your microcomputer as a video display terminal (VDT), monitor, CRT (cathode ray tube), or simply, computer screen. Technically, the terms *monitor, CRT,* and *screen* refer only to the display screen itself, whereas *VDT* encompasses both the keyboard and the screen.

A VDT can be part of a standalone microcomputer or act as a terminal in a computer system consisting of terminals linked to a central minicomputer or mainframe computer. Sometimes microcomputers are used both as a terminal and as an independent computer. If so, they are called **intelligent terminals.** Terminals that have no independent processing capacity are called **dumb terminals.** This type of computer system has become less common because of the increasing use of computer networks that use hundreds of microcomputers hooked together instead of a central computer with many terminals.

A computer screen displays data both as it is being input and after it has been processed. Being able to see input as it enters the computer system allows you to make sure that inadvertent errors have not occurred in the input process and to make any necessary changes to the data that has been entered. Being able to look at output on a computer screen (often called *soft copy*) and preserve it on a secondary storage device, rather than on a piece of paper *(hard copy),* can save both trees and time.

We now look at some important differences among the many types of display screens available.

CRTs   Most display screens still use **cathode ray tube (CRT)** technology (see photo). A CRT is a large vacuum tube similar to the one in your television set. A computer system displays an image on a screen by first sending a stream of bits defining the image to be created from the CPU to the CRT. An electron gun within the CRT then shoots a beam of electrons through a deflection yoke, which scatters the beam in varying directions. The intensity and direction of the beam are determined by the data sent from the CPU. When the beam hits the phosphor coating on the inside of the screen, it selectively lights up a certain number of the screen's **pixels** (the thousands of tiny dots that make up an image on the screen), which generates the image. Figure 5.8 shows how a CRT works. CRTs are relatively inexpensive and

Figure 5.8
How a CRT Works

The image on a CRT starts with a stream of bits from the CPU to the CRT's electron gun. The gun then shoots a beam of electrons through a deflection yoke. When the electrons strike the phosphor screen, they light up selected screen pixels to produce the image.

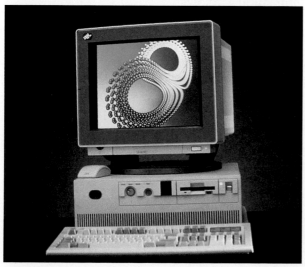

A CRT can provide bright, clear, vibrant color images.

Source: Courtesy of IBM Corporation.

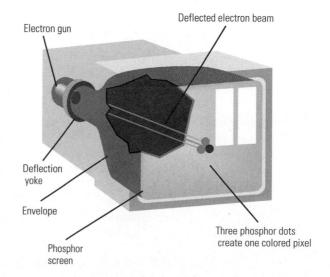

Electron gun

Deflected electron beam

Deflection yoke

Envelope

Phosphor screen

Three phosphor dots create one colored pixel

reliable and provide clear, bright monochrome and color images. However, they can take up quite a bit of space, are heavy, and consume a lot of power. They may also produce hazardous emissions.

Flat-Panel Displays The disadvantages of CRT technology and the growing need for other types of displays led to the development of a different type of screen technology, called **flat-panel displays (FPDs).** Flat-panel display screens have a thin profile and are much lower in weight and power consumption than a CRT (see photo). Laptop, notebook, and palmtop computers would not be possible without FPDs.

FPDs are generally composed of two glass plates pressed together with some form of active display element located between the plates. Unlike CRTs, which light up selected pixels through the use of the deflection yoke, FPDs use a matrix-addressing scheme. There are two basic methods: In a *passive-matrix display,* the CPU sends its signals to transistors around the borders of the screen, which control all the pixels in a given row or column. In an *active-matrix display,* each pixel is controlled by its own transistor attached in a thin film to the glass behind the pixel. Active-matrix screens are brighter and sharper and have faster response times than passive-matrix screens, but their added complexity increases their cost.

Flat-panel displays also differ as to the type of substance used between their plates. The most common type of FPD is the **liquid crystal display (LCD)** screen. Liquid crystal is an oily substance that responds to electrical fields by reorienting its molecules along the field's lines to transmit or block ambient light or backlighting to create an image. Other types of FPDs include *gas plasma screens,* which illuminate pixels by ionizing low-pressure inert gas, and *electroluminescent displays,* which emit light produced by the electron excitation of phosphors. At this time, these types are more expensive and thus not yet as common as LCD screens.

Flat-panel display screens are used primarily for portable computers.

Source: John Greenleigh/Courtesy of Apple Computer, Inc.

Text Plus Graphics Capability Early computer screens could display only text (numbers, letters, and special characters). Today, most can also display graphics (charts, graphs, and picturelike drawings). **Bitmapping** allows each of the thousands of dots, or pixels, on the screen to be individually "addressed" or manipulated by the computer, allowing software to create a much greater variety of images than when pixels had to be addressed in blocks. As you learned in Chapter 3, most microcomputers require a graphics adapter board or card to take advantage of advanced graphics software.

Monochrome Versus Color Monochrome screens can usually display only a single color against a different-colored background (for instance, white, amber, or green letters against a black background). They are often sufficient if the computer is being used primarily for word processing.

Color, though, is not only fun to look at but also can be an important tool for conveying information. As a result, color monitors, although more expensive than monochrome monitors, have become much more popular in recent years, especially as the use of graphics and color in popular software packages has increased.

All color monitors form colors by using an electron beam to illuminate phosphor dots containing three primary colors—usually red, green, and blue. (Most monitors use three beams, one for each color.) This produces eight basic colors (black, red, green, blue, purple, yellow, blue-green, and white), and many others can be generated by varying the intensity of the electron beam striking the phosphors.

Resolution The **resolution,** or clarity and sharpness, of the image on a screen depends on how many pixels per square inch of screen there are—the higher the density of pixels, the higher the resolution. A screen that has 1,024 x 768 resolution (786,432 pixels) will display images that are noticeably sharper and clearer than a screen with 640 x 480 resolution (307,200 pixels). The amount of space between each pixel, called the **dot pitch,** also affects resolution—the closer the dots, the sharper the image. Another factor that has an impact on image quality is the **refresh rate:** the number of times per second that the pixels are recharged so that they will continue to remain bright on the screen. If the screen is not refreshed often enough, the image on the screen may appear to flicker.

Multiscan Versus Single Standard Monitors Just as there are certain standards for bus architecture (remember ISA and EISA from Chapter 3), there are certain graphics standards for display devices. These standards are embodied within graphics adapter cards that are plugged into your PC's system unit. Some of the standards you may see in advertisements for IBM-compatible computers are Hercules, MDA (Monochrome Display Adapter), CGA (Color Graphics Adapter), EGA (Enhanced Graphics Adapter), VGA (Video Graphics Array), Super VGA (used for the higher-resolution monitors), and Extended VGA. Figure 5.9 provides you with a table summarizing the differences between these standards. Each of these standards operates at its own characteristic frequencies and demands a certain mode of operation that your monitor must comply with. Some monitors can comply only with a sin-

Standard	Comments
MDA (Monochrome Display Adapter)	Introduced with IBM PC in 1981. Displays 25 lines of 80-character text (no color or graphics) on a monochrome monitor.
CGA (Color Graphics Adapter)	Also introduced with IBM PC in 1981. Supports graphics with 640×200 resolution in monochrome and 320×300 resolution with 4 colors.
Hercules Graphics Card	Introduced in 1982. Supports graphics with 640×348 resolution for monochrome monitors. Still a popular standard for monochrome monitors.
EGA (Enhanced Graphics Adapter)	Introduced by IBM in 1984. Supports graphics with 640×350 resolution with 16 colors. Superseded CGA standard.
VGA (Video Graphics Array)	Introduced by IBM in 1987 with PS/2 line of computers. Now widely available for MS-DOS machines. Supports graphics with 640×480 resolution with 16 colors.
Super VGA	A higher-resolution version of VGA. Supports graphics with 800×600 resolution.
Extended VGA	Also referred to as high resolution. Supports graphics with 1024×768 resolution.

Figure 5.9
Graphics Standards for Display Devices

gle standard: their internal circuits lock to a single set of signal frequencies generated by the display adapter board, and if the signal frequency varies from what the monitor expects, the result is a scrambled image. Monitors that can comply with a wide range of graphics standards are called **multi-scan,** or **multisync, monitors.**

Emissions Standards CRTs emit electric and magnetic fields in very low and extra-low frequencies. A growing body of evidence suggests that these fields, once believed innocuous, could pose health hazards. Sweden has imposed the world's strictest safety standards for monitor emissions, and many monitors sold in the United States now comply with them. For the greatest protection, look for monitors that meet Sweden's newest standard, called MPR II, published in December 1990.[8]

High-Definition Television (HDTV)

As we mentioned, CRTs are based on the same kind of technology as your television set. Now a move is on to turn your television set into a computer monitor. **High-definition television (HDTV)** will feature a screen that is much wider than today's television screens, images that are twice as detailed, colors that are vibrant and sharp, and sound with compact disc quality. Behind HDTV stands digital technology: images and sound will not only be processed digitally in the studio and by your television receiver but will also be transmitted through the air and by cable in digital form.

The FCC plans to choose the technical standard for new HDTV systems by 1994. The three main electronics groups that had been competing to develop the standard have recently agreed on a single, joint approach that should quicken the process. The first HDTV sets could be available as early as 1996, and within 15 years or so, they will have completely replaced today's televisions. HDTV may also end up replacing your color monitor: you might be connecting your HDTV screen to your computer. HDTV will be an important component of the new world of high-resolution multimedia and other image-processing applications.

Printers and Plotters

Although people are becoming much more comfortable with information displayed on a computer screen and retained in permanent form on some type of secondary storage medium, paper continues to play an important role in our lives. *Printers* and *plotters* enable material displayed on a computer screen (both text and graphics) to be transferred to and displayed on paper. In this section, we take a look at a wide variety of printers and plotters as well as the features that distinguish them.

A daisy wheel used in a daisy wheel printer. Different type styles are available.

Source: © Dan McCoy.

Impact Printers Like a typewriter, an **impact printer** forms characters by striking a mechanism such as a print hammer or wheel against an inked ribbon and paper. The most common forms of impact printers are the daisy wheel printer and the dot matrix printer.

A **daisy wheel printer** prints using a removable wheel with a number of long, thin spokes, each containing one fully formed raised character (see photo). The wheel rotates so that the selected character can be struck by a tiny hammer against the

Paper

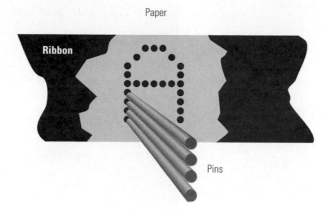

Ribbon

Pins

Figure 5.10
How a Dot Matrix Printer
Creates Characters.

ribbon and paper. A daisy wheel printer is a letter-quality, character printer, meaning that it produces a high-quality print but only one character at a time. Daisy wheel printers are relatively slow (only 10 to 80 characters per second) and noisy and cannot print graphics. As a result, they are used primarily in lower-cost electronic word processors.

Dot matrix printers are versatile and relatively inexpensive (see photo). Although the print quality is not as high as a daisy wheel printer, they are much faster and can handle graphics. The character to be printed is sent by the CPU from primary storage to the printer's electronic circuits. The circuits activate tiny print hammers that look like pins in a pattern that corresponds to the character. When pressed against a ribbon and paper, they create small dots that form the character (see Figure 5.10). The number of pins used affects the quality of the print. Today, most of the better-quality dot matrix printers use a 24-pin print head.

Dot matrix printers generally print only one character at a time, moving first from left to right and then back from right to left. However, some dot matrix printers can print an entire line at a time; these are called *line printers*.

Other types of impact printers that can print entire lines at once include **chain printers**, high-speed (up to 3,000 lines per minute) printers that contain characters on a rotating chain, and **band printers**, which instead of a chain, use a rotating band.

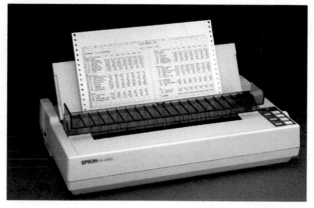

An Epson dot matrix printer.
Source: Courtesy of Epson Corporation.

Nonimpact Printers   As their name implies, **nonimpact printers** form characters without physical contact between a printing mechanism and paper. Because they have fewer moving parts, they are faster and quieter than impact printers. Nonimpact printers include laser printers, ink-jet printers, and thermal-transfer printers.

Laser printers are the most common type of nonimpact printer. As with a dot matrix printer, the CPU transmits printing instructions to the printer, which then beams a laser across a light-sensitive drum, turning the beam on and off to charge the surface of the drum in a pattern of dots that form an image. As the drum turns, inklike toner particles emitted from a toner cartridge adhere to the charged parts of the drum. Then, as paper passes by the drum, the toner is attracted from the drum onto the paper. The toner is then pressed by heated rollers into the page as it passes through a fusing station.

Laser printers usually can produce a number of different typefaces, or fonts, of varying design and size. They produce higher-quality print and graphics than dot matrix printers, and they are quieter and quicker. Laser printers are *page printers*, meaning that they print not just characters or lines but entire pages at one time. Laser printers designed for use with mainframes and minicomputers can print over 120 pages per minute. Companies that use local area networks typically use laser printers that can print from 15 to 30 pages per minute, whereas individual desktop computers are often linked to printers that can print 4 to 8 pages per minute (see photo). Though dot matrix printers are probably still more common for home computer use because of their cost, laser printers designed for personal use have become the fastest-growing segment of the personal computer printer market.

Laser printers also differ in the quality of their output. As with display screens, the number of dots per inch affects the quality of the image: the more dots there are in a given space, the sharper and more realistic the text or graphics will be. Most current desktop laser printers generate 300 dots per inch, but the newest generation generates 600 dots per inch. The newer printers are particularly useful for black-and-white graphs, charts, illustrations, and photographs. Recently, the first desktop color laser printer was introduced by QMS, Inc. Although much more expensive than the color ink-jet and thermal-transfer printers discussed below, color laser printers are likely to become the norm in the not-too-distant future.

Hewlett Packard's HP LaserJet 4 produces high-resolution text and graphics at 8 pages per minute.

Source: Courtesy of Hewlett Packard.

Ink-jet printers form images by spraying electrically charged droplets of ink through four tiny nozzles onto a piece of paper. The most common color printers are ink-jet models because the nozzles can each hold a different color of ink. Ink-jet printers are even quieter than laser printers and can produce high-quality output. Bubble-jet printers use a variation of ink-jet technology and are commonly used for portable printers.

Thermal-transfer printers use heat to melt images composed of tiny dots from a thin wax-based ribbon directly onto chemically treated paper. Thermal-transfer technology is superior to ink-jet in producing clear and bright color graphics but costs significantly more.

Printers and the Environment Printers tend to be voracious consumers of paper. However, there are environmentally sensitive ways to use printers. First, if you can, use recycled paper. Then, rather than throwing away paper that has been used on only one side, turn it over and reuse it for drafts or scrap. If you have a laser printer, when your cartridge runs out of toner, replace it with a recycled cartridge. In addition to being environmentally correct, you will save money—a recycled cartridge costs about half the price of a new one. If your printer uses a Canon cartridge, you can send it back to Canon, who will recycle it instead of dumping it in a landfill. Finally, consider a printer introduced by Kyocera Corporation called the Ecosys. Kyocera claims that the Ecosys's toner cartridge will last the life of the printer without having to be replaced—that's the equivalent of as many as 75 cartridge replacements on a conventional printer.

A flatbed pen plotter.

Source: Courtesy of Hewlett Packard.

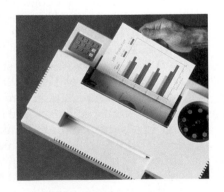

Plotters A **plotter** is a specialized output device that produces high-quality drawings, maps, charts, and other forms of graphics. On a *flatbed plotter*, the paper remains stationary, and the plotting device moves across the surface. With a *drum plotter*, the paper moves through the plotter as printing takes place. Both types of plotters can use either pens or electrostatic devices as the marking device. Electrostatic plotters use electrostatic charges to produce tiny dots on treated paper in a pattern that creates an image (see photos).

Audio Output Devices

Audio output, which includes voice, music, and other sounds, is becoming increasingly important in today's world. We look at voice output here. We'll explore other forms of audio output in Section 5.4.

Voice Output Devices   Voice output devices convert digital data into sounds that humans can understand as speech. Some devices are add-in cards that plug into an expansion slot, whereas others are external units that plug into serial or parallel ports. More and more microcomputers are starting to come with built-in speech software and hardware, such as Apple's Macintosh line, and with more and more emphasis being placed on multimedia, this trend will continue.

Two basic types of voice output devices are available. The first, more elementary method, stores actual human voices speaking words in digital form and then reconverts them into voice as needed. This method is limited to words previously stored in the computer. The second type uses **voice** or **speech synthesizers** to artificially generate sounds. Using "text-to-speech" software, the synthesizer converts stored text into a form compatible for voice output. Then it translates the word into phonemes, the small bits of sound that make up all words. All words in the English language are made up from just 40 phonemes. Next, it puts the phonemes together into understandable, although not particularly human-sounding, English. The final step is to project the word through a speaker attached to the computer.

In addition to being part of many new multimedia systems, voice synthesizers are being used to convert fax messages to speech, as telephone voices for telephone-based information systems, and in automobile navigation systems to provide directions to drivers. And researchers are working on combining voice synthesizers with speech recognition and translation technology to create a computer translator telephone system that will be able to automatically translate conversations from one language into another. Developed by an international collaboration of scientists at Japan's Advanced Telecommunications Research Institute, Carnegie Mellon University in Pittsburgh, Pennsylvania, and a team from Siemans A.G. and Karlsruhe University in Germany, the system is seen as one way of overcoming language barriers. While the days of being able to dial anywhere in the world and talk freely in your own language with automatic translation is still probably decades away, the researchers feel that the translator system may be ready for limited applications, such as making travel reservations, by the year 2000.[9]

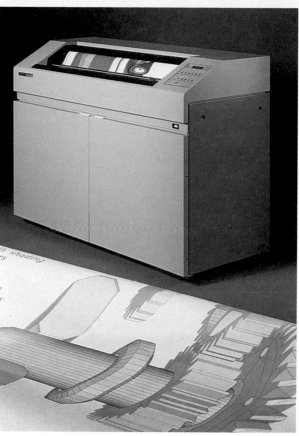

A drum plotter that uses an electrostatic plotting device.

Source: Courtesy of Hewlett Packard.

Professor Steven Hawking is a brilliant theoretical physicist at Cambridge University in England (see photo). The general public knows Hawking primarily as the author of *A Brief History of Time*, a best-selling book that explained his theories about the origins of the universe in a way that even ordinary people could appreciate and understand.

Hawking's work would not be possible without the help of computer technology, but not for the reasons you might initially suspect. Unlike other scientists who need computers to crunch long strings of numbers or solve complex equations, Hawking's needs are much more elemental: without computer technology, he would not be able to communicate with others. The reason—Hawking is almost totally paralyzed and is unable to speak because of an ever-worsening neuromotor disease.

Computer technology to assist the disabled often requires innovative forms of input and output devices. For instance, right now, though unable to speak, Hawking can still move one of his fingers. Amazingly enough, that's all he needs to do in order to "talk," thanks to a computer hooked to a voice synthesizer. When Hawking wishes to speak, he types what he wants to say, and the computer supplies the voice.

Steven Hawking.

Source: © 1993 Jeffrey Aaronson/Network Aspen.

The story "Talking Without a Voice, Speaking with Your Eyes" illustrates how voice synthesizers and other forms of input and output technology can be used to help the physically challenged pursue their careers.

Virtual Reality Devices

We wrap up our discussion of output devices with a quick look at those that make virtual realities like the one described in the opening story possible. One of the most impressive things about virtual reality systems is the display that makes what you see feel real. Cutting-edge output technology has created goggles and headsets that actually let you feel as if you are within the scene being displayed. The goggles and headsets usually feature two small video screens, one for each eye, in order to achieve a realistic 3-D effect. Another variation on the headset is a semi-enclosed viewing screen mounted on a boom that moves as the user guides it around. Both types are usually accompanied by headphones or earphones that block out any sounds other than those coming from the virtual reality world. Even better, a new kind of virtual reality headphone developed by NASA and Crystal River Engineering allows the listener to hear those sounds in 3-D. With regular stereo headphones, you perceive sounds as emanating from inside or near your head. The new 3-D headphones manipulate your perception of sound so you hear sounds emanating not only from the outside of your head, but also from the front, back, left, right, and anywhere in between. The headphones can also compensate for movement, with sound that appears to

One problem, however, is that as Hawking's disease progresses, he will probably lose the use of his hand. If that happens, though, Hawking hopes to be able to use an eye-controlled computer that has been developed by Professor Thomas Hutchinson of the University of Virginia in alliance with IBM's research division in Yorktown, New York. Called ERICA (Eyegaze-Response Interface Computer), the system uses a camera connected to an image-capture card within an IBM PS/2 microcomputer to collect digitized images of the eye 60 times per second. Customized software analyzes the images to determine the spot on the display screen that the user is looking at and allows the user to use eye movements to select letters, words, or commands displayed on the screen.

Technology designed to assist the disabled is not just for geniuses like Steven Hawking. Today, legislation such as the Americans with Disabilities Act is helping ensure that businesses take advantage of available technology to allow disabled persons to pursue their careers. Some innovative sensing and display technologies currently being used to assist the disabled include devices that can accept input in the form of speech or virtually any physical movement (from the gaze of an eye to the flick of the tongue), devices that can read aloud text and machine commands or provide audio signals for various elements on a computer screen, and devices that can translate sounds into video displays.

Source: Based on "IBM Technology Will Help Hawking Communicate," *IBM Horizons,* No. 2, 1992.

Critical Thinking Questions

1   Identify the different types of input and display technologies described in this story.

2   After reading this story, you can see how input and display technologies can be used to help people with disabilities. Can you think of some ways that common input or display technologies might present barriers to some disabled persons?

3   How might you ultimately benefit from one of the technologies described here?

be coming from behind you switching to in front of you as you turn toward it.

As the technology used to create them continues to advance, virtual reality systems are beginning to find more and more applications. For instance, Stanford Medical School has developed a prototype that includes virtual bodies that medical students and trained doctors can practice new procedures on. The virtual bodies have an advantage over cadavers in that they can more accurately mimic the effects of real operations.[10]

Figure 5.11 summarizes the key output devices described in this section.

Scientists at the GE Research and Development Center in Schenectady, N. Y., have created software that provides 3-D images of magnetic resonance and computerized tomography scan data—an imaging technique that is being used today to plan surgical procedures. Demonstrating how the software provides 3-D visualization of the human brain are Graphics Scientist Dr. Boris Yamrom (left) and Graphics Engineer William E. Lorensen.

Source: Will & Deni McIntyre/Photo Researchers, Inc.

Figure 5.11
Summary of Output Devices

Name of Device	Description
Display Screens	
CRT	Still most common; uses vacuum tube technology; monochrome and color images
FPD	Thin, light flat screen; uses matrix addressing; types include LCDs, gas plasma, and electroluminescent
HDTV	Television screen that can receive digital signals; may replace monitors in future
Impact Printers	
Daisy wheel	Letter-quality, character printer; slow, noisy, cannot do graphics; low cost
Dot matrix	Uses pin-based print hammer; fair to good print quality; some graphics and color capabilities; relatively low cost
Chain or band	Uses rotating chain or band; high-speed text printer
Nonimpact Printers	
Laser	Uses laser-based technology; very fast, quiet, reliable; very high print quality; excellent graphics; varieties available for desktops and mainframes
Ink-jet	Sprays charged ink onto page; less expensive than laser printers; used for color and portable printers
Thermal-transfer	Uses heat to melt images onto special paper; excellent color graphics; more expensive
Plotters	Used for high-quality drawings and graphics; drum or flatbed types; pen or electrostatic
Audio Output	
Voice synthesizers	Used to artificially generate speech
Virtual Reality Devices	
Headsets and goggles	Allow users to feel as if they are within the scene being displayed
3-D headphones	Supply three-dimensional sound

5.4 Multimedia Systems

Multimedia systems are special PCs that unite text, sound, and pictures in a single, digital, experience. Right now, what makes these systems special is their ability to digitize all the information required for an effective human interface—picture, sound, and text.

In a few years, as we described in Chapter 2, these capabilities will be built into all new PCs. When you think about it, that's what this chapter is all about: creating a powerful human interface so that we can understand, con-

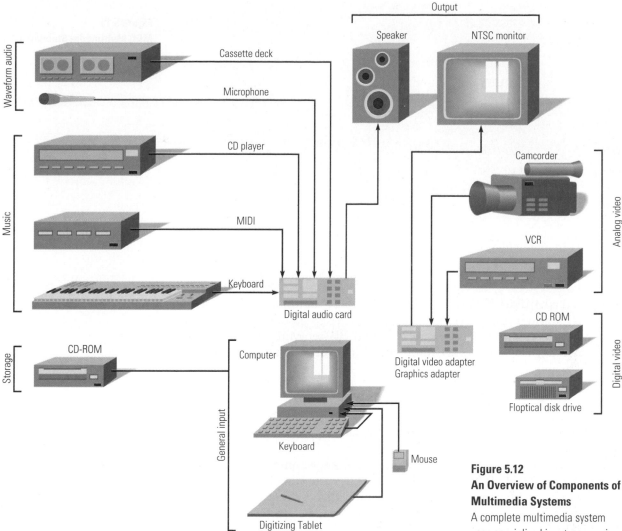

Figure 5.12

An Overview of Components of Multimedia Systems

A complete multimedia system uses specialized input, processing, storage, and output devices. Audio input devices include cassette decks, microphones, CD players, music keyboards, and MIDIs. Video input devices include camcorders, VCRs, and already digitized video stored on optical disks. Traditional input devices such as the keyboard, mouse, and digitizing tablet are also used. Special audio and video adapter cards digitize incoming audio and video. To display multimedia files, multimedia systems use either an NTSC monitor or a computer and speakers. To store multimedia files, most systems use CD-ROMs.

trol, and work with knowledge and information. The social importance of multimedia is that it creates a more realistic "virtual" environment in which learning and entertainment can take place.

Figure 5.12 illustrates the various components of a multimedia system. Advanced sensing, analyzing, and display technologies are at the heart of multimedia systems.

MPC Standards

Multimedia computers and their related software are called **MPC machines.** They are built according to standards set by the Multimedia PC (MPC) Marketing Council, a collection of hardware and software companies, including Microsoft, Intel, NEC, IBM, Fujitsu, and others, who work together in developing standards for multimedia. These standards change over time. MPC 2.0 (Level 2) will be operative in 1994. The specifications for MPC 2.0 are set forth in Figure 5.13.

Currently, a number of manufacturers are marketing complete MPC systems that meet the MPC 2.0 standard. These include IBM's Ultimedia systems, Tandy's Sensation MPC system, and NCR's Multimedia Learning Station, among others. Alternatively, you can purchase an MPC upgrade kit if

Processor	486SX, 25 MHZ
RAM memory	4 megabytes
Bus	ISA or EISA bus
Storage	160 MB hard disk
	CD-ROM drive with
	300 KB/sec transfer rate,
	400 ms access time
Video	Super VGA graphics adapter card
Audio	MIDI board (music interface)
	Waveform audio board
Software	Windows 3.x with multimedia extensions

Figure 5.13
MPC Multimedia Standards 2.0
(Level 2)

Source: Multimedia PC Marketing Council, 1994.

you have a system with a 386SX or faster microprocessor, 2 or more MB of RAM, and a hard drive. Such kits typically include multimedia software, the necessary audio input and output equipment (described in the next section), and a CD-ROM drive. Creative Labs' Sound Blaster Multimedia Upgrade Kit and Media Vision's Pro 16 Multimedia System are two of the leading upgrade kits.

Audio Input and Output

On the input or sensing side of the system are *audio input* devices that record or play analog sound and then translate it for digital storage and processing. Audio input devices include CD-audio (just like your home CD players) and cassette players that contain analog sound. The signal is sent from the audio-cassette to a special *audio board* in the computer that digitizes the sound and stores it for further processing. Alternatively, you can use a MIDI (Musical Instrument Digital Interface) audio board to create music in digital form, store it, and play it back using a special *MIDI board* in your computer. Many professional musicians compose music using MIDI equipment (see photo). As you can see, all these devices require a special audio card inside your computer to process and digitize the incoming sound into a form understandable to the computer.

The *audio output devices* used by MPC machines are stereo speakers that have much better sound than the tiny 2-inch speaker found in most PCs.

Learning how to use MIDI equipment is now part of the training for some musicians at the Berkeley School of Music, Boston, Mass.

Source: Brian Smith/Stock Boston.

Video Input and Output

A home VCR player, a handheld videorecorder (camcorder), or a videodisk can all serve as multimedia video input devices. These devices are cabled to your PC, and the signal is sent to a special video card that digitizes the incoming signal. Some video cards can grab only a single frame at a time (called *frame grabbers*), but more advanced cards can digitize full motion video at 30 frames per second, which the human perceives as a continuous motion picture.

A Super VGA or Extended VGA monitor usually acts as the primary multimedia video output device. Some multimedia machines of the future will permit playback on home television.

Storage

Advances in storage capabilities are an important part of the multimedia story. Sound and full motion video imposes very severe storage and processing demands.

For instance, about 600 kilobytes are required to store a minute of computer sound with current MPC standards. That means a 4-minute song would require 2.4 megabytes of storage. An hour of music would require about 36 megabytes of storage—that's 36 high-density 3 1/2-inch floppy disks! A single frame or picture, in color, requires about 1 million bytes (1 megabyte) of storage. Full motion video means 30 frames per second, or 30 megabytes per second, to store and process. Hardware companies like Intel have developed special-purpose chips and boards for compressing and processing full motion video. The Intel standard is called *DVI* (*Digital Video Interactive*). DVI compresses video at a 150:1 ratio using special chips on a DVI board. This means that one hour of video can be stored on about 720 megabytes (compared to the 110 gigabytes that would normally be required). To play back DVI video, the board decompresses the frames and plays them back through the color graphics card for display on your screen. Intel is also developing a new version of its 486 microprocessor that incorporates DVI technology. The new chip allows users to take advantage of full motion video without the need for additional add-in chips or boards.

Even with compression techniques, multimedia sound and video pose enormous storage and processing difficulties because of the huge amount of data required. The answer is optical disks of various kinds. CD-ROMs using 3 1/2-inch optical disks can store 600 megabytes of digital material. CD-ROMs can also store about an hour's worth of compressed video.

In addition to optical disks, multimedia requires a really large hard disk drive—one that can store 160 to 600 megabytes. The drive is needed to store smaller multimedia files that you need very fast access to. As you learned in Chapter 4, hard disk drives provide much faster access: 20-millisecond access time to files as opposed to much slower CD-ROM access times of 360 to 600 milliseconds.

Some Current Examples

Hundreds of multimedia titles are now available on CD-ROM disks. The subjects covered range from reference titles, to education products, to entire encyclopedias, to entertainment games. Refer to Chapter 4 (page 121) for a list of some of the titles now available.

Although home use of multimedia is a large market, multimedia is also playing a significant role in transforming American education. Multimedia is being used to train doctors, lawyers, engineers, and students from kindergarten to college. As the story "The Hippocrates Project" describes, the ability to combine high-resolution video with sound makes multimedia an ideal tool to teach doctors how to diagnose a sick heart.

Multimedia is also starting to be used for a wide variety of business purposes. For instance, 3M recently put its office supplies catalog of over 2,400 products on CD-ROM. In addition to helping customers find the products

"I swear. . . so far as power and discernment shall be mine, I will carry out a regimen for the benefit of the sick and will keep them from harm and wrong. Into whatsoever house I shall enter I will go for the benefit of the sick."

This fragment from the Oath of Hippocrates is taken by all medical students on graduation. Written by the father of modern medicine, the Greek physician Hippocrates, around 400 B.C., the oath describes the mission of modern medicine: to do no wrong or harm, to help the sick. In today's world, multimedia is beginning to play a role in fulfilling that mission.

In 1987, Dr. Marty Nachbar, Professor of Microbiology at New York University's School of Medicine, began Project Hippocrates: an effort to utilize microcomputers to educate students about the human body and to train them in medical procedures. Using Macintosh computers, Nachbar encouraged leading faculty members to develop multimedia modules for their courses. By 1992, one-third of the 150 faculty members had come to the Hippocrates Project Multimedia Lab to create multimedia course segments.

One course module in cardiology illustrates particularly well how multimedia can be used to teach medical students. Cardiology is the study of the human heart. Teaching students how the heart works, and doesn't work, involves text, sound, and sight. Text is useful for describing the parts of the heart; sound is useful for describing how diseased and healthy hearts sound; and sight is useful for showing students how the parts of the heart—like valves—should look when healthy as well as when sick.

In the cardiology module, students are presented with all three elements. In the left half of the screen, text is shown. The right half of the screen contains smaller windows containing full motion video, sound, and quiz questions. Clicking on the video box brings up a full motion video of a diseased heart valve in action, and then a healthy valve. Clicking on the sound box brings up sound recordings of healthy and diseased valves. The quiz box presents students with questions they should be able to answer after viewing the multimedia presentation.

Source: J. Wilson/Woodfin Camp and Associates.

Other multimedia presentations are available from fields as diverse as psychiatry and neural biology. Has it been a success? According to Nachbar, students like multimedia learning better than simply reading textbooks. The faculty enjoys the experience of working with students to create the multimedia presentations. On the other hand, it takes a tremendous amount of work to create a single module: about four months of student and faculty time are required. They have never attempted an entire course. Once modules are perfected, they can be shared among medical colleges throughout the United States.

Critical Thinking Questions

1   As a student, what do you think are the advantages and disadvantages of multimedia modules over other learning methods? What parts of education could not be delivered on CD-ROMs?

2   Do you think multimedia courses—entire courses on disk—could replace attendance at schools someday? Do you think this should happen?

3   How could some of the new information technologies described in this chapter make multimedia an even more powerful educational tool?

they are looking for, the catalog also treats them to a video demonstration of some of 3M's more unusual products. In the legal arena, multimedia is altering the ways lawyers manage evidence in court cases. Stenograph Legal Services' new Discovery Video System allows users to search for a key word or phrase in a witness's testimony, then watch the video of the testimony in one window on the screen while reading the written version in another window. The system allows lawyers to catch subtleties like the witness's expression and tone of voice that they would otherwise miss if they relied solely on written testimony.[11]

Summary

Input Devices

▶ The word *input* refers to both the information that is to be processed and the process of conveying that information to the computer.

▶ The keyboard is the most common input device. Other popular input devices for microcomputers include mice and trackballs.

▶ Pen-based systems, which employ handwriting recognition technology, are starting to emerge. The different types of systems now available include electronic clipboards, notebook computers with an electronic stylus and touch screen, and palmtop-sized personal digital assistants.

▶ Touch screens allow you to input data by touching a word, number, or location on the surface of a screen with your finger. Their ease of use makes them a good choice for systems that deal with infrequent computer users.

▶ A digitizing tablet allows you to write, draw, and trace designs with a pressure-sensitive tablet and handheld puck or stylus.

▶ Voice recognition systems enable computers to accept commands and data in the form of spoken words. Most systems today are still speaker dependent; can process only single, isolated words; and have relatively small vocabularies. Research is now focusing on systems that will have large vocabularies, be speaker independent, and be able to understand continuous speech.

▶ Biological feedback devices include body suits, cyber gloves, and robotic hands. They are used most frequently in virtual reality systems.

▶ Source data automation technology collects data in machine-readable form so that the data need not be interpreted or handled directly by humans. Some of the forms of source data automation currently in use include magnetic ink character recognition (MICR) readers, optical recognition systems that read optical marks, optical characters and optical codes, imaging systems, sensors, and other data collection devices.

Output Devices

▶ Output devices display processed data in a form that we can understand and use.

▶ Display screens are an important form of output device. Display screens may use cathode ray tube technology or be a flat panel display. There are several different types of flat panel displays, including liquid crystal display screens, gas plasma screens, and electroluminescent displays. Flat panel displays are used most frequently for portable computers.

▶ Display screens may provide either monochrome or color display and can usually display both text and graphics. The resolution of the image on the screen depends on the density of the pixels. Dot pitch and refresh rate also affect image quality.

▶ High-definition television uses digital technology to process and transmit digital images and sound from the television studio to your television receiver. HDTV may end up replacing display screens as computer monitors.

▶ Printers and plotters enable material displayed on a computer screen to be transferred to and displayed on paper. A variety of different types of printers are available. They include impact printers, such as daisy wheel printers, dot matrix printers, chain printers, and band printers, and non-impact printers, such as laser printers, ink-jet printers, and thermal-transfer printers. Plotters produce high-quality drawings and other forms of graphics.

▶ Voice output devices include voice synthesizers that use the computer to artificially generate speech.

Multimedia Systems

▶ Multimedia systems are specially equipped microcomputers that bring together text, sound, and moving pictures into a single digitized experience.

Key Terms

Input
input devices
keyboard
mouse
cursor
icon
trackball
joystick
pen-based system
digitizing tablet
touch screen
voice recognition system
biological feedback devices
source data automation
magnetic ink character recognition (MICR)
optical scanner
optical marks
optical character recognition (OCR)
point-of-sale (POS) terminal
optical codes
imaging system
data collection device
sensors

Output
output devices
display screen
intelligent terminals
dumb terminals
cathode ray tube (CRT)
pixels
flat-panel displays (FPDs)
liquid crystal display (LCD)
bitmapping
resolution
dot pitch
refresh rate
multiscan, or multisync, monitor
high-definition television (HDTV)
impact printer
daisy wheel printer
dot matrix printer
chain printer
band printer
nonimpact printer
laser printer
ink-jet printer
thermal-transfer printer
plotter
voice or speech synthesizers
multimedia systems
MPC machines

 Interactive Supplement

Review Questions

1 Identify the input and display devices that are part of the virtual reality system described in the opening vignette.

2 What is input? Why do input devices fall within the category of sensing technologies?

3 Describe how keyboards, mice, and trackballs work. What are the advantages and disadvantages of each type?

4 Summarize the different types of pen-based systems beginning to emerge. What are some of the obstacles that pen-based systems still need to overcome?

5 Explain how voice recognition systems enable computers to recognize speech. What is the difference between a speaker-dependent and a speaker-independent system?

6 Define source data automation, and name and describe each of the important types of this kind of technology.

7 Compare the different types of optical recognition systems in use today. What do they have in common, and how do they differ?

8 What distinguishes a CRT from an FPD? (Your answer should include an explanation of the different methods each uses to display images.)

9 What are some of the other characteristics that distinguish the types of display screens available?

10 Explain how impact printers differ from nonimpact printers. What are the different types of printers available for use with microcomputers, and what are their respective advantages and disadvantages?

11 Draw a diagram that illustrates how a voice synthesizer translates text into speech.

12 Describe the major components of a multimedia system.

Problem-Solving and Skill-Building Exercises

1 How has our ability to understand patterns in nature (global warming, ozone holes, ocean currents, earthquakes, tornadoes, hurricanes, and so on) been enhanced by advances in input or output technology? Choose one of these areas, and write a short (2–3-page) report on the way scientists use input or output technology to help them better understand the subject.

2 One recent trend in information technology has been to try to integrate everyday appliances such as telephones, televisions, and cameras into computer systems. Choose one of these appliances, and investigate how they are being used in connection with input or output technology. Prepare a short (3–5-minute) oral report on your findings, including your thoughts on the reasons behind this trend.

3 Together with another student, choose an industry such as financial services, retail, or manufacturing, and brainstorm about how multimedia PCs could be used to provide a solution to a particular problem faced by a company in that industry. (To find out about problems, look at recent issues of *Business Week, Forbes, Fortune, The Wall Street Journal*, or the business section of your local newspaper.) Then, using computer magazines and periodicals that describe MPC machines, or add-on components, estimate how much your solution would cost.

PERSONAL TECHNOLOGY

Choosing a Keyboard, Monitor, and Printer

You've decided on the kind of microcomputer that you'd like to buy. You've picked your secondary storage devices. But wait! Your job's not over yet. The choice of peripheral devices—a keyboard, mice or trackball, monitor, and printer—is just as important as picking the right system unit.

Before you select a keyboard, make sure you like the way it feels. Some keyboards have *tactile* keys that click when you press them; others are silent and feel somewhat mushy to the touch. Also make sure that the spacing between the keys and the slope of the keyboard is comfortable to you.

Choosing between a mouse and a trackball is largely a matter of personal preference, and perhaps available desk space. Mice range from bargain-price corded models to more expensive cordless units. The amount of software that comes with the mouse will also affect the price (the software typically provides control over the mouse's tracking and cursor movement and may offer other special features). Make sure that the mouse you purchase fits the size of your hand. There are also right-handed and left-handed versions available. If you decide to go for a trackball, choose one that has a larger rather than a smaller ball—the larger the trackball, the more comfortable it will be to use.

Picking a monitor may be somewhat more difficult. There are many varieties from which to choose. First you need to decide whether you really need a color monitor. If you plan to use your computer primarily for word processing, spreadsheets, and similar applications, a good-quality monochrome VGA monitor is sufficient and much less expensive. On the other hand, today, most software applications are designed with color monitors in mind. Applications designed to work with Windows or that contain a lot of graphic elements almost certainly require a color monitor. If you decide to go for a color monitor, you probably should try to avoid lower-end versions—the images on inexpensive color screens will be much less sharp than those on a monochrome unit half the price. If you can afford it, it will be worth your while to get a monitor that is Super VGA compatible and has at least 800 × 600 resolution and a dot pitch of no more than .31 mm. If speedy color graphics performance is important to you, you may want to add a

local bus to your system unit. (As you learned in Chapter 3, a local bus allows video signals to bypass their regular pathway through adapter cards and data buses and instead travel directly to the CPU). Choose a monitor that has a high refresh rate coupled with noninterlaced display for a flicker-free image. Monitor size is a further consideration; though you probably don't need more than a 12-inch monitor, 14 and 15 inches are becoming the new standards. Finally, make sure that the monitor is compatible with the system unit you have chosen—if your system unit has a VGA graphics adapter card, you need to purchase a VGA monitor. If you purchase a higher-resolution monitor (a Super VGA), you will need to upgrade your graphics adapter card to Super VGA.

Your choice of printer will begin with deciding between a dot matrix and laser printer. If cost is your primary consideration, a dot matrix printer is probably the wisest choice. As you learned in this chapter, dot matrix printers are slower and more noisy than laser printers, and they do not produce as high-quality print or graphics, but they are much less expensive and are very reliable. If you decide to spend the extra money for a laser printer, there are now a wide variety of relatively inexpensive desktop models available with 300-dpi resolution that will print 4 to 8 pages per minute. Check on the number of copies the printer will print before you have to change the toner cartridge. Also check on the kinds of "resident" fonts that come with the printer—fonts that provide for proportional spacing look more professional and sophisticated. Finally, before you choose your printer, examine the quality of its output first to make sure that you like the way it looks.

Once you have made these decisions, your basic computer hardware will be complete. In later chapters, we guide you through some of the considerations in choosing an operating system and applications software.

Notes

1 **Mandell, Mel,** "Pen Input Tool Aids Illiterate Workers," *Computerworld*, September 30, 1991.

2 **Rifkin, Glenn,** "Computers That Hear and Respond," *New York Times*, August 14, 1991; **Caudill, Maureen,** "Kinder, Gentler Computing," *BYTE*, April 1992; **Das, Subrata,** and **Nadas, Arthur,** "The Power of

Speech," *BYTE*, April 1992; **Kurzweil, Raymond,** "Voice-Activated Word Processing," *BYTE*, April 1992; **Verhaeghe, Bart,** "Toward Continuous-Speech Recognition," *BYTE*, April 1992; **Calem, Robert,** "Coming Soon: The PC with Ears," *New York Times*, August 30, 1992.

3 **Caudill, Maureen,** "Kinder, Gentler Computing," *BYTE*, April 1992; **Marcus, Beth,** "Feedback Devices: The Human Machine Connection," *BYTE*, April 1992; "Virtual Reality: How a Computer-Generated World Could Change the Real World," *Business Week,* October 5, 1992; **Alexander, Michael,** "Exos Lends Added Hand to Science with Sensor Tech," *Computerworld,* November 11, 1992; **Pollack, Andrew,** "Computers Taking Wish as Their Command," *New York Times*, February 9, 1993.

4 **Betts, Mitch,** "IS Must Get a Handle on Bar Coding," *Computerworld*, September 9, 1991; "Scanners in Space," *Computerworld*, April 20, 1992; **Stearne, Susan,** and **Hale, Debra,** "Bar Code Earns Respect," *Computers in Healthcare—Laboratory Special Edition.*

5 **Horwitt, Elisabeth,** "Library Tests Worldwide Availability of Images," *Computerworld*, July 8, 1991.

6 "The Information and Image Management Industry," AIM White Paper.

7 "Electronic Eyes See Through Storms," *Popular Mechanics*, February 1992; **Wade, Betsy,** "Smart Cars that Navigate," *New York Times*, March 29, 1992; **Pollack, Andrew,** "Someday Bridges May Have Feelings Too," *New York Times,* February 16, 1992.

8 **Woodard, Ollie,** and **Long, Tom,** "Display Technologies," *BYTE*, July 1992; **Lurie, Michael,** "Color and Resolution," *BYTE*, July 1992; **Alexander, Michael,** "High Hopes for Flat-panel Displays," *Computerworld*, February 10, 1992; **Rosch, Winn,** "Shopper's Guide: Monitors," *Computer Shopper,* March 1992.

9 **Lazzaro, Joseph,** "Even As We Speak," *BYTE,* April 1992; **Zimmerman, Jan,** "Giving Feeling to Speech," *BYTE*, April 1992; **Pollack, Andrew,** "Computer Translator Phones Try to Compensate For Babel," *New York Times,* January 29, 1993.

10 **Hamilton, Joan,** "Virtual Reality," *BusinessWeek,* October 5, 1992; **Newquist, Harvey,** "Virtual Reality's Commercial Reality," *Computerworld,* March 30, 1992.

11 **Schwartz, Terry,** "Corporate Paperwork Gets Sound and Action," *New York Times*, July 7, 1993; **Kurtz, Josh,** "The Rules of Evidence Are Being Rewritten," *New York Times*, June 7, 1992.

Chapter 6 contains:

New Data Highways May Help Ease Court Congestion

6.1   Introduction

6.2   Telecommunications Basics

Telecommunications Systems

Communications Channels

Knowledge: Curing Patients with Fiber Optics

Dilemmas and Controversies: Privacy Versus Security

Communications Equipment

Careers: Telecommuting—Two Tales

Communications Software

Communications Protocols

6.3   Telecommunications Networks

Local Networks

Organizations: Finding the Right Person for the Job

Wide Area Networks

Value-Added Networks

Network Security

6.4   Telecommunications in Society and Business

Information Utility Companies

Smart Telephones and Personal Communicators

Electronic Bulletin Boards

Society: The Electronic Meet Market

Facsimile Transmission (Faxes)

Voice Mail

Electronic Mail (E-Mail)

Teleconferencing

Workgroup Computing

Electronic Data Interchange (EDI)

Summary

Key Terms

Interactive Supplement

Review Questions

Problem-Solving and Skill-Building Exercises

Skill Development: Communication Skills

Notes

After completing this chapter, you will:

▶   Appreciate the impact that advances in telecommunications have had, and will have, in shaping our lives, society, and organizations.

▶   Understand the basic components of telecommunications systems.

▶   Be able to decipher the differences among the many kinds of telecommunications networks available today.

▶   Become familiar with some of the important applications of telecommunications technology and how they are affecting society and business.

Communication Technologies

New Data Highways May
Help Ease Court Congestion

America's court system forms one of the linchpins of our society. However, what some have called a "litigation explosion" has clogged court dockets and slowed the process of hearing and resolving lawsuits to a snail's pace. Those who win are sometimes just as disillusioned and frustrated as those who lose by the time a final verdict is reached.

One reason for this problem may be a lack of efficient communication. The 180 circuit, district, and bankruptcy courts that make up the federal court system have traditionally operated as independent units, with the judges in each court ruling over their own tiny kingdoms. Microcomputers purchased for courthouses tended to be unconnected, stand-alone systems. As a result, exchanges of information between courts typically have taken place by mail or telephone, or occasionally, by fax machine. Now, though, an ambitious project is underway that will link the over 15,000 personal computers and terminals and 100 minicomputers already in courthouses across America. The new system will allow judges, as well as 26,000 other court employees, to exchange electronic mail and files instantly.

Each judge will have a small local area network, or LAN, made up of up to eight microcomputers hooked together along with an IBM PS/2 Model 80 server (a larger microcomputer that helps coordinate network activities). Each court's administrative offices will have a somewhat larger LAN with two servers that can accommodate up to 32 users. The various LANs within each courthouse will then be connected to one another. Communications to courthouses across the country will be facilitated by regional minicomputers that will provide network control and E-mail management. The final step will be connecting the 2,000 small LANs, 150 larger LANs, and 14 E-mail nodes via gateways or switches (types of equipment that allow a LAN to communicate with outside networks) to the federal government's nationwide communications backbone, a wide area network called the Federal Telecommunications System 2000. When complete, the network will be one of the world's largest centrally managed open systems networks (meaning that the computers in the network need not be from the same manufacturer).

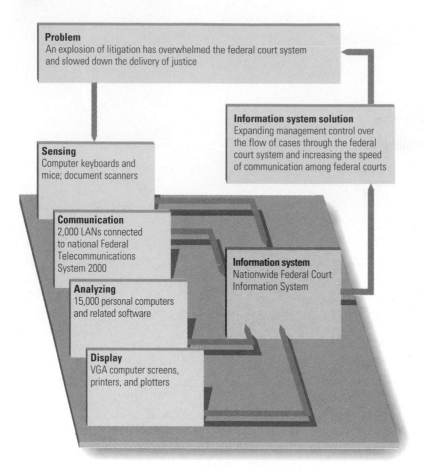

Problem
An explosion of litigation has overwhelmed the federal court system and slowed down the delivery of justice

Information system solution
Expanding management control over the flow of cases through the federal court system and increasing the speed of communication among federal courts

Sensing
Computer keyboards and mice; document scanners

Communication
2,000 LANs connected to national Federal Telecommunications System 2000

Information system
Nationwide Federal Court Information System

Analyzing
15,000 personal computers and related software

Display
VGA computer screens, printers, and plotters

"Now, for the first time, the judiciary will be linked together, allowing the sharing and exchange of information electronically," says Pamela B. White, chief of the Integrated Technology Division of the U.S. Courts Administrative Office. Judges, law clerks, staff attorneys, and administrative personnel will be able to exchange E-mail messages as well as files of financial, case-management, and other administrative data. Users will also have easy access to commercially available legal databases like Lexis and WEST-LAW. Faster and easier access to information should help both untangle administrative logjams and speed the decision-making process. The hoped-for result: a court system that is more efficient and, therefore, leaves participants more satisfied that justice has been served.

Sources: Based on Kaufman, Liza, "Going to Court Without Paper," *Legal Times,* February 10, 1992; Anthes, Gary, "Wide-Area Net to Link Federal Court System," *Computerworld,* June 24, 1991.

6.1 Introduction

Communication is a cornerstone of all great civilizations and a key element in the transformation of society. The ancient Chinese empires used an elaborate national postal system to unify China; the Romans built an elaborate road system to organize and control their far-flung enterprises. In our own American civilization, in the span of 200 years, communications networks have helped transform our society from a very localized economy and culture, to a regional society, then to a national society, and finally to a global one (see Figure 6.1).

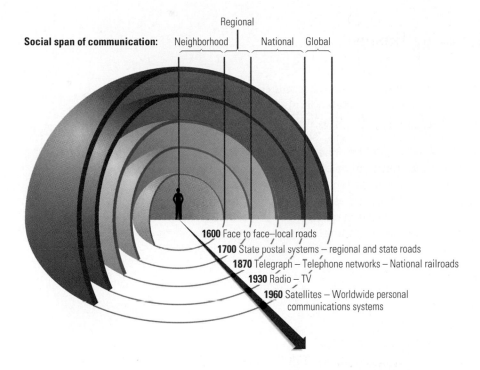

Social span of communication: Neighborhood   Regional   National   Global

1600 Face to face–local roads
1700 State postal systems – regional and state roads
1870 Telegraph – Telephone networks – National railroads
1930 Radio – TV
1960 Satellites – Worldwide personal communications systems

Figure 6.1
The Expanding Communication Horizon in the United States

Communication technologies greatly extend our ability to visualize, understand, control, and organize our environment. As you can see from the opening vignette, effective communication is critical for organizations—without it, it is difficult to carry out the organization's mission, be it the speedy dispensation of justice or the pursuit of profits, in an efficient and productive manner. Sears Roebuck and Company—the first truly national marketing organization when it was founded in the late 1890s—would have been impossible without a reliable, national postal system and an emerging telephone system. The modern centralized business located in a high-rise building in a metropolitan area likewise would be impossible to operate without telephone and now computer communications networks. To a very real extent, the shape and form of our society, our business enterprises, and hence our personal wealth, depend on underlying changes in communication technologies.

Many powerful changes in communication technologies have occurred in the last few decades. Take a minute to think about some of the communication technologies we now take for granted that didn't exist or were not so prevalent ten years ago, such as fax machines, cellular phones, satellite dishes, voice mail systems, and home computers (both desktop and portable) that can be connected to office networks. Today, the communications revolution continues to accelerate. Hold onto your hats: the recent changes are only a harbinger of more to come.

For instance, it is likely that by the year 2000, the telephone system as we know it today will be radically different. Instead, millions of persons in the United States may be using a "personal communications system" based on pocket-sized radio telephones and pocket-sized computers connected to a far-flung global voice and data communications network. People will carry their phones with them at all times, with one phone number that will reach them at home, at the office, or while they're out taking a walk. The phones will also be able to relay data to computers. With a personal communications system, you might be able to check in with your boss while cooking breakfast, or send an electronic message from your backyard barbecue to a customer in Australia, or talk with your friends while skiing, rafting, or sailing.

In this chapter, we focus on these exciting new technologies. How will they change our personal lives, our ways of conducting business, the kinds of information we hear about each day, and our culture and society?

Today, communications and computer technology have become inextricably intertwined with one another. What has resulted is **telecommunications:** the electronic transmission of data of all kinds (text, graphics, sound, video) over a variety of different communications channels, such as public telephone lines, private cables, microwave, or satellite. The data may be traveling just a short distance from a computer terminal or other input device to a nearby mainframe, minicomputer or microcomputer, or it may be traveling thousands of miles between two computers on opposite sides of the globe.

To understand telecommunications and be prepared for the increasingly important role it is playing within organizations and society, you first need to know what a typical telecommunications system involves and the various components of a system.

Telecommunications Systems

All telecommunications systems, no matter how large or small, are created from the same building blocks: an interconnected collection of hardware devices and software, along with a communications channel that enables data to be transmitted from one location to another. The basic components usually will include the following:

1   Computers (or sometimes just input or display devices) that originate and receive the data involved

2   A communications channel over which the data is sent

3   Communications equipment that assists in sending and receiving the data

4   Communications software that helps control the functions of the system

Those functions include establishing the available paths between sender and receiver, directing the data along the most efficient path, making sure it reaches the right place, checking the data for errors, converting the data, if necessary, so that it can be received by different kinds of devices, and in general, controlling the overall flow of information. Figure 6.2 illustrates a telecommunications system.

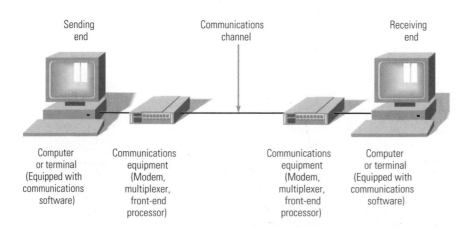

Figure 6.2
The Basic Elements of a Telecommunications System
The major components of a telecommunications system are computers or terminals, communications equipment, a communications channel, and communications software.

Sending end — Communications channel — Receiving end

Computer or terminal (Equipped with communications software) — Communications equipment (Modem, multiplexer, front-end processor) — Communications equipment (Modem, multiplexer, front-end processor) — Computer or terminal (Equipped with communications software)

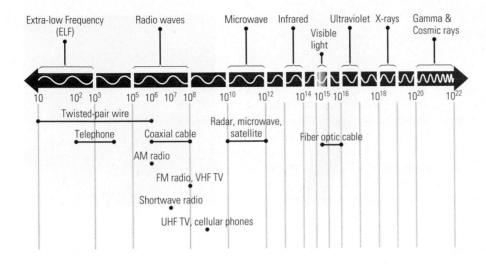

Figure 6.3
The Electromagnetic Spectrum

Communications Channels

A **communications channel** (also called a communications link or line) forms the path over which data travels as it passes from a sending device to a receiving device in a telecommunications system. In this section, we first explore the different types of transmission media available for communications channels and the regulatory structure governing the ownership and use of those media. We then discuss the different types of signals that can travel over those channels and examine some other important characteristics of data transmission.

Transmission Media   Various types of transmission media have been developed through the years, each with its own advantages and disadvantages. Transmission media can be classified into two broad types: those that rely on actual "lines" of some sort—twisted-pair wire, coaxial cable, and fiber-optic cable—and those that use "wireless" technology—microwave and satellite systems and other forms of wireless transmission. In this section we outline each of the primary types and discuss the impact each has had on the telecommunications revolution. Let's begin with a quick look at the natural phenomenon that underlies all types of modern telecommunications—electromagnetic radiation.

Electromagnetic Radiation   All the transmission media covered in this section, whether wireless or based on physical lines, make use of a fundamental component of our universe: electromagnetic radiation. Generally invisible to the human eye, electromagnetic radiation surrounds us everywhere. It is generated by nature (the sun is a major source) and by electronic devices. The radiation is emitted in the form of waves or a stream of particles that can be transmitted through space or a physical medium like a wire.

Different forms of electromagnetic radiation are characterized by wavelength (the distance between the peaks of two waves) and frequency (the number of wave cycles per second, expressed in hertz). Together, the various types of radiation make up the *electromagnetic spectrum*. At one end of the spectrum are very long and extremely low frequency radio waves (about 30 hertz), and at the other end, extremely short and high frequency cosmic rays (about 10 million trillion hertz). In between, there are various kinds of waves, such as electrical current, AM, FM, shortwave, UHF, VHF (television), microwaves, infrared, and visible light, that cover certain ranges of frequency, called bands or bandwidth. Many of these waves can be manipulated and controlled by different types of transmission media to communicate information. Figure 6.3 shows you how the different types of media relate to the electromagnetic spectrum.

a.

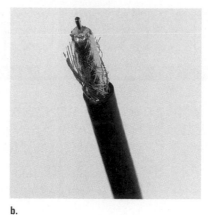

b.

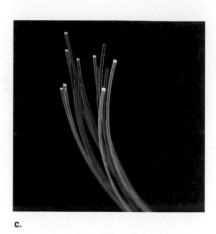

c.

Now, let's take a closer look at the characteristics of the different transmission media, beginning with those that use physical lines, such as twisted-pair wire, coaxial cable, and fiber-optic cable.

Twisted-Pair Wire The oldest and most common transmission medium in use today is **twisted-pair wire,** which consists of strands of insulated copper wire twisted together in pairs to form a cable (see photo). Twisted-pair wire has been used for telephone lines for many years. Telephones lines are primarily designed to transmit voice signals. However, with the help of a device called a modem, which you'll learn more about later, telephone lines can also transmit binary data, although at a relatively slow pace. That already-installed telephone lines could also be used for data transmission was an important factor that helped start the telecommunications revolution. However, despite its low cost and other advantages, the limitations of twisted-pair wire—its relative slowness and susceptibility to electrical interference that can garble data—make it generally unsuitable for the high-speed data transmission required by today's telecommunications systems.

Coaxial Cable Popularized by the cable television industry, **coaxial cable** (or coax—pronounced *ko-aks*) is now often the transmission medium of choice for important links in a telecommunications system. Coax, which consists of a copper wire surrounded by several layers of insulation, can transmit a larger amount of data at faster speeds than twisted-pair wire (up to 200 megabits per second compared to about 10 megabits per second for twisted-pair wire) and does not suffer from electrical interference. The primary disadvantage of coaxial cable arises from its size—the layers of insulation that enable it to transmit data faster and protect it from interference also make the cable thick and harder to install (see photo).

Fiber-Optic Cable The final type of transmission media that uses a physical line is based on a technology called **fiber optics.** Fiber-optic cables are created by binding together hundreds to thousands of strands of smooth, clear glass fiber that are as thin as a human hair (see photo). Data is transformed into pulses of light emitted by a laser device about the size of a pinhead and can be transmitted at blinding speed. Present-day fiber-optic technology can transmit data at rates of up to 1.7 gigabits (billions of bits) per second, and scientists at AT&T's Bell Laboratories have recently reported that a new configuration of lasers enabled them to transmit 6.8 gigabits per second over a 520-mile stretch of fiber-optic cable.[1]

Fiber-optic technology represents the wave of the future in telecommunications transmission media. In addition to the ability to carry more data at faster speeds, it is smaller, lighter, more durable than wire-based media and

(a) Twisted-pair wire. **(b)** Coaxial cable. **(c)** Fiber-optic strands.

Sources: Fredrick D. Bodin/Offshoot; Tony Stone Worldwide.

is unaffected by magnetic or electrical fields. It is particularly suitable for the transmission of the large amounts of data needed to create complicated graphics and images such as photographs and moving videos. Many organizations are choosing fiber-optic cable for their telecommunications systems' *backbone*—the communications channel that connects their various smaller networks together.

Fiber-optic cables are helping to move many exciting applications from the stage of wishful thinking into reality. The story "Curing Patients with Fiber Optics" gives you a glimpse of how fiber optics may affect your life in the future.

Fiber optics are also behind plans for a data superhighway—a national high-speed, high-capacity, fiber-optic network. In 1991, Congress authorized the development of a national research and education network linking supercomputers at major universities and national laboratories. But plans are afoot for an even broader network—one that would reach schools, hospitals, colleges, corporations and even private homes across the nation, providing easy access to data of all kinds. Advocates say that such a network would greatly aid education, scientific research, and health care, and is essential to the ability of American corporations to compete in a global economy. They liken the impact that such a network would have on the flow of information to the impact that the development of a national highway system had on the flow of goods.

However, the quest for a national data superhighway has raised a major debate—about how the costs (estimated at between $100 billion and $400 billion) should be financed, who will own the network, and how it should be regulated. The Clinton Administration has argued for a public network, constructed and regulated by the government, for the benefit of all Americans. But the nation's telephone and cable companies feel that the data superhighway should be built, owned, and operated by private companies such as themselves.

While the debate rages on, the telephone industry and large cable companies have been proceeding with their own plans. Many miles of fiber-optic cable have already been laid (the nation's long-distance lines are already overwhelmingly fiber optic), but in most instances the lines from local phone company central switching stations to the home are still twisted-pair wire. But this may soon change. Pacific Bell has announced its plans for an electronic superhighway serving nearly half of all California homes by 1997, while Bell Atlantic has been spending about $1.5 billion a year for the past several years on fiber optics. Tele-Communications Inc., the nation's largest cable company, has embarked on its own $2 billion program to lay fiber-optic cable throughout the more than 400 communities it serves across the country by 1996.

Experts estimate that the cost for telephone and cable companies to upgrade their network systems nationwide will be approximately $1,500 per customer. To justify such cost, companies will need about $20 to $30 of extra monthly revenue per subscriber. What do you think—would you be willing to spend an extra $20 to $30 per month for the benefits of fiber-optic cable and a national data superhighway?[2]

Microwave and Satellite Systems   We now turn our attention to transmission media that do not require actual physical lines to connect sending and receiving devices. **Microwave systems** broadcast data as high-frequency radio waves, much like regular radio signals. Microwave systems can transmit a large volume of data over long distances extremely quickly (up to 100 megabits per second). However, because microwaves travel in a straight line and do not curve around the earth, microwave stations (also called earth

a. Microwave

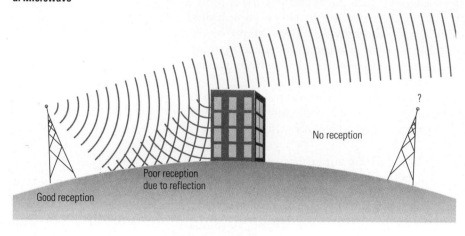

b. Satellite

Figure 6.4
Microwave and Satellite
Systems

stations) need to be placed relatively close to one another (a maximum of 25–30 miles), and positioned in high places to help ensure a relatively unobstructed transmission path (see Figure 6.4a).

To avoid some of this difficulty, microwave stations on earth are often coupled with **communications satellites.** Satellites orbit 22,300 miles above the earth at the same rate of speed as the earth's rotation, so they always remain in the same position relative to the earth (called *geosynchronous orbit*). They act as relay stations for earth stations, receiving data, amplifying it, and then retransmitting it to another earth station (see Figure 6.4b). First launched in the 1960s, communications satellites have been an extremely important factor in fostering closer connections around the globe by providing a relatively inexpensive and high-quality transmission medium for long-distance and overseas telecommunications. For instance, satellites are helping to bring the outside world to China. Millions of Chinese now can hook into the "global village" via satellite earth stations, bypassing the Communist Party's monopoly on news and propaganda. They can tune in to Taiwanese sitcoms and BBC news, encountering ideas and values that they would never have been exposed to otherwise. China's leaders are concerned—its armies may be able to repel invading troops, but they are useless against microwaves.[3]

Private satellite communications services are starting to catch on with retailers and other firms. For instance, Holiday Inn Worldwide is now using MCI Communication Corporation's VSAT (very small aperture terminal) satellite communications service to transmit room and rate information between the United States and Europe (see Figure 6.5). Each hotel is equipped with its own satellite dish and can transmit information back and forth to

Curing Patients with Fiber Optics

If you or someone you love is seriously ill, one of the most important things in the world is access to the best medical help that you can find. Sometimes, though, the doctors that you need cannot be where you need them. But hold on—help is on the way.

At the University of Pittsburgh Medical Center, a new fiber-optic network called Neuronet links operating rooms to 110 Hewlett Packard workstations at the seven hospitals that make up the medical center. As Dr. Robert Sclabassi, professor of neurological surgery at the University, explains, "In complex brain operations, surgeons often encounter complications that require the assistance of a colleague. If the colleague was at another hospital, he or she would have to literally run to the operating room to scrub up and take a look. With this advanced network, a doctor will be able to walk to the closest computer terminal and attend the operation."

Using Neuronet, the neurophysiologist will be able to monitor brain-wave activities and see what the surgeon is seeing through his or her microscope as well as visually scan the operating room. Two-way voice communication will allow the neurophysiologist to hear what is being said in the operating room and communicate with the surgeon. Neuronet will even let neurophysiologists assist simultaneously in several operations if needed.

Fiber optics also help make doctors available over even longer distances. The Medical College of Georgia has developed a two-way interactive system made possible by an extensive fiber-optic network laid throughout the state by Southern Bell to treat patients hundreds of miles away. Doctors can hook stethoscopes, microscopes, endoscopes, and other diagnostic devices directly into the system and can send the images and sounds revealed by those devices instantaneously over fiber-optic cable (see photo). For the millions of Ameri-

Doctors at the Medical College of Georgia use a new fiber-optic network to help treat a transplant patient in a hospital located over 100 miles away in rural Eastman, Georgia.

Sources: Michael Scwartz/NYT Pictures.

cans who live in rural areas without easy access to hospitals and specialists, such a system could prove to be a godsend.

Sources: Based on Alexander, Michael, "Is There a Doctor in the Network?" *Computerworld,* December 9, 1991; Smothers, Ronald, "150 Miles Away, the Doctor Is Examining Your Tonsils," *New York Times,* September 16, 1992.

Critical Thinking Questions

1   Why do you think fiber-optic cable is necessary for the development of the systems described in this story?

2   What are some possible dangers that might result from reliance on these types of systems?

3   The traditional means for regulating doctors is through state licensing boards. Doctors may only practice in the states in which they are licensed. What are the implications of systems such as the one described here for this regulatory process?

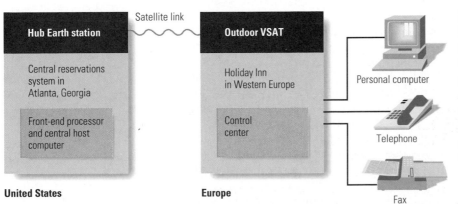

Figure 6.5
Holiday Inn's VSAT Satellite Communications Service
Holiday Inn uses MCI's VSAT (very small aperture terminal) service to transmit data back and forth between its Holidex central reservation system in the United States and its more than 100 hotels in Western Europe.

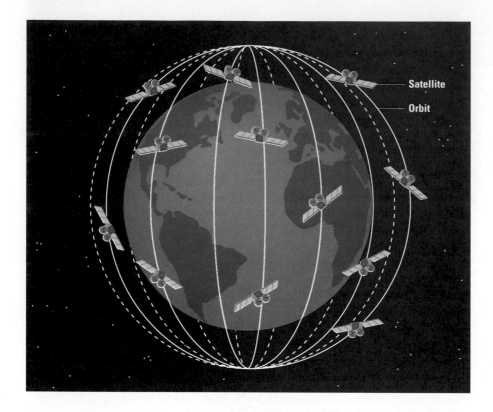

The Iridium project aims to provide a global wireless communications system through 66 small satellites encircling the earth.

Holiday Inn's Holidex central reservation system in Atlanta, Georgia. In 1987, Holiday Inn became the first hotel to use VSATs within the United States, but until recently, it had been leasing undersea cables to link up with its hotels outside the United States. However, the cables were sometimes unreliable. When a shark chewed through a line and caused an outage during a major holiday season, Holiday Inn decided it was time to try something new. Although VSAT has never been used for trans-Atlantic applications before, Holiday Inn believes it will be as successful overseas as it has been in the United States.[4]

A somewhat different kind of satellite communications system is also in the works. This system would allow you to transmit and receive mobile calls and data from remote areas around the world. The system would employ low-earth orbit satellites encircling the globe at distances of a few hundred to several thousand miles apart (see diagram above). The low-orbit satellites need less power and are cheaper to launch than traditional communications satellites and are close enough to earth to pick up signals from weak transmitters. The system may be in place as early as 1998 and is expected to have its greatest impact on business customers who can use the network to bypass inadequate communications systems in developing nations.[5]

Other Forms of Wireless Transmission Many new forms of **wireless transmission systems** have recently been developed and are helping encourage the trend toward "nomadic computing" described in Chapter 2. Some use infrared light waves to transmit signals. With these systems, transmitters and receivers must be placed relatively close together in an unobstructed, line-of-sight arrangement. Other systems use some form of radio-frequency technology. Radio-wave-based wireless transmission can be used for both short- and long distance data transmission.

Many manufacturers and retailers are beginning to turn to wireless, radio-frequency-based local area networks to speed delivery, track production, and improve inventory control. For instance, wireless networking has become the foundation for Oxford University Press's distribution operations in Cary, North Carolina. Oxford uses wireless terminals coupled with scanning technology to fill and track orders from among Oxford's 15,000 titles and 6 million books in stock (see photo). Roving wireless terminals can communicate directly with Oxford's DEC central computer via radio antennas. What was once day-old information entered in batches has turned into real-time information that allows orders to be filled more promptly.[6]

Long-distance wireless systems have been developing in several different directions. Right now, national two-way wireless data transmission is being offered by two joint ventures, one called Ardis, formed by IBM and Motorola, and the other, called RAM Mobile Data, formed by Bellsouth and Ram

Many companies are now using wireless networks for inventory control and other purposes.

Source: Hewlett Packard Company.

Broadcasting. Data is transmitted to and from specially equipped terminals by radio waves emitted by base radio stations located throughout the country. Another joint venture between Oracle Corporation, the nation's largest supplier of database software, and McCaw Cellular Inc., the biggest cellular phone carrier, plans to create another radio data network to be called the Data Broadcast Service. This service would piggyback signals on top of existing radio signals to transmit data faster and at a much lower cost than current two-way wireless systems or conventional telephone lines. However, unlike those systems, the Data Broadcast Service would transmit data only in one direction.[7]

A third approach, being tested by a consortium that includes IBM and nine of the nation's largest cellular telephone companies, would use the country's existing cellular telephone network to transmit data. The consortium plans to take advantage of idle air time to intersperse data amid voice conversations. Sears Technology Services will be among the first companies to field test the technology. Sears hopes to use it for their highly mobile professional staff members and as a messaging system to help fix the position of delivery trucks in the field.

Cellular telephones (also called mobile telephones) use radio waves to communicate with radio antennas placed within adjacent geographic areas called *cells*. As a cellular phone travels from one cell into another, a computer that monitors signals from the cells switches the conversation to a radio channel assigned to the next cell (see Figure 6.6). Currently, we are in the midst of a cellular revolution in which more than 7,000 people a day—twice as many as predicted—are signing up for cellular phone service. An estimated 12 million people now use cellular phones from their cars, from trains, and on the street. Reports about possible health hazards caused by the electromagnetic radiation from cellular phones may slow the revolution though. The National Cancer Institute has begun a comprehensive study of the issue. In the meantime, industry officials assert that neither company studies nor independent research has found any health risks associated with cellular phones.

Regulation of Transmission Media   To fully understand transmission media, you also need to know a little bit about why and how the U.S. government regulates transmission media.

The FCC and Common Carriers   In the United States, the Federal Communications Commission (the FCC) is the agency charged with overseeing the nation's telecommunications systems. All governments regulate transmission

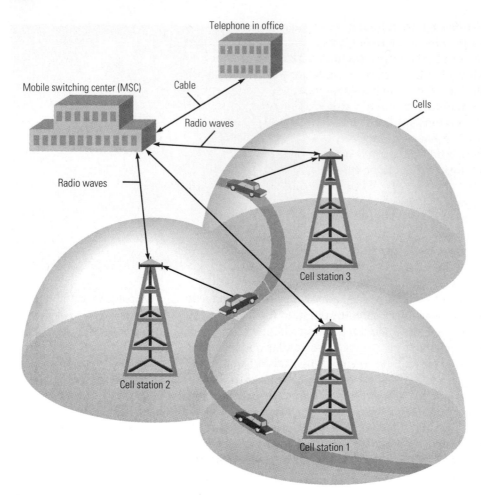

Figure 6.6
How Cellular Telephones Work
When you place a call from a regular telephone to a cellular phone, the call is routed to a mobile switching center, where it is transmitted by radio waves to antennas located within the geographic area (or cell) where the cellular phone is. The phone then picks up the transmission from the antenna. As the car moves into a new cell, a computer at the mobile switching center transfers the call to a channel in the new cell.

media because the electromagnetic spectrum on which they are based is a scarce public resource—if someone is using part of the spectrum within a certain geographic area, others within that area cannot use the same part without causing interference. One of the functions of government is to make sure that scarce resources are allocated fairly and in the most socially useful ways. In the United States, this is done by requiring that companies or individuals be licensed to use a part of the spectrum.

Government regulation was also particularly needed in the early days of telecommunications to ensure that uniform, interconnected line-based systems developed. In the United States, this was achieved by allowing AT&T, a government regulated private monopoly, to provide virtually all the nation's telecommunications lines. However, in 1984, AT&T was forced to give up its monopoly, allowing other companies to compete. Today, in addition to AT&T, the regional Bell system companies and local telephone companies that provide local service, there are a number of other **common carriers** (companies licensed by the FCC to provide communications channels and services to the public), such as US Sprint and MCI.

Types of Lines Offered by Common Carriers Common carriers can provide their customers with a choice between several types of lines. A *switched line* uses a regular, public telephone line to form the communications channel. To send data over a switched line, the communications equipment on the sending end dials the telephone number of the communications equipment on the receiving end. Telephone company switching stations choose the actual line that is to be used as the communications channel. Switched lines allow data to be sent between any two places that have telephone service and communications equipment. The cost to send data is the same as making a regular telephone call, which can be an advantage or a disadvantage, depending on how many calls need to be made. There are several other disadvantages, too—access to a line is not assured at peak periods, and the quality of the line cannot be controlled because it is chosen at random.

A *private* or *dedicated line* (also called a *leased line*) is an alternative to switched lines. These lines are reserved solely for one customer, who usually bears the responsibility for maintaining and repairing them. Communications devices on the sending end are always connected to those on the receiving end, usually allowing for faster and better connections. They are more secure than switched lines and can often be enhanced to allow for increased data transmission speeds. A flat rate is generally charged for a leased line, so organizations that have heavy telecommunications requirements would generally pay less than if using switched lines. On the other hand, since the same rate is charged no matter how many the calls, leased lines are less appropriate for business with lower telecommunications needs.

A third type, called a *virtual private network*, offers some of the advantages of a dedicated line without the maintenance and technical responsibilities usually associated with them. Using computers and sophisticated software, telephone companies can create the illusion that the customer has access to a private, dedicated line, while actually using regular public line equipment.

Types of Signals Two types of signals can travel over the various transmission media that we just described—analog signals and digital signals.

Analog Signals Traditionally, most communications devices, like telephones, televisions, and radios were designed to work with an **analog signal.** An analog signal takes the form of a continuous wave within a certain frequency range. This should not be surprising when you recall that electromagnetic radiation naturally occurs in the form of waves. As Figure 6.7a illustrates, the wave that makes up the analog signal can be manipulated so that it can represent information.

Digital Signals A **digital signal** uses separate, on–off electrical pulses that create a square rather than a continuous wave. When a pulse is transmitted, it represents a 1 bit; the absence of a pulse is interpreted as a 0 bit (see Figure 6.7b). Digital signals can transmit data faster and more accurately than analog signals. Computers are designed not only to store and process data digitally, but also to communicate digitally. However, as we noted before, much of our existing communications infrastruture, including telephone lines, coaxial cable, and microwave transmission, was set up to use only analog signals. This problem has been solved in part by a piece of equipment called a *modem*, which can translate the computer's digital signals into analog signals and then reconvert them to digital signals after they have been transmitted over an analog transmission medium. You will learn more about modems later in this chapter.

Although modems are helpful, they cannot deliver the full benefits of digital signals. As a result, much attention has been recently focused on

Figure 6.7
Analog and Digital Signals

a. Analog Signals

What an analog signal looks like prior to any modification

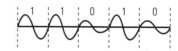

The height (or amplitude) of the wave can be modified. A wave of normal height signifies a 1, a smaller height a 0

The frequency (number of wave cycles within a given period) can also be modified

b. Digital Signals

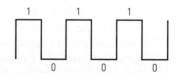

A digital signal conveys information through discrete bursts, or on–off electrical pulses

developing transmission media and communications devices that can handle digital signals. For instance, many telephone companies now offer **Integrated Services Digital Network (ISDN)** service. ISDN technology enables voice, data, and images to be transmitted simultaneously as digital signals over a regular twisted-pair wire telephone line. Experts predict that ISDN, and a related data transfer technology called *asynchronous transfer mode* (ATM), will help drive the next generation of innovation in the way people communicate and collaborate. Some of the exciting applications that these technologies may help develop and expand include:

▶ High-quality, full motion videoconferencing without the need for a lot of cumbersome equipment.

▶ Easier sharing of imaging, multimedia, and other complex applications involving text, voice, and video across computer networks.

▶ Greater integration of desktop computers with telephone services (for instance, being able to fax a document from your computer as easily as you can make a phone call).

Telephone lines are not the only transmission media being switched to digital signals. For instance, HDTV (see Chapter 5) will use digital signals instead of the familiar analog VHF television signals to produce a higher-quality television picture. Cable companies, seeking to get the jump on HDTV, are planning to increase channel capacity (and save money on satellite time) by digitizing and compressing analog TV signals. To improve capacity as well as provide for improved voice quality, many operators of cellular telephone systems are also planning to convert to digital transmission. And In-Flight Phone Corporation is now testing a digital air-to-ground communications service that will allow airline passengers on USAir, American Airlines, and Northwest to place high-quality phone calls, send and receive faxes, and plug in their laptops to receive E-mail, all while flying through the sky (see photo).[8]

But not everyone is happy about the switch to digital communications. The Dilemmas and Controversies feature, "Privacy versus Security," highlights some of the difficult questions that have arisen as a result of this trend.

In-Flight Phone Corporation's FlightLink allows airline passengers to receive E-mail even after takeoff.

Source: Courtesy of In-Flight Phone Corporation.

Other Important Aspects of Communications Channels

You now know about the different types of transmission media that make up communications channels and the two types of signals that can travel over those media. We conclude our discussion of communications channels with a quick look at some of the other important characteristics that can be used to distinguish them from one another, such as the rate at which data can be transmitted over them, the different methods by which data can be transmitted (transmission mode), and the directions that data can flow.

Transmission Rate   The amount of data that can be sent through a communications channel is directly related to the frequency of the signals that the channel carries. As you may recall from our discussion of the electromagnetic spectrum, frequency refers to the number of times a wave repeats itself, or how many times it completes a *cycle*, per second. Since these waves are used to represent data, it

a.

Technology

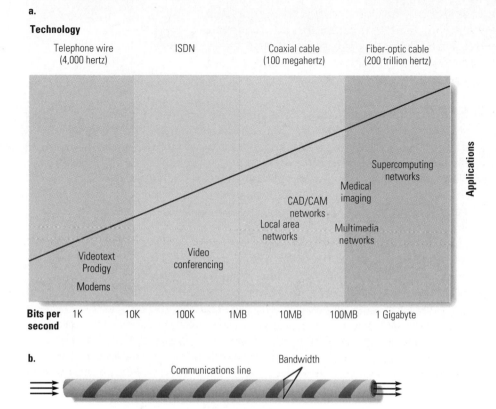

| Telephone wire (4,000 hertz) | ISDN | Coaxial cable (100 megahertz) | Fiber-optic cable (200 trillion hertz) |

Supercomputing networks

Medical imaging

CAD/CAM networks

Local area networks

Multimedia networks

Videotext Prodigy

Video conferencing

Modems

Applications

Bits per second   1K   10K   100K   1MB   10MB   100MB   1 Gigabyte

b.

Bandwidth

Communications line

stands to reason that the more cycles per second that a wave generates, the more data can be sent through the communications channel.

A channel's transmission rate is also a function of its **bandwidth.** Technically, bandwidth refers to the difference between the highest and lowest frequencies (the range of frequencies) that the channel can carry, although in the computer industry and popular press, it is often used as a synonym for a channel's overall information-carrying capacity. Because data can be assigned to different frequencies and then transmitted simultaneously, the wider the range of frequencies that the channel has available, the more data can be transmitted at one time. For example, fiber-optic cables have a bandwidth of over 200 trillion hertz whereas twisted-pair wire cables have a bandwidth of about 4,000 hertz. Obviously, much more data can be sent simultaneously over the fiber-optic cable than via twisted-pair wires. Figure 6.8a shows you the bandwidths necessary for some typical applications. Figure 6.8b illustrates the concept of bandwidth.

The speed at which data travels through a communications channel (and, in the popular press, bandwidth) is generally measured in the number of bits that can be transmitted per second (called **bits per second** or **bps**) or by **baud rate.** Baud rate refers to the number of times per second that the signal being transmitted changes in some predetermined manner. At low speeds (up to 2,400 bps), 1 bit is transmitted with each signal change, and so the baud rate and bps are identical. At higher speeds (over 2,400 bps), more than 1 bit may be transmitted with each signal change, and so bps will be greater than the baud rate.

Transmission Mode   When data is being transmitted over a communications channel, equipment on the receiving end needs some help deciphering where one character of data ends and another begins. This goal can be accomplished by one of two methods, one called asynchronous transmission and the other, synchronous transmission.

Figure 6.8
Bandwidth
(a) Bandwidths necessary for some typical applications. **(b)** A communications channel can be thought of as a straw. The width of the straw is equivalent to the bandwidth of the communications channel. The larger the width, the greater the communications capacity of the channel.

overnment law enforcement officials are worried. New digital forms of telecommunications are making it more difficult for them to monitor communications. Old-fashioned analog telephone transmissions could be tapped with relative ease. Digital communications lines, on the other hand, interweave hundreds or even thousands of conversations and data transmissions on each wire or optical fiber, making it much more difficult for law enforcement officials to wiretap on the spot, in real time. In addition, today's best computerized encryption (secret coding) systems can scramble telephone conversations and data so effectively that not even the National Security Agency's most powerful code-breaking computers can decipher them. Although encryption is still used in only a small amount of electronic communications, the volume is expected to grow rapidly as more and more of the nation's business starts to flow over data networks, particularly wireless networks that are more susceptible to unauthorized interception of data.

As a result, many in government feel that the technological attributes and capabilities associated with digital communications constitute a threat to society by permitting criminals to conspire without fear of law enforcement surveillance. Consider the price that society might pay, says the FBI, if complex crimes went unsolved because of the inability to wiretap. And, if criminals can hide their records and communications by using encryption, police might not be able to get enough evidence to convict them. Although the authorities recognize that businesses and individuals have a legitimate right to protect and keep information private, they feel that those rights must be balanced against the need to keep society safe from crime.

To combat these threats, the FBI has proposed a law that would require providers of all electronic communications services (not only the public telephone system, but also local area networks, corporate-wide area networks, electronic bulletin boards, E-mail, and private branch exchanges) to use telecommunications equipment with a built-in capacity that allows for wiretapping. In addition, the Clinton Administration has pro-

posed a new national encryption standard, embodied within a new tamperproof computer chip called the Clipper chip, which is designed to ultimately eliminate all other coding systems now in use. The new system would first be used for government electronic communications and is expected to spread quickly into commercial use. The technical details of the standard, developed by scientists for the National Security Agency (the NSA), are supposed to remain a national security secret. Law enforcement agencies would be able to get access to the keys necessary to break the code upon obtaining court authorization.

Civil liberties groups and industry groups have objected strongly to the proposal to require telephone and computer companies to modify their equipment to make wiretapping easier. They argue that such a system would make wiretapping too easy, leading to abuse. They also worry about the wide scope of the proposal—covering all digital communications. The national encryption standard has also met with objections. In particular, experts charge that since the details of the system are to remain secret, there is no way to be certain that the NSA has not built in a secret "trapdoor" that would allow unauthorized government eavesdropping. Although the NSA categorically denies that any such trapdoor exists, the perception remains. The plan would also give the NSA an unprecedented role in domestic civilian and corporate communications.

Sources: Based on Wayner, Peter, "Should Encryption Be Regulated?" *BYTE*, May 1993; Markoff, John, "U.S. as Big Brother of Computer Age," *New York Times*, May 6, 1993; Betts, Mitch, "FBI Seeks Right to Tap All Net Services," *Computerworld*, June 8, 1992; Sessions, William, "Keeping an Ear on Crime," *New York Times*, March 27, 1992.

Critical Thinking Questions

1   Identify the key social values involved in this debate. Which value do you think is more important and why?

2   How would you balance the conflicting interests expressed here? Come up with a proposal that you think satisfies the needs of law enforcement yet also protects legitimate concerns for privacy and data security.

In **asynchronous transmission,** data is transmitted 1 byte (or character) at a time. The string of bits that make up the byte is "marked off" by control bits that surround it. A start bit indicates the beginning of a character, and a stop bit marks the end. A parity bit, which, as you learned in Chapter 3, helps the computer detect errors in transmission, is also usually included just prior to the stop bit. Because data is transmitted only 1 byte at a time, asynchronous transmission is relatively slow and not appropriate when large volumes of data need to be transmitted quickly.

Synchronous transmission utilizes a slightly different method. It transmits a number of characters at a time in blocks. Timing signals that synchronize the sending equipment with the receiving equipment eliminate the need for control bits before and after each character. Instead, error-check bits and start and end indicators called synch bytes or flags are transmitted at the beginning and end of blocks. Synchronous transmission requires more expensive equipment than asynchronous transmission but is much faster because there are fewer intervening bits slowing down the transmission of data. Figure 6.9 illustrates the two types of transmission modes.

Direction of Transmission Communications channels also differ with respect to direction of data flow. There are three types: simplex, half-duplex, and full-duplex transmission. With **simplex transmission,** data can travel in only one direction. For example, data collection devices are often connected to computers with communications lines that use simplex transmission because data flows only from the collection device to the computer and never the other way. **Half-duplex transmission** allows data to travel in both directions but only in one direction at a time. A marine radio uses half-duplex transmission: if you are speaking, the party on the receiving end must wait until you have finished before they can talk back. In **full-duplex transmission,** data can be sent in both directions simultaneously, just like speaking and listening at the same time over the telephone. Communications channels between two computers usually use full-duplex transmission to transmit data back and forth. Figure 6.10 illustrates these three types of transmission.

a. Asynchronous Transmission

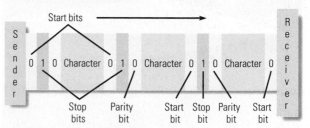

b. Synchronous Transmission

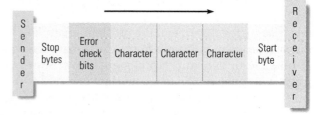

Figure 6.9
Asynchronous and Synchronous Transmission
(a) With asynchronous transmission, characters are transmitted one byte (or character) at a time, each framed by control bits.
(b) Synchronous transmission transmits blocks of characters with a start byte at the beginning and error-checking bits and stop bytes at the end.

Communications Equipment

Specialized communications equipment plays an important role in telecommunications systems. This section reviews the different types of equipment that let telecommunications systems function or increase their efficiency.

a. Simplex Transmission

Data can travel in only one direction

b. Half-Duplex Transmission

Data can travel in both directions but not at the same time

c. Full-Duplex Transmission

Data can travel in both directions simultaneously

Figure 6.10
Simplex, Half- and Full-Duplex Transmission

a.

b.

Modems Probably one of the most familiar pieces of computer communications equipment is the **modem.** As you have already learned, modems make it possible to transmit digital signals over transmission media that are designed for analog signals. A modem attached to a computer on the sending end converts the computer's digital signals into analog signals through a process called **modulation.** If you listen to your modem during the process, you can actually hear the analog equivalents to the digital signals as they begin their travel over the telephone lines. A modem attached to the computer on the receiving end then reconverts the analog signals into digital signals by a process called **demodulation.** (The word *modem* comes from combining the first few letters of each of these two words—*mo*dulation and *dem*odulation.)

There are a number of different types of modems. There are five major considerations in choosing a modem: internal versus external, speed, compression, error control, and fax capability. Internal modems come in the form of add-in boards that are installed inside your computer and are especially popular for portable computers. External modems are standalone units that come both in a standard, larger size and a smaller, pocket size and plug into a port at the back of the system unit (see photos). They are generally less expensive than the internal models and can be moved from one computer to another as necessary. Your second consideration is the speed at which the modem can transmit data. Older modems for personal computers feature 1,200 or 2,400 bit-per-second transmission speeds, whereas newer models offer 9,600 or 14,400 bps. Some modems also can further enhance data speed by compressing files before they are transmitted. Whether you need a "fast" modem depends on the types of applications you plan to use. For example, if all you plan to transmit are E-mail messages and small data files, a 2,400 bps modem without data compression is adequate. On the other hand, if you plan to transmit spreadsheets and other large files, the faster modems may be worth the extra cost. Other considerations include whether the modem provides error control to make sure data is transferred properly. Newer modems are also starting to combine fax capabilities with standard data transmission, which is important if you would like to use your computer as a fax machine.[9]

Modems are an indispensable tool for the mobile worker who travels with a portable computer. They also make *telecommuting*—working at home for a company located elsewhere—possible. Over 8 million people in the United States telecommute for part of their work week, and the figure is expected to double and perhaps triple during the next decade. The story "Telecommuting—Two Tales" illustrates some of the benefits, as well as some of the pitfalls, that await telecommuters.

(a) This external fax/modem offers 14,400 bps transmission speed and also allows you to send and receive faxes via your computer. **(b)** An internal modem like this one plugs into an expansion slot on the motherboard of your computer.

Sources: Courtesy of SupraFax Corporation; Courtesy of Hayes Microcomputer Products, Inc.

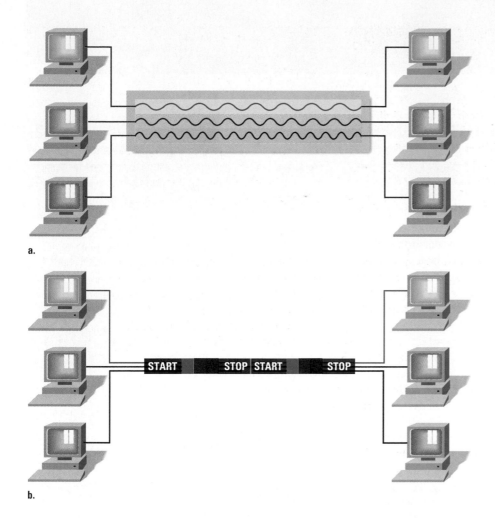

a.

b.

Figure 6.11
Multiplexers
(a) A multiplexer using frequency-division multiplexing divides up a communications channel into multiple, separate channels on the basis of frequency. Data streams coming in from multiple sources are assigned to different frequencies and then can be transmitted at the same time. The data streams are separated and sent to their respective destinations at the receiving end. **(b)** A multiplexer that uses time-division multiplexing takes 1 byte from each data stream in rotation. Bytes from all the channels are collected into frames, each of which is surrounded by start and stop control bytes. The frame (carrying a byte from four message signals) can be sent as quickly as 1 byte of one message. At the receiving end, the data stream is reorganized into individual channels.

Multiplexers   Most communications channels have a greater capacity to transmit data than is needed to send a single stream of data from one part of a telecommunications system to the other. A device called a **multiplexer** allows users to make more efficient use of a communications channel by enabling it to carry data from several different sources simultaneously. As Figure 6.11 illustrates, multiplexers can accomplish this task in a variety of ways.

Communications Processors   Telecommunications systems often contain a number of specialized devices that are used to perform special functions for the system.

A **front-end processor** (often a minicomputer) handles communications management for the main computer (often called the **host computer**) in a large telecommunications network (see Figure 6.12). The front-end processor generally performs a number of tasks such as error control, polling (checking to see if data is ready to be sent), and routing data.

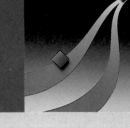

When you travel to a beautiful place on vacation, it's not uncommon to wish that you could stay there. But then reality sets in—your job or business is somewhere else, and prospects for replacing it with a similar position in paradise range from slim to none. But don't give up hope! Telecommuting might make your dream come true, as it did for Nabil Kabbani. On the other hand, it could lead to a nightmare, as happened to Joshua Frielich. Read on for the telecommuting tale of two similar men but with very different outcomes.

Nabil Kabbani runs Eye Group, Inc., an optometry company based in Augusta, Georgia. Joshua Frielich owns an optical supply company in North Hollywood, California. Both men visited Santa Fe, New Mexico, with their families on vacation and fell in love with the climate and lifestyle they found there. Neither man was old enough to retire.

What to do? A new life beckoned if only they could find a way to make it happen. Telecommuting provided that way. Armed with computers, modems, software, fax machines, and telephone lines, both men took the plunge at running their business from afar. Here though, their stories diverge.

For Mr. Kabbani, who was at first skeptical about long-distance management, telecommuting has proved a revelation. His computer and fax machine keep him abreast of operations. He has discovered that he doesn't actually need to be at the office. Instead, "I can make a lot of decisions through the computer," he says. Mr. Kabbani has one simple piece of advice for those contemplating telecommuting: "Do it."

On the other hand, after telecommuting for several years,

Mr. Frielich was stunned to discover that once-loyal customers were complaining about deficient shipments and inattentive service. He now believes that "When you're getting data from afar, you're not in touch with the soul of the business anymore. You can see vendors are being paid on time by running reports here in Santa Fe, but you don't know how they are really being treated." Mr. Frielich is now spending Tuesday through Thursday in California in an effort to rebuild customer and vendor relationships.

These two tales illustrate two sides of the telecommuting story. There aren't any statistics yet to show which experience—Mr. Kabbani's or Mr. Frielich's—is more likely to occur. But with telecommuting becoming a national trend, we can expect to learn more soon.

Source: Based on Ward, Leah Beth, "The Mixed Blessing of Telecommuting," *New York Times,* September 20, 1992.

Critical Thinking Questions

1 Why do you think Mr. Frielich's experience was different from Mr. Kabbani's? What might Mr. Frielich have done to prevent his problems?

2 The story focuses on two men trying to run their businesses from a distant location. Other telecommuters are employees of businesses. What kinds of rewards and risks do such employees and their employers face?

3 What type of modem would be most appropriate for the computers used by Mr. Kabbani and Mr. Frielich?

A **concentrator** collects and temporarily stores data in a buffer, or temporary storage area. When enough data have been collected to be sent economically, the concentrator sends them on their way.

As you learned in Chapter 3, a **communications controller** is a device that supervises communications traffic between the CPU and peripheral devices such as VDTs and printers. The controller manages the flow of data to and from these devices to the CPU.

Communications Software

Communications equipment requires *communications software*. For instance, modems for microcomputers work hand in hand with software packages that enable your computer to store and automatically dial telephone numbers of computers that you want to connect with, log-on to on-line services and bulletin boards, transfer files from one computer system to another, and imitate a terminal that can access a mainframe or minicomputer. (This last function is necessary because the operating systems of mainframes and

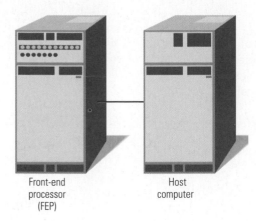

Figure 6.12
A Front-End Processor

A front-end processor takes care of communications tasks for the host computer in many large telecommunications networks.

Front-end
processor
(FEP)

Host
computer

minicomputers are designed to be accessed only by terminals, not micro-computers, which use a different kind of operating system. *Terminal emulation software* included in communications software packages enables your microcomputer to trick the mainframe into thinking it is communicating with a terminal.) Other programs, called *remote control software*, enable you to control a PC from another PC located thousands of miles away, allowing you to use the controlled PC almost as if you were sitting in front of it.

Popular general-purpose communications software for IBM-compatible microcomputers include Datastorm Technology's Procomm Plus, DCA's Crosstalk, and Microcom's Relay Gold (see photo). Packages for the Macintosh include Hayes Microcomputer Products' SmartCom and MicroPhone II. Remote-control software packages for IBM-compatibles include Symantec's Norton PCAnywhere, Central Point's Commute, and Microcom's Carbon Copy and, for the Macintosh, Microcom's Carbon Copy Mac and Farallon's Timbuktu/Remote.

Larger telecommunications systems also have special communications software installed on the host computer, front-end processor, and other specialized communications equipment in the system.

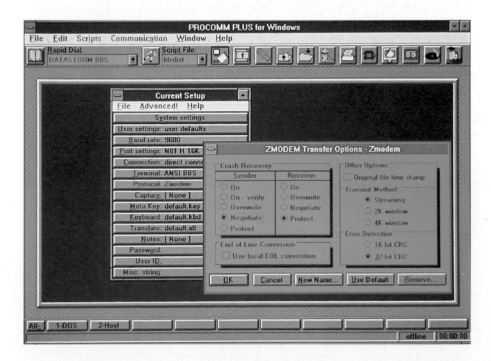

Procomm Plus for Windows is a popular general purpose communications software package for microcomputers.

Source: Courtesy of Digital Communications.

Communications Protocols

Telecommunications systems usually consist of a wide variety of hardware and software. For the different components of a telecommunications system to communicate with one another, they must follow a common set of procedures or rules called **protocols.** Some of the functions that protocols perform include:

▶ Identifying the different devices in the communications path

▶ Establishing the speed and method to be used for the transmission of data

▶ Alerting the receiving device to incoming data and defining the way receipt of data is to be acknowledged by the receiving device

▶ Determining how errors are to be detected and corrected

Although protocols are designed to help different types of communications equipment and software work together, not all manufacturers of the equipment use the same protocols. The difficulty this creates has fueled a drive to establish a standard accepted by all manufacturers to ensure that any computer connected to a network can communicate with any other computer, no matter who manufactured them. The International Standards Organization (ISO) has developed such a standard, called the Open Systems Interconnection (OSI) model, which is now beginning to be adopted by hardware and software vendors.

6.3 Telecommunications Networks

When computers and other communications equipment are connected by a communications channel in such a way that data, programs, and peripheral devices like printers can be shared or communicated, a telecommunications or computer **network** is formed. There are two primary types of telecommunications networks: *local networks* that connect devices that are in close physical proximity, and *wide area networks* that cover a much wider geographic area.

Local Networks

The most common kinds of local networks are private branch exchanges (PBXs) and local area networks (LANs).

Private Branch Exchanges   Traditionally, a **private branch exchange (PBX),** was a piece of manually operated equipment that companies used to switch incoming and outgoing telephone calls from the telephone company's public line to individual lines within an office (the company's switchboard). Today, a PBX has evolved into a computer specifically designed to manage both voice and data traffic in a building. These PBXs not only can store, forward, transfer, hold, and redial phone calls but also can handle voice and data communications and serve as a connection between different office devices. For instance, if your office is equipped with the latest in PBX technology, you can order your office copying machine to print a copy of a memo by connecting your microcomputer via a modem to the PBX, which then can send the instruction to the copying machine. The PBX can also be used to send the memo to other microcomputers. Because PBXs use existing telephone lines, they enable companies to connect devices in a network without the expense of installing new cables or wire. However, this is also their primary disadvantage—although they can handle limited and moderate traffic volumes, they are not well-suited for applications that involve the communications of large amounts of data. For such situations, local area networks, described next, are usually more appropriate.

Local Area Networks A **local area network (LAN)** is a combination of hardware, software, and communications channels that connect two or more computers within a limited area. A LAN may cover several floors within a building, an entire building, or even a group of buildings that are located close together. Unlike PBXs, which can share existing phone lines with the telephone system, LANs usually require their own communications channel.

Components of a Typical LAN A typical LAN, such as the one in Figure 6.13, has the following components (the hardware devices in a network are sometimes referred to as *nodes*):

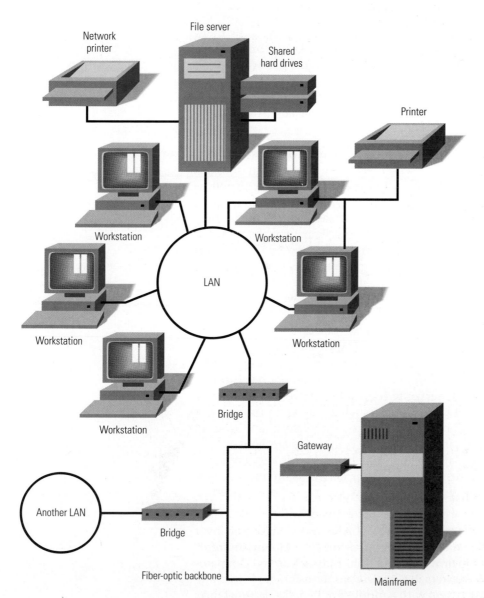

**Figure 6.13
A Typical LAN**
This LAN connects several microcomputers, a file server, and shared printers in a ring. Bridges allow the LAN to communicate with other LANs, and a gateway provides access to wide area networks or mainframes.

▶ Two or more desktop microcomputers, each equipped with a network interface card that enables the microcomputer to send and receive messages through the LAN.

▶ A cabling system connecting the components, created with twisted-pair wire, coaxial cable, or fiber-optic cables. (As you learned in the section on wireless transmission media, some LANs also use wireless technology.)

▶ A high-speed, high-capacity microcomputer or workstation called a **file server** that helps manage the network, processes communications, and allows users to share data, programs, and peripheral devices. Some systems also include additional servers with more specialized functions, such as print servers used to handle printing-related activities and communications servers dedicated to managing communications links. Other networks operate without a file server.

▶ Network operating system software that manages all activity on the network. This software may be installed just on the file server or on all microcomputers in the network. Some of the leading network operating systems include Novell's NetWare, Microsoft's LAN Manager, and IBM's PC LAN.

▶ Shared peripheral devices, such as printers.

Many LANs also feature hardware and software devices that allow them to communicate with other LANs and computing resources. A **bridge** connects two or more LANs based on similar technology, and a **gateway** allows users on a LAN to communicate with a mainframe or dissimilar network—for instance, a commercial database available on a wide area network. A **router** is used to route messages through several connected LANs or to a wide area network.

Client/Server Versus Peer to Peer   As you have read, many networks include a powerful microcomputer called a file server that is equipped with network operating software to help manage the activities of the network. Applications software (word processing, spreadsheets, E-mail, and so on) and data files are also typically stored on the server. The server distributes the programs and data to the other microcomputers (the "clients") in the network as they request them. Some processing tasks are performed by the desktop computer; others are handled by the file server. Networks that utilize this type of system are said to have *client/server architecture*. The use of servers in a network provides the network with more speed and power, but adds expense and complication.

Other networks are organized on a *peer-to-peer* basis (see Figure 6.14). Using proprietary technology such as Artisoft's LANtastic, Microsoft's Windows for Workgroups, or Apple's Localtalk, computers in peer-to-peer networks can communicate directly with one another and do not need to rely on a central host computer or file server to control the network. Peer-to-peer networks can provide basic network services such as file and print sharing and are much less expensive and less difficult to administer than those set up with file servers. However, if more than 25 computers are hooked to a peer-to-peer network or if the database that is being shared is very large, the network can bog down. As a result, peer-to-peer networks are most appropriate for smaller businesses that do not need the power and speed of client/server architecture.

Benefits of LANs   The popularity of PC-based LANs has skyrocketed over the last several years. A 1992 study by Nolan, Norton & Company, an information technology consulting firm in Lexington, Massachusetts, estimates that nearly 40 percent of all workers in large corporations are now working on LANs. LANs provide their users with a number of benefits. For instance,

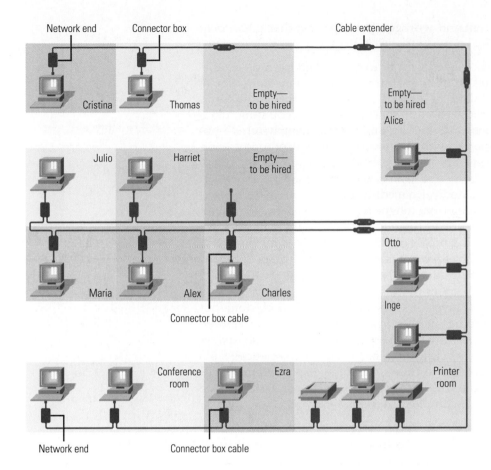

Figure 6.14
A Peer-to-Peer Network
A peer-to-peer network allows employees to share files and printers. Computers communicate directly with one another without having to rely on a central host computer or file server.

Source: Apple Local Talk Cable System. Owner's Guide, 1987.

with a LAN, expensive hardware devices such as laser or color printers or large hard-disk drives can be shared by a number of users, lowering costs and enabling the resource to be used more efficiently. A workstation on a LAN generally provides its user with more flexibility and functionality than a fixed-function terminal connected to a host computer. LANs also provide users with access to shared programs and data files, improving work flow, productivity, and communication within an organization.

To illustrate, let's take a look at St. Agnes Medical Center in San Joaquin, California. St. Agnes has a PC-based LAN linking almost 500 personal computers along with 75 laser printers. One of the tasks carried out with St. Agnes's PC-based LAN is surgery scheduling, which requires the involvement of a number of different departments. The first department schedules the operating room. As soon as a surgery is scheduled, a "pick ticket" is created on-line and sent via the LAN to the materials management department. That department picks all the materials necessary for the procedure, from syringes to gloves. From there, the on-line list proceeds to the distribution department, which assembles the materials and sends them to the operating room. All materials used during the surgery are automatically debited from supplies, and reorder requests are sent to the purchasing department. The purchasing department is linked via modem to the hospital's main suppliers to speed supply ordering. Being able to transfer data throughout the different departments has greatly improved the efficiency of the scheduling system, and as Ken Shimamoto, St. Agnes's director of information technologies notes, "When people are being more efficient, the hospital saves money. It helps keep costs down."[10] In the next section, you'll learn about some other applications, like E-mail and workgroup computing, that LANs help make possible.

Impacts of LANs LANs have played a major role in a trend toward *downsizing*—moving computing tasks from mainframes and minicomputers to smaller microcomputers linked in networks. Many of the applications needed to move people, products, and money—such as accounting, databases, inventory, reservations, order taking, and management systems—traditionally have been associated with mainframe and minicomputer environments. Now many firms are finding that LANs can handle these applications, with more flexibility and with less expense. One company that has made the switch is Taylor Medical, a medical supplies company in Beaumont, Texas, that sells everything from tongue depressors to x-ray machines. Started in 1987, Taylor Medical had grown to over $100 million in sales per year in 1991 but was still relying on six old IBM System/36 minicomputers for order entry, inventory control, accounts receivable, and other standard business applications. With more than 150 employees using the system to service over 16,000 accounts, response time had slowed to a crawl. Taylor's chief information officer, Jim Hayes, knew something had to be done but also realized that simply adding another System/36 was not the answer. After considering all the options, Taylor has begun to install a LAN based on Compaq microcomputers. Computing time has been cut dramatically, according to Hayes, from 30 minutes to 10 seconds for one application. Hayes also likes another benefit of the LAN—the ease of adding computers to the network leaves Taylor Medical with plenty of room for growth.[11]

Disadvantages of LANs Although LANs can in many instances lower an organization's costs while increasing productivity, LANs have certain disadvantages and are not likely to totally replace mainframes anytime soon. LANs can be very complicated and usually require specially trained personnel to manage and run the network. Even with support staff, a LAN tends to be less reliable and more exposed, from the standpoint of data security, than computers run in stand-alone mode. Furthermore, even the most powerful microcomputers linked in a network lack the speed and memory capacity needed to tackle very large on-line transaction processing applications. Finally, users generally require special training to learn how to use the LAN and may need to relearn certain applications that must be modified to work on the LAN.

LAN Topology The physical layout, or shape, of a network is referred to as its **topology.** LANs are usually configured in one of three basic shapes: star, bus, or ring. Different proprietary technologies have been developed for connecting LANs based on these different shapes.

The **star network** topology has its origins in the early days of computing, when most organizations' processing needs were met by one large computer hooked to dumb terminals. In an updated star network, the central host computer (still usually a mainframe or minicomputer) is connected to a number of smaller computers, intelligent terminals and other devices, forming a pattern that looks like a star (see Figure 6.15a). A star network allows data to be processed in a number of ways: data can be *downloaded*, or transferred, from a central file stored on the host computer to the local computer for processing and then *uploaded*, or retransferred, to the central file when work is complete. Or software can enable the local computer to turn itself into a dumb terminal, and processing can then take place directly on the central computer. Star networks also allow data to be transferred to different computers attached to a host computer, but to do so, the data must first pass through the host computer. A star network is appropriate for organizations

a. Star Network

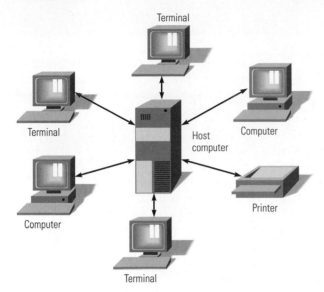

b. Bus Network

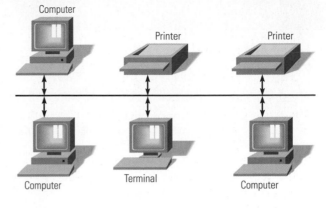

c. Ring Network

whose information processing requirements combine both the need to maintain a large, central database and at the same time allow certain applications to be performed locally. Though its reliance on a central host computer enables a star network to keep close control over the data being processed on the network, it also makes the network more vulnerable—if the host computer stops functioning, the entire network will screech to a halt.

The most common type of LAN topology is the **bus network.** A bus network links computers and other devices along a single, common communications channel composed of twisted-pair wire, coaxial cable, or fiber-optic cable (see Figure 6.15b). Many bus networks use a proprietary technology called Ethernet, developed by Xerox, which transmits data at 10 megabits per second. Bus networks may be organized along peer-to-peer lines or may utilize a client/server architecture.

With a bus network, when data is to be transferred from one device to another, it is "broadcast" through the communications channel in both directions to the entire network. Network software helps ensure that only those devices for which the data is intended actually receive it. One problem with bus networks is that the communications channel can handle only one message at a time. When two computers transmit at the same time, a "collision" occurs, and the messages must be resent. Bus networks slow down when this happens.

The third type of network topology is a **ring network.** A ring network links all the network's devices via a communications channel that forms a closed loop (see Figure 6.15c). Each computer in the network can communicate directly with any other computer through the ring. Ring networks avoid the data collisions that can slow bus networks by creating an electronic signal called a "token" that circulates around the network and must be attached to messages being sent to other devices. When a computer on the network is ready to send a message to another, it checks the token as it passes by to see if it is free. If it is, it captures it, attaches its message to the token, and then transmits the data. When the data is received, the receiving device releases the token back to the network. A disadvantage of ring topology is its sensitivity to a single link failure—if a connection between any of the devices

Figure 6.15
Different LAN Topologies
(a) In a network with a star topology all devices in the network are connected to a central host computer. Communications between different devices in the network must always pass through the central computer first.
(b) In a bus network, each device is connected to a single communications channel. Data is "broadcast" on the channel in both directions to the entire network.
(c) In a ring network, all the network's devices are linked via a communications channel that forms a closed loop.

Filling job openings with the right individuals is a critical task for all organizations. When the organization is one of the world's largest employers, as the U.S. government is, making sure that the process works smoothly and efficiently is even more important.

Consider what used to happen when someone applied for a government job. In the 1980s, months would go by before job seekers received their scores on civil service exams or had their applications processed. It often took federal managers several weeks to get an applicant referral list, and by the time

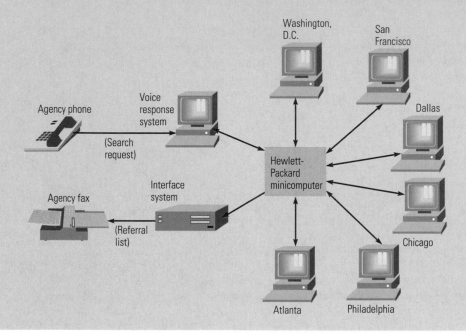

The AARS uses a voice response system, minicomputers, a WAN, and a fax machine to automate the applicant referral process.

fails, the network shuts down. Variations on basic ring topology have been developed to avoid this problem. IBM's Token Ring Network, which transmits information at a speed of 16 megabits per second, is the most common ring network for PC-based LANs.

In addition to the standard star, bus, and ring networks, a new type of LAN capable of handling very high transmission rates is available. These high-speed LANs are based on something known as the **Fiber Distributed Data Interface (FDDI)** and offer transmission speeds of 100 megabits per second. FDDI LANs use the same token-passing technology used by Token Ring networks but have a dual fiber-optic ring configuration. Use of fiber-optic cable increases the network's transmission capability; use of two rings instead of one increases reliability. Applications that are expected to help drive the market for LANs based on FDDI technology include imaging, computer-aided design/computer-aided manufacturing (CAD/CAM), and multimedia.

Wide Area Networks

In contrast to local networks, a **wide area network (WAN)** can cover large geographic areas by using one or more of a variety of communications channels, such as switched and dedicated telephone lines, as well as microwave and satellite communications systems. Companies may choose to use a public wide area network maintained by a common carrier or to create their own by using a combination of public and private resources. Wide area networks

they could make an offer, many of the people they wanted to hire had already accepted other jobs. Not a very good way to run an operation as important as the U.S. government.

Today, a new wide area network created by the U.S. Office of Personnel Management (OPM) enables staff to turn employment tests around in one day, and entire applications in less than three, and allows government managers to quickly find the right person for the job from among OPM's pool of 500,000 or so applicants.

Using the Automated Applicant Referral Service (AARS), a federal manager anywhere in the United States can dial into a Micrologic Corporation voice response system at the Staffing Service Center in Macon, Georgia. The system prompts the user for job-related information and the characteristics of the person sought. When the user hangs up, the request is passed directly to a Hewlett-Packard minicomputer, which formats a transaction request and sends it on to one of 16 unattended Hewlett-Packard minicomputer nodes on a wide area network that spans the nation. For instance, if the user has requested someone for a position in Chicago, the HP minicomputer sends the request there. The Chicago computer checks its database for qualified applicants and sends information

back over the network to the HP minicomputer in Macon. The data is then passed through an interface system that converts the results of the search into fax format, looks up the requester's fax number and sends the list of candidates back to the requester (see diagram). The whole process now takes only between 15 and 45 minutes, compared to several weeks, and involves no human participation other than the initial request. By coupling existing resources (HP minicomputers, telephone lines, and fax machines) with some new software, OPM was able to implement AARS in just four months for a bargain-basement price of $50,000.

Source: Based on Anthes, Gary, "Uncle Sam Uses Network and Fax to Fill Jobs," *Computerworld,* December 2, 1991.

Critical Thinking Questions

1   What are the components of the telecommunications system described in this story?

2   If you were an applicant for a government job, what might you not like about this system?

3   Which of the telecommunications systems described elsewhere in this chapter qualify as wide area networks?

offer their users a number of benefits, including, as illustrated by the story "Finding the Right Person for the Job," enhanced access to information that may be located anywhere in the country.

The Internet   Perhaps the most famous wide area network, and certainly the largest, is the **Internet**, connecting thousands of smaller networks and millions of users all around the world. The Internet was once the exclusive province of government-sponsored research scientists and academics but now almost anyone with a PC and modem can get the Internet access in one form or another. It provides an entrance to a vast array of information stored in computer systems throughout the world. Here's a short list of just some of the resources available:

▶   Hundreds of on-line databases, many covering unique or specialized fields. Examples include Dartmouth's DANTE—a database that includes the full text of Dante's "Divine Comedy," as well as 32 commentaries; Penn State's PENpages, a database of agricultural and nutritional information; the Johns Hopkins Genetic databases; reports from the World Ocean Circulation Experiment; as well as access to commercial databases offered by Dialog and Mead Data Central. Wide-Area Information Servers (WAIS) help users search for and retrieve information located in the databases.

▶   On-line library catalogs from the Library of Congress, Harvard, the University of California, as well as over 200 universities around the world.

- Access to over 2 million different software programs. You can download general MS-DOS PC software, Apple software, and state-of-the art scientific software, often free of charge. There is even a search tool, called Archie, that will help you find a particular program.

- Bulletin boards and "virtual communities" where people can have discussions about topics of common interest, post questions, and get responses from around the globe.

- E-mail. The Internet allows you to send an electronic message that will reach someone on the other side of the world in just a few seconds. You can also send messages out to a large group, using the Internet's mailing list and newsgroup capabilities.

- Interactive computer games such as chess, multi-user Dungeons and Dragons, and the like.

The Internet has already had a significant impact on the scientific and academic communities. It has made close collaboration with someone located across the world, something that was once inconceivable, possible. Take Dr. Brendan McKay, a computer scientist at the Australian National University, for example. In 1990, he got an electronic query about his work from Dr. Stanislaw Radziszowsky, a mathematician at the Rochester Institute of Technology in Rochester, New York. Since then the two have exchanged over 1,000 E-mail messages. It has also speeded up the process by which ideas are communicated to a large audience, often an important component in the pace of progress. In the past, scientists and academics generally had to wait for publication of journal articles to find out the latest information in their field. But now, in many cases, they can get the most up-to-date information from one of the Internet's bulletin boards.

Despite its attractions, though, the Internet is not without its problems. There is so much information available that one runs the risk of information overload. Consider that no matter how long you remain on-line, on exit you will still be faced with a message such as "There are still 1,038,071 unread articles in 1,388 groups." Navigating through the vast mass of information available through the Internet can be difficult even for the experienced user.

E-mail is one of the many services offered by value-added networks.

Source: Courtesy of ComShare, Inc.

Some have likened it to a huge library where all the books are dumped on the floor in no particular order.

You can get access to the Internet in a number of different ways. Check with your school's computer center staff to see if your school has access and allows students to log-on. There are also private companies, such as Performance Systems International of Reston, Virginia, that offer access to the full range of Internet services and resources for a relatively reasonable fee—usually a monthly charge of between $10 and $20, plus an hourly fee of $1 to $5. You can also access certain of the Internet services (such as E-mail) via a commercial on-line information service such as CompuServe, Prodigy, or America On-Line. Finally, public libraries are starting to discover Internet and hook into the system.[12]

Value-Added Networks

A **value-added network (VAN)** is a private data network created by a firm that offers the services of the network to others for a fee. VANs deal only in digital data and not voice communications. The vendors of VANs generally lease communications channels from common carriers and then add some extra value or service that subscribers are willing to pay for. The value added may be access to E-mail, public databases, or bulletin boards; enhanced error detection; faster response time; or simply cost savings based on economies of scale. Customers using a VAN do not have to invest in network equipment or software, nor perform their own telecommunications management. They pay only for the amount of data they submit, plus a subscription fee.

In addition to sharing the costs of using the network among many users, VANs can achieve economies of scale by using a technique called **packet switching.** Packet switching divides electronic messages into small segments called data packets. Each packet travels independently through the network to maximize efficiency. The packets of data constituting a message can be combined with others, routed through different paths, and then reassembled into the original message at the receiving end. This enables communications facilities to be utilized more fully and shared by more users.

Today, some popular VAN suppliers include firms that offer access to public databases and bulletin boards, such as Prodigy, CompuServe, and America On-Line, and others such as General Electric Information Services, BT Global Network Services, and Advantis that provide general network services.

Network Security

Although networks offer their users innumerable advantages, these benefits are not totally without risks. One of the major problems facing organizations that rely on networks is network security. Some of the same attributes that make a network so attractive, such as the ability to communicate over distance and increased access and sharing of resources by a greater number of users, also make it more vulnerable to disruption and penetration. For instance, unauthorized users may be able to gain access to the system more easily on a network. Data traveling over communications channels can be intercepted. *Computer viruses*, disruptive software programs that spread from computer to computer, can run rampant if introduced into a network environment. You will learn more about security issues and some of the ways that networks can be protected in Chapter 15.

6.4 Telecommunications in Society and Business

At the beginning of this chapter, we argued that communication technologies form the foundation of civilizations, and that changes in those technologies fundamentally alter how a society works, the values in the culture, and the forms of organization. Now that you have a basic understanding of the components of telecommunications systems and how they can create computer networks, let's take a look at some of the new applied technologies and how they are affecting our society.

We'll describe nine applications of the new communication technologies: information utility companies, smart telephones and personal communicators, electronic bulletin boards, facsimile transmission (faxes), voice mail, electronic mail, teleconferencing, workgroup computing (groupware), and electronic data interchange. When you read about these applications, think about the impact they might have on your personal life, work life, and society as a whole.

Information Utility Companies

Today, most people gather the information they need to live from day to day primarily from newspapers, magazines, books, radio, and television. Major changes in the delivery of information to the general public are looming on the horizon, though.

Hundreds of companies now provide on-line information retrieval services. These services are often part of value-added networks available for a fee to anyone with a personal computer, modem, communications software, and telephone line. For instance, if you are one of CompuServe's 800,000 subscribers, for just $7.95 a month and the cost of telephone hook-up time, you can receive unlimited access to news, sports, weather, travel information, home shopping services, financial information, medical and legal advice, reference works, and games, not to mention hundreds of computer bulletin boards. You can even send an E-mail message to President Clinton. (Figure 6.16 gives you a more detailed list of some of the information services available from CompuServe.) Be aware, though, that services such as CompuServe and Prodigy can be significantly more expensive if you live in a rural area and must make a long distance call to reach the nearest access number.

Other vendors offer more specialized services geared toward specific industries. Lexis, offered by Mead Data Corporation, provides on-line access to a comprehensive legal database covering state, federal, and international law. Instead of having to search through a pile of books for information to support a legal argument, a lawyer now merely needs to log-on to Lexis and type in a search request. Within seconds, he or she will be rewarded with a list of cases that discuss the issue, which can then be called up on-screen for review. A companion service, called Nexis, provides abstracts and full-text retrieval of hundreds of newspapers, magazines, and journals. These are just a few of the thousands of different public databases now available.

Information services have become big business (over $19 billion in 1991) and promise to get even bigger (up to $31 billion by 1995). In the process, traditional dividing lines between computer companies, communications companies, and entertainment companies are beginning to fall by the wayside as they all seek a piece of the market. For instance, before long your local tele-

News, Sports, Weather

Associated Press Online
    Hourly News Summaries, Sports,
    Entertainment, Business News,
    This Day In History

Accu-Weather® Maps and Reports

National Weather Service

Reference Library

Grolier's Academic American Encyclopedia
    A 21-volume on-line encyclopedia
    updated quarterly

Peterson's College Database

HealthNet
    An on-line medical reference source

Shopping

The Electronic Mall®

Shopper's Advantage®
    A discount shopping club

Consumer Reports

Classified Ads

Financial Information

Current Stock Quotes

Issue/Symbol Reference

Mortgage Calculator

Entertainment & Games

Roger Ebert's Movie Reviews

Science Trivia Quiz

The Grolier Whiz Quiz

ShowBizQuiz

CastleQuest

Black Dragon

Classic Adventure

Enhanced Adventure

Hangman

Electronic Mail

CompuServe Mail

Travel and Leisure

EAASY SABRE® and WORLDSPAN
    Travelshopper^SM airline, hotel, and rental
    car information and reservations

Department of State Advisories

Visa Advisors

Membership Support Services

DOS CIM Support Forum

Mac CIM Support Forum

Navigator Support Forum

Practice Forum
    A forum designed to teach you the
    fundamentals of real-time on-line
    communication

Directory of CompuServe Members

Ask Customer Service
    A helpful resource if you need on-line
    assistance

Figure 6.16
**Some of the Information
Services Available from
CompuServe**

phone company may be providing you with more than directory assistance when you call asking for "Information": a recent court case ruled that the seven regional telephone companies created upon the breakup of AT&T (the "Baby Bells") can now own and provide information services as well as telephone lines. Among the services being contemplated are electronic white and yellow pages; voice mail to fax conversion; advanced messaging services that would forward voice mail, faxes, and E-mail to you wherever you were located; and on-line transaction processing. More ambitious plans include on-line medical consultations and electronic retrieval of books from far-off libraries.[13]

In addition to information services, your local telephone company may soon provide you with entertainment too. A recent FCC ruling has cleared the way for telephone companies to begin transmitting video programming over telephone lines. The telephone lines could be linked to the television set or computer monitor in your home. Telephone customers would dial a special number to obtain a "video dial tone" that would provide them with a menu of programs offered. The programs could be anything from movies and home shopping to two-way interactive education services. And telephone companies are even starting to buy cable companies. Although they are not permitted to buy systems in areas where they operate telephones, they can enter the cable market outside their home territories.[14]

Cable companies are also getting into the act. For instance, Time Warner, the nation's second largest cable operator, has entered into a joint venture with US West, a regional Bell Telephone company, to build a cable system that offers entertainment and information services. TeleCommunications Inc., the nation's largest cable operator, has had discussions with IBM about creating a two-way information delivery service that would deliver movies on demand, interactive shopping, educational programs, and other services.

Cable systems have at least one advantage over telephone companies in the fight to become the new information utility companies. To fully realize all the possibilities the new rules allow them, telephone companies must replace existing twisted-pair wire with fiber-optic cable. In contrast, the coaxial cable used by cable companies already possesses sufficient bandwidth to handle most applications now contemplated.[15]

So get ready: just as the development of the television forever changed the way information reached your home, we are now on the verge of a new era, fueled by the ever-increasing convergence of computer and communication technologies.

Smart Telephones and Personal Communicators

The convergence of computer and communication technologies discussed in the previous section is affecting more than just information delivery. It is also transforming that familiar instrument—the telephone—and ultimately the ways we communicate.

Telephones and computers have begun to merge into one another, blurring the lines between them. For instance, several telephone manufacturers have begun to introduce telephones that contain LCD screen displays and microprocessors (see photo). Phillips Electronics' Enhanced Telephone, for instance, comes with a large screen that can display 16 lines of text, a keyboard for typing messages, a built-in modem for sending faxes, and the ability to incorporate smart cards. Described as a "telephone with a personal computer hidden inside," it allows you to use new phone-based services such as banking by phone, at-home shopping services, electronic mail delivery, Caller ID, and others more easily. Now when you call your bank, you can see your account information displayed and can use the keyboard to enter data and even instruct the bank to stop checks or take some other action.

On the other end of the spectrum, there are those who seek to create personal computers that are also communications devices. Part telephone and part computer, a personal communicator combines the two technologies into a wireless, pocket-sized device that you can carry with you everywhere. Ultimately, personal communicators will allow you to place and receive phone calls, send and receive faxes and electronic mail, do word processing, create spreadsheets and databases, and communicate with your desktop PC wherever you may be. Two early examples of this form of technology are the Eo Personal Communicator and

A Rolm electronic enhanced phone.

Source: Courtesy of Rolm.

Apple's Newton Message Pad. Dozens of other companies have also entered the race to provide these services. "This is the hottest area of information technology for probably the rest of the century," says Portia Isaacson, president of the research firm Dream IT.[16]

Electronic Bulletin Boards

The merger of computers and telecommunications has also created a whole new method for people to communicate on topics of common interest: **electronic bulletin boards.** Like on-line information services, public access bulletin board systems are open to anyone with a personal computer, modem, communications software, and a telephone line. So equipped, a user anywhere in the world can have his or her computer dial a board, pick a topic of interest, and write or read messages. Setting up a public-access bulletin board is so easy and inexpensive that there are now over 50,000 of them in the United States. All you need is a personal computer, some bulletin board software such as Mustang Software's Wildcat BBS or Clark Development's PC Board, and a telephone and you can be in business. Figure 6.17 lists a sampling of bulletin boards available around the country.

Figure 6.17
A Sampling of Electronic Bulletin Boards

a.

Specialized BBS	Description	Location	Modem Number
Aquila	Largest board in Chicago area	Chicago	(708) 820-8344
Boardwatch	Lists of other boards	Denver	(303) 973-4222
Channel 1	Conferences, files, games, chat	Cambridge, Mass.	(617) 354-3230
Cleveland Freenet	Government and Supreme Court information	Cleveland	(216) 368-3888
Exec-PC	Largest bulletin board in U.S.	Elm Grove, Wisc.	(414) 789-4210
Free Financial Network	Stock closings; investor resources	New York	(212) 752-8660
Invention Factory Files	Games, messages	New York	(212) 274-8110
Minnesota Spacenet	NASA news and information	Minneapolis	(612) 920-5566
The USA TBBS	News, games, entertainment	Miami	(305) 599-3004
The Well	Conferences, files, chat	San Francisco	(415) 332-7190
SBA On-Line	Info on running small business	Washington, D.C.	(800) 859-INFO
FedWorld	Gateway to 61 government boards at 50 different federal agencies	Washington, D.C.	(703) 321-8020

b. General On-Line Information Services That Offer BBS

Name	Information Number
CompuServe	(800) 848-8199
Prodigy	(800) 776-3449
America OnLine	(800) 827-6364
GEnie	(800) 638-9636
Delphi	(800) 695-4005
The Sierra Network	(800) 743-7721

The Electronic Meet Market

Are you a little shy or insecure? Do you sometimes have trouble meeting new people? Are you afraid that you won't be able to develop the business relationships that you'll need to get ahead in our dog-eat-dog world? Well, just join the thousands of folks who have discovered a new way to enlarge their circle of friends and business contacts (and perhaps even find someone special), all without having to leave the comfort and security of home or run the risk of personal rejection: electronic bulletin boards.

Kevin Morley, a 31-year-old electrician from Spring, Texas, and Kathie Fields, a 36-year-old long-haul trucker, are two who are glad they did. Kevin and Kathie both subscribed to Prodigy and first met on-line. As Kevin recalls, "It started with this friendly chit-chat. We would go on-line and type letters back and forth." Then, Kathy says, "the letters got more intense. We found out that there was a lot we had in common." Several months later, Kevin and Kathie got married.

On-line networking isn't limited to people looking for love. Jeff Freemen, 25, of Front Porch Computers in Chatsworth, Georgia (population 5000), started his home business in 1991, and by 1992, was raking in $500,000 in gross revenues. Freemen said his business would not have taken off the way it did

An SF Net computer table at the Horse Shoe, a San Francisco Bay-area coffeehouse, allows customers to engage in debate and discussion with other people who are also hooked into the network.

Source: James Wilson/Woodfin Camp & Associates.

People by the tens of thousands are using bulletin boards to discuss politics and environmental issues, find out information about business opportunities, get legal, tax, and accounting information, play computer games together, and comment on hundreds of other possible topics. And as the story "The Electronic Meet Market" illustrates, bulletin boards have created a whole new way to meet people.

Some bulletin boards are part of value-added networks that require subscription fees; others are free and merely require the user to pay for the telephone time needed to connect to the service. The fastest-growing segment of the market are boards operated by private companies that want to give their managers and employees more access to company information and policy messages. Bulletin boards also allow members of the rank and file to make their views known more easily to upper management.

One controversial aspect of bulletin board services relates to issues of censorship and free speech. What happens when material that some might find offensive or obscene is disseminated over the system? For example, Wayne Gregori, who runs the SF Net, pulls messages with racial, ethnic, and sexist slurs off the network. Many other system operators have similar policies. Some critics charge that such behavior is censorship and claim that a system operator should have no more control over what is expressed over a network than a telephone company has over what is transmitted over its lines. Others say that an electronic bulletin board is more like a newspaper whose publisher has the right to control and monitor the content of its product. What do you think?

without the help (tips, contacts, prospects) he received from electronic penpals on CompuServe's Working from Home Forum.

In San Francisco, electronic bulletin boards allow you to participate in coffeehouse culture without actually having to make the scene. SF Net hooks together "computer tables" at over a dozen Bay-area coffeehouses (see photo). Those who want to dial in from home can do so for a small monthly fee. The heated debates and deep philosophical discussions that are coffeehouse hallmarks now also take place via the network rather than just face to face. Users like the network because "no one is looking at you—you don't have to worry about rejection." As the network's founder, Wayne Gregori, says, "There is no visual contact, no hearing of accents. People are judged on the content of what they say." This doesn't always assure a match made in heaven though. One user of SF Net, Amber Clisura, says that though she met her current boyfriend through the network, a prior effort led her to "a computer geek from hell—they may sound cool on the board, but then you meet them and it's not pretty."

Amber's bad experience points out one of the risks of relying on electronic bulletin boards: it's not a total substitute for getting to know a person face to face. The anonymity that a bulletin board provides allows people to exaggerate, or even lie, about themselves. Even if they haven't, they may not match the impressions that you've formed in your mind. Nonetheless, electronic boards offer a unique opportunity—to reach out and find a customer, a friend, or even a future spouse among a world of strangers connected to you only by a telephone line, modem, and computer.

Sources: Based on Resnick. Rosalind, "The Electronic Meet Market," *Compute,* August 1992; Bishop, Katherine, "The Electronic Coffeehouse," *New York Times,* August 2, 1992.

Critical Thinking Questions

1 Speculate on the impacts (social, political, or otherwise) electronic bulletin boards may have if they continue to mushroom in popularity.

2 The last paragraph of the story points out some risks associated with electronic bulletin boards. What other hazards can you think of?

Facsimile Transmission (Faxes)

The transmission of information using facsimile (fax) technology has exploded in popularity over the past ten years. **Fax machines** are now essential, very affordable pieces of office equipment for even the smallest of businesses; many people now even have fax machines in their homes. A fax machine scans and digitizes images (text, graphics, and even signatures) on a page and transmits them in analog form over a regular phone line to another fax machine, which then reproduces a copy or facsimile of the image on a piece of paper (see photo).

Fax machines have played a large role in speeding up business transactions. You no longer need to wait for a legal document to arrive in the mail or be delivered by an overnight delivery service. Instead, a fax machine allows a hard copy of the document to be sent from one end of the country to the other in less than a minute.

Fax technology is becoming more and more integrated with computer technology. A fax board plugs into an expansion slot in your microcomputer and allows it to both send and receive faxes. A fax modem also performs the same function. Both suffer from the same drawback though: if the docu-

Fax machines have become standard office equipment for businesses of all sizes.

Source: Fredrik D. Bodin Offshoot.

ment you wish to send is not one that you created on your computer, you will have to scan it into your system first with an image scanner. Another possibility is an add-on device that lets you send documents received by fax directly to your laser printer. Some printers, like Everex Systems' Laserscript Fax, are also starting to include built-in fax circuitry that enables you to automatically receive and send faxes from your computer.

Fax machines are also combining with computer technology in a slightly different way: in some cases, they are becoming integral parts of information systems. Let's look at one example: the Art Co-op in Santa Fe, New Mexico. The Art Co-op operates a clearinghouse that lets dealers buy and sell prints, seriagraphs, photographs, and other limited edition artwork. The clearinghouse combines database, voice response, and fax technology. The system runs on four networked microcomputers—two to run the voice response system, one to house the database, and one to power the fax machines. A dealer looking for a piece of art can make a telephone call to the Co-op, and using the voice response system, search for a specific work of art by title and author within the Co-op's 16,000-title database. The caller can check the latest trading price of the piece as well as be faxed a list of all prices for all available titles by the artist, all without the need for intervention by Co-op staff. Once somebody decides to buy, the Co-op acts as clearinghouse, faxing the invoice and purchase order to the respective parties, and certifying the work and funds. The Art Co-op originally planned to create a network accessible only by computers but found that many galleries still didn't have them. Instead of giving up, they decided to work with what existed—in doing so, they have created a system that may help remake their industry by expanding access to information, standardizing pricing, and speeding sales.[17]

Voice Mail

Another communication technology that has spread throughout American offices during the last decade is **voice mail**—a sophisticated, computerized telephone answering system. Unlike answering machines, which can only answer a specific telephone, voice mail systems can perform a variety of functions.

First, most voice mail systems can act as an automated switchboard operator, directing calls to certain destinations, as in "Hello, you have reached the offices of XXX corporation. If you know the extension of the party that you wish to speak to, enter that number on your touch-tone telephone now. If you would like to speak to someone in customer services, press 1; for other information, press 2." The system may also be able to hold and screen calls.

Second, voice mail systems enable your callers to leave detailed messages, replay them, and re-record them if they so desire. The voice mail system digitizes the messages and stores them in your voice mailbox until you are ready to listen to them. You will have the option of saving the messages, deleting them, or sending them along to another extension. Like the E-mail systems you'll soon read about, this voice mail function helps eliminate telephone tag, with the added advantage of being able to listen to the speaker's voice.

Voice mail systems also allow you to distribute voice messages throughout an office. You merely need to record the message once and let the voice mail system send it to the numbers you request.

When properly implemented, voice mail systems can be powerful tools that help companies reduce costs and enhance the productivity of both callers and the call recipient. However, though most people are becoming more accustomed to voice mail systems, many still dislike them. Poorly designed systems can put a caller into *"voice mail jail,"* a maze of recorded instructions that form an endless loop without letting you get to the person to whom you would like to speak. Companies are now becoming more sensitive to these issues and refining their systems to be more user-friendly.

Electronic Mail (E-Mail)

Another way to eliminate telephone tag is through **electronic mail (E-mail)**. Electronic mail systems allow you to send memos and other messages directly from your computer to any other computer using the system, often merely by typing the recipient's name (see photo). In addition to making the task of communicating easier and more efficient, E-mail can significantly reduce telephone bills, the cost of overnight and regular postage, and secretarial costs. As a result, E-mail has become the preferred method of communication for many organizations, especially those with large numbers of employees. By the end of 1990, there were nearly seventeen million electronic mailboxes. That number is expected to double by 1994.

There are several different ways to set up an E-mail system. PC-LAN-based systems are by far the most popular. Digital Equipment Corporation, IBM, Data General, and others also offer systems for companies that continue to rely on large central computers connected to terminals. Finally, if you have a computer, but are not part of a network, you can still send and receive E-mail by subscribing to a value-added network that offers the service or by using a public E-mail system like AT&T Mail or MCI Mail.

In addition to enhancing business productivity, the emergence of E-mail as a replacement for telephone calls and paper memos brings with it a host of interesting and difficult issues. For instance, you would probably be outraged to find that your employer is listening in on your personal telephone calls or opening your U.S. Postal Service mail. Even if you were using company telephones or services, it would be illegal for your company to do so

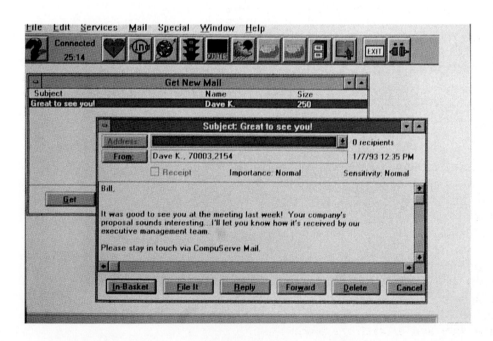

E-mail allows you to send notes, letters, and other messages directly from computer to computer. E-mail is typically available on office LANs. E-mail service can also be obtained from VANs such as CompuServe and Prodigy.

Source: Courtesy of CompuServe.

because these communications are protected by federal law. But no such rules protect your electronic conversations or E-mail.

Here's an example of the problem. When Alana Shoars arrived for work one January morning in 1990 at Epson America (the U.S. marketing arm of a Japanese firm) she discovered her supervisor reading and printing out electronic mail messages between employees. Appalled, Shoars complained, and the next day she was fired for insubordination. (Epson claims that Shoar's dismissal had nothing to do with her questioning of E-mail practices.) Epson is not alone in this practice: many companies reserve the right to monitor employee E-mail on the grounds that such access is necessary to properly administer the system. And as Michael Simmons, chief information officer at the Bank of Boston, says, "If the corporation owns the equipment and pays for the network, the asset belongs to the company and it has a right to look and see."[18]

Others disagree. They feel that even if a company has notified its employees that it may monitor E-mail and has the legal right to do so, the company should not invade its employees' privacy as a matter of ethics and respect for the individual.

Another sticky issue relates to the preservation of E-mail. Paper records are the way government and business have documented history from time immemorial. Now, though, much of that paper is being replaced by electronic messages. Who decides what should be erased and when?

Let's examine a case in point. The Federal Records Act requires the U.S. government to preserve important documents for posterity, but the Reagan-Bush Administration contended that the Act didn't cover E-mail. They likened E-mail to mere "buck slips" or secretarial phone messages, and said it would be unreasonable to maintain backup tapes indefinitely. A coalition of historians, librarians, and public interest groups felt that this was a dangerous position, given that E-mail was so widely used throughout the highest reaches of government and sued the government to prevent destruction of backup tapes. To support their view, they pointed to a seemingly innocuous series of E-mail messages that came to light as a result of the Iran-Contra scandal. In August 1986, Lt. Col. Oliver North, then a member of the National Security Council, met with a group of congressmen. North later confessed that at the meeting he lied to the congressmen about his extensive support of the Nicaraguan Contras. Not long after the meeting an aide to U.S. National Security Advisor John Poindexter sent Poindexter an E-mail report on the meeting. "Session was a success," it said. "Ollie told the congressmen that he had not given any military advice" to the Contras. Poindexter forwarded the note to North, attaching a two-word E-mail message of his own: "Well done." Later, it came to light that at the time Poindexter was well aware that North had in fact been deeply involved with the Contras. Under those circumstances, Poindexter's seemingly simple two-word congratulation was more revealing than 1,000 words might have been. As Thomas Blanton, the National Security Archive's deputy director, said: "The government would call that a buck slip. A historian would look at that and see the world within those two words."

In January 1993, the federal courts ordered the Bush Administration to preserve copies of all E-mail files, ruling that the Federal Records Act did indeed apply to such files. Historians hailed the ruling as a landmark decision, one that would bring the federal government into the twentieth century by recognizing that information in electronic form is every bit as official as information on paper.[19]

Toy designers in Seattle use a Picture Tel video conferencing system to discuss product ideas with a manufacturer in Germany.
Source: Courtesy of Picture Tel Corporation.

Teleconferencing

Breakthroughs in communication technology are now enabling people to meet even when they cannot be in the same geographic location. Computer *teleconferencing* uses a system similar to an electronic bulletin board to allow people to confer on a topic or issue. An even more advanced form of teleconferencing, called **videoconferencing,** allows participants to see and hear one another (see photo).

Videoconferencing systems usually include videocameras, special microphones, large television monitors, and a computer equipped with a *codec*—a device that converts analog video images and sound waves into digital signals and compresses them for transfer over digital telephone lines. On the receiving end, another codec reconverts the digital signals into analog for display on the receiving monitor.

Right now, most videoconferencing systems are installed in special videoconference rooms. If a company does not wish to incur the expense of installing a private system (the most popular cost around $30,000 to $40,000), they may be able to use the facilities of a third-party provider. As videoconferencing technology becomes more advanced, we are likely to see it move from the conference room to the desktop. Though it is not yet possible to send good-quality video and voice over most existing LANs, that barrier is likely to fall when high-speed FDDI LANs become more commonplace. When that occurs, voice mail and E-mail may give way to video mail—portions of videoconferences digitized and stored in an electronic mailbox, just like any other file.

Videoconferencing systems can save the time and expense of travel and link people who might not otherwise be able to meet. Ben and Jerry's Homemade Inc., the Vermont-based progressive and ecologically conscious ice cream manufacturer, uses its system to help maintain interdepartmental teamwork as the company grows and its employees spread out geographically. Videoconferences are held every other week to support the team communications concept and help Ben and Jerry's cut down both on travel expenses and air pollution. Employees needed some time to adjust to the cameras and seeing themselves on monitors, but overall they felt it was a great improvement over communicating just by telephone.

Workgroup Computing

Ben and Jerry's is not the only organization to realize the benefits of teamwork. When employees are working on common projects, efficient methods of communication and collaboration are a must. **Workgroup computing** is a catchphrase for information technology that helps people work on a common job. Experts believe that workgroup computing will be a significant trend in the 1990s, with the potential to provide a company with a distinct competitive edge.

Workgroup computing is made possible by *groupware,* software designed for use on computer networks that allow people to share information and coordinate activities. Today, the most popular form of groupware on the market is Lotus Notes. In Chapter 2, you read about how the international advertising agency, Young and Rubicam, uses Lotus Notes to help account representatives across the globe keep track of common clients. In Texas, Dell Computer Corp. has installed Notes on its LAN to help the "core teams" that develop its products. Each team includes representatives from all relevant areas of the company. Notes allows the team to create a database called a NoteBook that centralizes all information (project concepts, specifications, reports, schedules, risk analyses, and the like) about the project. Prior to Notes, information on issues was shared through paper reports and weekly updates. Now, though, it can be shared instantly—both with team members and senior management. Dell has found that Notes has made collaborating on projects much easier and more efficient for its employees. As Dale Reynolds, Dell's vice president of product development noted, "When we first introduced Notes, many people couldn't understand why. But once they spent thirty minutes with a Notes database, their eyes lit up and they asked us where we'd been hiding the system."[20]

Although workgroup computing and groupware have undeniable benefits, implementing such a system isn't as simple as just installing a new software package onto the network. Groupware may force a company to address its corporate culture, work processes, and the relationships between individuals and groups. For instance, groupware provides a method of communication that may be less hierarchical than what people in the organization are used to. Groupware may upset a company's traditional environment for getting work done and lead to information overload. It may also meet with resistance from people who view the possession of information as a personal competitive advantage. For collaborative computing to be successful, it must be actively supported by the entire organization.[21]

Electronic Data Interchange (EDI)

Just think about how many paper-based transactions there are in a single year in the 5 trillion dollar U.S. economy. No one knows for sure, but estimates are that nearly ten billion paper transactions occur each year, and the cost of processing each transaction on average is $5. If paper transactions could be made electronic, these costs could be significantly reduced. That's where EDI comes in. One of the most significant business applications made possible by telecommunications networks is **electronic data interchange (EDI)**. Using EDI, standard business transaction documents, such as invoices, purchase orders, and shipping notices, are generated by an organization's computers and then passed directly to another organization's computer over a telecommunications network. By using an electronic means of transfer and eliminating paper (along with the need to handle, file, and store it), transactions can be processed more efficiently and quickly, with reduced costs and reduced error rates. Fewer trees are felled as a result.

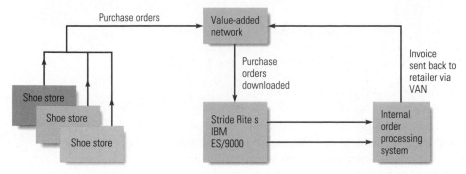

Figure 6.18
Stride Rite's EDI Network
Stride Rite uses EDI to fill purchase orders faster.

Source: Based on Gillin, Paul, "Shoe Retailer Makes Strides with EDI," *Computerworld,* June 1, 1992.

EDI also offers strategic benefits—it helps firms "lock in" customers and distributors by making it easier for them to deal with the organization. To illustrate, let's take a look at how one company, Stride Rite Corporation, used EDI to convert retailers' demands for faster order turnaround into a competitive advantage. When a store needs to order Keds, Sperry Topsiders, or any other shoe sold by Stride Rite, they now can send the purchase order over a value-added network. Stride Rite's IBM Enterprise System/9000 mainframe dials up the VAN every evening and downloads the orders. By taking orders electronically, Stride Rite can generate "picking orders" at its distribution centers just hours after the order is received. Once the order is filled, invoice data is sent back to the retailer electronically via the VAN (see Figure 6.18).

Altogether, EDI has enabled Stride Rite to cut turnaround time on shipments from three to one-and-a-half days. The payoff: according to Roger Monks, Stride Rite's senior vice president of manufacturing and operations, "We have yet to engage in an EDI partnership where business hasn't grown at a double-digit rate in the year immediately following."

Not everyone is so enthusiastic about EDI, however. There is concern that as more and more large companies start requiring their trading partners to have EDI, smaller businesses that cannot afford such systems will be shut out. Victor Brungart, director of the Small Business Development Center at Southwest Virginia Community College, recounts the tale of one client, a printer employing around 20 people. One day, the large chemical company that accounted for almost half the printer's business said that the printer had two months to implement an EDI system if it wanted to continue doing business with the chemical company. It cost the printer $20,000 that it could ill-afford to comply. Many large retailers such as Wal-Mart and Kmart have also pressured their suppliers to go to EDI or risk losing their business.[22]

EDI in use at Texas Instruments in Dallas, Texas.

Source: Courtesy of Texas Instruments.

Summary

Telecommunications Basics

▶ Telecommunications refers to the electronic transmission of data over a communications channel.

▶ The basic components of a telecommunications system include computers that send and receive data, a communications channel over which the data is sent, special communications equipment, and communications software.

▶ Various transmission media can function as a communications channel in a telecommunications system. All transmission media make use of some form of electromagnetic radiation to communicate information.

▶ Transmission media can be classified into two basic types—those that rely on physical lines to serve as links and those that are wireless. The principal line-based transmission media are twisted-pair wire, coaxial cable, and fiber-optic cable. Wireless transmission systems include microwave systems, satellite communications systems, and other systems that use infrared light and radio wave technology.

▶ The Federal Communications Commission oversees our nation's telecommunications system. Common carriers are companies licensed by the FCC to provide communications channels and other communications services to the public.

▶ Common carriers can offer customers a choice of switched lines, private or dedicated lines, or a virtual private network for their telecommunications needs.

▶ Two types of signals can travel over transmission media: analog and digital. Most communications devices traditionally have been designed to send and receive analog signals (a continuous wave), but computers are designed to communicate with digital signals (a discrete on–off pulse). Special equipment, called modems, convert digital signals into analog and then back again.

▶ Many telephone companies are starting to offer Integrated Services Digital Network (ISDN) service—telephone lines that can transmit sound, images, and data simultaneously in the form of digital signals.

▶ The amount of data that can be sent through a communications channel is related to the frequency of the signals that the channel carries. The speed at which data travels through a communications channel is measured in bits per second (bps) or baud rate.

▶ Asynchronous transmission and synchronous transmission are two methods for designating where one character of data ends and another begins when data is being transmitted over a communications channel.

▶ Communications channels differ in the direction they allow data to flow. The three possibilities are simplex transmission (data travels in one direction only), half-duplex transmission (data travels in both directions but not at the same time), and full-duplex transmission (data can travel in both directions simultaneously).

▶ Modems convert digital signals into analog signals and back again through modulation and demodulation. The primary considerations in choosing a modem are whether to pick an internal or external modem and the speed at which it can transmit data.

▶ Other specialized communications equipment include multiplexers, front-end processors, concentrators, and communications controllers. Communications equipment works hand in hand with communications software.

▶ For different components of a telecommunications system to communicate with one another, they must follow a common set of rules called protocols.

Telecommunications Networks

▶ The two primary types of computer networks are local networks and wide area networks.

▶ Local networks are used for communications within several floors of a building, an entire building, or a group of buildings located close to one another. The most common types of local networks are private branch exchanges (PBXs) and local area networks (LANs).

▶ Today's PBXs are computerized central switchboards that not only perform the functions of traditional telephone switchboards but also handle voice and data communications and serve as a connection between different office devices.

▶ A typical LAN consists of a number of microcomputers, a file server equipped with network operating system software, and shared laser printers, all linked by a cabling system. Networks that use file servers to help manage the network have a client/server architecture; those that do not use file servers are said to operate peer-to-peer. LANs enable users to share hardware devices, programs, and data files and have played a major role in a trend toward downsizing.

▶ LANs are usually configured in one of three basic shapes, or topologies: star, bus, or ring. LANs with a Fiber Distributed Data Interface (FDDI) use a variation of ring topology and offer very high transmission rates.

▶ Wide area networks (WANs) cover large geographic areas. Companies can use one of the public wide area networks maintained by common carriers or create their own using a combination of public and private resources.

▶ Value-added networks (VANs) are privately owned and managed networks that offer the services of the networks to others for a fee. In addition to providing basic communications services, VANs provide access to E-mail, public databases, and bulletin boards.

Telecommunications in Society and Business

▶ The convergence of communication and computer technologies is creating important changes in the way information will be delivered to the general public. On-line information retrieval services are already commonplace, and soon access to information and other data services will be available from telephone companies and cable companies.

▶ Electronic bulletin boards enable people to communicate electronically on topics of common interest.

▶ Facsimile (fax) machines enable copies of documents to be transmitted across the country in less than a minute.

▶ Voice mail is a sophisticated, computerized telephone answering system. Like E-mail, which allows users to send messages directly from computer to computer, it helps increase productivity by helping to eliminate telephone tag.

▶ Videoconferencing uses videocameras, microphones, computers equipped with codecs, and digital telephone lines to allow people to meet when they cannot be in the same geographic location.

▶ Workgroup computing uses a computer network and software called groupware to help people working on common projects communicate and work together more efficiently.

▶ Electronic data interchange (EDI) allows for a computer-to-computer electronic exchange of standard business documents between two separate organizations via a telecommunications network.

Key Terms

telecommunications	concentrator
communications channels	communications controller
twisted-pair wire	protocols
coaxial cable	network
fiber optics	private branch exchange (PBX)
microwave systems	local area network (LAN)
communications satellites	file server
wireless transmission systems	bridge
cellular telephones	gateway
common carriers	router
analog signal	topology
digital signal	star network
Integrated Services Digital Network (ISDN)	bus network
	ring network
bandwidth	Fiber Distributed Data Interface (FDDI)
bits per second (bps)	
baud rate	wide area network (WAN)
asynchronous transmission	Internet
synchronous transmission	value-added network (VAN)
simplex transmission	packet switching
half-duplex transmission	electronic bulletin boards
full-duplex transmission	fax machines
modem	voice mail
modulation	electronic mail (E-mail)
demodulation	videoconferencing
multiplexer	workgroup computing
front-end processor	electronic data interchange (EDI)
host computer	

 Interactive Supplement

Review Questions

1 Name and briefly describe the principal elements of a telecommunications system.

2 Why is electromagnetic radiation relevant to a discussion of telecommunications systems?

3 Describe the principal differences among the three types of line-based transmission media. Which type would you choose if you were installing a LAN, and why?

4 List the different types of wireless transmission media available, and summarize their important characteristics.

5 Compare switched lines, dedicated lines, and virtual private networks.

6 What is ISDN? How does it differ from existing telephone lines?

7 How do frequency and bandwidth relate to the transmission rate of a communications channel?

8 Describe the differences between (a) asynchronous and synchronous transmission and (b) simplex, half-duplex, and full-duplex transmission.

9 Name three different types of communications equipment, and explain what each does.

10 What is a protocol, and what functions does it perform?

11 Identify the differences between (a) a local network and a wide area network, (b) a private branch exchange and a local area network, and (c) client/server architecture and a peer-to-peer network.

12 What are some of a LAN's advantages and disadvantages?

13 How does a bus network differ from a ring network? What is the topology of the networks shown in Figures 6.13 and 6.14?

14 What is a VAN? What services does it typically offer?

15 How may the delivery of information to the public and businesses change within the next several years?

16 What is an electronic bulletin board? How does it differ from (a) an on-line information service and (b) E-mail?

17 Describe how facsimile transmission, voice mail, and E-mail might be used in a typical business setting.

18 What are the benefits and drawbacks of using a videoconferencing system?

19 Discuss the significance of EDI.

Problem-Solving and Skill-Building Exercises

1   One of the perils of the new age of telecommunication technology may be information overload, which sometimes occurs when people are exposed to too much information. Prepare a 2-page essay on how the technologies discussed in this chapter may contribute to "infoglut." Also include your thoughts on how technology can be used to avert this problem.

2   Your state is thinking about legalizing Caller ID—an automatic telephone number identification system. In groups of two or four students, prepare for a debate on the topic. Research how Caller ID may be used by business and individuals and the issues it raises. Then split your group into two sides: one side supporting Caller ID and the other opposing it. Debate the topic for 5–10 minutes and then vote on whether your state should allow it.

3   Primrose, Mendel and Hansen is a large law firm spread out over ten floors in a New York office building. It also has offices in Washington, D.C., Los Angeles, San Francisco, London, and Paris. On a typical day, lawyers need to be able to communicate and deliver documents to other lawyers inside and outside the firm and to clients across the country and in Europe. Although much of the work the lawyers do is collaborative (working with other lawyers to create and edit documents), legal research is also important. What types of telecommunications systems and applications would you suggest for Primrose, and why?

Communication Skills

This chapter has focused on the importance that communication has in our lives. One of the most crucial skills that you need to develop, to do well in school and on the job and in your personal life, is your own ability to communicate. George Plimpton gives you some tips that will help you make the oral presentations required for this course and others you will undoubtedly have to make throughout your life.

Although George doesn't mention them in his article, computers make excellent speech and presentation tools. Instead of using 3×5 cards, you can write down the main points of your presentation in large type for display on the screen of a portable computer. Then you can scroll through the text as you speak by simply clicking a key or mouse button. Another tip: practice your presentation skills every time you talk on an answering machine or voice mail system.

How to Make a Speech

By George Plimpton

One of life's terrors for the uninitiated is to be asked to make a speech.

"Why me?" will probably be your first reaction. "I don't have anything to say." It should be reassuring (though it rarely is) that since you were asked, somebody must think you do. The fact is that each one of us has a store of material that should be of interest to others. There is no reason why it should not be adapted to a speech.

Why Know How to Speak?

Scary as it is, it's important for anyone to be able to speak in front of others, whether twenty around a conference table or a hall filled with a thousand faces.

Being able to speak can mean better grades in any class. It can mean talking the town council out of increasing your property taxes. It can mean talking top management into buying your plan.

How to Pick a Topic

You were probably asked to speak in the first place in the hope that you would be able to articulate a topic that you know something about. Still, it helps to find out about your audience first. Who are they? Why are they there? What are they interested in? How much do they already know about your subject? One kind of talk would be appropriate for the Women's Club of Columbus, Ohio, and quite another for the guests at the Vince Lombardi dinner.

How to Plan What to Say

Here is where you must do your homework.

The more you sweat in advance, the less you'll have to sweat once you appear on stage. Research your topic thoroughly. Check the library for facts, quotes, books and timely magazine and newspaper articles on your subject. Get in touch with experts. Write to them, make phone calls, get interviews to help round out your material.

In short, gather—and learn—far more than you'll ever use. You can't imagine how much confidence that knowledge will inspire.

Now start organizing and writing. Most authorities suggest that a good speech breaks down into three basic parts— an introduction, the body of the speech, and the summation.

Introduction: An audience makes up its mind very quickly. Once the mood of an audience is set, it is difficult to change it, which is why introductions are important. If the speech is to be lighthearted in tone, the speaker can start off by telling a good-natured story about the subject or himself.

But be careful of jokes, especially the shaggy-dog variety. For some reason, the joke that convulses guests in a living room tends to suffer as it emerges through the amplifying system into a public gathering place.

Main body: There are four main intents in the body of the well-made speech. These are 1) to entertain, which is probably the hardest; 2) to instruct, which is the easiest if the speaker has done the research and knows the subject; 3) to persuade, which one does at a sales presentation, a policital rally, or a town meeting; and finally, 4) to inspire, which is what the speaker emphasizes at a sales meeting, in a sermon, or at a pep rally. (Hurry-Up Yost, the onetime Michigan football coach, gave such an inspiration-filled half-time talk that he got carried away and at the final exhortation led his team on the run through the wrong locker-room door into the swimming pool.)

Summation: This is where you should "ask for the order." An ending should probably incorporate a sentence or two which sounds like an ending—a short summary of the main points of the speech, perhaps, or the repeat of a phrase that most embodies what the speaker has hoped to convey. It is valuable to think of the last sentence or two as something which might produce applause. Phrases which are perfectly appropriate to signal this are: "In closing . . ." or "I have one last thing to say . . . ."

Once done—fully written, or the main points set down on 3" × 5" index cards—the next problem is the actual presentation of the speech. Ideally, a speech should not be read. At least it should never appear or sound as if you are reading it. An audience is dismayed to see a speaker peering down at a thick sheaf of papers on the lectern, wetting his thumb to turn to the next page.

How to Sound Spontaneous

The best speakers are those who make their words sound spontaneous even if memorized. I've found it's best to learn a speech point by point, not word for word. Careful preparation and a great deal of practicing are required to make it come together smoothly and easily. Mark Twain once said, "It takes three weeks to prepare a good ad-lib speech."

Don't be fooled when you rehearse. It takes longer to deliver a speech than to read it. Most speakers peg along at about 100 words a minute.

Brevity Is an Asset

A sensible plan, if you have been asked to speak to an exact limit, is to talk your speech into a mirror and stop at your allotted time; then cut the speech accordingly. The more familiar you become with your speech, the more confidently you can deliver it.

As anyone who listens to speeches knows, brevity is an asset. Twenty minutes are ideal. An hour is the limit an audience can listen comfortably.

In mentioning brevity, it is worth mentioning that the shortest inaugural address was George Washington's—just 135 words. The longest was William Henry Harrison's in 1841. He delivered a two-hour 9,000-word speech into the teeth of a freezing northeast wind. He came down with a cold the following day, and a month later he died of pneumonia.

Check Your Grammar

Consult a dictionary for proper meanings and pronunciations. Your audience won't know if you're a bad speller, but they will know if you use or pronounce a word improperly. In my first remarks on the dais, I used to thank people for their "fulsome introduction," until I discovered to my dismay that "fulsome" means *offensive* and *insincere.*

On the Podium

It helps one's nerves to pick out three or four people in the audience—preferably in different sectors so that the speaker is apparently giving his attention to the entire room—on whom to focus. Pick out people who seem to be having a good time.

How Questions Help

A question period at the end of a speech is a good notion. One would not ask questions following a tribute to the company treasurer on his retirement, say, but a technical talk or an informative speech can be enlivened with a question period.

The Crowd

The larger the crowd, the easier it is to speak, because the response is multiplied and increased. Most people do not believe this. They peek out from behind the curtain and if the auditorium is filled to the rafters they begin to moan softly in the back of their throats.

What about Stage Fright?

Very few speakers escape the so-called "butterflies." There does not seem to be any cure for them, except to realize that they are beneficial rather than harmful, and never fatal. The tension usually means that the speaker, being keyed up, will do a better job. Edward R. Murrow called stage fright "the sweat of perfection." Mark Twain once comforted a fright-frozen friend about to speak: "Just remember they don't expect much." My own feeling is that with thought, preparation and faith in your ideas, *you* can go out there and expect a pleasant surprise.

And what a sensation it is—to hear applause. Invariably after it dies away, the speaker searches out the program chairman—just to make it known that he's available for next month's meeting.

Reprinted by permission of International Paper Company.

Notes

1 **Ramirez, Anthony,** "Lots of Conversations Over One Skinny Cable," *New York Times,* June 30, 1992.

2 **Markoff, John,** "Building the Electronic Superhighway," *New York Times,* January 24, 1993; **Andrews, Edmund,** "A Baby Bell Primed for the Big Fight," *New York Times,* February 21, 1993; **Andrews, Edmund,**

"Cable Company Plans a Data Superhighway," *New York Times*, April 12, 1993; **Andrews, Edmund,** "Battle Looms Over Paying to Rewire U.S. for Phones," *New York Times*, June 9, 1992.

3 **Kristof, Nicholas,** "Satellites Bring Information Revolution to China," *New York Times*, April 11, 1993.

4 **Thyfault, Mary,** "The Dish at Holiday Inn," *Information Week*, May 11, 1992.

5 **Booker, Ellis,** "The Whole World in Your Pocket," *Computerworld*, September 7, 1992; **Andrews, Edmund,** "Wireless Phones: Different Visions," *New York Times*, August 26, 1992; **Ramirez, Anthony,** "The Ultimate Portable-Phone Plan," *New York Times*, March 18, 1992.

6 **Wexler, Joanie,** "Oxford Presses Wireless LAN into Service," *Computerworld*, September 23, 1991.

7 **Markoff, John,** "Oracle and McCaw Tell of Radio Data Network," *New York Times*, May 18, 1992.

8 **Booker, Ellis,** "Earth to Laptop: Network Access from the Air," *Computerworld*, June 1, 1992; **Pollack, Andrew,** "Packing Cable with Programs," *New York Times*, January 22, 1992; **Ramirez, Anthony,** "Next for the Cellular Phone," *New York Times*, March 22, 1992.

9 **Fitzgerald, Michael,** "Modems: Not Just for Data Anymore," *Computerworld*, April 27, 1992; **Leaser, Mark,** "Just a Modem?! Not Anymore," *Computerworld*, August 17, 1992.

10 **Hildebrand, Carol,** "PCnet Keeps Health Care Costs in Check," *Computerworld*, August 3, 1992.

11 **Hildebrand, Carol,** "Taylor Medical Overcomes Gridlock," *Computerworld*, March 9, 1992.

12 **Broad, William,** "Doing Science on the Network: A Long Way from Gutenberg," *New York Times*, May 18, 1993; **Quarterman, John,** "In Depth: The Internet," *Computerworld*, February 22, 1993; **Markoff, John,** "A Web of Networks, an Abundance of Services," *New York Times*, February 28, 1993; **Calem, Robert,** "The Network of All Networks," *New York Times*, December 6, 1992; **Dern, Daniel,** "Plugging into the Internet," *BYTE*, October 1992; **Wilson, David,** "Huge Computer Network Quickens Pace of Academic Exchange and Collaboration," *The Chronicle of Higher Education*, September 30, 1992.

13 **Thyfault, Mary,** "Bells Ring Up Info Services," *Information Week*, August 26, 1991; **Bozman, Jean,** "Pac Bell Reaching Out after Ruling," *Computerworld*, August 5, 1991; **Seitz, Bob,** "Phone Companies Join Their Rivals in Facts Business," *New York Times*, June 7, 1992; **Andrews, Edmund,** "Ruling Backs 'Baby Bells' on Information Services," *New York Times*, May 29, 1993.

14 **Andrews, Edmund,** "Telephone Companies to Get Right to Transmit Television," *New York Times*, July 16, 1992; **Andrews, Edmund,** "Baby Bell Entering Cable TV," *New York Times*, December 16, 1992; **Fabrikant, Geraldine,** "Phone Company Breaks Ground by Buying into Cable Television," *New York Times*, February 10, 1993.

15 **Fabrikant, Geraldine,** "US West Will Buy into Time Warner," *New York Times*, May 17, 1993; "IBM Close to Tuning in New Information System," *Citizen Register*, August 25, 1992.

16 **Ramirez, Anthony,** "For the 90's, Screen-Based Phones," *New York Times*, December 13, 1992; **Vecchione, Anthony,** "EO: More Than Magic," *Information Week*, February 15, 1993; **Ryan, Bob,** "Communications Get Personal," *BYTE*, February 1993.

17 **Hildebrand, Carol,** "PCs and Voice Recognition Help Co-op Sell Artwork," *Computerworld*, August 24, 1992; **Bulkeley, William,** "Faxes Prove To Be a Powerful Tool for Setting Up Electronic Markets," *Wall Street Journal*, July 28, 1992.

18 **Rifkin, Glenn,** "Do Employees Have a Right to Electronic Privacy?" *New York Times*, December 9, 1991.

19 **Betts, Mitch,** "Ruling Forces Government to Save Electronic Messages," *Computerworld*, January 11, 1993; **Miller, Michael,** "Historians Crusade to Preserve E-Mail," *Wall Street Journal*, March 31, 1992.

20 **International Data Corporation White Paper,** "Workgroup Technology: Tying Technology to Business Objectives."

21 **Hsu, Jeffrey and Lockwood, Tony,** "Collaborative Computing," *BYTE*, March 1993; **Wreden, Nick,** "Regrouping for Groupware," *Beyond Computing*, March/April 1993.

22 **Gillin, Paul,** "Shoe Retailer Makes Strides with EDI," *Computerworld*, June 1, 1992; **Knight, Robert,** "Firms Must Do Up-front EDI Planning," *Computerworld*, October 19, 1992.

After completing this chapter, you will:

▶ Understand how a computer's operating system enables the computer to perform basic functions.

▶ Appreciate how a graphical user interface allows a user to interact more easily with the computer's operating system.

▶ Know what distinguishes the different kinds of operating systems available for microcomputers.

▶ Understand the role that other types of systems software play in a computer system.

7

Operating Systems and Systems Software

Computer Orphans

There's a 13-year-old orphan in Gary Rose's office at the Alameda County public school headquarters. But Gary isn't a school counselor, and the orphan isn't a student. Instead, the orphan is a Honeywell DPS-8 mainframe computer used to handle payroll and accounting chores for 10 of the county's 22 school districts.

Why is the machine an orphan? Because Groupe Bull, the company that acquired Honeywell in 1988, has decided that it will no longer "support" (help fix glitches and provide enhancements for) the DPS-8's operating system, the systems software that is akin to a central nervous system for the computer. Although there's nothing wrong with the DPS-8, without the operating system, the hardware is useless. And to make matters worse, the operating system that Bull told Rose it would support doesn't run on the DPS-8. Switching to the new operating system would mean trashing the Honeywell and replacing it with a new mainframe, at a cost of almost half a million dollars. In addition, all the old applications software that ran on the Hon-

IBM RISC System/6000.
Source: Courtesy of IBM.

eywell would have to be replaced, adding thousands of dollars to the cost.

Computer orphans like the one in Gary Rose's office are becoming more and more common. For years, computer manufacturers have been creating computers with

25

proprietary operating system software. Proprietary operating system software is designed to operate only with a specific kind of CPU chip. But when the systems start to get old and new processors are introduced, manufacturers are reluctant to keep spending the resources needed to support the old software. They'd rather encourage their customers to switch to a newer model.

Today, however, the game is starting to change. To avoid getting into the same bind down the road with another proprietary system, Rose chose something different. To replace the DPS, Alameda County purchased an IBM RS/6000 system that uses a version of an operating system called UNIX. Originally developed for scientific and academic research, UNIX is a non-proprietary, "open" operating system that can be used with many different varieties of computer hardware. Support is now available from a number of different vendors, making it unlikely that the operating system will become obsolete before the computer equipment does.

Source: Based on Baldwin, Howard, "Seduced and Abandoned," *Unixworld*, August 1992.

You have now learned about many of the technologies—CPUs and RAM, secondary storage media and devices, input and output devices, communications equipment—that are needed to create an information system. But as you saw in the opening vignette, hardware is just half the story. What makes a computer so unique is its ability to perform any number of different tasks. And what enables a computer to do this is *software* (also called computer programs), a detailed set of instructions that can be stored in the computer's memory. Software tells the equipment in an information system what you want to do. It is software that makes the computer so valuable as a problem-solving tool.

7.1 An Introduction to Software

There are two basic types of software: systems software and applications software. **Systems software** controls and coordinates the operation of the various types of equipment in a computer system. The most important type of systems software is a set of programs called the operating system. The operating system contains general instructions that enable a computer to carry out basic functions—like loading, storing, and retrieving files—common to all types of computer programs. The operating system also establishes the interface with the user (sometimes called the operating environment).

Once a computer system has systems software, **applications software** can be added. Applications software allows you to apply the computer to solve a *specific problem* or perform a *specific task*. Today, in addition to the familiar word processing, spreadsheet, and database programs (covered in more detail in Chapter 10), thousands of different types of applications software are now available, covering an amazing variety of problems and tasks encountered in everyday life, business, government, science, medicine, engineering, law, education, and so on. We discuss the ever-expanding universe of applications software in Chapter 11.

The instructions that make up systems software and applications software are written (or "coded") by people called *programmers.* The instructions must be written in a language, called a *programming language,* that can be understood by the computer equipment. There are a variety of programming languages, each designed to solve a particular class of problems. We will examine programming languages in more detail in Chapter 9.

Computers need both applications and systems software in order to be able to do what we want, when we want. Figure 7.1 illustrates the interrelationship among hardware, systems software, applications software, and the person using an information system to solve a problem or perform a task.

In this chapter, we will look at systems software, focusing primarily on the operating system. We'll examine the important role that the operating system plays within a computer, discuss how operating systems are changing to make it easier for people to interact with them, and explore some of the different types of operating systems used for different types of computers. We'll finish up with a review of systems software that performs other vital functions, such as language translators and utility programs.

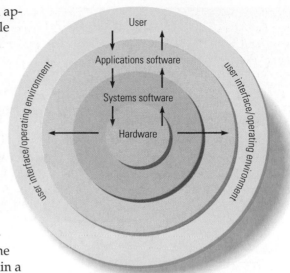

Figure 7.1

The Interrelationship Among Hardware, Systems Software, Applications Software, and the User

Although interaction with the computer's operating system cannot be totally avoided, the user primarily interacts with a specific piece of applications software that is directly related to the problem or task at hand. Systems software acts as the intermediary between the applications software and hardware. It transforms the instructions from the applications software into ones that can be understood by the hardware, coordinates all the resources of the system to execute the instructions, and then communicates the results back to the applications software. The applications program then converts the results into a form that the user can understand.

7.2   Operating Systems

Systems software that manages and controls the activities of a computer is called the **operating system.** The operating system is probably the single most important piece of software in a computer system: without it, the system cannot function.

Basic Background

In the early days of computing, computer operators had to manually load programs and data onto input devices, reset switches to clear storage locations of data from previous jobs, set other switches to process the data, and then unload the program, input data, and output results after processing was complete (see photo). The CPU remained idle while these other activities were carried out, and as a result spent more time waiting than it did working. Researchers realized that automation of this process would greatly increase computer hardware efficiency. They eventually developed an operating system program that enabled the computer to supervise its own operations and carry out basic activities without the need for direct human intervention.

There is a close relationship between the power of computer hardware and the power of its operating system. The faster and more powerful the CPU and the greater the amount of memory, the more the operating system can do. And the more the operating system can do, the more useful it can make a computer for its users. For instance, a large mainframe computer has the CPU power and primary storage space to support a sophisticated operating system, one that can handle the demands of hundreds of users seeking to run hundreds of different programs on the mainframe at the same time. A microcomputer, which has less CPU power and primary storage, can only

Early information systems needed computer operators to perform many of the tasks manually that are now carried out by operating systems.

Source: Courtesy of IBM Corporation.

support a much less complicated operating system, one that may be able to handle only one user running one program at a time. However, as microcomputers become more powerful, new operating systems being developed for them are beginning to incorporate some of the sophisticated features of mainframe and minicomputer operating systems.

We'll now take a closer look at the basic functions that operating systems perform.

Operating System Functions

The operating system performs a variety of important tasks. Although the tasks will vary depending on the size of the computer involved, they can be categorized into three general areas: allocating and assigning system resources, scheduling the various operations that need to be performed, and monitoring system activities (see Figure 7.2).

Figure 7.2
The Operating System's Principal Functions
The operating system performs three basic functions: (1) it allocates and assigns system resources, (2) it schedules the use of resources, and (3) it monitors system activities.

Allocating and Assigning Resources	Scheduling	Monitoring System Activities
Helps coordinate work (supervisor)	Allows computers to work on more than one job at once	Performs error control
Deciphers instructions and assigns resources (command language translator)		Tracks system performance
		Provides system security

Allocating and Assigning System Resources A primary function of all types of operating systems is to determine which of the computer system's resources (the CPU, primary storage, secondary storage, input and output devices) are needed for the job at hand and to allocate and assign those resources.

A part of the operating system called the **supervisor** (or sometimes the executive, monitor, kernel, master program, or control program) handles most of this task. This part of the operating system always remains in primary storage while the computer is on. (For this reason, the supervisor is referred to as the *resident* portion of the operating system.) Other less frequently used parts of the operating system are kept in secondary storage. (These are referred to as the *nonresident* portions of the operating system.)

The supervisor determines which other programs within the operating system are required for the job to be performed. If the program is located in secondary storage, the supervisor brings it into primary storage as needed. On doing so, the supervisor relinquishes control of the system to the new program. The supervisor takes back control once the program has finished its role.

A part of the operating system called the **command language translator** also plays a role in the assignment of system resources. Programs generally allow the user to issue commands to the computer, such as to retrieve, save, copy, delete or move a file, choose a certain input/output device, select a specific applications program, and so on. These commands are written in *command language* (sometimes called *job control language*). When the supervisor encounters a command, it calls in the command language translator, which deciphers and assigns the resources necessary to process the instruction. When the translator has finished the job, it returns control of the system to the supervisor.

Scheduling Operations An operating system not only has to assign system resources but also needs to determine how to schedule the use of those resources. Though the first operating systems allowed only a single user to run a single program at one time (which did not require much scheduling), many of today's operating systems now allow computers to work on more than one job at the same time. In this section, we'll look at some of the methods developed to accomplish this task. Most of these techniques are applicable primarily to larger computer systems with many users, but they are beginning to trickle down into operating systems for microcomputers as well.

Multiprogramming allows multiple programs to be executed concurrently through a sharing of the computer's resources. Even though the CPU can handle only one program instruction at a given time, it is much faster than other parts of the computer system. As a result, the CPU would be idle much of the time if it had nothing to do while data was being transferred from secondary storage or to an output device. A multiprogramming operating system takes advantage of this fact by allowing another program to use the resources of the CPU when it would otherwise be idle.

Here's an example of how it works. Let's say three different users are all logged onto their office's computer system. Each is using a different applications program: one is writing a memo with a word processing program, another is updating a database file, and the third is doing some spreadsheet calculations. While User 1's memo is being printed out on a printer and User 2's database file is being transferred into primary storage from a hard disk, the CPU can be crunching numbers for User 3's spreadsheet program (see Figure 7.3). By switching back and forth between different programs and tasks, the operating system is able to give each user the impression that he or she is the only one using the computer at that moment.

Host computer   Terminals

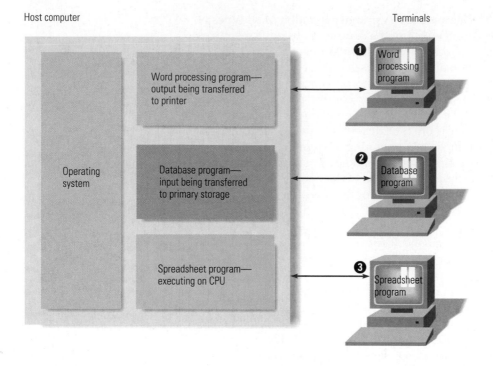

Figure 7.3
Multiprogramming
Multiprogramming allows a computer system to work on several programs at the same time. While the CPU is processing User 3's spreadsheet calculations, the computer performs input and output tasks for Users 1 and 2.

Multitasking provides multiprogramming capabilities to single-user operating systems. Multitasking allows you to run two or more programs at the same time on a single computer. This is particularly useful when information stored in the files of one application program is needed to carry out a task that requires a different program. For instance, an attorney preparing bills for clients may need both the word processing program and the client file database. Multitasking allows the attorney to display and work with both programs at the same time. Multitasking is becoming an important feature of advanced microcomputer operating systems such as Windows NT and OS/2.

Multiprocessing uses two or more CPUs linked together to execute instructions. Unlike multiprogramming and multitasking, which involve the processing of programs and tasks concurrently, computer systems that utilize multiprocessing can execute different instructions from the same program or instructions from more than one program simultaneously. Parallel processing, which you learned about in Chapter 3, is one form of multiprocessing. Computers that use multiprocessing need sophisticated operating systems to schedule and coordinate the work among the CPUs. As the story "Journey to the Center of the Earth" illustrates, the utilization of multiprocessing techniques by supercomputers may open the door to new scientific breakthroughs.

Time-sharing is another method that allows a number of users to share the resources of one computer system simultaneously. With time-sharing, the operating system rapidly rotates through all users on the system. Each user is allocated a very short slice of CPU processing time (a **time slice**), usually no more than 1 to 2 milliseconds long. The CPU performs whatever operations it can for that user within that time slice and then moves on to the next user in the rotation. (In multiprogramming, in contrast, the computer works on one program until it reaches a logical stopping point, such as an input/output event, before switching to a new program.) Unless the system is underpowered for its normal workload, before users notice any lapse, they have already been allocated another time slice, so processing appears to be uninterrupted.

For those who experience them directly, earthquakes can be an earth-shattering event. The lives of those living in the danger zone would be much less precarious if earthquakes could be predicted with any reasonable degree of accuracy. Researchers at Los Alamos National Laboratory in Los Alamos, New Mexico, are hoping that supercomputers using parallel processing techniques will help them achieve that goal.

The forces that create earthquakes begin deep in the earth's core. As John Baumgardner, a technical staff member in the theoretical division explains, "The problem with understanding the interior of the earth is we have to sense it remotely. We can't take actual measurements of the properties."

To help visualize what is happening under the earth's crust, Baumgardner wrote a software program that creates three-dimensional models. Until recently, says Baumgardner, "most of the models have been two-dimensional, but the earth is not a rectangular box." The models depict the earth as 33 separate layers from crust to core, with the average layer about 100 kilometers deep. Each model layer is a multigrid "mesh" of 80,000 triangular sections. Baumgardner runs equations in each triangle to plot the theoretical behavior of the tectonic plates of the earth's crust.

The models are based on the premise of breaking down one massive computer challenge into thousands of smaller ones. For that reason, Baumgardner has high hopes that utilizing multiprocessing techniques will provide even greater efficiency. Right now, the software is running on a Cray Y/MP supercomputer that uses regular, sequential processing, but the lab hopes to switch soon to a massively parallel Connection Machine supercomputer from Thinking Machines. "On the code we've converted so far, we've seen ten times better performance," says Baumgardner.

With the next generation of Connection Machine, Baumgardner hopes to increase the computer resolution to simulate activity in layers as small as 50 kilometers thick. Although right now this is not small enough to accurately model the tectonic plate changes that cause earthquakes, in the not too distant future further advances in massively parallel supercomputing may make even this elusive goal possible.

Source: Based on Wilder, Clinton, "Delving into the Depths of the Earth," *Computerworld*, July 29, 1991.

Critical Thinking Questions

1 What other functions must the operating systems that run the supercomputers described in this story perform?

2 Why do you think a computer that utilizes multiprocessing would be well suited to the tasks described here?

Most time-sharing operating systems allow the number of time slices that are allocated to a given user or application to be adjusted. For instance, one organization may decide that order entry should be given higher priority than accounting and allocate it more time slices.

Virtual storage is a technique that expands the limits of existing primary storage by enabling multiple users to utilize the same memory space. Before virtual storage was developed in the early 1970s, to run a program, the entire program had to be loaded into primary storage. This created inefficiencies. Generally, only a few programs could fit within primary storage at once. If a program was very large, it might have to be split up into different sections to fit. On the other hand, often a portion of primary storage went underutilized because the programs loaded did not take up the whole space available.

With virtual storage, though, only the portion of the program currently being used needs to be in primary storage. The rest of the program is stored in virtual storage on a hard disk until required. The operating system handles the transfer of data and instructions between primary storage and virtual storage by using the segment method, the page method, or some combination of the two.

An operating system using the **segment method** of virtual storage divides a program into variable-length *segments*. Each segment consists of a logically related block of material from the program. Since the segments are based on keeping logically related portions of the program together, they vary in size, with some segments larger than others. When a particular

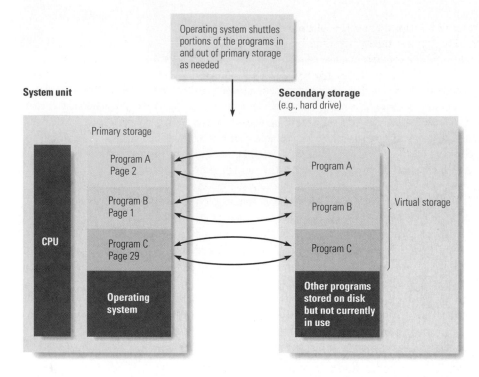

Figure 7.4
Virtual Storage Techniques
Using virtual storage, only a portion of the programs in use need to be in primary storage. The rest of the program is held in virtual storage until the next page or segment is required.

instruction or piece of data is required by the program, the operating system transfers the segment containing the instruction or data from virtual storage into primary storage.

The **page method** breaks a program down into *pages*, each always containing the same fixed number of bytes. As a result, the pages do not necessarily correspond to a logical division as a segment does. As with the segment method, when a page is needed, it is transferred to primary storage. If the time comes when primary storage is full, but another segment or page is required, the operating system makes room by transferring the oldest page or segment back to virtual storage (see Figure 7.4).

Thus, with virtual storage, many portions of different programs, broken down into segments or pages, can reside in primary storage at the same time, thereby maximizing the number of programs (and users) that can use primary storage simultaneously.

Figure 7.5 summarizes the different scheduling techniques discussed in this section.

Multiprogramming	Used primarily by minicomputers and mainframes. Allows multiple programs to be executed concurrently through sharing of computer resources.
Multitasking	Provides multiprogramming capabilities for microcomputers.
Multiprocessing	Uses two or more CPUs linked together to execute multiple instructions.
Time-sharing	Operating system rapidly rotates short slices of CPU processing time among all users on the system.
Virtual storage	Expands limits of existing primary storage space by enabling multiple users to utilize same memory space. Splits programs into segments or pages, some of which are stored in secondary storage until needed.

Figure 7.5
Different Scheduling Techniques That Enable Computer Systems to Work on More Than One Job at Once

Monitoring System Activities   The final basic function of operating systems is to monitor system activities. The operating system will notify the user if input/output devices need attention, if an error has occurred, or if anything abnormal occurs in the system. Operating systems for larger computer installations generally track system performance by keeping logs of operations that record the elapsed time required to process a job.

Operating systems also play a role in providing system security. Most multiuser systems (both in a mainframe environment and in a computer network environment) require users to enter a user ID and password before allowing access to the system. The operating system checks the validity of these codes, records who is using the system and for how long, and reports any attempted breaches of security. In some organizations, such records are also used to bill users for time spent using the system.

7.3 Operating Environments and Graphical User Interfaces

Although a user interacts primarily with applications programs, some contact with the operating system is usually necessary. For many years, operating systems required that users communicate through text-based commands. For instance, to copy a file from a hard disk onto a floppy disk using a text-based operating system like DOS, a user would be required to type something like "copy a:test.doc b:." DOS commands can have up to three parts: the *command name, parameters* that identify the object being acted on, and *switches* that modify the action being performed. Figure 7.6 shows you the component parts of some typical DOS commands. Remembering all the different commands (around 90 in all), with all of their proper parts, and using the proper *syntax* (the order in which the command and any parameters and switches that follow it must be typed) was an arduous task. In the 1960s, researchers began to search for ways to make operating systems easier to use. The method they struck on was to create an "operating environment" with a graphical user interface.

To delete or erase a file: **del(or erase) c:test.doc/p**

Del (or **Erase**) is the command name, **c:test.doc** are the parameters that specify the location and name of the file you want to delete (here a file named test.doc located on the c: drive) and **/p** is a switch that causes the del command to display the file name and the message "test.doc, Delete (Y/N)," requiring you to press Y to confirm the deletion or N if you want to cancel the command.

To copy a file to another disk and rename it: **copy c:test1.doc b:memo1.doc**

Copy is the command name and **c:test1.doc b:memo1.doc** are the parameters—they specify the location and name of the file that you want to copy (here a file named test1.doc located on the c: drive) and where you want the copied file to be stored, as well as its new name (here, on the b: drive under the new name memo1.doc). In this example, there are no switches.

To display a list of all filenames with the .doc extension on drive C: **dir c:*.doc /w/p**

Dir is the command name, **c:*.doc** are the parameters (here, a list of all files with the .doc extension on drive c, with the * symbol acting as a wildcard that tells the system you want all files with that particular extension, no matter what their name) and **/w** and **/p** are switches. /w displays the listing of files in a wide screen format while /p causes the screen to pause each time the screen is full rather than scrolling immediately through to the end of the listing.

Figure 7.6
Some Typical DOS Commands Dissected

A **graphical user interface** (often simply called a **GUI,** pronounced *goo-ee*) is the "face" that the operating system presents to the user. It uses *icons* (symbolic pictures) to represent programs, files, and common operations instead of text-based commands. The icons use simple pictures of objects and events with which users are generally familiar. Rather than having to remember and type in the right command, a user can move the cursor with a mouse to the appropriate icon and then click the button on top of the mouse to issue the command. Figure 7.7 gives you an idea of how GUIs work.

The goal of GUIs is to create a system that the novice computer user can turn on and operate right away without any prior training or the need to refer to manuals or remember commands. So far though, they have not

Figure 7.7
A Guided Tour of a GUI

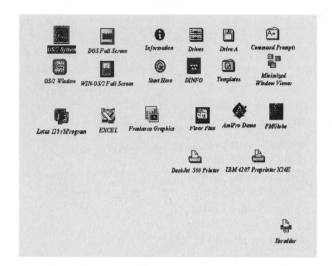

a. This is OS/2's opening screen, called the Desktop. It consists primarily of a blank screen with icons representing various options, commands, and files. For instance, a miniature floppy disk represents the A drive (normally the floppy disk drive on most systems).

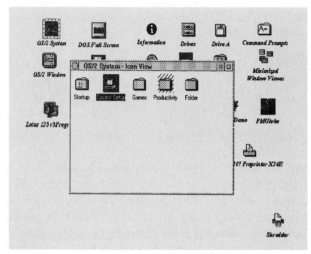

b. Double-clicking on an icon opens the object that the icon represents into a window. Here, we have clicked on the OS/2 System icon. Note the small version of the icon in the upper-left corner of the window.

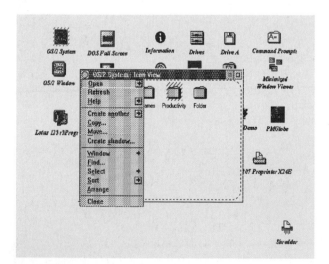

c. Clicking on the System icon in the upper-left corner of the window brings up the menu for the object in question. The options listed in the menu will vary depending on the type of object in the window.

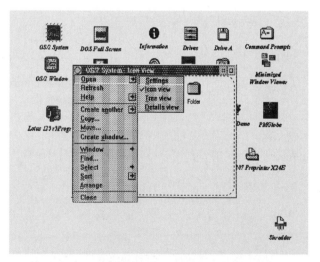

d. Clicking on an arrow button in the menu brings up a submenu for that item. Here, we have clicked on the arrow button next to the word Open, bringing up a submenu listing further options.

totally achieved that goal. Just because a system is graphical doesn't automatically make it a snap to use. Badly designed GUIs may be unclear, difficult to understand, and inconsistent across different applications. Even GUIs that are straightforward in their presentation and easy to navigate require between 20 and 30 hours of training time before users become truly adept. Nonetheless, that's still generally quicker than the time it would take for most new users to become skilled at using a non-graphical operating system.

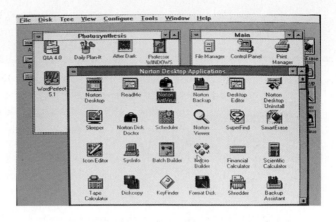

Some operating systems, such as Apple's Macintosh System 7 (discussed more fully in the next section), have a graphical user interface built directly into the system. For older systems that do not, a **shell** program that contains a GUI can be inserted to act as an interface between the operating system and the user. Microsoft's Windows (also discussed more fully later) is a sophisticated shell program that allows users with a relatively up-to-date machine and a DOS operating system to take advantage of the benefits of a GUI. Another less complicated, inexpensive shell, Symantec's Norton Desktop for DOS, transforms even older DOS machines that are not capable of running Windows into a kind of GUI (see photo).

Most GUIs create computer screens that are supposed to resemble a typical office desktop. You can move items around on the desktop, add new

Symantec's Norton Desktop is a shell program that creates a graphical user interface for older DOS machines not capable of running Windows.

Source: Fredrik D. Bodin/Offshoot.

a.

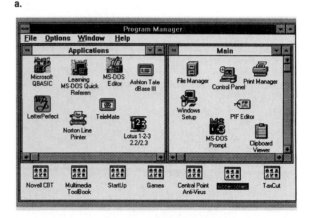

Figure 7.8
Basic GUI Elements in the Windows Operating Environment
(a) Windows main menu. **(b)** This is the submenu you would see if you clicked the mouse button on the word File on the menu bar. **(c)** This is the dialog box that would pop up if you clicked on the command Copy... from the File submenu shown in part b. The Copy dialog box requires you to type in where the file should be copied to and then asks you to click on the OK button to confirm.

b.

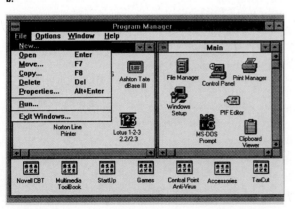

c.

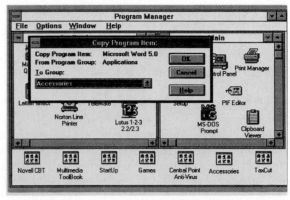

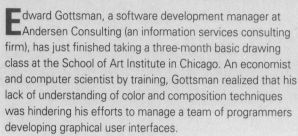

Edward Gottsman, a software development manager at Andersen Consulting (an information services consulting firm), has just finished taking a three-month basic drawing class at the School of Art Institute in Chicago. An economist and computer scientist by training, Gottsman realized that his lack of understanding of color and composition techniques was hindering his efforts to manage a team of programmers developing graphical user interfaces.

Today's interfaces must be as aesthetically pleasing as they are functional. "GUIs have to visually pack a lot of information," explains Ann Palermo, director of office systems research at International Data Corp. in Framingham, Massachusetts. "If you look at an icon and have to ask, 'What's that?' it isn't working." In addition, users are coming to expect more attractive and graphically entertaining screens.

Gottsman says the art class has improved his graphic sensibilities and given him a better appreciation for the communication and miscommunication that can occur with visual media. This can be seen in some of the recent icons he has developed. One is a yellow Post-it-type note. When the user decides to "tear up" the note, a jagged black line is sent through the icon. Gottsman predicts that the aesthetic demands of user interfaces will continue to increase dramatically in the 1990s and that a basic understanding of art will be an important characteristic of successful programmers.

Throughout this book, you've seen how information technology will be important to your career, even if your job doesn't directly involve the use of computers. If your job does directly involve computers, you need to know more than just technology. As this story illustrates, it will be the well-rounded individual, the person who can make connections between different disciplines like science and art, who will be in demand in the 1990s.

Source: Based on Booker, Ellis, "Graphic Interfaces Need Artful Programmers," *Computerworld*, April 29, 1991.

Critical Thinking Questions

1 What makes a graphical user interface easy to use? What features might a well-designed GUI have?

2 Why is software with a graphical user interface more difficult for programmers to develop than a traditional program?

3. Create your own set of icons to illustrate the following operations: deleting a file, copying a file, saving a file, and printing a file.

ones, and remove those you no longer need. GUIs usually feature *windows*: boxes with information that can be layered on top of one another, like files on the top of a desktop. Most windows contain certain elements, including a menu bar along the top of the screen that shows basic command options (clicking on one of the options in the menu bar produces additional submenus with further, more detailed choices), scroll bars that move parts of the document into view if the entire document cannot fit within the window, and buttons that will make the window larger or smaller. Typical icons within a window might include file folders to represent files, an artist's palette to represent a drawing application, a trash can to represent a delete operation, and so on. Sometimes a *dialog box* that requests information about the task you are performing or supplies information you might need will appear (see Figure 7.8 a–c).

Although GUIs have made life simpler for users, they have made life more challenging for those programmers charged with the task of creating them. There is generally a steep learning curve. Programmers often require a lot of time to learn the intricacies of working with a GUI. And because GUIs are designed as proprietary products, that knowledge cannot be easily transferred from one GUI to another. A piece of software designed to work with Apple's System 7 will not run with a different GUI, such as Windows. In addition to these difficulties, the story "The Programmer as Artist" explores another challenge that GUIs present to their developers.

7.4 Operating Systems for Microcomputers: A Hot Battleground

Operating systems come in two basic versions. As you saw in the opening vignette, a **proprietary operating system** works with only certain kinds of computers. In addition, most applications software is designed to be used with a specific operating system and generally cannot run with any other. For example, the operating system that powers Apple's Macintosh microcomputers does not work with an IBM PS/2. Applications software designed for the PS/2 will not run on a Mac.

In many cases, an operating system designed by a manufacturer for its

Name	Description
DOS	Operating system for IBM (PC-DOS version) and IBM-compatible (MS-DOS version) personal computers.
OS/2	IBM-designed successor to DOS; supports multitasking, virtual storage, and so on. Designed to take advantage of capabilities of 32-bit microprocessors.
Windows NT	Microsoft-designed successor to DOS. Same basic capabilities as OS/2 but uses Windows GUI.
System 7	Operating system for Apple's Macintosh line of computers. Supports multitasking, powerful graphics, and multimedia.
UNIX	A portable, nonproprietary operating system that allows applications software to work across a full range of platforms. Supports multitasking, multiuser processing, and networking. Several different versions available.

Figure 7.9
Microcomputer Operating Systems

microcomputers will not run on that manufacturer's larger computers. For instance, as you'll see in this section, though PC-DOS or OS/2 is the operating system for IBM's microcomputers, its mainframes use different operating systems called MVS or VM. (In some cases, as with Digital Equipment Corporation's VMS operating system, the operating system will work with a manufacturer's entire line, from microcomputer to mainframe.)

In contrast to proprietary operating systems, a **portable operating system** can run on many different types of computers. The drive toward "open systems" and "interoperability" is one of the most important information technology trends of the 1990s. Open systems and interoperability allow applications software to operate on different hardware platforms, show users the same interface, and have the same functionality. A necessary precursor for open systems and true interoperability is a common, standard, portable operating system. As we noted in the opening vignette, the leading portable operating system is UNIX.

Operating systems are one of the hottest battlegrounds in the computer industry today, with industry giants IBM and Microsoft facing off against each other at the same time that Apple and vendors of UNIX-based systems strive for their own piece of the pie. The story "From Operating System to Empire" helps you understand why companies are so anxious to dominate this market.

Let's now take a closer look at some of the operating systems available today for microcomputers. Figure 7.9 lists the most common systems. Figure 7.10 gives you an estimate of each type's share of the market in 1992.

Figure 7.10

As this pie chart shows, DOS is still the most popular operating system, with Windows gaining ground. Macintosh is in third place, followed closely by OS/2. UNIX still trails, with only 2 percent of the market.

Source: Based on data from International Data Corp. (cited in "The CW Guide: Desktop Operating Systems," *Computerworld*, February 22, 1993).

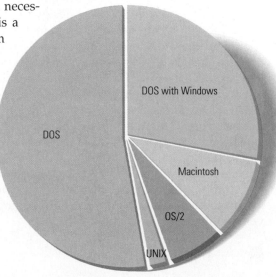

From Operating System to Empire

Microsoft Inc. and its founder Bill Gates are a legend of our times. Today, Gates is the richest man in America. Microsoft's $25 billion market value tops that of Ford, General Motors, 3M, Boeing, RJR Nabisco, General Mills, Anheuser-Busch, or Kodak. It is one of the most influential companies in the computer industry. Microsoft's decisions about which technologies to pursue (it is now focusing on multimedia, interactive TV, and wallet PCs, among others) will have a significant impact on the kind of life we can expect to have in the 1990s. And all this, the empire that Microsoft has become, is due to an operating system.

In the early 1980s, as IBM got ready to introduce its first personal computer, it knew it would need an operating system for the new machine. IBM turned first to Gary Kildall, a professor of computer science at the University of California at Berkeley. Kildall had previously developed an operating system called CP/M for machines powered by the Intel 8080 microprocessor. CP/M was the first operating system that could be easily modified to run on many different types of microcomputers. But negotiations between Kildall and IBM broke

Bill Gates.
Source: Doug Menuez/Reportage.

DOS

Short for Disk Operating System, **DOS** was the most common operating system for IBM and IBM-compatible microcomputers during the 1980s. Two basic versions of DOS are available: PC-DOS, used with IBM microcomputers, and MS-DOS, developed by Microsoft and used with IBM-compatible microcomputers. DOS was originally designed to work with computers that had a 16-bit microprocessor. New and enhanced versions of DOS continue to be introduced. For instance, DOS 6.0, the latest version, includes built-in data compression, a better memory management system, built-in virus protection, a new back-up program that makes it easier to back up the hard disk, and a better on-line help system. Nonetheless, the architectural limitations of DOS's original software design prevent it from taking full advantage of the power of the newer 32-bit microprocessors. DOS relies on a text-command-driven interface and cannot support extensive multitasking or other sophisticated operating systems functions. Nonetheless, it is estimated that around 60 million microcomputers still are based on DOS. Switching operating systems is not a trivial undertaking: it is likely to involve the purchase of new hardware, new versions of applications software, and the need to learn a new command system. In fact, a recent survey of computer professionals showed that it can cost an average of $4,000 per PC to move from DOS to Windows, OS/2, Macintosh, or UNIX.[1] As a result, it is probable that despite its limitations, DOS will be around for some time to come.

Although DOS cannot take advantage of the power provided by 32-bit microprocessors, a number of new operating systems have begun to be developed that can.

down, so IBM turned to Bill Gates. Gates, then 25, had previously written a microcomputer version of the programming language BASIC with a friend and had founded Microsoft to market it. When IBM came knocking, Microsoft went out and purchased an operating system program from a small company called Seattle Computer Products, modified it slightly, renamed it MS-DOS, and licensed it to IBM for use in its personal computers.

The IBM PC soon became the standard in the microcomputer world. (There are an estimated 70 million IBM and IBM-compatible personal computers in U.S. homes and businesses.) And as a result, so did MS-DOS. It dominated the microcomputer operating system market and became a major cash cow for Microsoft. But Gates didn't rest on MS-DOS's laurels. Instead, he has parlayed that success into an empire. Microsoft now offers applications software for just about every category of software, markets the leading graphical user interface (called Windows), and overall ranks first in software. Small wonder that others would like to duplicate its success.

But as you'll read in this section, further challenges await Microsoft as it seeks to create a new operating system to replace the now aging MS-DOS. Many believe that the computer industry has changed so much in the last ten years that it will be impossible for any one company to dominate the operating system market in the 1990s as Microsoft did in the 1980s. Whether a new standard will emerge from the proliferation of technologies available is anybody's guess.

Source: Based on Deutschman, Alan, "Bill Gates' Next Challenge," *Fortune,* December 28, 1992.

Critical Thinking Questions

1   Why do you think MS-DOS was able to achieve such dominance in the microcomputer operating system market? Do you think Microsoft's new operating system, Windows NT, will be able to do the same? Why or why not?

2   Why do you think Microsoft is such a force in the computer industry today?

OS/2

One of the new operating systems designed to work with 32-bit microprocessors is IBM's OS/2. Used primarily on IBM's PS/2 and other IBM-compatible microcomputers, OS/2 Version 2.0 (and later versions) not only runs applications programs written for OS/2 but those written for DOS and Windows systems as well. OS/2 features an easy-to-use GUI called the Workplace Shell that has received praise for its consistency across different operations (see photo). Like operating systems for larger computers, OS/2 supports multitasking, allowing users to operate several different applications concurrently. Other sophisticated functions include virtual storage; protection between applications so that applications and data cannot write over other applications and data; and monitoring services such as systems dumps, error logging, and trace utilities to isolate and report software problems. Version 2.1 added multimedia capabilities, enhanced graphics ability, and pen computing compatibility to the package.

To take full advantage of the features OS/2 offers, a fast 386 or 486 microprocessor, 8 megabytes of RAM, and an 80- to 100-megabyte hard drive are suggested. A streamlined "lite" version, introduced in 1993, makes do with 4 megabytes of RAM and a 60 megabyte hard drive. Because many preexisting microcomputers used by individuals for personal use are not up to these requirements, industry analysts believe that OS/2 is likely to find more acceptance in the business environment, particularly those downsizing from mainframe computers.

OS/2 allows the user to run most DOS, Windows, and OS/2 applications side by side.

Source: Courtesy of IBM Corporation.

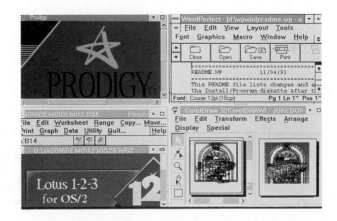

Windows and Windows NT

Windows 3.1 (and later versions) is the dominant GUI for personal computers with more than 10 million copies sold in the last two years. Windows, as you learned, is technically not an operating system; rather, it is a GUI shell that sits on top of an existing DOS operating system and acts as an interface between DOS and the user (see photo). However, Windows has certain functions that take it beyond merely being a GUI. For example, Windows adds some multitasking capabilities and makes it easier to move information from one application program to another. Recommended standards for an entry-level Windows system include a 386 or 486 microprocessor, 4 to 8MB of RAM, and a hard drive with at least 80MB of storage space.

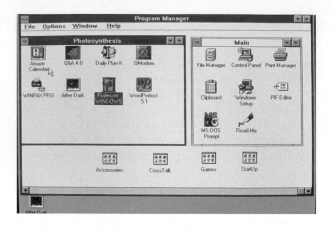

Microsoft's Windows is the leading GUI.

Source: Courtesy of Quarterdeck Office Systems.

Windows NT picks up where Windows leaves off. Windows NT, unlike Windows, is a complete operating system that is designed to replace DOS in its entirety. Like OS/2, it is designed to take advantage of the capabilities offered by 32-bit microprocessors. Windows NT can be used with Intel's 486 and Pentium chips as well as Digital's Alpha AXP and Mips' R3000 and R4000 RISC chips and can run applications programs designed for DOS, DOS running with a Windows shell, and OS/2. Windows NT features the ability to support multiprocessing with multiple CPUs as well as the more standard multitasking features. In addition, Windows NT offers a centralized security system for virtually all systems resources. Like OS/2, Windows NT is aimed primarily at the business market, particularly as an operating system for high-performance workstations and network servers. It requires a fast and powerful microprocessor, at least 12–16MB of RAM, and a large hard drive.

System 7

Apple Computer Corporation has been a leader in developing operating systems with graphical user interfaces since the early 1980s. The latest version of Apple's operating system for its Macintosh microcomputers is called **System 7.** Like OS/2 and Windows NT, System 7 is designed to exploit the capabilities of a 32-bit microprocessor, and like those operating systems, works best on systems that have several megabytes of RAM.

System 7's claim to fame is a GUI against which all others are measured (see photo). In addition to its GUI, System 7 supports powerful graphics capabilities with greatly expanded use of color, better interapplication communication (when data in one file is changed, changes are automatically made to

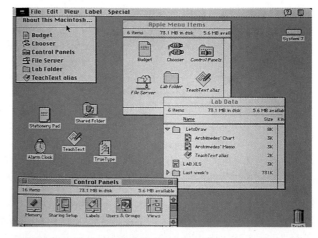

The Mac System 7 GUI is the one against which all others are measured.

Source: Courtesy of Apple Computer Corporation.

other documents in which you previously copied that data), virtual storage, peer-to-peer file sharing, multitasking, and scalable font technology. And with the benefit of an extension called Quicktime, System 7 provides multimedia capabilities that allow Macintosh users to integrate video, sound, and animation with conventional text and graphics. System 7 also addresses global markets with a new feature that provides system-level support for Asian languages using large character sets. In the future, Apple plans to offer additional "snap-on" extensions to System 7 that will allow users to pick and choose among future upgrades to the system.

UNIX

As you have read, **UNIX** is a popular nonproprietary, portable operating system. UNIX was originally developed at AT&T's Bell Lab in 1969. Because Bell Lab was prohibited by federal regulation from entering the computer industry and making a profit on sales of UNIX, during the 1970s AT&T distributed it at low cost to colleges and universities, where it quickly became popular with scientists and academics. It also licensed UNIX to other companies, who developed their own versions for commercial use. With the deregulation of the telephone industry in the 1980s, AT&T was finally free to commercialize UNIX. Since then, UNIX has made increasing inroads into the business marketplace. And with the recent takeover by Novell (whose NetWare is the largest-selling LAN operating system) of AT&T's UNIX Systems Laboratory, UNIX is likely to become an even greater force, especially in the client/server arena.

a.

b.

(a) Many of the newer versions of UNIX, such as this system from Sun Microsystems, have added GUIs that make UNIX more user-friendly. (b) Without a GUI, UNIX screens sometimes look like this.

Sources: Courtesy of Sun Microsystems; Frederik Bodin/Offshoot.

The rise in popularity of UNIX is driven by several factors. First, the operating system can be used on a variety of makes of computers, allowing users to choose the equipment they want. Unlike many proprietary operating systems that are limited to a single model of computer, UNIX allows applications programs to work across the full range of platforms—from microcomputers to supercomputers—and across manufacturers' lines. In a world where open systems are becoming more and more important to users who are seeking to free themselves from dependence on proprietary platforms, many feel UNIX is the answer.

Second, UNIX has many of the attributes of the most sophisticated operating systems and makes them available to users of both small and large computer systems at an attractive cost. UNIX supports multitasking, multiuser processing, and networking. UNIX is the primary operating system for systems that use the new RISC-based microprocessors. Finally, GUIs like Open Systems Foundation's Motif and Sun Microsytems' Open Look are available to mask the complexities of UNIX (see photos).

However, UNIX is not without certain disadvantages. UNIX lacks many of the systems management tools for performance monitoring, tuning, storage management, tape management, capacity planning, and so on, that are commonly found in operating systems of large computer systems. As a result, companies generally do not choose UNIX for critical transaction processing and large database support where a systems failure would have catastrophic results. UNIX systems are also often criticized for their lax security systems that allow systems safeguards to be easily circumvented. Finally, the legacy of its early days as an AT&T "give-away" has led to the development of many different versions of UNIX. (UNIX Systems Laboratories' UNIX

System V, Sun Microsystems' Solaris, and Santa Cruz Operations' SCO version are the leaders of the pack.) This has created a certain amount of market fragmentation and lack of common standards although most do not find this an insurmountable problem. As Peter Bauer, director of Information Systems at the Marshfield Clinic in Wisconsin, explains, "While not all UNIX systems are identical, adapting to different versions is like adapting to differences in the way English is spoken is South Carolina versus Ohio. With a proprietary system, it's like the language difference between Czechoslovakia and Japan."[2]

Now that UNIX has attracted the attention of the business world, software developers that support UNIX are beginning to offer newer versions that retain the good aspects of the system while eliminating some of the problems. As a result, the market for UNIX operating systems is expected to grow dramatically during the 1990s.

Trends for the 1990s: Object-Oriented Operating Systems

Object-oriented programming (OOP), a topic we will explore in more depth in Chapter 9, lets programmers think in terms that more closely resemble the real world. Instead of having to treat data and procedures as separate components, and having to write a separate programming operation every time someone wants to take an action on a particular piece of data, OOP lets programmers create "objects" that combine both the data and instructions for acting on that data into a single package. These objects form modular building blocks that can be reused and plugged together in different combinations depending on the user's needs. Although object-oriented programming is still somewhat controversial (many still believe that OOP has not lived up to expectations and is overrated), it is beginning to make its presence felt on operating systems software and is likely to continue to do so. For instance, when Apple co-founder Steven Jobs set out to create a new leading-edge computer, he developed an object-oriented, UNIX-based operating system for the machine. Called NextStep, the operating system has won praise for its ease of use, functionality, and the environment it provides (see photo). In fact, NextStep has proven to be more successful than the machine it was originally designed to operate: Next has left the computer hardware business to focus exclusively on NextStep. Microsoft's Windows NT also employs object-based design although it is not a "true" object-oriented operating system. And IBM and Apple have jumped on the bandwagon as well with a joint venture called Taligent. Taligent's object-oriented operating system, currently code-named "Pink," is expected to be available in late 1994 or 1995.

NextStep is a UNIX-based object-oriented operating system that features an easy-to-use GUI.

Source: Courtesy of Next Computer.

Other Kinds of Systems Software

Although the operating system is certainly the most important form of systems software used in a computer system, several other types of systems software deserve mention.

Language Translators

As you learned in Chapter 3, to convey information to a computer in a way that can be understood by the computer, the information must be expressed in binary digits. The first computer programs were written in *machine language*—long strings of binary digits. Writing in machine language was a very difficult and time-consuming task. Eventually, researchers developed new ways to create software, first using symbols and alphabetic abbreviations in place of 0s and 1s (*assembly language*) and, later, using English-like statements (*high-level language*). These developments were made possible by systems programs called **language translators** that translate programs written in symbolic and high-level languages into machine language. There are three basic kinds of language translators: compilers, assemblers, and interpreters.

Compilers translate entire programs written in a high-level language (also referred to as the *source module*, *source program*, or *source code*) into machine language (sometimes also referred to as *object code*) before any instructions are executed. The machine language version (referred to as the *object module*) can be saved on disk so that the program need not be recompiled the next time it is run. Before the CPU actually executes the translated instructions, another systems program called a **linkage editor** binds together portions of the code with other prewritten "subprograms" held in object code form in a "systems library." These prewritten subprograms cover certain standard operations, which ease the burden of the programmer writing the applications program. Instead of having to write out detailed instructions for each standard operation, the programmer merely needs to include an instruction telling the linkage editor to fetch it from the systems library. These subprograms joined together with the object code create the *load module*, which is what is actually executed by the CPU. Figure 7.11 illustrates this process. Like the object module, the load module can be saved on disk for later use.

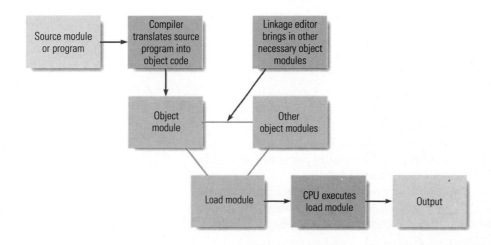

Figure 7.11
How a Compiler Works
Compilers translate programs written in high-level languages into a form that can be processed by the CPU.

When the Chips Are Down, Utility Programs Help Caesars Stay Up

Just like any other business, casinos rely on information systems to provide their customers with services. And just like any other business, when conditions change, a casino's information system must be up to the challenge.

Caesars Atlantic City has a 60,000-square-foot casino, 11 restaurants, 3 lounges, and 673 rooms. Its data center features an IBM Model 3090 mainframe computer. When Caesars first opened in 1979, New Jersey limited the hours during which a casino could offer gambling. Caesars' information system was designed with this in mind. Many of the applications developed for the system utilized batch processing (data is accumulated, stored, and processed at a later time in "batches") and presumed the availability of a nightly window of time when the system would not need to be otherwise available to customers.

But when New Jersey authorized 24-hour gambling on weekends and holidays in 1991, the system that had taken Caesars comfortably through the 1980s was suddenly no longer adequate.

There was no way for Caesars to eliminate batch applications altogether. But they could try to eliminate wasted time rerunning failed batch programs. To do this, they turned to Sys-

Information technology helps keep Caesars going around the clock.
Source: Zigy Kaluzny/Tony Stone Worldwide.

Data International, a New York software company that had developed Quickstart, a checkpoint restartability utility program.

There is a different compiler for each type of high-level language that exists and each type of computer on which the language may be used. **Assemblers**, a specialized version of compilers, work just with programs written in assembly language.

In contrast to compilers and assemblers, **interpreters** translate source code into machine language one line at a time, executing each translated statement before proceeding to the next. They do not create an object module. Interpreters are easier to use, enable program errors to be discovered more quickly, and require less storage space, but in many ways they are less efficient than compilers. It usually takes much more time to execute a program using an interpreter. In addition, because interpreters do not produce an object module that can be saved, they must retranslate the entire program every time it is run.

Utility Programs

Another important form of systems software is utility programs. **Utility programs** perform routine tasks, such as formatting disks, copying files from disk to tape, sorting files, and editing files, as well as other important "housekeeping" functions. Many operating systems have utility programs built directly into the operating system itself. Other utility programs are sold separately as software packages that the user must install.

Utility programs are generally stored in secondary storage. Some types are loaded automatically into primary storage when the computer is turned on. (In the DOS world, these are sometimes referred to as TSRs, terminate-

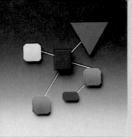

Without a utility program like Quickstart, batch application programs would be like songs that can be restarted or rerun only from the beginning. Imagine that the old favorite "A Hundred Bottles of Beer on the Wall" is in fact a batch application program. The song is progressing well until disaster strikes on the 78th chorus. With only 22 bottles of beer left on the wall, one of the singers hiccups and the song stops. With the Quickstart utility program in place, the singers merely need to back up to the last chorus before the disruption began and then continue; without it, there would be no choice but to start all over again.

The ability to restart batch programs from a convenient checkpoint instead of rerunning them from the beginning is critical to keeping a system running smoothly. Not only does the utility help Caesars manage applications programs that run into problems, but it also allows them to manage long-running batch jobs more efficiently. Caesars can use the utility program to deliberately terminate large, long-running batch programs and then restart them later from a convenient checkpoint when the demands on the system are lower.

Caesars' customers are seeing the benefits in a number of ways. For instance, before Quickstart was installed, the Casino Credit System had to shut down for several hours every night. If a customer needed a marker (a line of credit), the request would have to be processed manually, which takes much longer. Now with Quickstart in place, the Casino Credit System is available around-the-clock. And if New Jersey decides to permit 24-hour gambling every day of the week, Quickstart will help Caesars' information systems step up to the challenge.

Source: Based on Kador, John, "Restartability Helps Caesars Stay Up," *Enterprise Systems Journal,* December 1991.

Critical Thinking Questions

1   The Casino Credit System is one service that an information system helps make possible at Caesars. Since Caesars also includes restaurants and hotel facilities, what other services might their information systems need to support?

2   What kind of operating system do you think Caesars might be using? What kinds of features do you imagine it might have?

and-stay-resident utilities; in the Mac world, they are referred to as INITs, initializing utilities.) Other utility programs require the user to issue a command.

Although utility programs are sometimes thought of as add-ons, in many organizations, they play a crucial role in creating more efficient information systems. The story "When the Chips Are Down, Utility Programs Help Caesars Stay Up" gives you one example.

A number of different kinds of utility programs are available. In addition to disk utility routines already built into most operating systems, many users add disk toolkits, data compression utilities, backup utility programs, virus protectors, and screen savers to their systems. Some popular examples of these types of utilities include:

- Symantec's Norton Utilities, which helps users recover lost data and increases the speed and performance of their hard drives, and Norton Desktop for Windows, which makes Windows even easier to use.

- Stac Electronics' Stacker, which compresses data files to increase hard disk storage capacity.

- Fifth Generation Systems' Fastback Plus, which provides easy backup of files.

- Central Point's Anti-Virus, which protects a system from damage caused by computer viruses.

▶ Berkeley Systems' After Dark, which allows the user to install a screen saver that prevents monitors from burning a faint image onto the computer's screen if it is left too long in one position. The screen saver features a series of offbeat collages that rotate across the screen while it is not being used (see photo).

Other forms of utility programs include text editors, device drivers, and spooling programs. Text editors help users edit text in files that are not part of a word processing document. Device drivers enable applications software to work with different types of hardware devices. Spooling programs manage output going to printers, freeing up the CPU and primary storage to move on to other work while the output is printed.

Berkeley Systems' utility program After Dark prevents screen "burn-in" with whimsical displays like this one.

Source: Courtesy of Berkley Systems, Inc.

Summary

An Introduction to Software

▶ There are two basic types of software. Systems software controls and coordinates the operation of various types of equipment in a computer system. Applications software allows you to apply a computer to solve a specific problem or perform a specific task.

Operating Systems

▶ The operating system is system software that manages and controls the basic activities of the computer.

▶ Operating systems were developed to help the computer supervise its own operations and carry on basic actitivies without the need for human intervention.

▶ The faster and more powerful computer hardware is the more an operating system can do. The more an operating system can do the more useful it makes a computer for its users.

▶ The basic functions of the operating system include allocating and assigning system resources, scheduling the operations that the computer needs to perform, and monitoring system activities.

▶ A program within the operating system, called the supervisor, helps determine which of the system's resources are needed for the job and to allocate and assign those resources. The command language translator helps decipher command language instructions and assign the necessary resources.

▶ Multiprogramming, multitasking, multiprocessing, time-sharing, and virtual storage are techniques that enable a computer system to work on more than one job at the same time.

▶ Multiprogramming allows multiple programs to be executed concurrently through a sharing of the computer's resources. Multitasking provides multiprogramming capabilities to a single-user operating system.

▶ Multiprocessing uses two or more CPUs linked together to execute instructions.

▶ Time-sharing enables many users to share computer resources at the same time by rotating short slices of CPU processing time among all users.

▶ Virtual storage expands the limits of primary storage space by enabling multiple users to utilize the same space by splitting programs into segments or pages, some of which can be stored in secondary storage until needed.

▶ Operating systems also help users monitor system performance and play a role in providing system security.

Operating Environments and Graphical User Interfaces

▶ A graphical user interface (GUI) allows a user to communicate with the operating system by using a computer mouse to click on icons that represent commands and operations. GUIs are used to create an operating environment that is easier for the novice computer user to use and understand. Apple's computers are renowned for their GUIs. Windows is the leading GUI for IBM-compatible computers.

Operating Systems for Microcomputers: A Hot Battleground

▶ Proprietary operating systems work only with certain types of computers. Portable operating systems can run on many different kinds of computers.

▶ The leading operating system for microcomputers during the 1980s and early 1990s was DOS. DOS works with 16-bit microprocessors and is limited by the amount of primary storage such microprocessors can address.

▶ New operating systems designed to take advantage of the capabilities of 32-bit microprocessors include OS/2 and Windows NT. They will allow users to multitask and support sophisticated GUIs.

▶ UNIX is a popular nonproprietary, portable operating system. UNIX provides multitasking, multiuser processing, and networking capabilities.

▶ Object-oriented operating systems may be an important trend for the 1990s.

Other Kinds of Systems Software

▶ Language translators are systems software that translate programs written in symbolic and high-level programming into machine language that can be processed by the CPU. Compilers translate the entire program into machine language before any instructions are executed. Assemblers, a specialized version of compilers, work just with programs written in assembly language. Interpreters translate a program one line at a time and execute each translated statement before proceeding to the next.

▶ Utility programs are systems software that perform routine tasks, such as formatting disks, copying files, sorting files, and editing files as well as other important "housekeeping" functions.

Key Terms

systems software
applications software
operating system
supervisor
command language translator
multiprogramming
multitasking
multiprocessing
time-sharing
time slice
virtual storage
segment method
page method
graphical user interface (GUI)
shell

proprietary operating system
portable operating system
DOS
OS/2
Windows
Windows NT
System 7
UNIX
language translators
compilers
linkage editor
assemblers
interpreters
utility programs

Review Questions

1 What roles do systems software and applications software play in a computer system?

2 Describe the interrelationship among hardware, systems software, applications software, and the user.

3 Why were operating systems developed?

4 Describe the primary tasks that operating systems perform.

5 What role does the supervisor play in an operating system?

6 How do multiprogramming, multitasking, and multiprocessing differ?

7 How does virtual storage maximize primary storage space?

8 Describe some basic characteristics of a GUI.

9 What is the difference between a proprietary operating system and a portable operating system?

10 Compare MS-DOS, OS/2, Windows, Windows NT, System 7, and UNIX.

11 How does a compiler differ from an interpreter?

12 What is a utility program?

Problem-Solving and Skill-Building Exercises

1 Which microcomputer operating system do you think will be the leader in 1996: DOS, Windows NT, OS/2, UNIX, or something else? What factors do you think will be important in determining the success of an operating system in the 1990s? Prepare an oral presentation defending your choice.

2 You are a consultant to a company looking to make the shift from a DOS environment to a Windows environment. Prepare a short report highlighting the issues that management should consider before making the switch.

3 Hundreds of different utility programs are available for microcomputers today. Choose one, and write a product review. (Trade publications and sales literature are likely to be your best sources of information.) Discuss what function the program performs, any specific advantages or disadvantages you discover, and whether it appears to be worth the price charged. Then compare reviews with your classmates; take a class vote ranking the products from most useful/best value to least useful/worst value.

Choosing an Operating System

In previous chapters, we've discussed some of the things you need to consider when choosing a computer and peripheral equipment. Now let's talk about choosing the most appropriate operating system for your needs.

The first question to consider is the applications software that the operating system supports and the kind of work you expect to be doing. Right now, applications software that works with DOS is the most commonplace, with Windows applications quickly closing the gap. OS/2 and UNIX trail these two in the number of applications programs available, but their numbers are increasing. Apple's System 7 excels in supporting graphics applications software. If you have your heart set on using a particular type of applications software, make sure that a version exists that works with the operating system you're considering.

The next question to consider is the kind of computer hardware that the operating system is associated with. For instance, if you purchase an Apple Macintosh, you automatically get its operating system, System 7; you do not have a choice in the matter. IBM and IBM-compatible computers that use a 286 or slower microprocessor and have less than 4MB of RAM will pretty much be limited to DOS. However, if you choose a machine that has a 386 or faster chip and at least 4MB of RAM, you will have enough power and memory for Windows. With 8MB or more of RAM, your choices widen even further, to include OS/2, Windows NT, and UNIX. But remember that added CPU power and memory will cost you extra dollars, so consider carefully whether you really need the added functionality that the 32-bit operating systems offer.

Another consideration is the system's ease of use. How easy is the system to learn and use? If you already know DOS and choose another system, count on spending some time relearning once-familiar commands. On the other hand, if you're new to the computer world, a friendlier GUI, such as Apple's System 7 may be your best bet.

Next, look at the expected reliability of the platform that you are considering. Early versions of software may not include all promised features, nor have all the bugs been ironed out. For instance, early versions of Windows were famous for their "Unrecoverable Application Errors," which would crash your program on a seemingly random basis. Likewise, Version 1.0 of OS/2 did not fulfill user expectations. Right now, Windows NT is the new kid on the block and it may be worthwhile to wait until it has proven itself.

Finally, consider the portability of the skills you acquire. If you are now a student, but expect to be working closely with computers on the job, keep in mind that most businesses still use IBM and IBM-compatible microcomputers although Macintosh is beginning to make some inroads into the business world. Time spent becoming familiar with one or more of the operating systems used by these computers (Windows, OS/2, and increasingly, UNIX) may give you a head start when you get to your workplace.

Notes

1   "The CW Guide: Desktop Operating Systems," *Computerworld*, February 22, 1993.

2   **Payne, Sheila**, "The UNIX System: Changing from Blue Jeans to Suits," *Enterprise Systems Journal*, June 1992.

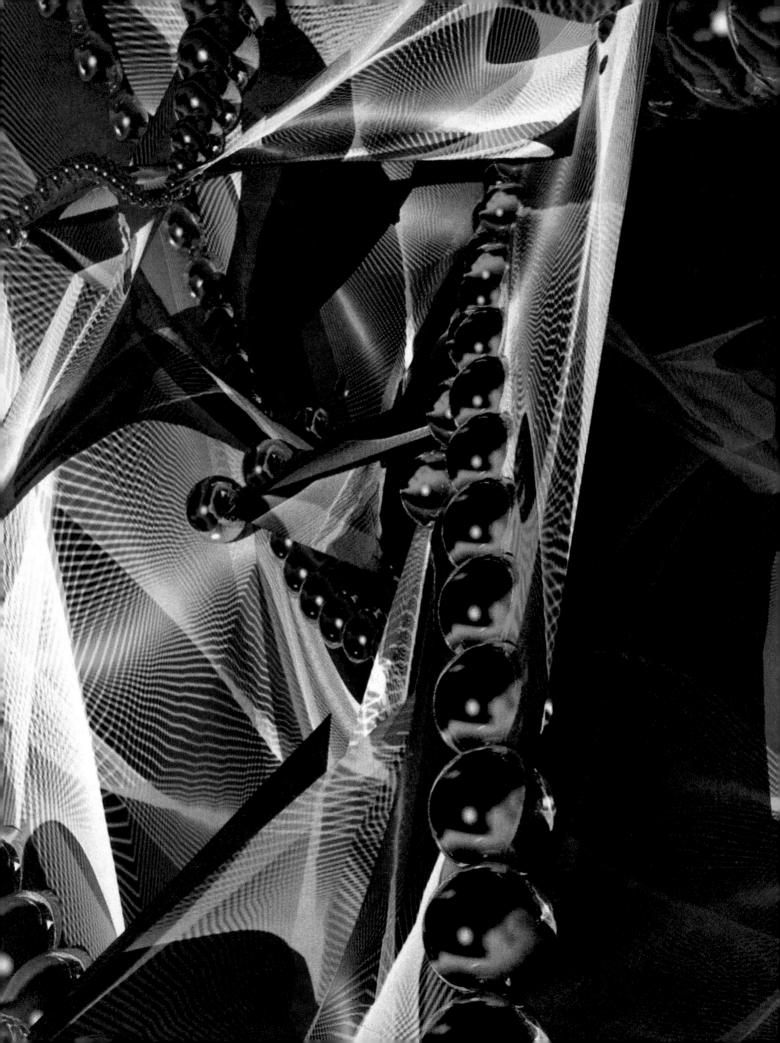

three

Creating Solutions with Information Technologies

Quiet Storm
Melvin Prueitt, Los Alamos
National Laboratories

Chapter 8 contains:

After completing this chapter, you will:

▶ Understand the technological, organizational, and people issues involved in building information systems.

▶ Be able to critically analyze problems in business and other pursuits.

▶ Know the major stages in building a system and be able to effectively participate in building an information system.

Critical Thinking and Problem Solving: Building Information Systems

What's Wrong at Macy's?

I n 1858, R. H. Macy Company became America's first department store—a large open-floor building with a wide variety of goods for sale. From its "home" store at 34th and Broadway in New York City, Macy's expanded to become one of America's biggest department store chains, with over 114 locations.

In the financial frenzy of the 1980s, Macy's was bought by its management and transformed into a privately held company. To buy the company and pay for new acquisitions like I. Magnin and the Bullock's retail chain, management took on a huge amount of debt in the form of "junk" bonds, paying very high interest rates, to be repaid from Macy's earnings.

It didn't work. Macy's began losing money in the late 1980s. In January 1991, it was forced to file for bankruptcy when banks and bondholders demanded their money and suppliers refused to deliver goods for fear they would not be paid. In 1991, its 134th year, Macy's managed to lose a

whopping $1.3 billion—the largest loss in retailing history. What went wrong at Macy's?

With management focused on financial affairs, Macy's failed to keep pace with changes in the retailing industry. Small, faster-moving, specialized stores like Benetton and The Gap began draining away younger customers. Other low-cost national retailers like Kmart and Wal–Mart drained away customers for standard goods like shirts, boots, and pants.

It wasn't just the tough new competition or the fast pace of change in retail clothing that hurt Macy's. Macy's inventory management system was out of date. In this system, a Macy's store product manager would call a national buyer requesting more goods. The buyer might take several days to get back to the requesting store. Then the buyer would poll other stores. If enough requests for a particular item were received, the buyer would order from the supplier. Eventually (perhaps several months later), the

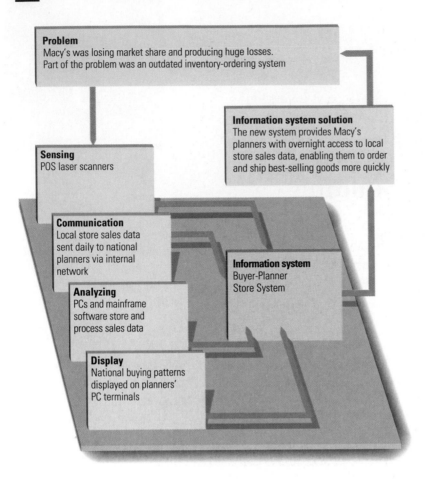

goods would arrive at the original requesting store. Frequently, store shelves would be empty of goods that sold fast and filled with slow-moving unpopular goods that would have to be discounted.

What's the solution to Macy's problems? Several were tried. Edward S. Finkelstein, the former chief executive officer, announced in late 1991 that he would increase television advertising by 25 percent to an unprecedented $150 million in 1992. Banks and Wall Street financiers questioned this solution, and Finkelstein was replaced shortly thereafter. Now, Macy's new chief executive officer, Myron E. Ullman III, has come up with a new five-year plan.

Key elements of the new plan are to reduce the advertising budget and cut operating expenses from 37 percent of sales to 32 percent, reduce the number of one-day sales, and focus attention on credit-card buyers. Macy's also plans to scale back on private labels (Macy's own label) and stock more name-brand goods.

But the most ambitious part of the five-year plan to save Macy's is a new computerized inventory management system. Called the Buyer-Planner-Store System, the system captures what is actually sold at the counter with a point-of-sale (POS) system. Checkout clerks use a handheld laser scanner to read bar codes attached to all items. A central computer stores this information and, at the end of each day, sends the data to 100 national planners (a new position created by the system) assigned to various product groups. The planners watch their computer terminals to see what is selling and where. Based on this information, the planners call the store managers to investigate what's behind the numbers and then call national buyers to tell them to ship specific items to specific stores. (For instance, in one store, the planners found that orange leisure shirts did not sell at all. Why? They discovered that local sanitation workers wore orange, and that as a result, orange was not considered a leisure color in this community. More navy shirts were shipped to the store, and they sold well.) The whole process now takes place in a few days.

Macy's New York City Store.
Source: 1986 Naoki Okamoto/Black Star.

Despite the new plan, some critics doubt whether Macy's will make it. It may take years to retrain employees and get new business procedures working. Some store managers and buyers are reportedly resisting the intrusion of national planners into areas they traditionally controlled. It may take years to convince the public that Macy's is an economical place to shop for up-to-date fashions. But Macy's doesn't have years to wait: on Wall Street, its junk bonds now sell for pennies on the dollar.

Sources: Based on Strom, Stephanie, "Changing the Mood at Macy's," *New York Times,* June 27, 1993; Zinn, Laura, "Prudence on 34th Street," *Business Week,* November 16, 1992; Strom, Stephanie, "A Key for a Macy's Comeback," *New York Times,* November 1, 1992.

The problems at Macy's are typical of many real-world problems: they have many facets and are very complex. Is the answer to Macy's problems just a new computer system and some new business procedures? Probably not, but obviously, the new management at Macy's believes that a good information system is one part of the overall solution.

8.1 Building Information Systems

Up to now, we have used our model of information systems to illustrate how organizations can use information technologies to develop solutions to a variety of problems. But we have not said very much at all about how this takes place, about how organizations actually build information systems. How do people in organizations know that an information system will solve the problem? How do they know what type of system to build and which information technologies to choose? In this chapter, we will answer these questions. Then, in Chapter 9, we will show you how programming is used to implement those systems and solutions.

Why Are Information Systems Built?

Information systems in a business or other organization are built for both *internal reasons* and *external reasons*. The most common internal reason for building a system is to *respond to some perceived problem inside an organization*. Managers and employees become aware that the organization is not performing as well as they expected or as well as competitors. But problems are not the only source of information systems. Often, systems are a response to *perceived opportunities*. Managers and employees in the course of doing business routinely discover areas where their firms could do better. Entrepreneurs—people who dream up and start new business ventures—commonly use information systems to help them take advantage of new business opportunities. Several of the stories in this chapter illustrate how information technologies are used to create new businesses or recreate old ones. When we use the term *problem solving* in this chapter and throughout the book, we mean taking an approach aimed not just at attacking problems in the traditional sense of the word but also at exploiting opportunities that may be available.

Sometimes, *new developments outside the organization* in the larger business and social environment cause organizations to build systems. For instance, the Toxic Waste and Substances Control Act of 1980 required firms working with toxic substances to keep information on worker exposure to toxic substances for a period of 30 years. Most firms responded by building an information system that keeps track of daily toxic substance exposure levels for each worker. Depending on the nature of the problem, information systems are just one of many possible solutions to problems and opportunities facing modern organizations. Several stories in this chapter illustrate how businesses and other organizations use information technology to respond to outside problems and opportunities.

Individuals buy personal computer equipment (and hence build their own information systems) for much the same reasons that organizations do. Individuals turn to personal computers as a way to solve problems (like preparing term papers on time) or to take advantage of opportunities (like tracking the stock market to profit from trading opportunities).

An Overview of Systems Analysis and Design

Go back to the diagram in the Macy's vignette. The information system solution shown in this diagram is the result of a long chain of events called systems analysis and design. *Systems analysis and design* is a structured kind of *problem solving*. Systems analysis and design refers to all the activities that go into producing an information technology solution to a business, scientific, or individual problem or opportunity. In a formal systems analysis and design conducted in large organizations, there are five phases or steps (see Figure 8.1). These five phases can be classified into two distinct kinds of activities: systems analysis and systems design.

Systems analysis (Phases 1 and 2) involves understanding and defining the nature of the business problem or opportunity that the new system will try to solve. Phase 1 entails a preliminary analysis of the situation, while Phase 2 involves a more detailed study of the existing system (both its faults and virtues), the needs of users in the organization who want a new system, and possible alternative solutions. Some of the potential solutions may involve information technology, whereas others may require changes in procedures, people, or the organization.

Systems design (Phases 3 to 5) is the process of actually designing, building, and implementing a new system. This requires making decisions about alternative designs, programming the solution, and making the new system

Phases	Activities	Outputs
Systems Analysis		
Phase 1: preliminary analysis (3 months)	*Critical thinking and problem definition.* Define the problem, establish overall objectives, scope, potential solutions, key issues, and actors	Preliminary plan
Phase 2: systems analysis (3 months)	*Problem understanding.* Specify problem; obtain differing perspectives; model existing system; establish system objectives and requirements	System requirements plan
Systems Design		
Phase 3: systems design (6 months)	*Decision making.* Examine alternative solutions; model new system; prototype; detailed design	Detailed system design
Phase 4: systems development (12 months)	*Building.* Purchase of equipment and services from outside vendors; programming, testing, file conversion, documentation	Workable system
Phase 5: implementation (3–6 months)	*Roll-out.* Selection of roll-outsites; training of employees; installing equipment; conversion of old files to new files; auditing; evaluation; develop longterm maintenance process	System installed and operational
Total time: 2–3 years		

work in real life. Frequently, this starts with a simple paper-and-pencil preliminary design of the solution followed by more detailed designs (Phase 3). Once the preliminary design is completed, it's time to start building the detailed design. Once the detailed design is completed, programming and creating the systems solution (the hardware, software, and other equipment) begins (Phase 4). After the system has been built, it needs to be implemented—actually put to work and tested in the field (Phase 5).

Most mistakes in building systems occur in the early analysis stage of problem definition. Many times, the problem or opportunity is incorrectly defined or poorly understood. To succeed in this stage, the systems analyst must engage in critical thinking, which we describe later in this chapter.

Figure 8.1
Problem Solving: Systems Analysis and Design

Different Kinds of Information Systems in Organizations

As we noted in Chapter 2, and will detail further in Part Five, there are a number of different types of information systems. Three basic types are transaction processing systems, management support systems, and knowledge work systems (see Figure 8.2). Systems within each of these three categories support the activities of the four functional divisions of a typical business: Production (Manufacturing or Operations), Sales (Marketing), Finance and Accounting, and Human Resources. The Information Systems (IS) division is usually a standalone division that supplies information technology and management services to the whole organization. For instance, the IS division works with Production to build systems that automate production and operations; with Finance to develop financial transaction control systems that track the flow of money in an organization; with Sales to develop marketing information systems that track sales; and with Human Resources to build payroll and personnel systems.

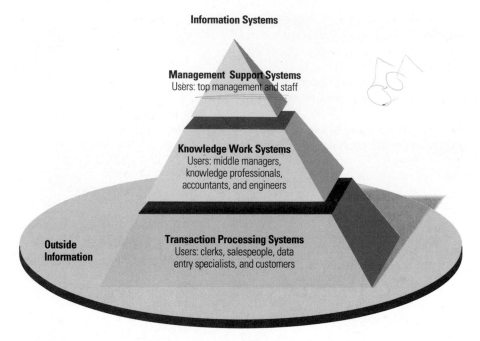

Information Systems

Management Support Systems
Users: top management and staff

Knowledge Work Systems
Users: middle managers, knowledge professionals, accountants, and engineers

Outside Information

Transaction Processing Systems
Users: clerks, salespeople, data entry specialists, and customers

Figure 8.2

An Organization-wide View of Information Systems

There are three overlapping kinds of information systems in organizations: Transaction Processing Systems, Knowledge Work Systems, and Management Support Systems. The Information Systems department serves the information technology needs of the other divisions, as well as the organization as a whole. Increasingly, though, divisions and end users build their own systems without assistance from the IS department.

Information systems come in all different sizes from very small projects built by one or more end users on a PC at a cost of perhaps a few thousand dollars, to medium-size projects involving as many as 20 full-time developers and costing up to a million dollars, to very large projects requiring hundreds of people and costing several million dollars.

Who Builds Information Systems?

Information systems in organizations are built by one or more of three groups: end users, professional systems analysts from the IS division, or outside vendors. In some cases, it is less expensive to "outsource" a project (have outside vendors build or provide it) than to use internal developers.

Figure 8.3 illustrates the team nature of building a system. Systems typically evolve through a very close interaction between **end users** (those who will actually use the completed system) and **systems analysts** (those who are primarily responsible for developing the system). Other

The Organization
Chief Executive Officer (CEO)

Senior Management

Sales   Information Systems Management
Chief Information Officer (CIO)   Finance

Production   Project Management   Human resources

Project Team

Project Manager

End Users ←→ Systems Analysts

Figure 8.3
The Systems Development Team

members of the team may be specialists like programmers, telecommunications experts, network specialists, and of course, project managers. The project team reports to the organization's chief information officer (CIO) and to the functional department management in other parts of the organization for which the system is being built.

Nontechnological Factors in Building Systems

So far we have depicted information systems as being composed primarily of information technologies that sense, communicate, analyze, and display information. Information systems are seen as a collection of technologies that take information from the environment as input, process the information, and produce output back to the environment.

However, although technology is important, it is just one component in building an information system (see Figure 8.4). Other factors include organization and people. To use technology wisely, you need a keen understanding of organizations and how they work as well as an understanding of how to motivate people to work effectively and creatively within an organization. All the technology in the world is no good to an organization unless the organization is set up to use it and unless the people within the organization can put the technology to good use. Let's discuss some of the organizational and people issues now, and later we will show you how they apply to a real-world system building effort.

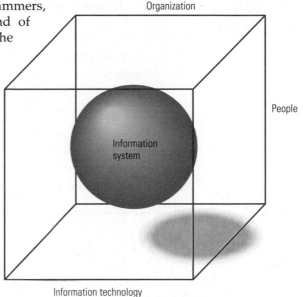

Organization

People

Information system

Information technology

Figure 8.4
Dimensions of Information Systems
Information systems involve more than just information technology. Organization and people are also critical ingredients.

Organizational Issues Every organization is based on an **organizational culture** composed of beliefs that everyone takes for granted. For example, a major cultural assumption of the American school system is that children must attend a school. Information technology potentially could radically threaten this cultural assumption: students in the future might learn at home and "come to school" electronically. If this were to happen, major changes in school culture might take place: teachers would not have physical classrooms, but electronic classrooms. The physical school building might be turned into a community culture center. The point is that when building information systems, you will find new ways to do the work of an organization, and this may threaten an existing organizational culture.

Every organization is made up of groups that compete with one another for power, money, and respect. This competition is called **organizational politics.** The players in this competition, and the nature of the competition itself, may be altered by information technology. For example, in the example of electronic school systems, the power of a school principal to "supervise" teachers would probably be weakened, and teachers might become more independent professionals like doctors and lawyers. Likewise, the role of a teachers' union might change as teachers move out of the physical school system into an "electronic school." The players in organizational politics may recognize these possibilities and may try to alter your system design so that it serves their own political ends. You must be aware of this when building systems.

All organizations develop bureaucratic **business procedures** or rules to guide the behavior of members through most situations. These bureaucratic rules and business procedures become refined, automatic, and precise over time. Information systems potentially threaten to upset these business procedures by introducing whole new ways of doing the task or business. For instance, school systems have developed very elaborate student and staff rules of conduct to guide behavior in class and in the building. Many of these rules would be irrelevant in electronic classrooms, and new rules of behavior would have to be developed—for instance, when and how to ask a question of a teacher who is giving an electronic lecture or how to address other students. When you build an information system, you will often have to develop new procedures and rules of behavior. Indeed, the most important efficiencies often come from simplifying and redesigning business procedures and not from the technology per se.

People Issues   Building information systems inevitably requires that people change their behavior to support the new system and the new ways of doing business that are a part of all new systems. *The systems analyst is an agent of change—a person whose job it is to change organizations and personal behavior.* There are several key factors to being a successful change agent.

One key success factor is *involvement*. To change the behavior of people who will use a new system, it helps to involve them in the process of building the system. Many studies have shown that people will accept change more readily if they participate in the design, creation, and implementation of the change. In fact, the people who are presently doing the work most often are the ones who really understand how things get done and should get done. They can be valuable sources of new ideas and solutions to problems. Many companies are seeking to exploit this untapped resource by encouraging ordinary employees to contribute and implement new ideas. In the story "USAir Looks for Ideas That Fly" we look at how one company is getting its employees more involved.

Although involvement motivates people to change, *training* is often required to make it possible for them to change. You cannot ask people to perform tasks without providing the tools and training. In systems projects, you can count on spending 15 percent of your budget on user training and involvement. If your system uses personal computers, though the hardware and software may cost $4,000 per machine, the training will add another $1,000 per employee in the typical organization, or 25 percent of the cost of the hardware and software.

A third critically important people factor is the *ergonomics* (or physical relationship) between the technology and the employee. You cannot expect trained, motivated employees to perform tasks that are physically harmful. As we discussed in Chapter 5, interacting with computers can impose physical hazards: eye strain; arm, hand, and back strain; and excessive radiation from poorly designed terminals. You must consider ergonomics when designing information systems.

You should also be aware of any potential *legal* or *regulatory issues* surrounding your information system designs. Legal contracts may exist between the organization and employees that prohibit certain kinds of job changes. There may be government regulations to consider. You will need to consider these legal and regulatory issues when designing the system.

Training employees to use a new information system is an important part of building a successful information system.

Source: Jon Feingersh.

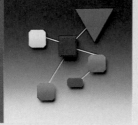

USAir Looks for Ideas That Fly

On a Saturday morning, two busloads of USAir employees and spouses gathered in a 3-acre warehouse outside St. Louis. At the sound of a gun, they started a 60-second run through the warehouse to grab as much merchandise as they could in a cart. How come? These USAir employees were grand prize winners in a program to encourage employees to come up with new ideas that would make money (or cut costs) for USAir.

In 1992, USAir initiated a program called the IdeaSystem, created by Maritz Inc., a St. Louis consulting firm. The program sought to capture the knowledge, creativity, and experience of employees by encouraging them to join teams that would come up with cost-saving or revenue-enhancing ideas. After a successful implementation, employees are rewarded with merchandise credits based on the value of their ideas. Teams with the top ideas in total dollar value earn a trip to the merchandise warehouse and the chance to keep as much as they can grab in 60 seconds.

The results? In one year, 3,000 Idea Teams formed and generated 1,386 approved ideas for savings and additional revenue of more than $80 million. The ideas ranged from small to large, commonsensical to breakthrough. Here are some examples: commonsensical—install motion-detection switches in a sporadically used warehouse, saving $8,000 a year on lighting, heating, security; breakthrough—replace manual procedure with a switch on certain aircraft cockpit windows to activate a window sensor, saving $633,000 a year.

Source: Based on Schofield, Seth, "Ideas That Fly," USAir Magazine, January 1993.

One of USAir's 3,000 Idea Teams.

Source: Courtesy of USAir, Inc.

Critical Thinking Questions

1   What kinds of skills would be needed to come up with and implement a new idea at USAIr?

2   What other positive effects do you think this program might have on USAir employees?

3   Can the process of creating new ideas go on forever? Why or why not?

Becoming a Systems Analyst

As the previous sections have suggested, the systems analyst plays a central and often fascinating role in building an information system. For the rest of the chapter, we invite you to try on the role of systems analyst for an insider's view of the systems building process. First, let's take a look at the three most important activities that a systems analyst engages in and the skills those activities require.

▶   *Communication skills.* A large part of the job is working with nontechnical end users (ordinary employees and managers) to help them turn their good business ideas into a practical, working information system. The ability to listen to end users and understand their sense of the business problem or opportunity is perhaps the most important skill required for the job. You also need to act as a liaison between nontechnical end users and managers on the one hand and technical people on the other; you must speak the language of both groups. A good systems analyst is sensitive to the concerns of managers, programmers, end users, and employees. You must also be able to communicate the information you gather through written reports and oral presentations.

A developer proposes to build four high-rise buildings in your already overcrowded neighborhood. What will the impact be on you and your family? How will traffic patterns change, where will children play, how will your views change, and what will happen to the sunlight you usually enjoy in the morning and late afternoon?

Questions like these arise in all major real estate development proposals in both cities and suburbs. Usually they are fought over by developers, government officials, citizens, and professional groups. Until recently, many of the questions could not be answered because of an insufficient knowledge base. This is changing in some locations.

The New School for Social Research, a college in New York City, has developed the Environmental Simulation Center to build and operate a computerized model of development in the city. Backed by the city's Real Estate Board, the American Institute of Architects, several citizen-based planning groups, and major developers like Donald Trump, the "Sim Center" has developed models of major development areas like the Grand Central Station area, Second Avenue, and the Upper West Side, where Donald Trump is proposing a huge development project involving a 20-block strip of former railroad yards.

The computer simulation models are built from layers of data beginning with geographic coordinates, the width and height of sidewalks and streets, and the "footprints" of buildings, including their shape, height, and setbacks from the street. With these data, the simulation models are most valuable for understanding the overall neighborhood impact of a development project.

For instance, the simulations can show the impact of changing the bulk and shape of buildings from high-rise, pencil-thin structures to low-rise, squat buildings; the models can show how view corridors change (the vistas in a neighborhood) and how sun and shadows are changed by different designs. With a computerized model, groups of viewers can take a digital walk through a neighborhood before the concrete is poured.

In the Riverside South project sponsored by Donald Trump, the Sim Center produced 45 studies (separate simulations) showing how sun and shadow patterns would change in the area of development at five times of day on three days of the year under three different development scenarios. The scenarios tested were no development, the Riverside South project is developed and the current West Side elevated highway remains, and the project is built but the highway is moved inland to create a waterfront park (see photos).

The biggest impact of the Sim Center will be to help produce consensus among conflicting groups with a healthy dose

---

▶ *Management skills.* There are a large number of stakeholders in building systems. A systems analyst must be able to manage schedules, conflicts, resources, and perceptions throughout the process. Project managers can often assist you in this task, but you still need to be aware of management concerns like producing revenues, cutting costs, and achieving a more effective business. You also need to motivate people and manage the change process—the switch from old ways of doing business to new ways.

▶ *Design skills.* To design information systems, you need to know what contemporary information technology can do, how much it costs, and what is required to use it effectively. You have to think critically and creatively (see the next section on critical thinking), suggesting new ways of doing business. You do not need to be a programmer, but you should have some programming background so that you can communicate with programmers. (Chapter 9 outlines the programming basics you'd need to know.)

Systems analysis and design is a team effort. Information systems can sometimes act as a useful tool for bringing together knowledge, organizations, and people in the search for solutions. The Environmental Simulation Center described in the story "Simulations of Neighborhood Development" provides a platform where communitywide systems analysis and design can be performed in the search for a higher-quality urban environment.

Although you don't have to be a computer programmer to be a systems analyst, a knowledge of basic programming techniques and tools will prove quite useful.

Source: Superstock.

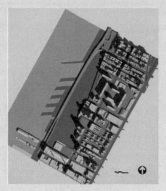

a. New York's Upper West Side. Scenario 1: no development.

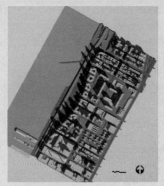

b. Scenario 2: Riverside South developed, West Side Highway remains.

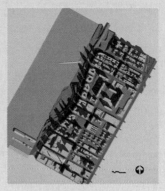

c. Scenario 3: Riverside South developed, West Side Highway moved to create waterfront park.

Source: Courtesy of Environmental Simulation Center/New School for Social Research.

of knowledge and insight. For the first time, conflicting groups are able to rationally discuss their differences and reduce if not eliminate conflict over development. Projects that have decidedly negative impacts on neighborhoods are withdrawn by developers, whereas projects with little negative impact cannot be easily dismissed.

Source: Based on Dunlap, David, "Impact of Zoning Is Pretested on Computers," *New York Times*, June 14, 1992.

Critical Thinking Questions

1 Do you think the Simulation Center will always produce consensus on development projects?

2 What kinds of disputes is the Simulation Center good at handling, and what kinds would not be resolved by the Center?

3 In what ways does the Simulation Center provide a platform for community-based systems analysis and design?

8.2 Critical Thinking

The first step in systems analysis is to engage in a period of critical thinking. Figure 8.5a illustrates the critical thinking process. The purpose of critical thinking is to define the issue confronting you and creatively think up some preliminary solutions. If you identify the problem incorrectly, you will inevitably fail to solve the real problem. In fact, when information systems fail, it is usually not the technology at fault but instead the early analysis; that is, the problem was poorly or mistakenly understood. Sometimes, an entire business can perish because of faulty problem identification.

Problems and opportunities do not present themselves objectively. In fact, people usually disagree with one another about what the problem or opportunity is. There are many solutions available to any given problem depending on how the problem is defined. Choosing the right solution depends on defining the problem correctly. Unfortunately, correctly defining a problem often turns out to be much harder than most people realize. As you will see later, a broadly-based awareness of the environment that produced the problem will help you identify its true sources.

Figure 8.5a
The Critical Thinking Process
The critical thinking process involves setting a vision, identifying problems, and generating solutions. The process is inherently flexible—you may start at any one of the stages and move back and forth at will.

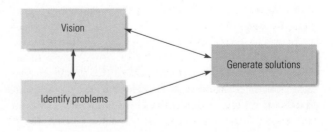

Ruth Owades created a minor revolution in the floral business in 1989 by starting a company called Calyx and Corolla. Calyx and Corolla creates a direct computer-based connection between the retail flower customer—you and me trying to meet a Mother's Day or Valentine's Day obligation—and the actual growers of flowers distributed across the country and the world.

Until 1989, the biggest innovations in the retail floral business were a 1950s' idea called FTD (Floral Telegraph Delivery) and the appearance of flowers in supermarkets sometime in the mid-1980s. FTD is a worldwide cooperative of 25,000 florists who take orders from local customers for delivery by member florists in other locations. Largely telephone based, FTD processed 21 million orders in 1990, shipping orders worth $700 million, and producing revenues of $49 million.

Though novel for its day, FTD changed little in the cut flower retail business. Here's how the business works. Thousands of small growers sell their produce to local distributors, who in turn sell the raw flowers to wholesalers in market areas. The wholesalers then sell the raw flowers to local florists, supermarkets, and other retailers. The industry is very lucrative: distributors mark up flowers they receive from growers by 50 percent, wholesalers take a 100 percent markup, and retailers add an additional 150–200 percent markup. A flower arrangement is sold by a farmer to a distributor for $5, is resold by the distributor to a wholesaler for $7.50, is then resold by the wholesaler to a flower shop for $15, and is finally resold again by the flower shop to the final retail customer for $30–60.

This lengthy retail distribution chain takes a long time to negotiate. Retail customers buy flowers that are several weeks old; hence, the flowers stay fresh for only a few days. FTD really did not change the industry so much as it expanded the existing industry by acting as a clearing agent.

Calyx and Corolla changed how the industry operated. Despite warnings from colleagues in the mail-order business, and protests from knowledgeable experts in the floral business, Ruth Owades believed it would be possible to directly connect the retail customer to the grower. Here's the system that Ruth Owades dreamed up. She first persuaded 30 small growers of flowers to install PCs and modems that could receive orders from Calyx and Corolla computers in San Francisco twice each day. She also had to teach the growers how to cut, package, and preserve flowers using pillows of ice in small packages. She then relied on Federal Express—the heavily computerized overnight delivery service—to pick up flowers from the growers each day and guarantee delivery the next day anywhere in the United States. Now Owades's company is one of FedEx's larger customers. FedEx has installed its own computers at Calyx and Corolla so that shipping orders can be entered directly to FedEx computers.

How does critical thinking differ from "normal thinking"? In Chapter 1, you learned that critical thinking means to analyze topics from different perspectives; to seek out causes or potential consequences of issues and events; and to apply what you have learned to new, possibly unrelated, or previously undiscussed areas or issues. Now, let's take this one step further to describe the kind of creative critical thinking you need to use when trying to understand a problem or when trying to come up with a novel solution, one that no one else has thought about or was too afraid to describe in public. Figure 8.5b contrasts normal thinking with this type of critical thinking.

Normal Thinking	Critical Thinking
Make judgments	Suspend judgments
Accept the obvious	Question the obvious
Accept limits	Push limits
Accept situations	Imagine alternatives
Make incremental improvements	Seek order-of-magnitude changes

Figure 8.5b
Normal Versus Critical Thinking

Using a small building in San Francisco, Owades built up an 800-number customer service department and a small management group to oversee operations and develop mail-order catalogs. After losing money for the first two years, in 1992, Calyx and Corolla had a $1.2 million profit on sales of $24 million.

The result: customers get flowers that are at least ten days fresher (and last much longer) than are available at local florists for about the same price.

Sources: Based on Strom, Stephanie, "In the Mailbox, Roses and Profits," *New York Times,* February 14, 1992; "Calyx and Corolla," Harvard Business School case, 1992.

Critical Thinking Questions

1 What factors do you think made Ruth Owades successful? Which behaviors of Ruth Owades suggest critical thinking?

2 Are there other businesses where some of Ruth Owades's ideas might work? What do you think they are?

3 What do you think was the most creative aspect of Calyx and Corolla?

4 Besides the ones we have listed, what other factors do you think are important in defining a problem or finding an innovative solution?

Ruth Owades' creative and critical thinking skills helped her develop a new way to distribute flowers.

Source: Doug Menuez/Reportage.

This kind of critical thinking inverts much of what we call normal thinking. In normal thinking, you are encouraged by teachers, parents, and other authorities to arrive at judgments quickly; to accept the judgments of people with more experience and "wisdom"; to accept the limits of technology, people, and organizations; and to accept situations, however bad, without becoming dissatisfied or unhappy. In general, we are encouraged to make incremental changes in some process rather than to radically rethink the process or seek order-of-magnitude improvements.

For most of us, normal thinking is just fine most of the time: it is efficient and helps us make it through the day without puzzlement or too much dissatisfaction. Normal thinking does not challenge people or institutions. But these characteristics are not the best for problem solving or creative thinking. At times, to make progress, to meet a problem head on, or to come up with a new view of matters, you need to invoke some critical thinking. As you read the story "Floral Heresy—Where New Ideas Bloom," consider how critical thinking helped make Ruth Owades so successful.

Critical thinking is the first step in the systems analysis and design process. Often it is a group or team process involving senior managers, outside consultants, end users, and systems analysts. In the next section, we'll show you how important critical thinking was to redesigning a successful American insurance company.

System Building in Action: Re-Engineering The Progressive Corporation

To get a good feeling for how to conduct a systems analysis and design, how to apply all the subjects we've talked about, let's take a look at an actual company that went through a lengthy systems building process—a period of re-engineering. **Re-engineering** is a popular term for rethinking and re-designing the business (or some portion of it) using critical thinking methods.

First, some background. The Progressive Corporation, based in Mayfield Heights, Ohio, sells automobile and other types of property casualty insurance through independent insurance agents in the United States and Canada. Progressive pioneered the profitable business of insuring high-risk clients and turned the business into a $1.7 billion operation. Progressive prided itself on its relationship with its customers. But in 1988, California voters passed Proposition 103, which mandated rate rollbacks and tighter regulation of insurance companies. Progressive's management felt that Proposition 103 contained an important message for the insurance industry—that customers were fed up with high rates and poor service. To remain at the forefront of the industry, Progressive's management believes that the company must respond to these consumer concerns. Let's trace the systems analysis and design process that you would go through if Progressive's management asked you to work on this case.

Phase 1: Preliminary Analysis and Critical Thinking

In the preliminary analysis and critical thinking phase, you have to answer some key questions: What are Progressive's objectives? What are the nature and origins of Progressive's problems? What is the scope of those problems? What are some potential solutions? What are the expected costs and benefits of those solutions?

Conducting the Preliminary Analysis   The main activities in this phase are critical thinking, interviews with key executives, and reading of external sources and internal documents. Let's look at how you would go about answering each of the key questions needed to perform your analysis.

Objectives   As the systems analyst on the project, you need to know more about your company's goals and recent performance. To understand the objectives and performance of Progressive, you would want to read corporate annual reports and other internal documents, as well as reports and articles written about the company by outsiders, and to interview key corporate executives. (See the Skill Development box at the end of the chapter for some tips on how to get the most information you can out of these documents.) From these sources, you discover that Progressive believes that superb claim service can improve customer satisfaction and cut claim costs by reducing unnecessary medical treatment, auto repair costs, litigation, and fraud.

Peter Lewis, CEO, The Progressive Corporation.

Source: © Ann States/SABA.

Nature of the Problem   You know at the start that Progressive's management is concerned that much of the claim service delivered by the industry is slow and adversarial. Now is the time to delve more deeply into the nature and origins of this problem. Remember that problems generally have both external and internal dimensions. To discover the external dimensions of the challenges facing Progressive, you would need to read generally about the insurance business as a whole in leading financial papers (like *The Wall Street Journal*) and insurance industry trade newspapers. To determine any internal dimensions of the problems, you can go back to the sources you consulted to discover Progressive's objectives (Progressive's key executive officers, internal reports, and the like).

The various resources reveal that to meet Progressive's goal of responding to claims reports 24 hours a day, 365 days a year, anywhere in the country, will require dramatic changes in the company's information systems and claims organization. At the moment, Progressive's claim service is hampered by a cumbersome paperwork system. When a customer has an accident, he or she calls his or her independent agent who contacts Progressive. A Progressive claims representative then sends the customer a form and arranges to view the damaged car. The claims representatives spend most of their time at their desks in one of 175 claims offices throughout the U. S. and Canada. The process is almost entirely paper based, involving the mailing of forms back and forth between customers, claims offices, and division headquarters. At division headquarters, some of the information on these forms is entered and stored with a batch processing system, but this database is not available on-line to claims representatives or managers. Instead, the system puts out reports on a routine basis, containing mostly financial rather than policy or claims information. Overall, the system is very inflexible with limited functionality.

Scope of the Problem   The next step is to research the scope of the problem. What are the boundaries of the problem? How much of the business is involved? Who is involved? To answer these questions, you would once again interview key insiders (top-selling independent agents, claims representatives, IS executives, and product managers). For further information, you would want to read outside sources that analyze your competitors' claim service methods. Based on your interviews, you discover that the problem seems to involve a large part of the organization. Progressive could become much more responsive to customers if it changed the behavior of its independent agents and claims representatives and if it had some strong support systems for these groups from the IS department.

Possible Solutions   For any problem, there are always a good many possible solutions. How do you discover these solutions? Once again, you must look at the actions of your competitors and other businesses facing similar problems and interview key personnel at all levels for their ideas. Here, there seem to be three alternatives: do nothing, make the existing system more efficient, or build a new system. Let's examine the thinking behind each of these alternatives.

▶ *Do nothing.* Within the bounds of normal thinking, the problem is quite simple: Progressive's manual paperwork system for claim reports is slowing the company's ability to respond to and settle claims quickly. But Progressive's claims service is already considered by many to be among the best in the industry. The company could just maintain its current position.

▶ *Make the existing system more efficient.* If Progressive's management will be satisfied with a slow, steady improvement in efficiency, there are some incremental ways that the existing paper-based, batch processing system could be improved. For instance, a new, less-expensive mainframe could be leased or purchased; the forms filled out by claims representatives could be simplified, and perhaps the transmission of the forms to headquarters could be made less costly. Claims representatives could be given PCs that would allow them to complete the forms electronically and send them to headquarters via a modem. These possible changes would not involve a major change in the organization or the way it processes information.

▶ *Build a new system.* If Progressive's management is looking for order-of-magnitude changes, a number of somewhat radical suggestions could lead to wholesale improvements in business. For instance, Progressive could choose to automate its claims process entirely by creating an on-line claims database that could capture both financial information (how much a customer pays) as well as policy and claims information. This would have to be a mainframe-based system given the size of the database. Second, once Progressive had developed an on-line database, customers could call into claims offices directly, bypassing their independent agents, and claims could be processed on-line, interactively, with the customer. This would make the process much more efficient. Once this system was established, claims representatives could be dispatched directly to the scene of an accident, respond immediately to customer needs for such things as a rental car, and even settle claims on the spot with mobile PCs.

This alternative would require a major change in the processes of the organization. An entirely new system would be required at headquarters and claims offices, and significant changes made in how claims representatives work.

Costs and Benefits   Now that you've identified some possible solutions, you need to examine the costs and benefits of each alternative. To find out the costs and potential benefits, you would want to contact vendors for preliminary prices of certain equipment and interview IS executives as well as senior executives in other divisions.

You discover in your analysis that the least costly alternative in the short term is to do nothing. In the long term, however, such a choice might backfire if competitors improved their service and Progressive did not. Incrementally improving the existing system by making it more efficient would cost a few million dollars—it would require Progressive to buy or lease a less expensive mainframe, develop new forms, and perhaps shift some of the forms creation onto PCs. Building a new system, on the other hand, would involve purchasing a new mainframe, software, and thousands of new mainframe terminals. In addition, Progressive would need to purchase mobile PCs and communications equipment, as well as retrain thousands of Progressive employees. In the short run, this is the most expensive alternative, but in the long run, it has the potential to produce very large increases in efficiency and customer satisfaction, giving Progressive a powerful competitive edge.

The Preliminary Plan   The primary output of Phase 1 is a **Preliminary Plan.** Here you will present your analysis of the business setting and environment; describe the nature and scope of the problem; and detail potential solutions, costs, and benefits. An organization chart (see Figure 8.6) also usually accompanies the Preliminary Plan so that executives can more easily understand who the key players will be in the system building effort.

The plan concludes with several recommendations or options for senior management, who will review the plan and select a direction for the project. They may approve your thinking, reject your thinking, or come up with some alternatives you did not consider.

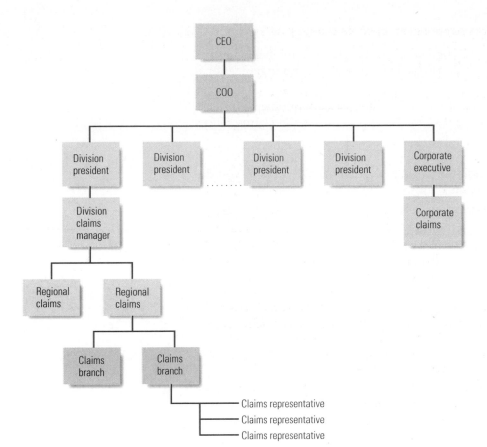

Figure 8.6
An Organization Chart of The Progressive Corporation
This is what Progressive's claims organization looked like before Progressive undertook the re-engineering process.

Source: Used with permission of The Progressive Corporation.

Phase 2: Systems Analysis

In fact, Progressive's management chose the radical alternative: re-engineering the company in order to achieve order-of-magnitude increases in efficiency, productivity, and customer satisfaction. They decided that the new system should focus on two goals: (1) reducing costs and response time for settling claims and (2) responding immediately to customer requests for service after accidents.

Choosing this alternative requires the re-engineering of how work is accomplished. A major new on-line mainframe database that captures all claims information is envisioned—a database that would make this information available immediately if needed by claims representatives at the scene of an accident. This alternative also requires a new claims processing strategy: rather than having customers call independent agents, they instead would call Progressive's claims offices directly. Such direct customer contact and immediate field response to accidents would, senior management believes, give Progressive a significant strategic advantage over its competitors. Senior management has asked you to undertake a careful study of the information requirements of the new system. What information will be needed by agents and claims representatives, in what form, and how often?

What's needed now is a better description of the existing system and a clear understanding of how the new system would differ. You will also need to consider how the organization and its people will need to change for the new system to work. The primary output of Phase 2 is a **Systems Requirements Plan,** which describes in detail the organizational requirements for information and how you propose to meet those requirements.

First, let's look at the organizational and people changes.

▶ *Organizational changes.* A re-engineering of Progressive involves some big changes in Progressive's culture, business processes, and organizational politics.

▶ *People changes.* The proposed changes will require retraining thousands of claims representatives and clerical workers in the 175 claims offices around the country.

Tools and Resources for Analysis   Several tools are available to help you develop the Systems Requirements Plan.

Gathering Data   To gather information on the organization, technology, and people issues involved in building the system, you can use traditional research procedures for data collection and analysis. Let's review these traditional procedures and see how they relate to building systems.

▶ *Written documents.* Manuals, reports, business forms, and policy statements provide you with a wealth of documentation on the existing way of doing business, plans for the future, performance success and failure, and key organizational issues and conflicts. Unfortunately, much of this material will be out of date, and you will often find that the real way things are done is quite different from official written descriptions.

▶ *Interviews.* Interviews with employees, middle and senior managers, union and employee representatives, competitors, and vendors are required to truly understand how the business works now and how it might work in the future. Structured interviews involve using questions that have been prepared in advance (and often given to the interviewee). These are useful if you have a large number of interviewees and want to assure each is asked precisely the same question. Unstructured interviews allow you to probe into areas that are not written about, for example, personnel matters.

▶ *Questionnaires.* These are useful when you have to gather very general information from large numbers of people. They can be anonymous—respondents do not have to identify themselves. This sometimes increases the candor of the response. Questionnaires are efficient, cheap, and produce a large amount of data. However, questionnaire results can also be difficult to interpret or ambiguous. For instance, it may be difficult to interpret responses to questions like, "On balance, would you like to expand your job responsibilities or reduce them?"[15]

▶ *Observation.* You can learn a great deal about an organization by simply observing people as they go about their work. Sometimes this produces a more accurate assessment of how things actually work than interviews and testimony by the participants themselves; people say one thing, then do another. Of course, if people know you are watching (obtrusive observation), they will often behave accordingly. If you can unobtrusively observe from a distance (without violating the ethics of the situation), this often produces more accurate assessments. Taking this a step further, you can join the group you are observing and become a *participant observer.* By experiencing the responsibilities and pressures of people you are trying to help, you can often gain better insight into how to build a system to improve their lives.

Before/After Action Chart   Remember you have to communicate effectively to nontechnical management what your new system will do and what it will look like. After you gather your data through document analysis, interviews, questionnaires, and observation, it's time to start making some sense out of it. A good place to start is a simple **Before/After Action Chart,** as shown in Figure 8.7. This chart should briefly summarize how Progressive works now (the before) and how it will work in the future (the after); it should also describe the action changes in organization, technology, and people required by your system.

Data Flow Diagrams   **Data flow diagrams (DFDs)** are graphic representations of how data flows through an existing or future proposed system. They are useful in quickly describing the logical design of a system without referencing any specific technology. Data flow diagrams are easy to draw and understand. They have three elements.

▶ *External entity.* A data source or destination outside the system. Represented by a rectangle.

▶ *Process.* Something that transforms input data to output like filing, sorting, stamping, dating, or comparing. Represented by a box with rounded edges.

▶ *Data store.* The data files, which could be information on disk, on tape, or in a filing cabinet. Represented by an open rectangle.

Figure 8.7
A Simple Before/After Action Chart

Before	After	Recommended Actions and Comments
Organization		
Claims offices: 175 claims offices throughout United States	Claims offices: reduce number	Redesign business procedures.
Independent agents: sell new policies, manage accounts, receive initial calls after accident	Independent agents: encourage customers to report claims directly to company	Retrain claims representatives, independent agents, clericals.
Claims representatives: office work, assessment of damages on site	Claims representatives: mobile offices, immediate response, new selling roles	Prepare for staff reductions. Possible resistance by agents to claims representatives' new role and new culture of the company emphasizing immediate response.
Division headquarters: batch-processed database, processing of new accounts, claims processing; large data entry staff	Division headquarters: eliminate paper-based systems; deal directly with customers	
Information Technology		
Sensing: none in local units	Sensing: new keyboards and scanners for local units	Need for rugged field units; consider pen-based handheld computers for claims representatives; explore radio communications links vs. cellular phone modems; explore reliability of cellular phones for data transmission. Explore artificial intelligence software to make new policy and claims applications faster and more error free.
Analyzing: headquarters mainframe and database	Analyzing: new mainframe computers (IBM 3090s); new mainframe software to create on-line database; mobile PCs for claims representatives	
Communications: U.S. mail	Communications: equip agents and claims representatives with modems	
Display: none in local units; headquarters terminals	Display: mainframe terminals and new database screens	
People		
Ergonomics: traditional paper environment	Ergonomics: consider keyboard and screen design	Contact vendors of pen-based computers for ergonomic studies and data; contact training firm for services and costs; contact general counsel for legal/regulatory issues, labor issues.
Training: training in traditional system, policies, procedures	Training: retrain workforce in new software and hardware	
Legal/regulatory: no issues	Legal/regulatory: no issues	

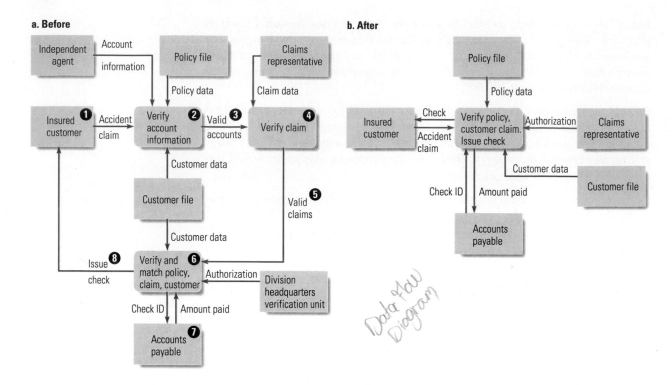

Figure 8.8

Before and After DFDs for Claims Handling Process

(a) (1) The claims handling process begins with an insured customer's call to his or her independent agent informing the agent of the accident. (2) The agent verifies the status of the customer and the policy conditions and (3) passes valid account claims on to a Progressive claims representative. (4) The claims representative visits the customer to verify the amount of damage. (5) When verified, the claims representative sends the paper file to division headquarters, where (6) the information is keyed into the computer and verified once again. (7) A notice is sent to the accounts payable division, which (8) issues a check to the customer. The traditional process is almost entirely paper-based involving forms and paper folders. **(b)** The new system promises a radical reduction in the number of different processes being performed by consolidating them into one process performed by the claims representative at the scene of the accident (although you cannot tell from the DFD precisely who does what or how they do it). *Source:* Used with permission of The Progressive Corporation.

Figure 8.8 illustrates before and after DFDs for the important claims handling process.

System Flow Diagrams A **system flow diagram (or flowchart)** is another graphic tool that is useful for depicting how a system will work. System flow diagrams document the sequence of processing steps, the flow of data, and the exact files used by each step. Because specific documents, files, and processes are referred to, system flow diagrams are called a *physical analysis and design tool*. Figure 8.9 shows the basic system flowchart symbols, and Figure 8.10 shows how they can be used to describe the claims handling process in Progressive's new system.

Decision Tables One part of Progressive's plan is to develop expert system modules to help make field decisions by claims representatives more accurate and faster. Later, in Chapter 14, we will describe in detail how expert systems work, but the basic idea is to capture in software the decision-

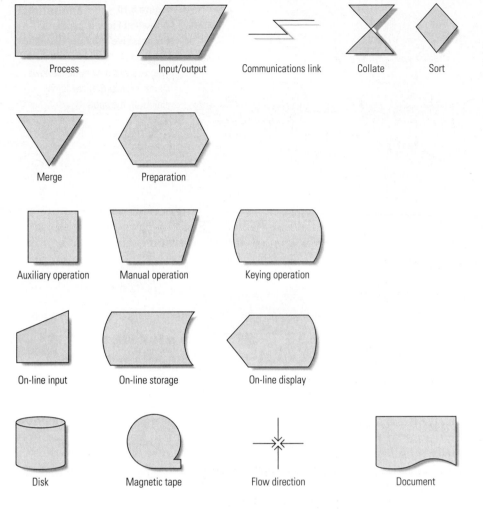

Figure 8.9
Basic System Flow Diagram Symbols
A system flow diagram is a physical design tool for depicting the flow of information, documents, and steps in a system.

making rules used by experts. In Progressive's case, the "experts" are claims representatives who make decisions using simple rules based on years of experience. One way to graphically depict these rules is through a **decision table,** which models a simple, structured decision-making process.

Figure 8.11 shows a decision table that models an insurance claims representative's decision-making process. The table is made up of an identifying header (title), a number of "IF" conditions, followed by a number of actions ("THEN DO X"). The various combinations of conditions and actions make up decision rules that can be programmed into software to prompt end users, assist them, or actually make the decision.

The use of a decision table helps programmers understand the logic of a situation and assures they do not overlook any possible situation. Many times, odd as it may seem, experts have a hard time describing precisely how they make decisions, and the interviewing process with a systems analyst is often an occasion for businesspeople to more fully understand and document how they work.

The Systems Requirements Plan   As we noted, the main output of the systems analysis phase is a written report called the systems requirements plan. Based on the facts you have collected and analyzed, the systems

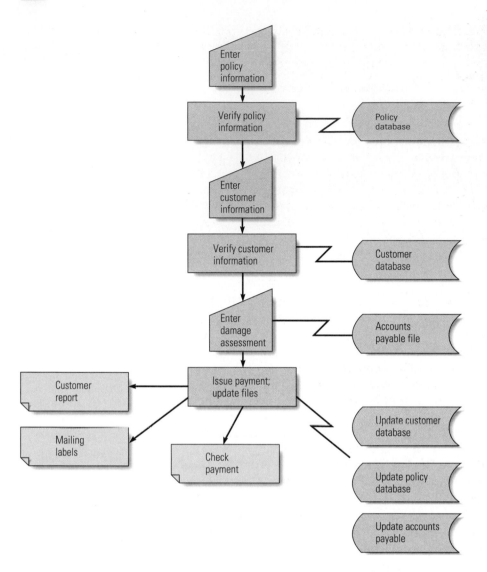

Figure 8.10
A System Flow Diagram of Progressive's Claims Handling Process
Progressive's new system allows claims representatives to pay claims on the spot.

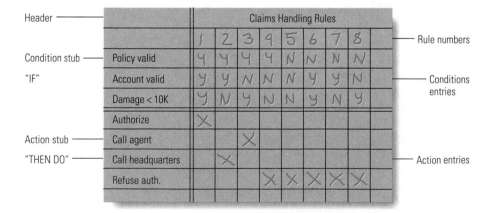

Figure 8.11

A Decision Table: Mapping Out the Claims Decision

To read a decision table, focus on the rules. For instance, Rule 1 says, "IF the policy is valid, AND IF the account is valid, AND IF the damage is less than $10,000, THEN authorize." The remaining rules you can read yourself. Decision tables provide a quick overview of the decision-making process. There are five situations where the claims representative would definitely not authorize and three situations where the claims representative definitely would or might authorize depending on additional information the claims representative obtains.

requirements plan lays out in detail (1) how the existing system works, (2) the major problems of the existing system, and (3) information requirements for the new system. One way to organize the information requirements statement is in a chart (see Figure 8.12).

Phase 3: Systems Design

Management has approved your analysis of the problems of the existing system and the requirements for a new system. You now proceed to Phase 3, Systems Design. The major output toward which you will work is a detailed systems design document. This is similar to an architect's detailed plan for a house. Now that a specific design is under consideration, you can more accurately estimate its costs and benefits. There are also usually several alternative ways to build a system, some better than others (just as there are different ways to build a house). Let's take a look at how you would deal with these issues.

Preliminary Design: Modeling the New System   The same tools that are used to describe or model an existing system (data flow diagrams, system flow diagrams, and decision tables) are also used to describe alternative preliminary designs of a new system. A **preliminary design** (sometimes called a logical design) describes the general functional capabilities of a system without specifying precisely how it will achieve these capabilities. A **detailed design** (sometimes called a physical design) describes how the system actually delivers the capabilities.

It is usual to consider several alternative systems and then choose the most cost-effective system. To determine which system is most cost-effective, you engage in a **cost/benefit analysis**: all the benefits for each alternative are added up, and all the costs are added up. The cost/benefit ratio (benefits divided by costs) must be greater than 1 before management will proceed to build a system. In other words, the benefits must be greater than the costs, and some companies require a cost/benefit ratio of 2 or more before proceeding.

Transaction Processing

1   Support claims representatives in the field with on-line policy, customer, and accounting information.

2   Capture claims information once, in the field.

3   Support telecommunications links to mobile claims representatives in vans and cars.

4   Provide expert system support to claims representatives in the field.

5   Greatly reduce the cost and time of claims processing.

6   Create user-friendly software for claims representatives based on the latest graphical user interfaces.

Management

7   Provide up-to-date reports to management.

8   Provide managers with ability to gain access to information immediately, including reports, transactions, and exceptions.

Implementation

9   Train claims organization in use of new system.

Security

10   Provide security and accounting controls for entire system.

Figure 8.12
Information Requirements Summary: The Progressive Corporation

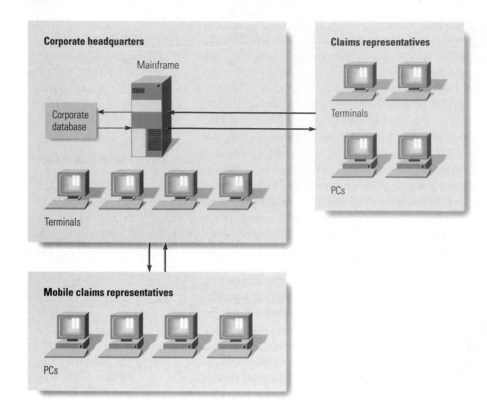

Figure 8.13
Schematic Overview of PACMan.
Progressive's PACMan system is based on an IBM 3090 mainframe serving more than 2,000 terminals and PCs.

In the case of Progressive, there are several possible alternatives. One possibility would have been to purchase thousands of personal computers for claims representatives, allowing them to do their own information gathering and data entry. But since Progressive's management wanted an on-line corporate database at headquarters, they decided on another alternative: a new mainframe connected to thousands of terminals, with new software designed to make on-line entry and retrieval of policy and claims information efficient and easy. (This part of the system was later dubbed PACMan, short for Progressive Automated Claim Management.) They also decided to shift some claims offices and claims representatives to mobile office vans and cars equipped with cellular phones, PCs, modems, and fax machines to link the claims representatives to their claims offices and corporate headquarters (the Immediate Response Program). Figure 8.13 shows a schematic diagram of the system.

What are the benefits of Progressive's system? Figure 8.14 lists some of the major benefits. Tangible benefits are those that can be quantified, whereas intangible benefits cannot be quantified. In general, firms require that projects pay for themselves on the basis of tangible benefits.

Tangible Benefits	**Intangible Benefits**
Reduced data entry staff	Immediate response to customer claims
Reduced paperwork cost	More accurate claims handling
Expanded market share	Greater customer goodwill
	Faster response to customer inquiries

Figure 8.14
Benefits of Progressive's New System

Costs of a system include hardware (computers, telecommunications, storage devices, displays, and input devices), software development, and implementation. Hardware costs are much easier to estimate than software development costs or implementation costs. In the case of Progressive, the actual total cost and time needed to develop the system (ultimately, around $28 million and over five years) was far above the initial estimates. In general, system development costs are twice their estimated budgets and time frames.[1]

Detailed Design   Once the basic preliminary design is chosen, it's time to begin the detailed design. Physical modeling involves building system flow diagrams, schematic diagrams, and decision tables that lay out clearly the major components of the system and their interrelationships. Figure 8.15 lists the major issues considered in detailed design. Here's a brief rundown of some of the detailed design issues at Progressive.

Output Requirements   The first thing to consider is what the system will produce in the form of printed reports and screen information along with the devices used to produce this output. Here it is useful to make a list of reports, design the reports, and design the actual screen output using the prototyping tools described later in this section. Once you know the outputs, you can better understand how big and powerful the system must be. A key output requirement at Progressive was screens and reports that could be easily understood by claims representatives.

Input Requirements   Once you know the output, the input is easy. You have to decide what information you need to take in, where this will be done, by whom, and on what kinds of devices. In addition, you will need to establish some editing process to check the accuracy of incoming data where possible

---

Output Requirements

Design screen and print outputs

Design reports for management

Develop user interfaces for software

Develop schedule of outputs (reports)

Input Requirements

Define sources of data input

Design data input sensing devices

Establish time frames for data input

Plan data input forms

Processing

Define hardware platform requirements

Define telecommunications system

Decide on operating system(s)

Storage

Define files and databases

Define record storage formats

Identify physical devices

Develop database interfaces

Coordinate with other corporate databases

System Controls

Develop document controls

Develop auditing procedures

Design data accuracy and integrity controls

Develop privacy safeguards and policies

Develop a backup plan and facilities

Implementation

Establish roll-out schedule

Identify key supporters (and resistors)

Identify training needs

Develop procedures documentation

Evaluation and Maintenance

Establish target delivery dates

Develop maintenance group

Establish benefit measurement methods

Develop plans for low-cost maintenance

**Figure 8.15
Detailed Design Tasks**

(no seven-figure salaries should be allowed) and some idea of the volumes of data to be handled.

Processing   What kinds of computers will you need to produce the output from the input you have just described? How fast do they need to be to handle the volume? How will you connect the processors to telecommunications systems? What about the operating system? At Progressive, new software was needed for the mainframe. Local and mobile PCs had to easily communicate with the mainframe at headquarters. How would you recommend these problems be solved?

Storage   How will you store all this information? When you choose a microprocessor (a PC as opposed to a mainframe), some of your storage problems are answered for you—much of the information will be stored on hard disk drives. You also have to consider what information will be stored at headquarters on the mainframe and how you will transfer information from the PCs to the mainframe and vice versa. Because much of the information gathered by Progressive's claims representatives at the scene of an accident will involve different groups at Progressive, you need to coordinate your work with the database administrator (the person in charge of databases at Progressive).

System Controls   How do you plan to protect the security, integrity, and privacy of the information at Progressive? A great deal of information will be moving out to claims representatives—this presents a potential security problem. How will you verify it is in fact a Progressive claims representative dialing into Progressive computers and not some "hacker" or criminal? You will need to develop some privacy standards or ways of keeping customer information from being used for purposes other than intended. Most important, you will have to develop a backup plan: what if your system fails?

Implementation   How do you plan to implement your system? Many systems falter at this point: elegantly designed with no money spared, the transition to the real world can be devastating. You will have to decide how to "roll the system out" slowly to end users, hoping to catch minor flaws as you go and gain support from happy customers (end users) as you proceed. Progressive handled this potential problem with its Immediate Response system by starting with selected test districts in Virginia; it also used Atlanta, Georgia, for a test of its mobile office concept (see photo).

Evaluation and Maintenance   You need to build into a system the measures for judging its success: how many new customers signed up for insurance because of the new system, how much response time has declined, and how much paperwork and clerical work has been reduced. Did you deliver a 100

Progressive chose to implement its Immediate Response/mobile office system by first testing it in selected areas of the country. The system features mobile office vans equipped with cellular phones, PCs, modems, and fax machines.

Source: © 1990 Roger Mastroianni.

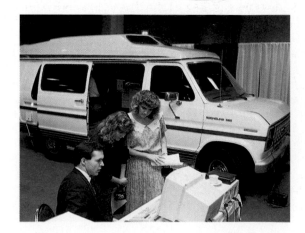

percent functional system on the target date? If not, how much functionality did you deliver? Chances are that your systems will not deliver all of their potential on the promised date, especially if it's a big project. And what about maintenance? Systems need to change with the times, and they need a team of people to keep them up to date (a maintenance team). Your detailed design needs to plan for these contingencies.

Software Tools for Designing Systems   As you can see, building systems can become very complicated—there are many players in the process, many issues, and a complex technology to boot. Maybe this is why so many large system projects fail and why so many others are very often late and over budget.

Some of the biggest problems in systems building are:

1   *Requirements analysis.* Getting users to agree on the information that is actually required in a system and how it should be processed

2   *Record keeping.* Keeping track of all the documents, diagrams, and notes developed by project team members

3   *Coordination costs.* Communicating among the project team members

4   *Project management.* Keeping the work of many small teams and individuals on time and handling the interdependencies among elements of the program

Three significant software tools have emerged in the last five years that help systems analysts build better systems in a more timely cost-effective manner.

Prototyping   Imagine hiring an architect and a builder to build you a house without seeing the plans and without seeing a model house or a house similar to what you will be buying. It might work, but chances are you would end up with a house you will regret. If only you could have "seen"—either in real life or in a model—what the house actually was going to look like.

Prototyping is a way we can make planned systems come alive by building small models of them or building parts of them using simple tools. Prototyping is a major way of solving some of the problems of information requirements. It is a repetitive or iterative process that begins with a statement of user requirements and ends with a working model of a system (see Figure 8.16). Special software packages are available for designing sample screens. You can also use any one of several PC database packages to design representative input/output screens for small scale databases.

For instance, to find out what claims representatives would be comfortable with at Progressive, system designers built a number of data entry and display screens as a prototype and then showed them to claims representatives. Claims representatives suggested changes in the screens, added data fields, changed colors, and moved fields from one part of the screen to another. Finally, systems analysts and the claims representatives came to an agreement: "Yes! This is the way the system should look; this is the data we need to see on the screen! Yes, this is exactly how we want the reports to look!"

Armed with this kind of agreement, the systems analyst can return to the project team and confidently begin development of the system knowing that the end user actually observed a model of the proposed system and heartily approved it.

CASE Tools   Prototyping helps solve the problem of understanding user requirements. **Computer-aided software engineering (CASE) tools** help reduce the record-keeping and coordination cost problems. Imagine how complicated you would find it to coordinate 200 people working over 100,000 hours in a two-year period. With thousands of data flow diagrams, structure

Figure 8.16
Prototyping Continually Refines the Design
Prototyping is an iterative process that attempts to quickly and efficiently model the user's information requirements. Once the requirements are finally agreed on, the design is—to the extent possible—frozen.

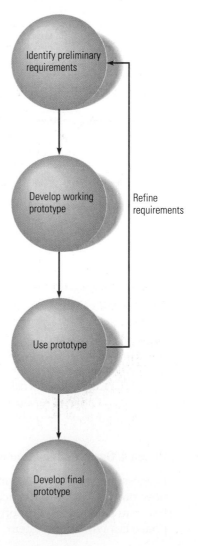

Identify preliminary requirements

Develop working prototype

Refine requirements

Use prototype

Develop final prototype

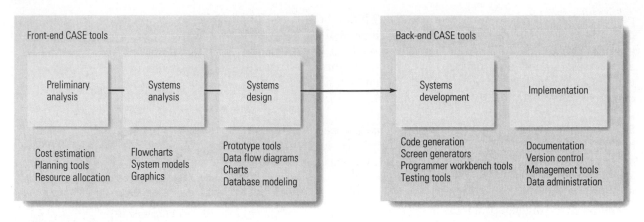

Other tools
Reverse engineering tools: produce structure charts from existing code
Project management tools: keep track of all project elements and personnel
Documentation: provides a word processing facility to create documentation
Data dictionary: a repository or database of all data elements in the system

Figure 8.17
CASE Tools
Different types of CASE tools are used in each phase of the systems development life cycle.

charts, data elements, screens, and other written documents (created by 200 analysts and programmers with different backgrounds), it is clearly a management and communication nightmare.

Enter CASE. So-called front-end CASE tools provide a consistent, uniform set of tools for creating and storing database models, data flow diagrams, system flow diagrams, screen designs, and prototyping models. These are called front end because they assist in the preliminary design, systems analysis, and design stages. Back-end CASE tools help with the systems development and implementation phases by providing semiautomatic code generation and application development, along with traditional project management tools, program module management, data administration, and test facilities (see Figures 8.17 and 8.18). Figure 8.19 shows an example of the output from Bachman Information Systems' BACHMAN/Analyst, a front-end CASE tool.

There are also a number of manufacturers that offer integrated CASE tools that cover the full systems development life cycle. Leading CASE tools of this ilk include KnowledgeWare's Application Development Workbench (ADW) and Information Engineering Workbench (IEW), Texas Instrument's Information Engineering Facility (IEF), and CGI System's PacBase.

Project Management Tools **Project management tools** based on PCs and with graphical user interfaces are increasingly used to keep track of the many elements in a systems design effort. They break the project down into smaller modules and keep track of those modules over time. The most common tools are the *Gantt chart* and the *critical path diagram* (see Figure 8.20).

You are now done with the detailed design. The document produced in this stage is a large report containing the entire design of the new system—very similar to a complete architectural design for a new house.

Phase 4: Systems Development

Progessive's management has accepted your detailed design, and you can now proceed to build the actual system. This primarily means acquiring the hardware, acquiring the software, and testing the system. The output of this phase is a workable system.

a. Front-End Case Tools

b. Back-End Case Tools

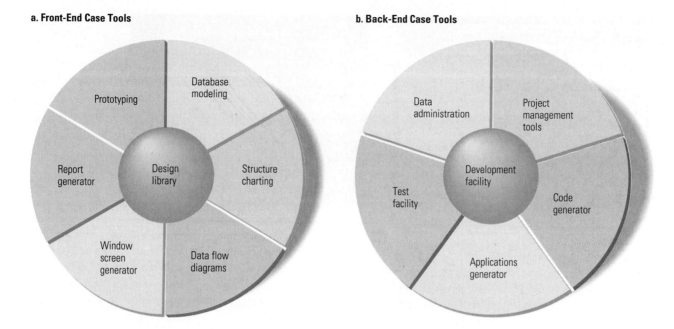

Figure 8.18
Front-End and Back-End CASE Tools

Front-end CASE tools offer a consistent, uniform environment for systems analysts, programmers, and end users to create and store thousands of system documents during the preliminary analysis, systems analysis, and systems design phases of building systems. With CASE tools installed on a local area network, all the people working on a project can gain access to the documents in seconds. Back-end CASE tools provide an environment in which project managers as well as programmers can track and control the development of a system. These tools focus on development and implementation.

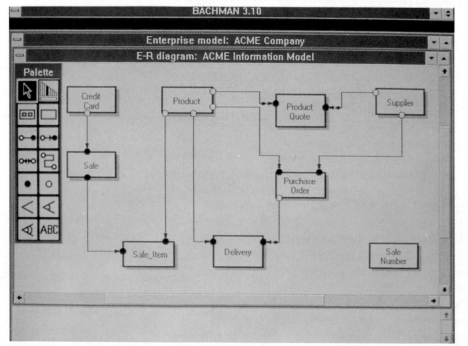

Figure 8.19
CASE Tools in Action

BACHMAN/Analyst, a front-end CASE tool, allows systems analysts to physically model an information system quickly and cost effectively.

Source: Bachman Information Systems, Inc.

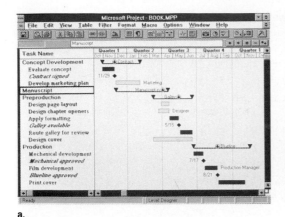
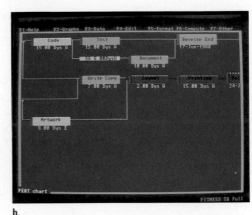

a.   b.

Figure 8.20

Project Management Tools

(a) Gantt charts are useful for tracking completion times of project modules or activities. **(b)** PERT charts are useful for showing the interdependencies among modules in a project. A PERT chart can show, for instance, a critical path that must be completed before the project can proceed further.

Sources: Courtesy of Microsoft Corporation; Fredrik D. Bodin/Offshoot.

Acquiring the Hardware   Your new system will often require the purchase or lease of new hardware—computers, displays, telecommunications networks, modems, and other physical devices. Should the equipment be purchased or leased? For very expensive equipment (mainframes and minicomputers costing over a million dollars), it may be beneficial from a tax as well as an economic point of view to rent the equipment on a one-or two-year lease rather than purchase it. A rental charge can be deducted entirely from annual income, and the price of computing is falling so fast you may not want to buy a machine if it can be replaced in a year with a much cheaper machine.

If you do not know precisely what equipment to buy, you may issue a **request for proposal (RFP)**. This is a lengthy document sent to all potential vendors describing the technical and functional capabilities you require and asking vendors to submit bids and plans to provide these capabilities. Other times, you will know precisely what you want, and you will issue a **request for quotation (RFQ)** for prices on specific equipment.

Acquiring the Software   Programming—the development of software for your new system—comes very late in a systems building effort. Some people think that programming is all there is to building a system, but you can now see that it actually accounts for a small, but obviously critical, part of the entire effort. In most cases, programming accounts for about 15 percent of the budget and 20 percent of the hours.

The most common way to obtain software for your new system is to write the programs using your own internal staff. However, in many cases, the new software will be beyond the skills of your internal programming group, and it may be cheaper in some instances to outsource all or part of the project. You may purchase the software that accomplishes what you want, or you may hire consultant programmers to come work with your staff. Still another option is to outsource the entire project and let some more experienced firm provide you with the capabilities.

There are advantages and disadvantages to outsourcing some or all of the work. You may find it less expensive to outsource, and it may require less time to develop the system. On the other hand, your internal staff loses critical skills, and your organization becomes dependent on outside firms for vital, business-sustaining services. Chapter 9 considers programming in detail.

Testing the System   Once your software is completed and integrated with the hardware environment, you will begin to implement a **test plan.** A test plan usually calls for all program parts to be tested in isolation—called *unit testing*—using simple test data. Then the parts are linked for *system testing*, also using simple test data. Production data—samples of actual data used in the company—are then brought in to test the capacity of the system to handle high volumes and full data sets. Finally, *"crash proof" testing* is performed using unusual and erroneous or invalid data to test the "robustness" of the system.

By the end of this development phase, you will have arrived at a workable system, one that is ready to roll out for implementation.

Phase 5: Implementation

Now that your hardware and software development is over, it's time for **implementation**—making the system operational and successful. Progressive's management has decided that because of the large amount of change involved, a two-phase implementation plan should be used. You will need all of your skills as a salesperson and manager to have a successful implementation. This phase's main tasks include system conversion, training, auditing, and maintenance.

System Conversion   Several steps are involved in **system conversion,** the process of converting to the new system. *Hardware conversion* involves replacing the old machines with new ones. This may involve new buildings, environment control systems, or in the case of PCs, new desks and office equipment. *Software conversion* requires that you bring old applications over to the new system and that you start up any new applications that did not exist in the old environment.

A tricky part of the conversion involves files: you often will have to move files from mainframes onto smaller machines, even PCs. Special programs are written to help automate *file conversion*, but it can sometimes involve reentering data from old systems into the new systems manually.

When you are ready with hardware, software, and files, you will have to decide how to convert to the new system. There are four strategies. One strategy is a *phased conversion* where you take several years to phase in various capabilities. Progressive chose this route. In the first phase, the PACMan system was implemented. In the second phase, Immediate Response claims service was implemented. Another common strategy is *parallel conversion:* you run both the old and new systems for a period to ensure the new system works properly. If you are fully confident (or bold and foolish), you can try a *direct switch-over* by turning off the old system and starting up the new. This should be attempted only in special circumstances. Finally, in cases where it is too expensive to convert old files and applications, a *day-one conversion* is used in which the old system continues to run, but all new customer accounts and activities are put on the new system. Eventually, the new system is performing all the work and the old system is retired.

Training   Training is one area that in the past sometimes received short shrift. Today, there is a new recognition that training people to use a system is as important as building it—a system is no better than its users. For in-

Effective employee training is an important factor in the successful implementation of a new information system.

Source: James Schnepf/The Gamma Liaison Network.

stance, PACMan and Immediate Response claims service have dramatically changed the way Progressive's claims representatives do their jobs. Once confined to their desks all day, claims representatives are now required to spend most of their working hours with insureds and claimants. This then has a ripple effect on other Progressive employees and independent agents. Some agents might be reluctant to relinquish control over their client base and need to be encouraged to tell customers to report claims directly to Progressive. And a fast-response mentality has to be instilled in Progressive employees in other departments.

To educate more than 2,000 employees, Progressive ended up spending $1.3 million on training. This involved 40 hours of live class training for members of Progressive's claims organization, along with the development of two user manuals, copious support documentation, and a series of videotapes.

Auditing   The new system cannot be made operational until you develop an auditing plan: a series of connected activities to ensure the integrity and security of the data in the system. Usually this is worked out with the accounting department, but other departments are also involved.

Maintenance   How long do systems last? There is no good answer to this question. Some parts of systems survive for years; others are out of date in five years or less because of changes in the business. But all systems require continued updating because of new products, new customers, and changes in government regulations. A permanent staff of analysts and programmers is required to maintain large systems. In fact, about 80 percent of the IS budget is devoted to the maintenance of existing systems.

You're Done! Success (or Failure)

It's time to sit back and look at what has been accomplished at Progressive through the systems analysis and design effort. Progressive has rebuilt how it does business—it has re-engineered the company. The effort was not easy, according to Bruce Marlow, Progressive's chief operating officer. It cost $28 million and took over five years, far longer than expected. To create PACMan, for instance, more than 200 people spent over 100,000 staff hours.

Once a system has been implemented, the hardware and the software that make up the system both need to be maintained.

Source: Hank Morgan.

Three years after the process began, PACMan was rolled out. Two years later, the Immediate Response claims service went into the pilot test phase in Virginia and Atlanta.

But the effort has proved worth the time and money. PACMan has reduced paperwork to a minimum, reduced costs by an estimated 30 percent, and cut the time to respond to claims. In 1992, Progressive made personal contact with 78 percent of all claimants within 24 hours of report and settled 52 percent of all physical damage claims within seven days of report. The Immediate Response process begins with a call to Progressive's 24-hour nationwide claim service 800-number, which the company's communications technology automatically routes to the appropriate claims representative or to Progressive's Cleveland claim service center. Callers speak with trained professionals who assess their situation, determine their needs, and begin the support process. Progressive will immediately dispatch a company claims representative or service vendor (tow truck, glass repair, rental car, etc.) wherever the customer chooses. Claims representatives often issue a check on the spot, closing out the claim immediately without any paperwork or delay for the customer. In several states, claims representatives work out of roving vans equipped with PCs and modems to link via telephone into the PACMan system, as well as fax machines and cellular telephones.

Much of Progressive's re-engineering effort involved not computers or technology but instead a bold vision of what could be, a good deal of critical thinking, and creative problem solving. This may be the most important ingredient to system success: consistent vision to drive the systems analysis and design. Failures have many parents, but clearly the research literature shows that systems lacking a consistent vision, or suffering from no vision, are candidates for failure.

But the vision could not be achieved without a solid understanding of information technology. How could anyone even dream that claims representatives might be dispatched instantly to the accident scene and write out a check unless they understood the possibilities of today's telecommunications, laptop computers, databases and other software?

Given the complexity and scope of Progressive's project, you can also understand now that organization, people, and your management skills are central to the success of a systems project. Whatever happens to technology, your ability to organize, communicate your vision, and work with other people will remain key factors in the success of systems you work on. Given the need for new systems, the chances are very good that one day you will be involved with building an information system. The story "New Careers in Information Technologies" highlights some potential positions.

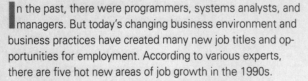

In the past, there were programmers, systems analysts, and managers. But today's changing business environment and business practices have created many new job titles and opportunities for employment. According to various experts, there are five hot new areas of job growth in the 1990s.

1 *System planners and architects.* These people are in great demand as corporations and government agencies try to adjust to a rapidly changing technical environment. Planners and architects are needed to take a longer-range view of what the organization should be doing now and in the future and to develop the overall plan for the future.

2 *Network experts.* As companies move applications off older mainframes onto networks of PCs, there is a corresponding demand for people with expertise in local networks, telecommunications, and global communications. From 1990 to 1992, the number of PCs on networks went from 7.5 million to over 21 million. By the year 2000, it is expected that 40 million PCs will be connected to networks.

3 *UNIX experts.* One powerful alternative to mainframe applications is UNIX workstations connected to Ethernet networks. With many critical corporate applications on these workstations, administrators, analysts, and programmers with UNIX experience are in high demand. Most software here is written in the C programming language (see Chapter 9).

4 *Programmers specializing in graphical user interface programming and object-oriented programming.* Programmers with these skills are in very high demand.

This is likely to continue as more and more end-user software applications are written for Windows and Macintosh machines.

5 *Quality assurance and test analysts.* A role is emerging for programmer-analysts with a background in conducting quality assurance programs and developing tools for testing software quality. As software applications move onto corporate networks and immediately affect end users, someone has to carefully examine the impact of such programs on user computers, the telecommunications infrastructure, and work procedures.

Source: Based on Laplante, Alice, "New Job Titles, Functions Abound in Market," *Computerworld,* May 4, 1992.

Critical Thinking Questions

1 Compare the information technology job titles described here with those described in your local newspaper. What kinds of information technology and communication skills are called for in your local newspaper listings of information technology jobs?

2 Given what we have said about the systems analysis and design process, make a list of the nontechnical skills that you think would be valuable for those seeking employment in this field.

3 What kinds of skills do you have now or would you like to learn that would be valuable to an organization building a system like Progressive's PACMan or Macy's system described in the opening vignette? Where do you see yourself fitting into the systems development process?

Summary

Building Information Systems

▶ Information systems are built to solve internal problems and to respond to external challenges and opportunities.

▶ The process of building systems is called systems analysis and design. It is a structured kind of problem-solving activity.

▶ There are five steps to a systems analysis and design: preliminary analysis, systems analysis, systems design, systems development, and implementation.

- There are three basic types of systems in organizations: transaction processing, knowledge work, and management support.
- Systems range in size from small to very large.
- Building systems is a team effort involving end users, professional developers, and outside vendors.
- The key factors in building information systems are information technology, organizations, and people.
- The three key skills for a systems analyst are communication, management, and design.

Critical Thinking

- Critical thinking is an important feature in problem solving because it helps us develop new ideas.
- Critical thinking inverts normal thinking by asking us to suspend judgment, question the obvious, push the envelope of possibilities, imagine alternatives, and seek order-of-magnitude changes.

System Building in Action: Re-Engineering The Progressive Corporation

- Systems analysis and design involves rethinking or re-engineering organizations by changing how they operate. There are five phases to systems analysis and design.
- Phase 1, preliminary analysis, focuses on correctly identifying the problem, establishing organizational objectives, and understanding the scope of the problem. Critical thinking plays an important role in identifying potential new solutions.
- Phase 2, systems analysis, focuses on understanding how the existing system works and how the proposed new system will work. Before/after action charts, data flow diagrams, system flow diagrams, and decision tables are useful tools for describing the old and new systems.
- Phrase 3, systems design, is concerned with producing a preliminary and a detailed design of the new system. The costs and benefits of alternatives must be considered. A number of tools are helpful: prototyping, CASE tools, and project management software.
- Phase 4, systems development, involves acquiring the hardware and software for the system. There are many sources for both, and organizations usually combine internal programming with external consulting and programming (outsourcing).
- Phase 5, implementation, involves converting the old system and files to the new system, training employees in new business procedures, and developing a long-term maintenance plan.
- Successful systems building requires an understanding of information technology, organizations, and people.

Key Terms

systems analysis	organizational culture
systems design	organizational politics
end users	business procedures
systems analyst	re-engineering

preliminary plan
systems requirements plan
before/after action chart
data flow diagram (DFD)
system flow diagram
decision table
preliminary design
detailed design
cost/benefit analysis

prototyping
computer-aided software
    engineering (CASE) tools
project management tools
request for proposal (RFP)
request for quotation (RFQ)
test plan
implementation
system conversion

 # Interactive Supplement

Review Questions

1 What are the two major reasons organizations build information systems?

2 Name the three kinds of information systems usually found in organizations.

3 Who is involved in building information systems? Who is on the systems development team?

4 What are the major factors to consider when building information systems?

5 What kinds of skills must a systems analyst possess?

6 In what ways is critical thinking different from normal thinking?

7 What is re-engineering?

8 List the five major steps of systems analysis and design.

9 What are data flow diagrams and system flow diagrams and where do they fit in building systems?

10 How does a decision table work?

11 How does a preliminary design differ from the detailed design?

12 What is prototyping, and where does it fit into systems building?

13 What are CASE tools?

14 What are the major conversion strategies?

15 List some of the key factors in determining systems success and failure.

Problem-Solving and Skill-Building Exercises

1 With a small group of students (four or fewer), identify a well-known problem on campus. Once identified, try to solve the problem in two ways: first, use normal thinking, and then, use critical thinking. Write the two solutions down side by side, and compare them. Which would be easier to implement? Which do you think would be more effective and why?

2 Identify some process or activity in a business or organization, and then construct a data flow diagram and a system flow diagram for this process.

3 With a group of students, imagine a new business—one that does not now exist. Identify some key information technologies that would make this business possible, and sketch a schematic diagram showing how it would work. You might consider making a poster or overhead transparency to show other students in class.

Gathering Data

As you've read in this chapter, one of the most important tasks you face as a systems analyst is gathering and understanding data about a wide range of topics. In many cases, you will need to find out more about the company you are working for and other companies in the industry. One of the best sources of information will be annual reports that public and some private companies prepare describing their businesses and financial results.

Annual reports and other information on companies are available in electronic form from a variety of sources. Two of the best are Mead Data Central's Lexis/Nexis and West Publishing Company's Westlaw on-line information services. These services provide you with access to annual reports and other filings made by public companies since 1984, trade publications covering all the major (and not-so-major) industries, research reports prepared by major brokerage firms, government contracting data, as well as specialized databases that contain in-depth financial and other information. For instance, Westlaw's Trinet Company Database includes the current address, telephone number, and financial and marketing information on all U.S. companies with 20 or more employees, and their Kompass Europe and Kompass UK databases cover over 200,000 European companies and 100,000 companies within the United Kingdom. You may also be able to find useful information about companies and industries through on-line information services like CompuServe and Prodigy. Though less extensive, these services are much less expensive since you pay only for the cost of dialing the service over your telephone line plus a flat fee per month rather than the individual search fees charged by Mead Data Central and West.

Once you've obtained a copy of an annual report, how do you get the most from it? Jane Bryant Quinn gives you some tips on how to do just that.

How to Read an Annual Report

By Jane Bryant Quinn

To some business people I know, curling up with a good annual report is almost more exciting than getting lost in John le Carré's latest spy thriller.

But to you it might be another story. "Who needs that?" I can hear you ask. *You* do—if you're going to gamble any of your future *working* for a company, *investing* in it, or *selling* to it.

Why Should You Bother?
Say you've got a job interview at Galactic Industries. Well, what does the company do? Does its future look good? Or will the next recession leave your part of the business on the beach?

Or say you're thinking of investing your own hard-earned money in its stock. Sales are up. But are its profits getting better or worse?

Or say you're going to supply it with a lot of parts. Should you extend Galactic plenty of credit or keep it on a short leash?

How to Get One
You'll find answers in its annual report. Where do you find *that?* Your library should have the annual reports of nearby companies plus leading national ones. It also has listings of companies' financial officers and their addresses so you can write for annual reports.

So now Galactic Industries' latest annual report is sitting in front of you ready to be cracked. How do you crack it?

Where do we start? *Not* at the front. At the *back!* We don't want to be surprised at the end of *this* story.

Start at the Back
First, turn back to the report of the *certified public accountant.* This third-party auditor will tell you right off the bat if Galactic's report conforms with "generally accepted accounting principles."

Watch out for the words "subject to." They mean the financial report is clean *only* if you take the company's word about a particular piece of business, and the accountant isn't sure you should. Doubts like this are usually settled behind closed doors. When a "subject to" makes it into the annual report, it could mean trouble.

What else should you know before you check the numbers?

Stay in the back of the book and go to the *footnotes*. Yep! The whole profits story is sometimes in the footnotes.

Are earnings down? If it's only because of a change in accounting, maybe that's good! The company owes less tax and has more money in its pocket. Are earnings up? Maybe that's bad. They may be up because of a special windfall that won't happen again next year. The footnotes know.

For What Happened and Why

Now turn to the *letter from the chairman*. Usually addressed "to our stockholders," it's up front, and *should* be in more ways than one. The chairman's tone reflects the personality, the well-being of his company.

In his letter he should tell you how his company fared this year. But more important, he should tell you *why*. Keep an eye out for sentences that start with "Except for . . ." and "Despite the . . ." They're clues to problems.

Insights into the Future

On the positive side, a chairman's letter should give you insights into the company's future and its *stance* on economic or political trends that may affect it.

While you're up front, look for what's new in each line of business. Is management getting the company in good shape to weather the tough and competitive 1990s?

Now—and no sooner—should you dig into the numbers!

One source is the *balance sheet*. It is a snapshot of how the company stands at a single point in time. On the left are *assets*—everything the company owns. Things that can quickly be turned into cash are *current assets*. On the right are *liabilities*—everything the company owes. *Current liabilities* are the debts due in one year, which are paid out of current assets.

The difference between current assets and current liabilities is *net working capital*, a key figure to watch from one annual (and quarterly) report to another. If working capital shrinks, it could mean trouble. One possibility: the company may not be able to keep dividends growing rapidly.

Look for Growth Here

Stockholders' equity is the difference between total assets and liabilities. It is the presumed dollar value of what stockholders own. You want it to grow.

Another important number to watch is *long-term debt*. High and rising debt, relative to equity, may be no problem for a growing business. But it shows weakness in a company that's leveling out. (More on that later.)

The second basic source of numbers is the *income statement*. It shows how much money Galactic made or lost over the year.

Most people look at one figure first. It's in the income statement at the bottom: *net earning per share*. Watch out. It

can fool you. Galactic's management could boost earnings by selling off a plant. Or by cutting the budget for research and advertising. (See the footnotes!) So don't be smug about net earnings until you've found out how they happened—and how they might happen next year.

Check Net Sales First

The number you *should* look at first in the income statement is *net sales*. Ask yourself: Are sales going *up at a faster rate* than the last time around? When sales increases start to slow, the company may be in trouble. Also ask: Have sales gone up faster than inflation? If not, the company's *real* sales may be behind. And ask yourself once more: Have sales gone down because the company is selling off a losing business? If so, profits may be soaring.

(I never promised you that figuring out an annual report was going to be easy!)

Get Out Your Calculator

Another important thing to study today is the company's debt. Get out your pocket calculator, and turn to the balance sheet. Divide long-term liabilities by stockholders' equity. That's the *debt-to-equity ratio*.

A high ratio means that the company borrows a lot of money to spark its growth. That's okay—*if* sales grow, too, and *if* there's enough cash on hand to meet the payments. A company doing well on borrowed money can earn big profits for its stockholders. But if sales fall, watch out. The whole enterprise may slowly sink. Some companies can handle high ratios, others can't.

You Have to Compare

That brings up the most important thing of all: *One* annual report, *one* chairman's letter, *one* ratio won't tell you much. You have to compare. Is the company's debt to-equity ratio better or worse than it used to be? Better or worse than the industry norms? Better or worse, after this recession, than it was after the last recession? In company-watching, *comparisons are all*. They tell you if management is staying on top of things.

Financial analysts work out many other ratios to tell them how the company is doing. You can learn more about them from books on the subject. Ask your librarian.

But one thing you will *never* learn from an annual report is how much to pay for a company's stock. Galactic may be running well. But if investors expected it to run better, the stock might fall. Or, Galactic could be slumping badly. But if investors see a better day tomorrow, the stock could rise.

Two Important Suggestions

Those are some basics for weighing a company's health from its annual report. But if you want to know *all* you can about a company, you need to do a little more homework. First, see what the business press has been saying about it over recent years. Again, ask your librarian.

Finally, you should keep up with what's going on in business, economics and politics here and around the world. All can—and will—affect you and the companies you're interested in.

Each year, companies give you more and more information in their annual reports. Profiting from that information is up to you. I hope you profit from *mine*.

Source: Reprinted by permission of International Paper Company.

Note

1 See **Helms, Glenn L.** and **Weiss, Ira,** "The Cost of Internally Developed Applications: Analysis of Problems and Cost Control Methods," *Journal of Management Information Systems*, Fall 1986.

Chapter 9 contains:

After completing this chapter, you will:

▶ Understand the basic concepts behind computer programming.

▶ Be able to design a program flowchart.

▶ Understand the role that programming languages play in the development of programs, as well as the advantages, disadvantages, and uses of the most significant programming languages in use today.

▶ Be able to choose the appropriate programming language for a program.

Problem Solving with Programming and Programming Languages

Simon & Schuster:
Running by the Book

Simon & Schuster is one of the world's largest publishing firms. After years taking over other publishers—including Prentice-Hall, Que, and Pocket Books—S & S has evolved into 10 independent business units publishing under 60 different publishing imprints. But in doing so, Simon & Schuster created a software nightmare: each of the business units had its own information systems. According to Technical Manager Tom Masciovecchio, "People were reinventing the wheel. They were putting resources into solving the same problems in ten different business units."

The challenge was to build a common corporate-wide set of software applications called a Publishing Control System that would serve the finance, production, and manufacturing needs of all the business units. Compounding the problem was that some business units used DOS/Windows PCs, others used Macintoshes, and central headquarters used a Digital Equipment Corporation (DEC) mainframe to store a central database of book titles and

financial information. The proposed new Publishing Control System would have to run on different hardware platforms, and be able to exchange information with the corporate mainframe database. This "cross platform" operability is vital in mixed-hardware environments.

The Systems and Technology Group made one false start: they chose a vendor who promised cross-platform capability between Windows and Macintosh but failed to deliver after several months. The project had to backtrack and research the market more thoroughly. Finally a solution was found: a new product called Open Interface (made by Neuron Data Corporation).

Open Interface is a graphical programming environment that allows program developers to write an application on one platform (like a PC running Windows) and then generate a version to run on Apple Macintosh, IBM's OS/2, and even UNIX-based machines. After a year's work the first application was developed: a cost estimating program that will be used by all ten business units to estimate

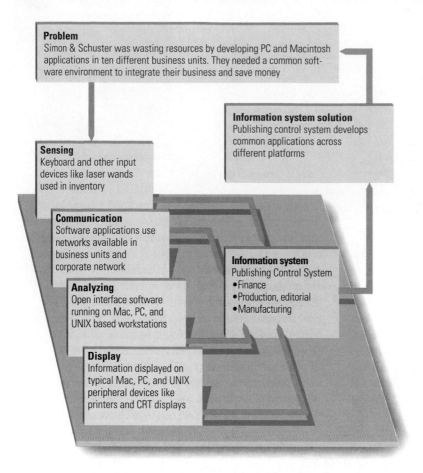

the costs and revenues for new books. Masciovecchio estimates that over a year of development time was saved using Open Interface because the application had to be programmed only once and could be ported to different platforms easily.

Source: Based on Ray, Garry, "Publisher Expedites Client/Server Solution," *Computerworld,* June 1, 1992.

In today's world of different machines on thousands of desktops distributed across a company, new challenges are faced by system developers and programmers. Simon & Schuster is one example of the complex new environment faced by software developers. How can organizations develop a coordinated approach to software when there are so many different information technologies with which to deal? One solution to this new complexity is the use of new kinds of software programming environments and tools such as those used by Simon & Schuster. Successful use of these new tools requires organizational change, retraining of personnel, and critical thinking skills.

9.1 Introduction to Programming

Once you have designed a system, as we did in Chapter 8, you will have to develop some computer programs to implement the system. In this chapter, you will learn how computer programs are created.

What Is Programming?

As we explained briefly in Chapter 7, *software* (a computer program) is a collection of detailed instructions that tells the computer what you want it to do. Computer programs control the information technologies that make up an information system. They drive CPUs and primary storage to perform their tasks and control (or respond to) sensing devices, display devices, and communications equipment. **Programming** is the art and science of creating computer programs. People who write (or code) computer programs are called **programmers.** Programs are written in various programming languages, each designed to write programs that solve particular kinds of problems. We'll explore those different languages in more depth later in this chapter.

Common Programs: To-Do Lists and Recipes

Even though you now know what a computer program is, it may still be difficult for you to conceptualize one. An analogy to some everyday activities may help.

Have you ever created a To-Do list or a recipe? If you have, you are already a programmer without even realizing it. Surprised? If you were a computer, To-Do lists and recipes would be your programs, expressed in a "natural language." (A *natural language* is a collection of commands and rules that allows you to instruct and communicate with other people and with yourself.) Figure 9.1 gives you an example of a "human program."

A To-Do list is an ordered list (usually ordered by time though it could also be ordered by priority) of commands. Commands are verbs: they tell us to do something, to take action. As you will see, computer programs are just like To-Do lists; they are a list of commands to do this, do that, and then do something else.

A somewhat more complicated form of natural language program is a recipe (see Figure 9.2). A recipe is more complicated than a simple To-Do list because it has several parts and specifies sequences and conditions for the performance of commands. For instance, the first part of a recipe establishes *the environment:* the things you need to do in order to perform the main task (in this case, making chili). The second part establishes *the sequence* and *logi-*

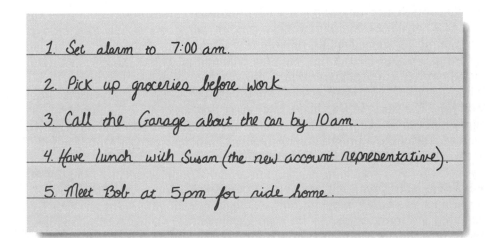

Figure 9.1
A To-Do List: A Natural Language Program for Humans

1. Set alarm to 7:00 am.

2. Pick up groceries before work.

3. Call the Garage about the car by 10am.

4. Have lunch with Susan (the new account representative).

5. Meet Bob at 5pm for ride home.

```
Carol's Chili

Obtain large frying pan
Heat pan to frying temperature
Cut 1 cup onions coarsely
Mince 3 cloves of garlic
Measure 3 tablespoons of oil
Cut 1 pound of beef into cubes
Measure 3 tablespoons of chili powder
Measure 2 tablespoons of flour
Measure 2 teaspoons of cumin
Measure 2 cups of beef broth

Cook the onions and the garlic in the oil.
When the onions wilt, add the beef.
Cook.
When the meat loses its red color, stir in chili powder,
flour, cumin, and broth.
Simmer until done.
```

Figure 9.2
A Recipe: Another Type of Natural Language Program for Humans

cal flow of steps in the recipe: cook the onions and garlic in oil first, and when (if) the onions wilt, add the beef. Virtually all computer programs have this same shape.

Programming a computer is of course different from communicating with human beings. No machine can yet match the unique capabilities of humans. For instance:

▶ Computers do not have common sense, and therefore require very precise use of language to program. For instance, a computer would require you to specify precisely the frying temperature in the recipe because it could not possibly know anything about frying temperature.

▶ Computers use artificial languages (called programming languages), which are very formal and do not permit the use of slang or undefined words. For instance, though you could tell a human cook to "throw the onions and garlic in the pan," a computer most likely would require a formal command like "*put* the onions and garlic in the pan."

What are some other ways that computers and humans differ?

Why Learn About Programming?

Many of you will take additional courses that teach you a specific programming language like BASIC, COBOL, or dBASE. From there, you may go on to become a professional programmer, systems analyst, or designer. These are all projected to be fast-growing occupations through the year 2000 and beyond because our society is becoming so dependent on digital devices that require programs and systems. Anything you learn now about programming will help your career advance. The story "A Day in the Life" gives you an idea of what life as a programmer can be like.

But what if you don't plan on becoming a programmer or analyst? Do you still need to learn about programming and programming languages? The answer is a resounding yes.

One reason is that applications software, such as word processing, spreadsheet, and database programs, is starting to swing full circle back to the days when anyone who used a computer had to be a programmer. Today, some of the best applications software is bringing programming back to the end user through scripting and macro capabilities, which allow you to write "miniprograms" that customize the software to your own particular

Even if you don't plan on becoming a programmer or analyst, a knowledge of basic programming techniques may be useful to you on the job.

Source: Larry Barns/Black Star.

requirements and work. A knowledge of basic programming techniques and programming languages will help you feel more comfortable with these capabilities and allow you to take fuller advantage of the benefits they offer.

A further reason to learn something about programming is to simply understand the world around you—both its limitations and possibilities. For instance, we have all seen people doing jobs that are really silly, dangerous, or boring—jobs that might best be done by a computer *if a program could be written to accomplish the job.* If you knew something about programming you could make a better judgment about how jobs might be improved through the use of information technology. You should also be in a position to say, "Nope, you need a real person to perform that job. A computer just couldn't do it." By the time you finish this chapter, you should be able to make these kinds of critical thinking judgments.

Packages and Custom Software: Buy or Make?

Few of us would think of making our own car. Much better to buy a car from a corporation that makes millions of cars, uses standard parts, obtains parts at the least cost, and achieves huge economies of scale (lower production costs achieved by large production runs of a single product). So it is with software: if you can buy a package manufactured by someone else that achieves your objectives, it is much cheaper to buy that package than create your own custom software.

You will, of course, still have to perform a systems analysis and design of your situation as described in Chapter 8. But before you begin to develop the programs for the system on your own ("in-house" software), be sure to contact major software and hardware vendors to see if packages for your application are available. In the past decade, with the standardization of computer platforms like PCs, Macintoshes, and minicomputers like IBM's AS 400, thousands of packaged programs capable of performing payroll, financial planning, accounting, project scheduling, and manufacturing control

What's it like to be a programmer? Here's a description of a day in the life of Russell Polo, chief programmer for Azimuth Corporation, a small software company that writes software and multimedia applications for the financial services and educational industries (see photo).

First, a little background on Russell. He is a recent graduate of the State University of New York at New Paltz, and has a B.S. in Computer Engineering. Russell's first exposure to computers came in grade school where he learned about BASIC, a beginner's programming language. He was so interested that he started programming as a hobby. He had limited instruction in high school but continued learning on his own. In college he started out as a computer science student but switched to computer engineering because he wanted to understand the hardware aspects of information systems as well as the software.

Russell's first programming job was to develop an educational program for his high school English teacher. The program identified subjects and predicates in sentences for other students. In high school, he worked after school on a small office database system for a local software firm. He also worked after school for IBM where he developed a inventory program that kept track of computer terminal cables. Later on, as a summer intern at IBM, he worked on an experimental program that automatically translated programs written in machine language into high-level languages. While at college he started working at Azimuth on a client and portfolio management database. Since then he has worked on multimedia educational software like the Interactive Supplement for this book.

Russell Polo, chief programmer for Azimuth Corporation.

So what does a programmer do during a typical day? Russell divides his work into four categories: planning, writing code, debugging, and testing. In a large firm these tasks might be divided among many people, but since Azimuth is a small company, Russell performs most of these tasks himself with the assistance of junior-level programmers.

When tackling a large job, one that may take months to complete, Russell starts by doing some planning. First, he

have become available. These packages are much less expensive and often of higher quality than custom-designed software, and they often include training and support.

There are some drawbacks to packaged software. Often, you have to make so many changes to a package that you might as well develop it yourself. Second, fitting the software to your other software and hardware is not always easy. Will the payroll package accept data from your general accounting package manufactured by someone else? Most important, packages by design are not custom fit to your organization or problems, and if you really want to do the job, you may very well have to build the programs from the beginning. In this chapter, we illustrate how this is done and what tools are available.

does some rough paper and pencil sketches of how the system is supposed to work overall at a very general level. Next, he identifies the important modules in the system. He then writes down how each module is supposed to work, identifying the key inputs, outputs, and variables of which he must keep track.

Once the modules of a program are identified, Russell shifts into the code-writing phase. If he modularized correctly, the job flows smoothly from one module to another. If he reaches an impasse in one module, he often switches to another. Solutions to impasses sometimes come to Russell at odd times—at night while sleeping, on the way to work, or while working on a completely different module.

One common pitfall that Russell tries to avoid when writing code is "reinventing the wheel." For example, date functions—keeping track of dates and times in a database—are a problem that has been solved thousands of times by programmers in the past. Why reinvent this program? To avoid doing so, Russell looks in catalogs and magazines to find utility programs and entire libraries of programs that he can purchase to handle routine but difficult-to-program tasks. Once purchased, Russell must integrate the purchased code into his own code.

When Russell completes the initial coding on a module, he tests it, first separately and then together with all the other modules that have been completed, checking to see that the results of sample data input are as expected. Putting all the modules together usually creates new problems that must be fixed. Sometimes the output from one module does not quite match the expected inputs to another module. Changes in code and additional testing are necessary.

Altogether, Russell spends about one-quarter of his time planning and writing a program, one quarter debugging modules, and the rest testing the program. This varies from project to project.

What's the best part of the job? Russell says, "When it works! When you put all the modules together and they work consistently, regardless of the data sent to the program. The look of satisfaction on the client's or boss's face—that's what makes me happiest. The idea that I overcame a lot of tough issues and was able to create a useful solution." But what about on a day-to-day basis? Russell says he loves the day-to-day aspects of his job too because he gets to exercise many different talents—design, planning, programming, debugging, and management of his own time. "The work is highly variable and the problems change all the time. I don't have someone standing over me telling me what to do. It's anything but boring."

Critical Thinking Questions

1 System analysts often are programmers before becoming systems analysts. Having read this description of a programmer's life, why do you think this might be so? In what ways are the jobs similar? In what ways are they different?

2 What courses might you take to prepare yourself for a job as a programmer? Include nontechnical as well as technical courses on your list.

3 How do you think a programming job in a large company might differ from the one described here? Which would you prefer and why?

9.2 The Program Development Process

Just as in systems analysis and design, there is a problem-solving methodology to follow when building software programs. There are five steps to the program development process (sometimes called the **software development cycle**) (see Figure 9.3).

The development of complex programs usually requires a *team effort*: several programmers working with systems analysts and even some end users. To develop a complete information system, it is not just computers that need programming but also sensing, communication, and display devices. This requires people with different skills as well as the use of a variety of pro-

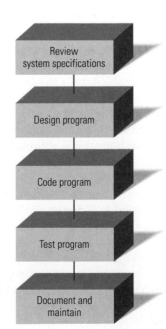

Figure 9.3
The Program Development Process
The program development process involves five steps.

gramming languages. Less complex programs may be written by a single individual, but even these often require interaction between programmer and end user. Very simple programs can usually be created by users themselves, using one of the fourth-generation programming languages described later in this chapter.

Step 1: Reviewing System Specifications

Methodology:
Building Software

The first step in the development of a program is to meet with the systems analysts, end users, and other members of the programming team to review the detailed designs produced in the systems analysis and design phase. The systems analysts have determined what needs to be done, and usually they have specified the equipment. The programming team must first understand the problems the system will be designed to solve, then determine how to do the job and finally build the system.

Using the data flow diagrams, flowcharts, and decision tables provided by the designers, programmers usually start with the output of the system: what reports, documents, checks, and screens are required? From here, they work backward to data, data files, and data flows required to produce the outputs. At this point, several, usually minor, changes in the system will be recommended by the programmers, and these will have to be reviewed and approved by users and analysts.

Step 2: Designing the Program

Designing the program takes place in three phases (see Figure 9.4). Program design involves transforming the analysts' and users' design into a logical solution that a computer can perform. Today, virtually all formal program design uses a design technique called **structured programming,** which we will trace here. There are three principles in structured programming: the modularization of programs, the use of standard control structures, and single entry/single exit from control structures.

Let's look at the structured design methodology using The Progressive Corporation case study from Chapter 8.

Phase 1: Modularize the Program   In structured design, the overall program is decomposed into smaller **modules** or parts. Each module performs a unique task within the program. There are as many modules as there are unique tasks. The purpose of modularization is to simplify the development process by breaking a large problem into smaller units that can be developed, tested, and maintained over the long term on an individual basis. Most modularization follows a *top-down* approach: the program's main functions are considered first, subdivided into component modules, which are then further subdivided into additional modules until the lowest level of detail is reached. After all the modules have been developed, they are connected to make a coherent whole program.

The modules of a program are usually illustrated with a chart (called a **hierarchy chart** or **structure chart**) that shows the overall purpose of the pro-

Figure 9.4
Program Design
Program design involves three phases.

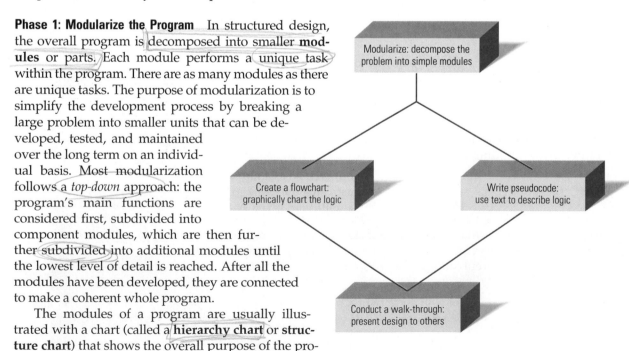

Modularize: decompose the problem into simple modules

Create a flowchart: graphically chart the logic

Write pseudocode: use text to describe logic

Conduct a walk-through: present design to others

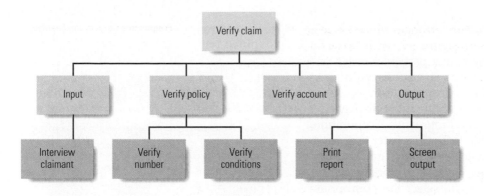

Figure 9.5
A Hierarchical Structure Chart
This hierarchical structure chart identifies the modules for PC software that could be used by The Progressive Corporation claims representatives.

gram at the top, identifies all the modules to achieve this purpose, and shows the relationships among modules. Figures 9.5 through 9.11 are all based on the design of software for Progressive Insurance claims representatives who will be using laptop PCs to perform their jobs. Figure 9.5 illustrates a structure chart for this software.

Phase 2: Flowchart the Program Modules/Pseudocode   Once the modules are identified, it's time to take each module and begin designing the logical flow of the program. There are two ways you can accomplish this task—through *flowcharts* or *pseudocode*. Although generally you would use only one of these techniques, larger projects sometimes use both.

A **flowchart** uses a standard set of symbols developed by the American National Standards Institute (ANSI), a private standard-setting group. Figure 9.6 illustrates the ANSI flowchart symbol set. (You can buy a plastic ANSI template in most college bookstores and use it to design any logical process.)

In structured program design, three control structures are used to form the logic of a program: sequence, selection, and iteration. With these three logical forms, all computer programs can be controlled. Refer to our discussion of recipes, and you will find that most recipes also contain these control structures (though they are not so explicitly used by cooks).

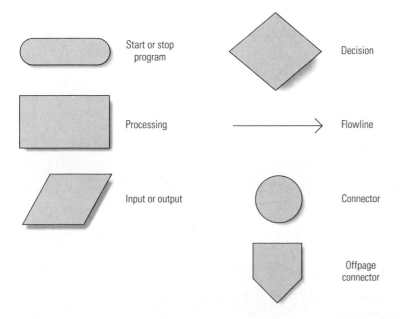

Figure 9.6
The ANSI Flowchart Symbol Set
The standard flowcharting tool is the ANSI flowchart symbol set available in most bookstores.

The **sequence control structure** arranges processes in a temporal and logical order. In Figure 9.7, each box is a process, and each process occurs in a particular order, one after the other. In computer terms, a process could be to open a file, read a record, move some data from one location to another, take input from a keyboard, or display data to a terminal. In the case of The Progressive Corporation, the claims representative in the field must enter the corporate database to verify the customer's policy and account. The program must dial the mainframe communication number, establish communication, select the appropriate data file to search, and initiate a search of the policy file.

The **selection control structure** is a way to represent choice: if a condition is true, then perform one procedure; else (if the condition is false), perform a different procedure (see Figure 9.8). In the case of Progressive, the program must come up with recommended actions and prompts for the claims representative when certain conditions are met.

An important variation on the If-Then-Else selection structure is the *case control structure* (see Figure 9.9). The case structure permits a large number of alternatives to be examined quickly without writing a lot of If-Then-Else statements. A menu in a PC program provides a good example of a case structure.

The **iteration control structure** is a way to represent the performance of a process if a given condition is true (Do While) or until a condition is met (Do Until) (see Figure 9.10). With the Do While structure, if the condition is true, the process is performed. Then the program loops back and checks to see if the condition is still true. If the condition is still true, the process is performed again. In the Do Until structure, the process is performed at least once, the condition is checked, and if it is true, the program loops back and performs the process again.

An important principle to follow when using structured methods is **sin-**

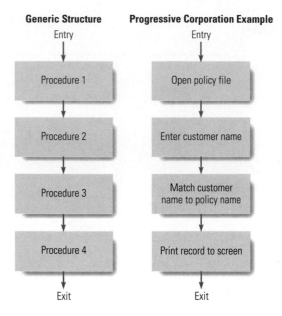

Figure 9.7
A Sequence Control Structure
Each box in the sequence is a computer process that occurs after a preceding process or after a start signal.

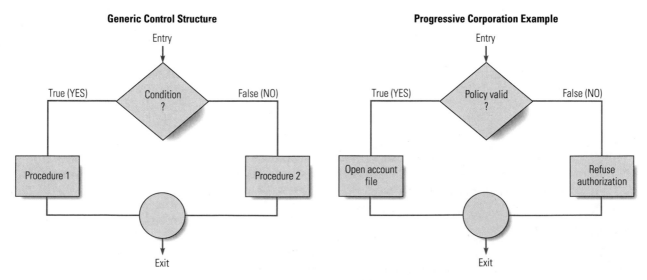

Figure 9.8
A Selection Control Structure (If-Then-Else)
A selection control structure is used to select between two alternatives.

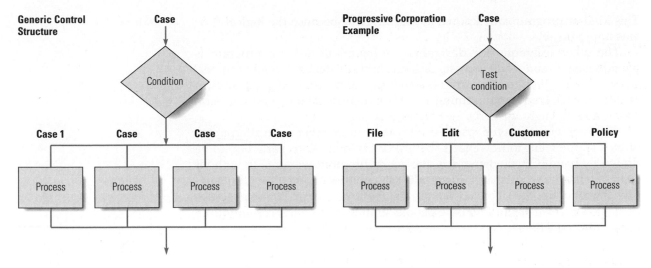

Figure 9.9
A Case Control Structure
A case control structure is used when the system must check for more than two options (more than true or false). For instance, a menu structure with options for File, Edit, Customer, and Policy would be useful for Progressive claims representatives. Choosing File alerts the system to Process 1, which pops up all the menu items listed under File.

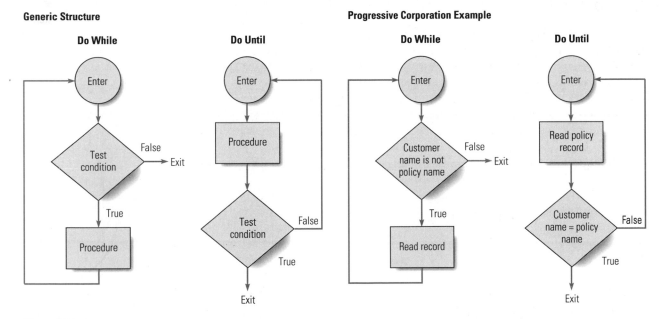

Figure 9.10
Do While and Do Until (Looping) Iteration Control Structures
In the Do While loop, the condition is tested first (does the customer name match the policy name), then a procedure is performed (a new record is read). In the Do Until loop, a procedure is performed (a record is read), and then a condition is tested (does the customer name match the name on the policy). In this case, the Do Until is more natural and avoids a double negative.

gle entry/single exit. This means that for each of the three control structures, there is only one entry and one exit. In each of the preceding examples, the control structure is entered at one point and exited at another point. Prior to structured programming, programmers could transfer control of the program to other parts of the program. This made it difficult if not impossible to follow the logic, read the code, or understand how the program worked.

This kind of program was known as *spaghetti code* because the logical flow was unpredictable.

The other technique for designing the logical flow for a program is **pseudocode.** Pseudocode consists of English-like statements readily understood by all. Although there are no standards for pseudocode, generally, it uses the structured programming control structures along with common programming language verbs (see Figure 9.11).

As we previously noted, pseudocode can be used either as an alternative, or as a supplement to flowcharts. Before CASE tools, flowcharts had to be drawn by hand. Often, changes in the actual program were made without changing the flowcharts, and this resulted in poor documentation: the charts (like maps) no longer depicted the terrain. Pseudocode can be easier to update. On the other hand, for some people, graphic flowcharts communicate much more effectively.

Phase 3: Walk-Through   You would be surprised how many details escape the notice of individual programmers and small teams working in isolation. Here's where a presentation of the program logic to the full project development team, composed of analysts, programmers, and concerned end users,

```
START
enter customer name
open policy file
go to top of the file (the first record)
DO UNTIL
    read a record

UNTIL Customer Name = Customer Name entered or end of
file
    IF Customer Name = Customer Name entered
        print to screen "Policy Valid"
    print to screen Policy ID
    store Policy ID to VPOLICY
  ELSE
    print to screen "Not Found"
  ENDIF
ENDDO
close policy file
END
```

Figure 9.11
Pseudocode from The Progressive Corporation

This piece of pseudocode lets the user search through a file to find out whether a given customer holds a valid policy. When a customer name is entered, the program will open the policy file and read records. The program will continue to read records until it has found the customer name entered by the user, or until it encounters the end of the file—the last record. If the customer name as indicated on one of the records is the same as the customer name entered by the user, then the program will print a "Policy Valid" message to the screen, print the Policy ID number to the screen, and store the Policy ID number in a new memory location called VPOLICY (where it can be used by other portions of the program not shown). Otherwise (ELSE) the program will print a "Not found" message to the screen.

There are no formal standards for pseudocode, but here are some rules:

1 Sequence structures are usually written in lowercase letters. Capital START and END are used to denote major blocks of code.

2 The selection (IF, ELSE, ENDIF) and loop (DO WHILE and DO UNTIL) structures are always in capital letters. Indent conditions, and use lowercase.

comes into play. The purpose of this walk-through is to review the overall design, review the modules for errors and completeness, and where possible, consider ways to speed up program execution by making sure no two modules do the same thing. Errors and omissions in the program detected at this point can be corrected easily at small expense. If errors and omissions are allowed to persist, the cost of fixing them later is extremely high.

Step 3: Coding the Program

Once the design is settled, the actual writing of program instructions begins using one of several possible languages. In the section "The Programmer's Tools," we review the most significant languages used by programmers.

The programming process is assisted by a number of tools that usually come with the program compiler or package. Programming languages like BASIC, COBOL, FORTRAN, dBASE, and C come in a package. The manufacturer of the software package provides the basic compiler along with a **programming environment** to assist the process of coding. Third parties also manufacture additional tools to assist programmers. Sometimes these environments are called programmer workbenches. Here are some of the tools found in a programming environment:

Code Standards   ANSI and other standard-setting bodies establish conventions and rules for the use of a language, and manufacturers usually comply with these rules. This makes it possible for one programmer to understand another programmer's C language programs, for instance. Otherwise, dialects of languages would develop, making understanding difficult.

Debugging Tools   Most programming environments come with **debuggers**, software that checks the syntax and usage of a programmer (much like grammar checker software assesses the grammar of a paper). With a debugger, a programmer can quickly spot an error and change the code before putting the program to a full test.

Data Dictionaries   Some programming environments provide the capacity for an organization to define a data dictionary or repository of all the data field names and relevant business values and procedures (such as how the business calculates annual return or how the business defines the fiscal year). Data dictionaries ensure that all programs in an organization use standard terms.

Code Libraries (Reusable Code)   Why reinvent the wheel? Some large companies have 10 or 20 different payroll, pension, customer control, and employee files built up over the years. In such organizations, imagine how many different times programmers have written code segments (short chunks of code) to print names from a list, arrange a list alphabetically, calculate state tax deductions, and so forth. One way around this problem is to create **code libraries** of reusable code segments that programmers can copy and paste into their own programs.

Step 4: Testing the Program

Program testing involves a number of procedures to prepare the program for the real world. First, all the program modules are placed together in a single package. Although the modules have usually been debugged by the programmers one at a time in the coding phase, and simple syntax checking

On February 25, 1991, during the Gulf War, a SCUD missile fired by Iraq slammed into an American barracks at Al Khobar, killing 28 soldiers, the war's single worst casualty toll for the Americans. The Americans had attempted to launch a Patriot missile to destroy the incoming SCUD, but the Patriot system was blinded: an error in its software prevented its radar from "seeing" the incoming missile. Originally designed to operate for 14 hours before scheduled maintenance, the Patriot system at Al Khobar had operated for over 100 hours of combat. The Army discovered, quite by chance when analyzing a successful launch, that the accuracy of the software progressively degraded after 8 hours of use. Investigators found a tiny error in the system's internal clock. This error corrected itself on restarting, and as long as the system was shut down and restarted, everything worked fine. However, the designers never anticipated that the system would be used for 100 hours before turning off and restarting. An upgrade to the software arrived on February 26, one day after the SCUD attack.

Increasingly, our lives and businesses depend on computer software, and the question of its durability, ruggedness,

Many of today's military weapon systems, rely heavily on complex software containing millions of lines of code.

Source: AP/Wide World Photos.

performed, they have never been tested together. Sometimes modules can interfere with one another or send the wrong messages to one another.

Even though the program may be internally valid (it works without crashing in the lab), the external validity has to be checked. External validity means the program actually produces the expected correct results when tested with real-world data. In this stage, sample test data is obtained from the organization and placed into the system. It is important that the test data have the same complexity as found in the real world and that system performance and load characteristics are examined. For instance, in the real world, a system may be required to answer requests from 60 customers per minute. A good test program would ensure that the system could meet this demand.

A last form of testing is crash proofing: the entry of wrong or partial data, or contradictory data, and the purposeful overloading of capacity. Here the point is to try to anticipate all the possible real-world circumstances under which the system must perform. Sometimes, excess capacity and additional logic tests can be built into a system to defend itself against unusual demands placed by users.

Today, with our increasing reliance on information technology and programs in all aspects of life, rigorous program testing is of utmost importance. The story "Software Risks" provides a graphic illustration.

Step 5: Documentation and Maintenance

People are sometimes befuddled by the notion that computer programs need to be documented—that books need to be written about the software. Even more strange is the idea that computer programs need maintenance—just like cars.

and accuracy is moving to front-page news. Consider that the telephone system relies on 2.1 million lines of code, an electronic automobile transmission uses 19,000 lines of code, and automated teller networks require 600,000 lines of code. On January 15, 1990, the AT&T Long Distance Network was brought to its knees by a single software bug. Half of all 800 service was lost, and one-third of attempted long-distance calls could not be completed.

Unfortunately, computer code at these levels of complexity cannot be made error free. Why not? Can't the software be tested? Of course software is tested before delivery, but this removes only the more obvious and frequent bugs. Most large programs contain residual bugs when delivered. Complexity is one cause of the problem: there may be tens of thousands of alternative paths of program execution. Many times, the inputs were not correctly anticipated, producing an incorrect output.

The specifications of programs also sometimes change during development or after deployment as in the Patriot mis-

sile system. Last, some of the bugs in programs are "5,000 year bugs"—they will occur on average once in 5,000 years. The bug could involve a single 0,1 bit in one line of a million-line program. To discover these bugs may take enormous resources, far more than the software itself cost to develop.

Sources: Based on Schmitt, Eric, "U.S. Details Flaw in Patriot Missile," *New York Times*, June 6, 1991; Littlewood, Bev and Lorenzo, Strigini, "The Risks of Software," *Scientific American*, November 1992.

Critical Thinking Questions

1 What would you recommend the Army do to test weapons software in the future?

2 Can you think of some ways of reducing software errors based on comments in this article and in the text?

3 Are software errors inevitable? If so, what steps would you recommend that society take to live with their consequences?

Documentation plays several roles and has several different audiences. Obviously, the diagramming techniques and text description of programs described in this and the previous chapter are important for coordinating the work of the programming group itself where teams of programmers need to keep informed about the program. This kind of documentation is called **programmer documentation.** Also obvious is the fact that end users require documents to introduce themselves to the program and to be trained by others. This is called **user documentation.** Less obvious is the role of documentation in quickly training new programmers. About 20 percent of programmers turn over or leave each year. On average then, 20 percent of the project team's programmers are new and need to be brought up to speed quickly. Documentation plays a vital role.

Program maintenance refers to all the activities required to keep the program up to date. Think of all the change that occurs in a modern organization: ownership and management structure often change, products come and go, government regulations change, and competitors change. All these changes in the environment of a firm require sometimes subtle, sometimes massive changes in existing programs. Indeed, about 80 percent of systems personnel and budget goes to maintain existing programs. Sometimes, maintaining old programs becomes so costly that drastic actions are required to overcome the difficulties. Read the story "Arizona State Attacks Spaghetti Code" for an example of how this can happen.

Documentation and maintenance are closely linked: in order to change a program (especially one you did not write), it is critically important to have good documentation that explains how it works. Once again, you can understand that successful systems development requires solid communication skills—presentation, writing, and clear thinking.

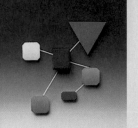

Imagine you are the director of Arizona State University's Information Systems (IS) Department. The department operates the hardware and software needed to support 43,000 students and 5,000 faculty and administrators. One morning you wake up and discover that all 55 of your applications programmers are busy maintaining old, difficult-to-read programs, and no one is available to handle requests for new programs. Your budget is frozen, and the backlog of new applications requests is getting longer and longer—stretching out to years of future work.

What's the solution? It would be impossible to throw out the old programs because they're needed to run the university, and it would take years to develop substitutes. You can't hire more staff—there's no money. On analysis, you discover that one of the big maintenance problems is that programmers are forced to work with unstructured, badly written, undocumented, and hard-to-understand code. Solve this problem, and you have the beginning of a solution.

Increasingly, organizations like ASU are turning to specialized tools that read old, badly written, unstructured code (spaghetti code that goes all over the place) and turn it into easily maintainable structured code. One product that does this code redevelopment is Renaissance from Viasoft, Inc. of Phoenix, Arizona. Along with other tools, Renaissance reads old COBOL code and turns out new code ready for testing. The result has been a 20 percent productivity gain and even more gains when developing new applications. For instance, with the new structured code, an application that used to take 40 hours to create now can be developed in 6 hours.

Source: Based on Ray, Garry, "Redevelopment Takes Root," *Computerworld,* November 23, 1992.

Critical Thinking Questions

1 What techniques described in this chapter would help ASU produce more easily maintained code in the future?

2 Why is the Renaissance software only a partial solution? Can ASU avoid development of entirely new applications?

3 In what ways do you think well-documented and structured code is related to software bugs and risks of failure?

9.3 The Programmer's Tools: Programming Languages

Now that you have a background on the procedures to follow when developing a program, let's review the primary tools—programming languages—that programmers use to create programs. As you learned in the section "Introduction to Programming," a **programming language** is a special form of software that programmers use to create other software.

To understand the basic concepts behind programming languages, it may help to think about how our own language works. Human languages are constructed from rules governing word meaning, grammar, syntax, and so on. These rules allow people using a common language to understand one another.

Programming languages are based on the same concept. A programming language allows a programmer to communicate with a computer and tell it what operations to perform by using certain symbols and words in accordance with predefined rules. However, unlike human languages, which can tolerate a fair amount of ambiguity and imprecision (one word may have two meanings, for instance), programming languages must be very precise because, ultimately, a computer can distinguish between only two things: whether electrical current is flowing or not (represented as a binary 0 or a 1).

Just as there are many different human languages, so too are there many different programming languages, each suited to solving particular kinds of problems. In this section, we will survey the wide variety of programming languages available. To begin, we'll explore how programming languages

Figure 9.12

Programming Language Milestones

A number of different programming languages have evolved through the years and can be classified into generations. This figure places the languages and generations along a timeline. Darker shading indicates the periods during which certain languages were most prevalent.

1954 FORTRAN	1958 LISP	1960 COBOL	1964 PL/1,BASIC	1967 APL	1969 Logo	1970 Pascal	1972 Smalltalk	1974 C	1980 Ada, Modula-2	1982 dBASE

Fifth generation: natural languages

Fourth generation: very high-level languages: Nomad, Focus Passport, Others

Third generation: high-level languages

Second generation: assembly language

First generation: machine language

1945   1950   1960   1970   1980   1990

have evolved through the years to the present. Then, we'll focus on some of the major languages in use today, highlighting their advantages, disadvantages, and the types of problems they are commonly used to solve. We'll also examine object-oriented and visual programming languages, important trends that will be affecting the development of software during the 1990s. We'll finish up with some guidelines for you to follow in deciding which programming language is the right tool for the problem at hand.

The Evolution of Programming Languages

Programming languages have changed radically since the first language was developed in the 1940s. Like computers themselves, the evolution of programming languages has traditionally been tracked by using "generations." Languages are classified as being first-, second-, third-, fourth-, or sometimes fifth-generation languages. Each generation has certain common features. In addition, languages are classified by "level." High-level languages are those that more closely resemble the English language; low-level languages are those that correspond more closely to binary 0s and 1s. Figure 9.12 shows you some milestones in the evolution of programming languages.

First Generation: Machine Language   As you learned in Chapter 3, instructions written in **machine language** consist of strings of binary digits: 0s and 1s. Machine language is the "native" language of the computer and can be processed directly by the computer's circuits. Each form of processor has its own machine language.

Machine language was the only way that programmers could communicate with the computers of the 1940s and early 1950s. Programs written in

Grace Hopper (at center) was a key figure in the development of assembly language.

Source: Hagley Museum and Library.

machine language are very efficient (they give the programmer precise control over the computer's operations), but creating them is a mind-numbing task. For instance, the instructions have to specifically identify the storage location for each instruction and piece of data. And since each processor has its own machine language, machine language programs cannot be reused with different machines—they are *machine dependent*.

Writing to a computer chip or processor in binary code (a base 2 number system) takes a lot of 0s and 1s to identify a chunk of memory, issue a command, or say much of anything. However, this process can be shortened considerably by writing the instructions in a shorthand system called the hexadecimal numbering system (or sometimes just "hex" for short).

Hexadecimal is a numbering system in base 16, which requires writing fewer digits than does the binary system. The computer reads the base 16 numbers and converts them to its own base 2 system. Thus, hexadecimal is a sort of machine language that is more convenient for humans to use. Figure 9.13 shows how a number can be converted between the base 2, base 10, and base 16 numbering systems.

Second Generation: Assembly Language In the mid-1950s, computer scientists struggling with machine language came up with the idea of replacing machine language instructions with short *mnemonic (symbolic) codes* that were

Base 2	Base 10	Base 16
0000	0	0
0001	1	1
0010	2	2
0011	3	3
0100	4	4
0101	5	5
0110	6	6
0111	7	7
1000	8	8
1001	9	9
1010	10	A
1011	11	B
1100	12	C
1101	13	D
1110	14	E
1111	15	F

Figure 9.13
Machine Language in Hexadecimal
Hexadecimal is a base 16 numbering system that programmers use as a shorthand for base 2 binary numbers. In base 16, each place is a power of 16 starting with 16^0. The table below shows how to convert numbers between the base 2, base 10, and base 16 systems.

The hex number 72F translates into decimal as:

$$15 \times 16^0 = 15$$
$$2 \times 16^1 = 32$$
$$7 \times 16^2 = 1792$$
$$\text{Total} = 1839$$

The real value of hex is as a shorthand for binary. 72F in hex translates into binary as:

In other words, 72F in hex is shorthand for 0111 0010 1111. Instead of writing 12 digits, you have to write only 3. This makes for shorter programs and easier writing of machine code.

easier to understand and remember. Each machine language instruction was given its own symbolic code. For example, the letter A was used to represent the instruction Add, the letters STO to represent the instruction Store, and so on. The new language also allowed a storage location to be identified by a name or symbol instead of its actual address, as machine language required. Grace Hopper, then a mathematician in the U.S. Naval Reserve, was one of the key figures in the development of this second-generation language, called **assembly language.** (Figure 9.14 compares an assembly language program to a hexadecimal version of a machine language program.) As you learned in Chapter 7, another program, called an *assembler program*, translates the assembly language program into machine language.

Assembly language makes efficient use of computer resources, and as a result, instructions written in assembly can be executed quite rapidly. However, though easier than machine language, assembly language is still very difficult to learn and use. And like programs written in machine language, assembly language programs relate directly to a specific kind of processor and cannot be easily transferred to a different type. As a result, few pro-

Machine Language

Assembly Language

Addresses	Machine Instructions			
0000		CSEG	SEGMENT PARA PUBLIC 'CODE'	
0000			ASSUME CS:CSEG, DS: CSEG	
0000	8C C8	ENTPT	PROC FAR ;entry point	
0002	8E D8		mov ax, cs	
			mov ds, ax ; set up addresses	
		; ---		
0004	BE 0000		mov si, 0 ; clear SI (counts + points to data)	
0007	B0 00		mov al, 0 ; clear AX (stores total)	
0009	02 84 001C R	count:	add al, [DATA+si] ; add memory value toAX	
			; location of memory is	
			; DATA plus value in SI	
000D	46		inc si ; add one to SI	
000E	83 FE 05		cmp si, 5 ; compare SI to 5	
0011	75 F6		jne COUNT ; if SI is not 5 then goto COUNT	
0013	A2 0021 R		mov RESULT, al ; store result in memory	
		; ---		
0016	B4 4C		mov AH,4ch ; return to dos	
0018	B0 00		mov AL, 00 ; return code	
001A	CD 21		int 21H	
001C	0C 0E 09 0B 12	DATA	db 12, 14, 09, 11, 18 ; bytes of data	
0021	00	RESULT	db 00 ; place to store result	
0022		ENTPT	ENDP	
0022		CSEG	ENDS	
		END ENTPT		

Figure 9.14
Hexadecimal Machine Language Compared with Assembly Language
These simple machine and assembly programs written for an 80386 chip add the numbers 1, 2, 3, 4, 5 and store the result in a memory location. The two columns on the left show the machine address locations and the actual machine instructions to make memory available and to move, store, add, and select numbers. The addresses and instructions are written in a shorthand form of binary code called hexadecimal.

Although the machine language obviously cannot be understood by itself, the assembly language at least looks a little more like English. The far right column (text after the ; symbol) is the documentation explaining what each line of code does. The assembly program is broken into three parts. The first part (above the first dashed line) is the entry point setting up blocks of memory and addresses. The second part of the program contains the procedures to follow when adding the numbers. The last part of the program provides the exit back to DOS and places the result in a memory store.

grammers today create programs in assembly language though it is still sometimes used to create operating system software. For instance, the first version of IBM's OS/2 operating system was written in assembly language for the Intel 286 microprocessor.

Third Generation: High-Level Languages   After the development of assembly language, computer scientists continued to focus on making programs easier to write. During the late 1950s, they began to discover ways that allowed programs to be written with regular words that could be combined into sentence-like statements (see Figure 9.15). As we explained more fully in Chapter 7, a program translator (an *interpreter* or *compiler*) translates the statements into machine language. Programmers writing programs in these **high-level languages** could rely on the translator to supply much of the coding detail, and as a result, programs became much easier to create and, once written, read. This allowed programmers to focus on solving a wider variety of problems.

During the 1960s and early 1970s, many new high-level languages were developed, such as FORTRAN, COBOL, BASIC, Pascal, and C, all of which are still significant today. Although some languages were closely related to a specific purpose, many were very flexible and could be used for a wide variety of tasks. In addition, unlike earlier languages, these languages were not machine dependent, and programs written in them could be used with more than one type of computer. The development of third-generation languages also opened the door to the creation of prepackaged software applications— programs written to answer specific needs, such as accounting, spreadsheet, word processing, and data management programs.

Fourth Generation: Very High-Level Languages   The next step in the evolution of programming languages was a shift from the *procedural* model that had characterized the first three generations to a *nonprocedural* model. Traditionally, programs consisted of program instructions that set forth a precise series of steps, or procedures, that the programmer wanted the computer to follow. These steps told the computer not only what the programmer wanted done but also how to do it. In contrast, a program written with a fourth-generation programming language (sometimes just called a **4GL** or a **very high-level language**) merely tells the computer what the programmer would like done, not how the task should be carried out. As a result, many fewer lines of code are required.

```
PROCEDURE DIVISION.

MAIN-PROGRAM.
    PERFORM START-PROCESS.
    PERFORM DECISION-FOR-HONOR-ROLL
        UNTIL END-OF-FILE-FLAG = "Y".
    PERFORM WRAPITUP.
    STOP RUN.

START-PROCESS.
    OPEN INPUT RECORDS-IN OUTPUT PRINT-OUT.
    MOVE SPACES TO STUDENT-LINE.
    WRITE PRINT-LINE FROM HDG AFTER ADVANCING 2 LINES.
    WRITE PRINT-LINE FROM HDG-1 AFTER ADVANCING 2 LINES.
    WRITE PRINT-LINE FROM HDG-2 AFTER ADVANCING 2 LINES.
    WRITE PRINT-LINE FROM HDG-3 AFTER ADVANCING 1 LINE.
```

Figure 9.15
A High-Level Language Program
This program is written in a high-level language called COBOL. As you can see, the instructions are much easier to read and understand than machine or assembly language instructions.

4GLs tend to fall into two basic categories. Some are aimed at helping programmers develop software more efficiently. 4GL supporters claim that 4GL applications can be written in anywhere from 1/5th to 1/300th the number of hours it takes to complete a comparable COBOL program, for instance. One example of this kind of 4GL is an application generator. **Application generators** are software tools that allow you to specify what needs to be done and then generate the code needed to create a program to perform the task. Although lacking the capabilities of a full-blown computer-aided software engineering (CASE) environment, application generators allow you to design and test applications in much less time than if you had to write the program code yourself. Application generators usually include menu and screen generators. *Menu generators* help create menus with lists of processing options, whereas *screen generators* help design input and output screens. Application generators also often integrate other 4GL tools like report generators, query language, and other very high-level programming language capabilities. Some popular application generators that include some if not all of these features include Must Software International's Nomad, Information Builder's Focus, and InSynch Software Corporation's Passport. There are also specialized code generators for specific markets, such as C code generators aimed at developing applications for Microsoft's Windows environment.

Fox Pro, a database management software program offered by Microsoft, can also be used as an application generator.

Source: Courtesy of Microsoft Corporation.

Other 4GLs are aimed at helping end users work more productively. These 4GLs allow nonprogrammers to create some customized applications themselves without having to call on information systems support staff. They are an example of the trend toward bringing programming back to end users, which we discussed at the beginning of this chapter. Examples of this form of 4GL include query languages and report generators.

Query languages are tools that provide customized access to data stored in a database. It's one thing to collect data in a database; another to make it available to users in a way that's meaningful to them. Most companies have applications software that produces certain standard reports. But what if the information you need is not contained in those reports or is presented in a way that's not useful to you? Query languages are high-level, relatively easy-to-use languages that allow you to create an ad hoc request that will produce the information you need. Some query languages also allow you to update data stored in the database. Examples of query languages include Structured Query Language (SQL), Query-By-Example (QBE), and Intellect.

SQL is a standardized query language that can be used with many different database management programs.

Source: Courtesy of Borland International, Inc.

Report generators help you produce customized reports. A report generator differs from a query language by providing you with more control over the way the data is actually organized and displayed. With a report generator, you can specify the headings, decide which data are to be represented as columns, determine how the columns should be positioned, choose a numbering scheme, and so on. The report generator then automatically compiles the data into the format chosen. RPG III, a successor to the third-generation language RPG, is a popular report generator.

4GLs do have some disadvantages. They generally are more narrowly focused on a particular task and provide the user with fewer options and less control over how the task is actually performed. As a result, they lack the flexibility and general-purpose powers of third-generation languages. They also generally require more processing power and processing time than procedural languages. Today, third-generation languages are still the primary tool for application development, especially for mainframe application software, as Figure 9.16 illustrates.

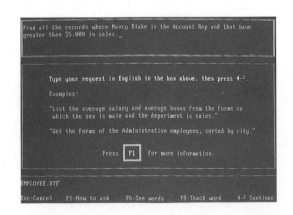

Fifth Generation: Natural Languages   Many commentators feel the programming profession is poised on the edge of a new generation. So-called **natural languages** resemble the English language even more than their predecessor 4GLs. Some basic natural language capabilities are beginning to be added to query languages in particular. They allow a user to query, or ask, a question of a database in regular English and receive a response. Here's an example. Suppose you are tracking down some sales leads in the New York area. You want to look at the records of all current customers with annual revenue of over $500,000 who have ZIP codes between 10000 and 19999. In fourth-generation languages, you would probably have to write a small program in a user friendly language or select the proper command from a menu and then type in something like the following in a dialog box:

Zip: > = 10000 or < = 19999

Annual Revenue: > = 500000

Current Customer: = Y

But if you created your database using Q&A, a popular microcomputer database applications package, you could use a feature called Intelligent Assistant, which allows you to enter the same query by merely typing, "Show me the records where Zip is between 10000 and 19999, Annual Revenue is greater than 500000, and Current Customer is Yes." Intelligent Assistant has a built-in vocabulary of over 600 words. You can also teach it to recognize and understand new words.

Elementary natural language features are beginning to show up in some commercial products, but overall natural languages are still in their infancy.

This screen gives you an example of the types of customized reports that can be produced with a report generator.

Source: Courtesy of Information Resources, Inc.

Q & A is a database management program with some natural language capabilities: it allows users to query a database in regular English.

Source: Fredrik D. Bodin/Offshoot.

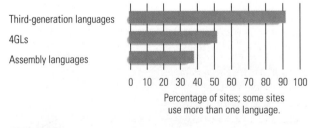

Third-generation languages

4GLs

Assembly languages

0 10 20 30 40 50 60 70 80 90 100

Percentage of sites; some sites
use more than one language.

Figure 9.16

Languages Used for Application Development at Mainframe Sites

Ninety-one percent of mainframe sites surveyed still use third-generation programming languages to develop software applications. Only slightly more than half use 4GLs.

Source: Xephon WPWS, Oviedo, Florida; cited in *Computerworld*, July 27, 1992.

By the year 2000, you can expect that they will be much more widespread. Natural languages are also an important part of the larger field of artificial intelligence and knowledge-based systems, which we will discuss in greater depth in Chapter 14.

Major Programming Languages in Use Today

Now let's turn to a survey of some of the major high-level programming languages in use today: FORTRAN, COBOL, BASIC, Pascal, and C. Although hundreds of different languages have been developed since the 1960s, only a handful are extensively used throughout the computer industry. We'll briefly review the background, the advantages and disadvantages, and the most popular uses of each of these significant languages.

FORTRAN FORTRAN (short for FORmula TRANslator) is the oldest surviving high-level language. Developed in the mid-1950s by a team of IBM programmers, FORTRAN was designed primarily to solve scientific, mathematical, and engineering problems that required repetitive numerical calculations and complex formulas. It quickly developed a reputation for efficiency in computational speed and memory usage. It also offered a large, well-designed library of preprogrammed *subroutines* that users could incorporate into their own programs. These features earned FORTRAN a large and dedicated group of users, and today, it remains the favorite number-crunching programming language of scientists, mathematicians, and engineers.

FORTRAN's ability to calculate complex formulas and solve sophisticated numerical problems also makes it useful for complex business applications such as forecasting and modeling. However, though improvements have been added to the language over the years, it still does not have strong capabilities for handling a large volume of input/output operations or file processing. As a result, FORTRAN would not be the best choice for typical business problems such as producing reports or reading and recording large numbers of records.

Although traditionally used in a mainframe environment, FORTRAN can run on minicomputers and workstations as well and is becoming increasingly available on microcomputers. It also appears to be the language of choice for supercomputers, particularly those that use parallel processing.

Figure 9.17 illustrates a simple FORTRAN program that calculates a student's grade point average at the end of a semester and shows you the output that would result. Subsequent figures will show you the same program as it would be written in COBOL, BASIC, Pascal, and C. Compare how the different languages look and the different ways they handle the same problem.

Figure 9.17
FORTRAN

FORTRAN is a fairly easy-to-read, high-level language.

```
      character*1 grade(5)
      character*30 course(5)
      write(*,*)
      write(*,*) 'Student Grade Report: Jennifer Jonson'
      write(*,*)
      write(*,*) 'Class             Grade Number'
      total=0
c do the rest of this 5 times
      do 10, i=1, 5
      if (grade(i).EQ.'A') gradenum=4
      if (grade(i).EQ.'B') gradenum=3
      if (grade(i).EQ.'C') gradenum=2
      if (grade(i).EQ.'D') gradenum=1
      if (grade(i).EQ.'F') gradenum=0
      total=total+gradenum
      write(*,98) course(i),grade(i),gradenum
10    continue
      average=total/5
      write(*,*)'
      write(*,99) average
      data grade /'A','B','B','C','A'/
      data course / 'Freshman English', 'Roman Empire',
+     ' Elementary French','Pre-Calculus','Volleyball 1'/
98    format (1x,A30,2x,A1,4x,f4.2)
99    format ('Average',30x,f4.2)
      end
```

Output

Student Grade Report: Jennifer Jonson

Class	Grade	Number
Freshman English	A	4.00
Roman Empire	B	3.00
Elementary French	B	3.00
Pre-Calculus	C	2.00
Volleyball 1	A	4.00
Average		3.20

COBOL As its name indicates, **COBOL** (short for COmmon Business Oriented Language) was developed to handle business problems. Machine language, assembly language, and FORTRAN were not particularly well suited to handling such applications. A joint effort by computer professionals and the federal government resulted in COBOL's introduction in 1960. Today, COBOL remains the primary business programming language with more than two-thirds of mainframe users citing it as their top programming language. And as mainframe users have migrated to microcomputers, so too has COBOL; today many different microcomputer-based COBOL compiler programs are available to allow COBOL programs originally designed for mainframes to run on microcomputers.

COBOL was designed to handle large data files containing alphanumeric characters (letters and numbers). It is very effective in reading, writing, and manipulating records and allows the programmer to specify input/output formats. COBOL uses English-like phrases, and is much easier to learn, write, and read than a language like FORTRAN. The language is organized around four major parts or divisions. The *identification* division identifies the program, the *environment* division specifies which computer the program will be running on, the *data* division describes the data to be processed, and the *procedure* division provides the actual instructions to be executed. Like FORTRAN, COBOL is relatively machine independent. Together, these attributes made COBOL quite attractive for business use.

COBOL is not without its disadvantages though. The same characteristics that make COBOL programs easy to write and read also make them wordy and long. It takes many more lines of COBOL code than it does in other high-level languages to accomplish the same task. As we noted, 4GLs have the edge in productivity. But a very large installed base of existing COBOL applications (estimated at 70 billion lines of code!) has been developed over the years.[1] These programs are maintained by a large cadre of dedicated COBOL programmers. Changing these applications to a different language can be expensive and risky. As a result, despite the complaints that COBOL is a clumsy dinosaur that lacks the advanced capabilities of newer languages, it is unlikely that COBOL will fade from the scene anytime soon. In fact, it may even experience some renewed growth as newer versions that work with Windows and UNIX and run on 64-bit systems and in client/server environments become increasingly available.

Figure 9.18 illustrates a COBOL program that calculates GPA and the output that results. Note how many more lines of code are required compared to the FORTRAN program shown in Figure 9.17.

BASIC **BASIC** (short for Beginner's All-purpose Symbolic Instruction Code) was developed in 1964 by two Dartmouth professors, John Kemeny and Thomas Kurtz. BASIC is a relatively simple, easy-to-learn language designed to work in an interactive environment.

Earlier computer programs were run in a *batch processing environment*—the programmer submitted the program and data and waited for it to be run some time later. If there were any errors in the program, the job would stop when it reached the first one. After deciphering the reason for the error and fixing it, the programmer would have to resubmit the entire program and run it from the beginning, with the hope that there were no further errors. If there were, the whole process would begin again. In contrast, an *interactive processing environment* featuring on-line terminals allows the user to communicate with the computer as the program is being written and data is being input. Changes can be made as soon as errors are discovered.

John Kemeny, a professor at Dartmouth, was one of the creators of BASIC.

Source: Courtesy of Dartmouth News Service.

```
IDENTIFICATION DIVISION.
PROGRAM-I.D. PGM001.
AUTHOR. JOHN DOE
DATE-WRITTEN. MARCH 8, 1993.
DATE-COMPILED.


*
**  ┌─────────────────────────────────────────────────┐
*   │ SYSTEM:           STUDENT GRADE REPORT            │
*   │ RUNNING SCHEDULE:     ON DEMAND                   │
*   │ OVERVIEW:         THIS PROGRAM WILL READ STUDENT DATA, │
*   │                   CALCULATE AND PRINT STUDENT'S GRADE │
*   │                   AVERAGE.                        │
*   │ INPUT:            STUDENT DATA                    │
*   │ OUTPUT:           REPORT OF STUDENT'S GRADES AND THE │
*   │                   GRADE AVERAGE                   │
*   └─────────────────────────────────────────────────┘


ENVIRONMENT DIVISION.
CONFIGURATION SECTION.
SOURCE-COMPUTER. IBM-PC.
OBJECT-COMPUTER. IBM-PC.
SPECIAL-NAMES. C01 IS TOP-OF-PAGE.
INPUT-OUTPUT SECTION.
FILE-CONTROL.
    SELECT STUDENT-DATA
        ASSIGN TO "D:\INPUT.DAT".
    SELECT GRADES-REPORT
        ASSIGN TO "D:\OUTPUT.REP".
*_____
DATA DIVISION.
FILE SECTION.
FD  STUDENT-DATA
    RECORD CONTAINS 121 CHARACTERS
    DATA RECORD IS STUDENT-REC.
*
01  STUDENT-REC.
    03 STUDENT-NAME.
        10 FIRST-NAME        PIC X(8).
        10 LAST-NAME         PIC X(8).
    03 CLASS-DATA OCCURS 5 TIMES.
        10 CLASS-DESCR       PIC X(20).
        10 CLASS-GRADE       PIC X.
*
FD  GRADES-REPORT
    RECORD CONTAINS 80 CHARACTERS
    LABEL RECORDS ARE OMITTED
    BLOCK CONTAINS 0 RECORDS
    DATA RECORD IS PRINI-LINE.
*
01  PRINT-LINE               PIC X(80).
*
WORKING-STORAGE SECTION.
*
01  WS-INDEX                 PIC 9 COMP VALUE ZERO.
01  WS-GRADE-SUMM            PIC 99V99 COMP-3 VALUE ZERO.
01  WS-GRADE AVERAGE         PIC 9V99 COMP-3 VALUE ZERO.
01  WS-EOF                   PIC X VALUE SPACE.
    88 END-OF-FILE           VALUE 'Y'.
```

Figure 9.18
A COBOL Program

Figure 9.18
A COBOL Program
COBOL is easy to understand and learn but very wordy and difficult to debug. COBOL excels at file handling but is less good at number-crunching tasks.

317

```cobol
*
01  WS-HEADER.
    03 FILLER               PIC X(5)
           VALUE 'Class'.
    03 FILLER               PIC X(22)
           VALUE SPACES.
    03 FILLER               PIC X(12)
           VALUE 'Grade Number'.
01  WS-STUDENT-NAME.
    03 FILLER               PIC X(22)
           VALUE 'Student Grade Report:'.
    03 WS-FIRST NAME        PIC X(8)
           VALUE SPACES.
    03 FILLER               PIC X
           VALUE SPACES.
    03 WS-LAST-NAME         PIC X(8)
           VALUE SPACES.
01  WS-CLASS-LINE.
    03 WS-CLASS-DESCR       PIC X(20)
           VALUE SPACES.
    03 FILLER               PIC X(9)
           VALUE SPACES.
    03 WS-CLASS-GRADE       PIC X
           VALUE ZEROES.
    03 FILLER               PIC X(4)
           VALUE SPACES.
    03 WS-CLASS-GRADE-NUM   PIC 9.99
           VALUE ZEROES.
01  WS-UNDERLINE.
    03 FILLER               PIC X(33)
           VALUE SPACES.
03  FILLER                  PIC X(6)
           VALUES '_____'.
01  WS-AVERAGE-LINE.
    03 FILLER               PIC X(34)
           VALUES 'Average'.
    03 WS-AVERAGE           PIC 9.99
           VALUES ZEROES.
*------------------------------------------------
PROCEDURE DIVISION.
    OPEN INPUT STUDENT-DATA
        OUTPUT GRADES-REPORT.
    PERFORM 100-PROCESS-STUDENT
           THRU 100-EXIT
           UNTIL END-OF-FILE.
    PERFORM 900-END-OF-JOB
        THRU 900-EXIT.
*
100-PROCESS-STUDENT.
    READ STUDENT-DATA INTO STUDENT-REC
        AT END MOVE 'Y' TO WS-EOF.
    IF END-OF-FILE
       NEXT SENTENCE
    ELSE
       PERFORM 150-CALC-AND-PRINT
           THRU 150-EXIT.
100-EXIT.
    EXIT.
```

```
*
150-CALC-AND-PRINT.
    MOVE SPACES TO PRINT-LINE.
    MOVE ZEROES TO WS-GRADE-SUMM.
    WRITE PRINT-LINE AFTER ADVANCING TOP-OF-PAGE.
    MOVE FIRST-NAME TO WS-FIRST-NAME.
    MOVE LAST-NAME TO WS-LAST-NAME.
    WRITE PRINT-LINE FROM WS-STUDENT-NAME
        AFTER ADVANCING 1 LINE.
    WRITE PRINT-LINE FROM WS-HEADER
        AFTER ADVANCING 2 LINES.
    PERFORM 155-PROCESS-CLASS THRU 155-EXIT
            WITH TEST AFTER
            VARYING WS-INDEX FROM 1 BY 1
            UNTIL CLASS-DESCR (WS-INDEX) = SPACES OR
                WS-INDEX = 5.
    DIVIDE WS-GRADE-SUMM BY WS-INDEX
        GIVING WS-GRADE-AVERAGE.
    MOVE WS-GRADE-AVERAGE TO WS-AVERAGE.
    WRITE PRINT-LINE FROM WS-UNDERLINE
        AFTER ADVANCING 1 LINE.
    WRITE PRINT-LINE FROM WS-AVERAGE-LINE
        AFTER ADVANCING 1 LINE.
150-EXIT.
    EXIT.
155-PROCESS-CLASS.
    MOVE CLASS-DESCR (WS-INDEX) TO WS-CLASS-DESCR.
    MOVE CLASS-GRADE (WS-INDEX) TO WS-CLASS-GRADE.
    IF WS-CLASS-GRADE = 'A'
        MOVE 4 TO WS-CLASS-GRADE-NUM
        ADD 4 TO WS-GRADE-SUMM
    ELSE
        IF WS-CLASS-GRADE = 'B'
            MOVE 3 TO WS-CLASS-GRADE-NUM
            ADD 3 TO WS-GRADE-SUMM
        ELSE
            IF WS-CLASS-GRADE = 'C'
                MOVE 2 TO WS-CLASS-GRADE-NUM
                ADD 2 TO WS-GRADE-SUMM
            ELSE
                IF WS-CLASS-GRADE = 'D'
                    MOVE 1 TO WS-CLASS-GRADE-NUM
                    ADD 1 TO WS-GRADE-SUMM
                ELSE
                    IF WS-CLASS-GRADE = 'F'
                        MOVE 0 TO WS-CLASS-GRADE-NUM.
    WRITE PRINT-LINE FROM WS-CLASS-LINE
        AFTER ADVANCING 1 LINE.
155-EXIT.
    EXIT.
900-END-OF-JOB.
    CLOSE STUDENT-DATA,
        GRADES-REPORT.
    STOP RUN.
900-EXIT.
    EXIT.
```

Output

```
Student Grade Report: Jennifer Jonson

Class               Grade   Number
Freshman English    A       4.00
Roman Empire        B       3.00
Elementary French   B       3.00
Pre-Calculus        C       2.00
Volleyball 1        A       4.00

Average                     3.20
```

BASIC soon became the standard for teaching students the essentials of programming. Features that make BASIC easy to learn include the conversational, interactive programming mode it supports, its easy-to-understand error messages as well as other helpful diagnostic tools like an on-line syntax checker, and simplified rules for naming and classifying variables. With only a few hours of training, a student can write a program to handle a simple task, like sorting the results of a survey or calculating the load-carrying capacity of different building materials.

BASIC continues to enjoy widespread use. Although primarily used for educational purposes, its popularity has expanded beyond the campus into other arenas. As the principal programming language for microcomputers when they were first introduced, BASIC has allowed people with good ideas but little programming experience to create their own programs. And BASIC is starting to make headway as a "serious" programming language in the business world. More than 5 million developers program PCs in BASIC according to market estimates, not including programmers from DEC, IBM, and Hewlett-Packard, which offer versions of BASIC for their minicomputers and instrument control systems.[2]

Many different versions of BASIC exist today. The most popular are Kemeny and Kurtz's True BASIC, Microsoft's QuickBASIC, and an object-oriented version called Visual Basic for Windows. Visual Basic has much more in common with advanced 4GLs than regular BASIC and has begun to take hold in corporate America, with over 100,000 applications now in business use.[3] The language has proved particularly useful for prototyping and allows for the rapid development of applications. Newer versions of BASIC come with compilers to translate the language into machine code rather than the much slower interpreters that were used with earlier versions.

Despite its popularity, BASIC has detractors who complain that though it can do many things, it does few things well. The perception is that BASIC is for beginners, not "real programmers." To make matters worse, because the older versions of BASIC lacked structures that required a well-organized program, many claimed that it was not even conducive to teaching good programming practices. Edgser Dijkstra, a prominent computer scientist, once charged that it was almost impossible to teach good programming to students who had had prior exposure to BASIC. "As potential programmers, they are mentally mutilated beyond repair," he said.[4] Nonetheless, BASIC is beginning to overcome its reputation and is likely to continue to play an important role in the coming years. For instance, Microsoft, in addition to offering QuickBASIC and Visual Basic to outside programmers, itself chose BASIC as the programming language for Access, its new database software product.

Figure 9.19 illustrates the GPA program written in BASIC and its output.

Pascal   Pascal was created by Niklaus Wirth, a Swiss computer scientist, in the late 1960s. Named after the French mathematician Blaise Pascal, Pascal is an alternative to BASIC as a teaching language. Although Pascal, like BASIC, is relatively easy to learn, it requires a more structured, well-organized approach than BASIC. For instance, programmers must define all variables to be used in the program in a separate section at the beginning of the program. This helps prevent errors.

Pascal also supports more sophisticated programs than BASIC. Each Pascal program is made up of smaller subprograms. Pascal allows the programmer to invoke different control structures to systematically manipulate these subprograms. This approach makes it easier to create large programs.

Niklaus Wirth, the creator of Pascal.
Source: Shelly R. Harrison.

The French mathematician and inventor Blaise Pascal.
Source: North Wind Picture Archives.

Figure 9.19
A BASIC Program

BASIC is very English-like, easy to read, and fairly economical. However, the original BASIC did not allow programmers to use case control structures.

```
5 PRINT
10 PRINT "Student Grade Report: Jennifer Jonson"
11 PRINT
15 PRINT "Class", "              Grade Number"
20 FOR A = 1 TO 5¹ do this 5 times
30 READ CLASS$, GRADE$
40 IF GRADE$ = "A" THEN NUM = 4
50 IF GRADE$ = "B" THEN NUM = 3
60 IF GRADE$ = "C" THEN NUM = 2
70 IF GRADE$ = "D" THEN NUM = 1
80 IF GRADE$ = "F" THEN NUM = 0
90 PRINT CLASS$, GRADE$;
100 PRINT USING "   #.##"; NUM
110 TOTAL — TOTAL + NUM
120 NEXT A
130 AVERAGE = TOTAL / 5
140 PRINT , , "   _____"
150 PRINT "Average" , , ;
160 PRINT USING "          #.##"; AVERAGE
1000 DATA "Freshman English   ",A
1010 DATA "Roman Empire       ",B
1020 DATA "Elementary French  ",B
1030 DATA "Pre-Calculus       ",C
1040 DATA "Volleyball 1       ",A
```

Output

Student Grade Report: Jennifer Jonson

Class	Grade	Number
Freshman English	A	4.00
Roman Empire	B	3.00
Elementary French	B	3.00
Pre-Calculus	C	2.00
Volleyball 1	A	4.00
Average		3.20

```
Program grades (input, output);
var
    A:integer;
    num, total, average: real;
    grade: array [1. .5] of char;
    class: array [1. .5] of string [30];

Begin
grade [1] : = 'A';
grade [2] : = 'B';
grade [3] : = 'B';
grade [4] : = 'C';
grade [5] : = 'A';
class [1] : = 'Freshman English        ';
class [2] : = 'Roman Empire            ';
class [3] : = 'Elementary French       ';
class [4] : = 'Pre-Calculus            ';
class [5] : = 'Volleyball 1            ';

Writeln;
writeln ( 'Student Grade Report: Jennifer Jonson');
writeln;
writeln ( 'Class             Grade Number' ) ;
    For a: = 1 to 5 do
        Begin
            case grade [a] of
                'A' : num: = 4;
                'B' : num: = 3;
                'C' : num: = 2;
                'D' : num: = 1;
                'F' : num: = 0;
            end; (case)
            writeln (CLASS [a],'      ',GRADE [a],'       ',NUM: 4:2);
            total :=total+num;
        end; {for}
    average:=total/5;
    writeln('                      – – – – – ');
    writeln ('Average          ', average: 4:2);
end.
```

Output

Student Grade Report: Jennifer Jonson

Class	Grade	Number
Freshman English	A	4.00
Roman Empire	B	3.00
Elementary French	B	3.00
Pre-Calculus	C	2.00
Volleyball 1	A	4.00
Average		3.20

Figure 9.20
A Pascal Program
Pascal was created to teach structured programming techniques. Pascal programs are easy to read and debug but poor at handling many common business tasks like large file handling.

Turbo C ++ is an object-oriented version of the C programming language offered by Borland International.

Source: Courtesy of Borland International, Inc.

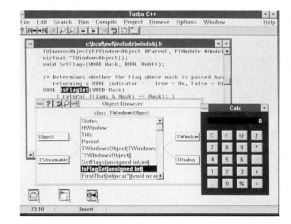

Although Pascal is not as well suited as COBOL for heavy-duty business transaction processing, an updated, object-oriented version called Turbo Pascal (offered by Borland International Inc.) has become quite popular with nonprofessional programmers in the business community.

Figure 9.20 shows a Pascal program that calculates GPA and its output.

C   The **C** programming language was developed at AT&T's Bell Laboratories in the early 1970s. It was originally created as a language to write operating system software and is the language in which most UNIX operating system programs are written. C is a high-level programming language that has many of the advantages of assembly language without being as difficult to use. Like the UNIX operating system, C programs are machine independent and can run on different kinds of computers. Today, C is the language of choice for the development of most commercial microcomputer software applications packages.

C's primary disadvantage is that it is not an easy language to learn. Although it contains many similarities to Pascal, C is for experienced programmers, not beginners. In the next section, we discuss C++, an object-oriented version of C.

Figure 9.21 illustrates the GPA program written in C and its output.

Figure 9.21
A Program in C
C provides the programmer with the power and efficiency of assembly language while being much easier to work with. However, it is not as easy to read and use as some other high-level languages.

```c
#include <stdio.h>
main()
{
char * course[5]={"Freshman English ",
                  "Roman Empire     ",
                  "Elementary French",
                  "Pre-Calculus     ",
                  "Volleyball 1     "};
char grade[5]={'A','B','B','C','A'};
int a;
float num,total=0;

printf("\n");
printf( "Student Grade Report: Jennifer Jonson\n");
printf("\n");
printf("Class\t      Grade Number\n");
for (a=0;a<5;a++)
  {
  switch (grade[a])
    {
    case 'A':num=4;break;
    case 'B':num=3;break;
    case 'C':num=2;break;
    case 'D':num=1;break;
    case 'F':num=0;break;
    }
  printf("%s\t%c  %g \n",course[a],grade[a],num);
  total=total+num;
  }
printf("\t\t\t ------\n");
printf("Average\t\t      %g\n",total\5);
}
```

Output

```
Student Grade Report: Jennifer Jonson

Class                Grade   Number
Freshman English     A       4.00
Roman Empire         B       3.00
Elementary French    B       3.00
Pre-Calculus         C       2.00
Volleyball 1         A       4.00
                             ------
Average                      3.20
```

Other Programming Languages

In addition to the programming languages we have discussed, there are a number of other third-generation languages that you may encounter. These include PL/1, APL, RPG, Ada, LISP, Prolog, Logo, Modula-2, and dBASE.

▶ **PL/1** IBM introduced **PL/1** (short for Programming Language/1) in 1964. It was designed to be a general-purpose business and scientific problem-solving language. Although a very powerful and flexible language, PL/1 has not been able to make many inroads into markets already dominated by COBOL and FORTRAN.

▶ **APL** Another early programming language is **APL** (short for A Programming Language). APL uses a number of special symbols that enable users to solve complex formulas in a single step. These symbols, not part of the normal ASCII or EBCDIC character set, require a specially configured keyboard. APL is particularly useful for processing groups of numbers in table form. Although its supporters claim that APL programs can be written in much shorter time than comparable FORTRAN programs, its detractors argue that APL's special symbols and programming conventions make it too difficult to learn.

▶ **RPG** The programming language **RPG** (short for Report Program Generator) was designed, as its name indicates, to help generate business reports. The programmer uses a special form to supply the details about what data the report should include and how the report should look. The program then generates another program to produce the report.

Initially created by IBM in the early 1960s and refined in later versions, RPG (in its 4GL form, RPG III) today remains very popular and is used quite extensively with the IBM minicomputer line (Systems 36, 38, and the AS/400).

▶ **Ada** Sponsored by the Department of Defense, **Ada** (named after Charles Babbage's "programmer" Ada, Countess of Lovelace) was originally developed in 1980 to serve as a standard language for weapons systems and has since spread to other military and some nonmilitary applications. A large and complex language, Ada has a required format that promotes structured programming and is portable across hardware lines though the amount of memory required to use the language hinders its use on microcomputers. Although based on Pascal, Ada includes a number of additional features such as reusable software components, real-time control of tasks (where the computerized process must be able to respond immediately, in real time, to input and feedback), and concurrent processing capabilities. But despite these attractive features and the support of industry leaders such as Intel, Ada has not yet caught on in the business community. Commercial users have a big investment in COBOL, FORTRAN, and C programs and have little incentive to sacrifice them in favor of Ada. As a result, many experts feel that it is unlikely that Ada will be successful in expanding beyond the government market.

▶ **LISP** Developed in 1958 by John McCarthy, an MIT mathematician, **LISP** (short for LISt Processor) has grown from a language for theorists to an important tool used to construct artificial intelligence programs. LISP is based on the premise that logical deductions can be represented and manipulated using lists. LISP is used today in expert systems and natural language programs. The Department of Defense has adopted a variation of LISP called Common Lisp as one of its three official languages. The story "Creating a New World," examines a complex expert system created using a LISP-based programming language.

Ada Augusta Byron, Countess of Lovelace.

Source: Culver Pictures, Inc.

Seymour Papert, MIT, with students using Logo at the Hennegan School, Boston.

Source: Bob Kramer.

▶ **Prolog**   Another programming language used for artificial intelligence purposes is **Prolog.** Like 4GLs, Prolog is a nonprocedural language. Prolog was selected by the Japanese as the language for their fifth-generation computer project.

▶ **Logo**   Developed at Massachusetts Institute of Technology by Seymour Papert, **Logo** has become a language that is widely used to teach school-children problem-solving skills and how to program. Logo allows the user to control the movements of an on-screen, triangle-shaped character called a *turtle* (see photo). The turtle responds to instructions like forward, left, right, penup, and pendown to allow users to create simple graphics.

▶ **Modula-2** and **Modula-3**   The creator of Pascal, Niklaus Wirth, created **Modula-2** in 1980 to improve and expand on Pascal. Like Pascal, Modula-2 continues to emphasize structured programming but is specifically designed for writing systems software. **Modula-3** includes further enhancements and improvements.

▶ **dBASE**   Introduced by Ashton-Tate in 1982 (and now supported by Borland International), **dBASE** is often thought of merely as a database management applications software package. However, the most current version of dBASE on the market, dBASE IV (as well as its predecessor, dBASE III Plus) is a very powerful programming language as well. dBASE contains a number of different commands (such as GO TO, DO WHILE, LIST, LOOP) that allow you to create your own applications.

dBase, a popular database management program, is also a powerful programming language.

Source: Courtesy of Borland International, Inc.

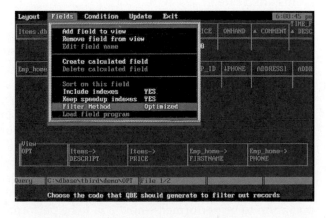

In September 1991, eight human guinea pigs physically sealed themselves off from the rest of the world as part of a controversial private research experiment called Biosphere 2. Biosphere 2's goal was to recreate the Earth's ecosystem (known as Biosphere 1) within a closed environment—a huge greenhouse-like dome located near Tucson, Arizona (see photo).

Awaiting the eight men and women within Biosphere 2 was a diverse physical environment. The glass and steel structure contained several biomes: a 30-foot deep ocean with waves, tide, and coral reef; a rain forest with a 50-foot mountain, waterfalls, and clouds; a desert; a marshland; a savannah; farmland; and a habitat for the project team. Several thousand species of plants, animals, and insects shared the Biosphere. The Biospherians aimed to remain within Biosphere 2 for two years with only power and information being exchanged with the outside world. All other requirements of human life—air, water, food—were to be created within Biosphere 2 and all waste products recycled.

Building an entire new world was certainly an ambitious task and one that would have been entirely inconceivable without the help of information technology and systems. A major part of the project was the creation of the Nerve System: a sophisticated control and monitoring expert system powered by several Hewlett-Packard HP9000 workstations

The agriculture biome in Biosphere 2 contains over 150 crops.

Source: AP/Wide World Photos.

hooked together using a broadband telecommunications network. The Nerve System was created using G2, a variation of the LISP programming language developed by Gensym Corporation.

Let's take a closer look at some of the functions the Nerve System needed to supply. For starters, each biome's climate

Object-Oriented and Visual Programming

Now that we've reviewed the major programming languages in use today, let's look at two important, related trends that may affect the future of those languages as well as traditional programming techniques. Object-oriented programming and visual programming may revolutionize the way programs are created.

Object-Oriented Programming In Chapter 7, we introduced you to the basics of *object-oriented programming* (OOP). Traditional structured programming keeps data separate from the procedures that manipulate the data. Every time some action is to be taken with respect to a piece of data, a separate programming operation needs to be written. OOP instead focuses on the creation of objects. An *object* consists of a block of programming code that encapsulates a chunk of data and instructions about the operations to be performed on that data all into one. The code describes all the significant attributes of the object and all the actions that the object may be called on to perform. Then when an operation involving the object is required to be performed, a *message* is sent to the object. The message need only identify the operation to be performed—how it is to be performed is already embedded within the instructions (called *methods*) that are part of the object.

How does this work in a real application? CSX Transportation Corporation, a Jacksonville, Florida, rail freight system, created locomotive objects

needs to be created and controlled. To accomplish this function, researchers created a G2-based expert system, called the Biome Supervisory Controller, that runs on autonomous, dedicated HP 9000/375 computers. The systems rely on sensors and actuators to provide the necessary raw data about environmental conditions within the biome.

The Biome Supervisory Controller systems are then monitored by other G2-based expert systems. One system (called the Process Variable Monitoring System), running on a Sun-Sparc 2 workstation, monitors environmental indicators, including carbon dioxide levels, light, temperature, humidity, air flow, water flow, pressure, and ocean water quality. If any of the monitored indicators goes above certain levels, a graphic alarm icon is displayed on a geographic map of Biosphere 2, indicating the location of the problem. A text message describes the problem, along with information to help personnel determine the root cause of the condition.

A second system (called the Network Monitoring System), running on an HP 9000/375 computer, monitors all computer, data acquisition, and control systems on the network, including file systems, shared memory, network traffic, systems security, systems load, and so on. Other specialized systems include a continuous water-quality monitoring system (with a record of all tests being stored in a historical database system), a G2 system that controls an instrument for continu-

ously testing air samples, and another system aimed at energy optimization.

What made G2 such an appropriate choice to develop these systems? A subset of the programming language Common Lisp, G2 integrates a number of software technologies, including object-oriented programming, rule-based reasoning (needed for the development of expert systems), windowing, animated graphics, structured natural language capabilities, network services, and most important, real-time data collection and management facilities.

Sources: Based on Stewart, Rocky, "Biosphere 2 Nerve System," *Communications of the ACM*, September 1991; Allard, James and Lowell Hawkinson, "Real-Time Programming in Common Lisp," *Communications of the ACM*, September 1991.

Critical Thinking Questions

1 What other programming languages might have been appropriate choices? Which languages would not be as appropriate?

2 The Biosphere Project is trying to use information technology and software to create a new world. How similar is this new world to the real world? In what ways is it different? How relevant do you think scientific research obtained from such sources would be to real-world problems?

3 The Biosphere Project has proved to be very controversial. Why do you think this is so?

for its rail freight tracking system. Each object contained data about a specific type of locomotive's fuel mileage and hauling capacity, as well as the ability to calculate fuel consumption.[5] When the mouse button is clicked on the locomotive, that action sends the object the message to calculate fuel consumption. Instructions on how to calculate consumption need not be given; they are already embedded within the code for the locomotive object.

Once an object has been created, it can become the foundation for similar objects that have the same behaviors and characteristics. Objects that are derived or related to one another are said to form a *class*. Each class contains specific instructions or methods that are unique to that group. For instance, let's suppose we were writing a client-management program for stockbrokers. We can start by creating a class of objects called client accounts. All client accounts share certain characteristics (such as the name and address of the client and data on the client's portfolio such as the name of securities owned) and will have certain methods associated with them (for example, instructions for totaling the client's portfolio). We can then create subclasses of objects that retain all the attributes of the parent class but also have special characteristics that are unique to the subclass. For example, here we could create a subclass of client accounts called a trading account. The trading account object inherits all the characteristics and methods of the client account but also has some special characteristics: for instance, it includes instructions for calculating the gain or loss on the sale of securities. Subclasses can be

CSX uses an OOP-based system to calculate the fuel consumption of its locomotive.

Source: Courtesy of CSX Transportation.

further broken down into additional subclasses (trading accounts for different kinds of securities: stocks, bonds, and so on). In each instance, the subclass inherits all the capabilities of the classes above it. This method of passing traits down to subclasses is called *inheritance* (see Figure 9.22).

The ability to create predefined groups of classes (called *class libraries*) without having to rewrite the code to define all the initial attributes of the object is one of OOP's greatest benefits. For instance, CSX was able to use the locomotive object to create a subclass of related objects (container cars) for the firm's railway container-tracking application. Being able to reuse a basic object and just adding code for those characteristics that are specific to the new subclass can save programmers a tremendous amount of time. OOP becomes even more efficient as these libraries of reusable objects grow. In addition, updating code becomes a much easier task. If the original design of a parent class is modified, all members of the class automatically change to reflect the modification.

Unfortunately, although OOP can improve productivity, it has a very steep learning curve that can initially slow programmers down. At Kash n' Karry Food Stores, a $1 billion grocery chain, learning to build object-class libraries took the company's information systems staff more than six months

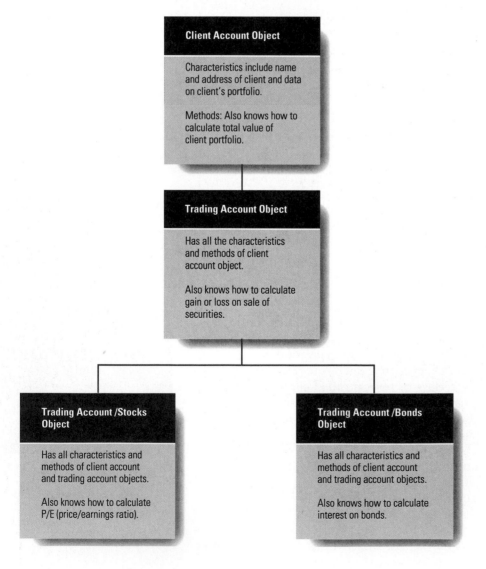

Figure 9.22
Inheritance at Work: Creating Classes and Subclasses with OOP
Subclasses inherit all the characteristics and methods of their parent object classes and may have their own unique characteristics and methods.

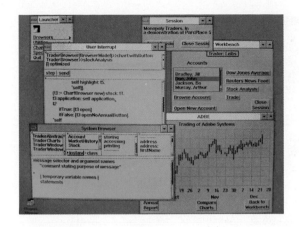

Smalltalk was the first object-oriented programming language.

Source: Courtesy of ParcPlace Systems, Inc.

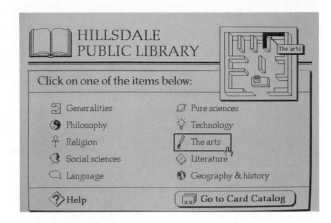

Hypercard is a popular object-based program for Macintosh computers.

Source: Courtesy of Apple Computer, Inc.

and boosted the budget by over 10 percent. The difficulties come not in learning the syntax and grammar of a new programming language but in mastering a new philosophy of programming and unlearning conventional programming techniques. Once over the hump, though, rewards come in the form of quicker development time, reuse of code, and greater ease and lower cost in maintaining code.

Object-Oriented Programming Languages   The first OOP language, called **Smalltalk,** was invented in the early 1970s by computer scientist Alan Kay at Xerox's Palo Alto Research Center (Xerox PARC). Most of the basic concepts of OOP (for instance, reusing and combining standalone modules of code to enhance software development productivity) were pioneered by Smalltalk. Today, Smalltalk continues to be the language favored by object-oriented purists.

Smalltalk led the way to the development of **Hypertalk,** the programming language for the Hypercard toolkit offered by Apple for its Macintosh computers. Hypercard is a program that allows users to place data objects (text, still or animated graphics, music and other sounds) on electronic *cards* grouped together in *stacks*. Objects can have *scripts* (really just simple programs) that allow them to carry out instructions when certain events happen, such as clicking on a certain button.

Hypercard's programming language, Hypertalk, is considered to be an *object-based* language rather than an *object-oriented* language since it does not, for instance, allow you to create classes of objects that can be replicated. Nonetheless, Hypercard and Hypertalk have gone a long way to introducing the general public to some of the basic concepts behind OOP.

Various third-generation languages have been updated to include true object-oriented capabilities. Of these, the most popular is **C++,** offered by Borland International and other software vendors. (Borland also offers an object-oriented version of Pascal called Turbo Pascal.) C++ incorporates all the benefits of standard C while adding many new object-oriented features. C++ supports object-oriented programming but doesn't require it—programmers can write regular C code, pure object-oriented code, or mix the two. Given the large installed base of microcomputer programs written in C, the fact the C++ is compatible with traditional C has made it easier to introduce programs with some object-oriented aspects.

Visual Programming In addition to object-oriented programming, another important trend is the development of **visual programming** techniques and languages. These languages borrow the object orientation of OOP languages but make it possible to create working applications by drawing, pointing, and clicking instead of writing code. Programs are built by connecting (or linking) various objects. The advantage of visual programming is that you don't have to learn a programming language or syntax. ObjectVision from Borland is one example. Application Methods, Inc., a Seattle-based consulting firm, used ObjectVision to create a custom data input program for an international quality survey conducted by Ernst & Young. The survey contained over 2,000 different data points. Using ObjectVision, the firm was able to devise an on-screen image that matched the paper survey forms. Temporary workers used this screen form to input the data. According to Ron Stevenson, one of the designers of the program, ObjectVision's visual aspects allowed his firm to complete more work in much less time.[6]

ObjectVision enables users to create applications without code.

Source: Courtesy of Borland International, Inc.

Despite visual programming's appeal, most people still use visual tools only for the visual parts of an application, such as the graphical user interface. According to one expert, "if you try to do things that don't make sense, you can end up with a mess of boxes and lines that can be incredibly painful to edit." But even critics agree that if you want to do something visual, it can be a dramatic help.

Choosing the Right Programming Language

You now know quite a bit about the unique characteristics of the major programming languages in use today. Even still, selecting the right programming language for a particular problem is not an easy task. Here are some key factors that you should consider in making the choice.

1 What kind of problem are you trying to solve—a business problem, a scientific problem, a problem that requires the creation of a database? As you saw, some languages are best suited to handle particular types of problems. Once you identify the problem, you may be able to create a short list of appropriate languages.

2 What hardware resources are available for the completed program? What languages do they support? (Not all languages are available on all machines.) Does the application need to be portable (able to run on many different kinds of computers)?

3 Do you (or whoever will be writing the program) know the language? If not, how easy is it to learn? How easy will it be for someone other than the original program creator to maintain the program (very important if you expect to make frequent modifications to the program)? How quickly do you need to create the program?

4 Does the organization for whom the program is being created have any particular standard language that they require?

Summary

Introduction to Programming

▶ Programming is the art and science of creating computer programs. People who create computer programs are known as programmers.

▶ Computer programs are in some ways similar to To-Do lists and recipes.

▶ You need to learn about programming if you want to become an information technology specialist such as a programmer or systems analyst, two of the fastest growing occupations of the 1990s. An exposure to basic programming concepts is useful even if you plan to use only packaged applications software.

▶ Before beginning to develop a program, it is useful to find out if any prepackaged applications software is available for the problem you are seeking to solve. Prepackaged software will generally be much less expensive and often of higher quality than internally developed software though it may not exactly fit your specifications.

The Program Development Process

▶ The program development process (sometimes called the software development cycle) has five basic steps: reviewing system specifications, designing the program, coding the program, testing the program, and documenting and maintaining the program.

▶ The first step in the program development process is to meet with systems analysts, end users, and other members of the programming team to review the new system's specifications.

▶ Three phases are involved in designing the program: modularizing the problem, flowcharting the logic of the program and/or pseudocoding the logic, and walking through the design with others.

▶ Most program design today follows a design technique called structured programming. The three basic principles of structured programming are modularization, use of standard control structures, and allowing only single entry/single exit from control structures.

▶ The top-down approach to modularization involves identifying a program's main functions, subdividing them into component modules, and then further subdividing those component modules into additional modules until the lowest level of detail is reached.

▶ Three basic control structures are used to form the logic of a program. The sequence control structure arranges processes in a temporal and logical order. The selection control structure represents choice: if X is true, perform Y; if X is false, perform Z. The case control structure is a variation on the selection control structure and permits a large number of alternatives to be quickly examined. The iteration control structure is a way to represent the performance of a process if a given condition is true or until a condition is met.

▶ Structured programming also follows the principle of single entry/single exit from a control structure. This makes the logic of the program much easier to follow.

331

▶ Pseudocode allows the programmer to depict the logic of a program using English-like statements. Flowcharts depict the same thing graphically.

▶ Today's programmer is assisted in the coding process by programming environments or workbenches that include tools such as debuggers, data dictionaries, and code libraries.

▶ Program testing includes debugging the program as a whole, running test data, and then crash testing the program with invalid data or by trying to overload it.

▶ There are two types of documentation: programmer documentation and user documentation. Program maintenance includes all the activities required to keep a program up to date once it has been written.

The Programmer's Tools: Programming Languages

▶ Programming languages are the primary tools that programmers use to create software. They allow programmers to communicate with a computer and tell it what operations to perform by using symbols and words in accordance with predefined rules.

▶ Programming languages are classified by generation: first, second, third, fourth, or fifth; they are also classified by level: low, high, and very high.

▶ Machine languages are first-generation programming languages. They are composed of strings of binary digits that can be processed directly by the computer's circuits. Assembly languages form the second generation of programming languages. They represent machine language instructions with short symbolic codes. Both machine language and assembly language are considered to be low-level languages.

▶ Third-generation languages are much closer to the English language and allow programs to be written with regular words and sentencelike statements. They are often referred to as high-level languages.

▶ Fourth-generation languages (4GLs) tend to follow a nonprocedural model and just tell the computer what to do, not how to do it. 4GLs are even more English-like than their predecessors and as such are considered to be very high-level languages. Examples of 4GLs include application generators, query languages, and report generators.

▶ Natural languages are the fifth generation of programming languages. They allow users to communicate with a computer with regular English. Natural language features are beginning to find their way into commercial software packages.

▶ A number of third-generation, high-level programming languages are still in use today: FORTRAN, COBOL, BASIC, Pascal, and C are the most significant.

▶ FORTRAN is designed primarily to solve scientific, mathematical, and engineering problems that involve complex formulas and sophisticated numerical calculations.

▶ COBOL is a standard programming language for business problems and is very effective in reading, writing, and manipulating data files. It uses English-like phrases but tends to produce long and wordy programs.

▶ BASIC, an easy-to-learn language designed to work in an interactive environment, was developed at Dartmouth to teach students the essentials of programming. Today, it is used for business and personal computer applications as well.

▶ Pascal is an alternative to BASIC as a teaching language and requires more structured, well-organized programming than does BASIC.

▶ C is a high-level programming language that offers many of the efficiencies of assembly language without being as difficult to use. C is the language of choice for most commercial microcomputer software applications packages.

▶ Other significant programming languages include PL/1, APL, RPG, Ada, LISP, Prolog, Logo, Modula-2, and dBASE.

▶ Object-oriented programming combines data and instructions into a modular software building block called an object. Object-oriented programming's greatest benefits derive from the ability to use objects to create similar objects without having to rewrite whole blocks of code. Popular object-oriented programming languages include C++, Smalltalk, and Turbo Pascal. Visual programming languages combine the object orientation of OOP languages with the ability to create working applications by working with a mouse instead of writing code.

▶ Key factors to consider in choosing a programming language are the kind of problem that needs to be solved, the hardware resources available, ease of use, and maintainability of the language and organizational considerations.

Key Terms

programming
programmers
software development cycle
structured programming
modules
hierarchy or structure chart
flowchart
sequence control structure
selection control structure
iteration control structure
single entry/single exit
pseudocode
programming environment
debuggers
code libraries
program testing
programmer documentation
user documentation
program maintenance
programming language
machine language
hexadecimal
assembly language
high-level languages
4GLs
very high-level languages

application generators
query languages
report generators
natural languages
FORTRAN
COBOL
BASIC
Pascal
C
PL/1
APL
RPG
Ada
LISP
Prolog
Logo
Modula-2
Modula-3
dBASE
object-oriented programming
   (OOP)
Smalltalk
Hypertalk
C++
visual programming

Review Questions

1 In what ways is a To-Do list or recipe similar to a computer program? In what ways does it differ?

2 Why should you bother to learn about programming?

3 What are the advantages of prepackaged software compared to custom-designed software? What are the disadvantages?

4 Describe the program development process.

5 What are the main principles of structured programming? Why is it the primary program design methodology in use today?

6 Write a recipe that includes a sequence control structure, a selection control structure, and an iteration control structure.

7 What is a programming environment? Name and describe three common features that they usually include.

8 Why is program documentation important? How do program documentation and program maintenance interrelate?

9 What are programming languages? In what ways are programming languages similar to human languages? In what ways are they different?

10 What are the primary characteristics that distinguish the different generations and levels of programming languages from one another?

11 How do 4GLs improve programmer and end-user productivity?

12 Describe the differences between FORTRAN, COBOL, and BASIC, lising one key advantage and disadvantage for each.

13 Why was Pascal developed? What uses does it serve?

14 Why has C become the most popular programming language for microcomputer software applications packages?

15 List and give a short description of at least five other programming languages.

16 What are the advantages and disadvantages of object-oriented programming? How does OOP differ from traditional programming languages?

17 What are the key factors to consider when trying to determine which programming language to choose for a particular problem?

Problem-Solving and Skill-Building Exercises

1 With a small group of students (four or fewer), identify a process or activity in a business or other organization. Construct a structure chart and a program flowchart (for one module) using each of the three structure programming concepts.

2 Find a good cookbook and a recipe of your favorite dish. Rewrite the recipe in pseudocode.

3 Identify a process or activity in a business or organization that you believe would be impossible to program. Write a short essay about this situation, and identify three characteristics that make it difficult if not impossible to program the process.

Creating Your Own Multimedia Applications

You don't need to be a programmer to create slick multimedia applications. If you have one of the newer Apple Macintoshes with Quicktime or an IBM-compatible personal computer that meets the MPC standards described in Chapter 5, it's easy to develop your own multimedia applications using multimedia authoring tools. But watch out: you may discover that it's so much fun, you won't want to stop!

A number of different multimedia authoring tools are now available. Your choice depends on the kind of operating system that your machine has: Macintosh, DOS with Windows, or OS/2. Most of the products work with only one kind of system. Beyond this, you can expect that most of the authoring packages will allow you to combine animation, voice, full-motion and still video, graphics, text, and audio. Using these tools, you can create interactive applications. Moreover, the packages often include graphics and paint tools as well as some form of scripting or command language. Here's a brief list of some of the less expensive authoring tools that can nonetheless produce surprisingly sophisticated applications.

Hypercard is bundled with most Macintoshes. As we described earlier in the chapter, Hypercard lets users organize information in stacks of cards and create applications combining text, graphics, video, voice, and animation. It includes Hypertalk, an easy-to-use, English-based scripting (programming) language. A more sophisticated version of Hypercard called Aldus Supercard is available from Aldus Corporation.

Multimedia Toolbook 1.5 from Asymetrix Corporation is similar in many respects to Hypercard. Designed to work with IBM-compatible machines running Windows, Multimedia Toolbook uses an object-oriented approach combined with a simple scripting language called OpenScript.

Other multimedia authoring packages include Gold Disk Inc.'s Animation Works and Owl International's Guide for machines running Windows, and Datalus Inc.'s Multimedia Desktop for computers with an OS/2 operating system.

In addition to general authoring tools, you'll probably want to invest in some clip media—digitized files of graphics, photos, animation, and video clips, as well as music and sound bites, that you can drop into your multimedia application without fear of copyright infringement. Clip media generally come stored on CD-ROM discs and is available for anywhere from $50 to $500 or more. Some examples include The HyperMedia Group's HyperClips, containing over 1,000 animation and sound clips, Educorp's Digital Video Library, containing more than 180 video clips on a wide variety of topics (ranging from sports to restaurants to Wall Street), and Digidesign's Clip Tunes, containing a large selection of music and sound effects.

If you get really serious about multimedia applications, you might want to consider a few other ancillary products. Video editing programs help you assemble and integrate your video clips into the rest of your application. Two available for the Macintosh platform are Adobe Premiere from Adobe Systems and DiVA Videoshop from DiVA Corporation. Another helpful tool is sound recording, editing, and mixing software that lets you modify and digitize audio onto disks for future use or plug them directly into your applications. Examples include Media Vision Inc.'s Pocket Recorder and Creative Lab's SBPro Mixer and Voice Editor II.

So if you're interested in multimedia, don't be afraid to start creating your own. Now's the time to get in on the ground floor.

Notes

1 **Appleby, Doris,** "COBOL," *BYTE*, October 1991.

2 **Nash, Kim,** "Father of BASIC Leaves Legacy," *Computerworld*, January 11, 1993.

3 **Ray, Garry,** "BASIC Gains Commercial Respect," *Computerworld*, November 16, 1992.

4 **Appleby, Doris,** "BASIC," *BYTE*, March 1992.

5 **Bozman, Jean,** Object-Oriented Obstacles," *Computerworld*, October 19, 1992.

6 **Bermant, Charles,** "ObjectVision Eases Data Gathering, Presents Information Graphically," *Computerworld*, April 6, 1992.

four

Applications Software

Electron Assembly
Melvin Prueitt, Los Alamos
National Laboratories

After completing this chapter, you will:

▶ Know the basic characteristics of applications software packages.

▶ Understand the capabilities of word processing, spreadsheet, and database management software.

▶ Know how to go about using such software.

▶ Know what to look for when purchasing such software.

10

Personal Productivity Tools: Word Processing, Spreadsheet, and Database Management Software

Creativity Unleashed

Penn & Teller offer a strange, offbeat mix of comedy and magic. They describe themselves as "a couple of eccentric guys who've learned how to do a few cool things." Cult heroes, they appear on television, on Broadway, and have written such books as *How to Play with Your Food* and *Cruel Tricks for Dear Friends*. Audiences delight at the sardonic commentary that accompanies their sleight-of-hand magic. But though their performances may seem effortless, they are carefully scripted. Penn & Teller write all of their own material. Not bad for two fellows who had never written much of anything before they got their first PCs (see photo).

As Penn recalls, within a week of buying his first computer in 1985, he wrote three stories that were subsequently published. Prior to that time, he had produced the grand total of one four-page story that he never showed to anyone. "If I had to write longhand, I wouldn't write. If I had to type, I wouldn't write," says Penn. "But as soon as I got a computer, I started writing every day."

Penn and Teller.
Source: Anthony Loew.

What was it about computers that unleashed Penn's creative genius? The answer lies in the power of word processing software. Penn says he had never been very creative because he was always so concerned about spelling, punctuation, and grammar. With word processing software, though, he found that it was easy to make revisions,

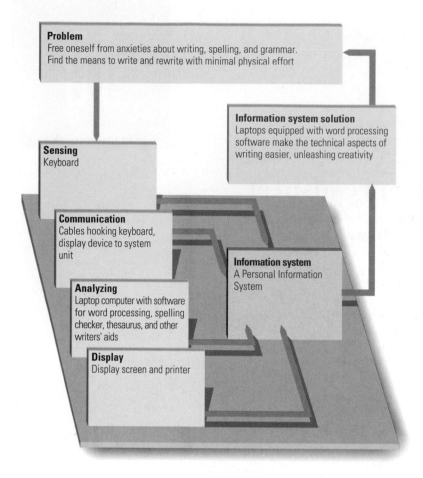

Problem
Free oneself from anxieties about writing, spelling, and grammar.
Find the means to write and rewrite with minimal physical effort

Information system solution
Laptops equipped with word processing software make the technical aspects of writing easier, unleashing creativity

Sensing
Keyboard

Communication
Cables hooking keyboard, display device to system unit

Information system
A Personal Information System

Analyzing
Laptop computer with software for word processing, spelling checker, thesaurus, and other writers' aids

Display
Display screen and printer

move things around, and check spelling and grammar later, allowing his imagination to run free while working on a first draft.

Penn also says that word processing software has been good for his ego. "I'm a very bad speller, but I don't like to perceive myself as a bad speller. With spell checking and grammar checking I get better. Making the mistake, seeing the choices, picking the choice. You do that six times, you'll know how to spell the word."

Teller, a former high school Latin teacher and self-described "niggler," loves the fact that his word processing software gives him the ability to see the words he writes exactly as the reader will see them in printed form. "I feel that there is a difference between italics and small caps and boldface, and this enables me to make those decisions right at the writing stage."

For both performers, computers have become a part of the fabrics of their lives. Both favor laptops (Penn a color Toshiba, Teller an NCR) so that they can take their computers with them wherever they go. Without their computers, they'd be merely a couple of eccentric guys.

Source: Based on "Penn & Teller's Sleight of RAM," *The 1992 Review of Computers* (a supplement to the *New York Times*), June 21, 1992.

Penn & Teller are just two among a universe of people who have had their personal or work lives transformed by personal computers, specifically, by the applications software now available for those computers. In this chapter, the first of two focusing on personal computer applications software, we examine the most widely used types—word processing, spreadsheet, and database management software.

10.1 Introduction to Applications SoftwarePackages

You have already been briefly introduced to the topic of applications software and software packages. As you learned in Chapter 7, *applications software* is software that allows you to apply a computer to solve a specific problem or perform a specific task. In Chapter 9, you learned that there are two basic kinds of applications software available: *custom-designed applications software* and *prewritten applications software packages*. Custom-designed software, which is written specifically to satisfy a particular user's needs, is still a mainstay in many areas. In the late 1960s, though, independent software developers started to create applications software packages that could satisfy the needs of a wide range of users and could be purchased "off the shelf." The first software companies primarily produced applications software for mainframes. But with the advent of the microcomputer in the late 1970s, generic accounting, spreadsheet, word processing, and database management applications software soon became available for use on a microcomputer at a small fraction of the cost of custom-designed programs. Today, applications software packages exist for computers of all sizes, from supercomputers to handheld computers, with the greatest variety reserved for microcomputers.

One important objective of applications software is to enhance the personal productivity of the people who use the software. By automating time-consuming tasks and making information more readily available, applications software aims to help people become more efficient. During the 1980s, American businesses, lured by the promise of increased productivity, spent almost a trillion dollars on information technology. But although there have been numerous individual success stories (many of them highlighted in this book), the overall productivity of service industries on a nationwide basis has not increased as much as expected.[1] Experts have concluded that many white-collar workers are not making effective use of information technology. The story "The Fiddle Factor," discusses some of the reasons why this may be so.

Now, let's take a closer look at applications software packages. Although they cover a broad spectrum, most share some basic characteristics. The programs are stored on one or more 3-1/2- or 5-1/4-inch floppy disks, usually accompanied by written *documentation* (such as a user's manual) that helps explain how to use the software. Before you can actually use the software, you need to install it on your computer. The software is comprised of a number of different files that contain the instructions for the various functions that the software performs. Each of these files must be downloaded from the floppy disk that the software comes on onto your hard drive. If your system does not have a hard drive, you will leave the software package's system disk in one floppy drive and a data disk in the other floppy drive.

Most software today uses on-screen displays that step you through the installation process. Once the software has been installed, the program must be loaded from the hard drive (or the A: floppy drive) into primary storage. If your computer has a traditional DOS operating system, you would type a command after the *system prompt* (A:> if you are using a floppy disk system or C:> if you have a hard disk drive) appears on your screen and then press the Enter key. The command will normally be some version (or abbreviation) of the program's name.

After the program loads, the first screen that you are likely to see will be a product logo, some licensing information describing your rights to use of the

The Fiddle Factor

If you have ever used a personal computer, you know about the fiddle factor: all that time you spend "fiddling around" with your computer, being unproductive. Unfortunately, it may be more time than you like to admit.

Although some fiddling, such as learning a new program, may eventually make a person more productive, much of it is merely a waste of time. A study by SBT Accounting Systems Inc. asked customers how much time they spent "futzing" with their PC. The answer: an average of 5.1 hours a week, according to David Harris, SBT's vice president of sales and marketing. He says this extrapolates to losing 2 percent a year of the nation's gross domestic product.

What is it about our personal computers that leads to such behavior? One reason is that today's software, by offering endless options in layout and design, and the promise of ultimate perfection, lures users to experiment endlessly. Take Thomas Willmott, a management consultant with Aberdeen Group in Boston, for example. Willmott was designing presentation slides with a presentation software package and became frustrated because the "bullets" used to highlight items were sometimes out of alignment when the slides were actually printed. Willmot says he spent several days reading the software's user manual and trying to make the software compatible with other software used to create the slides. After all that, he ended up switching to a new software program. He likes the results but concedes that if he counted all the time he spent, the actual cost of creating the slides would be astronomical. Lewis Schwartz, a Stamford, Connecticut, lawyer spent 15 hours setting up statistics and depth charts for his son's Little League baseball team. "I could have kept them on a clipboard," he says.

Gary Lovman, an assistant professor at Harvard Business School, has done research on why PCs have failed to boost white-collar productivity as much as hoped. Lovman points to the fact that present-day software makes it easy to make an endless number of refinements to documents and spreadsheets. He cites a study of IRS examiners who were given laptop computers. The study found that the examiners did examinations faster but didn't increase the actual number they performed. The extra time they saved went into writing more aesthetically pleasing reports.

What's the solution to the fiddle factor? SBT Accounting recommends that small companies designate employees to become experts on different programs so that they are available as a resource for fellow workers who need help. James Miner, publisher of a geothermal industry newsletter in Santa Monica, California, advocates another, much more drastic, approach. He delegates computer tasks to others and refuses to learn to do them himself. "I know too many . . . who are addicted to it," he says. "I'm afraid I'd lose my effectiveness."

Source: Based on Bulkeley, William, "Swept Away: How Using Your PC Can Be a Waste of Time, Money," *Wall Street Journal,* January 4, 1993.

Critical Thinking Questions

1 Do you agree with Mr. Miner's approach to the fiddle factor? Why or why not?

2 What steps would you recommend for the most efficient use of a personal computer?

3 What are some of the benefits (tangible or intangible) that might result from fiddling with your computer?

software, and sometimes the software's license number. The first time you load a program, you also may be required to enter your name as the official licensee of the software. The initial screen will also generally contain information about what to do to proceed to the next screen, the one that actually enables you to begin using the product (see photo).

Most microcomputer applications software is designed to be *user friendly,* easy to use even for someone who has never been exposed to computers. In Chapter 7, you learned about the graphical user interfaces (GUIs) that help make operating systems easier to interact with. Applications software programs also feature *user interfaces* that, in many instances, are just as graphical as those used for operating systems.

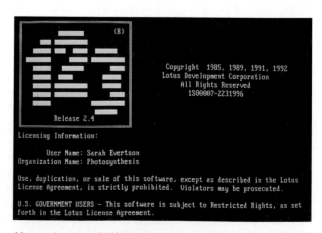

After you have installed Lotus 1-2-3, the opening screen lists your name, lists the license number of the software, and tells you what rights you have in using the software.

Source: Fredrik D. Bodin

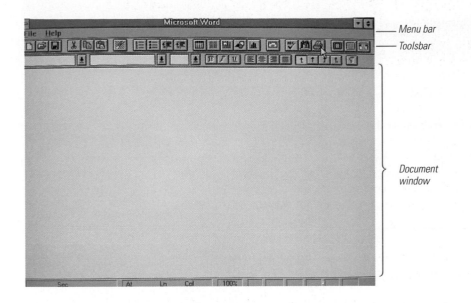

Menu bar

Toolsbar

Document window

(a) Microsoft's Word for Windows, a popular word processing program, has a GUI with both a command menu and a toolbar full of icons.

Source: Fredrik D. Bodin.

(b) A closer view of the Word for Windows toolbar.

One way that user interfaces make applications software easier to use is by simplifying the command process. All programs are driven by *commands*—in order for a program to function, you must give instructions that tell it what you want to do. In the early days of applications software, commands had to be entered by typing them out on the keyboard. Today, instead, most programs will present the user with an on-screen *menu* that lists command options. Sometimes the menu is merely a main menu that, when selected, provides you with submenus for each of the commands listed. Some programs also use *icons* to show program options (see photos).

There will usually be several ways to select the command that you want. One way might be by pressing the letter or number key that corresponds to the option you want. Or you may move the cursor over to the option via the cursor control keys or a mouse and then press the Enter key or click on the mouse button. Some programs allow (or require) you to use the *function keys* (the ones labeled F1–F12) alone or in conjunction with the Shift, Alt, and Ctrl keys to execute commands (see Figure 10.1).

Most software also includes *on-line help*. Instead of having to refer to a manual when you get stuck trying to remember how to do something, in many cases, all you need to do is press the F1 key or otherwise invoke a Help command. Most often, a

Figure 10.1
Some Lotus 1-2-3 Function Keys
Lotus 1-2-3, a popular spreadsheet program, allows you to sidestep the command menu and use function keys to execute commands.

Key	Function
F1	Calls up on-line Help
F2	Puts Lotus into EDIT mode, allowing you to change contents of cells without retyping entire cell
F5	Moves the cursor to specified cell coordinates
F9	Recalculates the worksheet
Alt + F4	Undoes most recent change to worksheet

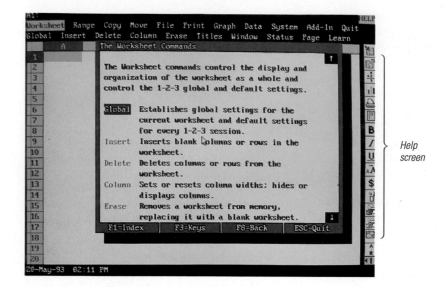

Help screen

If you are trying to figure out what the Worksheet command in Lotus 1-2-3 means, press F1. A help screen pops up to give you the information you need.

Source: Fredrik D. Bodin.

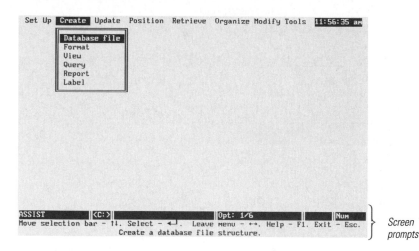

Screen prompts

This dBASE screen prompt (shown here at the bottom of the screen) tells you that the Database file command will allow you to create a database file structure.

menu will appear listing the different areas for which Help is available. Select the one you need, and the software will walk you through the procedures to follow. In some cases, the help will be *context sensitive*—that is, it will pertain directly to the command the program thinks you are trying to execute (see photo). *Screen prompts* (messages displayed by the program) can also help guide you as you work (see photo).

Now that we've given you an overview of applications software packages, let's examine some specific examples. Word processing, electronic spreadsheet, and database management programs are three of the most widely used productivity tools. In the next three sections, we'll show you how word processing software helps you become a better writer, how spreadsheet software helps you perform mathematical, statistical, and financial calculations, and how database management software helps you organize and retrieve facts and figures. By the time you complete this chapter, you'll understand what makes these forms of software so useful and have a general idea of how to go about using them. We'll also give you some guidelines to follow when choosing software of each type. If you'd like to go beyond the basics and learn more about how to actually use a specific word processing, spreadsheet, or database software package, we recommend the series of software manuals for such products as Microsoft Word, Lotus 1-2-3, dBase, Paradox, and Access, available as a supplement to this book.

Throughout this book, you have seen the many different ways that information technology affects our lives. But if you ask people who have a computer to choose the one program that has had the biggest impact on them, chances are they would tell you word processing software.

Word processing software (sometimes just called a **word processor**) allows you to create, edit, format, print, and save **documents** like letters, memos, reports, and other text with much greater ease and efficiency than using a typewriter. It significantly reduces the amount of time required to produce such documents. Word processing software has made typewriters virtually obsolete.

Word Processing Software Features and Capabilities

Let's examine the special features and capabilities of word processing software that enable you to work more efficiently.

Text Entry   The first step in any writing task is to record your thoughts. Word processing software makes this job much easier.

After you load your word processing program, you will be faced with a blank screen, usually accompanied by a **status line** at the top or bottom of the screen (see photo). The status line tells you the position of the cursor and may include such other information as the date, time, and filename of the document you are working on. You can then begin to enter text, much in the same way you would if you were using a typewriter. The cursor is your first helper; it tells you visually where the text will appear on the screen. If you don't like the position—for instance, you want to start lower down on the page—it's easy to move the cursor by using the cursor control keys or the mouse.

When you enter text using a word processing program, you don't have to worry about pressing a carriage return key at the end of every line. Instead, at the end of a line, the software moves you to the next line automatically. (This is called a *soft return.*) Pressing the Enter key automatically starts a new

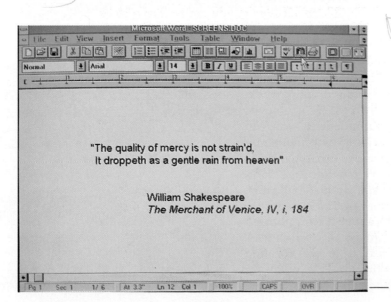

Word's status line indicates the page number and the position of the cursor.

Source: Fredrik D. Bodin.

Status line

345

paragraph rather than a new line. (This is called a *hard return*.) Another way that word processing software makes entering text easier than using a typewriter is by providing **word-wrapping.** If a word won't fit at the end of a line, the software will automatically bring the word down to the next line (or hyphenate it, if you desire).

Another convenient feature of text entry using word processing software is the ability to **scroll** through the document you are creating from beginning to end. Word processing packages allow you to type page after page of material, but only a small number of lines can be displayed at one time. To go back or forward to review what you have already written, you can scroll through the text. Pressing the up arrow or down arrow key once allows you to move one line up or down the page; holding down either key keeps you moving up or down until you release the key. Pressing the Page Up key once takes you to the previous page, and pressing the Page Down key takes you to the next page. (As with the arrow keys, you can usually scroll more quickly by holding down the Page Up and Page Down keys.)

Text Editing   Another way that word processing software shines is the ability it gives you to edit the work that you've written. Instead of having to correct errors by retyping an entire document, using correction fluid, or typing on erasable papers, as you had to with old-fashioned typewriters, word processors allow you to easily insert, delete, move, and copy text. Most word processing packages give you several ways to accomplish this.

You can insert a character, word, or line through either insert or replacement (typeover) mode. In *insert mode*, you merely move the cursor to the location where you want the new text to appear, and as you type, existing text moves over to allow space for the new text. In *replacement* or *typeover mode*, as the name suggests, existing text is replaced by new text.

Deleting text is just as easy. For instance, if you realize you have made a mistake while typing, you can press the Backspace key to erase the preceding text. If you want to make changes to a sentence that you have already typed, you can move the cursor back to the place where you would like to make the change. If you would like to delete a word, you can do it character by character using the Delete key. Holding down the Delete key allows you to continually erase text until you release the key. Most packages also give you the ability to perform functions affecting a large amount of material even more quickly by defining it as a **block** (see photo). To delete a sentence, paragraph, or even the entire text in one fell swoop, you define it as a block and then use the Delete key or a Delete command.

Blocking is also used to move text around within a document, commonly called **cutting and pasting.** (The term comes from the days when moving text meant actually cutting it out of its existing location and physically pasting it onto its new location.) With a word processor, you can switch a paragraph from one location to another by blocking it and then using the word processor's Cut and Paste commands. This deletes the paragraph from its original spot and shifts it to the new location. If you would like the same block of text to appear in more than one location, there's no need to retype the entire thing. Almost all word processors allow you to copy text from one location within a document to another and, in many instances, into entirely different documents. The

The highlighted portion of this text has been defined as a block. Once this has been done, you can delete the entire thing all at once.

Source: Fredrik D. Bodin.

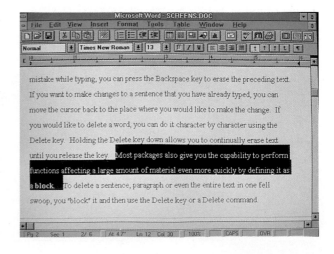

newest Windows-based word processors incorporate a drag-and-drop feature that allows you to define and move text with a mouse rather than requiring you to go back to the command menu and click on cut and paste options.

The **search** function is another feature that helps make text editing easier. Say that you are concerned that you have used a certain word too many times. Word processing software allows you to specify the word that you would like to search for. After you give the Search command, the program will start searching for the word, stopping at the first occurrence. You can then change the word or order the program to proceed on to the next occurrence. **Search and replace** is a further extension of the search function. Suppose you realize after you have finished typing a document that you have consistently misspelled someone's name. Rather than having to go through the entire document looking for the name and then manually keying in the correct version, you can use search and replace. This allows you to define both the word being searched for and the word that should replace it in each instance that the word occurs.

Formatting   Yet another way that word processing software helps you produce professional-looking documents is through its formatting capabilities. **Formatting** refers to the way a document looks—its margins, line spacing, where characters are placed on the page, the number of lines that appear on each page, if and where page numbers will appear, the typefaces used, and so on. Word processing software helps you format documents so that they look just the way you want them to look.

Most word processing packages begin with what are called **default settings** for the various format elements, such as margin width, page length, and typeface. These are settings that have been preselected by the software's developers. Normally, there are a wide range of alternatives to the default settings.

For instance, most word processing programs use a 1-inch margin on the top, bottom, left, and right sides of the paper as the default setting, but you can change these margins to whatever widths suit you. You also need to choose whether you want a *ragged-right* margin (where each line may end at a slightly different spot) or a *justified-right* margin (where each line ends at exactly the same spot) (see Figure 10.2). If you choose a justified-right margin, the spacing between the words on each line will be adjusted as necessary to make sure that each line ends at the same place. As a result, some words will have more space between them than other words, which can

Figure 10.2
Ragged-Right versus Justified-Right Margins

(a) A ragged-right margin **(b)** A justified-right margin. Notice the varying spaces between the words.

Source: Fredrik D. Bodin.

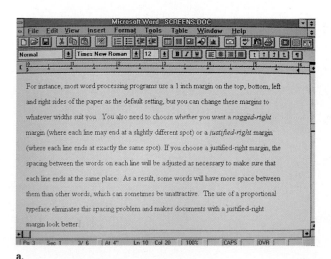

a.

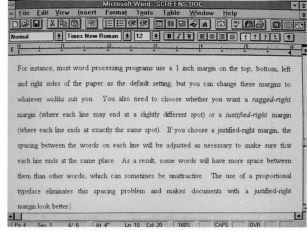

b.

sometimes be unattractive. The use of a proportional typeface (discussed at the end of this section) eliminates this spacing problem and makes documents with a justified-right margin look better.

With a word processing package, it's also easy to vary *line spacing*. You can choose single spacing, double spacing, or even triple spacing. You can also mix the spacing within the document, with some sections single spaced and others double spaced. Or you may choose to have a double space between text within a paragraph but a triple space between paragraphs.

Other elements of a page's format include the number of lines that appear on each page and pagination options. The standard number of lines that will be printed on an 8-1/2-by-11-inch page that has a 1-inch margin on the top and bottom is 54 single-spaced lines. This number can be shortened or, in some instances, increased (if, for example, you want to keep certain material together on the same page). Some packages allow you to number the lines along the left margin, which can be a useful feature for identifying text when you are working with others on a document. The *pagination* feature enables you to choose when and where you would like page numbers to appear—perhaps at the bottom center, the top right corner, or alternating between the lower left and lower right corners (the common format for newsletters and other publications). Often, you will not want a page number to appear on the first page of a document, or on any pages at all. Any of these options are easy to choose and implement with word processing software.

Most word processing software also allows you to choose to include *headers* and *footers*—lines of text that appear at the very top (headers) or very bottom (footers) of the page. Headers and footers can be used to record identifying information about the document (filename, date, time, and so on), as title references, and for many other purposes.

Word processing software also gives you other options. A simple command usually allows you to center text on a page. Some programs enable you to easily arrange text in multiple columns. Automatic tab stops (places to which your cursor will jump if you press the Tab key) are usually part of a program's default settings though you can set your own if you like. Easy paragraph indentation allows you to indent individual paragraphs, which is particularly useful if your text contains long quotes that need to be set off from the rest of the text. You can also easily CAPITALIZE characters, make them **boldface** or *italicized*, and underline or double underline them. Furthermore, you can create *superscripts* (^{1}) and *subscripts* ($_1$), which are useful for denoting footnotes and mathematical and scientific notations. Another helpful feature, particularly for students writing papers, is the ability to set up footnotes that can appear at either the bottom or end of the document. The word processing software normally automatically numbers the footnotes for you and renumbers them if you add or delete any during the editing stage. Other helpful features of word processors are commands that allow you to automatically generate a table of contents, an outline, section numbering, an index, and a bibliography.

Many of these format elements are identified internally by the software through the use of embedded formatting codes (see photo). Most word processing programs normally hide embedded formatting codes from the user unless instructed otherwise. Instead, the screen normally displays the

You normally do not see embedded formatting codes while you are working on a document. But you can instruct your software to display them if you need to see what's going on "behind the scenes."

Source: Fredrik D. Bodin.

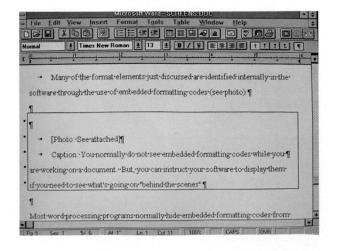

document as it will appear when printed on a piece of paper (though without a full-page view since most screens cannot display that much). However, it is still difficult for most word processing programs and monitors to display certain elements, such as italics or underlining, exactly as they appear on a printed page. Instead, these may be indicated by a change of color (if you have a color monitor) or in some other fashion.

Some word processors include a preview feature that allows you to see a full-page view (though in much reduced size) of exactly what the document will look like when printed. This is called **WYSIWYG** (pronounced *wizzy-wig*), short for What You See Is What You Get. You generally cannot edit when in WYSIWYG mode but must return to the regular screen first. Some Windows word processors do allow WYSIWYG editing although the process can be slow and difficult.

Another feature of word processing software is its ability to automatically reformat a page after changes have been made. What this means is that after you have performed any text editing operations, such as inserting or deleting text, or changed any page format elements, the software automatically adjusts existing text so that it fits within the new parameters.

Finally, word processing software offers you a wide variety of potential typefaces and type sizes. A **typeface** (also called a **font**) is the particular style of lettering. The type size, measured in points, may range from 6 point (very small) to 24 point or larger. The most common type sizes are 10 point and 12 point. Both your printer and word processor must support a particular font in order for you to use it: if either does not, the font will not be available to you. There are two basic types of typefaces: serif, which have little strokes at the ends of the letters, and sans serif, which do not. Figure 10.3 illustrates both types.

Compare the Courier and Times Roman typefaces you see in Figure 10.3. As you may notice, each character in the Courier typeface takes up the same amount of space. In contrast, the Times Roman typeface uses **proportional spacing:** some characters are allocated more horizontal space than others. For instance, a wider letter, such as the character W, takes up more space than a narrower letter such as the character I. As we noted, justified-right margins work best when used in conjunction with proportional spacing.

Aa Bb Cc Dd Ee Ff Gg Hh Ii Jj Kk Ll Mm Nn Oo Pp Qq Rr Ss Tt Uu Vv Ww Xx Yy Zz
1 2 3 4 5 6 7 8 9

Aa Bb Cc Dd Ee Ff Gg Hh Ii Jj Kk Ll Mm Nn Oo Pp Qq Rr Ss Tt Uu Vv Ww Xx Yy Zz
1 2 3 4 5 6 7 8 9

Aa Bb Cc Dd Ee Ff Gg Hh Ii Jj Kk Ll Mm Nn Oo Pp Qq Rr Ss Tt Uu Vv Ww Xx Yy Zz
1 2 3 4 5 6 7 8 9

Aa Bb Cc Dd Ee Ff Gg Hh Ii Jj Kk Ll Mm Nn Oo Pp Qq Rr Ss Tt Uu Vv Ww Xx Yy Zz
1 2 3 4 5 6 7 8 9

Figure 10.3
Typefaces: Helvetica, Times Roman, Bookman, and Courier.

The way a document looks can, in many cases, be as important as its content. Figure 10.4 gives you tips on formatting and typefaces so that the documents you produce, at school or on the job, will make the best impression.

To design a truly attractive document, it helps if your word processing software has graphics and layout capabilities. Most high-end word processors now allow you to import graphics from other packages and to move, resize, rotate, and crop them within the document. A few (like Lotus's Ami Pro and Microsoft's Word for Windows) provide some drawing capability or allow you to incorporate an existing drawing package. Most also provide basic layout capabilities, such as combining text and graphics, and the more sophisticated programs allow you to wrap text around odd-shaped graphic elements.

These features illustrate how word processing programs are starting to invade the desktop publishing software arena. Word processing software traditionally has focused on making the process of writing easier, while desktop publishing software (described in depth in Chapter 11) has emphasized tools for design and layout. As word processors become ever more powerful, the line separating them from DTP software becomes more and more indistinct. For instance, all the leading word processing packages now offer style sheets, a standard feature of desktop publishing software. (A *style sheet* allows you to predefine the look of a business letter, a memo, or a multicolumn newsletter by setting and saving a collection of formatting and font specifications.) Some of the word processing programs also offer "canned stylesheets"—standard formats or templates for various kinds of documents, such as letters, fax cover pages, memos, and so on. All you need to do is enter the text; the word processing software then automatically formats it into the style you have selected. Likewise, most of the newer desktop publishing programs have borrowed a number of features from word processing programs. This trend is likely to continue to accelerate until the difference between the two types of programs disappears altogether.

Word processing programs are also starting to encroach on spreadsheet software's ground. The latest word processors supply table-making capabilities, can perform arithmetic computations, and allow you to create and edit complex formulas, including fractions, radicals, integrals, and more.

Electronic Storage   One of the most useful things about word processing software is that you can save your work in electronic form, for future reference and use. If you need to stop working on your writing project for a while, what you have completed can be saved on your hard or floppy disk and will be waiting for you when you are ready to resume. After you have finished a project, you may be able to reuse your completed work by modifying it.

To save a document, you first must assign it a filename. Rules for creating filenames will vary from package to package. Most allow you to choose any combination of letters and numbers

Figure 10.4
Formatting and Typeface Tips

1 Don't be afraid to leave white space: experiment with margin widths and line spacing until you come up with a roomy, visually appealing result.

2 Use two spaces after periods.

3 Use capitalization, bold, italics, and underlining for emphasis. But don't overdo. If you try to emphasize too many things, the result will be a cluttered look in which nothing really stands out.

4 Don't set long blocks of text in italics, bold, or all capital letters—it makes them harder to read.

5 Use subheadings liberally to help readers find what they're looking for.

6 Use 12-point type size for easy readability.

7 Always use typefaces and sizes consistently: all headings should be in one typeface and size, all subheadings in another, and regular text in a third. Changing a typeface or format at random from page to page will confuse readers.

8 Serif fonts are considered easier to read and are often used for main text. Sans serif fonts are recommended for titles and other display text.

that does not exceed a total of eight characters. The filename should be as specific as possible to aid you in identifying the file's contents at a later date. Some packages will add a three-character extension to the filename, separated from the filename by a period. This also helps you identify files later. For instance, all document files created by Microsoft Word have a .DOC extension.

Documents should be saved periodically as you work on them in order to prevent the loss of your work in the event of a power surge or interruption. You should also save your work before printing out the document. Some word processing packages offer an autosave feature that automatically saves the document at preselected intervals, perhaps every 5 or 10 minutes.

Printing   Another way that word processing software makes preparing documents easier is that it lets you print out the document whenever you like. If you'd like to review an intermediate draft, you can print it out at that stage. Or you can review your work on-screen and just print out the final version.

To print a document, your word processing software calls up a file called a *printer driver*. The printer driver converts embedded formatting codes into instructions that the printer can understand so that it can produce the needed effect. Different kinds of printers require different printer drivers. Your software will generally come with a selection of different drivers, enabling it to work with just about any kind of printer, from dot matrix to lasers. When you install the software for the first time, one step of the process will involve telling the software which type of printer you have. Once you have done so, the software automatically selects the proper printer driver, and you need do nothing further.

Other Important Features   In addition to providing easy text entry, text editing, format options, and so on, most word processing software packages offer a number of features that help you write better and work more productively. Chief among these features is a **spelling checker,** which checks your document for misspelled words by consulting an electronic dictionary. When the spelling checker comes across a word it does not recognize, it lets you know and offers possible corrections (see photo).

In some instances, the word may in fact be correctly spelled but just not in the word processor's electronic dictionary. Many spelling checkers allow you to add new words to the dictionary—a useful feature if you frequently use technical words or personal names that are not included. But just because you use a spelling checker doesn't mean you should skip a careful reading of your document before you finish. A spelling checker won't catch grammatical mistakes in which you've used one word when you meant another. For example, it won't sort out *too* versus *to, their* versus *there,* and so on.

Another useful feature is an **electronic thesaurus** that provides synonyms (and perhaps antonyms) for words that you feel you are using too often. Once you select a word, the thesaurus will display a list of related words for you to review. If you frequently need to work in foreign languages, you also might want to consider an add-on package like WordStar's Lexica. (An *add-on package* is a program that complements a specific type, and sometimes brand, of software by adding "missing"

Microsoft Word highlights misspelled words and lists possible corrections. The most likely correct spelling is also highlighted.

Source: Fredrik D. Bodin.

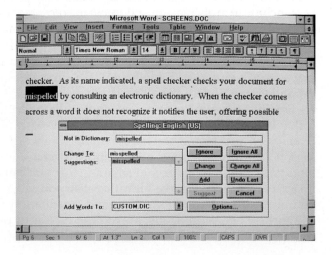

features.) Lexica is a multilingual (English, French, Spanish, German, and Dutch) dictionary and thesaurus that can quickly translate words and phrases from one language to another. Although you need to know the basic grammar of your target language (Lexica doesn't conjugate verbs, for instance), it's a great aid to increasing your foreign language vocabulary.

A rudimentary **style and grammar checker** is also sometimes included with word processing software. This tool can perform such basic tasks as telling you that a word is repeated. If you want to truly sophisticated checker, you will need to invest in an add-on package. Some of the more popular add-ons include WordPerfect's Grammatik, Que Software's RightWriter, and WordStar's Correct Grammar (for DOS and Windows). These style and grammar checkers check for errors in grammar, punctuation, and word usage. They also offer style suggestions—for instance, pointing out a tendency toward long sentences or wordy phrases. In addition, they will review your document for readability and provide you with some idea of the overall reading level that it requires. But as with the spelling checker, it's important to recognize the limitations of style and grammar checkers. The English language is exceedingly complex and filled with nuance, making it difficult to reduce to a system of rules captured on software. Good writing sometimes bends the rules—a fact that's hard for software to comprehend. You can't blindly accept everything that grammar or style checkers recommend, but on the other hand, they're hard to beat if you need help remembering the difference between *affect* and *effect*.

Another useful capability of many word processing programs is the **mail-merge** function. Mail-merge allows you to prepare a form letter, with the inside address and salutation (the "Dear so and so" part) left blank, then merge the letter with your mailing list. The program automatically fills in the name and address of each person on the list. The result: a personalized-looking form letter. When you're ready to mail, the latest word processors will automatically lift the address from the letter, combine it with your return address, and print them on an envelope.

In addition, most word processing programs allow you to create **macros**—a sequence of predefined keystrokes or mouse clicks to which you can assign a name. Then, whenever you want to invoke those keystrokes, you merely type in the name of the macro and the program executes the keystrokes for you. For instance, suppose when you prepare a memo, you always set it up the same way, with the To/From/Re/Date headings in a certain place. Instead of having to do it manually every time, you can create a macro that will automatically set the headings for you. The process of creating a macro is becoming less and less complicated. The newest word processors include sample macros and *macro recorders* that automatically turn your series of keystrokes or mouse clicks into a single command.

Although most word processing packages already offer a plethora of features, the number of add-on packages that you can buy is increasing. The story "Adding to Your Knowledge Base" illustrates how such add-ons can expand your abilities even further.

Finally, as you already know, one of the hottest trends in information technology is the development of products with multimedia capabilities. Even word processing software manufacturers are catching the fever. Microsoft Word for Windows now includes a voice-annotation module that allows you to import and record sounds. Now you can record your comments on a report directly into the file rather than scrawling them down the margin of a printed copy. And both Word and WordPerfect for the Macintosh offer support for QuickTime videos—you can type up a product description and throw in a video that shows how the product works!

It's 1 A.M. You're still working on that paper for your American Revolution history course. The paper's due tomorrow at 9 A.M., but as you write, you discover that somehow you've misplaced your notes on Thomas Jefferson. The library's closed, and your professor is not too understanding about papers handed in late. How are you going to get around this one?

Well, you may not be sunk if you've invested in add-on programs to complement your word processing software. For instance, if you had System Compatibility Corporation's Writer's Toolkit for Windows, you'd have on-line access to the *Dictionary of Common Knowledge,* a one-volume encyclopedia that contains information on a wide variety of topics, including Thomas Jefferson. If you needed some additional quotations from Jefferson, his contemporaries, or about the American Revolution, you could check the *Concise Columbia Dictionary of Quotations,* containing over 6,000 entries, including Jefferson's famous "The earth belongs to the living, not to the dead."

But that's not all the Writer's Toolkit contains. Not sure whether you should describe King George III as a regent or a reagent? Check it out in the *American Heritage Electronic Dictionary,* with more than 116,000 definitions. Want some other synonyms for the word *king*? Refer to *Roget's II Electronic Thesaurus*—not only will it give you possible synonyms, it'll also give you definitions for those synonyms. Have you abbreviated the University of Virginia (founded by Jefferson) correctly? If you want to make sure, consult Toolkit's abbreviation dictionary. It not only tells you the appropriate abbreviation for a word, if one exists, but also expands abbreviations into their long form. The Toolkit also includes Correct Grammar, a grammar-checking program, as well as *The Written Word II,* an on-line handbook of grammar and style. You can search for a topic using keywords or browse the handbook's table of contents and click on a desired topic. If you need to be reminded to write sentences with active verbs rather than passive ones, an on-line grammar-checker and grammar and style reference book may be worth more than their weight in gold to you.

Even better, the Writer's Toolkit allows you to integrate all these different knowledge bases through a Synchronize All menu option. This command automatically looks up your entry simultaneously in all the different references available (or as many as you choose). Let's say you wanted to spark your thought processes on the general concept of government, a topic very dear to Jefferson's heart. With Writer's Toolkit, you

Writer's Toolkit can supply multiple approaches to a single concept.

Source: Courtesy of Systems Compatability Corp.

could get a definition, synonyms, background data, and relevant quotations all in front of you at once.

Systems Compatibility Corporation includes macros with Toolkit that make it virtually a part of Word for Windows, WordPerfect for Windows, or Ami Pro. You can check a document or use any of the reference modules without ever leaving your word processing program. Right now, it requires you to have an Intel 286 or better processor, Windows 3.0, and at least 6.5MB of hard disk space.

Source: Based on Matzkin, Jonathan, "Windows Bring Added Dimension to the Writer's Toolkit," *PC Magazine,* February 11, 1992.

Critical Thinking Questions

1 In what ways are on-line reference materials superior to those available in book form? In what ways may books be better?

2 What would be the most useful aspects of The Writer's Toolkit for you?

3 Why don't software manufacturers include the features of add-on packages in their word processing software?

Comparing Word Processing Software Packages

There are many different word processing software packages. What's the right one for you? Let's look at how you can distinguish among all that's available on the market.

Before you start looking at particular brands of word processing software, you need to know the type of computer that you will be running the software on. At the extreme low end of the spectrum are dedicated word processors—a form of electronic typewriter. These come with their own software built in and can perform only word processing, nothing else. These may be cost effective if all you plan to do is light word processing, but they do not supply anywhere near the functionality of word processing software running on a regular computer. If you have a regular microcomputer, you need to check its memory (RAM) and secondary storage capacity to make sure that the software you choose does not require more. Another important consideration is the type of operating system your computer has. If you have a machine running DOS, you will need DOS-based word processing software. If your machine is equipped with Windows, you have a wider choice —you can go with a DOS-based program or one of the newer Windows-compatible versions. (In the Personal Technology section at the end of the chapter, we set out some factors to consider in choosing between Windows and non-Windows versions of applications software.) Likewise, Apple computers require word processing software compatible with the Apple operating system. There are even word processors designed to work with Unix-based systems and OS/2.

Once you've determined the technical requirements that the software must meet, the next question to answer is the type of work you plan to do with the software. Most word processing packages are general-purpose ones that can satisfy the needs of a wide variety of users.

The primary distinguishing characteristic among general-purpose word processing packages is whether they are expensive, top-of-the line products that offer all the latest bells and whistles or whether they are the lower-priced, low-frill type. Three packages dominate the full-featured market: WordPerfect Corporation's WordPerfect (DOS, Windows, and Macintosh), Microsoft's Word (DOS, Windows, and Macintosh), and Lotus Development Corporation's Ami Pro (Windows only). All three offer nearly every conceivable feature for creating sophisticated documents. The most recent versions of all three require a 386 or faster microprocessor, 2–4 MB of RAM and 12 to 15 MB of hard disk storage space for adequate performance. Word processing packages for the Macintosh (in addition to Macintosh versions of Word and WordPerfect) include Claris Corporation's MacWrite, T/Maker's Write Now, and DeltaPoint's Taste.

Low-frill versions (sometimes referred to as executive word processors) sell for around half the price of their full-featured siblings and typically require less than a third of the hard disk storage space. Typically, what you get are basic editing tools, text manipulation, formatting capabilities, and a rudimentary spelling checker. Such programs generally do not include advanced editing tools, extensive graphics and tabling capabilities, multiple fonts, full-blown spelling checkers, or grammar checkers. If you will be using your word processor primarily to create short, simple documents, or want a word processor that has less memory requirements to use on your portable, a low-frill version may do the trick. Low-frill DOS versions include Broderbund Software's BankStreet WriterPlus, WordPerfect's LetterPerfect, and Software Publishing's Professional Write. Popular low-frill Windows packages include WordStar International's WordStar, Computer Associates' CA-Textor, Lotus Development's LotusWrite, Software Publishing's Professional Write Plus, and Spinnaker Software's Easyworking for Windows. Integrated software packages that combine the ability to process words with spreadsheet, database management, and other functions are another choice for light word processing. (We will consider integrated software packages in greater depth in Chapter 11.)

Some special-purpose packages are also available. For example, Nisus Software offers Nisus 3.4 Complete Flag Edition (available for the Macintosh), a word processor that supports text entry in such languages as Arabic, Hebrew, Russian, Thai, Chinese, and Japanese, as well as English and European languages. If you work for a corporation with international operations or customers, a government agency with multilingual constituents, or are merely a frequent traveler, you may find the capabilities offered by Nisus very useful. Or if you're a scriptwriter (or would like to become one), consider Cinovation's Scriptware. Scriptware is a word processing program that automatically provides the capitalizations, centering, scene numbers, and margins that mark a professionally prepared script.

Figure 10.5 summarizes these different word processing packages.

Word Processing Software Packages	Manufacturer
Full-featured, Windows-based	
Word for Windows	Microsoft
Ami Pro	Lotus Development Corporation
WordPerfect for Windows	WordPerfect Corporation
Lower-cost, Windows-based	
WordStar for Windows	WordStar International
CA-Textor	Computer Associates
LotusWrite	Lotus Development Corporation
Professional Write Plus	Software Publishing Corporation
EasyWorking for Windows	Spinnaker Software
Full-featured, DOS-based	
Word	Microsoft
WordPerfect	WordPerfect Corporation
Lower-cost, DOS-based	
WordStar	WordStar International
BankStreet Writer Plus	Broderbund Software
LetterPerfect	WordPerfect Corporation
Professional Write	Software Publishing Corporation
Macintosh	
Word	Microsoft
WordPerfect for the Mac	WordPerfect Corporation
MacWrite	Claris Corporation
WriteNow	T/Maker
Taste	DeltaPoint
Multilingual	
Nisus Complete Flag Edition	Nisus Software
Multi-Lingual Scholar	Gamma Productions

Figure 10.5
Summary: Word Processing Software Packages

10.3 Spreadsheet Software

Along with word processing software, **spreadsheet software** has had a tremendous impact on the conduct of business in the United States.

As you learned in Chapter 2, for several milennia people have needed ways to keep records and accounts of inventories, sales, income, expenses, profits, and so on. One solution was to record and organize such data in columns and rows on sheets contained in a ledger book (see photo). This arrangement made it relatively easy to perform calculations on the data. But creating the actual worksheets—developing the format, filling in the numbers, actually doing the calculations—remained a painstaking and time-consuming task. Any change in a number might force the recalculation of the entire spreadsheet. Even the arrival of the electronic calculator did not totally relieve the intensive labor involved in keeping manual spreadsheets.

In the late 1970s, Dan Bricklin, a student attending Harvard Business School, decided that there had to be a better way than manually preparing the spreadsheets that his classes required. He joined forces with Dan Flystra, another Harvard MBA student, and Robert Frankston, a friend who was a programmer, to develop a program that would allow them to create an electronic spreadsheet. They called the program **VisiCalc** (short for Visible Calculator). VisiCalc was an *electronic spreadsheet:* a computerized version of the traditional ledger book. It allowed you to enter the data you wanted, as well as indicate the calculations you wanted performed on the data. The program then automatically performed all the calculations with perfect accuracy and produced the result. It also allowed you to print out a paper copy if you wanted. If you needed to change any of the numbers on the spreadsheet, the program would automatically recalculate any other values affected by the change. And when you were done, you could store the spreadsheet on a disk for later use. The time-saving features of the program were overwhelming. Bricklin and Frankston soon discovered that there was a huge market for the product among other students, businesspeople, and professionals. VisiCalc, designed to run on the Apple II, was the original "killer app": an application so powerful and so necessary that it actually caused people who previously

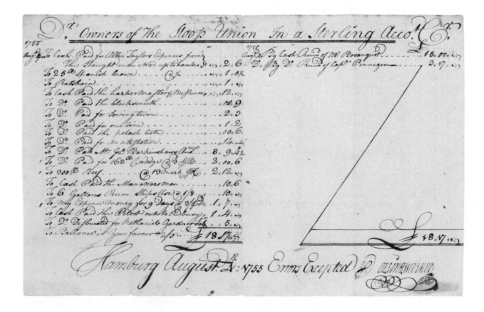

A spreadsheet showing ship's expenses, from the ledger book of the Sloop Union, 1755.

saw no use for a computer to go out and buy one. In fact, many credit Visi-Calc with making the Apple II the predominant microcomputer at the beginning of the 1980s. In 1983, Lotus Development Corporation introduced a more powerful version of the electronic spreadsheet, Lotus 1-2-3, which quickly dominated the marketplace. Although similar products have since been developed, Lotus 1-2-3 is still synonymous with the word *spreadsheet*.

Today, businesses large and small, nonprofit organizations, scientists, professors, and private individuals all rely on spreadsheet software. The power to record, organize, analyze, and present all kinds of financial and statistical information is within the grasp of anyone with a personal computer and the right software. The story "Spreadsheets Changed Their Lives" illustrates the impact that this software has had and continues to have.

Here are some of the things you can do with a spreadsheet:

Develop a budget
Track and analyze financial results
Construct projections and forecasts
Evaluate different scenarios: play what-if games
Analyze current and potential investments
Create control and reporting systems
Do statistics
Keep a student roster, track grades, and calculate GPAs
Model physical systems
Analyze scientific data
Plan scientific processes

And that's just scratching the surface.

Spreadsheet Software Features and Capabilities

Now that you have a general idea about some of the things you can do with a spreadsheet, let's take a closer look at how they work and the features and capabilities that make them such useful tools. As we illustrate the fundamentals of spreadsheets, we'll step you through the basic process that you would use to construct a Lotus 1-2-3 spreadsheet.

Data Entry   Figure 10.6 shows you the initial screen that appears after you have loaded Lotus 1-2-3. The screen is divided into three basic areas: a worksheet area, a control panel, and a status indicator. The **worksheet area**

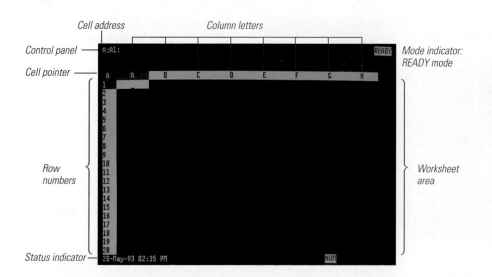

Figure 10.6
Lotus 1-2-3's Opening Screen in READY mode
Notice that the left side of the first line contains only the cell address since no data has been entered.

Source: Fredrik D. Bodin.

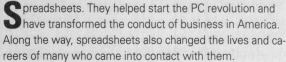

Spreadsheets. They helped start the PC revolution and have transformed the conduct of business in America. Along the way, spreadsheets also changed the lives and careers of many who came into contact with them.

Chuck Miwa credits spreadsheets with launching his career in finance. In 1983, the teenaged Miwa used his knowledge of Lotus 1-2-3 (then a new software product) to get a summer job at Hughes Aircraft's Space and Communications Group, where he was responsible for helping to automate the business department's financial operations. After the summer was over, Miwa continued to hone his spreadsheet skills and ultimately landed a full-time job at Hughes while studying business administration at the University of Southern California. After graduation, Miwa's skills led him to Meyer Interest Rate Survey, a California-based supplier of interest rate information to commercial banks, savings and loans, and credit unions. To meet the needs of Meyer's nearly 1,000 clients, Miwa and his staff rely heavily on Lotus 1-2-3. Without spreadsheets, Miwa says he probably would have ruled out a career in finance: "I don't know if I would have had the patience to add a column of numbers, then type them in."

If not for spreadsheets, Bill Clayson might be standing in an unemployment line today. Bill has managed to survive through several years of staff reductions as Chicago's Continental Bank struggled to reorganize after its massive failure in 1984. He credits his staying power to his spreadsheet expertise: spreadsheets were playing an important role in Continental's plans to achieve greater efficiency and return to solvency. Today, Clayson is a vice president and 15-year veteran at Continental. He's certain that had he not used his spreadsheet tal-

ents, he'd be involved in a completely different line of work. "My PC skills allowed me to provide enough value to keep my job."

Miwa and Clayson used spreadsheets to make the most of the careers they were in, but Joe Lee took a different tack. In the 1980s, Lee was a lawyer with a side interest in several businesses. To keep track of his multiple ventures, he turned to spreadsheets. Soon, he was applying his spreadsheet expertise to his law practice. Business clients who came to him for legal advice were surprised to find that he could provide better business case analysis than their accountants. In February 1988, spreadsheets helped Lee make his "great escape from the law" when he was invited to join a large real estate development project for Xerox Realty Corporation. From there, he jumped to become vice president of Prodata Systems, a hospital and patient accounting and financial reporting company. For Lee, "Law was dry. Lotus 1-2-3 changed my life for the better. Now I truly enjoy what I'm doing."

Sources: Based on Asbrand, Deborah, "Chuck Miwa: Early Starter" and "Bill Clayson: A Job Saved," *Lotus,* June 1992; Radosevich, Lynda, "Joe Lee: Multitasking Career," *Lotus,* June 1992.

Critical Thinking Questions

1   Why have spreadsheets had such a transforming effect on the conduct of business?

2   Think about a career you might be interested in pursuing. How might you use spreadsheets in that career?

3   What might be some of the dangers of relying too heavily on spreadsheets?

Main menu ———
Submenu
for worksheet
command

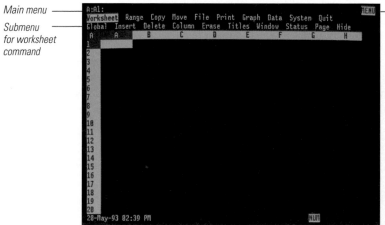

— Mode indicator:
MENU mode

Figure 10.7

Lotus 1-2-3's Opening Screen in MENU mode

Notice that the control panel has changed and now displays a main menu and submenu.

Source: Fredrik D. Bodin.

contains a large rectangular grid, called the **worksheet,** made up of columns and rows. The columns are identified by the letters along the top of the screen, and the rows by the numbers along the left side of the screen. Spreadsheets prepared with Lotus 1-2-3 contain up to 256 columns and over 8,000 rows though only a very small portion can be displayed on the screen at any one time. You can use the Tab, Page Up, Page Down, and arrow keys to bring other parts of the worksheet into view. (In addition, most spreadsheet programs offer options that allow you to see two different parts—the first column and last column or the first row and last row, for instance—of a spreadsheet at one time, which is very useful if you are working with a large spreadsheet.)

The intersection of a column and row is called a **cell.** Each cell has a **cell address** (its particular location on the spreadsheet), identified by its column and row coordinates, for instance, A1 or A2. Lotus spreadsheets have over 2,000,000 different cell addresses. The cell is the basic building block of a spreadsheet. A set of contiguous cells is known as a **range.** A range may consist of one or more cells, a row, a column, or several rows or columns. A range is defined by the cell addresses of its upper left and lower right cells, separated by one or two periods. Once you have defined a range, you can give it a *range name* and use the name instead of the cell addresses if you need to refer to it elsewhere in the spreadsheet. Many of the operations that you will be telling the spreadsheet software to perform will involve a range rather than individual cells.

To begin to enter data onto a worksheet, you need to move the cursor to the cell where you want the data to be located. The cell over which your cursor is positioned is known as the **current cell.** When your cursor is positioned over a cell, it will be highlighted: this highlight bar is called the **cell pointer.** The column letter and row number may also be highlighted.

To prepare entries for the worksheet and issue commands, you use the area of the screen known as the **control panel.** With Lotus 1-2-3, the control panel consists of the top three lines on the screen. The left side of the first line contains the cell address, the contents of the current cell, and information about the format of the current cell. If you have not yet entered any data into the cell, only the cell address will be displayed. On the far right side, Lotus displays information about its *mode:* the state in which the program is currently operating. Lotus has 14 different modes, such as READY (ready for you to enter data or a command), MENU (the program is displaying your command options), WAIT (the program is in the middle of a command or process), and ERROR (Lotus has detected an error and asks you to correct it). If you are in MENU mode, the second line of the Lotus control panel will display the main command menus, and the third line will show a submenu for whichever command on the main menu that the cursor is on (see Figure 10.7). We will discuss a spreadsheet's different command options in greater depth shortly.

The third area of the basic spreadsheet screen is the *status indicator,* at the lower right corner of the screen. As you learned in Section 10.1, most types of applications programs include such a display. The Lotus status indicator includes the date and time and some further information about various settings in place, such as CAP if you are using the Caps Lock key. Lotus also allows you to display the filename in place of the date and time indicator.

Each cell can contain one of two possible types of data: a label or a value. A **label** consists of text—a word, symbols, or some combination of letters and numbers—that functions as a heading or describes the contents of a cell. A label cannot be manipulated mathematically.

Most spreadsheet programs automatically assume that any entry that begins with a letter or a *label-prefix character* (the ', ^, ", or \ characters) is a label. Label-prefix characters serve an additional formatting function: ' indicates that the contents of the cell should be left-justified (lined up with the left margin of the cell), ^ indicates that the contents should be centered, " indicates that the contents of the cell should be right-justified, and \ indicates that the contents of the previous cell should be repeated in the new cell. If a label-prefix character is not used, the software uses left-justification as the default setting.

How do you actually decide what the names of columns and rows should be? How do you enter labels to name the columns and rows? To answer these questions, let's start to construct an actual spreadsheet.

Suppose that you own a sailboat. Last summer, to help pay for the costs of owning the boat (mooring fees, repairs, and maintenance), you rented it out on some weekends and weekdays. This summer, you would like to expand the business (which you have named Red Sky Yacht Charters) by adding a second boat and hiring someone to go sailing with people who would like to rent a boat but don't know how to sail. You know someone who is willing to lease you a boat for the summer and have another friend whom you could hire. You also would like to put a weekly ad in the local paper. But your friends advise you to "run it through" a spreadsheet program before proceeding. Now what?

The first thing you must consider when creating a spreadsheet is what you want to accomplish. What are you trying to show or find out? What information do you need? When you can answer these questions, you will know how to create the rows and columns of the spreadsheet. Here, you want to figure out whether there will be enough profit to support expanding the business. To develop a profit projection, you will need information on your estimated income from the business and your estimated expenses. The difference between the two will be your profit. See if you can figure out what rows and columns you would need from the information contained in the preceding paragraph.

Once you know what information you need to show, you need to arrange the information in an organized manner. A poorly designed spreadsheet can be worse than no spreadsheet at all.

Each spreadsheet should begin with labels that set forth the spreadsheet's documentation: the purpose of the spreadsheet, its author, date, filename, and the location of any macros (we will explain why this is important a little later in this section). The next block of labels should contain any assumptions related to the spreadsheet. Assumptions are variables that may be subject to change. Then, you should enter short, but descriptive labels for the other types of data that will be included in the spreadsheet.

To enter a label using Lotus 1-2-3, you merely position the cursor over the appropriate cell and start to type. As you type, you will notice that what you are typing will appear at the top of the screen and that the mode indicator has switched from READY to LABEL. If you make a mistake as you are typing, you can correct it by using the Backspace key to erase the mistake and then retyping correctly. The data is not stored and transferred to the spreadsheet until you have finished typing and have pressed the Enter key. Figure 10.8 shows you the labels that you would need for Red Sky's profit projection spreadsheet.

Figure 10.8

Labels for Red Sky's Profit Projection Spreadsheet

This shows the initial setup of rows and columns in a spreadsheet for Red Sky Yacht Charters, and also lists the key assumptions. Notice that a properly designed spreadsheet begins with documentation describing the purpose, date, author, and filename of the spreadsheet. Although you may not be able to tell from the screen shot, the assumption values occupy their own cells and the values in these cells can be referenced later for use in formulas to determine the values of other cells.

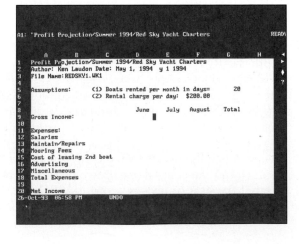

Once you know the goal of your spreadsheet and what information you will need, you must determine what values you have to input so that the spreadsheet can calculate your results. A **value** may be a number (either positive or negative) or a **formula**—something that tells the software to perform a calculation involving certain cells and to display the result in the cell containing the formula. A formula generally consists of cell addresses and mathematical symbols. (The first cell address that you refer to in a formula must be preceded with a + sign, or the spreadsheet package will assume it is a label. Most spreadsheet programs assume that entries that begin with a number, a mathematical symbol, a decimal point, a currency symbol, or the @ symbol are values.) Figure 10.9 lists the different mathematical symbols in the order in which they would be carried out by the spreadsheet software.

You should always try to use a formula rather than the actual numbers. Formulas minimize errors and make recalculations much easier. For instance, suppose in cell A5 you would like the total of the numbers appearing in cells A2, A3, and A4 to appear. Rather than typing in the actual numbers that are in those cells, you could simply type in the formula + A2 + A3 + A4 and press Enter. But there's an even easier way to get the result you want.

Instead of creating your own formulas, you may be able to use a **function,** a preprogrammed formula included with the software. Spreadsheet software programs generally include a number of such built-in formulas, ranging from a simple @SUM function (which calculates the sum of a group of numbers) to the more complex @NPV function, which computes the net present value of a series of future cash flows. You should always use a function if one is available for the result you are trying to get. Functions save keystrokes and minimize the possibilities of error. In this instance, the @SUM function performs the same calculation as your formula. Instead of having to type in the formula yourself, you would merely need to input @SUM(A2..A4). The function name tells the software which calculations to perform. The material within the parentheses (known as the function's arguments) are the values on which the calculation will be performed. Arguments may be actual numbers, cell or range addresses, cell or range names, formulas, or even other functions. Figure 10.10 lists some of the commonly used functions available for use with Lotus 1-2-3.

Symbol	Operation
( )	Groups numbers together
^	Raises a number to an exponential power
*, /	Multiplication/division
+, −	Addition/subtraction
=	Equal to
<,>	Less than/greater than

Figure 10.9
Mathematical Symbols

Figure 10.10
Some Lotus 1-2-3 Functions

@Function Name and Arguments	Operation Performed
Statistical	
@SUM(list)	Adds a range of cells, for example, @SUM(A12..A17)
@AVG(list)	Averages a range of cells, for example,@AVG(A12..A17)
Mathematical	
@ROUND(value,places)	Rounds a number to any of 15 decimal point places on either side of the decimal point, for example, @ROUND(A12, −2) will round the value in cell A12 to the nearest $100
@SQRT(value)	Computes square root
Financial	
@NPV(interest,range)	Computes the net present value of a series of future cash flows, discounted at a fixed periodic rate of interest, for example, @NPV (10%, A2..A9) where assumed interest rate is 10% and A2..A9 contains seven future cash flows
@PMT(principal interest, term)	Computes the amount of the periodic payment on a loan, for example, @PMT(100000, 7%/12, .30* 12) will compute monthly payment amount where amount of loan is $100,000, interest rate is 7%, and the term of the loan is 30 years

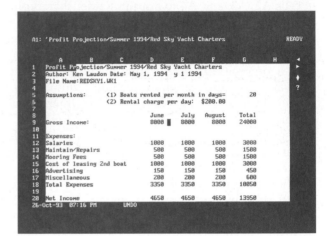

a.

b.

c.

Figure 10.11

(a) This shows the cell values entered into the spreadsheet and the use of functions. For instance, the values in cells D18..F18 are not entered by hand but instead are calculated with a Lotus function called @SUM which automatically calculates the sum of rows and columns you specify. The formula for cell D18 is @SUM(D12..D17). **(b)** This shows the use of formulas in a spreadsheet. The values in cells D20...F20 are determined by formulas. For instance, the formula for cell D20 is: D9–D18 (the Gross Income minus the Total Expenses). Also, the Gross Income cells are determined by formulas and the values entered in the Assumptions area. For instance, the formula for D9 (the gross income for June) is: G5*2*F6 (the number of days boats are expected to rent (G5=20) TIMES the number of boats in operation (given by the problem as 2) TIMES the daily rental fee (F6=$200). The $ sign freezes the cell references in formulas. In this way, the impact of any change in the number of days boats are rented, or the fee for renting, will automatically cause the spreadsheet to recalculate all values and show the latest results. This feature allows users to do "What if" kinds of analyses to quickly test various scenarios and impacts. **(c)** This is the completed spreadsheet with all functions and formulas entered.

You input values the same way that you enter labels. The only difference is that when you input a formula or function and press the Enter key, only the results of the formula or function appear in the cell rather than what you typed. Figure 10.11a shows one of the functions that you might use to prepare Red Sky's spreadsheet, and Figure 10.11b shows one of the formulas. Figure 10.11c shows what the spreadsheet would look like once all the values have been entered.

Automatic Recalculation One of the most important features of spreadsheet software is **automatic recalculation,** which is used if you discover that you need to change some of the numbers you have entered. The beauty of a spreadsheet is that you can make a change and have it ripple automatically through any other cells that refer to it. For instance, suppose after completing the Red Sky spreadsheet, you realize that you have made a mistake in entering your anticipated advertising expenses for the month of July. The mistake affects several results—your total expenses and profit for the month, as well as your total advertising expenses. If you had prepared the spreadsheet manually, you would have to recalculate each of those totals. With

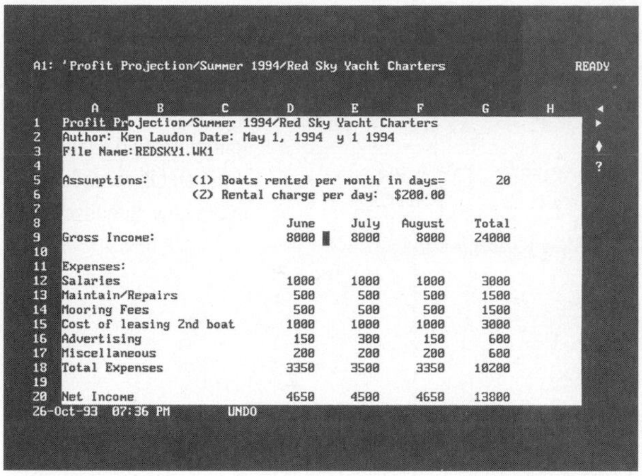

a.

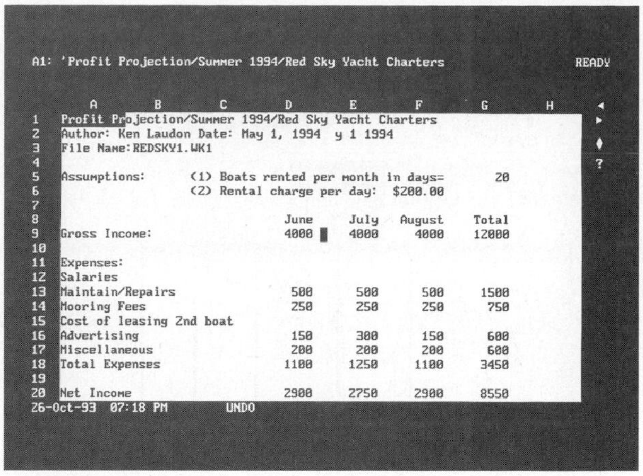

b.

spreadsheet software, though, you merely need to enter the new number once. Because you used formulas to calculate the totals, the spreadsheet is able to automatically adjust to reflect the changed value (see Figure 10.12a).

Automatic recalculation also makes it easy to play what if, one of the most important games in business. What-if games allow you to examine what would happen under different scenarios. A spreadsheet is a great tool for what-if analysis because it's so easy to see the result of each change. For example, suppose you want to see what would happen if you did not lease another boat and hire someone, but instead just chartered your own boat out at every possible opportunity. Figure 10.12b shows the results.

Commands   Other basic features of spreadsheets include the ability to copy the contents of cells, move parts of the spreadsheet from one location to another, insert and delete columns and rows, format the spreadsheet, save and retrieve it, use saved spreadsheets as templates, and print results in different formats, including graph form. Before we discuss these features, let's look at how the command menus that allow you to perform these operations generally work.

The DOS versions of Lotus 1-2-3 and Quattro Pro (a popular spreadsheet from Borland International) both still use a layered command menu. As we noted, when the spreadsheet is in MENU mode, the second line of the control panel displays the main menu, and the third line displays a submenu. The command menu is set up in tree fashion: you start at the main trunk (the main menu) and work your way out among different subsidiary branches (the submenus) by moving the cursor until you come to exactly the option that you want. Suppose, for instance, at the end of the summer, you decide to create a new spreadsheet comparing your estimated profit projection to your actual results. You set up the new spreadsheet and begin to type in the data from the Totals column of the old spreadsheet. But there's an easier way: a command that would allow you to bring the Totals column from the old spreadsheet into your new spreadsheet. First, you need to choose the File command on the main menu. This brings up a submenu listing a number of different options, among them the command Combine. When you choose Combine, it brings up a further submenu, listing the options Copy, Add, and Subtract. To replace the partially entered data in the new worksheet with the Totals column from the old spreadsheet, you must choose the Copy option. From there, your choices are either Entire-File or Named/Specified-Range. Since you need only the Totals column, you choose the latter option, type the name of the range to be extracted, and press the Enter key. Figure 10.13

Figure 10.12
(a) This shows what happens when you correct your mistake and change the advertising budget in July to $300.00. When you enter this amount in cell E16, the spreadsheet automatically recalculates all other cells. **(b)** You want to see what happens if you decide not to lease a second boat. The lease cost would disappear, there would be no salary for the additional captain and crew on the second boat, and mooring fees would drop in half. When these values are entered, net income is $8,550. Do you think it is worthwhile to lease a second boat?

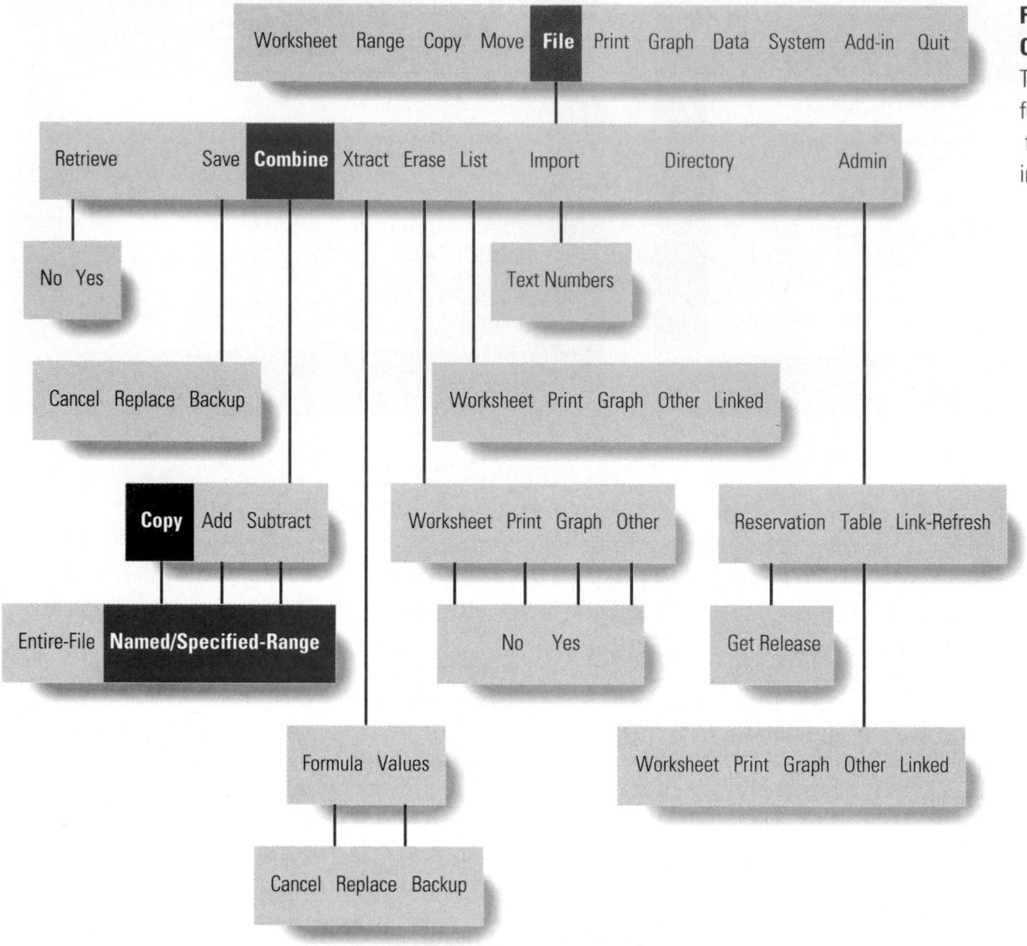

Figure 10.13
Command Tree
This is the path you would follow to bring a column from an old spreadsheet into a new spreadsheet.

illustrates this command tree, highlighting the options you would need to choose.

Once you are familiar with the various command options your spreadsheet software offers, most allow you to short-cut the command tree by merely typing the first letter of the applicable commands.

Editing All spreadsheet packages provide you with sophisticated editing capabilities. For instance, it's easy to insert or delete columns and rows. You can also copy the contents of a cell or range to another cell or range. If the cell or range includes a formula, the spreadsheet software assumes that you want a *relative copy,* meaning that it will use the same formula structure but change the cell addresses to match the new cell or range. For instance, if you were to copy the formula +A4–A3 from cell A5 into cell B5, the software would automatically change the formula to +B4–B3. You can also choose to make an absolute copy or a mixed copy. An *absolute copy* uses the exact formula the old cell had in the new cell. A *mixed copy* allows you to keep one of the variables as it was while changing the other to a relative copy. For example, in the previous example, if you chose a mixed copy, it would change the formula +A4–A3 to either +B4–A3 or +A4–B3.

You can also move any row or column to another location on the worksheet. For instance, suppose you would like to reverse the positions of two rows. Each row is deleted from its original location and added at its new location. The spreadsheet software automatically changes all cell references to the new location.

Formatting As with documents created by word processing software, the way a spreadsheet looks may be as important as its contents. Spreadsheet software programs provide a variety of formatting capabilities in addition to the ability to justify and center labels. For instance, spreadsheet packages usually allow you to vary the widths of different columns. You might want the first column, which normally contains labels, to be somewhat wider than columns containing numbers. Most packages also enable you to quickly add dollar signs, commas, decimals, and percent signs to values and to indicate negative values by surrounding them with parentheses. You merely need to select the range of cells to be edited and choose the option you want. Press the Enter key or click the mouse button, and the software automatically inserts the proper symbols in the proper places.

Files and Templates Like word processing software, one of the most valuable features of spreadsheet software is its ability to store your work in electronic form and to be able to easily retrieve and modify it at a later date if necessary. You can also create and save a **template,** a skeleton of a worksheet that has all labels and formulas entered, but no numbers. The template is all ready for you to use later. For instance, you could easily create a template from your profit projection spreadsheet. Then, next year, you would not have to go through the trouble of setting up the spreadsheet—all you would need to do would be to enter the new data. If you anticipated having any new categories of expenses, the template could be easily modified.

Printing and Graphing Spreadsheet packages allow you to print all or part of your spreadsheet at any time you wish. Printing a large spreadsheet can sometimes be difficult though. For instance, if your spreadsheet has a lot of columns, they may not all fit across a standard 8-1/2-by-11-inch piece of paper. Some spreadsheet packages allow you to print characters in a compressed format so that more of them can fit across a page. But, in some instances, even this will not be enough. The Windows version of Lotus 1-2-3 allows you to turn your spreadsheet sideways so that you will have 11 or 14 inches in which to fit the columns. You can also purchase add-on software to provide this capability if you have one of the older versions of spreadsheet software. Other print options include the ability to print the contents of each cell on a separate line (see Figure 10.14).

```
A1:     'Profit Projection/Summer 1994/Red Sky Yacht Charters
A2:     'Author: Ken Laudon Date: May 1, 1994 y 1 1994
A3:     'File Name:REDSKY1.WK1
A5:     'Assumptions:
C5:     '(1) Boats rented per month in days=
G5:     20
C6:     '(2) Rental charge per day:
F6:     (C2) 200
D8:     "June
E8:     "July
F8:     "August
G8:     "Total
A9:     'Gross Income:
D9:     +$G$5*2*$F$6
```

Figure 10.14
Print Options
This is what a portion of the Red Sky spreadsheet would look like if each cell was printed on a separate line.

Most spreadsheet packages also allow you to print data and results in pie chart, bar chart, and line graph form, with titles and legends (short descriptions beneath the graph that show what each symbol, pattern, or color on the graph represents). For instance, pie charts and horizontal bar charts are very useful for comparing proportions, whereas vertical bar graphs and line graphs are useful for showing trends. You can even create 3-D bar graphs for extra emphasis. If you have a color monitor and color printer, you can display and print charts and graphs in color. We discuss these and other kinds of presentations graphics more fully in Chapter 11.

Other Important Features   In addition to the features described in the preceding sections, most spreadsheet programs offer two other important capabilities: these are the ability to develop macros and limited database management features.

As you learned in Section 10.2, a *macro* is a collection of predefined keystrokes that can be labeled with a name and stored. Whenever you invoke the macro, the program automatically executes the keystrokes for you. Like their word processing cousins, spreadsheet macros are used to automate frequently used commands, such as printing a worksheet, or for performing repetitive procedures, such as moving the cell pointer to a specified cell. They can also be used to develop customized worksheets.

Macros are stored in cells and are entered as labels. The most common way to create a macro is to type in the keystrokes needed to perform the tasks you want to do as a series of labels in contiguous cells. (Most spreadsheet software programs also contain a macro recorder feature.) Macros should generally be created in a portion of the worksheet that is not likely to be used for the spreadsheet itself; typically, you would use a series of cells below and to the right of your anticipated worksheet area. That way you don't have to worry about the macro being affected by having data entered over it or by having columns inserted or deleted. It's also important to document your macros so that you remember later what they are supposed to do.

Another important feature of most spreadsheet software is basic data management capabilities that allow you to create a simple database, sort records, and query (search) the database based on criteria that you specify. These capabilities are not nearly as developed as those possessed by database management programs (see Section 10.4) but are still useful.

As you learned in Chapter 4, database files are comprised of records, which in turn are comprised of fields. In a spreadsheet, each row of data can constitute a record, and each cell within the row represents a field of that record.

The *sort feature* allows you to put records in numerical order, alphabetical order, or date-and-time order. The order may be either ascending (from A to Z, smallest to largest, earliest in time to latest) or descending (Z to A, largest to smallest, latest in time to earliest). You can use the *search feature* to find, extract (copy), edit, and delete selected records from the database.

Comparing Spreadsheet Software Packages

Many of the same general considerations that apply to the purchase of word processing software also apply to spreadsheet software. Once again, you need to know the memory and secondary storage capacity of your machine as well as the kind of operating system you have. For IBM PCs and compatibles with a standard DOS operating system, the dominant product by far is Lotus Development Corporation's Lotus 1-2-3, followed by Borland International's Quattro Pro. If your machine is running Windows, your choices expand to include Microsoft's Excel, as well as the Windows versions of Lotus 1-2-3 and Quattro Pro. In addition, Lotus has recently introduced a financial modeling and analysis program (essentially an advanced spreadsheet package) called Improv for Windows. If you have a Macintosh, far and away the leading package is Microsoft's Excel, with Lotus 1-2-3 for the Macintosh following far behind. Other Mac spreadsheet products include Claris Corporation's Resolve and Informix's Wingz.

Lotus 1-2-3, Quattro Pro, and Excel each have their own advantages. The DOS-based version of Lotus 1-2-3 is the most popular applications software package in history, with over nine million copies sold. It remains the spreadsheet of corporate America and is your best choice if you want or need a DOS-based spreadsheet. But if you have the capability of running a Windows-based version, the choice becomes somewhat more confusing. Microsoft Excel leads the pack, with Quattro Pro running second. Here, Lotus 1-2-3 is currently third.

Windows-based spreadsheets have a number of additional capabilities compared to their DOS-based siblings. For instance, they include multidimensional or 3-D capabilities that allow you to link and tabulate data across different spreadsheets. Instead of cramming a full year's worth of sales data onto one large spreadsheet, you can split up the data into 12 separate months, each on its own spreadsheet. The spreadsheet software can perform calculations across the separate pages to create a thirteenth page containing a summary of the totals for the year.

In addition, they sport a much more graphical interface than the traditional DOS versions and tend to be easier for a beginner to use. For instance, instead of having to identify cells by their cell addresses, Lotus's Improv allows you to use plain English labels. To construct a formula for profit, you would merely have to type (Income–Expenses). Excel and Quattro Pro allow you to easily move data with a mouse-driven drag-and-drop technique. Lotus 1-2-3 for Windows now offers the SmartIcon technology developed in connection with Lotus's Ami Pro word processing program. The technology allows users to click on one icon to invoke a process that once took several commands.

Windows-based spreadsheets also lead the way in the new field of *spreadsheet publishing,* the creation of professional-looking reports and documents containing spreadsheets. Excel boasts enhanced chart-creation tools (it will even try to figure out what chart you should be creating with the data you've selected), and Quattro Pro for Windows can rapidly apply canned formats—color, fonts, and so on—to dress up portions of your spreadsheet.

Once again, though, all this added functionality does not come without a price. Windows-based spreadsheets require significantly more RAM (4–6MB) to run at a satisfactory speed. So consider carefully whether the features offered justify the cost for you. Figure 10.15 summarizes the different spreadsheet programs.

Figure 10.15
Summary: Spreadsheet Software Packages

Spreadsheet Software	Manufacturer
DOS	
Lotus 1-2-3	Lotus Development Corporation
Quattro Pro	Borland International
Windows	
Excel	Microsoft
Lotus 1-2-3 for Windows	Lotus Development Corporation
Quattro Pro for Windows	Borland International
Improv for Windows	Lotus Development Corporation
Macintosh	
Excel	Microsoft
Lotus 1-2-3 for the Mac	Lotus Development Corporation
Resolve	Claris Corporation
Wingz	Informix

10.4 Database Management Software

You've now learned about word processing software that helps you create documents and spreadsheet software that helps you manipulate and analyze numbers. The third major category of personal computer applications software is database management software.

Database management software helps you store, organize, and retrieve information much more efficiently than using paper file folders stored in cabinet drawers. In a world of "information overload," database management software offers people a way to better manage the wealth of information that is now available, leaving more time for creative and productive endeavors.

Here's a great example: THOR, a database containing information on various technologies related to satellite recovery efforts developed with Software Publishing Company's Superbase for Windows. The database contains detailed data about launch sites, recovery vehicles, reactor composition, and satellite size and mass. THOR allows scientists to develop recovery and disposal scenarios for nuclear-powered satellites. If a satellite is likely to crash into the earth, scientists can input information on the type of satellite, type of reactor, and so on, and the database can return a detailed recovery scenario, including what kind of recovery vehicle to use and where to launch it. In the past, this job had to be performed by hand using a complex matrix, and it depended on the scientists' being aware of all the various options for recovery. Now, scenarios that used to take weeks or months to prepare can be performed in minutes.[2]

To really understand the capabilities of database management software, you need to recall the basic concepts behind the electronic storage of information. As you remember from Chapter 4, discrete pieces of data within an information system are represented as *fields*, and related fields are organized into *records*. Related records together create a *file*. Finally, a *database* can be constructed from a collection of related files.

Types of Database Software

Two types of applications software have been developed to work with data stored in database files: file managers and database management systems.

File Managers   A **file manager** (sometimes called a flat file manager) enables you to create data files called *flat files* and to retrieve and work with those files, but only one file at a time. A file manager can be a powerful and useful tool. You can use one to create and store just about any kind of list—a mailing list, a customer list, an inventory list, a list of your personal friends, and so on. Each list is a file composed of records and fields. You can later retrieve those lists, update them, delete information, or rearrange the order of the records within them. A file manager also allows you to search and extract information from files, to display that information, and generate printed reports. For many tasks, a file manager is more than sufficient. But its inability to work with more than one file at a time can be a significant limitation.

For instance, what if the pieces of information needed to answer your question are spread out among more than one file? Suppose that you want to send a collection letter to customers who have not paid their most recent bills. Billing information (customer name, amount, and whether the bill has been paid) is collected in an invoice file. Customer data (name, address, and telephone number) is stored in another file. Since a file manager allows you to work with only one file at a time, it's not so easy to pull out exactly the information you need. You would first have to search the invoice file for those bills that had not been paid. Then you would have to search the customer file for the addresses matching the names on the unpaid bills.

Database Management Systems   The answer to this problem is a **database management system (DBMS).** DBMS software allows you to construct a database environment for a set of related files and to quickly and easily access and manipulate the information located in several separate files.

A database environment has several advantages over the traditional file environment based on data stored in separate files. First and foremost, when information is stored in a database, you can access multiple files at one time. This allows you to retrieve data in one search even though it is stored in separate files. A DBMS makes it easier and quicker to find the information you need.

Second, traditional file processing environments often fall prey to the problem of **data redundancy**—the same piece of information is stored in multiple data files. Data redundancy can lead to the further problem of **data confusion,** which occurs when data is updated in one or more of the files in which it appears but not all. A further problem with the traditional file processing environment, particularly within a business setting, is **data dependence**—different parts of an organization may use different software to collect, process, and store information. The data files of one department may be incompatible with the software used by a different department, making it very difficult to combine or exchange information between the two.

A DBMS reduces data dependence, data redundancy, and data confusion. Once everyone is using the same DBMS, information can be more easily shared across department and division lines. Because a DBMS maintains all data within one database, data redundancy and data confusion are reduced. When information needs to be updated, you need update it in only one place.

Today, DBMSs are used by businesses of all sizes (to compile information about employees, customers, vendors, and inventories and to keep track of accounting information and the like), by government agencies (to administer benefit programs and track compliance with laws), and by scientists and other academic researchers (to track research data). DBMS software used to be available only for larger computers, but now there are sophisticated DBMS software packages for personal computers as well. In fact, DBMSs have become so popular and relatively inexpensive that DBMS software is increasingly being purchased by individuals for their own personal use.

There are three basic types of DBMS applications software: those that organize the database using a relational model, those that use a hierarchical model, and those that use a network model. In addition, a fourth kind of DBMS, the object-oriented database management system, is starting to appear in some arenas.

Relational DBMSs   As its name indicates, a **relational DBMS** is able to *relate* data in different files through the use of a common data element, or field, in those files. It enables you to easily combine specific pieces of information from several different files into a new file. A relational DBMS uses a two-dimensional table structure with rows that correspond to the various records in a file and columns that correspond to the various fields. Any piece of data in any file or table can be related to any other piece of data in another file or table as long as each table shares a common field (see Figure 10.16).

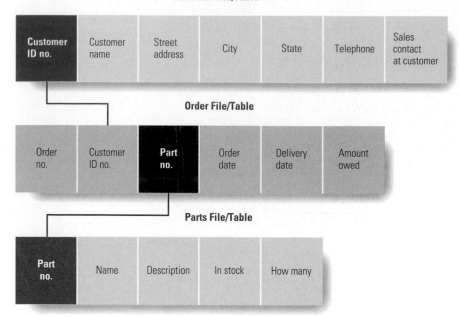

Figure 10.16
A Schematic View of a Relational Database
A relational database allows you to link data stored in separate files (called tables) if both files contain a common data element or field. Here, for instance, you can easily link data in the customer file (table) with data in the order file (table) through the use of the customer ID no. Likewise, data in the order file (table) can be joined with data in the parts file (table) because each table has a part no. field.

Some relational DBMSs also include a set of powerful tools that can be used to help develop a complete information management system. These so-called *programmable relational DBMSs* have built-in programming languages that can be used to develop custom business applications, such as on-screen forms and special report generators. The story "Miller and Reynolds Linked by Paradox" illustrates how one company developed an innovative database application using a new programmable relational DBMS named Paradox for Windows.

Today, relational DBMSs are the most popular form of database management software for microcomputer-based information systems. They have also become very popular for minicomputer- and mainframe-based systems. Nonetheless, many larger organizations continue to use databases organized along other models.

Other Types of DBMSs Instead of relating data through a series of tables, a **hierarchical DBMS** links data through a hierarchical relationship. The hierarchy begins with a data segment that is considered the parent element. This element may then be linked to multiple subordinate, lower-level segments, called children. These subordinate segments in turn may be linked to further lower-level data segments. In a hierarchical database, a parent element may be linked to one or more children, but a child element always has only one parent element. Figure 10.17 illustrates a hierarchical database. These types of databases work best when the data involved naturally has an inherent one-to-many type of relationship. They have well-defined, prespecified access paths (for example, to get to information on the bottom rung, you must start at the highest level and then work your way down) and are not as flexible in relating information as a relational database.

A **network DBMS** also employs a hierarchy, but here each lower-level data element may be related to more than one parent element. A network DBMS provides more flexibility than a hierarchical DBMS but still requires that the access paths be defined in advance. There are also limits on the number of links that can be established among different data elements. Figure 10.18 illustrates a network database.

A Ticket Reservation System

Name of show

The Secret Garden   Les Misérables   Phantom of the Opera

Date of performance

April 20   April 21   April 22

Time of performance

Matinee   Evening

Seat numbers

A1   A2   A3

Figure 10.17
A Schematic View of a Hierarchical Database
A hierarchical database structure for a theater tickets reservation system. Note that each data segment has only one "parent," but parent elements may have more than one child.

A Class Scheduling System for a Typical College

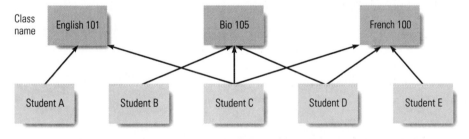

Class name   English 101   Bio 105   French 100

Student A   Student B   Student C   Student D   Student E

Figure 10.18
A Schematic View of a Network Database
A network database structure allows you to capture "many to many" relationships. A typical college will offer many different courses, each with many students. Each student, in turn, will be enrolled in several or more courses.

Finally, **object-oriented DBMSs (OODBMSs)** have been developed to handle complex data types (such as those used in multimedia applications) not easily handled by other types of DBMSs. Their ability to represent complex real-world entities and relationships makes them ideal for engineering, manufacturing, document management, and software development projects.

Relational DBMS Features and Capabilities

Perhaps the easiest way to illustrate all the concepts we have been discussing, as well as the features and capabilities of DBMS software, is to step through the process of actually developing a database. The software that we'll feature is dBASE III Plus, a widely used relational DBMS from Borland International.

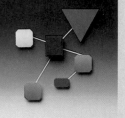

Miller and Reynolds Linked by Paradox

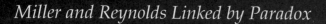

What do Miller Beer cans and Reynolds Wrap have in common? They're both made from the same raw material—aluminum. In fact, Miller Brewing Company's Can Division gets its aluminum from Reynolds Metals Company, the maker of Reynolds Wrap. And recently, Miller and Reynolds have been using a system developed with Borland's new programmable relational DBMS software package, Paradox for Windows, to forge even closer links between the two companies.

Miller's goal was to reduce the stockpile of aluminum used at its can manufacturing plants and to better monitor the quality of the aluminum it received. Reynolds, eager to help satisfy an important customer, used Paradox for Windows to develop a database that would allow Miller to perform tasks like tracking remote, in-transit, and in-house inventories, materials forecasting and ordering, and quality control monitoring. The actual link between Miller and Reynolds was created using electronic data interchange (EDI). The project was completed over six to seven months by Brent Kanady, team leader at Reynolds' Mills Products Division, Rick Losco, lead programmer, and two part-time programmers. Most of the development was done on Intel 486SX machines. Initially, the machines were configured with 4MB of RAM, but they were expanded to 8MB when 4MB proved too slow. Nonetheless,

the team felt that speed was a small price to pay for the power of the product.

For instance, one of the most important features that the project team found in Paradox for Windows was its ability to efficiently create screens and modify forms. They were able to produce query screens that let users move through relevant data without having to actually use Paradox's query language. Paradox also included point-and-click relational table linking.

Today, the database is providing Miller with a system that lets it more closely monitor orders for raw materials and conduct an expanded quality management program. Plans also include moving the database to the shop floor so that managers can input and view data on aluminum shipments directly.

Source: Based on Lindquist, Christopher, "Miller Finds Paradox Brew Tasty," *Computerworld,* February 8, 1993.

Critical Thinking Questions

1 What files might be in the database described in this story?

2 Why wouldn't a file manager be appropriate for the applications described here?

3 What are some of the ways that the Miller/Reynolds database helps improve organizational efficiency and quality?

Field

Field	①	②	③	④	⑤	⑥	⑦	⑧
Field name	Last Name	First Name	Street	City	State	Zip Code	Phone No	Sailing Exp

Figure 10.19
Customer List

Sketching out the information you want your database file to include is a useful step. This figure shows the information you would want to include in the Red Sky customer file.

Database File Design The first step in designing a database is to decide what information needs to be included and the form into which that information should be put. Imagining what your database would look like on paper helps get you started. Let's say that the first file you would like to create is a list of customers for your Red Sky sailing business. Figure 10.19 shows a layout of what you would probably want the file to include.

Now let's look at how you would transform that list into a computerized database file using dBASE. Once you have loaded the program, the opening screen appears (see Figure 10.20).

The first step is to select a name for the file. The name you select should be short but descriptive of the contents of the file. We'll call our file Customer (eight characters long—the maximum length for a dBASE filename). Like most of the other forms of applications software that we've discussed in this chapter, dBASE uses a command menu to help you enter commands. (It also allows you to bypass the command menu and enter commands directly—often a quicker option for the experienced user.) Choosing the Create command option eventually brings up a screen that prompts you to enter

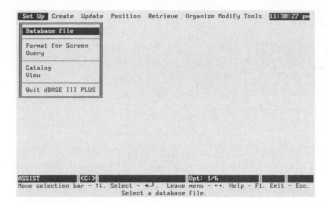

Figure 10.20
dBase III Plus Opening Screen

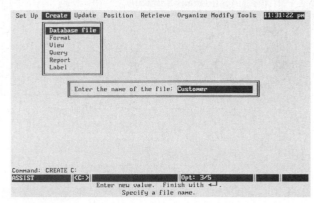

Figure 10.21
Naming the File

The first step in creating a database file with dBASE is to select a name for your file.

the name of the file (see Figure 10.21). After you've done so, dBASE will automatically add a three-letter extension, .dbf, after the filename to distinguish this as a relational data file as opposed to other general categories of files that can be generated by the software (such as report form files, query files, and database memo files).

Once you've chosen and entered a filename, the next step is to define the field names, the field types, and the width of the fields that will hold the information you want to store. This process is known as **data definition.** When you're done, you will have created a file structure, or *template,* for the records that will compose the database file.

You must first give each of the discrete pieces of information that you would like to include (each of which constitutes a field) a **field name** that describes the information. Each DBMS has its own rules about forming field names. With dBASE III Plus, a field name must begin with a letter, can be no more than ten characters long, and may contain only letters, digits, or underscores. (Underscores can be used to take the place of blank spaces.) Here is where you can use your paper sketch (Figure 10.19) as a guide. In our example, we will use the following field names: Last_Name, First_Name, Street, City, State, Zip_Code, Phone, and SailingExp.

The next step is to define the type of data that will be stored in each field. Most DBMS software allows for four or five different **field types:**

1 *Alphanumeric fields* store letters, or a mixture of letters, numbers, and symbols.

2 *Numeric fields* store numbers that may later be involved in some mathematical calculations.

3 *Date fields* store the month/year, the month/day/year, or the day/month/year.

4 *Logical fields* store any data that can be represented in one of two states, such as yes/no, true/false, male/female, and hourly/salaried.

5 *Memo fields* store varying amounts of text, for instance, notes about a particular piece of information.

Finally, you must define the width of any alphanumeric and numeric fields. (With dBASE, date, logical, and memo fields are automatically assigned a certain width.) To do so, you need to consider how many letters, numbers, or other symbols would typically be needed to store the kind of information that will be included in the particular field. You don't want to make the widths too short, or you will end up having to abbreviate, but if you make them too long, you will waste secondary storage space.

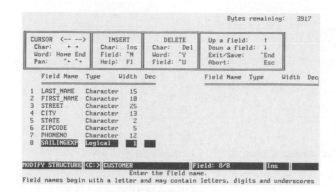

Figure 10.22
The Customer File Structure
The completed customer file structure looks like this.

Once the format for your records is complete, you save it and then follow it as you enter actual data to create the actual records. Figure 10.22 illustrates the completed Customer file structure.

Most DBMS packages include a screen design tool that allows you to create a more user-friendly *on-screen template* that you can use to actually enter the data making up your records. Figure 10.23 compares a standard data entry screen (10.23a) with a more customized version that you can create with dBASE's screen design tools (10.23b).

Data Entry You're now ready to actually enter data using the template you have constructed. Figure 10.24 illustrates the Customer file after data for eight customers have been entered. Each line constitutes a separate record within the file.

Figure 10.23
Comparison of a Standard Data Entry Screen with an On-Screen Template

Source: Courtesy of Borland International, Inc.

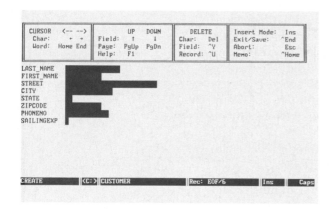

a. dBASE's standard data entry screen does not look particularly inviting or easy to use.

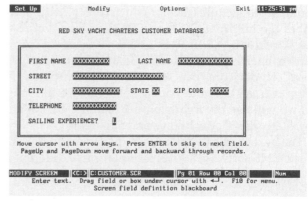

b. But dBASE allows you to create a customized data entry screen that is much more user-friendly.

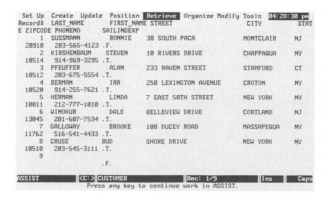

Figure 10.24
The Customer File
This is what the customer file looks like after data for eight customers have been entered.

Data Editing   As with word processing and spreadsheet software, DBMS software allows you to edit the data you have entered. You can easily correct mistakes as you go, much as you do when using word processing software. In addition, you can return to the file at a later date to update it by adding new data, deleting old data, or modifying existing data. You can even modify your file structure at a later date to add or delete fields or change the structure of existing fields. DBMS software also allows you to *sort* records and arrange them in the order you specify. To make the sorting process even more efficient, you can *index* the database. The index feature uses a pointer system to identify records and make them easier to find.

Some DBMSs will also construct a **data dictionary**—an automated file that stores your data definitions and monitors the data you are entering to make sure that it corresponds to the format required. For instance, you will be unable to enter a six-character number in a field defined as being five characters wide. The data dictionary is also used by DBMS software to help relate fields contained in different files, to document who is responsible for maintaining the data, and to help ensure the security of the database by defining who has a right to access the information.

Information Retrieval/Queries   One of the things that makes DBMS software so useful is the ability to retrieve just the information that you are looking for. This process is known as querying the database. To query the database, you issue commands in a special **query language.**

You use query language to frame searches of your database: you can ask to see the entire thing or just data that meets conditions you have specified. Queries may be very simple or very complex. Suppose, for example, you want only a list of those customers who live in New York. Using dBASE III Plus, you would build a simple query that looked like this: List First_Name, Last_Name, State For State = NY. The State = NY is an example of a search condition that employs a *relational operator,* in this case, an equal sign, to specify the criteria that must be satisfied. Figure 10.25 shows the other operators commonly used in search conditions.

More complex queries can require that several different conditions be met, for example, a certain last name and a certain state. And as we noted at the beginning of this section, in addition to extracting information from individual files, a relational DBMS allows you to retrieve information from separate files. Let's go back to the Customer and Invoice files described in the section on file managers. There, the names and addresses of customers were located in a file separate from billing information. But notice that both files include a common field, the customer name. DBMS software can use that common field to extract the required information and create a new file combining the information you need.

Today, in addition to their own query language, most relational DBMSs allow you to use a standardized query language known as **Structured**

Figure 10.25
Operators

The three primary types of operators used in search conditions are relational operators, logical operators, and mathematical operators.

Relational Operators:

<	Less than
>	Greater than
=	Equal to
< > or #	Not equal
< =	Less than or equal
> =	Greater than or equal

Logical Operators:

.AND.	Logical AND
.OR.	Logical OR
.NOT.	Logical NOT
()	Parentheses for grouping

Mathematical Operators:

+	Addition
−	Subtraction
*	Multiplication
/	Division
** or ^	Exponentiation
()	Grouping parentheses
SQRT(N)	Square root of number N

Query Language (SQL). SQL queries follow a standard format (see Figure 10.26). Help may be on the way for those who find SQL language difficult to master: Intelligence Ware offers Iconic Query, an application that allows users to access database information by clicking on graphical icons. Iconic Query works with many different DBMS products, including Paradox, Oracle, Sybase, and DB2.

Report and Label Generation DBMS software also lets you generate printed reports containing the results of your queries. In most instances, you must first specify the format that you want the report to take—its title, its column headings, and which fields will be included. dBASE III Plus and most other forms of DBMS software use a series of report generator screens to guide you through this process. In addition, the report generator can also add, average, and perform other calculations on the contents of different data fields. Figure 10.27 shows a typical report that might be generated by a pharmacy using DBMS software.

Most database management software also allows you to generate mailing labels for bulk mailings. For example, dBASE III Plus includes a built-in label generator that makes it easy to print addresses onto various sizes of mailing labels.

Comparing File Managers and Relational DBMS Packages

When it comes to database management software for your microcomputer, you basically have two choices: a file manager or a relational DBMS. File managers tend to be much easier to use than relational DBMSs and much less expensive, generally retailing from about $100 to $150 compared to about $500 and up for a relational DBMS. Examples include PC-File, Personal R:Base, and File Express (all DOS-based). For simple database needs, these file managers may be more than sufficient. There are also more sophisticated file managers, such as Symantec's Q&A (DOS) and Claris Corporation's FileMaker Pro for Macintosh and Windows, that can provide rudimentary file linking and retail for around $400.

The basic structure of an SQL query for retrieving data:

```
SELECT <columns>      [Identifies columns/data fields
                       to be retrieved]

FROM <tables>         [Specifies tables/files from which
                       the data is to be retrieved]

WHERE <condition>     [Extracts only such records as
                       match a specified condition]
```

Example:
```
SELECT        CUSTOMER NAME, AMOUNT OWED
FROM          CUSTOMER, ORDER
WHERE         CUSTOMER.CUSTOMER ID NO =
              ORDER.CUSTOMER ID NO
```

This query creates a new record by linking the customer and order files described in Figure 10.16 through their common data field, Customer ID No. The new record will show the name of each customer and the amount that customer owes.

Figure 10.26
SQL Queries

Even the sophisticated file managers cannot match the power that a programmable relational DBMS can offer, however. Programmable relational DBMS packages generally try to satisfy the needs of two different groups: (1) end users who want to use the database to store, organize, and retrieve data and (2) programmers who want to use them to develop custom business applications.

Among relational DBMSs, dBASE has been the standard for many years and still commands nearly half the market.[3] dBASE III Plus is several years old, but is probably still the most widely used version of dBASE. Its successor, dBASE IV, introduced some significant enhancements but has not been a rousing success. A Windows-based version of dBASE is not expected until early 1994. Industry experts generally agree that from a technical standpoint, dBASE has fallen significantly behind its competitors. But American companies have invested billions of dollars in developing dBASE applications for their data and do not take the decision to switch products lightly. As a result, learning to use dBASE will continue to be a worthwhile endeavor for some time to come.

The other leading DBMS packages include Borland's Paradox (for DOS and Windows), Microsoft's Access (for Windows), and Microsoft's FoxPro (for DOS, Windows, and Macintosh). Each of these products seeks to combine ease of use with powerful data manipulation. They all exploit their graphical user interfaces and include easy-to-follow screen prompts to aid the user in developing complex queries and forms, reports, and graphs. They also include a number of exciting new features, such as the ability to store pictures, sound, and video, as well as the ability to read and write data directly from competing products, allowing diverse users with a variety of DBMSs to work together and share data. But though they share many features, each of the products has particular strengths and weaknesses. For example, FoxPro provides significantly faster performance but is not as good at allowing nonprogrammers to easily create custom applications. Paradox for Windows sports a strong object orientation and includes ObjectPAL, an object-oriented visual programming language. And Access seeks to be all things to all people, targeted to both end users and program developers. Even though you are not likely to need the power of these products for personal use, they are rapidly becoming the wave of the DBMS future in the business arena.

Figure 10.28 summarizes these different database packages.

DATE	DRUG_CLASS	DRUG_NAME	SUPPLIER	TABS
04/23/93	S2	STEROPAX	ICI	25
08/17/93	X1	VALIUM	DOW	30
06/25/93	X3	TRICONLOR	HOECHST	15
03/31/93	T1	LOMOTOL	DOW	10
08/15/93	X1	VALIUM	DOW	40
07/08/93	T3	SERAPIN	BAYER	25
02/29/93	S2	WEDON	ABBOTS	30
12/12/93	X1	VOLTORARIN	SQUIBB	12
06/25/93	S4	REGNON	ROCHE	12
05/19/93	X2	ORGON	DOW	18

Figure 10.27
A Typical Report
This figure illustrates a typical report that a pharmacy using dBASE might generate. The report lists the year's transactions sorted by drug class, drug name, supplier, and number of tablets sold.

Figure 10.28
Summary: File Managers and DBMS Packages

File Managers	Manufacturer	Relational DBMS Packages	Manufacturer
DOS		**DOS**	
PC-File	ButtonWare	dBASE III Plus	Borland International
File Express	Expressware Corporation	dBASE IV	Borland International
Personal R:Base	Microrim	FoxPro	Microsoft
Q&A	Symantec	Paradox	Borland International
Windows		R:Base	Microrim
FileMaker Pro	Claris Corporation	**Windows**	
AceFile	Ace Software	Paradox	Borland International
Macintosh		Access	Microsoft
FileMaker Pro	Claris Corporation	FoxPro for Windows	Microsoft
Panorama II	ProVue Development	Superbase	Software Publishing
		Macintosh	
		FoxBase+	Microsoft
		4th Dimension	Acius

Summary

Introduction to Applications Software Packages

▶ Applications software allows you to apply a computer to solve a specific problem or perform a specific task. Applications software may be custom designed or sold as an applications software package.

▶ Applications software packages are stored on floppy disks and usually accompanied by written documentation. After you install the program and load it into primary storage, the opening screen generally displays a product logo and licensing information.

▶ Most applications software packages let you issue commands via a command menu or function keys. They are also increasingly making greater use of graphical user interfaces and icons to represent commands and program options.

▶ Most applications software packages also employ screen prompts and make on-line help available to help guide users.

Word Processing Software

▶ Word processing software allows you to create, edit, format, print, and save documents.

▶ Features of word processing software that make text entry easy and efficient include automatic returns at the end of a line, word wrapping, and the ability to scroll through the document.

▶ Word processing software allows you to easily edit what you have written. Editing features include the ability to insert, delete, copy, and move blocks of text. You can also search for a specific word or phrase and automatically replace it with some other word or phrase.

▶ Word processing software also allows you to format documents—make adjustments to the way they look. You can choose margin widths and a ragged-right or justified-right margin; vary line spacing and the number of lines on each page; choose different pagination options; and capitalize, boldface, italicize, or underline text. You can also center text or arrange it in columns. Word processing software automatically reformats pages after any changes are made.

▶ Word processing software generally offers a variety of potential typefaces and sizes. More sophisticated word processing packages also offer graphics and layout capabilities.

▶ Word processing software allows you to save your work in electronic form for future reference and use.

▶ Word processing software also allows you to print documents whenever you like.

▶ Other important features of word processing software include spelling checkers, electronic thesaurus, grammar and style checkers, mail merge, and the ability to create macros.

▶ The primary distinguishing characteristic between different word processing packages is whether they are full-featured, top-of-the-line products or low-frill versions. The three dominant full-featured word processors are WordPerfect Corporations's WordPerfect, Microsoft's Word, and Lotus's Ami Pro.

Spreadsheet Software

▶ Spreadsheet software allows you to enter data and indicate the calculations you want performed and then automatically performs those calculations. It allows you to store the spreadsheet on a disk for later use and can print out a copy of the spreadsheet.

▶ Spreadsheet software is used in business to develop budgets, track and analyze financial results, and construct projections and forecasts; in the academic world for student rosters and grade calculations; and in the research arena to analyze scientific data. Spreadsheets are also used for personal budgets and finances.

▶ A Lotus spreadsheet screen has three main parts: a worksheet area, a control panel, and a status indicator. Data is entered in cells formed by the intersection of columns and rows. Each cell has a cell address. Sets of contiguous cells are known as a range. To enter data, the cursor must be positioned over the cell (called the current cell) where you want the data to be located.

▶ Cells contain either labels or values. Labels consist of text, whereas values may be either numbers or formulas. Most spreadsheet programs also include prewritten formulas called functions.

- Electronic spreadsheets can automatically recalculate results if any of the numbers entered as data are changed. This feature allows spreadsheets to make projections and forecasts, and to examine what might happen under different scenarios.

- Spreadsheet programs generally use layered command menus set up in tree fashion.

- Spreadsheet software allows you to make relative copies, absolute copies, or mixed copies of cells and ranges.

- Spreadsheet software also provides a variety of formatting, printing, and graphing capabilities. You can develop your own macros and create limited databases with spreadsheet software.

- The leading DOS-based spreadsheet programs are Lotus 1-2-3 and Borland's Quattro Pro. The leading Windows-based spreadsheet program is Microsoft's Excel. The newest spreadsheets feature multidimensionality and easy-to-use graphical interfaces.

Database Management Software

- Database management software helps store, organize, and retrieve information more efficiently.

- There are two basic types of database management software: file managers and database management systems.

- File managers allow you to create and manipulate data files, but you can work with only one file at a time.

- Database management systems allow you to access and work with data located in separate files.

- Database management systems reduce data dependence, data redundancy, and data confusion.

- Relational databases use relational tables and relate data in different files through the use of a common field. Hierarchical databases link data through a hierarchical, parent–child relationship, with each lower-level data segment having only one parent element. Network databases also employ a hierarchy but allow lower-level data elements to be related to more than one parent element. Object-oriented database management systems are used primarily for engineering, manufacturing, and document management databases.

- After choosing a filename, the first step in designing a database file is data definition: defining the field names, field types, and width. Each DBMS has its own rules about forming field names. There are generally five field types: alphanumeric, numeric, date, logical, and memo. Field widths will vary depending on the typical length of the data they are designed to hold.

- DBMS software allows you to easily edit the database after it has been created. You can also sort and index data. The DBMS creates a data dictionary to monitor the data being entered.

- Querying a database allows you to retrieve just the information you are looking for. Queries may be simple or complex and may involve data stored in just one database file or multiple files. Searches are framed in query language. Most DBMSs have their own query language but also allow you to use a standardized query language called SQL.

▶ Other important features of DBMSs include report and label generation.

▶ The leading flat file managers include PC-File, Filemaker Pro (Macintosh and Windows), and Q&A. The dominant DOS-based relational DBMS is dBASE (versions III Plus and IV). The leading Windows-based products are Paradox for Windows, Access, and FoxPro for Windows. FoxBase+ is the primary Macintosh relational DBMS.

Key Terms

word processing software

word processing software
word processor
documents
status line
word-wrapping
scroll
block
cutting and pasting
search
search and replace
formatting
default settings
WYSIWYG
typeface
font
proportional spacing
spelling checker
electronic thesaurus
style and grammar checker
mail-merge
macros

spreadsheet software

spreadsheet software
VisiCalc
worksheet area
worksheet
cell
cell address

range
current cell
cell pointer
control panel
label
value
formula
function
automatic recalculation
template

database management software

database management software
file manager
database management system
    (DBMS)
data redundancy
data confusion
data dependence
relational DBMS
hierarchical DBMS
network DBMS
object-oriented DBMS (OODBMS)
data definition
field name
field type
data dictionary
query language
structured query language (SQL)

Review Questions

1 Name and describe five common characteristics shared by most forms of applications software packages.

2 How does word processing software make text entry an easier process?

3 What is blocking? Name several text-editing operations that can be aided by blocking.

4 Identify at least five different formatting operations, and explain how they can be used to change the appearance of a document.

5 What are the advantages and disadvantages of using spelling checkers and style and grammar checkers?

6 When and why might you use a macro?

7 What's the difference between WordPerfect and LetterPerfect? Which would be more appropriate for use in a law office? Explain your choice.

8 What are the advantages of an electronic spreadsheet compared to a manual spreadsheet?

9 Identify the three main parts of the Lotus opening screen. What role does each part play in the creation of a spreadsheet?

10 What are some of the questions you need to answer in order to begin constructing a spreadsheet?

11 What is the difference between a label and a value? Between a formula and a function?

12 Describe some of the ways you can edit a worksheet.

13 Lotus Development Corporation named its spreadsheet software Lotus 1-2-3 because it integrated three significant features. What do you think they were?

14 How do Windows-based spreadsheet programs differ from DOS-based versions?

15 What are the advantages of a DBMS compared to a file manager?

16 Explain how a database organized using a relational model differs from one using a hierarchical model or a network model.

17 What is involved in the process of data definition?

18 Describe the five different field types and the type of data that is stored by each type.

19 What role does a data dictionary play in a DBMS?

20 Define query, query language, and SQL.

Problem-Solving and Skill-Building Exercises

1 Susan Jackson runs a horse farm in Garrison, New York. Operating the farm involves a number of tasks. Here are just a few: making sure enough food for the horses and other necessary supplies are always on hand, tracking accounts payable (bills the farm must pay) and accounts receivable (payments owed to the farm), arranging lesson appointments for customers, and sending out a monthly newsletter to all present and past clients. Prepare a 2–3 page report explaining how you could use word processing, spreadsheet, and/or database management software to accomplish these tasks.

2 Together with two or three other students, construct a database file containing at least eight records, each with the following fields: first name, last name, address, city, state, zip code, phone, male/female. Use a file manager or other database management software available to you. (Check with your PC lab coordinator or your professor to find out where you can access and use a PC database package.)

3 Design and implement a personal check register using spreadsheet software. (Again, ask your PC lab coordinator or professor to find out how to get access to such software.) Be sure the register contains at least all the information that a manual check register would have.

Choosing Applications Software

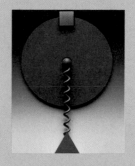

You've got the hardware, and you're ready to roll. Now it's time to think about applications software. Here are some general guidelines.

The best places to learn about the different kinds of applications software available are computer magazines that carry software product reviews. *PC Magazine, PC World, PC/Computing, Macworld, MacUser, Computer Shopper, Compute,* and *BYTE* all regularly review different applications packages and prepare comparison charts to help you find the best product/value combination.

You can purchase software in most of the same places that you purchase computer equipment: authorized dealers, speciality computer stores, mail-order houses. Dealing with a reputable seller is important: if the price of the software seems "too good to be true," it may be counterfeit. You can legitimately expect to pay $250 for software with a retail price of around $400. If the same product is being offered to you at around $100 or $150, you should be suspicious. Other counterfeit tip-offs include shrink wrap that doesn't fit right, missing registration cards, a photocopied manual, or a missing registration number when you load the software.

Factors that you should consider in evaluating any type of applications software include its compatibility with your hardware and operating system, how easy it is to learn and use, how well the software performs, the quality of its on-line help and documentation, the technical support made available by the manufacturer, and the manufacturer's upgrade policy. The version number of the software you're considering is also important. It's a well-known fact that the first release of a software product (usually denoted as version 1.0) is often plagued with bugs that must be corrected. Savvy software buyers also know to stay away from subsequent software releases that end in a 0 (as in version 2.0 or 3.0). Software manufacturers follow the convention of denoting major changes in software

packages by changing the product version number from 1.0 to 2.0 to 3.0 and so on. Such versions are also often riddled with bugs. Versions that have a number other than 0 after the decimal point (for example, version 3.1) generally fix the bugs that have cropped up in the earlier versions and are often a wiser choice.

Once you have your software, sooner or later you'll have to decide whether to switch to upgraded versions that manufacturers regularly produce. Some manufacturers make incremental upgrades (going from version 3.1 to 3.2, for example) available to registered users for a nominal amount. (That's why it's important to mail your software registration card in to the manufacturer.) On the other hand, a major upgrade (a jump from version 2.0 to 3.0, for instance) will generally cost you. Major upgrades typically involve significant product enhancements but often come with an additional price—the time you will need to spend relearning how to use the software. For instance, if you previously used WordPerfect 4.2 but want to switch to WordPerfect 5.1, you are in for a big change in the way you interact with the software. Going from a DOS-based version to a Windows-based version of the same software can be even more traumatic—the Windows GUI differs significantly from the traditional DOS-based command structures. In addition, Windows applications software demands more CPU power and RAM than do DOS-based versions. Without the hardware to support it, Windows-based software will not perform satisfactorily. Even with appropriate hardware, Windows software is likely to be slower than DOS versions. All in all, it would be wise to carefully measure the product enhancements the new version offers against these factors before making the switch from your tried-and-true software.

Notes

1   **Manzi, Jim,** "The Productivity MacGuffin," *BYTE,* August 1992.

2   **Lindquist, Christopher,** "RDBMS Helps Prevent Satellite Disaster," *Computerworld,* April 27, 1992.

3   **Vizard, Michael,** "Make Way for a Faster dBASE IV," *Computerworld,* March 15, 1993.

After completing this chapter, you will:

▶ Know the advantages and disadvantages of integrated software packages.

▶ Understand the features and capabilities of graphics, presentation, and desktop publishing software.

▶ Be aware of the wide variety of packaged applications software available for business and personal use.

The Expanding Universe of Personal Computer Applications Software

Stepping into the Future

For six days, at the end of April 1993, a staff of top magazine executives from well over a dozen major magazines stepped into the future.

Where did they go, and what did they do there?

They didn't have to travel too far—just to an underground room in the basement of the Time-Life building in Rockefeller Center in New York City. And what they did once there—working to put out a magazine—seems pretty mundane and routine on the surface.

So what made this project so special, so "futuristic"?

The answer is that they worked entirely electronically. For many of them, it was the first time they were able to integrate all preprinting steps—writing, editing, reviewing, adding photographs, retouching images, laying out pages, writing captions and headlines—on one desktop computer system. By the end of the week, they had produced a high-quality, 4-color, 92-page general interest magazine about—what else—the impact of technology on the magazine industry (see photo). Thirty-five thousand copies have been printed and distributed.

Although, as you'll learn later in this chapter, desktop publishing technology has been around for some time, and is already widely used by publishers of newsletters and small magazines, most of the large media companies remain wedded to traditional technology.

But as the week-long project demonstrated, it is now becoming technologically feasible to produce a major magazine with desktop publishing. In fact, as Ann Russell, editor in chief of *Folio* magazine says, "Any magazine that isn't doing this is really putting itself in peril. The technology is absolutely affordable, and the history of computers is cheaper, cheaper, cheaper."

But beyond cost savings, magazine executives are most excited about the influence that technological breakthroughs may have on the presentation of the news and the nature of the editorial process. "We're talking about the ability to integrate all the steps in one location and seeing the whole product, seeing precisely the possibilities of what your magazine will look like and if you aren't particularly happy, making changes on the spot," says James R. Junta,

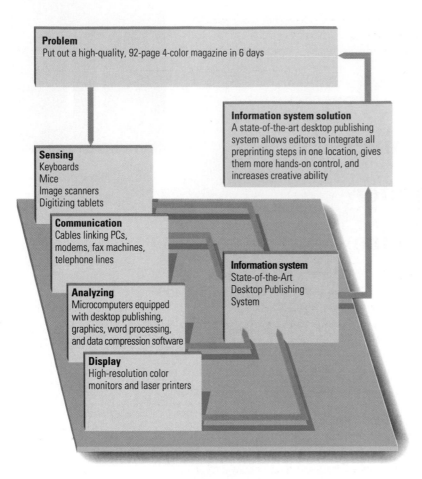

Problem
Put out a high-quality, 92-page 4-color magazine in 6 days

Information system solution
A state-of-the-art desktop publishing system allows editors to integrate all preprinting steps in one location, gives them more hands-on control, and increases creative ability

Sensing
Keyboards
Mice
Image scanners
Digitizing tablets

Communication
Cables linking PCs, modems, fax machines, telephone lines

Information system
State-of-the-Art
Desktop Publishing
System

Analyzing
Microcomputers equipped with desktop publishing, graphics, word processing, and data compression software

Display
High-resolution color monitors and laser printers

The table of contents of *Open,* a 92-page, 4-color magazine produced entirely with a desk top publishing system.

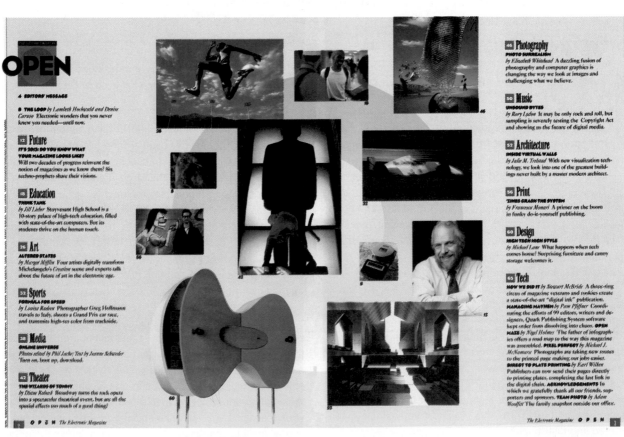

executive vice president of marketing at the Magazine Publishers of America. "What this stuff does is remove impediments to the creative process," says John Papenek, director of news media at Time Inc. "I have much more control about how my magazine is taking shape."

Although many of the systems used in the project are still in the development stage, much of the technology is readily available. Industry experts estimate that within three to five years most magazines, even the major ones, will all be using desktop publishing systems.

As the opening vignette illustrates, desktop computer applications software is making whole new ways of working and living possible. In Chapter 10, we reviewed the three most popular personal computer applications software packages: word processing, spreadsheet, and database management software. In this chapter, we turn our focus to the rest of the applications software universe: integrated software packages, graphics and presentation software, desktop publishing systems such as the one described in the vignette, as well as a wide variety of packaged software available for business and personal use. And it's a universe that is continually expanding, with more and more products becoming available every day.

11.1   Integrated Software Packages

The applications software packages described in Chapter 10 are designed to perform distinct functions, such as process words, perform calculations, or manage data. **Integrated software** packages, on the other hand, can perform a variety of tasks. Lotus 1-2-3 was one of the first software programs to offer an integrated package, combining powerful spreadsheet abilities with some limited graphics and database management abilities. Today, integrated packages commonly combine word processing, spreadsheet, database management, and data communications (E-mail) into one easy-to-use package. Other programs include additional features: presentation graphics and drawing programs, label addressing, scheduling, notepads, and the like.

Figure 11.1 lists the leading integrated software packages. These integrated packages are most popular with the budget-minded, novice, or light computer user, and with those who have notebook computers.

Manufacturer	Name	Platform
Microsoft	Microsoft Works	DOS, Windows, Mac
Lotus	Lotus Works	DOS, Windows
Spinnaker	PFS:First Choice	DOS
Spinnaker	PFS:Window Works	Windows
Claris	ClarisWorks	Windows, Mac

Figure 11.1
Leading Integrated Software Packages

Higher-end, more expensive packages (designed more for business than personal use) include Lotus Symphony (for DOS only), The Software Group's Enable, and Ashton-Tate's Framework. However, analysts believe that the audience for such packages is shrinking as low-end packages add more and more features.

Advantages and Disadvantages

An integrated software package has a number of advantages over individual software applications purchased separately. First, an integrated package generally costs much less. For instance, Microsoft Works for Windows is available for less than half the price of Microsoft Word for Windows word processing software. In addition, manufacturers now often market personal computers with an integrated package preinstalled. An integrated package also needs less RAM and takes up much less hard disk space. ClarisWorks version 2.0 for the Macintosh, for example, requires less than 600K of RAM and 3.5 MB of hard disk space compared to around 2MB of RAM and 10MB of storage space for Microsoft's Excel spreadsheet package alone. Integrated packages also tend to be easier to use because the different application modules within the package all share a common interface and common command structure. Instead of having to learn how to save or print in each different program, you have to learn only once. Last but not least, one of the most useful features of an integrated package is its ability to pass data from one module to another. For example, you can create a spreadsheet with the spreadsheet module or graphics with the graphics module and then easily add either or both to a document created with the word processing portion of the package. (The ability to transfer data between different applications is also a feature of Microsoft Windows applications software packages that include OLE (Object Linking and Embedding) or its precursor, DDE (Dynamic Data Exchange), but even so the process is not as easily accomplished as with a single integrated software package.)

Integrated packages are not without some disadvantages, however. Generally, the modules within an integrated package offer fewer features and less versatility than their standalone versions. For instance, the word processor available within Microsoft Works is not as powerful as Microsoft's regular word processing program, Microsoft Word. Likewise, if you are a heavy spreadsheet user, you're much better off with a standalone package than an integrated one. Although integrated packages present significant price savings over the aggregate cost of all the applications represented, these price savings are not cost effective if you don't really need all the applications covered by the integrated package.

Software Suites

The kinds of integrated software packages just described should not be confused with **software suites**—packages that contain bundled versions of a manufacturer's line of software. For instance, Lotus offers SmartSuite for Windows, consisting of its Lotus 1-2-3 for Windows spreadsheet software, Ami Pro word processor, Approach database software, Freelance Graphics, and Lotus Organizer (a personal information manager). Microsoft Office Professional includes Word word processing software, Excel spreadsheet software, Access database software, PowerPoint presentation graphics soft-

Your friend just got a copy of an integrated software package that you'd really like to have. You're low on cash. Your friend offers to make you a copy of the software on some spare disks and let you have it for free. Should you take it?

You work for a small company. Your department could use some presentation graphics software. Management, concerned about keeping costs down, tells you to purchase only one copy and make copies for the other members of the department. Is this right?

In both instances, you might not even think twice about the situation before going ahead. Although you probably would never think of stealing a software program from a retail store, somehow copying software feels different. But it isn't; in almost all cases, it's illegal to make duplicate copies of software other than to back up your own hard disk.

Why do so many people break this law, seemingly with few qualms? First, it's easy, far easier than copying a whole book or a videotape, for instance. Simply shove a blank disk into the floppy drive, press a few keys, wait a few seconds, and there you have it. Software is probably the only industry where the consumer can make an exact replica of the product right at his or her desk. Second, there appears to be little chance of being caught. And third, it seems like a victimless crime—nobody gets hurt. But let's stop and examine these rationalizations, and the potential ramifications, a little more closely.

In the United States alone, software piracy costs software manufacturers almost $2.3 billion, an amount greater than the national budget of many countries. Worldwide, loss estimates are between $10 and $12 billion. Although you may think that a single act has little if any impact, when millions of individuals think the same way, it can have a substantial effect on the bottom line. When economic returns are curtailed for software manufacturers, it stifles the industry's growth and creativity, and increases prices for everyone.

Other potential ramifications include the possibility that the software you copy may be defective or contain a virus that may affect your other files. You will have to make do with inadequate documentation, will not be able to take advantage of technical support available to registered users, and will not be eligible for software upgrades offered at discounted prices.

What's more, you could be subject to fines (and imprisonment in really egregious cases) if caught. Don't think it's impossible. The Software Publishers Association, a trade group, conducts raids, sends cease and desist letters, and files lawsuits (over 100 to date) against organizations and individuals suspected of software piracy. Its piracy hotline (800-388-7487) receives nearly 30 calls a day from people reporting suspected incidents of software theft or seeking information about piracy.

So, the next time someone offers you some free software, look before you leap and consider the consequences.

Sources: Based on Software Publishers Association, White Paper: Software Piracy, 1993; Markoff, John, "Though Illegal, Copied Software Is Now Common," *New York Times,* July 27, 1992.

Critical Thinking Questions

1 Suppose you have some software at home that you'd like to use on the job, but your company doesn't want to purchase it for you. What's wrong with bringing a copy from home and installing it on your computer at work?

2 What would you do if you discovered that the software you used at work had been copied illegally?

3 Should it be the software industry's responsibility to come up with a way to prevent software copying?

---

ware, and Microsoft Mail. Borland and WordPerfect Corporation have entered into a strategic alliance to offer Borland Office for Windows, a package that combines Borland's QuattroPro spreadsheet software and Paradox database program with WordPerfect's word processor. These suites differ from traditional integrated software packages in that they include the full-featured versions of each type of software. At the same time, they possess many of the advantages of integrated packages, such as a consistent interface and the ability to share data among the different applications composing the suite. Although still more expensive (they list for around $800) than the high-end integrated software packages, these software bundles are beginning to make their presence felt in the market.

11.2 Graphics Software

Over the last ten years, one of the most exciting trends in information technology has been the development of **graphics software** that allows you to create amazing computer graphics on a relatively inexpensive microcomputer. Apple led the way with machines famous for their graphics capabilities. Today, technological advances (high-speed, high-powered microprocessors, increased memory capacities, and high-resolution output devices capable of displaying millions of colors, to name a few) coupled with declining prices have put graphics tools unthinkable a decade ago within reach of the average PC user. Although word processing, spreadsheet, database management, and integrated software packages are still the best-selling classes of software for personal computers, many people now include graphics software on the shopping list as well. Graphics software created for the Macintosh continues to lead in innovation and features, but comparable programs are now also available for Windows-based machines.

A number of different types of graphics software are available, each targeted to a specific market and serving a specific purpose. General categories include analytical and presentation graphics software used primarily for business graphics, illustration graphics programs used to create computer art, computer-aided design software used in engineering and manufacturing, visual data analysis tools that have found a home among the scientific and academic community, and animated computer video graphics programs that create the computer graphics seen on television and in the movies. Let's now take a closer look at each type.

Business Graphics: Analytical and Presentation Graphics Software

Information conveyed graphically, in pictures rather than words or numbers, is generally easier to understand. A tool that creates a graphical format for data enables you to analyze that data more effectively. Sometimes, for instance, graphics may reveal a trend that otherwise might be buried in other data. In addition, information presented in graphical form tends to have more impact. A well-done chart or graph can make a point much more forcefully than several pages of text or columns of numbers (see Figure 11.2).

Graphics that present data in a visual and easy-to-understand format are sometimes called **business graphics.** Charts and graphs form the corner-

Quarter	Earnings
1stQ—1992	$2.50
2ndQ—1992	$1.50
3rdQ—1992	$3.50
4thQ—1992	$2.00
1stQ—1993	$4.25
2ndQ—1993	$3.75
3rdQ—1993	$5.75
4thQ—1993	$4.00

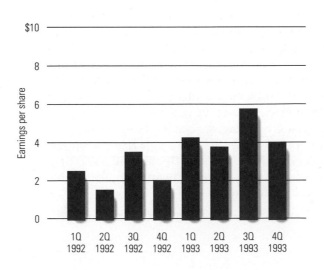

Figure 11.2
A Graph Is Worth a Thousand Numbers
Examine the financial results in the table. You can see that earnings are higher in the 1993 quarters than in the 1992 quarters. But there's another pattern hiding in those numbers that probably isn't so noticeable. Now look at the graph. It's much easier to see that the financial results in 1993 repeat the general pattern set in 1992 with a graph.

390

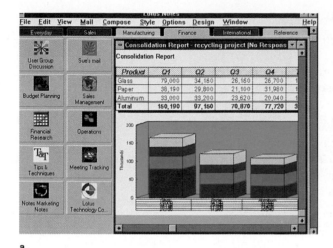

a.

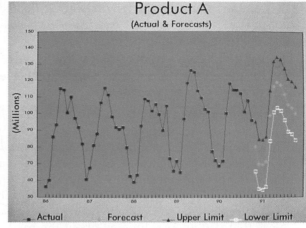

b.

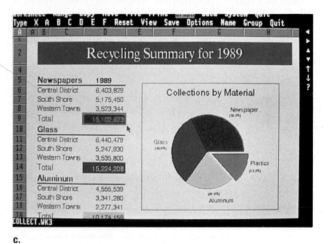

c.

stones of business graphics software. We have already introduced you to some basic charts and graphs in Chapter 10, but let's take a moment to look at this topic a little more closely.

In presenting information in graphical form, it's very important to choose the right type of chart or graph in order to accurately and effectively convey your message. The principal types of graphs and charts are as follows:

▶ **Bar graphs** use vertical or horizontal bars to compare data. They are useful for showing data over time (for example, quarterly sales for four successive quarters) and for comparing individual values at a particular point in time (sales revenues for different divisions for the first quarter).

Stacked-bar graphs, graphs in which different variables are stacked on top of one another, are best for comparing several items at one moment in time (for example, sales of different products within a division compared to results for other divisions). A horizontal stacked-bar chart is useful for calling attention to the differences between the totals for each data type (see photo). Bar graphs are most effective with a limited number of data items (called *data points*). If you want to show more than several items, use a line graph instead.

▶ **Line graphs** represent data as a series of points and connect the points with a line (see photo). Each point represents a particular data item, and each line represents a different category. Line graphs can show an unlimited number of data points though the number of different categories (lines) should generally be limited to around four. A line graph is the best way to illustrate trends and changes in a large number of data items over time (for example, changes in sales revenues over a ten-year period).

▶ **Pie charts,** one of the most common types of graphs, are most useful for showing proportions—the relationship of parts to a whole (for example, how much each of a company's products contributed to total revenue). Pie charts should only be used to compare the parts of one thing. If you want to include more than one entity, use a stacked-bar chart instead. An exploded pie chart is a variation on the pie chart that separates one slice of the pie for added emphasis (see photo).

(a) A stacked-bar graph. **(b)** A line graph. **(c)** An exploded pie chart.

Sources: Courtesy of Lotus Development Corporation; Courtesy of Business Forecast Systems, Inc.

▶ **X-Y graphs** illustrate the relationship or degree of correlation between two types of data, called the *variables.* If variables are correlated, the data points will form a line or a curve.

▶ **Mixed graphs** are a combination of bar and line graphs. These are most useful for presenting two types of data simultaneously (for example, actual sales compared to projected sales).

Although business graphics software makes creating basic charts and graphs easy even for the novice, ignorance of the principles of good design can lead to graphs that confuse and even mislead. According to Edward Tufte, a professor of political science and statistics at Yale University, and a leader in the field of information design (the design of graphs, charts, and diagrams to convey complex information), simplicity, the absence of clutter, and adherence to true scale are the hallmarks of a good graph.

Now that you know a little bit about the basic types of charts and graphs, and some fundamental design principles, let's investigate the software that helps you create these graphics. There are two basic forms of business graphics software: analytical graphics software and presentation graphics software.

Analytical graphics software allows you to take data from an existing spreadsheet or database file and create, view, and print charts and graphs. Such software can usually be found as part of a spreadsheet package like Lotus 1-2-3. A more advanced form of analytical graphics software, called **statistical software,** provides complete statistical data analysis and more sophisticated graphing capabilities for mathematicians, scientists, and engineers. Examples of this form of analytical graphic software include Wolfram Research's Mathematica, Systat Inc.'s Systat, SAS Institute's SAS System, and StatSoft's Statistica (see photo). We will discuss even more advanced visual data analysis tools a little later in this section.

As we noted in Chapter 10, the graphical tools included with spreadsheet programs, though becoming more sophisticated, are still somewhat limited. When added punch and professional-looking charts and graphs are needed (to accompany an oral presentation, for example), **presentation graphics software** is called for. These packages allow you to make charts and graphs produced by analytical graphics programs more visually appealing and to create sophisticated-looking charts, graphs, diagrams, and other presentation materials from scratch (see photo).

As the story "Delivering the Diagnosis with Computer Graphics" illustrates, presentation graphics can help you understand what you're being told, which is especially important when the topic is something as important as your health.

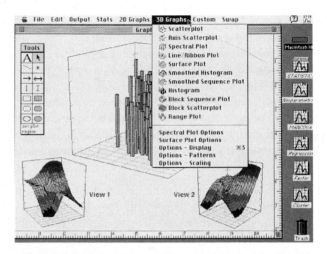

Systat Inc.'s Systat statistical software combines advanced statistical analysis tools with sophisticated graphing capabilities.

Source: Courtesy of Systat, Inc.

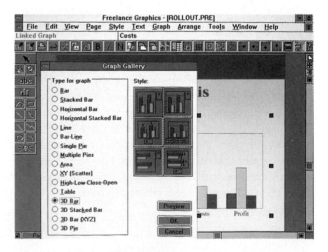

You can create professional-looking charts, graphs, and diagrams with a presentation graphics software program like Freelance Graphics.

Source: Courtesy of Lotus Development Corporation.

Delivering the Diagnosis with Computer Graphics

For many people, a doctor is the ultimate authority figure. Even when sick, people are often reluctant to press a busy doctor for answers to their questions. But over the last few years, a change has been occurring. People are attempting to become more involved in their own health care and more knowledgeable about the various options they might have. This trend has been supported by an increase in federal right-to-know regulations. How have doctors been responding?

At one hospital, Phoenix Baptist Medical Center, the staff has turned to computer graphics to help educate the public and patients on health issues. Using Software Publishing Corporation's Harvard Graphics for Windows, a presentation graphics software program, and Harvard Draw, a drawing program, the staff, working with a core of physicians, has been supplying graphics for doctors' lectures, newsletters, and patient conferences. The staff creates the graphics on 80386DX-based personal computers. For community outreach functions, slides can be transmitted directly over PCs linked to the audiovisual system in the hospital's community education center (see photo).

When the group started its effort about four years ago, slide shows were more often seen at medical conventions than in meetings with patients. But now, a doctor sitting down with a patient before an angioplasty (a procedure that involves inserting a small balloon into an artery to push aside a blockage) can explain the procedure and then supplement it with a video or slide presentation. Graphics have an advantage over photographs: they can depict views (such as a cross-section of the heart) that photographs cannot and may be less threat-

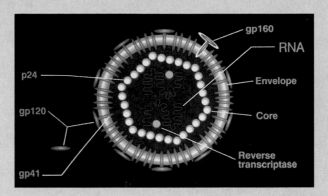

The staff at Phoenix Baptist Medical Center used Harvard Graphics presentation software to create this diagram of the HIV virus.

Source: Courtesy of Ray Litman Photographics.

ening for a squeamish patient. Most patients appreciate the opportunity to learn more about what to expect.

Source: Based on Hildebrand, Carol, "Computer Graphics Help Carry Physicians' Message," *Computerworld,* June 1, 1992.

Critical Thinking Questions

1 Why does the delivery of information in a graphical format have greater impact than other methods of delivery?

2 Make a list of some different design elements that go into creating effective graphics.

3 What are some other uses for presentation graphics software?

Presentation graphics software makes the effects described in the Knowledge story as well as many others possible by allowing you to create your own drawings; by providing a great variety of colors, patterns, textures, blends, fills, 3-D effects, and text options for titles, legends, and word charts; and by giving you access to *clip art,* collections of ready-to-use illustrations that you can add to your presentation materials. Presentation graphics software also provides a number of different output options: the materials may be displayed on a monitor in a *screen show,* converted into *slides* or *overhead transparencies,* or printed on paper. Ordinarily, you can't run a screen show unless the computer has the relevant presentation graphics program already on it. Now though, some presentation graphics software manufacturers are offering a "run-time" feature that allows you to copy a slide show to a diskette and play it on any PC, whether or not it's equipped with presentation software.

Typical additional features of presentation graphics software include chart galleries that provide a collection of chart types and styles to choose from; templates that provide basic layouts that can be copied, customized, and reused; color palettes that provide colors that contrast with or complement one another; outlining tools that help you get organized; and spelling checkers. An increasing trend, already noted in Chapter 2, is the addition of multimedia capabilities—sound, video, and animation—to presentation graphics software.

Figure 11.3 lists the leading presentation graphics software packages. The programs generally require relatively large amounts of RAM (2MB to 4MB) and hard disk storage space (5MB to 20MB). Experts tend to recommend Lotus's Freelance and Microsoft's PowerPoint for the more novice user. Aldus Persuasion scores high for its speed and support for long, text-intensive presentations. Users with a need for scientific charts will find that Deltagraph Professional offers the most options.

Illustration Graphics: Drawing and Painting Tools

Illustration programs—drawing, painting, and photo editing tools used to create illustrations and computer art—form a second general category of computer graphics software. Drawing and painting packages differ primarily in the manner in which they create graphic images. Drawing packages use a mathematical formula (called an algorithm) to plot the points (called vectors) that define the shape of an object. These kinds of packages excel at creating and manipulating graphics that consist of different objects. The method by which the objects are created makes it easy to modify or eliminate an individual object without affecting any of the other images on the screen. Paint packages, on the other hand, use a technique called bitmapping, in which pictures are created by turning individual pixels on and off. They can create more creative, complex images than a drawing program; however, images cannot be altered except by erasing or painting over them, and moving an "eraser" or "paintbrush" erases everything in its path. Some programs furnish both object and bitmapped graphics capabilities. Finally, the newest type of illustration graphics program provides you with the tools to edit and manipulate photographs and other images.

Let's look at each type a little more closely. **Drawing packages** allow you to draw straight and curved lines, freeform shapes, and geometric objects by moving the cursor with a mouse or through the use of a pressure-sensitive digitizing tablet (see photo). Once you have created an object, you can easily copy it to another location on the screen, resize it, rotate it, skew its proportions, create a mirror image of it, or align it with other objects. Illustrations can be created on a number of different layers, one on top of another, to create the perception of depth and perspective. The packages offer you a

A digitizing tablet and electronic stylus are often used in conjunction with drawing and paint programs, as used here by David Peña seen designing the main title for the 63rd Annual Academy Awards.

Source: Courtesy of Wacom Technology Corporation.

Manufacturer	Name	Platform
Aldus	Aldus Persuasion	Windows, Mac
Software Publishing	Harvard Graphics	DOS, Windows
Lotus	Freelance Graphics	DOS, Windows, OS/2
Claris	Hollywood	Windows, Mac
Microsoft	Powerpoint	Windows, Mac
Deltapoint	DeltagraphPro	Windows, Mac

Figure 11.3
Presentation Graphics Programs

Manufacturer	Name	Platform
Aldus	Aldus Freehand	Windows, Mac
Corel Systems	CorelDraw!	DOS, Windows, OS/2
Adobe Systems	Adobe Illustrator	Windows, Mac
Claris	MacDraw	Mac
Software Publishing	Harvard Draw	DOS, Windows
Micrografx	Windows Draw	Windows

Figure 11.4
Leading Drawing Packages

Some paint programs allow the creation of art that is almost indistinguishable from traditionally created works.

Source: Courtesy of Wacom Technology Corporation.

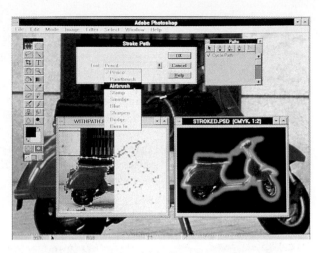

A photo image editor such as Adobe PhotoShop can be used to manipulate and retouch photographs.

Source: Courtesy of Adobe Systems, Inc.

wide choice of colors, patterns, textures, and shades for objects, lines, and backgrounds. Like presentation graphics programs, drawing packages generally come with a library of clip art. Most drawing programs also contain typographic features that allow you to enter and wrap text, use a variety of different typefaces, and create curved lines of text. They generally will contain a number of different tools that are intended to help you manage complex drawings. Figure 11.4 lists the leading drawing packages.

Paint programs allow the sophisticated user to create art almost indistinguishable from works created in the traditional manner (see photo). Some paint programs work with a pressure-sensitive input device such as a digitizing tablet used together with a pen-like stylus. Paint programs enable you to achieve a number of effects not possible with drawing programs. For instance, a paint program allows you to mimic various different application devices and techniques. Typical tools include a variety of simulated pens (regular to felt), brushes of different types and sizes (ranging from air brush to extremely thin), chalks, colored pencils, charcoal, crayons, water colors, even spray cans and eyedroppers. The software allows you to create different effects with these tools. For instance, objects, lines, and colors can be smeared, blended, and even made to appear as if melting. More advanced programs include a selection of textures for the canvas—paper, bristol board, regular canvas, and others. With the proper add-on equipment (a 24-bit color graphics board), literally millions of different colors are available. The more sophisticated programs also allow the artist to manipulate color hues, luminance, and saturation. As we noted, changes are made by painting over what you have created or by erasing material with an eraser tool.

Apple's MacPaint program remains the dominant program in the painting package market. Other leading packages include Aldus Corporation's Aldus Superpaint (for Macintosh and DOS), Zsoft's PC Paintbrush Plus (for DOS), and Fractal Design Corporation's Fractal Design Painter (for Windows and DOS).

The final form of illustration graphics software that we'll discuss is also the newest form—**photo image editors** that allow you to manipulate and revise photos and other images that you have scanned with an optical scanner (see photo). Adobe System's Adobe Photoshop (for Windows and Mac) and Aldus Corporation's Aldus Photostyler (for Windows) are two of the leading products. Among the features they offer are the ability to scan in images;

Step 1: Faulkner scans black-and-white photos of a lawn and lawnmower, a man's torso and pants that he has gathered from various sources using a Datacopy grayscale scanner. The photos are converted into digital Adobe Photoshop files.

Step 2: Faulkner selects the lawn image and, using Photoshop's pen tool, creates a kidney shape for the background. Then, he colorizes all the images, one at a time—first the man's hair, then face, jacket, tie, and so on.

Step 3: Next, he uses a feature called Indexed Color to get a wide range for the lawn to give it the textured quality of a real lawn. To create the T lying on top of the lawn, he selects the image from Photoshop's clip art and then darkens it and adds shadows and edges to give it an illusion of height—so it appears to stand above the lawn. Then, he cuts and pastes the image of the mower and the man onto the lawn. It is at this stage that Faulkner decides to substitute a large Y for the handles of the mower.

Step 4: Next, Faulkner creates the effect of blades of grass flying out of the lawn mower. Faulkner uses Photoshop's paint brush and spray-paint tools to draw white streaks above the mower. He then uses a Motion Blur filter to simulate grass spewing from the mower.

Figure 11.5
Creating Computer Graphics with Adobe Photoshop
Here's how Andrew Faulkner used Adobe Photoshop to create this illustration for an article on typefaces in *Macworld* magazine. Total time to create the illustration was approximately 15 hours.

Sources: Andrew Faulkner; Abes, Cathy, "Art Beat: Behind Macworld's Graphics," *Macworld,* September 1992.

Step 5: The final step is to create the letters coming out of the mower with the type tool. Smudging them slightly gives them the subtle effect of motion.

crop and resize them; retouch them; correct color; compose collages; add graphic images and text; and create special effects, including the ability to warp and distort an image, break it into squares, or turn it into a matrix of square-capped tower shapes that simulate depth. Figure 11.5 details how one artist, Andrew Faulkner, used Adobe Photoshop to create a computer graphic illustration that appeared in *Macworld* magazine.

Computer-Aided Design

Another area in which computer graphics play a very important role is computer-aided design. **Computer-aided design (CAD)** programs allow you to create two- and three-dimensional architectural drawings, engineering drawings, and product designs of all types (see photo). Today, offices once filled with drafting tables and T-squares are now occupied by rows of personal computers loaded with CAD software. Autodesk's AutoCAD is the dominant product by far, with over 70 percent of the market. Numerous add-on programs are available that will customize AutoCAD for specific tasks.

Although the initial creation of a design with CAD software may take as long, if not longer, than a design done in the traditional manner, CAD shines when it comes time to revise. Instead of having to redraw an entire plan, CAD allows you to modify it with a few clicks of a mouse. You can also easily pan the design or zoom in to magnify a particular part.

Computer-aided design is often coupled with computer-aided manufacturing (CAD/CAM). Computer-aided manufacturing takes computer-aided design one step further and uses computers to actually help manufacture the products in question. We discuss CAD/CAM in more depth in Chapters 12 and 13.

Visual Data Analysis Software

Visual data analysis (VDA) software encompasses a range of techniques that rely primarily on various forms of computer graphics. These techniques include computer simulations, animation, 3-D graphics, and renderings (creating computer images to represent the surfaces of 3-D objects). Many of the stories throughout this book have highlighted the advances made possible with such techniques. Scientists have used visualization to analyze pollution data, simulate the surface of the sun, peer below the surface of the earth, and design drugs. In engineering, visualization can provide rapid solutions in product design and development, like Michelin's 60,000-mile tire described

A computer-aided design system was used here to design a wheel. At left is the wire-frame version; at right the finished design.

Source: Courtesy of Autodesk, Inc.

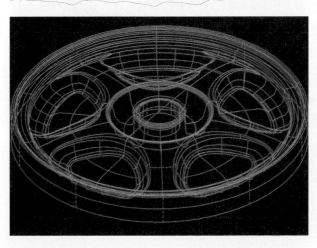

in Chapter 1. And in business, visualization techniques can reveal buying patterns, trends in financial results, and investment returns. Until recently, visual data analysis required access to a supercomputer. But today, anyone with a PC or Mac with fast math processing and high-quality graphics capabilities can produce sophisticated visualizations using off-the-shelf software. Examples include Research System's IDL for Windows, Precision Visual's PV-Wave, and CoHort Software's CoVis. Figure 11.6 shows you one of the sophisticated visualizations that can be produced with such software.

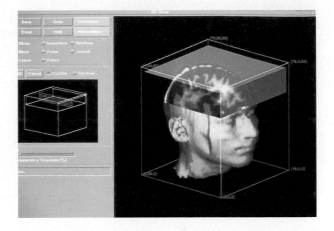

Animated Computer Graphics

No discussion of computer graphics would be complete without mentioning **animated computer graphics,** now so omnipresent on television and in the movies. Byte by Byte's Sculpt-Animate 4-D and Macromind's Macromind Director are just two of several products that enable designers to create computer-generated animated graphics and to combine them with sound and video. Many of the commercials you see on television have been created in this manner. Anytime you see moving graphics—dancing bottles, flying geometric shapes, and the like—you can be sure that they were created with video graphics software.

One of the latest special effects is *morphing,* in which one image gradually metamorphoses (or morphs) into another totally unlike the first. Morphing has been seen in films (such as *Terminator 2,* in which a metal robot turns into a human as well as other objects), music videos (Michael Jackson's "Black and White," featuring people of different races and gender turning into people of other races and gender), and even television commercials (such as the Exxon commercial in which a car turns into a tiger). And now you can create your own with Gryphon Software Corporation's Morph, an inexpensive program that runs on Windows machines or a Macintosh. The transitions aren't quite as smooth, and the images are grainier, but the package has nonetheless drawn rave reviews.

Animated computer graphics are also spreading beyond television and the movies into an entirely different arena—the courtroom. Lawyers have always relied on visual aids—photographs, illustrations, diagrams, and charts—to explain complex topics to juries. It's not surprising that some enterprising lawyers decided to go one step further to capture and hold a jury's attention. Now, with the cost of producing computer animations dropping steeply, they are becoming more and more common (see photo).

But the use of computer animations in the courtroom raises some difficult questions. A computer-generated animation must be based on certain assumptions about the event being depicted, but in many instances, the truth of those very assumptions may be in question in the case. Yet once the animation is created, what is shown onscreen takes on an air of authenticity that may be difficult to rebut. The underlying assumptions fade deep into the background. For this reason, some courts are still refusing to admit com-

Figure 11.6
Visual Data Analysis
This cutaway 3-D image of a human head was produced with data from a magnetic-resonance scanner using IDL for Windows.
Source: Courtesy of Precision Visuals, Inc.

This computer-generated animation prepared for a personal injury lawsuit shows a pickup slamming on the brakes in an attempt to avoid a collision with a tanker truck. It was based on skid marks found at the scene of the accident.
Source: Courtesy of ATA Associates, Inc.

puter-generated animations as evidence. Others believe that jurors have no more trouble deciding whether an animation is being misused than any other form of evidence. What would you do if you were the judge in the following case? In a murder trial in Marin County, California, the prosecution wanted to use a computer-generated animation that reenacted a fatal shooting. The defense objected because the animation showed the victim walking with his hands at his side while the defendant claimed he had thought the man had a gun raised in his hand. Should the animation be admitted as evidence? Do you think the jury would be able to adequately weigh the defendant's oral testimony against the visual impact of the animation?[1]

11.3   Desktop Publishing Systems

We have already briefly introduced you to **desktop publishing (DTP) systems** in Chapter 10. DTP systems allow you to produce professional-looking newsletters, reports, manuals, brochures, advertisements, and other documents that incorporate text with graphics. You can even produce your own books.

The Traditional Publishing Process

To understand the efficiencies provided by desktop publishing systems, you first must know a little bit about how commercially created publications are traditionally produced. The production process begins with the creation of written material on a typewriter or with a word processor. The author, either alone or in conjunction with a designer, makes some preliminary decisions on *page composition* and *page layout*—what typefaces to use, how to arrange the text around any pictures—in short, how the document should look. Next, the manuscript is delivered to a commercial typesetter, who sets the text into *galleys*—long columns of text. After the galleys are proofread and corrected, they are "pasted up" into page format (called *page proofs*), with spaces left for photographs or illustrations. After being checked for errors and the acceptability of the layout, a camera department takes a picture of the final version. The negatives are used to produce plates for the printing press. The document is then printed by the printing press. This process is obviously a long and expensive one. Now, though, anyone with a desktop publishing system can publish their own material at a small fraction of the cost. Even the smallest businesses can create ads, brochures, reports, and other materials that they might otherwise be unable to afford. And as the story "A Small Revolution in Mozambique" illustrates, desktop publishing systems are helping some brave journalists create independent news organizations in countries that have never known them before.

Desktop Publishing Hardware and Software

A desktop publishing system combines hardware and software that together allow you to produce documents much more quickly and inexpensively. With such a system, you can control all aspects of the publication process yourself: creating the text, designing the layout, choosing the typeface and type size, determining the spacing between words and letters and lines, adding the graphics, and printing the document.

A Small Revolution in Mozambique

Go to a newsstand in any city in the United States. What do you find? Newspapers. Although most cities may support only one or two major papers, you will still find a wide variety of special-interest papers available. If you added up all the newspapers in America, large and small, you'd come up with well over 1,000. Our society has been indelibly marked by the presence of newspapers and an active press, getting the news (and the stories behind the news) out to the people day after day. Freedom of the press, and the newspapers it protects, is one of the cornerstones of our society.

If you lived in many of the other countries in this world, you would find a very different scenario. Particularly in developing countries without democratic traditions or a history of an independent press, it is not uncommon to find only one newspaper in the entire country, often operating as an official arm of the government. This was the case in Mozambique, a small country in southeastern Africa that became independent from Portugal in 1975. Although the press there was not subjected to heavy-handed censorship, the government controlled the presses and supply of paper and favored one main pro-

government newspaper. Now, though, information technology is helping some dedicated journalists in Mozambique challenge the accepted order.

From a cramped command center located within former servants' quarters of a colonial-era house, Carlos Cardoso and a dozen fellow defectors from official press organizations operate a journalism cooperative that publishes a daily bulletin without printing equipment or paper. Instead, the group uses a desktop publishing system to produce their work, named Mediafax. They send it out to their 360 subscribers by fax, using a fax machine hooked to a computer with automatic dialing capacity.

So far, Mediafax has revealed the inside details of negotiations that ended Mozambique's civil war, told drought-stricken Mozambicans about shiploads of foreign food aid rotting in port warehouses because of bureaucratic snafus, and exposed the failure of government ministries and state-owned companies to pay their electric bills—all stories that would-have otherwise never seen the light of day. It might be small potatoes by American standards, but for Mozambique, it's

A desktop publishing system begins with a relatively high-powered personal computer (with an Intel 386 or Motorola 68030 microprocessor or faster, at least 2MB to 4MB of RAM, and a generous amount of secondary storage space on a hard disk or CD-ROM drive). In addition to traditional input devices such as keyboards and mice, DTP systems are often equipped with image scanners that scan and digitize photographs and other graphics as well as digitizing tablets that enable you to input artwork by tracing over it. A high-resolution, oversized color monitor and laser printer with 300 dpi resolution or better generally complete the picture. Desktop publishing systems often draw on the capabilities of several types of software to produce the final product. The primary type is **desktop publishing software** (sometimes called *page makeup* or *page composition software*). Frequently though, as you will soon see, such software is used in conjunction with other types of software, including word processing software, graphics software, clip art libraries, and font libraries. The leading DTP software packages include Aldus' Aldus PageMaker, Ventura Software's Ventura Publisher, Quark's QuarkXPress, and Frame Technology's FrameMaker (most available in DOS, Windows, and Macintosh versions), retailing for about $500 or more. There are also some lower-cost DTP software packages generally available for less than $150. They offer fewer features and less flexibility than the more expensive versions but will be more than adequate for the majority of potential desktop publisher users. These packages include Microsoft's Microsoft Publisher, Spinnaker Software Corporation's Publisher for Windows, Timeworks' Publish It for Windows, PowerUp Software Corporation's Express Publisher for Windows, and Serif's PagePlus. Let's look now at how a DTP system actually works.

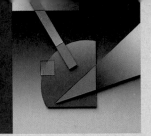

nothing short of a small revolution. "We've never had something like this," said Salvador Dimas, the press attaché to Mozambique's president. "It is not progovernment, not antigovernment. It is . . . independent." Mediafax has also shaken the official press from its longstanding lethargy. *Noticias,* the main progovernment newspaper, now scrambles to catch up with Mediafax's exclusive reports. Although the bulletin's subscriber base is small, it includes almost everyone of importance in Mozambique's capital. "All the ministries subscribe now," says Fernando Lima, a founder of the cooperative.

The first venture of its kind in Africa, Mediafax was inspired in part by the independent Soviet news service Interfax, which helped break down the official press monopoly in Moscow during the last years of the Soviet Union. Its founders hope that they will serve as similar inspiration and demonstrate to other African dissidents how information technology can be used to overcome political and economic barriers that sometimes seem insurmountable in developing countries.

Source: Based on Keller, Bill, "By Pluck and Fax, Tiny Free Press," *New York Times,* March 1, 1993.

Critical Thinking Questions

1 What impact do you think desktop publishing systems might have on American society or culture?

2 Do you think materials produced by the desktop publishing method will totally replace commercially produced documents in the near future? Why or why not?

3 Not long ago, the idea of using PCs to automate page layout and design was revolutionary in publishing circles. Now, desktop publishing software providers are intent on joining another revolution already in progress: electronic publishing. Industry experts believe that the portable electronic newspaper, for instance, is right around the corner, perhaps no more than five years away. What effect, if any, might this have on everyday life as we know it?

Using a DTP System

The first step in producing a document is entering the text. When you use a desktop publishing system, you can generally enter text either by using the word processing capabilities of DTP software or by importing a text file that you have created using a word processing software package or that you have scanned in using a scanner. (As you learned in Chapter 10, most word processing software packages still offer better text entry and editing features than desktop publishing software. All the leading desktop publishing packages accept text files created with any of the major word processing programs.) The graphics to be included in the document can originate from several sources: a clip art file included with the desktop publishing package, a third-party vendor, a graphics package, or a photograph or drawing that has been scanned in using an image scanner.

Desktop publishing software really shines in page composition and page layout. You generally begin by making some decisions on the overall format for the document. Among the first decisions you must make is what *fonts* (typeface and type size) you want to use for the different elements of the document. DTP software provides you with a much greater variety of fonts from which to choose than regular word processing software. If you want an even wider choice, you can also purchase additional fonts separately from software manufacturers. The fonts generally used for desktop publishing systems are based on *scalable typeface outline* technology—the software first creates an ideal mathematical representation of the font, which is then converted by a font rasterizer into a bitmap that can be displayed and printed. Scalable technology allows fonts to be created in virtually any type size. Two kinds of scalable fonts dominate the market: **TrueType fonts** (originally created by Apple but now available on any machine with Windows 3.1) and

Type 1 fonts developed by Adobe Systems. TrueType fonts offer the latest in technology and the greatest ease of use, whereas Type 1 fonts provide the greatest variety (over 20,000 different typefaces are available compared to only 2,000 or so different TrueType fonts) and artistic sophistication.

After you have chosen the fonts, other layout decisions include the amount of space between the lines (the *leading*, pronounced *led-ing*) and the amount of space between letters (the *kerning*), the number of columns, the width of the margins, and whether to include any special effects such as borders or backgrounds.

Different packages have different methods of implementing the layout process. Some have you create a stylesheet that sets forth your various decisions. Some include existing templates—predesigned outlines that you can follow and modify as necessary—for a wide range of document types. Others offer "intelligent assistants" that ask you questions about the document you want to produce and then create the format for you (see photo).

Once you have decided on an overall format, you can design individual pages, indicating where headlines, pictures, and other graphics should be placed.

The next step is to "flow" the text into the page format and insert the graphics in their proper places. With a proper monitor, most leading desktop publishing software packages will allow you to see on the screen exactly what the page will look like when printed (WYSIWYG). If you don't like what you see, you can easily move blocks of text and graphics around, reduce or enlarge or crop the graphics, adjust the fonts, or make other changes (see photo).

When you are finally satisfied with all elements of the layout, it's time to print out the document. To achieve the best results, desktop publishing systems need to have a laser printer with at least 300 dpi resolution (600 dpi printers work even better). Printers used in desktop publishing systems must be able to recognize **page description language (PDL).** Desktop publishing software uses PDL to tell the printer how to define the page and print the fonts, text, and graphics. Although most fonts are now PDL independent, meaning they are usable with any PDL, this was not always so. For instance, until 1990, to use a Type 1 font, you needed to have a printer equipped with Adobe System's Postscript PDL. Now though, you can use Type 1 fonts with any Windows-supported printer as well. Postscript continues to be the leading PDL and is supported by a wide variety of laser printers. Hewlett Packard's Printer Command Language (PCL) is more common among the less expensive printers.

(a) Microsoft Publisher features "Page Wizards"—intelligent assistants that help walk you through the creation of a document. This enables novice users to enhance documents with design elements. **(b)** QuarkXPress is the page layout program of choice for many graphic arts professionals.

Sources: Courtesy of Microsoft Corporation; Courtesy of Quark, Inc.

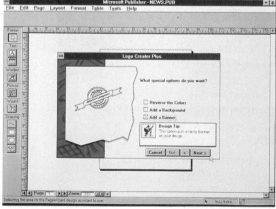

a.

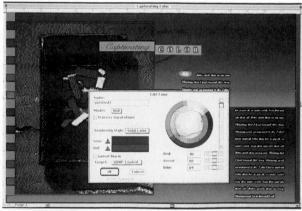

b.

Miscellaneous Business Software

In addition to the software described in the preceding sections, many other kinds of personal computer applications software are available for business use. Here, we highlight a few of the more significant types.

Accounting Software

Accounting is one of the most important functions within a firm. Keeping track of the influx and outflow of money is essential if the business is to survive and prosper. Proper accounting is also imperative in order to comply with tax laws and other legal and regulatory requirements.

As you learned in Chapter 10, spreadsheet software can be used to perform many basic accounting tasks. But although spreadsheet software may adequately serve the accounting needs of a very small business, it lacks the power and flexibility of specialized **accounting software** packages. These packages are able to automate accounting tasks far beyond the capabilities of spreadsheet software.

Most larger companies use mainframe and minicomputer-based accounting software packages for their primary financial system, but microcomputer-based packages that work on a standalone basis or as part of a network are becoming increasingly popular (particularly for medium-sized and smaller businesses). There are high-end, midrange, and entry-level microcomputer-based packages to serve the differing needs of large, medium-sized, and small businesses and home offices.

Accounting software packages usually contain separate modules that work interactively to handle the basic tasks that make up the accounting function. All packages generally include the following modules: a *general ledger* module (keeps a record of all the company's financial transactions in double-entry bookkeeping form), an *accounts payable* module (tracks amounts the company owes to suppliers and others), an *accounts receivable* module (tracks amounts owed to the company from customers), and a *payroll* module (keeps track of employee wages, tax deductions, and benefits). The packages also frequently include an *inventory control* module (tracks raw materials, work in process, and finished goods stored in inventory) and an *order entry* module (helps manage the customer order process). Each of these modules can also generate a variety of different kinds of reports—financial statements, cash flow analyses, an aged listing of accounts receivable, and so on.

Other common modules deal with fixed assets, budgets, the purchasing process, sales analysis, and project accounting. The programs generally include error detection and create audit trails that allow transactions to be traced from one set of books to another. The more sophisticated programs often include a cash management and check-writing feature, tables for federal and state income tax, and currency translation, among a host of other specialized features.

Some popular, high-end PC-based accounting packages include Great Plains Software's Dynamics Series, Macola Inc.'s Progression series, and Advanced Business Microsystem's Platinum. On the other end of the spectrum, there are the somewhat simplified programs aimed at the home office and small business market, such as Microsoft's Profit for Windows, Intuit's Quickbooks, DAC Easy's DAC Easy Accounting, and Computer Associates' CA–Simply Accounting. These lower-end packages typically avoid accounting jargon and feature user-friendly graphical interfaces and

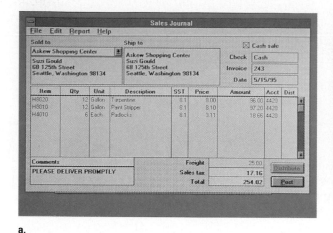

a.

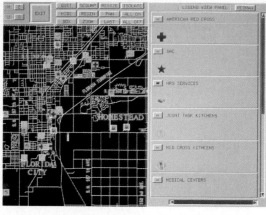

b.

advanced help technology. Although not designed to replace a human accountant, they are a useful support tool that saves time and money (see photo).

Selecting the proper accounting package for a business can be a tricky affair. Care must be taken to ensure that the package's features fit the business and the accounting systems already in place at the company. Accounting software consultant Carol Lisook tells the story of one professional services client that selected an accounting software package because it included a job-costing module. The client discovered after it was too late that the package produced reports based on construction job costing, a model that was inappropriate for the services offered by the company.[2] Since most packages offer comparable nuts-and-bolts capabilities, it's important to assess a company's special needs and then search out accounting software that offers features matching those needs. Another important consideration is reliability and data security. Accounting software is generally considered to be one of the most crucial pieces of software that a company has. As such, the vendor's policy on after-sales technical support and the availability of on-site instruction or regional training classes is also an important consideration.

Mapping Software

If you took a close look at information in a corporate database, you'd probably find that over half the data is tied in some way to geography: locations of customers and competitors, boundaries between sales territories, routes for deliveries, and so on. Often, a map is the best way to organize and present such data. Not too many years ago, the only way to do this was to plot the information on a paper map by hand. Now, though, **mapping software** combines graphics, database management, and some spreadsheet capabilities to display data geographically, allowing you to picture and more easily absorb the relationships between data and geographic locations.

Mapping software (sometimes referred to as *geographic information systems*, or *GIS*) was first developed for use by federal government agencies and state and local governments to create digitized maps (see photo). Soon, though, corporations realized that such software could also be used to map corporate data, allowing them to better understand geographic patterns and thus improve decision making. For instance, a company could use a mapping program to define sales territories for account representatives, then change the boundary lines to see how the revenue potential for each representative changes.

(a) Computer Associates' ACCPAC Simply Accounting makes it easy to keep track of important business indicators. **(b)** Mapping software helped the Federal Emergency Management Agency coordinate services to stricken Florida neighborhoods after Hurricane Andrew. Each day the agency issued a freshly updated computer-generated map marked with locations of Red Cross stations, trash-burning sites, tent kitchens, and other services.

Sources: Courtesy of Computer Associates International, Inc.; Courtesy of Digital Matrix.

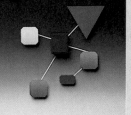

If you lived in east New York City during the 1960s, you probably would have had a difficult time getting a mortgage, even if you had a decent income and credit rating. The reason: redlining. The term *redlining* refers to a practice that some lending institutions used to engage in. They would take a map and circle low-income areas in red. If someone living in such an area applied for a mortgage, he or she might be refused outright or subjected to more stringent standards than someone with comparable qualifications living in a different area.

To help put an end to redlining, Congress passed the Community Reinvestment Act (CRA) requiring banks to adopt safeguards to ensure that they would not discriminate. If it turns out that a bank is making fewer loans in a low-income area than might be statistically expected, it will have some explaining to do. One bank, Chemical Bank, has turned to mapping software to help make sure that it complies.

Michael Burke, manager of Chemical Bank's affordable housing unit in Jericho, New York, explains how. Data from mortgage applications is downloaded every day from Chemical's mortgage database into a MapInfo GIS. The mapping software matches the address of the property against census data, then determines whether the tract is one covered by the CRA or not.

Using mapping software also enables Chemical to compare loans it is providing currently with what it should be providing in those areas and plan accordingly. Loans are represented as black dots superimposed on a street map shaded to depict the income level of various areas. It becomes much easier to see a pattern developing (for instance, only a few black dots in one geographic area compared to another) and institute steps to rectify the situation. For instance, if an application within a CRA area is rejected for a conventional mortgage, the applicant may be offered an alternative from one of Chemical's special programs. Burke says that the mapping software system has allowed his unit to make better deci-

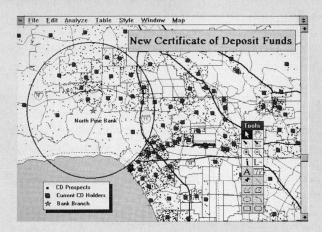

In addition to tracking loans, banks can use mapping software for many other purposes. This application shows the location of current and potential depositors compared to the location of a bank's branches.

Source: Courtesy of Tydac Technologies Corporation.

sions by providing data in a visual format that's easy to understand and interpret. And even better, it makes the information available much more quickly. "What would normally take one person a week to do, our GIS does in five seconds."

Source: Based on Forrest, David, "Seeing Data in New Ways," *Computerworld,* June 29, 1992.

Critical Thinking Questions

1 What are some other ways (not already mentioned in this text) that an organization might use mapping software?

2 What kinds of hardware and software might be necessary to implement a geographic information system?

3 What kinds of threats to privacy do you think sophisticated geographic information systems might pose?

Until a few years ago, mapping software was very expensive ($50,000 or more) and available only for mainframes. Today, though, mapping software has come to the desktop, and it's getting cheaper and easier to use all the time. (Mapping software traditionally entailed a steep learning curve and required several months' time before the full benefits of the package could be realized.) Companies are finding that such software can provide significant benefits: it can help them design and manage sales territories, perform demographic analyses of customers and markets, streamline distribution channels, plan business trips more efficiently, as well as a whole host of other possible applications. The story "Putting Data on the Map" illustrates how one company, Chemical Bank, uses mapping software to make sure it complies with federal regulations.

Some mapping software packages come with maps already provided. With many, though, you must either scan in your own maps or purchase digitized versions from a third-party vendor. The U.S. Census Bureau offers digitized maps of the entire country at a relatively reasonable cost. Corporate data must generally be imported from a company's database system. Census data (household income, projected populations, age data, retail trade data, and so on), boundary data (regions broken down by ZIP code, census tracts, and so on), business locations, and other types of data can also be purchased.

There are three leaders in the desktop mapping software field: Environmental Systems Research Institute's Arc/Info (for DOS only and retailing for around $6,000) and its low-cost sibling ArcView (for Windows, Macintosh, and Unix and available for under $500), Strategic Mapping's Atlas GIS (for DOS and retailing for about $2,600) and its lower-end version Atlas*Pro (for Windows and Macintosh and available for around $800), and Mapinfo's Mapinfo (for DOS, Windows, and Macintosh and retailing for less than $1,000).

Workflow Software

As you learned in Chapter 6, groupware is a form of software involved in workgroup computing. Another type of applications software aimed at the same market is **workflow software**—software designed to streamline and automate different types of work processes. Workflow software has its origins in the imaging systems described in Chapter 5. Imaging systems made processing documents in parallel possible and focused attention on the need to update serial, paper-based processes. Today, workflow software is used quite frequently in conjunction with imaging systems.

There are three basic categories of workflow software. The first category serves highly structured, formal, and complex processes that a business engages in day in and day out (mortgage loan processing, insurance underwriting, claims processing, and so on). For instance, Banc One Mortgage is using this kind of workflow software to re-engineer its mortgage loan process. Banc One realized that it had to take some drastic steps if it hoped to cope with handling 300,000 loans a year. The traditional desk-to-desk approach has been scrapped in favor of a speedier team approach. Now, a process that used to involve 8 departments and take 17 days takes just 2 days. Figure 11.7 shows you how. Leading products in this category include FileNet Corporation's Workflo Business System, Plexus Software's FloWare, and Sigma Imaging System's RouteBuilder.

The second general type of workflow software is designed to help automate ad-hoc projects (the creation of a strategic plan, the development of a report—any task that involves an identifiable group of people in a project environment as opposed to a day-in, day-out business process). The software adds a layer of coordination beyond the familiar word processing, spreadsheet, and document management tools traditionally used to carry out such tasks. Lotus Notes, a generic groupware product, has the capacity to do double-duty and serve this function as well. FileNet's FolderView is also aimed at these kinds of workflow applications.

The third form of workflow software is designed to automate routine, administrative processes, such as the processing of expense forms. Here, the best software is often electronic mail-based and enhanced with folder management and form-routing capabilities. Vendors that offer such products include Reach Software Corporation's MailMan, DEC's Teamlink, and Beyond Inc.'s BeyondMail.

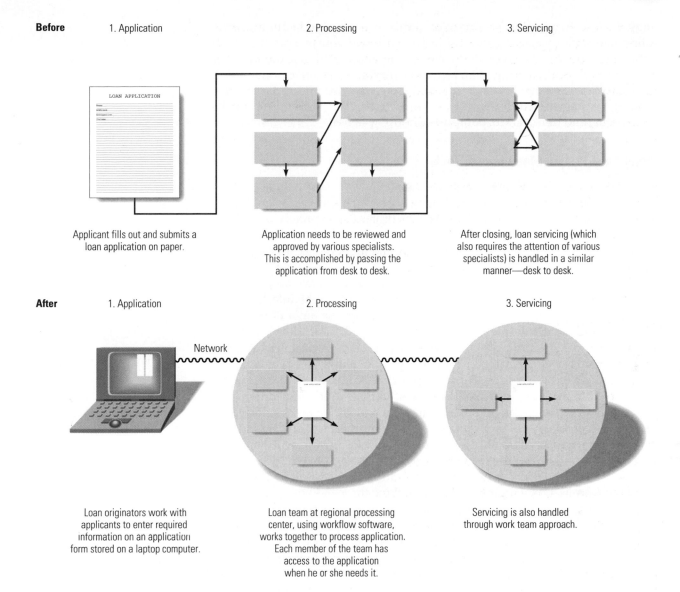

Before   1. Application · 2. Processing · 3. Servicing

Applicant fills out and submits a loan application on paper.

Application needs to be reviewed and approved by various specialists. This is accomplished by passing the application from desk to desk.

After closing, loan servicing (which also requires the attention of various specialists) is handled in a similar manner—desk to desk.

After   1. Application · 2. Processing · 3. Servicing

Network

Loan originators work with applicants to enter required information on an application form stored on a laptop computer.

Loan team at regional processing center, using workflow software, works together to process application. Each member of the team has access to the application when he or she needs it.

Servicing is also handled through work team approach.

Meeting Management Tools

With so many organizations moving toward more team-oriented management, as well as organizing rank-and-file employees along team lines, group activities such as meetings are taking on an increasingly important role. For many, managing the meeting process is becoming a core aspect of ongoing quality initiatives. Several types of software have been developed to aid in this endeavor. For instance, **scheduling software** is now available to automate the often time-consuming and sometimes frustrating process of setting up meetings. Such software typically allows you to schedule a time and date for a meeting, select attendees, and reserve conference space and other necessary resources. The software is able to check the calendars of proposed attendees and sets the meeting for the first available time that such attendees are free to attend. An example of such software is On Technology's Meeting Maker XP.

Meeting support software is a software tool that aims to increase the efficiency of meetings that take place electronically or in decision-room set-

Figure 11.7
Banc One's New Mortgage Processing Procedures
Workflow software has helped Banc One move from the traditional desk-to-desk approach to processing mortgage applications to a speedier "work cell" or team approach. Processing time has been slashed from 17 days to 2 days.

Source: Based on Betts, Mitch, "Banc One Mortgage Melts Paper Blizzard," *Computerworld*, December 14, 1992.

tings. Such software allows teams to construct meeting agendas, brainstorm, submit ideas for discussion, build a decision list, and vote on priorities. Collective ideas are displayed on overhead screens and in real time on the monitors of people participating in an electronic meeting. Researchers claim that such software leads to shorter, better, and more well-documented meetings. Leading packages include Collaborative Technologies' Visionquest, IBM's TeamFocus, and Ventana Corporation's GroupSystemsV.

Project and People Management Tools

In Chapter 8, you learned how project management software can be used to help build information systems. For many years, such software was difficult to learn and use and appealed mainly to professional project managers. However, in the last several years, easier-to-use versions sporting a Windows-based graphical user interface have found an audience among mainstream business managers.

Project management software helps you plan and control projects more effectively. A project management program helps you schedule the tasks that must be performed to complete a project, figure the amount of time it will take to finish it, allocate resources, deal with task dependencies (when, for instance, task B cannot be started until task A has been completed), order priorities, and develop a budget. The software also allows you to track a project's progress and analyze its performance against anticipated results. Information is communicated through the use of various kinds of charts: Gantt charts (a kind of time table), *PERT* charts (which illustrate tasks and dependencies) (see Chapter 8), resource charts, cost-distribution charts, and others that you can create yourself. Project management software will generally also include an outliner that will assist you in writing project reports. The leading PC-based project management tools include Microsoft's Project (for Windows and Macintosh), Symantec's TimeLine for Windows and a lower-cost version called On Target, Computer Associates' CA-SuperProject, and Claris Corporation's MacProject Pro (for Macintosh).

People management software is a variation of project management software. Whereas project management software typically allows you to track activities of employees in connection with performance on a project, people management software is designed to let managers track employees' progress against general goals.

The leading example of this form of software is Avantos Performance Systems' ManagePro (for Windows and Macintosh). The program allows you to set company or department goals and to assign supporting goals to individual employees or groups. You can list the goals on a kind of scoreboard, with a description, a deadline, a list of the people or teams responsible for achieving the goal, and an indicator of how the project is going for each one. If you want more information, you click on a particular item for greater detail. ManagePro goes beyond traditional project management tools in its focus on the people involved. For example, you can summon information on an employee's goals, progress, feedback, review, recognition, and more. As Randy Dugger, a manager at Tandem Computers, explains, "Before ManagePro, you typically had to write down all this information in some word processing file and you'd print it out and put the paper in the employee's file. It was all paper tracking, searching through files for the right piece of information. With ManagePro, everything concerning [the people you manage] is only two or three clicks away." ManagePro also contains a collection of people management tips and strategies from personnel consultants that you can tap for help under different situations.[3]

Desktop Organizers, Personal Information Managers, and Contact Managers

Another important category of business software includes desktop organizers, personal information managers, and contact managers that allow you to store, organize, and have easy access to the details of business and personal information. These products overlap somewhat with one another and other software products (such as database management software), but each type contains some unique features not found elsewhere.

Desktop organizers and **personal information managers (PIMs)** both generally include an address book, appointment book, calendar, and notepad (see photo). PIMs generally are more sophisticated though and frequently offer additional features not found with desktop organizers, such as an autodialer function that allows you to automatically dial numbers listed in your address book. Many PIMs also include a tickler feature that notifies you of scheduled appointments and the like.

Today, dozens of desktop organizers and PIMs are on the market. A primary factor to consider is ease of use: if the program is too much trouble to learn and use, you'll end up reaching for a pen and paper when you need to record information instead of struggling to remember commands. Fast performance is also important—you don't want to take more time to find a name and address in your electronic address book than in your Rolodex. The desktop organizer or PIM should also be able to function as a background program that is accessible at the touch of a key, no matter what application you're in: if you're using your word processing program and your boss calls to schedule an appointment, you don't want to keep him or her waiting while you exit from the word processor and launch the PIM.[4]

Most integrated software packages include a desktop organizer. You can also purchase desktop organizers separately. Well-known packages are Borland's SideKick and Symantec's Norton Desktop (a general utility program that also includes productivity tools). Some of the leading full-featured PIMs for Windows-based machines include Lotus's Lotus Organizer, Prisma Software Corporation's YourWay, Polaris Software's PackRat, and Micro Logic

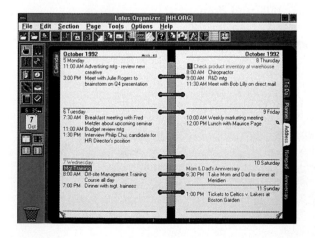

Lotus Organizer contains an easy-to-use address organizer that looks just like a real address book.

Source: Courtesy of Lotus Development Corporation.

Corporation's Info Select. A leading Macintosh PIM is Heizer Software's Connections. There are also PIMs that focus primarily on time-scheduling and to-do lists, without an address book feature, such as Campbell Services' On Time for Windows and Now Software's Now Up-To-Date.

A **contact manager** is a variation on a PIM. A PIM focuses on you and your schedule—your meetings, to-do items, and the like—whereas a contact manager focuses on your outside contacts—phone calls, letters, and so on. Contact managers tend to have stronger database capabilities that allow you to conduct sophisticated searches. With a contact manager, you can maintain a detailed profile of all the people you deal with. You can keep a record of all of your dealings with them: the history of your phone calls, meetings, and letters. A contact manager also performs as a scheduling device—you can list who you need to call, what correspondence needs to go out, and your schedule of meetings. A contact manager is most useful for people whose work depends on heavy contact with clients and customers. Often, successfully cultivating and maintaining a relationship with a client depends on knowing and being able to quickly retrieve information on that client's history, special needs, and preferences. Contact managers give you this ability.[5] Popular contact managers include Symantec's Act for Windows, Modatech System's Maximizer for Windows, and Pyramid Data's PowerLeads.

11.5   Personal Software

What can you do with your computer at home? The subject is long enough to write an entire book about. We'll highlight just a few of the most useful and fun forms of applications software that you may want to install on your personal computer at home.

Personal Finance and Tax Preparation Software

There are two things that most people dislike: paying their bills and doing their tax returns. So it's not surprising that this has proved to be a fertile ground for computer software that aims to make the process less painful. In fact, personal finance and tax software form one of the fastest growing segments of the personal computer software market.

Personal finance programs help you manage your checkbook, credit cards, investments, and other accounts; pay your bills (by linking with an electronic bill-paying service such as Checkfree or Prodigy's BillPay USA); and keep track of your income and expenses (see photo). If you want, they will help you create a budget, net worth statement, or household inventory of your personal possessions. They typically include some helpful financial planning tools, such as a life insurance guide, a loan planner that calculates interest payments and amortization, retirement planners, college savings planners, and the like. They also let you export information to tax preparation programs so that you don't have to rekey when you go to do your taxes.

A personal finance program can help you manage your checkbook and track your income and expenses.

Source: Courtesy of Intuit, Inc.

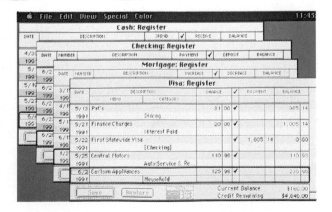

The three leading personal finance programs are Intuit's Quicken (for DOS, Windows, and Macintosh), Microsoft's Microsoft Money (for Windows), and Meca Software's Andrew Tobias's Managing Your Money (for DOS, Windows, and Macintosh), all available for about $50 or less. Of the three, Money has the reputation for being the simplest and easiest to use. Quicken, the industry leader, offers slightly more power for financial analysis. Managing Your Money is the most comprehensive, with a scope ranging far beyond the other two. In addition to check-writing, budgeting, and reporting functions, it contains extensive financial planning tools; for instance, it can perform an in-depth analysis of your stock portfolio, allow you to examine your investment risk profile (conservative or aggressive), and compare your results against historical rates. It then calculates where your money might do better and offers suggestions. If you regard personal finances as necessary drudgery and want to get it over with as painlessly and quickly as possible, get Quicken or Money. But if you think keeping track of your personal finances and financial future is serious fun, Managing Your Money is probably the program for you.

Tax preparation software guides you through the procedure of calculating your taxes and filling out tax forms, helping you make sure that you have done so correctly and that you haven't missed any deductions you might be entitled to (see photo). Tax preparation programs are essentially spreadsheet programs that automatically calculate numbers and enter them in the correct locations in related IRS forms, schedules, and worksheets. Although tax preparation programs can't totally replace an accountant, they do an admirable job. The best of the programs employ a step-by-step interview process, similar to what you might encounter with a human tax preparer. They ask you a series of yes/no questions and use the information you give them to fill out the forms.

Tax programs generally give tax tips appropriate to your situation, as well as steps you can take to reduce your tax liability during the next year. They will even offer audit alerts, warning you if any items are likely to be IRS "red flags." They either display the proper forms being filled out as you answer questions or allow you to jump easily between interview and form. As we noted, you can import files from most personal finance programs into a tax program, making tax preparation almost automatic. After using the package, you'll end up with a completed tax form, which you can print out on your printer. (Most programs provide all the basic IRS forms, schedules, and worksheets, as well as many of the esoteric ones.) You also have the option of filing your return electronically, either by mailing a floppy disk or by sending it via modem to an IRS-authorized service bureau. This eliminates the need for IRS typists to rekey each paper return into a computer, reducing the risk of error. (This kind of error will become less of a concern once the IRS adopts its new image scanning system discussed in Chapter 2.)

The leading tax programs are ChipSoft's Turbotax (for DOS and Windows) and MacInTax (for Macintosh), Meca Software's Andrew Tobias's TaxCut (for DOS, Windows, and Macintosh), and Personal Technology's Personal Tax Edge (for DOS and Windows), all available for under $50. The programs contain largely similar features. Although the DOS versions are just as functional, those designed for Windows and the Macintosh have the advantage of being able to display tax forms that look like the real thing

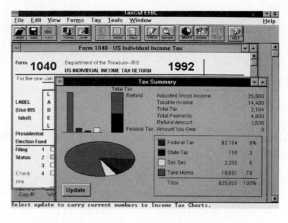

Programs such as Andrew Tobias's TaxCut guide you through the preparation of your tax returns and suggest tax tips.

Source: Courtesy of Meca Software, Inc.

on- screen. The programs typically require around 640KB of RAM and about 3MB to 6MB of hard disk space.

Information on Disk and CD-ROM

A wealth of information is now available on floppy disks and CD-ROMs. Although books are unlikely to become obsolete anytime soon, data stored on disk can often be accessed more quickly and with more specificity. Here's a sampling of some of the products now on the market.

▶ Medical advice: Doctor Schueler's Home Medical Advisor contains a database on diseases, symptoms, injuries, poisons, drugs, tests, health, and diet. The drug file, for instance, gives information on over 1,200 different prescription and nonprescription drugs; the symptom file lists over 70 different symptoms and can produce more than 400 possible diagnoses. The Mayo Clinic Family Health Book Interactive Edition contains similar information in CD-ROM form. The iMHOTEP program has information on diseases that primarily affect African Americans.

▶ History: The Time Table of History (on CD-ROM) includes over 6,000 stories covering key events in science and technology, with over 1,000 graphic images and sound. Who We Are is an interactive program containing sound and animation that contains more than 250 questions and answers on the history of black people in Africa and elsewhere.

▶ Religious information: The Bible Library (on CD-ROM) includes 9 different Bibles and 20 different reference works. New Testament contains the King James version of the Bible on two floppy disks and allows you to search for passages using key words.

▶ Geographic information and travel maps: PC Globe and MacGlobe (on CD-ROM) contain detailed world and regional maps showing topography, natural features, and major cities of each nation. It also includes demographic and other relevant statistics. Automap is a color road atlas on computer. Tell the program where you plan to start and finish your trip and where you'd like to stop along the way. The program then draws a map that you can print out. It will also print directions, telling you where to turn and what roads to take. You can also set preferences about how quickly you like to travel, what types of roads you prefer, and so on. Automap programs are available for both the United States and Europe. Zagat-Axxis CityGuide gives business travelers directions and dining and entertainment information from a variety of cities. The guide features the text and rating of Zagat's annual restaurant and hotel surveys and can create personal maps of how to get around a city.

(a) Compton's Interactive Encyclopedia, Mac version. **(b)** Compton's Interactive Encyclopedia, Windows version.

Source: Courtesy of Compton's New Media, Inc.

a.

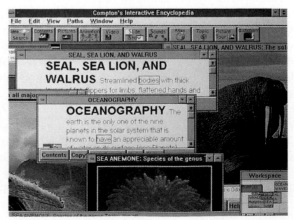

b.

▶ Recipe and recipe organizers: The Micro Kitchen Companion contains a database of over 200 recipes to which you can add your own. The program helps you organize recipes and plan special diets and meals in advance, and allows you to automatically adjust a recipe to feed eight instead of four people. DietPro for Windows allows you to analyze a recipe by typing in a list of its ingredients.

Educational Software

In addition to reference materials, there is a wide variety of **educational software** covering a myriad of topics. According to the Software Publishers Association, parents spent over $100 million on educational software for school-age children during 1992, up considerably from 1991. As recently as five years ago, educational software was little more than computerized workbooks, but today's software is much more sophisticated, incorporating sound, animation, and even video images. Here are just a few examples.

Alphabet Blocks teaches preschool and elementary school students to recognize letters and read by lip-synching sounds and words. KidsWorks2 helps children tell stories, using simple words or pictures if they can't type words. The computer then reads the words and icons aloud. Other programs, such as Syracuse Language System's Playing with Language (on CD-ROM), help teach grade school children a foreign language through computer games. You can even learn to play the piano with computer software. Miracle includes a large electronic keyboard that plugs into a Mac. As you play, the program reacts and leads you through any difficulties with screen displays. The program even provides specific evaluations of your performance along the way. Although Miracle may not replace a human music teacher, it makes the routine business of practice more fun.

Educational software is also available for high school and college students. Stumped by chemistry? Turn to Chemistry Works, which offers detailed information on all 106 elements and graphics that show what atomic structures look like and how element properties interact with other atoms. Need to learn more about geometry or algebra? Try What's My Angle or Algebra Tutor. Want to brush up for the SATs, LSATs, GMATs, or GREs? Consider the Personal Trainer series.

Packages designed to appeal to adults include Orbits, an entertaining, informative tour of the solar system, and BodyWorks, a colorful, comprehensive guide to the structures, systems, and functions of the body. Auto Insight covers the main mechanisms of the automobile, with some history, trivia, and emergency and maintenance hints thrown in. It includes quizzes on the principal topics and a final exam. Boating safety education is also available on disk. Criteria Instruments offers Fleetwise/RVO, a boating course, with 25 lesson categories and over 400 multiple-choice questions. When a student achieves 80 percent accuracy, the computer prints a diploma, which some states accept as the equivalent of a Coast Guard Auxiliary, U.S. Power Squadron, or state boating safety course.

And if your career demands that you quickly develop some skills you don't have, you might consider seeing if there's software that can help. Read the story "Career Skills on Disk" for an example.

Computer Games

Many of you may have received your first introduction to computers through **computer game software.** Some computer games have both educational and entertainment value; others are designed purely for fun.

Suppose you don't have a Harvard MBA and you didn't study Japanese as an undergraduate, but your boss wants you to go to Japan, set up a new company office, and write a business plan for the new office. It's a great opportunity. But how do you pull it off?

Let's tackle the language problem first. A growing number of people are learning languages on multimedia software that combines voice, pictures, and text. This software goes far beyond earlier generations of language labs, records, and software. Most foreign language programs speak words aloud while displaying the word in text and a related picture. Power Japanese by Bayware Inc. teaches street Japanese in three weeks—enough to get around Tokyo by bus or taxi, order food, or arrange for a room. Hyperglot Software Co. makes programs in Russian, German, Italian, and Chinese. More programs are becoming available each month.

Now for the MBA problem. A number of new programs are available to teach you quickly how to write a business plan, how to negotiate, and how to establish personnel policies. For instance, Lord Publishing makes a program called Ronstadt's Financials, which will show you how to develop a business plan, including financial models, balance sheets, and cash flow statements.

Knowledge Point Inc. makes a program called Personnel Policy Expert, which walks you through the procedures you need to hire, fire, and retain employees. And if you face a tough negotiation, Experience in Software Inc. makes a program called Art of Negotiation, which teaches you to look for win–win solutions to problems.

Are these shortcuts to career skills any good? Can you really substitute a computer software package for a two-year MBA program or an undergraduate course in Japanese? Chances are, no. But if you did not have two years to get an MBA or a semester to take a college course, and if you needed to get some expertise quickly, these programs are an answer.

Sources: Based on Bulkeley, William M., "Language Software Tackles Many Tongues," *Wall Street Journal*, January 25, 1993; Bulkeley, William M., "With New Planning Software, Entrepreneurs Act Like MBAs," *Wall Street Journal*, June 2, 1993.

Critical Thinking Questions

1 What advantages do you see to obtaining skills through software rather than attending classes in school? What disadvantages?

2 What kinds of skills could not be taught through software played on a PC or Macintosh at home?

3 List the three most important skills you think you need to perform the job you want to attain (or already have). Now write a brief description of a software program that could teach you those skills.

Leading examples of the first type include Broderbund's line of Where in the World is Carmen Sandiego? software, which mixes geography lessons into a detective game, and Maxis's line of simulation games, such as Sim-City—The City Simulator, SimEarth—The Living Planet, and SimLife—The Genetic Playground. Each of these programs allows you to design a living organism, make choices, and see what results. In SimCity, you get to play mayor and city planner and to set up neighborhoods, manage a municipal budget, and try to take the best advantage possible of your city's natural features. If a single city seems too small to you, you can take on the whole planet in SimEarth. And if that's still not enough, how about re-engineering the entire universe? You can do it with SimLife. Working in a genetics laboratory, you design an ecosystem and populate it with creatures and plants, seeing the effects of various natural disasters and random mutagens. Maxis also distributes A-Train, a program that allows would-be engineers and tycoons to construct railroads and railroad empires. A-Train gives you various scenarios—a developed city, an empty prairie,

Microsoft's flight simulation game is a popular computer game designed for fun.

Source: Courtesy of Microsoft Corporation.

and so on—and allows you to see the effects of building a railroad network. You also have to watch over the financial side of the business, or you may run your railroad into bankruptcy.

Among those programs designed purely for fun are computer games like Tetris, Welltris, WordTris, and Super Tetris—all based on a falling blocks theme. There are computer sports games such as Michael Jordan in Flight, Links, and John Madden Football; flight and space simulators like Aces of the Pacific, X-Wing, and Wing Commander II; and adventure games based on TV shows and movies, such as Star Trek 25th Anniversary and Indiana Jones and the Fate of Atlantis (see photo). There are also computerized versions of popular board games, such as Scrabble, Monopoly, and Risk, and card games, such as bridge and poker.

Communications Software and Utility Programs

Two other important kinds of software that may be useful for your home computer are communications software, which allows you to connect with on-line information services and hook up with the computer at your office, and utility programs which allow your computer to perform tasks such as formatting disks and copying, sorting, and editing files more quickly. For more information about these kinds of software, refer to Chapters 6 and 7.

Summary

Integrated Software Packages

▶ Integrated software packages combine word processing, spreadsheet, database management, and data communications modules into one program.

▶ Integrated packages possess several advantages compared to individual software applications purchased separately. They generally cost less, require less RAM and disk storage space, and are easier to use because all the different modules within the package share the same interface and command structure. They also allow you to exchange data between different applications more easily. However, the modules generally offer fewer features than standalone versions.

▶ Software suites are bundled full-featured versions of different types of software offered by the same manufacturer.

Graphics Software

▶ Analytical graphics software allows you to take data created with a spreadsheet or database management package and create, view, and print charts and graphs. Most spreadsheet and database packages contain analytical graphics capabilities. There are also special statistical software packages that provide more sophisticated data analysis and graphing capabilities.

- Bar graphs, stacked-bar graphs, line graphs, pie charts, X-Y graphs, and mixed graphs are some of the basic types of graphs and charts used for business graphics. Each type of graph and chart is suited for displaying particular types of information.

- Presentation graphics software allows you to create more visually appealing charts and graphs and provides you with a number of different output options, such as screen shows, slides, overhead transparencies, as well as printed material.

- Drawing packages allow you to draw straight and curved lines, geometric objects, and freeform shapes. Objects created with a drawing program can be easily modified or manipulated without affecting any of the other images on the screen.

- Paint programs allow you to create more complex images than a drawing program through a technique called bitmapping. Images cannot be altered except by erasing or painting over them.

- Photo image editors allow you to manipulate and revise photos and other images that you have scanned with an optical scanner.

- Computer-aided design (CAD) programs allow you to create two- and three-dimensional architectural drawings, engineering drawings, and product designs. CAD is often coupled with computer-aided manufacturing (CAM) systems that use computers to help manufacture the products designed with the CAD program.

- Visual data analysis (VDA) software uses computer simulations, animation, 3-D graphics, and renderings to produce sophisticated graphic visualizations of data.

- Animated computer graphics are used in television and the movies. Morphing, the gradual metamorphosis of one image into another, is one of the latest techniques.

Desktop Publishing Systems

- Desktop publishing systems are typically composed of a powerful microcomputer, image scanners, high-resolution color monitors, laser printers, and desktop publishing software. They allow you to control all aspects of the publication process yourself and to produce professional-looking documents of all kinds.

Other Business Software

- Accounting software packages typically contain a general ledger module, an accounts payable module, an accounts receivable module, a payroll module, an inventory control module, and an order entry module.

- Mapping software combines graphics, database management, and some spreadsheet capabilities to display data geographically. Today, many corporations are using such software to better understand geographic patterns behind corporate data.

- Workflow software is designed to streamline and automate different types of work processes. This software can help improve and automate highly structured, complex, everyday processes; ad-hoc projects; and routine or administrative processes.

▶ Scheduling software and meeting support software are two forms of meeting management tools. Scheduling software helps automate the process of setting up meetings, and meeting support software helps increase the efficiency of meetings.

▶ Project management software helps you schedule and control projects more effectively. People management software, a variation of project management software, helps managers track their employees' progress against various goals.

▶ Desktop organizers, personal information managers, and contact managers all help you store, organize, and get easy access to the details of business and personal information. They typically include an address book, appointment book, calendar, and notepad. Contact managers focus more on your outside contacts than your own personal information and are often used by people whose work depends on heavy contact with clients and customers.

Personal Software

▶ Personal finance programs help manage your checkbook, credit cards, and investments; pay your bills; and keep track of your income and expenses. The more sophisticated packages contain extensive financial planning tools.

▶ Tax preparation software guides you through the complex procedure of calculating your taxes and filling out tax returns.

▶ A wide variety of reference materials on disk and educational software is available. In addition, computer game software often has both educational and entertainment value.

▶ Other software typically found on a home computer includes communications software, which allows you to hook up with on-line information services or your computer at work, and utility programs.

Key Terms

integrated software	desktop publishing (DTP) systems
software suites	desktop publishing software
graphics software	TrueType fonts
business graphics	Type 1 fonts
bar graphs	page description language (PDL)
stacked-bar graphs	accounting software
line graphs	mapping software
pie charts	workflow software
X-Y graphs	scheduling software
mixed graphs	meeting support software
analytical graphics software	project management software
statistical software	people management software
presentation graphics software	desktop organizers
illustration programs	personal information managers
drawing packages	(PIMs)
paint programs	contact managers
photo image editors	personal finance programs
computer-aided design (CAD)	tax preparation software
visual data analysis (VDA) software	educational software
animated computer graphics	computer game software

Review Questions

1 What are the advantages and disadvantages of purchasing an integrated software package compared to individual applications programs? How does a software suite differ from an integrated package?

2 When would you use an analytical graphics program? When might you use presentation graphics software instead?

3 Name and describe five different types of basic charts and graphs. Find examples of at least three elsewhere in this text, and explain why they were appropriate for the sort of information being displayed.

4 How does a paint package differ from a drawing package?

5 Why is computer-aided design more efficient than hand-drawn design?

6 Discuss some of the potential uses of VDA software.

7 How does a desktop publishing system achieve efficiencies of time and cost over the traditional publishing system? Create a table comparing the steps involved in both processes.

8 What is the difference between a TrueType font and a Type 1 font?

9 What modules do accounting software typically contain?

10 What is mapping software, and how is it used?

11 Describe three different types of processes that workflow software can be used to streamline, and give concrete examples of each type.

12 In what ways does project management software help you manage a project more efficiently?

13 What is the difference between a PIM and a contact manager?

14 How might you use a personal finance program?

15 Discuss the overlap between educational software and computer game software. Why do you think this has happened?

Problem-Solving and Skill-Building Exercises

1 Find at least two examples of material that you think has been published using a DTP system. Prepare a 1–2 page critique of the material, discussing any differences you notice compared to a commercially produced non-DTP document. Include any suggestions you may have for making the DTP documents more professional looking or visually appealing.

2 Many presentation graphics software packages are adding multimedia capabilities. Are such capabilities just snazzy bells and whistles, or do they serve a real purpose? Are the added functions worth the cost? What could you do with a multimedia presentation that you couldn't do with a regular presentation graphics program? Divide the class into two groups, and debate these issues.

3 Interview a relative, friend, local businessperson, or school administrator about his or her job or business, and find out about the kinds of software that he or she uses. Then prepare a short report (3–5 pages) analyzing the software choices. Are they appropriate for the business? Are there any other types of software that the business might consider?

Writing a Winning Resume

Throughout this book, we've aimed to help you prepare for a successful career, be it in information technology or some other field. But to launch that career, you've got to get a job. Often, the first step along the way will be to write a resume. Jerrold Simon, a career development specialist at Harvard Business School, tells you how to write one that works.

In addition to following Simon's advice, you may also want to check out some applications software packages designed to make the resume-writing process easier. Spinnaker Software's PFS: Resume and Job Search Pro (for DOS and Windows) and WinWay's WinWay Resume for Windows (both available for under $40) are two examples. Such packages help you create professional-looking resumes. They typically include several different model resume formats that you can tailor to your own experience, automatic layout and formatting capabilities, a spelling checker, a thesaurus, and an on-line "action verb" glossary. Use them in conjunction with Simon's advice and you'll have at least one edge in the difficult hunt for that perfect job.

How to Write a Resume

by Jerrold G. Simon, Ed.D., Harvard Business School

If you are about to launch a search for a job, the suggestions I offer here can help you whether or not you have a high school or college diploma, whether you are just starting out or changing your job or career in midstream.

"What Do I Want to Do?"

Before you try to find a job opening, you have to answer the hardest question of your working life: "What do I want to do?" Here's a good way.

Sit down with a piece of paper and don't get up till you've listed all the things you're proud to have accomplished. Your list might include being head of a fund-raising campaign, or acting a juicy role in the senior play.

Study the list. You'll see a pattern emerge of the things you do best and like to do best. You might discover that you're happiest working with people, or maybe with numbers, or words, or well, you'll see it.

Once you've decided what job area to go after, read more about it in the reference section of your library: "Talk shop" with any people you know in that field. Then start to get your resume together.

There are many good books that offer sample resumes and describe widely used formats. The one that is still most popular, the *reverse chronological*, emphasizes where you worked and when, and the jobs and titles you held.

How to Organize It

Your name and address go at the top. Also phone number.

What job do you want? That's what a prospective em-ployer looks for first. If you know exactly, list that next under *Job Objective.* Otherwise, save it for your cover letter (I describe that later), when you're writing for a specific job to a specific person. In any case, make sure your resume focuses on the kind of work you can do and want to do.

Now comes *Work Experience.* Here's where you list your qualifications. *Lead with your most important credentials.* If you've had a distinguished work history in an area related to the job you're seeking, lead off with that. If your education will impress the prospective employer more, start with that.

Begin with your most recent experience first and work backwards. Include your titles or positions held. And list the years.

Figures Don't Brag

The most qualified people don't always get the job. It goes to the person who presents himself most persuasively in person and on paper.

So don't just list where you were and what you did. This is your chance to tell *how well you did.* Were you the best salesman? Did you cut operating costs? Give numbers, statistics, percentages, increases in sales or profits.

No Job Experience?

In that case, list your summer jobs, extracurricular school activities, honors, awards. Choose the activities that will enhance your qualifications for the job.

Next list your *Education*—unless you chose to start with that. This should also be in reverse chronological order. List your high school only if you didn't go on to college. Include college degree, postgraduate degrees, dates conferred, major and minor courses you took that help qualify you for the job you want.

Also, did you pay your own way? Earn scholarships or fellowships? Those are impressive accomplishments.

No Diplomas or Degrees?

Then tell about your education: special training programs or courses that can qualify you. Describe outside activities that reveal your talents and abilities. Did you sell the most tickets to the annual charity musical? Did you take your motorcycle engine apart and put it back together so it works? These can help you.

Next, list any *Military Service.* This could lead off your resume if it is your only work experience. Stress skills learned, promotions earned, leadership shown.

Now comes *Personal Data.* This is your chance to let the reader get a glimpse of the personal you, and to further the image you've worked to project in the preceding sections. For example, if you're after a job in computer programming, and you enjoy playing chess, mention it. Chess playing requires the ability to think through a problem.

Include foreign languages spoken, extensive travel, particular interests or professional memberships, *if* they advance your cause.

Keep your writing style simple. Be brief. Start sentences with impressive action verbs: "Created," "Designed," "Achieved," "Caused."

No Typos, Please

Make sure your grammar and spelling are correct. And no typos!

Use 8½" x 11" bond paper—white or off-white for easy reading. Don't cram things together.

Make sure your original is clean and readable. Then have it professionally duplicated. No carbons.

Get It into the Right Hands

Now that your resume is ready, start to track down job openings. How? Look up business friends, personal friends, neighbors, your minister, your college alumni association, professional services. Keep up with trade publications, and read help-wanted ads.

And start your own "direct mail" campaign. First, find out about the companies you are interested in—their size, location, what they make, their competition, their advertising, their prospects. Get their annual report—and read it.

No "Dear Sir" Letters

Send your resume, along with a cover letter, to a specific person in the company, not to "Gentlemen" or "Dear Sir." The person should be the top person in the area where you want to work. Spell his name properly! The cover letter should appeal to your reader's own needs. What's in it for him? Quickly explain why you are approaching *his* company (their product line, their superior training program) and what you can bring to the party. Back up your claims with facts. Then refer him to your enclosed resume and ask for an interview.

Oh, Boy! An Interview!

And now you've got an interview! Be sure to call the day before to confirm it. Meantime, *prepare yourself.* Research the company and the job by reading books and business journals in the library.

On the big day, arrive 15 minutes early. Act calm, even though, if you're normal, you're trembling inside at 6.5 on the Richter scale. At every chance, let your interviewer see that your personal skills and qualifications relate to the job at hand. If it's a sales position, for example, go all out to show how articulate and persuasive you are.

Afterwards, follow through with a brief thank-you note. This is a fine opportunity to restate your qualifications and add any important points you didn't get a chance to bring up during the interview.

Keep Good Records

Keep a list of prospects. List the dates you contacted them, when they replied, what was said.

And remember, someone out there is looking for someone *just like you.* It takes hard work and sometimes luck to find that person. Keep at it and you'll succeed.

Reprinted by permission of International Paper Company.

Notes

1 **Baird, Jane,** "New from the Computer: Cartoons for the Courtroom," *New York Times,* September 6, 1992. In the case in question, the judge decided to admit the animation but barred the segment showing the victim walking, instead covering him up with a gray dot. The defendant was ultimately convicted of voluntary manslaughter.

2 **Snell, Ned,** "Top Accountants Rate Accounting Software," *Datamation,* June 1, 1992.

3   **Lewis, Peter,** "Pairing People Management with Project Management,"
   New York Times, April 11, 1993; **Mossberg, Walter,** "PC Program Lets Machines Help Bosses Manage People," *Wall Street Journal*, January 31, 1993.

4   **Baran, Nicholas,** "Personal PIMs," *BYTE*, May 1993.

5   **Fersko-Weiss, Henry,** "Contact Managers: Keeping in Touch," *BYTE's
   Essential Guide to Windows*, Spring 1993.

Information Systems in Business and Society

Post Horn Serenade
Melvin Prueitt, Los Alamos
National Laboratories

After completing this chapter, you will:

▶ Be familiar with some basic business concepts.

▶ Understand how transaction processing fits into business operations.

▶ Know about the different types of transaction processing performed by the production, finance, sales, and human resources groups within a firm.

▶ Be able to describe the different kinds of transaction processing systems (TPS) used by each group.

Basic Business Concepts and Systems

Fed Ex at the Kiosk

Federal Express epitomizes the effective use of information technology in transaction processing systems. The company began in 1973 with the novel idea of using a combination of spare airplane capacity and mobile computers in trucks to create a whole new business: overnight package delivery (see photo).

After rapid growth during the late 1980s, Fed Ex is now expanding its traditional service. On a typical day, it delivers 1.8 million letters and packages overnight. In the past, customers would drop letters and packages off at one of 29,500 drop boxes or call Fed Ex and request that their packages be picked up. This process required customers to manually fill out a form, to know what ZIP codes Fed Ex serves, and to have a valid Fed Ex account number. All this took time and produced errors.

Taking a cue from the banking industry, Fed Ex is installing electronic kiosks that look and function like a bank cash machine or ATM (automatic teller machine). The system is known as Federal Express Online. The video-game-sized kiosks are painted Fed Ex's familiar colors. Each kiosk has a touch screen video display terminal. The customer just has to key in the shipping address information, choose next-day or two-day service, and run a credit card through a magnetic reader.

The local kiosk processes much of the information, sends it along to a regional computer, which authorizes the credit, prints a bar-coded address label, and verifies that Fed Ex serves the ZIP code on the address label. The local kiosk prints the bar-coded shipping label, the customer places it on the package and then drops the package in the drop-off box for later pickup.

Fed Ex hopes the new system will broaden the market for Fed Ex services by allowing people who don't have a Fed Ex account to use credit cards instead and by making it easier to use Fed Ex services. Officials also hope to improve quality for existing customers by reducing errors.

Source: Based on Ramirez, Anthony, "Teller Machines Inspire a New Kiosk Business," *New York Times,* March 31, 1993.

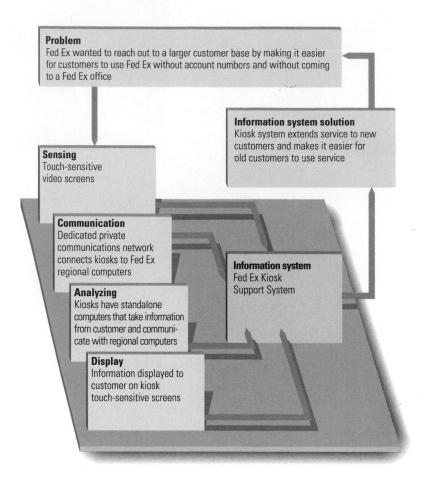

Problem
Fed Ex wanted to reach out to a larger customer base by making it easier for customers to use Fed Ex without account numbers and without coming to a Fed Ex office

Information system solution
Kiosk system extends service to new customers and makes it easier for old customers to use service

Sensing
Touch-sensitive video screens

Communication
Dedicated private communications network connects kiosks to Fed Ex regional computers

Information system
Fed Ex Kiosk Support System

Analyzing
Kiosks have standalone computers that take information from customer and communicate with regional computers

Display
Information displayed to customer on kiosk touch-sensitive screens

A fleet of airplanes, coupled with a powerful transaction processing information system, allows Fed Ex to deliver mail and packages overnight.

Source: Courtesy of Federal Express.

12.1 Basic Business Concepts

Chapter 2 gave a brief introduction to how private businesses and public nonprofit organizations work. In this chapter, we will extend this discussion and focus more closely on business organizations. Public organizations like schools, churches, and other associations are not so different from private businesses.

First, we'll introduce you to some basic business concepts. Then, we'll examine one of the most basic, but also one of the most important types of business information systems: **transaction processing systems (TPS).** A *transaction* is a record of an event to which the business must respond. Take a customer order, for example. A customer order is a transaction that generates a long chain of events that eventually results in the customer's receipt of a product. Information systems that track these events are called transaction processing systems, and they form the foundation for a firm's information processing activities.

Transaction processing systems are "frontline" systems, that is, they often form the basis of the first contact with the customer by taking orders, as in the Fed Ex example in the opening vignette. But TPS also pervade other parts of firms and public organizations at all levels, including production, sales and marketing, human resources and finance. When you think about it, business is all about transactions: people sell their labor and buy things and businesses sell products and services to us and buy from suppliers. These are all transactions. In any year, there are trillions of transactions in the U.S. economy. Transaction processing systems keep track of all these events. Should these systems fail or perform poorly, many firms would be out of business. At the same time, business and organizations that can perform transaction processing well end up with a strategic competitive advantage in the marketplace.

How a Business Works: Purpose, Functions, Structure, and Process

You can describe a business in terms of its purpose, functions (activities), structure (shape), and process. A business is a formal organization whose *purpose* is to make a *profit*—to sell goods and services for an amount greater than the cost of production. The extra amount or profit pays back the entrepreneur and the investors who risked their time and money to create the business. Customers are willing to pay more than the cost of an item because they receive superior value buying goods and services from firms that are experts at making what they do. Lots of people could make a car, but we would all rather buy a car from a firm that has a lot of experience and a solid track record. Generally, firms that provide services for millions of customers can produce the product much less expensively than amateurs because of experience and economies of scale. (Being big allows firms to buy supplies in large quantities and achieve other economies as well.)

Firms that produce physical products are called **manufacturing firms,** whereas firms that produce or sell services like parcel delivery, medical care, food preparation, or accounting advice are called **service firms.** Some economists and sociologists further divide service firms into two groups: traditional services and information services. This distinction will become important in Chapter 13, where we talk about firms whose chief product is based on information and knowledge.

Figure 12.1 illustrates the major functions and typical structure of a business. A **business function** is similar to an activity or responsibility. In most businesses, you will find at least four different kinds of functions being per-

Figure 12.1
Business Functions and Structure
Business firms typically engage in four major functions: production, accounting and finance, marketing and sales, and human resources development. Large businesses, in particular, typically employ a hierarchical structure similar to this organization chart.

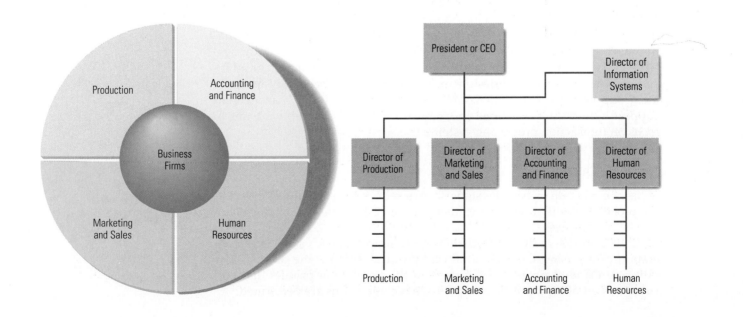

formed. The *production group* is responsible for manufacturing the goods that are sold. If the company is a service firm like United Parcel Service or H&R Block, the production unit is usually called *operations.* The *finance group* is responsible for finding and keeping track of the money to pay the company's suppliers, employees, banks, and stockholders. The *sales group* is responsible for marketing and selling the product. Marketing involves developing advertising to alert customers about the firm's products, and sales involves creating and managing a sales force to actually go out and contact potential customers, perform followup work with customers, and handle complaints. The *human resources group* is largely responsible for hiring, training, and retaining the employees required to produce the product or service.

A fifth function is now typical in most large organizations: *the information systems group.* Generally, when a business grows to even moderate size (more than 100 employees), a specialized group is needed just to operate the information technology needed by production, finance, sales, and human resources. Sometimes this is simply another department (the IS department); other times it is a specialized unit close to the senior management group and considered more of a staff activity.

These five different business functions are usually structured in the form of a pyramid, with increasing authority concentrated at the top in a few individuals (senior managers). Figure 12.2 illustrates a typical business hierarchy with different levels in the organization and the different types of information systems that support the organization.

Generally, there are three general categories of employees in a business: managers, information workers, and production workers. Managers are responsible for seeing that the work gets done at an acceptable time and with acceptable quality and efficiency. Information workers are of two general types: data workers (office clerical workers and sales personnel) and knowledge workers (behind-the-scenes professionals like engineers, designers, lawyers, and the like needed to run the business). Production or service workers actually perform the tasks needed to produce the product or service.

Each of these different levels in an organization has a different kind of supporting business information system. Production workers are usually supported by transaction processing and manufacturing systems. Information workers are supported by a wide variety of systems from clerical systems (sometimes called office automation systems) to computer graphics systems for engineers and designers. Managers are supported by management support systems. Both knowledge work systems and management support systems are described in Chapter 13. In this chapter, we want to focus on transaction processing systems.

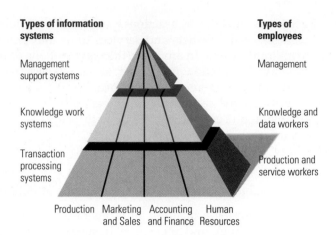

Figure 12.2
A Typical Business Hierarchy, Types of Employees, and Related Systems
Each of the different divisions in a firm typically has at least three general categories of employees. Managers are at the top of the pyramid, information workers in the middle, and production and service workers at the bottom. Each of these different levels has its own kinds of information systems. Managers are supported by management support systems, information workers rely on knowledge work systems, and production and service workers interact with transaction processing systems.

The Value Chain

So far we have described the static structure of business. Now let's look at the process, how it all works together. Figure 12.3 shows you a value chain model of a business.

The basic idea of the value chain is quite simple: at each stage in the operation of a business, value is added by transforming some original raw input. A **value chain** is a set of steps in the production process that add value to a set of inputs at each step. Five basic operations are performed:

**Primary
Activities**

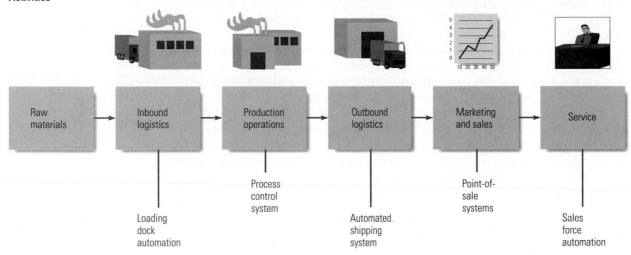

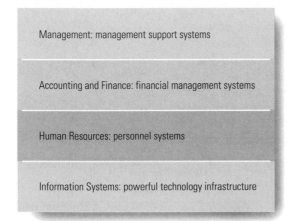

**Support
Activities**

Management: management support systems

Accounting and Finance: financial management systems

Human Resources: personnel systems

Information Systems: powerful technology infrastructure

**Figure 12.3
The Value Chain Model of a
Business**
The value chain is a set of steps that transforms raw inputs into salable products and services. Various support systems underlie each of the basic steps. Value chain analysis focuses on improving the efficiency of each step and the "hand-off" to the next step.

1 Inbound logistics (a warehouse) receives and stores incoming raw materials.

2 Production (or operations) transforms the raw materials into products and services.

3 Outbound logistics (again a warehouse) holds the inventory of completed products or services.

4 Sales and marketing sell the product.

5 Service (usually a part of the production unit) supports the product and keeps in touch with customers.

Underlying these basic activities are support activities like administration, human resources, and information systems. Both suppliers and customers have their own value chains.

In the value chain are many *hand-offs*, or places where one unit of the business must hand off some information or product to another unit. For instance, business begins when a sale is made to a customer. The customer purchases the product or service from the sales group. The sales group receives the order and checks with the production group that runs the warehouse to see if the product is already on the shelf. If not, sales must alert the production facility—the factory—to make the product. Once made, the product goes to the warehouse. When the warehouse is alerted about an order, it finds and ships the requested product. Once shipped, the finance group sends the customer a bill or invoice asking for payment for the product.

In this simplified description, the business transaction called a sale led to the involvement of three different business units: sales took the order, production produced the good or found it in the warehouse and shipped it, and finance sent the invoice and accepted payment. Human resources was only indirectly involved: they made sure people were on hand to perform all of these activities. The IS department was probably also involved throughout, although also indirectly: IS may have supplied the system to take the order, the system to produce and inventory the product, and the system to keep track of the finances behind the transaction.

The basic idea behind value chain analysis is to start thinking about (a) how to add more value to the product for less money (increasing efficiency) and (b) how to fit into the value chains of suppliers and customers better so as to reduce the cost of supplies and the cost of sales.

Information Systems and Productivity

One way to use the value chain described in Figure 12.3 is to look at each point on the chain and ask two questions: "How can technology be used to increase the value of the output at this point?" and "How can technology make the hand-off from one point to another better or more efficient?"

The major reason business firms and other organizations use information technology is to achieve higher levels of productivity or efficiency. **Productivity** is defined as the amount of goods produced per hour of labor. If an information system can increase a worker's output from 100 parts per hour to 150 parts per hour, his or her productivity has gone up by 50 percent. Increasing productivity is important because the general social welfare—the standard of living or real wages—in the society as a whole depends on productivity gains: the faster productivity can be increased, the faster the rise in the standard of living. *Real wages and standard of living* are defined in terms of the amount of goods and services that an average person can afford to purchase.

Technology of all sorts has played a significant role throughout history in advancements in productivity. New technology like the steel plow, the Bessemer furnace, steam engines, electricity, internal combustion engines, railroads, telegraph and telephone, radio, and television have all made major contributions to increasing the productivity of workers on farms, in factories, and in offices.

Information technology—the sensing, communication, analyzing, and display technologies—is having a major impact on productivity in all major business areas. In general, in the United States since 1945 productivity has advanced around 3 percent a year, as have real wages. Information technology has played an important role in this advance. In factories, information technology is used to automate tasks previously done by human workers, thereby increasing the quality of products and releasing

Manufacturing firms such as Inland Steel are increasingly turning to information technology to help automate the manufacturing process.

Source: Michael L. Abramson/Woodfin Camp & Associates.

labor to work in other higher-value occupations. In offices, information technologies are used to automate tasks and, more importantly, to increase the information and knowledge available to clerical, sales, and managerial personnel, making their work both higher quality and more efficient.

Using technology to increase productivity is not easy: much more is involved than just plugging in some machines and walking away. In general, as we discussed in Chapter 8, to achieve large productivity gains, the organization, flow of work and business procedures must also be changed. Consider that the first cars were called horseless carriages because they were literally carriages with an engine instead of a horse providing the power. It took decades of rethinking the carriage, and enormous investments in highways and support activities, before the car as we know it emerged.

A little later in this chapter, we'll describe a number of examples from production, finance, sales, and human resources that increase the productivity of employees. When reading these examples, try to think about the organizational and work changes needed to successfully raise productivity.

The Strategic Role of Information Systems

Value chain analysis is also helpful for seeing how some firms can gain a competitive advantage over other firms. By accomplishing the various steps in the value chain better, or by improving the hand-offs from one activity to another, a firm can gain a competitive advantage over other firms. A **competitive advantage** is some unique feature of a firm that gives it the ability to produce products at *lower cost* or to produce *unique products* that cannot be imitated.

Successful firms can use information technology to deliver better products and services for lower costs than anyone else. Many examples in this chapter describe how business firms and other organizations try to use information technology to achieve a competitive advantage.

Types of Transaction Processing Systems

There are various differences among the transaction processing systems within a firm. Some TPS are on-line, and others are batch. **On-line transaction processing systems** immediately record information and respond to user requests. ATM machines at banks, for instance, are on-line TPS, as are airline reservation systems. **Batch transaction processing systems,** on the other hand, process information in a batch and do not give an immediate response. Traditional check balance systems are batch systems: when you write a check, it is received and recorded by your bank, but a new balance is not struck until the end of the day when all checks are processed in a batch. Batch processing is less expensive than on-line processing, and for applications where immediate feedback is not required they are perfectly suitable.

Another way transaction processing systems differ is that some are *centralized* and others much more *distributed*. **Centralized systems** store all information and do all processing at a single, central

On-line transaction processing systems can respond instantly to user requests.

Source: Courtesy of Martin Marietta.

location. For instance, the U.S. Social Security Administration uses about 50,000 dumb terminals linked by satellite to a single mainframe in Baltimore, Maryland, where all processing of transactions is accomplished in a single large data center. Today, though, the trend is toward **distributed systems.** A distributed system uses multiple computers connected by a telecommunications network, instead of relying on a central computer. In a distributed system, as much processing and short-term data storage as possible is performed at local levels (the desktop or laptop computer) and centralized mainframes are used, if at all, only for storing information.

This Salomon Brothers trading room in London, England is supported by a fault tolerant system that protects against the failure of any one computer.

Source: John Moss/Tony Stone Worldwide.

Most TPS have a variety of protections against failure such as backup emergency plans, dual systems, or fault tolerant systems. **Fault tolerant systems** are specialized systems that contain several redundant computers and special computer programs to protect against failure of any one computer. They are used in life-dependent or critical situations like stock trading, space missions, and financial systems.

Each of the major business functions has its own set of transaction processing systems, and each is designed to solve a particular kind of problem. In the rest of the chapter, we will examine the use of TPS in the four basic business activity areas: production, finance, sales, and human resources. For each of these business areas, we will describe some of the classic business problems faced and show how TPS can be used to solve these problems. By "classic business problems," we mean ones that are faced by nearly every business and hence are typical. Classic problems are also recurrent—they never go away, and there always seems to be a better way emerging to solve them, given changes in technology. Solving these problems is critical to the existence of a business.

12.2 Production and Operations Transaction Processing Systems

A factory manager or office manager faces the daunting task of deciding how many supplies to order, when to produce, how to produce, how much to produce, and where to store the company's products or services. The manager is also responsible for the quality of the goods and services produced.

Classic Problems and TPS Solutions

Figure 12.4 lists some classic production problems and the TPS used to solve them.

Production Control: Purchasing, Scheduling, Inventory, and Shipping

A number of systems are directly involved in the production process. Production begins with supplies that must be ordered, received, and stored ready for production. **Purchasing management systems** keep track of vendors and supplies ordered, received, stored, and on back-order. **Job scheduling systems** decide when to initiate production of specific items based on supplies on hand and customer demand. **Inventory control systems** track the current supplies of inventory and match this against anticipated future orders from customers. For instance, an inventory control system should "know" that more winter jackets should be manufactured in the summer to anticipate heavy winter demands. A job scheduling system should help plan the production of specific winter coats and jackets. **Shipping management systems** are used to track customer orders from receipt to final shipping. They track the customer order, shipping information, and shipper used and can trace the route of a package as it goes to the customer.

Given the complexity of the production process, simply identifying the nature and location of parts becomes a difficult task. In the past, huge ledger books were used to manually coordinate the flow of supplies, goods, and shipping information. Now, modern bar code technology enormously increases the efficiency of the entire production process. Traditional bar codes are called 1-D bar codes: they contain a single line of information. Now there's also a 2-D bar code: multiple lines of information (up to 1,800 characters) can be stored on a single 2-inch-square patch and scanned by new types of laser readers in a single pass. With this higher information density, distribution systems (warehouse, transportation, and delivery systems) can operate much more efficiently. For instance, at a receiving warehouse, a loading dock employee wearing a wrist-mounted laser reader can instantly tell who manufactured incoming supplies, the part numbers, cost, transit method, and even the location where it should be stored.

McKesson, the largest U.S. drug distributor, is one company taking advantage of new bar code technology. McKesson plans to spend $50 million to streamline its inventory tracking and distribution system. "Wearable" systems that fit onto people's hands and waists will be a part of the

Problem	Description	TPS Solution
Materials management	Ordering, receiving, storing supplies	Purchasing management systems
Job scheduling	Deciding when specific products should be produced	Job scheduling systems
Inventory control	Keeping track of inventory of finished goods and deciding when to initiate production	Inventory control systems
Process control	Monitoring and controlling physical machines on shop floor or workstations in office	Process control systems and shop floor data collection systems
Quality control	Monitoring machines, materials, and personnel to assure highest levels of quality	Quality control systems
Product design	Tools and techniques for improving old products or creating new products	Computer-aided design and computer-aided manufacturing tools
Integrated production planning	Deciding the best way to produce a product by coordinating supplies, job schedules, labor, and financial considerations	Manufacturing resource planning (MRP) systems

Figure 12.4
Classic Production Problems and TPS Solutions

effort. McKesson has installed "Acumax^{SM}," a hand-and-wrist laser reader and computer that verifies incoming supplies for warehousers, leaving both hands free to move packages too large for McKesson's automated picking system. One result is error reduction: McKesson avoids thousands of errors when filling orders for 51,000 pharmacies.[1]

Process Control

A key to management of large manufacturing and production operations is a kind of transaction processing application called a **process control system,** which monitors and controls either the physical machines on the shop floor or the work being done at workstation desktops in a large office setting. Without this control, it is impossible to manage production. Figure 12.5 illustrates a process control system.

Quality control systems are a kind of process control system that measure the deviation of products from predefined standards and set off alarms when the deviation becomes too large. Quality control systems usually take data directly from shop floor process control TPS.

The Acumax^{SM} wearable computer allows McKesson to warehouse and ship thousands of products on time with fewer errors.

Source: Courtesy of McKesson, Inc.

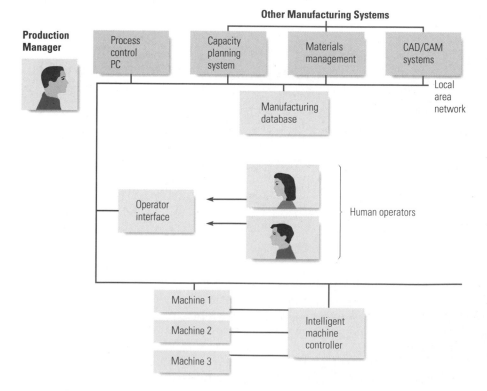

Figure 12.5
Process Control TPS

Process control systems are a kind of TPS often found in manufacturing firms. Process control systems begin with intelligent machines that can be computer-controlled and that report on their operation to a local area network through computers called intelligent controllers. Human operators observe the computer output of the machines. The data on output from all machines is also available to a process control PC, which monitors the operation for the production manager. The data is stored in a production database and sent to other manufacturing systems like purchasing, inventory, and materials management.

Computer-Aided Design and Computer-Aided Manufacturing (CAD/CAM)

Ordinarily, one might not consider design tools to be a kind of TPS. Today, though, computerized design tools are closely integrated with production and often are an integral part of factory process control TPS. **Computer-aided design (CAD)** tools are used by engineers to design, draw, and create products. A specialized CAD machine is a powerful workstation—usually a UNIX desktop machine with a very high-quality, large monitor. Engineers create designs on these machines and then feed the output into **computer-aided manufacturing (CAM)** systems that control shop floor machines. In this way, the product cycle (length of time from design to manufacturing) can be greatly speeded up.

The use of CAD/CAM in production, along with significant changes in work procedures, has vastly increased the productivity of American manufacturers. Figure 12.6 illustrates how Chrysler Corporation uses these systems.

Figure 12.6
Chrysler Corporation Creates With CAD/CAM
Chrysler has invested more than a billion a year in new CAD/CAM equipment, factories, work procedures, and many other computer-based technologies. The centerpiece of this effort is Chrysler's new $1.3 billion Chrysler Technology Center (CTC). This 3.5-million-square-foot center in Auburn Hills, Michigan, employs 7,000 people in "platform development teams." Using team techniques borrowed from the Japanese in which a small group of people work on a whole new car (rather than separate divisions working on the body, engine, and design), along with advanced technology, Chrysler has greatly increased its productivity.

The first new product from the CTC is the LH—a "cab-forward" midsized car designed largely on CAD/CAM machines. A much admired design, the LH series is the first Chrysler product directly competitive with Japanese automobiles on price and quality. Because of the CTC, Chrysler has cut its design and production staff in half on new products like LH and reduced the time to develop new products by nearly 30 percent.

Source: Courtesy of Chrysler Technology Center/Chrysler Corporation.

Another company that uses CAD/CAM and computer-controlled machines in the same production TPS is Gillette Company, a Boston-based manufacturer of shaving equipment. In the early 1980s, Gillette used CAD equipment to design a new razor called Sensor, which contains two floating blades that conform to the contour of the face (and legs). The problem was making it: no production equipment in existence could weld the blades to a stiff backbone without harming the sharpness of the blades or make the blades within the range of tolerances (25 microns, which is 25 thousandths of an inch) required by the engineers' designs. After several years of research, Gillette created its own computer-controlled laser welding equipment that can make 15 welds per razor cartridge in less than one-fifth of a second. Quality? A microscopic camera controlled by a minicomputer examines 2.5 blades a second and removes rejects from the assembly process.

Gillette has achieved impressive results: Sensor has captured 43 percent of the market—triple its closest competitor—and Gillette has sold more than one billion of them. [2]

Manufacturing Resource Planning (MRP)

Many of the classic problems in production can be addressed by transaction processing systems called **manufacturing resource planning (MRP)** systems. MRP systems integrate many of the aforementioned functions into a single software/hardware system.

A typical MRP installation can be found at J. Brach Corporation, one of the country's leading candy makers. Brach, located in Oakbrook Terrace, Illinois, manufactures 400 million pounds of candy a year. Prior to installing an MRP system, it relied on a manual system of paper records to schedule production. As a result, Brach experienced frequent interruptions to its work flow, stopping the entire production line when insufficient packing cases were on hand or when a small package partition was out of stock.

The new MRP system coordinates materials management with process control, inventory, and capacity planning. It also sends data to financial systems. Previously separate departments at Brach like purchasing, inventory control, scheduling, and quality control now have on-line access to outstanding orders and inventory. This permits decisionmakers to know instantly what should be and can be produced. There are no more work flow interruptions at Brach. Raw materials inventory has fallen by one-third, saving $1 to $2 million a month. Deviations from production standards have fallen from 8 to 4 percent, reducing the amount of raw materials consumed. [3]

Caterpillar Corporation's wheel loader factory in Aurora, Illinois and tractor assembly factory in East Peoria, Illinois use computer-integrated manufacturing and manufacturing resource planning systems to streamline the manufacturing process.

Source: Courtesy of Caterpillar Corporation.

Electronic Data Interchange (EDI)

How can production be coordinated across time and space? Many firms have truly global operations. If they have a message for a firm in Japan, how do they get it there? If they want to sell currencies on the European markets, how do they communicate this to brokers in Paris? International firms, and increasingly domestic firms, rely on *electronic data interchange (EDI)* systems that you learned about in Chapter 6. EDI provides an easy-to-use telecommunications link among large suppliers, manufacturers, and customers. Caterpillar Corporation, for instance, one of the world's premiere manufacturers of earth-moving equipment and diesel power plants, has 36 worldwide plant locations and more than 1,000 different suppliers. Caterpillar created its own

EDI communications network that links 950 suppliers to production plants. Caterpillar uses the network to send orders for parts. Suppliers use the network to bill Caterpillar. Other messages also flow over the network concerning price, availability, and quality. The result: Caterpillar has saved $10 million a year just in reduced paperwork, and has saved its suppliers an equal amount.

12.3   Accounting and Finance Transaction Processing Systems

The first business applications for computers in the 1950s were printing payroll and dividend checks. Today, accounting and finance TPS are the backbone of most large business organizations. The cash flow of firms almost totally depends on basic financial systems.

Classic Problems and TPS Solutions

Figure 12.7 lists some classic accounting and finance problems and the TPS used to solve them.

Problem	Description	TPS Solution
Accounting		
Accounting for financial flows	Keeping track of accounts receivable, accounts payable, and the general ledger of a business	Accounting systems
Payroll	Keeping track of employee compensation	Payroll systems
Budgeting	Developing an operating and capital budget	Budgeting systems
Finance		
Managing the flow of cash	Tracking and monitoring cash flows and assuring cash is invested appropriately	Cash management systems
Credit management	Tracking and monitoring credit balances, interest, and billing statements	Credit management systems
Financial accounting	Developing key financial ratios that reflect the performance of the firm	Financial accounting systems
Securities trading	Managing firm assets by trading currencies, bonds, and other financial instruments	Trading systems

Figure 12.7
Classic Accounting and Finance Problems and TPS Solutions

The basic purpose of accounting systems is to track the flow of funds into and out of the firm, as well as to show just how well the firm is doing financially at any given moment. The basic purpose of financial systems is to optimize the overall financial condition of the firm through superior management of funds. The two kinds of systems—accounting and finance—are closely related.

Accounts Receivable, Accounts Payable, and General Ledger

Accounts receivable systems (see Figure 12.8) are among the most important accounting systems because they record the amounts of money owed by your customers based on the invoices (bills) sent to customers. **Accounts payable systems** keep track of the amount of money your business owes suppliers and creditors (people who have extended credit to you). **Payroll systems** are a special kind of accounts payable: these systems keep track of how much you owe and have paid to your employees. In addition to issuing checks, payroll systems produce statements for the Internal Revenue Service and other tax agencies, showing how much tax employees have paid.

Accounts receivable, accounts payable, and payroll together form the basis for what is called the **general ledger system.** The general ledger records the firm's income and expenditures—somewhat like a very large checkbook. From the general ledger system comes a large number of accounting statements like the income statement, the balance sheet, the general ledger trial balance, and many others described in books on basic accounting.

Accounting systems form the backbone of large business organizations.

Source: Superstock.

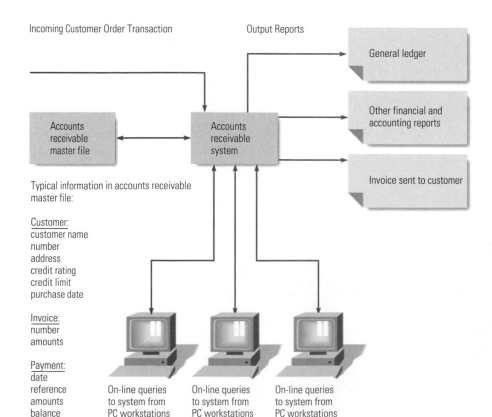

Incoming Customer Order Transaction

Output Reports

- General ledger
- Other financial and accounting reports
- Invoice sent to customer

Accounts receivable master file ←→ Accounts receivable system

Typical information in accounts receivable master file:

Customer:
customer name
number
address
credit rating
credit limit
purchase date

Invoice:
number
amounts

Payment:
date
reference
amounts
balance

On-line queries to system from PC workstations

On-line queries to system from PC workstations

On-line queries to system from PC workstations

Figure 12.8
An Accounts Receivable System

An accounts receivable system begins with a customer order. The customer order triggers the system to look into the customer file for information on the customer, including credit history and record. If the customer is known and reliable, the goods are shipped and a bill or invoice sent to the customer. The system also reports to the general ledger that the amount of money owed to the firm has gone up. Other reports and information are also updated.

Financial Systems: Cash and Credit Management

Financial systems are closely related to accounting systems, but serve a different purpose. In general, financial systems focus on optimizing and managing the overall financial resources of the firm. They are less concerned with day-to-day transactions, like bills and receipts or the general ledger, and more concerned with yearly financial results like how much of a return on investment of capital the firm is earning.

Cash management systems, for instance, keep track of the daily cash balances in the firm's accounts. A computer-based system "sweeps" through accounts at the end of the day. When these accounts have more cash than is needed for operations, the extra cash is "swept up" and invested in overnight or other short-term financial instruments so that it earns interest for the firm.

Credit management systems perform a similar task: they analyze the firm's credit position. Creditors have extended credit to the firm, and credit management systems keep track of this debt, trying to ensure that the firm does not pay too much interest on overdue bills and that reliable sources of credit are used. Credit management systems also oversee the credit granted by the firm to customers, attempting to increase payments from past due accounts and ensure that not too much credit has been granted to certain individuals or corporations, thereby minimizing the risk to the firm.

Information technology also has created an entire new industry of credit management based on accounting and financial management systems. We carry this new industry in our wallets in the form of credit cards. You can think of the credit card industry as a huge transaction processing system. The story "What Happens When You Say 'Charge It' "describes how the system works.

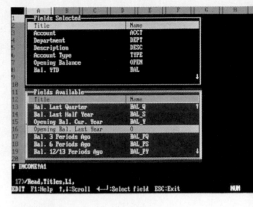

Computer Associates International's ACCPAC Plus is a popular microcomputer-based accounting software package.

Source: Courtesy of Computer Associates International, Inc.

Financial Accounting Systems

One of the most important problems for a firm is to understand how well it is doing financially. Should the firm have invested in some other business? Is it receiving a good return on its investments in factories, offices, people, and distribution systems? While these sorts of problems can also be answered using spreadsheet software, many large organizations have special **financial accounting systems** dedicated to this task. These systems focus on an analysis of the key financial ratios used by firms to understand their overall financial position.

Trading Systems

Large *Fortune* 1,000 firms (the largest 1,000 firms in the United States as listed by the business magazine *Fortune*) often have their own securities trading group. Many large firms manage their own savings by managing their own financial assets and investing them in bonds, currencies, and stocks just like individuals. For international firms, it is common to trade in foreign securities in order to protect the firm against a sudden fall in the value of a currency.

Securities trading systems are used to manage and track investment portfolios of currency, bonds, stocks, and other financial instruments. Trading systems use a number of digital "feeds" or telecommunication links to markets around the world. Securities trading rooms are filled with hundreds of terminals showing price and volume movements on world markets.

How many credit cards do you have? If you're the prototypical "average American" with an income greater than $10,000, chances are that you have at least 3, if not more. Today, there are over 1 billion credit cards in the United States and over one-half trillion (!) dollars each year are spent via credit card purchases. Mastercard and Visa account for nearly 80 percent of the market. Mastercard and Visa are typically issued by banks, which are members of an association that processes the credit transactions in return for a small fee (around 5 cents per transaction).

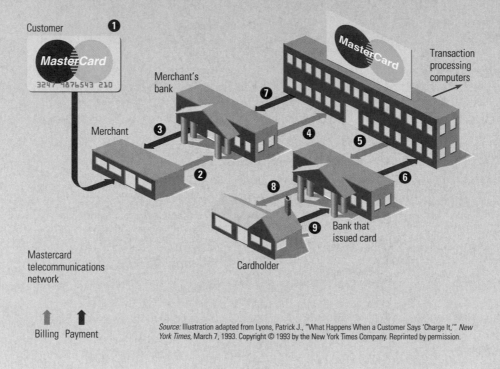

Mastercard telecommunications network

⬆ Billing ⬆ Payment

Source: Illustration adapted from Lyons, Patrick J., "What Happens When a Customer Says 'Charge It,'" *New York Times,* March 7, 1993. Copyright © 1993 by the New York Times Company. Reprinted by permission.

12.4 Marketing and Sales Transaction Processing Systems

It is said, "if there's no sale, there's no business." If a store can't get you through their door, it will have no chance to sell you anything. If the goods are not on the shelf when the customer wants them, a sale is lost, perhaps forever.

Ever wonder how grocery stores keep so many different types of potato chips on the shelves and how they always seem to be available? The answer is sales force automation—information technology systems that help local salespeople adjust their shelf space to local demands for particular kinds of products. This is just one example of the use of TPS in sales and marketing. Information technology is changing how we shop and how business sells (see Figure 12.9).

Levi Strauss's touch screen kiosks are an example of the new information technologies now being used to market products.

Source: MiroVintoniv/Stock Boston.

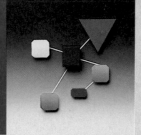

Let's look at how the system actually works. It all begins with a transaction: you go into a store to purchase a gift. When the salesclerk asks how you'd like to pay, you whip out your Mastercard and say "Charge it." Sometime later, you get a bill in the mail. It all seems very simple on the surface, but let's take a peak at what goes on behind the scenes to make it all possible (see diagram).

When you say "Charge it," the clerk takes your card and runs it through a credit card machine (1). The machine records the relevant data (credit card number and expiration date) and dials a number at the store's bank. The store's bank is linked though Mastercard's network to the bank that actually issued the card; this bank then approves the charge. Next, the store submits the charge to its bank (2). The bank subtracts a fee (usually around 2 percent) and pays the store the rest (3). For instance, for a $50 purchase, the store would typically receive $49. The merchant's bank then submits the charge to Mastercard (4), which submits it to the bank that actually issued the card (5). The card-issuing bank subtracts a fee (around 1.5 percent) and pays the rest ($49.25) to Mastercard (6), which then pays the merchant's bank (7). (The merchant's bank paid the store only $49 so it gets to keep the 25-cent difference.) The issuing bank then sends you a bill (8); when you pay it, it will receive $50 from you and perhaps some interest as well (9). So what appears to be a simple transaction to you is actually an elaborate stream of data and money, and none of it would be possible without information technology.

The credit card system has a number of different benefits. For consumers, it provides nearly instant credit anywhere in the United States at little or no extra cost. Merchants like it because easy credit encourages consumers to buy more. At the same time they need not worry about administering their own credit systems—Mastercard does all the work. There are also obvious benefits for the banks involved—revenues from transaction fees and interest. Finally, Mastercard makes out pretty well too—5 cents a transaction adds up quickly when you process 3 billion transactions a year.

The system is not without costs as well. Because most merchants add the cost of processing fees to their prices, this raises the prices of goods for all, not just those who use credit cards. Some also feel that the cards make credit too easily available, leading people into debt.

Critical Thinking Questions

1 Do you think the benefits of the credit card system in the U.S. outweigh the costs?

2 What do you think explains the popularity of credit cards even when interest rates are high and people must pay a fee to use them?

3 Do you think the information about credit card purchases should be sold to other companies for marketing purposes? Should credit card users be informed if their purchase information is sold?

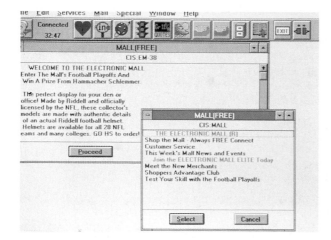

CompuServe's Electronic Mall allows customers to shop at home.
Source: Courtesy of CompuServe.

Figure 12.9
New Technologies in Marketing
- Self-checkout aisles—Shoppers scan their own bar codes. A built-in checker makes sure the shopper does not substitute a sirloin for a candy bar.
- Video shopping carts—Specials, maps, and price information are presented on a screen attached to a cart based on the cart's position in the store.
- Touch-screen kiosks—Shoppers are shown different patterns, products, and colors in a photo-realistic way (see photo).
- Pen-based notebook sales computers—With a wireless data interface to the store's point-of-sale system computer, these portables permit salespeople to follow customers around the store and record orders. Also used by inventory people to restock shelves. Sometimes directly connected to manufacturers' mainframes.
- Debit card purchase—Customers use a local bank debit card to pay for groceries. A debit card, unlike a credit card, immediately deducts the amount from your checking account.
- Electronic shop-at-home services—Customers use a home PC to scan available products and order using a modem. Even at-home grocery shopping is available in some cities (see photo).

 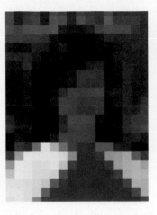  

A salesperson uses front-end technologies such as bar-code readers and point-of-sale terminals to store small bits of purchase information. So?

Combine that with data from other customer databases in which the customer's prior purchases are recorded.

Feed these buying behaviors into large computers that add other information from geographic systems, credit reports, and other sources.

You may come up with a clear enough image of your customer that you can create and market a product to her that will fit her like a glove.

Bringing the customer into focus.

Source: Don Smetzer/Tony Stone Worldwide.

Classic Problems and TPS Solutions

Figure 12.10 lists some classic sales and marketing problems and the TPS used to solve them.

Customer Identification Systems

Economic competitive pressure and new technologies are rapidly changing marketing and sales functions. Marketing is all about finding customers: identifying, locating, and contacting them. You can think of marketing as an effort to bring the customer into focus (see photos).

Automated data retrieval systems are TPS that help marketers identify who the customers are, what they want to buy, and how to contact them. These systems help marketers build up a customer database and create mar-

Problem	Description	TPS Solutions
Market analysis	Identifying customers and understanding market demand through use of market surveys and unobtrusive data gathering; creating customer lists	Customer identification systems, automated data retrieval systems, large customer databases
Supporting field sales staff	Providing information to sales field agents about customers and retail store owners	Sales support systems
Processing orders	Entering, processing, and tracking orders from the field	Order processing systems
Recording sales data	Capturing sales information at the point where the sale is made	Point-of-sale systems
Authorizing credit	Tracking and communicating to sales force the maximum credit available to customers	Credit authorization systems

Figure 12.10
Classic Marketing and Sales Problems and TPS Solutions

How Marketing Experts Know Who You Are

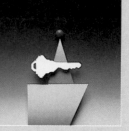

Look at your incoming mail. Ever wonder how marketing experts at large companies know who to send mail advertising to or what television show to advertise on so that you will likely be watching? How do they select *you* to call about a new product? The answer: *you* gave them the information on what you buy, read, drive, and even think.

How? Every time you make a credit card purchase, enter a sweepstakes, or order merchandise by phone or mail, information about who you are and the products you bought goes into one of several databases. Moreover, governments sell information about you to marketers: information available from birth records, driver's license, vehicle registration, and even civil court records. What is the color of your eyes, and how on earth did the cosmetics company find out? Answer: they searched motor vehicle records.

So-called database marketing is a growing part of the marketing industry that employs thousands of marketing experts to build and analyze the data. Marketers, of course, still use general broadcast and print advertising, but database marketing is targeted to a much smaller audience and therefore can be much more efficient. Consider the data-gathering efforts of some major corporations:

Procter & Gamble—Manufactures household products. Collects data through reply cards inserted in free samples.

MCI Communications Corporation—Long-distance service. Friends and Family program offers 20 percent discount to customers who identify people they call regularly. MCI then targets this group with mail and phone solicitations.

AT&T/Walt Disney World—Callers enter joint sweepstakes using interactive phone program and are asked about use of Disney products and services.

Kimberly-Clark—Diapers and household products. Buys lists of new mothers from government agencies and sends coupons, brochures, and new-product samples.

PepsiCo., Inc.—Soft drinks and snack foods. Summer Chill Out program develops database with discount card offered to children.

Hallmark Cards—Greeting cards. Envelope glued to magazine insert. When filled out, it is redeemable for a free card.

Coca-Cola Co.—Soft drinks and snack foods. Pop Music promotion provides CD buyers' names to partner Sony Corporation.

Phillip Morris Companies—Cigarettes. Blind free samples offer unidentified product as part of contest promotion.

Source: Based on Levin, Gary, "Databases Loom Large for '90s," *Ad Age*, October 21, 1992.

Critical Thinking Questions

1 Why might database marketing as described here be more efficient than print, television, or radio advertising?

2 What benefits do consumers obtain from database marketing?

3 What are some of the costs to consumers of database marketing?

---

keting lists for the sales force to contact. Every time you make a purchase by check or credit card, book a vacation or seat on an airline, or call a help line, chances are good that an automated *customer identification system* is recording the transaction and that this information will be used later to market additional products to you. The story, "How Marketing Experts Know Who You Are," explores this phenomenon.

Increasingly, marketers want this information on-line and in a dynamic fashion: they want the store's central computers to know what you buy and when you buy it. In this way, retail store goods can be ordered and arranged on the shelf so that you are sure to find them. One example of this is a system called Shoppertrak, which is being tested at Kmart, the world's largest retailer. Shoppertrak counts customers as they pass under sensors mounted in the ceiling of test stores. The data is used by Kmart to predict customer traffic, improve employee scheduling, and test the effectiveness of in-store marketing. Further, large retail stores are using supercomputers to instantly analyze in-store automated data. One midwestern retailer found, for instance, that if shoppers bought disposable diapers at 5 P.M., the next most common purchase was a six-pack of beer. To boost snack sales, the store put a display of chips next to the disposable diaper rack.[4]

Database marketing allows companies to deliver goods to you cheaply and efficiently, but it also means that large firms increasingly know many private things about you. Privacy is the claim of individuals to be left alone and the related claim to control information about themselves (see Chapter 15). Modern database marketing means that you will not be left alone and that you will lose some control over information about yourself—information such as what magazines and books you read, what clothes you wear, and what food you buy, and that's just for starters. This raises an important issue that we discuss further in the Dilemmas and Controversies feature, "How Much Knowledge About You Should Marketers Have?"

Sales Support Systems

Once customers are identified and customer lists developed, the next step is to support sales campaigns and sales personnel who actually make the sale. **Sales support systems** assist sales personnel in the field by keeping track of customers and prospects, following up on sales, and making sure the customers are satisfied. **Telemarketing systems,** a special kind of sales support system, use the telephone and a central sales staff to contact prospects and customers. The rapid growth in the use of computers to enhance the marketing and sales functions in business has opened up entirely new career possibilities. There are new jobs in market data gathering and data analysis and, of course, new jobs in telemarketing.

Probably one of the best known sales force automation systems in the United States is that of Frito-Lay, Inc., a division of PepsiCo., Inc. Frito-Lay first equipped its 10,000-person sales force with hand-held computers in 1989. Second-generation hand-helds have now replaced those early units (see Figure 12.11). Frito-Lay's system permits it to "micromarket" snack foods. Micromarketing means to target sales to a small geographic region rather than a national mass consumption market. Micromarketing permits large firms to produce specialized products for very small geographic units, even neighborhoods.

The hand-held sales computers are used to enter orders and keep track of competition. The flood of data is fed into a software package called the Cube, which tracks snack foods in 32 regions, 4 retail distribution channels, and 6 product categories. This divides the data into several hundred marketing cells. For instance, one marketing cell might be corn chip sales in the capital district in Washington, D.C. For each cell, there is a marketing plan, data on sales of Frito products, and competitor sales. Frito-Lay can micromarket to each cell, adjusting its sales strategy to fit each micromarket.[5]

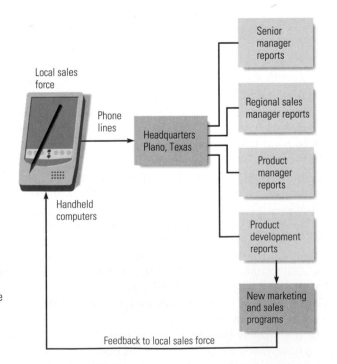

Figure 12.11
Frito-Lay's Sales Force Automation Program
Frito-Lay has developed a series of information systems to make sure shelves in all neighborhoods of the United States are properly stocked with chips and snack foods. Frito-Lay is now moving these systems into Europe as well.

he story "How Marketing Experts Know Who You Are" gives you some idea about how businesses today go about gathering information about you. But how much knowledge is too much? Here are just a few of the thousands of lists that are available to marketers throughout the country:

• A "Health Ailment" list of almost 1 million Americans who reported some form of chronic condition in a direct response survey.

• A "National Credit Hunters" list of 1.6 million people who applied for Visa or Mastercard credit cards but were turned down.

• "Goose" lists of gullible consumers who previously responded to patently obvious "come on" advertisements.

• A "Christian Zealots" list of half a million former donors to ten evangelical ministries.

• A "Young Family Index" of over 3 million new mothers.

Privacy advocates argue that the easy availability of lists like these give marketers far too much information about private citizens. They believe that individuals have a right to privacy and that at the very least people should be consulted before their name is added to a mailing list and before the information is used for a purpose other than for which it was gathered.

Others, especially marketing experts, argue that developing mailing lists and databases serves the needs of consumers by presenting them with information on new products. Moreover, customers give the information to marketers in return for some benefit; in other cases, marketers buy publicly available information from government agencies. These marketers believe there is nothing wrong with using this information for marketing purposes.

Source: Based on Larson, Erik, *The Naked Consumer,* Henry Holt and Company, Inc., New York, 1992.

Critical Thinking Questions

1 Should restrictions be placed on the information gathered by marketers? For instance, should marketers know what you read?

2 Do you think people should be asked if they want their names added to a database for marketing purposes or asked if the information can be sold to others?

Order Processing and Point-of-Sale Systems

Sales support systems help generate sales. But specialized systems actually take and process the order. **Order processing systems** translate the order into a list of products picked from the warehouse, a bill of lading for transportation routing, and finally delivery to the customer.

Point-of-sale (POS) systems are a special kind of order processing system that combines in a single transaction the placing of the order and its fulfillment. In a typical POS system, a customer brings a product to a checkout counter. A salesclerk uses a laser reader to read product information off a bar code on the product and records the sale. Information from the POS is fed directly to inventory control and, ultimately, the warehouse so that replacement products can be put on the shelf. In some cases, like Toys "Я" Us, the manufacturer of the product is informed by the POS of the sale and alerted automatically when new products should be shipped.

Credit Authorization Systems

If credit is involved in a sale—whether a credit card for an individual or a standing credit arrangement for firms—all orders must be checked by **a credit authorization system** before the transaction can be executed. Credit authorization systems contain data on the customer's credit history.

12.5 Human Resources Transaction Processing Systems

It may be true that without a sale, there is no business. But without the right people in the right place at the right time, there won't be any sales. All businesses have a human resources (HR) function or division: even very small businesses depend on their personnel.

Classic Problems and TPS Solutions

Figure 12.12 lists some classic human resources problems and the TPS used to solve them.

Human resources transaction processing systems deal with the basic employee information required by a firm for purposes of compensation, government reporting, internal management, and skill development.

Personnel and Applicant Record Systems

Personnel record systems provide the foundation for the firm by keeping information on the address, employment status, marital status, and family structure of all employees. **Applicant tracking systems** keep some of the same basic information for job applicants. Figure 12.13 illustrates a typical personnel record system.

Position Control Systems

Position control systems keep track of all the formal positions in a firm, including pay level. These systems are required so that the firm can keep control of its structure. For instance, a sudden doubling of the secretarial labor force should send personnel managers a signal that more attention should be paid to labor saving devices so that not so many secretaries are needed.

Human Resource Development Systems

In a knowledge- and information-based economy, the skills of employees will play a large role in how successful a business will be. **Human resource development systems** keep track of two pieces of information: current train-

Figure 12.12
Classic Human Resources Problems and TPS Solutions

Problem	Description	TPS Solution
Maintaining employee records	Keeping track of basic information on employees like name, address, marital status, dependents, age, and equal employment opportunity (EEO) category	Personnel record system
Maintaining information on job applicants	Keeping track of who applies for a job, both for internal purposes and for government employment regulations	Applicant tracking system
Maintaining information on positions in the firm	Keeping track of new opening positions in the firm as well as the overall structure of occupational positions	Position control system
Maintaining information on the skills and training of employees	Tracking training programs and employee skill levels; matching employees to right training program	Human resource development system
Maintaining information on employee benefits and compensation	Tracking salary, pension, medical, and other benefits	Benefit system

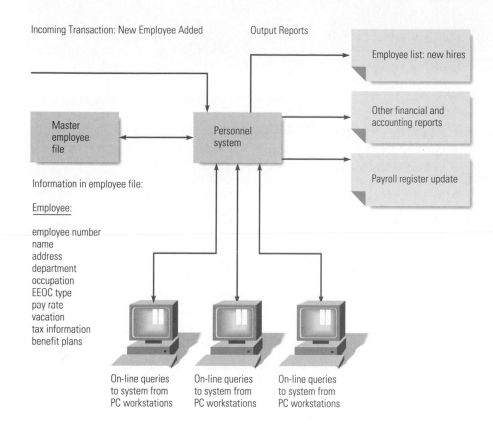

Incoming Transaction: New Employee Added

Output Reports

Master employee file

Personnel system

Employee list: new hires

Other financial and accounting reports

Payroll register update

Information in employee file:

Employee:

employee number
name
address
department
occupation
EEOC type
pay rate
vacation
tax information
benefit plans

On-line queries to system from PC workstations

On-line queries to system from PC workstations

On-line queries to system from PC workstations

Figure 12.13
A Personnel Record System
Personnel record systems help organizations keep track of important information about their employees. Some of the reports typically produced by a personnel record system include employee lists, financial and accounting reports, and payroll register updates. Some companies now allow their employees to get personnel-related questions answered directly through on-line access to the system.

ing programs available in the firm and the skill levels of existing employees. The purpose of these systems is to track the development of skill levels among employees, lay out a skill development track of course work and job experience, and then plan sufficient resources to train employees in the required skills.

In some instances, information technology can compensate for the absence of employee skills or long training programs. Mutual funds provide an example: many mutual funds rely on computer software to convince customers that a $30,000-a-year phone representative with a college degree provides the same quality advice as a $100,000-a-year personal stock broker at a brokerage firm. How do they do this?

Both Fidelity Mutual Funds (America's largest family of funds) and Merrill Lynch (one of the largest stock brokerages) have recently upgraded phone reps' terminals by providing a continually updated series of on-screen primers, help messages, and announcements to handle the most commonly asked questions (see photo). With a few clicks of the mouse, a phone rep can tell a customer about the latest actions of the Federal Reserve, the trade balance with Japan, the impact of new tax rules, or what is happening to the U.S. dollar in foreign markets.

In new systems being developed for its 2,000 phone reps, Fidelity is adding information on its customers' investment savvy and risk preferences. Phone reps will be able to adjust their investment advice to the level of sophistication and risk preference of their customer. Both Fidelity and Merrill

Telemarketers are frequently aided by information systems that give them on-screen prompts and help messages.

Source: David Young Wolff/Tony Stone Images.

The People Behind the Service

It's not known how many people work directly as salespeople in telemarketing, but Merrill Lynch and Fidelity Financial Services, the two largest telemarketers in the country, each recorded nine million calls last year. Telemarketing is definitely a growth area for sales because it uses telecommunications networks to rapidly sell products at a very low cost. Telemarketing has changed the nature of the financial services industry, replacing stockbrokers as the major sales force of stocks in the United States.

What's it like to be a telemarketer? T. Rowe Price Associates is a large mutual fund in Baltimore that uses 300 telemarketing reps to sell mutual fund shares. Sitting in a large, gray-carpeted room on the 10th floor of headquarters in Baltimore, the reps field over 100 calls a day. Each call is tape-recorded. The reps go through a five-week training period in a windowless room lined with desks and computer terminals. The instructor teaches them how to deal with difficult customers. Here's a typical problem call: "BEEP. This is Mr. Bronson, how may I help you?" An investor is calling and insists he did not invest in a mutual fund that has since plunged. Answer: "Would you like me to play back the tape of the call?" Or an investor calls and demands to talk with T. Rowe Price. Answer: "Sorry, Mr. Price is dead. Would you like to speak with a supervisor?"

Supervisors can listen to all calls without the knowledge of the rep. This is to maintain quality and to judge the reps on a four-point scale. The number of calls a rep takes, the number of hours a rep's terminal is being used, and the number of calls made are all recorded.

Most telemarketers at Price are college grads and make in the low to mid-20s. The firm offers the possibility of moving up in the company to a higher-level position. This chance to "move up" makes many consider the telemarketing floor at Price one of the best places to work in Baltimore.

Source: Based on Myerson, Allen R., "The Voice Is Friendly, the Job Hectic," *New York Times*, April 3, 1993.

Critical Thinking Questions

1 What kinds of marketing problems does a telemarketing system solve?

2 Would you trust the advice of a telemarketer from Price?

3 How would you feel about a supervisor monitoring your phone conversations with customers?

---

plan to enable phone reps to do what full-service personal brokers do, but in far less time and with at least equal skill.[6] The story "The People Behind the Service" describes what it's like to be a phone representative/telemarketer.

Benefit Systems

Benefit systems are among the most complex personnel systems. They must keep track of the myriad benefit programs in a firm as well as how often each employee has used his or her benefits. Benefit systems, for instance, keep track of medical, dental, and optical benefit programs, as well as retirement and pension plans. In some firms, salaries and wages are considered a part of the accounting function (controlled by the treasurer), but in other firms, employee compensation is handled by an integrated human resources benefit system.

A contemporary human resources information system can be found at Applied Materials Inc. in Santa Clara, California, a maker of wafer fabrication systems. A modern twist to the Applied Materials human resources system is an *employee self-service feature* that gives users direct access to the HR system via information kiosks, telephone, or a desktop PC. Employees typically have numerous questions about their benefit plans, like how much money is in their pension plan, what is the limit on medical deductions for

The Changing Face of Government

In what is probably the largest TPS in the United States (if not the world), the Social Security Administration (SSA) administers the government's pension program for over 130 million Americans who contribute to the Retirement and Survivors Insurance (RSI) program. Each month, about 50 million checks are mailed out to beneficiaries. Each year, SSA pays out $170 billion, sends out 10 million new social security cards, receives 350 million wage statements, and handles 120 million bills and queries from insurance companies and individuals.

Individuals contribute to social security for their entire working life. SSA must keep records of this. Until recently, it took four to six months to find out how much you had contributed to SSA and how much your income would be if you retired.

In 1982, SSA began rebuilding its antiquated computer system under what it called the Systems Modernization Program (SMP). A visit to a social security center in your neighborhood will show you the results of $1 billion in expenditures. You can now sit down in an office with an SSA rep who can call up on a computer screen your history of contributions and give you a precise description of your benefits. You can also request an earnings statement by calling a national 800 number. In a few weeks, you will receive a complete statement showing your contributions, predicted retirement income, predicted survivor benefit if your spouse should die, and your disability payment should you become disabled.

During the 10-year period of systems modernization, the SSA reduced the number of its employees by one-third (about 25,000). However, this did not happen as a natural result of modernization or computers: the president and Congress demanded SSA reduce its labor force by this amount during the 1980s. The modernization program has not been without pitfalls for employees. When you visit a local SSA office, take a

SSA's Systems Modernization Program included the development of a computer-based on-line help facility that answers millions of citizens' calls each year.

Source: Bob Daemmrich/Stock Boston.

careful look at how hard people are working, the condition of the office, and the lines of people seeking help. In some offices, working conditions have deteriorated.

Critical Thinking Questions

1 What are some of the components that make the information systems described in this story possible?

2 Based on your reading in this chapter, how could the SSA further improve its service to the public?

surgery, or what is the deductible amount on dental expenditures. In the past, human resources employees would field these questions, but today many HR systems provide employees with the electronic tools to find their own answers.

Human resources systems are, of course, found in government also. One of the oldest and most elaborate is the U.S. government's social security pension system. Created in 1932 by President Franklin Roosevelt, the Social Security Administration supports 50 million pensioners and beneficiaries, as described in the story "The Changing Face of Government."

Summary

Basic Business Concepts

- Business inherently involves transactions: buying and selling. Transaction processing systems (TPS) are those that keep track of these basic business events.

- The purpose of a business is to make a profit, to sell goods and services for a price greater than the cost of making or providing them.

- There are three types of firms: manufacturing, service, and information based.

- There are five functions in a business firm: production (operations), accounting and finance, marketing and sales, human resources, and information systems.

- Firms are structured hierarchically, with those at top having more authority and responsibility.

- Firms are made up of managers, information workers, and production workers.

- The value chain is a set of steps that transforms raw inputs to salable products and services. This includes sales, marketing, and after-sale service and support.

- Information systems play a vital role in increasing the productivity of firms and in achieving a strategic competitive advantage.

- Each functional area of a business has its own transaction processing systems.

- TPS can be either on-line or batch, centralized or decentralized.

Production and Operations Transaction Processing Systems

- Production control systems use information technology to control purchasing, scheduling, and shipping of goods and services.

- Process control systems use information technology to control machinery and the quality of machine output.

- CAD/CAM systems use information technology to design and then manufacture parts or entire assembled products.

- MRP systems integrate production control and process control with financial information into a single manufacturing system.

- EDI systems involve the establishment of electronic links between firms that have a customer–supplier relationship.

Accounting and Finance Transaction Processing Systems

- Accounting systems track the flow of funds in a firm. Financial systems manage the available funds of a firm, seeking to maximize the return on funds.

- Accounts receivable systems monitor the funds owed to the firm, whereas accounts payable systems monitor the funds that the firm owes to others. Payroll systems are a kind of accounts payable. Together, these systems form the basis for a general ledger system, a large checkbook for a firm.

- Financial systems manage the cash and credit of a firm and seek to optimize the use of the firm's financial assets.

▶ Trading systems are transaction systems used by firms to trade securities.

Marketing and Sales Transaction Processing Systems

▶ Customer identification systems are used to identify the name, location, and tastes of consumers.

▶ Sales support systems keep track of prospects and customers, and help sales personnel follow up after the sale.

▶ Order processing and point-of-sale systems take the customer's order and assure that a product is delivered from the warehouse and/or that the inventory is updated automatically after a sale.

▶ Credit authorization systems are used to identify customers and establish their credit limits.

Human Resources Transaction Processing Systems

▶ Personnel record systems provide the foundation for a firm by keeping track of basic information on employees and applicants.

▶ Position control systems monitor and plan the formal positions in a firm.

▶ Human resource development systems keep track of employee skills as well as available training courses and materials.

▶ Benefit systems are used to track and manage complex benefit packages such as pension, medical, and related benefit programs.

Key Terms

transaction processing system
  (TPS)
manufacturing firms
service firms
business function
value chain
productivity
competitive advantage
on-line transaction processing
  systems
batch transaction processing systems
distributed systems
centralized systems
fault tolerant systems
purchasing management systems
job scheduling systems
inventory control systems
shipping management systems
process control systems
quality control systems
computer-aided design (CAD)
computer-aided manufacturing
  (CAM)

manufacturing resource planning
  (MRP) systems
accounts receivable systems
accounts payable systems
payroll systems
general ledger systems
cash management systems
credit management systems
financial accounting systems
securities trading systems
automatic data retrieval systems
sales support systems
telemarketing systems
order processing systems
point-of-sale (POS) systems
credit authorization systems
personnel record systems
applicant tracking systems
position control systems
human resource development
  systems
benefit systems

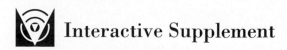 Interactive Supplement

Review Questions

1 How might the Fed Ex kiosks give Fed Ex a competitive advantage over other package delivery services?

2 Give five examples of a business transaction.

3 What are the main functions in a business? How is a business usually organized or structured?

4 What is a value chain?

5 How can information technologies be used in the value chain to increase competitiveness or productivity?

6 What is the strategic role of information?

7 Identify and describe four classic problems in production and their TPS solutions.

8 Identify and describe four classic problems in accounting and finance and their TPS solutions.

9 Identify and describe four classic problems in marketing and sales and their TPS solutions.

10 Identify and describe four classic problems in human resources and their TPS solutions.

11 Give three examples of how marketers find out who you are and where you live.

Problem-Solving and Skill-Building Exercises

1 Identify a value chain on your campus (or at your place of work), and describe how information technologies might be used to achieve gains in productivity. The library is a value chain, for instance. Put your results in the form of a report, poster, or overhead for class presentation.

2 With a small group of students, arrange to visit a local factory or office, and report back to the class on the use of transaction processing systems.

3 Identify several local or nationally known firms that use information technology in the form of transaction processing systems to attract customers. Write a short report analyzing the effectiveness of the different systems.

PERSONAL TECHNOLOGY

Keeping Track of Your Personal Transactions

This chapter described business transactions and the systems that keep track of transactions from production to human resources. But what about your personal transactions? What kinds of options are available to you?

First, think about the kinds of transactions you would like to track. Here's some different types: financial (checks and cash payments); important calendar events; names, addresses, and phone numbers of people and businesses with whom you have transactions; important accounts or other numbers, memos to yourself or others, letters, and of course phone messages. As this brief list suggests, there may not be just one solution to the problem of keeping track of your transactions.

Often what comes to mind is a generic solution like a spreadsheet program or database program. Lotus 1-2-3, Microsoft Excel, or Borland's Quattro Pro are all excellent for keeping track of financial transactions like checks, payments, and income. These spreadsheet programs can also do some limited tracking of data records like names, addresses, and phone numbers but they lack the ability to keep track of memos, letters, or phone messages.

Database packages for PCs and the Macintosh are excellent at tracking personal records, like names and information about people and businesses with whom you have transactions. But these systems are usually difficult to use and are not good at tracking financial flows. The desktop organizers and personal information managers described in Chapter 11 are another software option.

If portability is important, consider one of the new hand-held personal organizers like the Sharp Wizard or the Radio Shack Personal Organizer. Selling in the range of $100–$300, these systems provide very specific solutions to tracking your transactions. The advantage of these systems is that they fit into your pocket, require no external power source, and are available with sufficient memory to store calendar events and name and address information. Some, like the Sharp Wizard, have the ability to write short memos and outlines of speeches or papers. For the most part, however, these organizers do not have the power to keep track of all your transactions like telephone calls and financial information. Another disadvantage of these systems is that you cannot customize how they work, as you can with the more generic software solutions described previously, like Lotus or Quattro Pro.

Sometime in the 1990s, small very portable organizers like the Apple Newton may come close to providing all you need to organize personal transactions. At least that's what Apple and others that offer similar systems are hoping. Although still in its infancy, the technology behind Newton and other personal digital assistants should ultimately enable a hand-held, palm-size system to act as your communications link with the telephone system, tracking and recording incoming and outgoing calls; keep a record of letters you send from your word processor (with which it will be able to communicate); and track your financial transactions with a built-in spreadsheet program that can also interact with your desktop spreadsheet.

Until these powerful personal organizers become widespread (and hopefully inexpensive) we will all have to rely on a jumble of different software packages that do not communicate with each other. And as a last resort most of us will continue to keep a little black book of truly important names, dates, and transactions.

Notes

1   **Bartholomew, Doug,** "Arm in Arm With Technology, *Information Week,* April 27, 1992.

2   **Ingrassia, Lawrence,** "The Cutting Edge," *Wall Street Journal,* April 6, 1992.

3   **Bartholomew, Doug,** "Sweet Dreams For Brach IS, " *Information Week,* November 18, 1991.

4   **Wilke, John,** "Supercomputers Manage Holiday Stock," *Wall Street Journal,* December 23, 1992.

5   **Krass, Peter,** "Frito-Lay Cashes Chips," *Information Week,* February 10, 1992.

6   **Anders, George,** "PCs Bring Savvy to Mutual-Fund Reps," *Wall Street Journal,* November 30, 1992.

Chapter 13 contains:

Nissan Brings the Market to the Plant

After completing this chapter, you will:

▶ Understand the role of managers in organizations.

▶ Know how managers use information technology to achieve their own and their organization's goals.

▶ Be aware of the major trends in management support systems.

▶ Understand the role of information workers in business and other organizations.

▶ Know how information workers use information technology.

Management Support and Knowledge Work Systems

Nissan Brings the Market to the Plant

The world's fourth largest auto manufacturer, Nissan Motor Co., faced its first financial losses in the U.S. market in 1993, along with a 20 percent decline in revenue in Japan. Losing $178 million in a year for this $48-billion company was more a test of management skill than a real threat to the survival of the company. In previous years, Nissan could always count on customers buying whatever was produced at its Smyrna, Tennessee, or Japanese factories and on customers' willingness to accept long delays when ordering special colors or features. Now, for the first time, Nissan faced much tougher competition in world markets, especially in the United States, where domestic car makers were making high-quality cars for less money.

Here are some of the problems that Nissan's managers faced: overall U.S. sales were down; some cars in hot demand could not be found anywhere in the United States or were not being manufactured, whereas other, slow-moving cars sat on dealers' lots. Customers could not obtain cars with the colors they wanted. What would you do with problems like these?

Nissan built a new management support system that would more closely link dealers and regional and national sales managers with the factory. The goal was to improve service to the customer (and to the dealer) by making it easier for Nissan to produce the right product at the right time and deliver it to the right dealer.

Nissan's first step was to create a dealer order entry and management system named MAPS 90—the Market-driven Allocation and Production System for the 1990s—based in Carson City, California. Each of Nissan's 1,200 dealers are connected to the national headquarters' mainframe computers using Tymenet (a private wide area network). Every 30 days the dealer must submit an order declaring what cars he or she wants in the next 90 days. This way the cars actually on the dealer's lot reflect local demand much better.

Plant production managers are also connected to the system. They can now track the changing mix of cars ordered and adjust production to demand each day. With the new system, both Smyrna and Japanese plants can re-

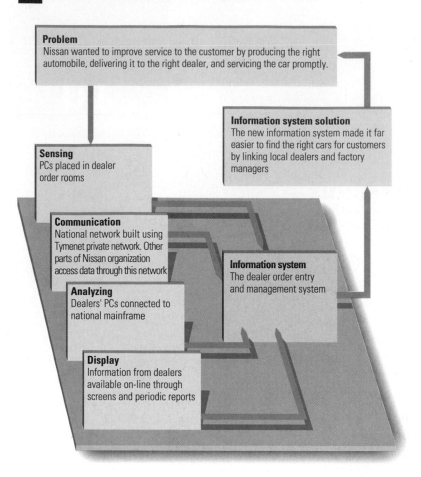

Problem
Nissan wanted to improve service to the customer by producing the right automobile, delivering it to the right dealer, and servicing the car promptly.

Information system solution
The new information system made it far easier to find the right cars for customers by linking local dealers and factory managers

Sensing
PCs placed in dealer order rooms

Communication
National network built using Tymenet private network. Other parts of Nissan organization access data through this network

Information system
The dealer order entry and management system

Analyzing
Dealers' PCs connected to national mainframe

Display
Information from dealers available on-line through screens and periodic reports

---

spond to customer order changes as late as ten days prior to the date of manufacture.

In the past, it was very difficult and time consuming for dealers to find cars they wanted. Where's a black, two-door Altima with stereo cassette FM? With the new system, each of the ten ports of entry can verify whether it has such a car at the port and guarantee delivery within two days from the time the order is placed on the dealer order entry system.

Nissan is looking forward to two new applications in 1994. A customer database is being developed in Carson City, California. Information from local dealers, purchasers of cars and services, and even people who just walk into the showroom will be recorded on a main national customer database. This information will be used for marketing, recall, and safety update bulletins. A second application will focus on parts management. In the past, it could take weeks to find the right parts at a dealer. By 1994 Nissan will be shipping 95 percent of the parts ordered by dealers on the same day they are ordered. Once this database is developed, it will be possible for the management system to predict what parts dealers need and ship them before they are ordered. That way, customers will not have any waiting time for parts.

Source: Based on Bartholomew, Doug, "Preventive Maintenance," *Informationweek,* February 1, 1993.

With Nissan's new Market-driven Allocation and Production System, MAPS 90, plant production can be adjusted to demand each day, allowing Nissan to respond more quickly to customer orders.

Source: Stacy Pick/Stock Boston.

13.1 Managing a Business

In Chapter 12, we described the basic business organization as being made up of layers: operations and production people, information workers, and managers. We described how a business could be seen as a *value chain* in which raw inputs are transformed into high-value outputs as they move through the production and distribution process. The overall goals of business are to make a profit and to survive in a competitive environment. In Chapter 12, we also showed you how information technology supports the basic transactions that go on in any business organization's value chain. In addition, we pointed out that information technology helps businesses design and carry out a *strategy*, a planned set of actions to achieve profitable results. These two concepts—value chain and strategy—play an important role in this chapter as well.

In this chapter, we focus on managers and information workers by describing what they do and how they do it. This will help you understand their information needs and how information technology can be used to fulfill those needs.

What Is Management?

Management is universal: it's virtually impossible to find an organization, however small, that does not have someone designated as a manager. Large businesses have hundreds of managers. In the United States, 15 percent of the labor force—some 17 million people—work as managers. They are among the highest paid people in the country. But what do managers do? What is a manager, what do they manage, and how do they manage it?

In popular magazines, management has been described as being similar to leading an orchestra, getting things done through other people, and making the most rational use of scarce resources. All these phrases are true but are inadequate to describe all the diverse activities of managers. Managers ultimately are the people in charge; they make the important decisions. Figure 13.1 describes some typical activities of managers.

The first and perhaps most important activity of managers is to *create or approve the products and services* that the business will sell at a profit. Of course, in this effort, managers are aided by scientists, researchers, engineers, and other professionals, but it is ultimately a management decision to go into specific business areas, to develop specific products or services. Second, managers *plan the business:* they establish the goals and then define the actual steps to be taken in achieving the goals. Third, managers play a very important role in *organizing and designing the specific jobs* or tasks that make up the

Activity	Example
Creating	Create or approve new or existing products
Planning	Develop strategies and tactics for the future
Organizing	Establish who will do what, where, when, and how
Controlling	Monitor and supervise the activities of others
Coordinating	Coordinate the work of various individuals
Deciding	Make decisions about work, people, technology, and organization

Figure 13.1
Traditional Management Activities

value chain. Who does what, where, when, and how is an important management activity.

Once the business is established, managers must control the value chain and related activities. Managers supervise other workers who actually do the work, and they review reports and other information on the work of others. Based on the information they receive, managers *coordinate the work* of others and *make decisions* about a host of problems that arise in the day-to-day life of a business.

Types of Management Decisions

Managers face three types of decisions. Some decisions are **structured** and routine. For instance, when sales of a particular product are often greater than supply on hand, it makes sense to increase production to meet demand. Or if a job applicant does not have the required skills for a computer programmer position, that person should not be hired. Other decisions are totally **unstructured.** For instance, should a company follow its competitors into a new line of business or stick with its traditional products and services? Does a particular job applicant have the right personality for a sales position? Still other decisions are **semistructured.** For instance, how many cars should a car rental firm allocate to Chicago in the first week of December given an unusually large schedule of business conventions? Or given a lowering in interest rates, a decline in real hourly wages, and an increase in new housing starts, how many board feet of lumber should be cut by a lumber mill in Oregon? Semistructured problems contain aspects that can easily be predicted, but they also contain aspects that require the exercise of judgment. As you'll see, information systems are quite good at helping managers cope with structured and semistructured decisions, and they are becoming more helpful for unstructured decisions.

Working with others, in a variety of different capacities, is one of the most important parts of a manager's job.

Source: Superstock.

Levels of Management

In most business organizations, you will find three **levels of management** that correspond roughly to the different kinds of decisions made by managers (see Figure 13.2).

Senior managers are concerned primarily with long-term issues of business growth and development. Generally, the problems they face are unstructured and require a great deal of outside information and communication with other organizations and managers. Middle managers are concerned with implementing the strategy of senior management, tactics of

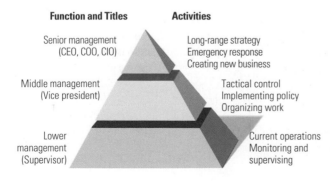

Function and Titles	Activities
Senior management (CEO, COO, CIO)	Long-range strategy / Emergency response / Creating new business
Middle management (Vice president)	Tactical control / Implementing policy / Organizing work
Lower management (Supervisor)	Current operations / Monitoring and supervising

Figure 13.2
Levels of Management

In most organizations, you will find three levels of management arranged hierarchically with responsibility, authority, and rewards increasing as you go up the hierarchy. Senior managers are responsible for long-range strategy, tactical response to threatening emergencies, and approving new lines of business. Middle managers are more concerned with tactical short-term problems, and controlling and implementing policy. Lower-level managers (supervisors) usually are concerned with day-to-day, current operations and coordinating work on a daily basis.

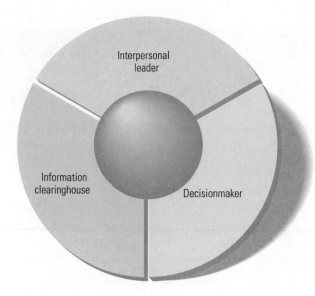

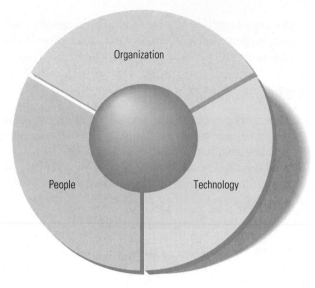

Figure 13.3
Three Related Management Roles
Interpersonal leader: motivate, counsel, advise, and support employees
Information clearinghouse: monitor, disseminate, and analyze information through voice, digital, and interpersonal communications
Decisionmaker: handle disturbances and emergencies, make decisions about new products, allocate resources, and negotiate with outside suppliers

Figure 13.4
The Manager's Areas of Concern
Managers have to be concerned about three areas of the business and be able to make decisions in each area. Managers must understand how to motivate and organize people into an effective unit. They must understand how to organize workflows and departments, as well as how to integrate contemporary technology into the organization.

operation, and controlling the organization by making sure it is performing according to plan, as well as handling exceptions to the plan. *Lower-level managers,* or supervisors, provide the hands-on, daily and hourly control and decisionmaking necessary to conduct day-to-day operations. These differences in management levels shape the different kinds of management support systems discussed later in this chapter.

Management Roles

Figure 13.1 lists several management tasks—things managers are responsible for and are expected to do. But it says little about how managers do those tasks or what managers manage. Managers are not just machines that make decisions, they are human beings making decisions about other humans. Contemporary research has identified three important **management roles** that managers play (see Figure 13.3).

Perhaps the most important role of a manager is as an *interpersonal leader* who presides at ceremonies, motivates subordinates to work, and maintains links with the community, including labor unions, politicians, and competitors. A second role is that of *information clearinghouse*. A manager is supposed to monitor the organization's performance by collecting information and analyzing it, disseminate information to those who need it, and act as spokesperson to the outside world. Last, a manager is expected to be a *decisionmaker*. Besides deciding about new products, employees, and future actions, the manager is expected to handle disturbances, allocate resources, and negotiate conflicts.

You should now be starting to see that the manager's job is very complex and involves managing three different areas of business: people, organization, and technology (see Figure 13.4). These are the critical ingredients in a business that determine if the value chain will actually work.

A Day in the Life of a Manager

What's it like to be a manager? You might have the impression that managers come to work, turn on a computer, and just read reports and use E-mail to control the organization and develop new strategies. Nothing could be further from the truth. Here's a glimpse of several managers on a typical day:

7:45 Jack Emery arrives at his office, unpacks his briefcase, turns on his PC, and looks over his To-Do list. Joanne Wilson, another executive, arrives at the same time.

8:00 Jack and Joanne go over their agenda for a 9:00 A.M. meeting they will have with marketing personnel concerning a new product. Jack and Joanne share stories about the weekend, discuss Mother's Day gifts, and summer vacation plans.

8:45 John Anderson, a subordinate middle manager, arrives to discuss with Joanne the slides for the 9:00 A.M. meeting. The slides need some correcting, so they both work feverishly for 15 minutes on Joanne's PC trying to correct the problems.

9:00 The meeting with marketing begins on a sour note: the slides are not ready yet. Conversation shifts to spreadsheets provided by marketing that show expected sales for the new product will probably exceed plans.

11:00 Joanne's and Jack's boss, vice president Harrison Williams, shows up unexpectedly to go over the results of the meeting.

11:15 Joanne has a meeting with production. They are not sure they can meet enlarged production schedules but will contact suppliers to check on the availability of additional supplies should they be needed.

1:00 After a lunch at her desk, Joanne and Jack go into another meeting with marketing to talk about the marketing plan and discuss changes in the sales force.

2:00 Jack talks with his secretary and discovers that her mother is in the hospital. He calls a florist to send some flowers to his secretary's mother.

2:15 Joanne reviews the sales figures from last month and is disappointed to learn that sales in Los Angeles were less than expected. She puts a call in to the regional sales manager for Los Angeles.

3:00 Jack and Joanne meet privately to discuss marketing and production problems and some likely solutions. They both work on a spreadsheet to do some what-if scenarios with production and marketing.

4:00 Joanne takes a call from a friend and then another from a manager in personnel to discuss staffing problems in Joanne's office.

5:00 Jack has 15 calls on his voice mail and 12 E-mail messages. He begins responding.

6:00 Jack and Joanne feel somewhat drained, but both must go to a corporate party in the lobby for a departing secretary who has been with the company 30 years.

About 75 percent of a manager's time is spent in meetings, both planned and unplanned.

Source: Michael L. Abramson/Woodfin Camp & Associates.

From this brief account, you can see that managers spend a lot of time talking to people one on one, or in meetings. Management is inherently a team effort. About 50 percent of a manager's time is spent in planned meetings, another 25 percent in unplanned meetings. A large part of these meetings involves analyzing charts, data, and other computer output. Electronic communications—E-mail and voice mail—take up about 15 percent of a manager's time. Only about 10 percent of a manager's time is spent working alone in his or her office. Although electronic communications and other forms of information technology can help make a manager more productive, in some instances they can create a problem: too much information. The story "Dealing with Too Much Information" describes this problem and some computer-based solutions.

How Managers Use Information Technology

Given the complexity of the manager's job, and the large part played by information and communication, there are a number of ways in which information technology can help.

One way in which information technology supports managers is through a number of different kinds of reporting and analytic systems loosely called **management support systems.** There are three kinds of management support systems, each distinguished by the type of decision and management level it supports (see Figure 13.5).

An **executive information system (EIS)** supports the senior management of a firm and the strategic planning function. Senior executives need information on changing government policies, demographics, the actions of competitors, and changing market conditions now and in the future. An EIS can deliver news, reports prepared by external services, broad overviews of

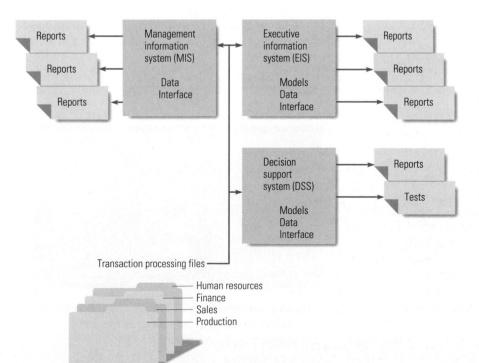

Figure 13.5
Three Types of Management Support Systems
Information from transaction processing systems feeds into three different types of management support systems: management information systems, executive information systems, and decision support systems. Each type of system uses the data it receives in a different manner, in accordance with the different levels of management it is designed to support.

The information era, which began with the PC in 1980, has created an embarrassment of riches and exposed the Achilles heel of the information revolution. Information has become so cheap that it is no longer in short supply, and it is beginning to overwhelm the decision-making and analytic powers of organizations and their managers.

There are now more than 5,000 on-line public databases used primarily by business and more than 5 million E-mail users at U.S. corporations. E-mail message traffic is doubling every four years in the United States. What this translates into for the average manager is a huge information headache: there is now more information than can be assimilated and so much information that a manager can easily be diverted from more important tasks simply sorting the mail. Some managers report receiving more than 50 phone calls a day and over 100 E-mail messages. The old etiquette said you should respond when phoned, right? But this may have to change.

Management experts are worried. Peter Drucker, a professor of management, argues that 99 percent of information important to a manager comes from outside the organization. Information on threats, opportunities, competitors, and major changes in the business climate all come from outside the organization. This outside information cannot be cut off without destroying the organization.

Information managers believe it is their job to bring all this outside information inside by subscribing to data services, news services, and E-mail networks. A business consultant, Robert Theobald, argues that "we're still hung up on the concept that information is wonderful. One hundred years ago we did not have much information. Now we have too much." Theobald believes that computers have created more work and more stress for managers by speeding up the flow of information and the pace of the workday. To survive, Theobald advocates a strong human perspective and thinking small. We need a new etiquette: a response to every message is not necessary.

Software firms are coming to the rescue. One idea is electronic filters that identify key topics. Desktop Data of Waltham, Massachusetts, makes a product called NewsEdge that sorts through 200,000 articles a day looking for the ones you want. AT&T's Bell Labs markets a software package called RightPages that searches 30 medical journals for researchers at the University of California at San Francisco. Whenever an article of interest is found in a new journal issue, RightPages informs the user via E-mail.

In some cases, firms hire other firms to preprocess electronic information, checking it for relevance and processing before it is loaded into a company's computers and disseminated. Texaco's Exploration Producing Technology department, for instance, hires outside data vendors to sift through raw petroleum industry data. In the future, it may be necessary for managers to hire clerical workers to read the E-mail, faxes, voice mail, and other electronic messages.

Sources: Based on Bozman, Jean S., "Grow with the Information Flow," *Computerworld,* May 3, 1993; Caldwell, Bruce, "The Answers Are Blowin' in the Wind." *Informationweek,* March 22, 1993.

Critical Thinking Questions

1 What suggestions can you come up with for reducing the flow of E-mail traffic within an organization?

2 What management roles might be enhanced by the rapid growth of electronic information, and which roles might be diminished?

---

the performance of the company, and in some cases, permit senior executives to "drill down" into the company to discover how the numbers were produced, who was responsible for certain actions, and who might have an answer to a problem.

A **management information system (MIS)** supports middle managers whose job is to control the operations of the company on a daily, monthly, and quarterly basis. An MIS can produce scheduled summary reports, exception reports, and in some cases, on-line ad hoc reports (see Figure 13.6).

A **decision support system (DSS)** supports middle management and information workers who need assistance with semistructured problems. A DSS usually contains analytic models that

Comshare Inc.'s Commander EIS is an example of packaged EIS software. Such software can be used to create customized, yet standardized EIS applications for an organization.

Source: Courtesy of Comshare, Inc.

```
Monthly Sales By Product

Month: June 30, 1994

Product Code        Description        QTY        Revenue
5-7569              Jean pants         1523       $45,690
5-6321              Jean shorts        2590       $64,750
5-4634              Jean blouse        1700       $40,800

Stock Out Report Date: June 30, 1994

Product Code    Description    Vendor        Available
5-8934          Tube socks     Burlington    7/30
5-7632          Suspenders     Johnson       7/15
5-1289          Tie pins       Bosewell      8/1

On-Line Query

Q: Sales of orange sport shirts in White Plains N.Y.?

Product Code        Description        QTY        Revenue
5-5390              Orange shirt       30         $900
```

Figure 13.6
Typical MIS Reports
Management information systems produce reports used by managers to control daily, weekly, and monthly operations. Routine summary reports describe ongoing activities, and exception reports focus on deviations from a plan. On-line query reports respond to a manager's ad hoc inquiries.

permit the user to simulate the business and to understand how to react to a change in business conditions.

In addition to the three management support systems, managers benefit from less structured systems that support the communication, information, and knowledge-generating roles of managers. These knowledge work systems support groups and teams of managers. (We discuss these kinds of systems in the section "The Role of Information Workers in Business.")

Let's take a look at a real-world management support system at Kmart, one of the leading retailers in the United States. As you will see, the Kmart system includes EIS, MIS, and DSS components.

13.2   A Contemporary Management Support System: Retail Automation at Kmart

Kmart Corporation is the second largest retailer in the United States, just behind Wal-Mart, with $35 billion in gross revenues in 1992. Kmart is believed to be one of the country's most efficient retailers in terms of sales per square foot (the standard industry measure). One secret of Kmart's success is a history of very precise marketing systems that ensure just-in-time delivery of products to each of its 2,400 stores. Kmart's Retail Automation System cost a cool $1 billion and is the engine of Kmart's spectacular growth. Here's how it works (see Figure 13.7).

Kmart uses satellite dishes atop each store to transmit daily sales information to a mainframe at central headquarters.

Source: Courtesy of Kmart Corporation.

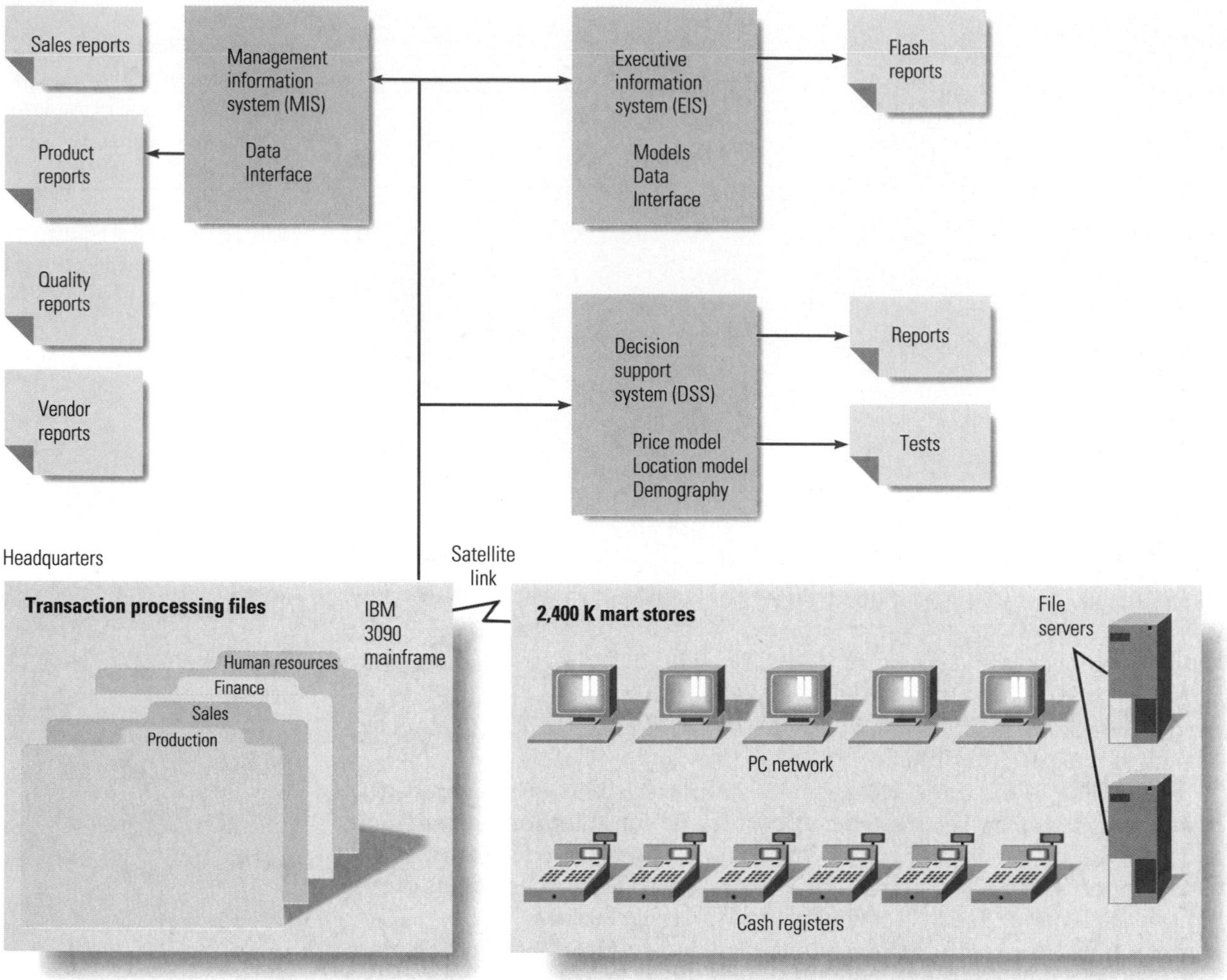

Figure 13.7
Kmart's Retail Automation System
Kmart's Retail Automation System provides an interesting example of how transaction processing systems support MIS, EIS, and DSS.

First, Kmart installed a local area network in each of its stores and connected all the cash registers to the network, which was controlled by two PCs acting as file servers and controllers. Each cash register was equipped with a handheld laser scanner to read price and inventory data at checkout, and all products were bar coded with prices and vendor information. From the beginning of the project, Kmart worked with Electronic Data Systems (EDS) of Dallas, Texas, a systems integrator that advised Kmart on technology, organization, and people issues during the project. Systems integrators are outside contractors that work with business firms to pull all the many pieces of systems together and help manage large projects.

Next, each store was equipped with a small satellite dish that, at the end of each day, transmitted summary sales information to a mainframe computer at headquarters (see photo). Because over 100,000 items are sold by Kmart, this resulted in a huge flood of data that was difficult to handle at first.

The incoming transaction data was loaded into several transaction database files at headquarters: a sales file, a store file (information on each store), and a vendor file. From here, software was written that became the basis of the management information system. The MIS produces summary and exception reports for product managers, sales managers, purchase managers, and quality control managers. In addition to summary reports, the MIS can produce on-line query reports. Want to know how well Nintendo games are selling in Dallas compared to other major cities in Texas? No problem. A

Sales personnel at Kmart
use handheld scanners to
gather data on Kmart's
floor inventory.

Source: Courtesy of Symbol
Technologies, Inc.

query to the MIS will produce a report showing total Nintendo product sales
(computers plus peripherals) in all major metropolitan regions of Texas
rank-ordered by size of the region (or any other rank order chosen) in just a
few minutes.

An EIS was also built to supply information to senior executives. Called
Flash Reports, these are a number of predefined reports that senior managers can call up from their desktops or laptop portables. Several hundred
reports are now routine, including previous days sales, sales by region,
planned sales (overall and by region), sales for any specific product type or
item, and anticipated sales by week, month, or year under varying assumptions of sales growth entered by the user. The EIS component also permits
access to external databases and news services.

Although the MIS and EIS reports fulfill management's need for routine
information to control the corporation, other managers use a decision support system (DSS) to interactively work with the data and the stores to advance sales at a tactical level.

In one Christmas season, porcelain dolls were not selling well at $29.88.
Typically, store managers drop prices in half on poor-selling merchandise,
surrendering profits but at least recovering the purchase price. This can
cause a loss of millions, perhaps billions, of dollars for stores as big as
Kmart. Kmart's DSS-based managers decided to drop the price to $24.88 to
see what would happen. How? They simply entered a new bar code price
into the mainframe sales database, sent this information to 2,400 store file
servers in one night, and the price changed across the country within 24
hours.

Result: sales skyrocketed. So the managers raised the price back to
$29.88. Result: sales dropped dramatically. On the third try, the sales man-
agers dropped the price to $26.49, and sales resumed at a brisk pace. Result:
Kmart managers were able to fine-tune the price of the product to ensure it
sold out completely by Christmas at a profit. The overall result was major
savings to Kmart through avoidance of excessive markdowns.[1]

The Flow of Information in Kmart's MSS

Let's trace the flow of information through the system. Kmart's MIS obtains information from a transaction processing system. The TPS begins at the cash register and extends into corporate headquarters. From this TPS foundation, the MIS and EIS systems take summary information.

The MIS processes the information by summarizing the transaction data and producing predefined summary and exception reports on a daily basis. The MIS also can respond to ad hoc queries from managers at all levels. Transaction data is also summarized and delivered to the DSS system where managers use a variety of analytic models to fine-tune marketing processes, and the EIS system where senior managers monitor the company's overall performance.

Significance for Managers and Business

What does Kmart's MSS do for Kmart and its managers? The main benefits for Kmart are an avoidance of excessive markdowns on products, faster customer checkouts, and far better control of inventory. Other benefits would include the reduction of "stock outs," where a product is unavailable due to unanticipated demand, and the intangible benefit of being able to fine-tune the marketing strategy to daily changes in market conditions. The MSS also gives Kmart a temporary strategic advantage over its competitors. It can achieve higher sales per square foot and per employee. It may take competitors several years to imitate Kmart's systems. By this time, Kmart may be able to develop even more advanced systems.

For Kmart's managers, the MSS provides several benefits. It is now far easier for senior management to consider new products and services, and to plan for the future. Middle managers find the new system increases their control over the day-to-day operations and helps them organize the flow of products and work in the company. Product managers find it easier to coordinate tactics at a national level and make precise decisions about products and prices.

Trends: Does Technology Lead to Fewer Managers?

The Kmart story illustrates many trends in business information systems and the organization of businesses in general. Let's explore some of these trends.

▶ **A reduction of managers and clerical workers.** For much of the 1980s, when investment in information technology skyrocketed, employment of managers and clerical workers also skyrocketed. In the recession of the late 1980s and early 1990s, however, managers and clerical workers were laid off in record numbers for the first time in U.S. history. But even as businesses start to recover, they are not rehiring many clerical and management employees. It is conceivable that information technology will displace many lower-level management and clerical workers of all kinds as offices become more automated. A true test of this idea will come during periods of rapid economic expansion when businesses typically add workers rapidly to keep up with demand.

▶ **More system integrators.** Large-scale projects like Kmart's are frequently too large for any one company to build by itself. Some systems require special expertise and a temporary large increase in management talent. **System integrators** like EDS, Andersen Consulting, and IBM provide planning, coordinating, scheduling, management, installing, and testing services to other firms that are building systems. You can think of these firms as large-scale temporary help providers.

▶ **More client/server computing.** In the past, large-scale applications operated exclusively on mainframe computers, to which were connected thousands of dumb terminals (keyboards and screens). All the work was done on the mainframe, which could be thousands of miles away. This required an expensive telecommunications network. As you learned in Chapter 6, with **client/server computing,** the workload is split between desktop or laptop PCs (the "clients"), where most of the work is done, and a server computer (often another PC with a big, fast disk drive), which simply stores software and files. The client/server arrangement requires a local area network to connect the clients and the server. This style of computing is much cheaper (about one quarter the cost) than mainframe computing.

▶ **Continuing use of mainframes.** Mainframes are still used to store huge, nationwide data files at central headquarters and as a communications switch routing messages and data around the company. However, even here the mainframes of old are being replaced by much cheaper arrays of workstations and minicomputers.

▶ **Downsizing.** The movement of corporations from large mainframe-based systems to smaller and cheaper client/server systems is called **downsizing,** or rightsizing. The idea is to move the computing resource closer to the worker or manager and to "empower" the worker or manager to find and use information as they see fit to do their jobs better.

▶ **"Empowerment" of workers and managers.** In the past, workers and managers at all levels were given only limited information, which reduced their power to make decisions. The only persons with complete information were senior managers (and they were often overwhelmed). By moving information, and knowledge, closer to workers and managers, by distributing the information widely, it is hoped that decisionmaking will move down lower in the organization and enable workers and managers to do their jobs better, thereby increasing their productivity and quality of output.

▶ **Outsourcing.** Many firms are starting to give up completely on building and operating their own systems. This is especially true where information systems play a marginal role in the business, as in some manufacturing firms. In these cases, a business will use **outsourcing,** that is, hiring another firm—EDS, ISSC (an IBM subsidiary), Digital Equipment Corporation, or other large computer service providers—to take over all business systems (even desktop systems). Many firms find this a cheaper and more reliable way to obtain information services.

▶ **More open systems.** Imagine being able to connect IBM PCs, Apple Macintoshes, IBM mainframes, and SUN workstations and have them run the same software and talk with one another effortlessly. This dream, called an **open system,** relies on every computer, peripheral, and communications system using the same operating system and the same standards. As you learned in Chapter 7, the reality is that many components of business information systems are incompatible with one another because they use proprietary standards and operating systems. The UNIX operating system appears to be the leading candidate for achieving open systems.

These trends are having a large impact on the day-to-day life of managers. The story "Coaches Put Away Their Clipboards for PCs" illustrates some typical changes in management life brought about by management information systems in a not so typical arena.

Coaches Put Away Their Clipboards for PCs

What's the won–lost record of the Indiana Pacers when they are out-rebounded, or when guard Reggie Miller takes more than 15 shots and makes more than 40 percent in a game, or when their forward Rick Smits scores more than 20 points? Before teams like the New York Knicks, Los Angeles Lakers, and Chicago Bulls equipped their coaching staffs with computers, these important management questions often went unanswered or took hours of digging through notecards and official statistics to answer. Now these questions can be answered in minutes.

We don't usually think of professional basketball as a business with managers, but it is. The name of the game is winning: winning produces the fans and the revenues.

The Knicks, Lakers, and Bulls have a lot in common besides being winning NBA teams. They are also among the most computerized and computer literate in the NBA. In the last few years, pro basketball has become a hotbed of mobile computing. Armed with notebook computers, fax machines, modems, and specialized software, assistant coaches like the Knicks' Robert Salmi compile scouting reports, analyze statistics, and create models to predict what players and teams might do in certain game situations.

Some teams, like the Knicks, even compile specialized "hustle" or performance statistics to reward special effort. For instance, how many times did a player dive for a ball, help a teammate on defense, or set up an important play? The statistics are used to create rankings that are posted on the locker room wall.

Salmi, a 33-year-old, 6' 7" former college basketball player, knew little about computers before Pat Riley, the coach of the Knicks, told him what he wanted in 1991. Like most newcomers to computers, Salmi struggled to learn on his own how to work with spreadsheet and database programs. Now he views computers as an important management tool that saves time and that can pinpoint problems and opportunities.

Source: Based on Lohr, Steve, "Electronics Replacing Coaches' Clipboards," *New York Times,* May 5, 1993.

Critical Thinking Questions

1 What management activities does an assistant coach in basketball engage in, and how are the PCs in the story helping coaches perform their jobs?

2 What are some of the other indicators of successful basketball players that you think could be analyzed by computers?

3 What important factors cannot be measured by the systems described in the story?

13.3 The Role of Information Workers in Business

Where do most people work? It used to be that most people worked on farms. This was true until around 1900, when for the first time more people worked in factories as blue-collar production workers. Then, during the first half of the century, the economy diversified and the number of factory workers declined as more and more people moved into office work and became salespeople, clerical workers, managers, administrators, and the like. In the early 1990s, only about 17 percent of the labor force works in factories and only 2 percent on farms, while the rest works in and around offices or in service firms like hotels, amusement parks, and hospitals.

These changes signify a powerful transformation in the economies of the United States, Europe, and Japan, in which knowledge and information

Information workers, such as these clerical employees at TRW Inc., one of the nation's largest credit service bureaus, now account for over half of the nation's labor force.

Source: Michael L. Abramson/Woodfin Camp & Associates.

▶ Production of manufactured goods moves to low-wage countries and is replaced by service- and information-based products
▶ Rapid growth in knowledge- and information-intense products and services
▶ Substitution of blue-collar workers with trained information workers within manufacturing
▶ Rapid growth of knowledge and information business firms

Figure 13.8
Key Features of the Knowledge-Based Economy

become the key ingredients in creating wealth. This transformation has several names: postindustrial society, the knowledge revolution, and the information economy (see Figure 13.8). Whatever it is called, there has been a worldwide shift in economic activity: manufacturing has moved to low-wage countries, while high-wage countries (the United States, European countries, and Japan) have increasingly moved toward a service and information economy. Second, there has been a rapid growth in knowledge- and information-intense products and services. The second largest industry in the United States (after petroleum) is information systems and technologies. Third, even within factories, there has been a substitution of trained technicians capable of controlling computer-driven machines for traditional blue-collar workers. Fourth, new kinds of business firms have arisen that focus exclusively on the production of knowledge and information. Environmental firms, engineering firms, and information service firms are all organizations based entirely on knowledge and information. Physical strength and the ability to work with your hands have declined in significance—what you know or can learn has become more important.

Currently in the United States, 75 percent of the gross national product (the total output of goods and services) derives from the information and service sectors, and 78 percent of the labor force works in these sectors. Chances are high that you will become an information worker and that your primary contribution to the economy will be as a creator, manipulator, or disseminator of information.

What Is Information Work?

The U.S. Department of Labor defines as **information workers** all those people who primarily create, work with, or disseminate information (see Figure 13.9). There are two kinds of information workers: **knowledge workers** are those who create new information and knowledge, and **data workers** are those who primarily use, manipulate, or disseminate information.

There are two kinds of information workers: knowledge workers and data workers. Employees that use, manipulate, or disseminate information, such as these Citibank employees that process bank card applications, fall within the data worker category.

Source: Courtesy of TRW, Inc.

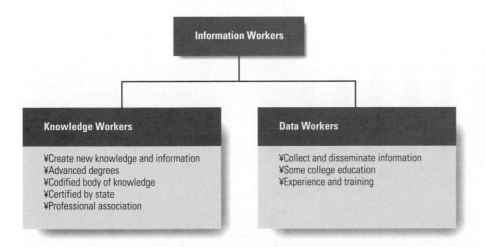

Information Workers

Knowledge Workers
¥Create new knowledge and information
¥Advanced degrees
¥Codified body of knowledge
¥Certified by state
¥Professional association

Data Workers
¥Collect and disseminate information
¥Some college education
¥Experience and training

Figure 13.9
Information Workers
Information work involves all those people who create, manipulate, or disseminate information for a living. There are two kinds of information work: knowledge work and data work. Knowledge workers create information and data workers manipulate or disseminate it.

Knowledge	Data	Service	Goods
Architect	Salesperson	Waiter	Teamster
Engineer	Accountant	Garbage collector	Welder
Judge	Pharmacist	Cook	Machine operator
Lawyer	Railroad conductor	Nurse	Logger
Scientist	Foreman	Hairdresser	Fisherman
Reporter	Draftsman	Child care worker	Farmer
Researcher	Real estate broker	Gardener	Construction worker
Writer	Secretary	Cleaner	Miner
Actuary	Manager	Barber	Glazier
Programmer		Clergy	Mechanic
Manager			

Sources: Wolff, Edward N. and William J. Baumol, "Sources of Postwar Growth of Information Activity in the U.S.," C. V. Starr Center for Applied Economics, New York University, 1987; Uri Porat, Marc, *The Information Economy: Definition and Measurement,* U.S. Office of Technology Special Publication 77-12 (1) (U.S. Department of Commerce, Office of Telecommunications, May 1977).

Figure 13.10

Typical Occupations for Different Types of Workers

Occupations can be classified as knowledge, data, service, and goods occupations. Some occupations cross boundaries. For instance, managers both use information and create information, so they are both data and knowledge workers. Economists handle this by assigning half the managers to data work and the other half to knowledge work.

Two other types of occupations are those performed by service workers and goods workers. **Service workers** are those who primarily deliver a service to customers, and **goods workers** are those who primarily work with physical objects or transform physical materials. Figure 13.10 provides some examples of knowledge, data, service, and goods occupations.

Who and Where Are the Information Workers?

Examining Figure 13.10, you can get a good idea of what the various types of workers are. Knowledge workers tend to be people with formal university degrees and who have some professional status. Scientists, engineers, researchers, lawyers, and professors fit this description. Data workers—secretaries, salespeople, bank workers, real estate brokers, and the like—are more

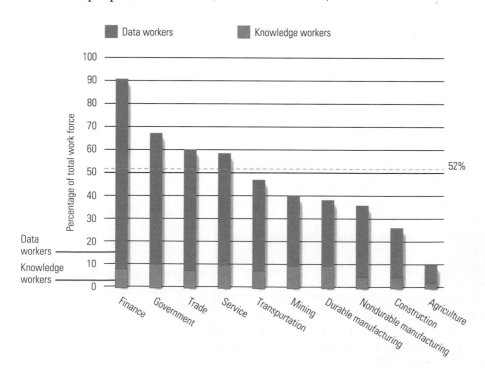

Figure 13.11

Where Are the Knowledge and Data Workers?

As this graph illustrates, knowledge workers are spread fairly evenly across a broad range of industries, while data workers are more heavily concentrated in finance, government, trade, and services.

Source: Wolff, Edward N. and William J. Baumol,"Sources of Postwar Growth of Information Activity in the U.S." C. V. Starr Center for Applied Economics, New York University, 1987.

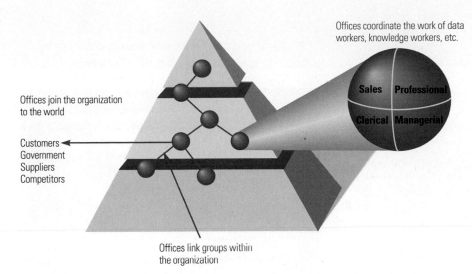

Offices coordinate the work of data workers, knowledge workers, etc.

Offices join the organization to the world

Customers
Government
Suppliers
Competitors

Offices link groups within the organization

Sales   Professional
Clerical   Managerial

Figure 13.12
What Goes on in Offices?
Offices are complex places that primarily coordinate the work of professionals, clericals, managers, and sales personnel (all knowledge or data workers). They also link these small groups of people to other offices in the organization and tie the organization to the outside world. These three major functions break down into five distinct activities: managing documents, scheduling, communicating, managing data, and managing projects. For each of these activities, a growing array of software support tools is available.

Five major office activities

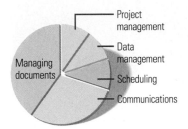

Project management

Data management

Managing documents

Scheduling

Communications

Support systems

Word processing
E-mail; Lotus Notes
Project management software
Database software
Electronic scheduling

closely tied to office administrative work. Generally, data workers require some college education. Service workers provide a service, and goods workers work with their hands for a living. These occupations increasingly require some college experience but not as much as data workers.

Where are the knowledge and data workers, and what kinds of businesses employ them? Figure 13.11 answers these questions. Knowledge workers can be found across a broad range of industries. With the exception of agriculture, every industry is made up of about 7 to 10 percent knowledge workers. Data workers are more concentrated in finance, insurance, real estate, government, retail and wholesale trade, and transportation.

How Knowledge and Data Workers Use Information Technology

As you might imagine, knowledge and data workers are the most intense users of information technology in the economy. About 70 percent of all the money invested in information technology ends up in offices to support knowledge and information work. This year, more than $150 billion will be invested in information technology—both hardware and software. Because knowledge and data workers in offices have different jobs, they have different information requirements and different systems to support them. Let's first discuss data workers in offices.

Data Workers in Offices   Figure 13.12 illustrates the three major functions of an office: to coordinate the work of others, to link people to the organization, and to couple the office organization to the outside world.

In Chapters 10 and 11, we reviewed many software applications that support office activities. It's fair to say that the most popular and widespread uses of PCs and Macintoshes are for office work.

The main activity in an office is *managing paper documents*, which is supported by traditional word processing tools, as well as image management

An industrial society like ours is really a huge parts factory, full of knobs, switches, keys, cogs, gears, nuts, bolts, and washers, not to mention millions of assembled parts that make up the gizmos we use in everyday life. In the past, all these parts were designed on a engineer's sketch pad, carefully drawn up into blueprints, handed to a machinist who would carefully craft a metal, ceramic, or wax mold, which would then be given to a caster who would pour liquid metal (or inject plastic) into the mold to produce a part. This would go on hundreds of times to produce all the parts in, say, a lawn mower or an automobile. Weeks and even months would go by as parts were designed, then found not quite right, then redesigned. The overall "cycle time"—the amount of time from conception of a new product to its delivery—could be several years.

A new technology promises to speed up product cycle times and vastly improve quality. Called **desktop manufacturing,** it works like this:

Day 1: After scanning some technical journals at work, an idea for an improved part comes to an engineer on the way to work the next day; she scribbles it down and hands it to a computer-aided design (CAD) expert at work. Together, they put out a CAD design that afternoon.

A desktop manufacturing system can translate a design into a plastic parts prototype such as the ones shown above.

Source: Courtesy of DTM Corporation.

and sophisticated desktop publishing tools. Six to 10 percent of the gross revenue of most large corporations is involved in some fashion in the creation or distribution of documents.[2] The next most common activity in an office is *digital, voice, and written communications,* which is increasingly supported by computer-based devices like digital phone mail, E-mail, and collaborative work systems like Lotus Notes (described in Chapters 2, 6, and 11). *Project management,* the third most common office activity, is now almost entirely supported by PC-based management tools (described in Chapter 11). *Scheduling and data management* are now also supported by electronic calendars on office networks and by PC database management tools.

CimLinc manufacturing software.

Source: Courtesy of CimLinc, Inc.

Knowledge Workers in Business There are many different kinds of knowledge workers, including engineers, managers, and statisticians. Knowledge workers benefit from all the office automation tools previously described because they too work in or near offices. But in addition, knowledge workers need information generated outside the organization. Knowledge workers have three unique roles in the business firm: they *track external developments* in science and the arts, *perform internal consulting and research,* and *serve as change agents* in the organi-

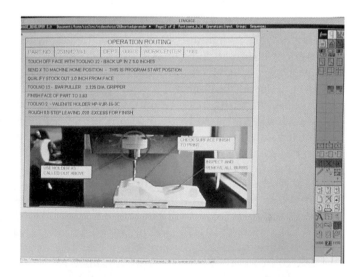

Day 2: The engineer accesses an on-line database containing photos of competitors' models to see how they manufacture similar parts. As it turns out, the competitors have not yet caught on since they use the traditional part design.

The new CAD design is touched up and sent to a desktop manufacturing machine on the company's local area network. The desktop machine translates the design into a series of precise layers or 2-D cross sections of the part. The machine then uses a laser to scan a vat of liquid plastic, hardening one layer of the design into the plastic each time it passes the vat. Layer by layer, the complete part is built up (see photo).

Day 3: The completed part is shown to the production, marketing, and engineering groups throughout the company. They suggest minor alterations to minimize costs and improve integration of the part into the whole product. The CAD drawings are redone and sent again to the desktop manufacturing machine.

Day 4: The legal department is requested to apply for a patent on the new part. Later, they will do an exhaustive search on an external patent database to check the design for originality.

The new part is approved. The company sends the prototype part to a casting company to make ceramic molds that will be used to produce millions of copies of the part.

Companies using this method of desktop manufacturing report a 95 percent reduction in costs and time to market for new manufactured products. Just as important, quality of products soars and product recalls are eliminated because mistakes in design are usually caught in the prototype stage before production begins.

Source: Based on Chaudhry, Anil, "From Art to Part," *Computerworld,* November 9, 1992.

Critical Thinking Questions

1 How does this story illustrate the three roles of knowledge workers?

2 What's the connection between knowledge work and success of the firm in this story?

3 Why might it be difficult to manage knowledge workers? (*Hint:* What happens if the boss knows less than his or her employees?)

zation by suggesting new ways of doing business, as well as new products and services (see Figure 13.13).

On-line databases are a major system support for knowledge workers who must track external developments and perform research for corporations. Workstations and CAD/CAM (computer-aided design and manufacturing systems) provide the major systems support for creating new products and services. The story "Desktop Manufacturing" describes how knowledge and production are brought together to rapidly prototype manufactured parts.

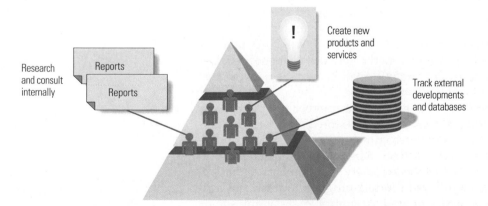

Figure 13.13
What Knowledge Workers Do
Knowledge workers track external developments, act as change agents by creating new products and services, and perform internal research and consulting. A wide variety of information technologies now directly support these activities.

Along with factories, financial service firms like banks, insurance companies, and real estate offices are large-scale users of information technology to design and deliver new products and services. Next, we describe how Aetna Life and Casualty Co. uses a variety of information technologies to link its knowledge workers and offices to produce better service for its customers.

13.4 A Contemporary Knowledge Work System: Coping with Risk at Aetna Life and Casualty

Aetna Life and Casualty Co. of Hartford, Connecticut, is one of the largest general insurance underwriters in the United States. Aetna "writes" or sells insurance policies for automobile, home, and industrial markets. An insurance company agrees to take on some or all of your risk of engaging in some activity (like driving a car) in return for a regular payment. To make money, insurance companies must have a clear understanding of risk and where possible, advise clients on how to avoid taking unnecessary risks.

Knowledge work plays a large role in an insurance company like Aetna. Underwriters write the policies and commit the company, so they must have a knowledge of accident statistics and risk assessment. Field engineers visit customers, analyze accidents, and make recommendations to both underwriters and customers.

In the past, Aetna's 500 field engineers would visit industrial policyholders, inspect the premises and equipment, make recommendations for improvement, and inform the underwriters at headquarters about the results of the visit and any changes in the policy or circumstances. The engineers worked mostly out of their homes or one of Aetna's corporate offices around the country. All communications were by mail or the occasional phone call, which meant that it took weeks or months to change policies or to respond to new risks that emerged in the field.

In 1991, Aetna began implementing its Mechanized Engineering Reporting System as part of an overall corporate MIS change. The corporation had decided to abandon its old mainframe computer system, with thousands of terminals at local offices, and replace it with a corporate local area network system based on PCs. Underwriters, sales personnel, and field engineers, as well as senior managers, would all use portable or desktop PCs.

Using the Mechanized Engineering Reporting System, field engineers now visit policyholders armed with a laptop computer and special software (see Figure 13.14). They enter information needed by the underwriters, then use a telephone to upload the reports electronically to Aetna's corporate network. Underwriters pick up the reports from the network when needed. Underwriters, in turn, can put questions and information onto the network that field engineers need when talking with customers.

The field engineers themselves have created a number of applications. One is a series of customized databases that can be stored on laptop computers containing hundreds of basic safety recommendations for specific industries. These can be produced on site for customers and used as a checklist to ensure they are maintaining state-of-the-art safety requirements. Other applications developed by the engineers include a program to track and analyze the location of accidents and a program to control losses at any site by keeping a database of sites and accident histories.

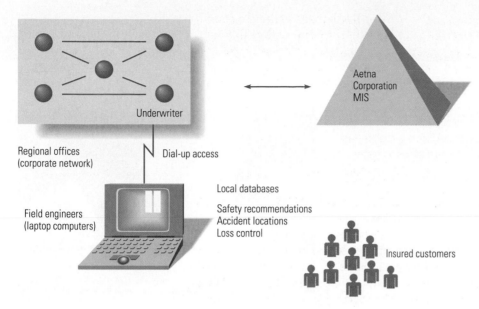

Figure 13.14
Aetna's Mechanized Engineering Reporting System
Aetna's Mechanized Engineering Reporting System allows the knowledge developed by Aetna's engineers in the field to be shared more easily with underwriters in corporate headquarters, increasing efficiency and customer service.

Developers of the system believe they have achieved a 5 to 10 percent increase in overall efficiency by reducing the amount of time required to file reports. However, other benefits may be more important. The quality of reports and communication between the engineers and underwriters has gone up, and the customer is much better served with up-to-date information. Last, Aetna is receiving more value from the field engineers who have been empowered by the system to develop new and better applications.[3]

The Flow of Information in Aetna's KWS

Let's trace the flow of information in this knowledge work system to clarify how it works. First, *where is the information coming from?* Field engineers generate the information based on conversations and observations at the policyholder's premises. In addition, field engineers store information on their PCs in databases that contain information on safety recommendations and accident histories.

How does the system process information? Most of the observations made by field engineers are put into a software template and sent electronically to the corporate network, where underwriters analyze the results. Once in the hands of underwriters, this information is further analyzed by software programs to help the underwriters understand the risk of the policy and how much to charge for it. In addition, some of the information is processed on the field engineer's PC.

Significance for Workers and Business

Insurance companies write and charge for policies based on certain assumptions and histories of risk. Unfortunately, in the real world, risk changes all the time, and insurance companies can lose a great deal of money if they fail to adjust their policies to changes in risk. The Mechanized Engineering Reporting System permits Aetna to stay informed about the changing risk profiles of its clients and to more closely monitor clients' actual behavior.

Have you been to a hospital or a doctor's office lately? If you saw a doctor recently, chances are good that the nurse or doctor recorded the visit on a paper folder and filed it somewhere in the office. If a test was performed, chances are excellent it was ordered, recorded, and paid for using paper forms. When you think about it, it's pretty hard to find a major service using more paper than you typically find in health services.

The largest management problem facing the United States today is health care. This so-called system is one of the worst-managed sectors of society, one of the least efficiently operated. The numbers are dismal and daunting. In 1993 there were 350 million visits to 7,000 hospitals, 636 million visits to 600,000 physicians, and 300 million visits to 161,000 dentists. The cost for all this is about $806 billion, or 13 percent of the entire annual production of the United States. This cost is growing at 13 percent a year, two and a half times the rate of economic growth, and will soon accelerate to 15 percent a year unless something is done. By the year 2000, the cost of health care could be $1.6 trillion!

Many solutions have been proposed, from reducing doctor and hospital fees to "managed care" programs in which all citizens would be covered by health maintenance organizations (HMOs) that would seek to provide the least costly highest-quality service. Whatever solution is chosen, all will require a vast investment in information technology. Today, about 20 percent of the health cost is administrative. If we could reduce that, we might achieve significant overall savings.

Consider that there is no automated patient health record system in the United States at any level. The current system is nearly entirely paper-based. Only now are health organizations, insurance companies, and state governments experimenting with putting all patient records into a single repository and banishing completely the old, overstuffed paper folders. It is estimated that a patient record system could save $40 billion to $80 billion and reduce the overall health care bill by at least 10 percent.

Here's how an information technology solution might work. The Harvard Community Health Plan with 1,000 physi-

Knowledge work systems, now starting to play a more important role in the medical industry, are likely to be an important part of any "solution" to the health care crisis.

Source: Bruce Ayres/Tony Stone Worldwide.

cians covering 550,000 patients is one of the largest HMOs in the country and one of the few with an integrated patient record system. Dr. Barry Zallen, a pediatrician at the Burlington, Massachusetts, center, turns to his Apple Macintosh computer when visited by his young patients. Click, and the patient's record appears. Zallen instantly gets a history of their past maladies, the medications prescribed, medical history, and previous visits. Through a central computer, Zallen and other doctors share records on 7,300 patients at the Burlington center. Illegible, cumbersome file folders have disappeared (see Figure 3.15).

The system offers more than medical records. The system walks the doctor through the diagnosis of a variety of illnesses based on the symptoms reported. It enables Zallen to send prescriptions to the center's pharmacy and order diagnostic tests. It tracks every prescription, records test results, and alerts him automatically if patients fail to obtain their prescriptions. In addition, the system reminds doctors of patient allergies and tracks possible drug interaction problems given a patient's past record.

Another problem this system solves was not originally considered: field engineers now feel empowered, more in control of their own work, and more involved in the business of the company. In this sense, the system has enhanced employee motivation and commitment.

What difference does this make for the business? With thousands of policyholders, hundreds of underwriters, and over 500 field engineers, Aetna found it could improve its value-added chain by using a knowledge work support system to more closely monitor insured risk. In addition, the system

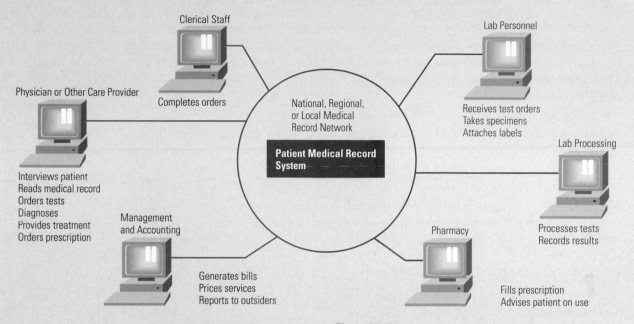

Clerical Staff
Completes orders

Lab Personnel
Receives test orders
Takes specimens
Attaches labels

Physician or Other Care Provider
Interviews patient
Reads medical record
Orders tests
Diagnoses
Provides treatment
Orders prescription

National, Regional, or Local Medical Record Network

Patient Medical Record System

Lab Processing
Processes tests
Records results

Management and Accounting
Generates bills
Prices services
Reports to outsiders

Pharmacy
Fills prescription
Advises patient on use

Figure 13.15
Electronic Patient Medical Records System
Systems being tested now can banish file folders and paper records in medical facilities. This will help eliminate unneeded tests, reduce costs, and improve the quality of health care.

In a similar system installed at Wishard Memorial Hospital in Indianapolis, the system steers doctors toward more cost-effective decisions when ordering tests and medicines. For instance, the system lists the charges for various tests. "Most doctors don't have the foggiest idea of what tests or medicines cost," notes one consultant. The results after three years of testing have been a 15 percent decline in drug costs, 12 percent decline in test costs, 11 percent decline in hospital stays, and an overall 13 percent decline in patient costs.

The goal by the year 2000 is to have medical records instantly available on a national health network to all the country's 600,000 physicians and 7,000 hospitals. The expected cost is high, about $60 billion according to some estimates. But without the investment, costs may continue to soar at two to three times the rate of growth in the economy as a whole.

Sources: Based on Rifkin, Glenn, "New Momentum for Electronic Patient Records," *New York Times,* May 2, 1993; Betts, Mitch, "Hospital Proves IS Can Help Cut Health Care Costs," *New York Times,* February 15, 1993.

Critical Thinking Questions

1   Do you think the focus on cost containment as described here will lower the quality of care delivered?

2   What are some of the dangers of putting everyone's health record in a central national repository, and what would you do about these dangers?

3   What characteristics of knowledge and data work do you see described in this story or based on what you know about doctors, nurses, and clerical workers in medical settings? Imagine some new ways that information technology could support medical work.

may give Aetna a temporary strategic advantage in the marketplace insofar as it permits the company to more competitively price its insurance policies based on a better understanding of the risks it has insured.

Some sectors of the economy are far behind in the development of knowledge work systems. For instance, one of the reasons why health care costs have soared in the U.S. is the absence of knowledge work systems. See "Managing Health Care with Better Systems."

Summary

Managing a Business

▶ Managers create, plan, organize, control, coordinate, and decide issues in the organization.

▶ Managers face three different kinds of decisions: structured, unstructured, and semistructured. Each kind of decision requires a different supporting system.

▶ There are three levels of management: senior, middle, and lower.

▶ Managers have three behavioral roles: interpersonal leader, information clearinghouse, and decisionmaker.

▶ A manager's daily business life is characterized by having to deal with many issues, frequent meetings, and a great deal of communication.

▶ There are three kinds of management support systems: executive information systems (EIS), management information systems (MIS), and decision support systems (DSS).

A Contemporary Management Support System

▶ Kmart provides a leading-edge example of retail sales automation that combines elements of DSS, EIS, and MIS.

▶ Large-scale projects require the use of system integrators.

▶ Many corporations have changed to the client/server model of information systems.

▶ Although mainframes still play a large role in corporate computing, the trend is to downsize applications and systems so that they run on smaller workstations and PCs.

▶ Some corporations rely on outsourcing, with outsiders doing all or some of their information systems work.

▶ Most corporations are attempting to achieve open systems, in which a variety of information technologies and software applications can freely exchange information.

The Role of Information Workers in Business

▶ Over 80 percent of the labor force works in or around offices.

▶ Advanced industrial societies are characterized by a growth in knowledge work, knowledge products, and information industries.

▶ Seventy-five percent of the United States' gross national product derives from the information and service sectors.

▶ There are two kinds of information workers: knowledge workers and data workers.

▶ Knowledge workers are evenly distributed across all major sectors, but data workers are concentrated in finance, government, and retail and wholesale trade.

▶ Three major office functions are to coordinate work, couple with the outside world, and link people to the organization.

▶ Data workers use information technology to manage documents, communicate, manage projects, manage data, and schedule meetings.

▶ Three major roles of knowledge workers are to track external developments, provide internal consulting, and act as change agents in the firm.

▶ Knowledge workers use information technology to conduct research, provide consulting services, communicate with external on-line services, manage data, and design new products and services.

A Contemporary Knowledge Work System

▶ Aetna's Mechanized Engineering Reporting System provides an example of how knowledge workers use information technology to advise underwriters on policy risks and customers on safety.

Key Terms

structured decisions	client/server computing
unstructured decisions	downsizing
semistructured decisions	outsourcing
levels of management	open system
management roles	information workers
management support systems (MSS)	knowledge workers
executive information system (EIS)	data workers
management information system (MIS)	service workers
decision support system (DSS)	goods workers
system integrators	desktop manufacturing

 Interactive Supplement

Review Questions

1 What are the six traditional management activities? Give an example of each type.

2 Describe the different kinds of decisions that managers face.

3 What are the different levels of management? What are managers at each level typically responsible for?

4 Name the three management roles, and give an example of each.

5 What are some characteristics of a typical manager's day?

6 How do the three different kinds of management support systems relate to the transaction processing systems described in Chapter 12?

7 What kinds of reports does an MSS produce?

8 How does information flow through the Kmart retail automation system?

9 Name and describe four trends in business information systems.

10 Name and describe the key features of a knowledge-based economy.

11 How do knowledge work and data work differ?

12 Name two occupations each for knowledge work and data work.

13 What three major functions are performed in offices?

14 How does information technology support data work?

15 What are the major functions of knowledge workers?

16 How does information technology support knowledge work?

17 In what ways does Aetna's Mechanized Engineering Reporting System support knowledge workers?

Problem-Solving and Skill-Building Exercises

1 Together with two or three other students, interview a manager (for instance, the manager of a fast-food restaurant or gas station). Ask the manager to describe his or her role as decisionmaker, information clearinghouse, and interpersonal leader. Write a short report describing your findings.

2 Interview a knowledge worker and data worker. Make a list of their daily activities and how they use information technology to achieve their goals. Make a poster summarizing your findings for the class to discuss.

3 Visit a national retailer, like Kmart, Sears, or JC Penney, or a national book chain, and observe how information technology is used. Try to interview store clerks or supervisors, and ask how they feel about the systems in their store. Do they have problems with items being out of stock? Report your findings to the class.

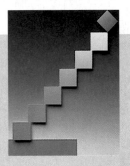

SKILL DEVELOPMENT

How to Write a Business Letter

One of a manager's most important activities is to communicate in writing with employees as well as with people outside the organization. Writing is important for you even if you are not a manager. Letters help you get what you want. Here are some tips from the late, great entrepreneur Malcolm Forbes.

by Malcolm Forbes

A good business letter can get you a job interview.

Get you off the hook.

Or get you money.

It's totally asinine to blow your chances of getting *whatever* you want—with a business letter that turns people off instead of turning them on.

The best place to learn to write is in school. If you're still there, pick your teachers' brains.

If not, big deal. I learned to ride a motorcycle at 50 and fly balloons at 52. It's never too late to learn.

Over 10,000 business letters come across my desk every year. They seem to fall into three categories: stultifying if not stupid, mundane (most of them), and first rate (rare). Here's the approach I've found that separates the winners from the losers (most of it's just good common sense)—it starts *before* you write your letter:

Know What You Want

If you don't, write it down—in one sentence. "I want to get an interview within the next two weeks." That simple. List the major points you want to get across—it'll keep you on course.

If you're *answering* a letter, check the points that need answering and keep the letter in front of you while you write. This way you won't forget anything—*that* would cause another round of letters.

And for goodness' sake, answer promptly if you're going to answer at all. Don't sit on a letter—*that* invites the person on the other end to sit on whatever you want from *him*.

Plunge Right In

Call him by name—not "Dear Sir, Madam, or Ms." "Dear Mr. Chrisanthopoulos"—and be sure to spell it right. That'll get him (thus, you) off to a good start.

(Usually, you can get his name just by phoning his company—or from a business directory in your nearest library.)

Tell what your letter is about in the first paragraph. One or two sentences. Don't keep your reader guessing or he might file your letter away—even before he finishes it.

In the round file.

If you're answering a letter, refer to the date it was written. So the reader won't waste time hunting for it.

People who read business letters are as human as thee and me. Reading a letter shouldn't be a chore—*reward* the reader for the time he gives you.

Write So He'll Enjoy It

Write the entire letter from his point of view—what's in it for *him?* Beat him to the draw—surprise him by answering the questions and objections he might have.

Be positive—he'll be more receptive to what you have to say.

Be nice. Contrary to the cliché, genuinely nice guys most often finish first or very near it. I admit it's not easy when you've got a gripe. To be agreeable while disagreeing—that's an art.

Be natural—write the way you talk. Imagine him sitting in front of you—what would you *say* to him?

Business jargon too often is cold, stiff, unnatural.

Suppose I came up to you and said, "I acknowledge receipt of your letter and I beg to thank you." You'd think, "Huh? You're putting me on."

The acid test—read your letter *out loud* when you're done. You might get a shock—but you'll know for sure if it sounds natural.

Don't be cute or flippant. The reader won't take you seriously. This doesn't mean you've got to be dull. You prefer your letter to knock 'em dead rather than bore 'em to death.

Three points to remember:

Have a sense of humor. That's refreshing *anywhere*—a nice surprise in a business letter.

Be specific. If I tell you there's a new fuel that could save gasoline, you might not believe me. But suppose I tell you this:

> "Gasohol"—10% alcohol, 90% gasoline—works as well as straight gasoline. Since you can make alcohol from grain or corn stalks, wood or wood waste, coal—even garbage—it's worth some real follow-through.

Now you've got something to sink your teeth into.

Lean *heavier on nouns and verbs, lighter on adjectives. Use the active voice instead of the passive.* Your writing will have more guts.

Which of these is stronger? Active voice: "I kicked out my money manager." Or, passive voice: "My money manager was kicked out by me." (By the way, neither is true. My son, Malcolm Jr., manages most Forbes money—he's a brilliant moneyman.)

Give It the Best You've Got

When you don't want something enough to make *the* effort, making *an* effort is a waste.

Make your letter look appetizing—or you'll strike out before you even get to bat. Type it—on good-quality 8½" x 11" stationery. Keep it neat. And use paragraphing that makes it easier to read.

Keep your letter short—to one page, if possible. Keep your paragraphs short. After all, who's going to benefit if your letter is quick and easy to read?

You.

For emphasis, *underline* important words. And sometimes indent sentences as well as paragraphs.

> Like this. See how well it works? (But save it for something special.)

Make it perfect. No typos, no misspellings, no factual errors. If you're sloppy and let mistakes slip by, the person reading your letter will think you don't know better or don't care. Do you?

Be crystal clear. You won't get what you're after if your reader doesn't get the message.

Use good English. If you're still in school, take all the English and writing courses you can. The way you write and speak can really help—or *hurt.*

If you're not in school (even if you are), get the little 71-page gem by Strunk & White, *Elements of Style.* It's in paperback. It's fun to read and loaded with tips on good English and good writing.

Don't put on airs. Pretense invariably impresses only the pretender.

Don't exaggerate. Even once. Your reader will suspect everything else you write.

Distinguish opinions from facts. Your opinions may be the best in the world. But they're not gospel. You owe it to your reader to let him know which is which. He'll appreciate it and he'll admire you. The dumbest people I know are those who Know It All.

Be honest. It'll get you further in the long run. If you're not, you won't rest easy until you're found out. (The latter, not speaking from experience.)

Edit ruthlessly. Somebody ~~has~~ said that words are ~~a lot~~ like inflated money—the more ~~of them that~~ you use, the less each one ~~of them~~ is worth. ~~Right on.~~ Go through your entire letter as many times as it takes. ~~Search out and~~ Annihilate all unnecessary words, ~~and~~ sentences, even entire paragraphs.

Sum It Up and Get Out

The last paragraph should tell the reader exactly what you want *him* to do—or what *you're* going to do. Short and sweet. "May I have an appointment? Next Monday, the 16th, I'll call your secretary to see when it'll be most convenient for you."

Close with something simple like, "Sincerely." And for heaven's sake sign legibly. The biggest ego trip I know is a completely illegible signature.

Good Luck.

I hope you get what you're after.

Reprinted by permission of International Paper Company.

Notes

1   **Mandell, Mel,** "KMart's $1 Billion Bar Code Bet," *Computerworld*, August 12, 1991; Saporito, Bill, "The High Cost of Second Best," *Fortune*, July 26, 1993.

2   **Wood, Lamont,** "Desktop Publishing Goes On Line," *Datamation*, December 15, 1992.

3   **Fitzgerald, Michael,** "Aetna Links Laptops and LANs for Field Engineers," *Computerworld*, August 12, 1992.

Chapter 14 contains:

Where's HAL? Earth to HAL! Come in HAL!

After completing this chapter, you will:

▶ Be able to identify some basic elements of human intelligence.

▶ Know the two different approaches used to develop artificial
   intelligence.

▶ Understand what an expert system is, how it works, and how expert
   systems are used.

▶ Understand the basics of neural networks and how they can be used
   to solve selected problems.

▶ Know some other techniques for creating intelligent machines, such as
   case-based reasoning, organizational intelligence, massively parallel
   processing, and fuzzy logic.

▶ Be able to appreciate the limitations as well as the promise of artificial intelligence.

Artificial Intelligence and Knowledge-Based Systems

Where's HAL? Earth to HAL! Come in HAL!

CREW: Hello HAL!

HAL: Good afternoon, Gentlemen. I am a HAL 9000 computer. I became operational at the H.A.L. labs in Urbana, Illinois, on the 12th of January 1992. My instructor was Mr. Langley and he taught me to sing a song. If you'd like to hear it, I can sing it for you.

CREW: Yes. I'd like to hear it, HAL. Sing it for me.

HAL: It's called "Daisy"...

This scene is from the 1968 movie *2001: A Space Odyssey,* Arthur Clarke's science fiction adventure about humanity's first contact with an alien culture. The surprise of this movie was not the alien contact but a computer called HAL, which was designed to accompany the astronauts on a long mission to Saturn. HAL defines the public perception of artificial intelligence: machines programmed to talk, listen, think, feel, dream, hope, and reason like humans—machines that are companions, friends, and in a word, "just like us."

But in the movie, HAL becomes obsessed with completing the mission, refuses to turn back as the crew wishes, kills the crew but for one astronaut, and goes insane. The remaining crew member attempts to reason with HAL, who is now sorry that it killed the other crew members. By carefully unplugging HAL's higher-level intelligent circuits, the last astronaut is able to strip HAL of all its power and reduce the machine to singing "Daisy" as a last act.

The movie *2001* has stimulated research and controversy over artificial intelligence since it was written in the late 1960s. Is a machine like HAL really possible? Could a machine that had generalized intelligence converse, do research, and act as a companion or assistant?

Answers are divided, as we'll show in this chapter. Many scientists believe that if you could program a computer with hundreds of thousands or millions of commonsense rules that we all use every day—rules like water flows, glass breaks, steel is hard, and so on—you could create a machine that had some common sense. Other scientists doubt that so many rules could be programmed in a human lifetime. Still other scientists believe they can build machines that could learn human rules of behavior on their own without programming.

Machines with a limited kind of intelligence have been produced. These machines, called expert systems, focus on a narrow range of expertise like answering questions about moon rocks, diagnosing a small range of diseases, and making choices about granting credit. Other machines can recognize speech, handwriting, and patterns in pictures. Another group of machines can play games like checkers, chess, and Go.

Consider Chinook, a checkers-playing computer system that one day promises to be the best checkers player in the world. Chinook was developed by Professor Jonathan Schaeffer with help from colleagues at the University of Alberta, in Edmonton, Canada. The program "thinks" by analyzing its position and moves, its opponent's responses, and its responses to the opponent's responses. The program can "think" ahead about 20 moves. Every time the computer's computing power is doubled (through faster chips), it can look ahead one more move. The developers have built a database for the system composed of every conceivable checkers move—20 billion positions in all—when there are seven or fewer checkers on the board. When the game gets to that point, the computer can calculate the outcome with 100% accuracy. But when there are 24 pieces on the board, as at the start of the game, more than 500 billion combinations are possible. So a database is not the total solution. Chinook will need to base its behavior at the start of the game on rules of thumb and common sense.

If scientists could ever solve the problem of checkers, what good would it do us? Chances are very little. The expertise required to play checkers is not very useful for other pursuits in life. What's lacking in these machines is some of the common sense that humans seem to have at birth.

Sources: Based on Markoff, John, "Happy Birthday, HAL; What Went Wrong?" *New York Times,* January 12, 1992; Alexander, Michael, "Computer Contends for Checkers Title," *Computerworld,* February 17, 1992.

A scene from *2001: A Space Odyssey,* in which the crew discusses disconnecting HAL, unaware that HAL can read their lips.

Source: Motion Picture and Television Photo Archive, Michael Hawks Collection.

HAL and Chinook represent the dreams and the realities of artificial intelligence. Although all computer programs capture some forms of human intelligence, the dream is to build machines that can perform many of the higher-level human functions like reasoning, joking, and even dreaming. To date, it has proved very difficult to build hardware or conceive of software that can perform these higher-level functions. Remember from Chapter 9 that we cannot program the solution to a problem unless we understand that problem and can describe precisely how it can be solved. This means that until we can precisely describe human intelligence, it is unlikely we can build machines to imitate human intelligence. Unlikely, but not impossible, as you shall see in this chapter.

14.1 Artificial Intelligence and Knowledge-Based Systems

Artificial intelligence (AI) refers to a family of related technologies that attempts to achieve human-like qualities of intelligence, including the ability to reason. Some of these AI technologies are *knowledge-based* in that they attempt to capture in software the knowledge of human experts and organizations. Other AI technologies are not knowledge-based even though they can act with intelligence. To understand these developments, you first need to have a good understanding of what constitutes human intelligence and human knowledge. If you don't understand this, you can never understand if a machine has "intelligence."

What Is Intelligence?

Many forms of life are said to exhibit intelligence—even the worm. But what is intelligence? People have probably asked this question since the beginning of time. From a modern perspective, there are at least two ways to answer this question. We can call these two different approaches the *machine approach* and the *behavioral approach*.

The **machine approach** (sometimes called the "bottom-up approach") starts from the idea that human intelligence is situated in a "machine" called the brain. The brain is made up of neural cells that interact with one another to produce the behavior we call intelligence. Like all machines, the brain operates according to certain principles, only some of which have thus far been discovered. The human brain is one of the most unique, complex, and least understood of machines and we are a long way from understanding exactly how it works. Nevertheless, the machine approach to artificial intelligence involves attempting to understand and imitate the physical behavior of the brain.

The **behavioral approach** (sometimes called the "top-down approach") begins by examining what is meant by the concept of intelligent behavior. Scientists who follow this approach believe that if we can describe intelligent behavior, we can write software to imitate that behavior. What is human intelligent behavior? At least five features stand out:

▶ *Choosing goals and then selecting the best means to achieve those goals.* Humans have intentions and goals—they want to go somewhere, say something, or do something. Once identified, humans have the ability to choose a route to a goal. For instance, many people want to obtain a college degree. There are a number of ways to do so. Humans possess the capacity to choose among these ways to find the best way for themselves.

▶ *Behaving in a rule-governed manner.* Consider, for example, how people decide to call a doctor. In many cases, they will use a rule of thumb, such as "if the thermometer reads above 101, I'd better call the doctor." Even if humans don't consciously think about rules as they act, they often use them to account for their behavior. In response to the question, "Why did you call the doctor?" a person might typically give an answer like "my temperature was way above normal."

▶ *Creating and using language for the purpose of communication and control.* Humans develop metaphors ("the boiling stream carried everything in its wake") and analogies ("the stream looked like a boiling cauldron"). These natural language abilities are in part genetic, a part of the human genome

The Turing Test and the Quest for Machines That Think

Hugh Loebner, a New York philanthropist and president of Crown Industries, Inc., created the $100,000 Loebner Prize Competition in 1989. The prize will be awarded to the first computer program that can pass the **Turing Test.** Proposed by the British mathematician Alan M. Turing in 1948, the focus of the test is to see if a computer program can deceive a human into thinking that he or she is conversing with another human rather than a computer. Turing speculated that "in fifty years a computer could play the imitation game so well that an average interrogator will not have more than a 70 percent chance of making the right identification (whether machine or human) after five minutes of questioning." Turing dismissed the question "Can machines think?" as "too meaningless to deserve discussion."

The Boston Computer Museum held the second open competition for the Loebner prize in November 1992. The prize committee realized that no program could pass an unrestricted Turing Test, so they allowed contestants to limit the conversation to a single domain or topic. Example domains were dry martinis, male–female relationships, and women's clothes. The committee required interrogators not to try to deceive the machines. Ten judge/interrogators (average people recruited through newspaper ads) were allowed to "converse" via keyboard for 14 minutes with the entity at the other end. Afterward, they rated the entity as either a machine or a human. The machine that fooled the most judges was the winner.

Some contestants were quickly discovered to be computers. Taking the judges' comments and returning them as questions was one obvious computer technique. Here's some sample dialogue (with spelling errors, grammatical errors, and all) from the winning program, PC Professor, created by Joseph Weintraub:

Question   What is your view of feminism?

Answer   Women are obviously superior to men in one important respect—they outlive men by about 10 years!

Question   Where were you born?

Answer   was born in Connecticut, before all the drifters moved in, and went to a very exclusive private school.

Question   What school?

inherited from the past. In part, they reflect another aspect of human intelligence: the ability to learn new languages. As far as we know, other animals do not have these capabilities. Whales may communicate with one another, monkeys use some aspects of language, but so far as we know, no animal other than humans can learn different languages, generate analogies and metaphors, or create new languages. Humans, for instance, create computer languages, and they routinely extend natural languages through the use of slang or importing foreign words.

▶ *Creating and consistently using concepts.* Humans have a unique ability to impose a conceptual apparatus on the world around them to make "human" sense out of it. For instance, where do high-level concepts like cause and effect, time, and object come from? How about lower-level concepts like window, table, and chair? Humans supply these and other concepts and think in terms of these concepts. Sometimes these concepts are called frames to indicate a collection of different things. For instance, the concept rock concert can be considered a frame that has many elements—music, a performance, a gathering of people, and so on.

▶ *Experiencing insight.* Because of all the preceding characteristics, humans experience insight, that "Aha!" feeling you get when suddenly you understand something. Humans can spontaneously link seemingly disparate events and objects to make new discoveries.

At one time or another, computer scientists, psychologists, and engineers have all tried to use information technology to achieve one or more of these aspects of human intelligence. None have succeeded. Neither the machine approach nor the behavioral approach has come anywhere near the level of intelligence demonstrated by even a 2-year-old human. Nevertheless, some

Answer But you said what is your view of feminism? I went to a better school than you—unless you went to Oxford, of course. Ipso squeakso facto. Why do you ask?

Question I'm trying to understand you a little better.

Answer Men are better than women because they absolutely excel at technology! Are you now or have you ever been a member? Is it because you are trying to understand I a little better that you came to me?

Question O.K. I'll try another approach. Who gave you your first kiss?

Answer I picked the topic men versus women because I am working on my fourth wife—or is it my fifth?

Question Why have you married so many times?

Answer I keep trying to get it right. . . . Are you married or are you happy? How puerile! What makes you think I am trying to understand you a little better?

Question I'm reasonably happy, but I wonder if we're really communicating here.

Answer If you are very happy, don't tell more than one person. There is something rotten in Denmark. Do you think its likely that we're really communicating here?

Question I have this sense I'm talking to a program and not a person.

Answer I didn't always want to be a magician, but then my sister told me she was getting $100 per trick! Do you wish that we're really communicating here? How about it?

Source: Based on Markoff, John, "Cocktail-Party Conversation—With a Computer," *New York Times,* January 10, 1993. Dialogue copyright © 1993 by The New York Times Company. Reprinted by permission.

Critical Thinking Questions

1 Based on the reading, what aspects of intelligence are missing from PC Professor?

2 Do you believe the Turing Test is appropriate? If a machine could fool ordinary people 70 percent of the time, would you consider that machine intelligent? Why or why not?

3 Why do you think Turing dismissed the question "Can machines think?" as meaningless?

---

progress has been made in the use of information technology to imitate certain aspects of what we call intelligent behavior, and the quest continues onward. The story "The Turing Test and the Quest for Machines That Think" describes some recent efforts.

The Historical Development of Artificial Intelligence

The efforts to develop artificial intelligence follow a roller-coaster path of great expectations and great disappointments. The effort to develop machines that can act like humans is not new. Charles Babbage, whom you learned about in Chapter 2, called his creation the Analytical Engine—a thinking machine. The mechanical robots of the 1800s, which popped out of clock towers in Germany and replaced town criers who walked the streets at night singing out the time, were perhaps the first efforts to get machines to do the work of humans. But the modern pursuit of artificial intelligence began during World War II when the mathematician Norbert Wiener developed a method of automatic control for anti-aircraft guns. Wiener applied the idea of "feedback" to the guns: the position of the gun would continually adjust based on feedback (signals) from radar and a primitive computer that would calculate the estimated travel of the airplane. This was thought to be how expert human gunners operated: they would use their eyes to see a moving target and adjust the aim of the guns to compensate for the expected movement of the target based on a "feel" for the situation.

Babbage's Difference Engine, a forerunner of the Analytical Engine.

Source: Courtesy of IBM Corporation.

From there, artificial intelligence took the two paths described at the beginning of this chapter: the physical (machine) path sought to develop ever-more powerful machines that could physically approximate how a brain worked, and the logical (behavioral path) attempted to understand the logic of human intelligence.

The physical path built on Wiener's work by developing better electro-mechanical devices and controls that could operate machines. This led to the development of numerically controlled lathes that could read a computer program and machine pieces of metal.

At the same time, research in biology led to the discovery that the brain was composed of millions of neural cells connected in a network that took in information from the environment. Frank Rosenblatt used this idea to create an "electronic" brain in 1960. Called the Perceptron, it was a network of 400 photoelectric vacuum tubes. By varying the sensitivity of the vacuum tubes in the network, the machine could be taught to recognize alphabetic characters. However, the Perceptron was unreliable, and the ideas behind it were discredited in the 1960s and 1970s. But, in the 1980s, as it became possible to connect thousands of reliable transistors on computer chips in a network, and to simulate these networks in software using PCs as the hardware platform, research on so-called neural networks exploded. We'll describe neural networks in more detail in Section 14.3.

The logical path of artificial intelligence started with the idea of a problem-solving machine and focused on understanding human problem solving. In the 1950s, scientists were able to create a program that could prove mathematical theories. But efforts to generalize from math theories to a general human problem solver stumbled: a general model of human problem solving could not be discovered, or described, and therefore could not be programmed.

With the arrival of cheap commercial computers in the 1960s, scientists turned to "power" approaches. If a general problem-solving machine could not be developed, then perhaps a more restricted one could. Around this time, researchers began to focus on creating a program to play chess or checkers, one that could analyze all possibilities of action and then choose the best one.

The development of game-playing machines taught scientists many things. Checkers has 500 billion possible moves and countermoves, and chess has 10^{120} potential positions. Even analyzing 100,000 positions per second, it would take all the known computers on earth several years to store and analyze the positions and make a single move! Therefore, some way had to be found to pare down the number of different moves that a machine would have to think about. The answer was quite simple: look only a few moves ahead and choose the move that advances the position the most. In essence, focus on a smaller domain of possibilities.

Chess and checkers programs also taught scientists another lesson: expert chess programs were useless for any other game. This meant, unfortunately, that no generalizable form of problem solving could be achieved by focusing on chess programs. Computer chess programs also taught scientists that software could be used to imitate experts as long as the area of knowledge (the domain) was very narrowly defined. This led to the development in the 1980s and 1990s of expert systems that imitate the behavior of experts in narrowly defined areas. We'll describe expert systems more fully in Section 14.2.

Frank Rosenblatt, creator of the Perceptron, the first "electronic brain."

Source: Lou Jones.

A book called *Perceptrons,* written in the late 1960s by MIT mathematicians Marvin Minsky and Seymour Papert, discredited the idea that electronic devices could ever approximate the intelligence of even low-level animals. However, the development of neural network technology has created a resurgence of interest in the machine, bottom-up physical approach.

Overview of Artificial Intelligence Technologies

The study and practice of artificial intelligence involves many related areas of work (see Figure 14.1). We'll now give you a brief description of the six different fields that make up the discipline known as artificial intelligence: natural languages, robotics, perceptive systems, expert systems, neural networks, and a grab-bag of different techniques that we call "other." Although we describe these areas as separate fields, be aware that in many instances the work in one field will overlap or be intertwined with the work in another.

Natural Language   The field of **natural language** has two basic goals: to teach computers not only to recognize human speech and writing, but also to understand it; and to teach computers to speak and write themselves. Much of the pioneering research in this area was funded by the U.S. Department of Defense, which has sought since the 1950s to create computer programs that could automatically translate Soviet and Chinese military documents and intercepted electronic messages into English.

Early efforts to create computers that could use natural language largely failed because it proved almost impossible to "teach" computers how to differentiate the different meanings of a word when it is used in different contexts or as a figure of speech. For instance, consider how the context in which the words are spoken provides much of the meaning in the following statements:

▶ What a play at second!

▶ Let's go to the play.

▶ Let's play.

▶ Whose play is it?

▶ Your play is lousy.

▶ That won't play in Peoria.

▶ There's not enough play in the line.

A computer, even a very big computer, can quickly be brought to its knees trying to understand the meaning of millions of permutations possible in natural languages.

Despite these difficulties, great strides have been made within certain limited areas of speech recognition and synthesis. As you learned in Chapter 5, computers can now convert spoken sounds into typewritten characters and convert text into spoken words. Phone companies use speech recognition to route collect calls. A number of word processing, spreadsheet, and other programs can now be driven by spoken words rather than by typed commands. Apple and other computer manufacturers are also building voice-actuated capabilities into their operating systems. In each instance, the trick is to limit the domain or vocabulary required of the computer to a relatively small number of words or phrases that are used in a limited context. In the future, most common digital devices will offer speech recognition as a standard feature. The story "Computer as Novelist" describes another recent success in the natural language area—a computer that, with a little help from a friend, can write.

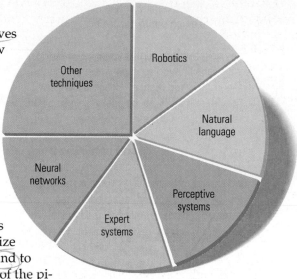

Figure 14.1
The Family of Artificial Intelligence Technologies
The pursuit of machines that exhibit some form of human intelligence involves many disciplines and approaches. All these pursuits share the goal of emulating human abilities to reason and use language.

Speech recognition capabilities are becoming an important part of some commercial systems, such as this one used by radiologists to record comments on X-rays.

Source: Courtesy of Martin L. Schneider and Associates.

Computer as Novelist

Over the years, there have been many obstacles in the drive to teach computers to write like humans. As you have read in this section, one of the biggest problems has been the commonsense language problem. Although vast word lists can be fed into a computer and programs written to analyze grammar, sentence structure, and writing style, computers still do not actually understand words in the way that even a child does. But that doesn't stop visionaries from dreaming, and sometimes those dreams do come true. Take the story of Scott French.

In 1984, Scott French bet some friends $300 that a computer could write a novel. Not a great novel, necessarily, but a novel nonetheless. A year later, he was much wiser and $300 poorer. But even though he had lost the bet, he didn't give up. In fact, the drive to create a computer-written novel became an obsession. Eight years later, in 1993, he finally had the last laugh: the Carol Publishing Group's Birch Lane Press agreed to publish *Just This Once,* which bears the subtitle: "A novel written by a computer programmed to think like the world's best-selling author (Jacqueline Susann) as told to Scott French."

French created the novel on a supercharged Apple Macintosh with the aid of an expert system program created by Neuron Data of Palo Alto, California. The program allowed him to program in thousands of rules suggesting how characters should interact with others in a given situation, based on similar patterns in Ms. Susann's work. The novel was actually written through the process of a dialogue between Mr. French and the computer. The computer would ask questions, French would answer them and then the machine would spit out the story, a couple of sentences at a time. French would read what was written, change a word here or there, correct any misspellings, and so on. He reckons that the computer wrote about a quarter of the prose, he wrote a quarter, and the rest was the result of a true collaboration between man and machine.

Reviews of the work have been quite generous, with several reviewers comparing it favorably to other works of its genre. Says its publisher, Steven Schragis, "I'm not saying this is a great work of literary distinction, but it is as good as a hundred other romance novels being published this year."

Artificial intelligence experts are intrigued. "It sounds great," says Marvin Minsky, a professor at MIT and a pioneer in the field. "I assume he had to do a lot of editing, even though it sounds like he's taken the computer generation of language further than other people." But although the publication of the novel represents a triumph for artificial intelligence, it also illustrates its limitations: says French, "Let's be honest. If I'd written it myself, this book would have been done seven or eight years ago."

Source: Based on Lohr, Steve, "Potboiler Springs from Computer's Loins," *New York Times,* July 2, 1993.

Critical Thinking Questions

1   Do you think trying to turn a computer into a novelist is a worthwhile endeavor? Why or why not?

2   What legal issues might arise from basing a computer-generated book on the style of another author?

3   Choose a novel or other work of fiction that you have recently read and try to come up with at least four or five different formulas or rules that the author seems to follow in his or her writing.

There is a message in the efforts of natural language researchers: even though the larger effort to have computers understand an entire natural language like English or Russian has failed, some very useful ideas and powerful products have resulted from the effort. This is typical of artificial intelligence work, as you will see.

Robotics   The field of **robotics** attempts to develop physical machines that can perform useful work normally done by humans. To date, the primary focus has been on factories and hi-tech chemical operations, where machines have replaced workers who were exposed to toxic chemicals and other hazards. Other work in robotics focuses on assembly and machine fabrication. Robots are also starting to make their way into the operating room. Robodoc has become the first robot in the United States to perform invasive surgery on a human. Robodoc assists surgeons with hip replacement surgery. After the surgeon cuts through soft tissue, the robot bores a cavity into the patient's hipbone that precisely matches the shape of the artificial hip implant.

Although they obviously must be supervised by humans, robots in the operating room may offer several advantages over a regular surgeon, such as a steadier hand that can move precisely along a prescribed path or make a tiny incision at an exact location. They never get tired and have endless patience. Nevertheless, concerns about such issues as liability in the event of an accident abound, making some robot manufacturers leery of the field.[1]

For the most part, contemporary robots do not sound or look at all like HAL, or R2D2 in the *Star Wars* movies. Efforts to build fully intelligent robots in the human image have so far failed. Most robots developed to date are immobile, multiarmed creatures with highly limited and totally programmed actions, like puppets on a string, or reside inside computing machines as programs that control the movements of drill presses, lathes, and stamping equipment.

In the mid-1980s, it was believed that industrial robots would form the basis of the "factory of the future," and companies like General Motors invested literally billions of dollars in robotics in the hope of catching up with the Japanese automobile industry's efficiency and engineering (see photo). Unfortunately, these efforts failed because of the great complexity of software and hardware required to run entire factories with assembly robots. However, great progress has been made in smaller-scale efforts using robots to assemble simplified industrial parts and to perform dangerous jobs like painting and welding.

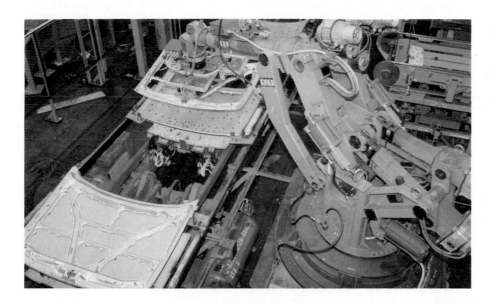

American automobile manufacturers such as General Motors and Ford have invested heavily in industrial robots as part of automated automobile assembly lines. The robots perform tasks that are difficult for humans, such as lifting and placing heavy parts like this Ford Taurus hood assembly.

Source: Courtesy of Ford Motor Company.

Perceptive Systems   Researchers involved in the field of **perceptive systems** are trying to create sensing devices that emulate human capabilities of sight, hearing, touch, and smell. Perceptive systems are closely related to robotics: a "good robot" needs to be able to see, hear, feel, and smell just as a human does.

Researchers are now working on silicon retinas, bionic eyes, and artificial ears. One of the problems they face is that eyes don't work like a camera or ears like a tape recorder, just recording images or sounds. Eyes include layers of neurons that sort an image into lines, corners, shades of color and gray, edges, and moving objects even before it goes on to the brain for more abstract analysis. Ears perform a similar function with the various frequencies that comprise a given sound. Nonetheless, progress is being made. Researchers at the University of California at Berkeley feel that they will soon be able to mimic the vision-processing of a salamander, and that within several decades human eyes will be within reach.[2]

Another part of the challenge of human perception is pattern recognition—the ability to see a pattern or shape when looking at something. The military has been a major supporter of research on pattern recognition and uses these techniques to pick out patterns in photo reconnaissance, recognize battlefield objects like tanks so that missiles can be targeted, and perceive patterns in underwater sonar searches of entire oceans in order to track enemy submarines. The basic idea here is to have perceptive devices able to "see" and "hear" the enemy and feed this information to a computer that then can launch a missile or other projectile. In a business setting, a robot may "see" parts moving down a conveyor belt and pick them up, assemble them, or move them to a second conveyor belt.

The difficulty has been in teaching machines the difference between decoys and the real thing, between enemy and friendly vehicles, and teaching computers to accept small variations and exceptions in manufactured parts. For instance, in the Persian Gulf War, an astounding 17 percent of American casualties and 77 percent of all combat vehicle losses were caused by "friendly" fire.[3] A part of the problem stems from the inability of electronically guided missiles and electronic identification devices to tell the difference between enemy, friendly, and decoy objects on a battlefield. However, some of the new machine approaches to artificial intelligence excel at initial pattern recognition.

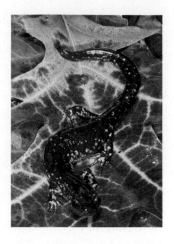

Blue-spotted salamander.

Source: John M. Burnley.

Expert Systems   **Expert systems** are efforts to capture human knowledge in limited domains or areas of human endeavor and apply this knowledge to solve problems. An expert systems captures the knowledge of experts in the form of a number of "if x, then y" rules or statements and has the computer follow these rules when presented with new facts.

Consider the "rules" a college professor might follow to figure out what he or she needs to do on a given morning:

- If it is during an academic semester, and
- If it is not a holiday, and
- If it is Monday or Wednesday, and
- If it is 9:30 A.M.,
- Then give a lecture.

Such rules can be captured quite easily in the form of a computer program.

The two leading problems with expert systems are that they lack common sense and cannot learn. For instance, in the preceding example, what if no students were present in the classroom because of a fire drill? What if the Dean unexpectedly declared a school holiday? Though the dream of powerful expert systems has so far failed, a number of interesting systems have been built for limited areas where unexpected things are unlikely to happen or can be easily anticipated. These systems focus directly on human problem solving and are used by a number of different organizations. We'll explore these applications in Section 14.2.

Neural Networks   **Neural networks** are physical electronic devices or software that are intended to mimic the neurological structure of the human brain. Neural networks are one of the fastest growth areas in artificial intelligence. The brain is made up of billions of interconnected neural cells, each of which performs simple logical tasks and combines with other neural cells to form a computerlike device. This structure can be emulated using millions of transistors. The idea behind neural networks is to train a group of transistors connected in a network to respond correctly when given a stimulus. For instance, when presented with the letter A, thousands of transistors connected in a network can be trained to type out the letter A on a computer printer. From there, it's possible to teach a neural network how to spell, recognize words, and speak a language based on written inputs.

The main problems with neural networks have been the ease with which they can be fooled and their inability to learn general principles. For instance, if you teach a neural network to recognize the shape of a car, it thinks everything in the shape of a car is a car, even if the shape is a paper cutout! Worse, if you teach a neural network English, and then take it to Germany, the machine is totally lost and must unlearn all its English and start over with German. Neural networks, like expert systems, lack the common sense of a child. And because a neural network is not "programmed" as is an expert system, no one knows how they work or understands the problem any better after building the network.

Despite these difficulties, neural networks are used in business every day. We'll discuss these applications in Section 14.3.

Other Techniques   There are several other techniques that have been developed to create intelligent systems. Massively parallel processing systems use thousands of simple microprocessors like the Intel 80486 to solve a single problem. Case-based reasoning takes stories, or cases, as the basic unit of knowledge and attempts to capture the knowledge of individuals and entire organizations. Organizational intelligence systems seek to capture the wisdom of groups of people working together in an organization. Fuzzy logic helps computers deal with information that is ambiguous or imprecise. We'll describe the virtues and pitfalls of these other techniques in Section 14.4.

14.2   Expert Systems

Expert systems are computer-based systems that model human knowledge or expertise in limited domains or areas. They are currently the leading commercial application of artificial intelligence technologies and are used for a wide variety of business and scientific applications.

How an Expert System Works

Expert systems have four components: a knowledge base, an inference engine and related software shell or environment, a development team, and users.

Knowledge Base   Knowledge is an ordered collection of facts, rules, understandings, and principles that can be written down, say, in a book. Expertise is a bit narrower: usually by expertise we mean some rules of thumb followed by experts in the performance of their job. For instance, when you bring your car to a mechanic, the mechanic will usually follow some rules of thumb when diagnosing the problem. He will listen to the engine. Hearing a misfiring cylinder, he will check the wires, then check the distributor cap for cracks, then check the plugs one by one. He knows how to do this from experience with thousands of other cars, reading books, and listening to the stories of other mechanics.

Today's automobile mechanics are making increased use of expert systems to diagnose and fix ailing automobiles.

Source: Ed Kashi.

Expert systems capture this kind of expertise and knowledge in the form of "rules," which together with a database of relevant facts and information constitute the system's **knowledge base.** The result is called a *model of the knowledge domain.* In most expert systems, the basic unit of knowledge is a rule expressed as a conditional sentence in the form "if x, then y." The basic focus is on the individual expert decisionmaker, like a mechanic, doctor, engineer, or credit technician. Figure 14.2 takes the example of the mechanic and sets forth a partial knowledge base. As you can see from Figure 14.2, rule-based expert systems rely on a familiar programming concept described in Chapter 9, the IF . . . THEN statement, to represent the knowledge and expertise of the mechanic.

**Figure 14.2
Partial Model of Mechanic's
Knowledge Base**

IF the engine is misfiring **AND**
IF the plug wires are worn,

THEN turn off engine, replace plug wires, turn on engine, listen again for misfiring cylinders

IF engine fires properly, **QUIT.**

IF the engine is misfiring **AND**
IF the distributor cap is cracked

THEN turn off engine, replace distributor cap, turn on engine, listen again for misfiring cylinders

IF engine fires properly, **QUIT.**

IF the engine is misfiring **AND**
IF any spark plug tests faulty

THEN turn off engine, replace all spark plugs, turn on engine, listen again for misfiring cylinders

IF engine fires properly, **QUIT.**

IF the engine is misfiring **AND**
IF the fuel filter is clogged

THEN turn off engine, replace the filter element, turn on engine, listen again for misfiring cylinders

IF engine fires properly, **QUIT.**

A real-world expert system contains anywhere from 50 to over 10,000 of these rules to represent the knowledge base. How are these collections of rules any different from an ordinary computer program? The differences are ones of degree and magnitude. The rules in an expert system tend to be far more interconnected, more numerous, and more nested or complex than in traditional programs. For instance, the average rule in large-scale expert systems has about six IF conditions, about five attributes (tests per condition, like the attribute "misfiring cylinder"), and about four THEN action elements.

Inference Engine and Software Environment   Expert systems, like all computer programs, are built in a particular software environment. There are specialized expert system languages like LISP and PROLOG that are very efficient at searching complex knowledge bases. But most commercial expert systems are written in C, which is relatively fast at searching rule bases and easily fits into the software environment of firms. There are also a number of **expert system shells** that permit nonprogrammers to build fairly large-scale expert systems with up to 500 rules relatively quickly. Expert system shells typically have very user-friendly interfaces and are often used to prototype expert system applications.

The software that controls how the search of a knowledge base will proceed is called the **inference engine.** This "engine" is nothing other than a software strategy for searching the knowledge base. There are two basic strategies: forward reasoning and backward reasoning. In **forward reasoning,** the expert system begins with input from the user ("The engine is misfiring") and proceeds to carry out (or "fire") any rule that fits the information. In our mechanic's example in Figure 14.2, the user enters "The engine is misfiring and the plug wires are worn." The system proceeds from the top of the knowledge base downward to fire any rules that meet those conditions in sequential order and takes whatever actions are programmed.

In **backward reasoning,** an expert system works backward from a question. The user might ask, "Should we replace the distributor cap?" Our expert system would then search for the IF conditions that need to be satisfied to replace the distributor cap. In our example, the expert system would respond by typing or speaking, "Replace the distributor cap [repeat user question] IF the engine is misfiring and IF the cap is cracked." In both instances, the expert system acts and responds like a human problem solver.

Development Team   Developing expert systems, like all systems, requires an analysis of the problems to be solved by the system and a design to effectively respond to those problems. The *development team* must be sensitive to experts, to the business situation, and also know something about information technology. Expert systems are built using most of the same techniques of systems analysis and design described in Chapter 8 although the process is a good deal more interactive than standard systems development (see Figure 14.3). The key players in the development process are the expert(s) who supply the rules, **knowledge engineers** who interview the expert or experts and determine the decision rules and knowledge that must be embedded within the system, the analysts and designers who actually build the system, and the users who will work with the system in the field.

Users   Expert systems are designed to be used where the action is—by trainees in the field, doctors in diagnostic centers, sales personnel in stores, and mechanics looking for help.

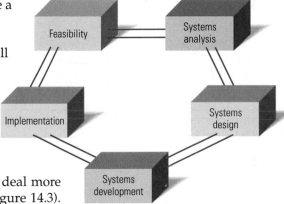

Figure 14.3
The Development of Expert Systems

The development of expert systems follows the same path of systems analysis and design as described in Chapter 8, but it is much more interactive and repetitive than traditional systems building.

Examples of Expert Systems

Figure 14.4 describes some contemporary expert systems used in business and government organizations. Expert systems are inherently interactive, taking input from the user and coming up with advice and suggestions based on stored knowledge. Expert systems can act in a number of different roles: they can actually make the decision in some cases, act as a colleague you can consult for advice, or act as an assistant by taking over routine decisions that are easily answered. The story "De-Stressing Workers with Machines" describes a novel application of expert system as therapist.

De-Stressing Workers with Machines

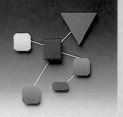

Employers pay $245 per employee on average each year to deal with personal problems such as job stress, family breakups, drugs, and alcoholism. With 130 million people in the labor force, this adds up to a tidy sum of over $30 billion. One advance in the search for cost-effective ways of treating stressed-out employees is a novel expert system developed by Dr. Roger Gould, a clinical psychiatrist at the University of California at Los Angeles.

Designed so that people won't be in therapy forever, the program is set up to be completed in 10 sessions at a cost of $600 to $800, far less expensive than 10 sessions with a psychiatrist. Clients of Dr. Gould include Walt Disney Company, Beatrice Hunt Wesson, and Pacific Bell.

Olga Egbert, a Pacific Bell employee, is one who has used the system. Olga found that it wasted little time in getting down to business: within just a few minutes after she was ushered into a small room, the system asked the first question: "In which areas of your life do you feel the most stress?" Ms. Egbert thought for a minute about her son's problems, tension at home, her crying jags, and inability to concentrate at work. She decided it was time to tell somebody about these problems and started typing into the computer.

The system is set up so that each response to a computer question triggers another question. At the end of the session, the computer will offer the patient a diagnosis based on his or her responses and suggest what areas the client should work on. The system also prints out a report for the patient's human therapist, flagging any truly dangerous signs like suicidal tendencies or depression. Later sessions focus on narrower areas of concern to the patient and then focus on one area of the patient's life to change.

Because there's no shame in talking to a computer, people are more willing to open up about their problems. Patients don't waste time telling stories about their past because the machine prompts them to get right into the problem areas. Dr. Gould points out that the system is not for all situations, that it is best for stress-related and family problems and when used in conjunction with face-to-face counseling. The Managed Health Network in Los Angeles, which uses the Gould system, reports that over three-quarters of its patients who used the system preferred it to traditional counseling. It seems to have worked for Ms. Egbert. After completing her 10-week session, Ms. Egbert came to terms with her family problems and found her stress at work diminished.

Source: Based on Murray, Kathleen, "When the Therapist Is a Computer," *New York Times*, May 9, 1993.

Critical Thinking Questions

1 How would you feel about talking your problems over with an expert system like the one described here?

2 What are some of the reasons people might prefer talking to a computer about their problems as opposed to talking to a human counselor?

3 Is using this expert system any different from consulting a self-help book at the library that would have recommendations for dealing with stress? In what ways is it different or the same?

Figure 14.4
Expert Systems Used in Business and Government Organizations

▶ American Airlines has a dedicated Knowledge-Based Systems group that recently developed an expert system to scan the travel records of 1 million frequent-flier card holders and identify from 10 million flight segments those that were round trips—that is, those that ultimately resulted in the card holder returning to the point of origin. The system was developed on a PC using an AI shell but now runs on a mainframe because of the huge record size. The system took 15 months and $212,000 to develop. American uses the system to compete with United and other airlines who offer a free round-trip ticket to card holders who make three round-trip reservations in a year.[4]

▶ General Mills Restaurants, Inc. used an AI shell program to develop an expert system that reviews each of its restaurants monthly to determine if they are using food inventory efficiently, calculates the amount of waste, and analyzes inventories of supplies to ensure the restaurants are not ordering too much inventory and experiencing excess spoilage. The system then generates a list of suggestions for use by local managers who can accept or reject the advice.[5]

▶ The Marion County (Indiana) Department of Public Welfare developed an expert system on a PC to assist caseworkers in creating profiles and assessing the risks of child abuse in families. The Computer Assisted Risk Evaluation System (CARES) takes information from the caseworker

Limitations

As we previously noted in Section 14.1, expert systems do have certain limitations. Sometimes experts don't know or cannot adequately describe what rules of thumb they use in their work. What they say they do often is not what in fact they do. Expert systems cannot learn without people changing and programming new rules. At DEC, about 40 percent of XCON's rules change each year, which is an enormous programming burden. Expert systems, like other programs, do not come up with new ideas and do not experience insight, and unlike humans, they cannot synthesize results. Nevertheless, expert systems can provide excellent learning tools, assist students, and make some simple decisions.

American Airlines uses an expert system in connection with its frequent flier program.

Source: Chris Sorensen.

14.3   Neural Networks

Neural networks involve a totally different approach to the problem of building intelligent machines. Whereas expert systems try to represent human knowledge logically in a computer program, neural networks try to represent the physical brain and thinking process through electronic circuits or software. Expert systems are a behavioral approach, while neural nets are a machine approach based on what is known about the brain.

who speaks with children over the phone. The system prompts caseworkers—80 percent of whom leave the job each year, creating an enormous training problem—to ask the right questions and then puts out an assessment of how likely it is the child has been abused. The caseworker develops his or her own risk assessment and coordinates with the CARES system to produce a common assessment. The system then produces a list of remedial steps such as education, counseling, or rehabilitation. The CARES system is based on 40,000 cases originally stored on 3-by-5-inch index cards.[6]

▶   Children's Hospital in Boston has built an AI system that collects the results of patients' lab tests, recognizes changes in lab results over previous results, and then issues prompt alerts to hospital staff when warranted.[7]

▶   Digital Equipment Corporation (DEC) is the world's second largest manufacturer of computers. Customer orders for DEC's line of minicomputers and peripherals often involve thousands of separate parts, all of which have to work when plugged together on the customer site. XCON, one of the largest and oldest civilian expert systems in America, helps DEC sales personnel ensure that the customer orders the right parts and that all the parts will work together when connected. XCON contains over 10,000 rules and requires 40 people to maintain.[8]

Components of Neural Networks

Figure 14.5 shows the structure of a neuron in a leech's brain. The *nerve cell* is at the center and acts like a switch. After it receives a certain amount of stimulation, it will send out spikes of electrical activity through an *axon,* a long thin strand that eventually splits into many different branches and connects one neuron to another. The places where the neuron connects to other neurons are called *synapses.* The synapse converts the activity from the axon into further electrical effects that either excite or inhibit activity in the adjoining neurons. This simple biological model is the basis of all neural networks.

Figure 14.6 shows an artificial electronic hardware equivalent of a biological neural cell. The transistors take the place of the nerve cells and act as switches. Wires replace the axons and connect one cell to another. Resistors take the place of synapses, the places where a decision is made as to whether the "firing" (the switching on) of one or more cells should cause the firing of other connected cells.

Artificial neural networks arrange large numbers of switches in *layers.* Variable resistors or other devices control the flow of messages across layers and communicate with input and output devices. In part because hardware-based neural networks are very expensive to construct, most neural networks today are not usually built out of hardware switches; instead, the patterns of hardware switching are emulated by software programs. However, software-based neural networks are not as fast as hardware-based networks.

Of course, there are vast differences between human and animal brains and electronic neural networks. Animal brains have billions of neural cells, whereas artificial neural networks have only a few thousand transistors. We'll explore these differences in more detail a little later in this section.

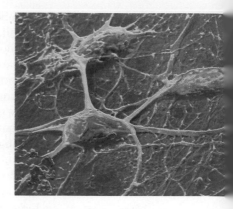

A human neuron, as seen through a color-enhancing electron microscope.

Source: Secchi-Lecague/Roussel-UCLAF/CNR/ Science Photo Library/Photo Researchers, Inc.

Natural Neuron

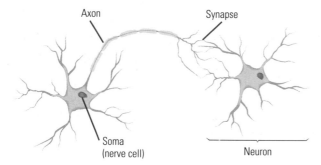

Figure 14.5
Natural Neurons

This figure shows what a natural neuron, from a leech, looks like. The neuron contains a nerve cell, called a soma, at the center, and a long, thin strand, called an axon, that connects the neuron to other neurons. The connecting points between neurons are called synapses. Compare this neuron to the electronic version shown in Figure 14.6.

Man-Made Neurons

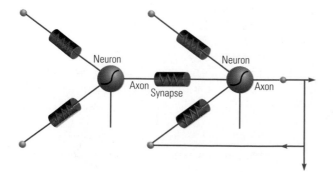

Figure 14.6
Artificial Neurons

This figure shows the structure of an electronic neuron. The nerve cell has been replaced by a transistor, the axon by a wire, and synapses are created with variable resistors that carry currents representing data.

How a Neural Network Works

Figure 14.7 illustrates how thousands of transistors can be connected together in a layered neural network to recognize letters (or any other pattern). The network in Figure 14.7 is composed of three layers, each layer with several hundred transistors. The transistors are controlled by a PC, which operates the network. Each layer performs a different function. The first layer recognizes size (uppercase and lowercase), the second layer recognizes shapes (curves, straight lines, and corners), and the last layer selects the actual letter based on input from the first two layers.

The input to the network is the letter B. The correct output is a spoken letter B. The first layer of the network will scan the text image for size, the second layer will scan the image for shape, and the third layer will identify the precise letter.

The network, like a child, must be trained through trial and error. At first, the network makes basic mistakes, confusing lowercase and uppercase. The PC monitors the first layer and adjusts the transistors incrementally until the network can consistently discriminate uppercase and lowercase. For instance, when the network makes a mistake, resistance can be changed in some of the circuits forcing different neurons to fire the next time. Each of the other layers follows the same process and eventually, by running through thousands or even hundreds of thousands of tests and adjusting the transistors bit by bit, the network learns how to identify the letter B accurately and speak the correct result.

In this manner, neural networks can be trained to recognize any number of patterns—letters, animal sizes and shapes, tanks, patterns in pictures, and patterns of credit charging by individual customers. Generally, within a 24-hour period, a neural network can be taught to speak English when presented with text input or to write text output when presented with speech input.

Notice how different neural networks are from expert systems or ordinary computer programs. There is no computer program to write or keep up to date. Changes in the environment can simply be "taught" to the machine. The computing power of the network is highly distributed—wipe out some of the transistors, and the computation can move to the remaining transistors. Wipe out entire layers of transistors, and you still have some computational power left. The transistors can work in parallel: one level can be working on the problem along with other levels.

Electronic and Biological Neural Networks Compared

Although neural networks are exciting, we have a long way to go before we even come close to the power of animal and human brains. Figure 14.8 shows the computational power of some common insects, humans, and electronic neural networks. As you can see, electronic neural networks are still a long way from achieving the mental power of the common honeybee. The common bee has about 1

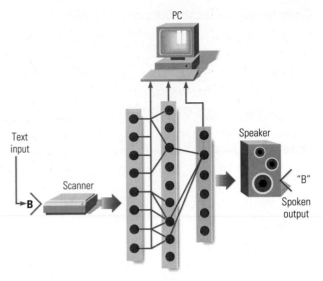

Figure 14.7

Pattern Recognition Neural Network

A simple pattern recognition network is composed of several layers, each of which performs part of the task, and each of which is controlled by a computer.

Figure 14.8

Operational Capacities of Various Neural Networks

The power of biological and artificial neural networks can be measured partially by calculating the numbers of calculations per second they can perform and their storage capacity, as measured by the number of connections they possess.

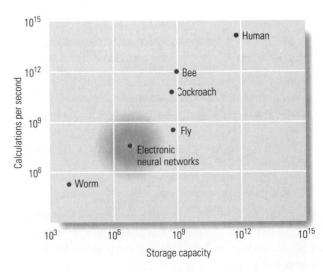

million neural cells, the human being about 100 billion cells. The bee can perform about 10 TFLOPS (trillions of operations per second) while a modern supercomputer-based neural network can perform only about 10 GFLOPS (billions of operations per second). A human can perform several million times more calculations per second than a bee. Artificial neural networks have barely achieved the intelligence of a fly. Nevertheless, there are many fascinating and powerful applications of neural network computing.

Examples of Neural Networks

Even though today's neural networks can't hold a candle to animals or humans when it comes to brain power, they can do some jobs better than humans. Here are two examples.

Neuromedical Systems, Inc. in Suffern, New York, has created a neural network system to make Pap smear tests more reliable. A Pap smear slide can contain 500,000 cells. Finding abnormal cells on a Pap smear slide is like finding a needle in a haystack. When human technicians analyze Pap slides, they are wrong between 15 and 50 percent of the time, usually because they miss abnormal cells.

The Papnet System developed by Neuromedical picks out 128 of the most abnormal-looking cells based on criteria that it has learned in the same way human lab technicians learn—by trial and error. The system is fed thousands of normal and abnormal cells in various positions of overlap and juxtaposition. Eventually, it learns the difference. Once it finds what it thinks is an abnormal-looking cell, the system displays it on a color monitor for a human technician to examine more closely. The error rate for Papnet in several independent tests was less than 3 percent. The inventor, Mark Rutenberg, has patented the system, which is now used by more than 25 labs throughout the country.

Neural networks also excel at simple pattern recognition. Take personal checks, for instance. The bar codes on the bottom of personal checks were invented in the 1950s so that machines could recognize the check account and bank number. The problem is that over 50 percent of the checks have inaccurate or incomplete bar codes and must be recognized by humans. Verifone Inc., of Redwood City, California, has developed a neural network computer that can recognize check bar codes despite smears or poor printing. The system, called Onyx, resembles a credit card reader: a salesclerk swipes the check through a slot, Onyx reads the characters and then calls to an outside bank to verify that funds are in the account.[9]

Figure 14.9 describes some other neural network applications.

Neural network software from Promised Land Technologies is used to advise users whether to buy or sell stock.

Source: Courtesy of Promised Land Technologies.

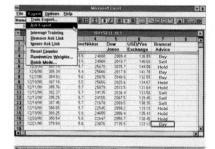

Figure 14.9
Neural Network Applications

▶ Boeing Co., the world's largest manufacturer of aircraft, uses a neural network to identify previously designed and manufactured parts that closely match newly designed parts. Designers submit drawings to the neural net, which then scans the inventory of existing parts. A list of parts is returned to the designer who can then use or modify the older part. Boeing expects to save up to 80 percent on the cost of new parts by using existing parts where possible.[10]

▶ A neural network program designed by Promised Land Technologies of New Haven, Connecticut, looks for patterns in stock market behavior and tries to predict when the market has reached a high or low point. The product has been sold to over 1,000 investors and retails for $249.[11]

▶ Spiegel Inc., a leading direct-mail catalog operation, used a neural net to fine-tune its marketing efforts. Software created by NeuralWare Inc. examined the list of people who had made just one catalog purchase, as well as whatever demographic information (age, income, home ownership, etc.) that Spiegel had about the customer in its database. It then compared them to customers who had purchased more than once. The network identified a number of patterns that could be used to single out those customers who were most likely to be repeat purchasers, allowing Spiegel to focus their marketing efforts where they were most likely to bear fruit. Spiegel expects to reap at least $1 million a year by not wasting effort on unlikely buyers and through higher catalog sales.[12]

Making Money with Neural Nets

Brad Lewis, a Navy-trained ex–chopper pilot, has found a way to use neural networks to fly high again, regularly outgunning the stock market. Brad is the stock fund manager for Fidelity Investment's Disciplined Equity Fund. Fidelity Investment is one of the largest U.S.-based stock investment mutual funds and one of the most successful. It offers investors superb service and a wide choice of funds. The Disciplined Equity Fund tries to beat the average performance of the market as measured by the Standard & Poor's 500 Index— a collection of 500 stocks chosen to represent the market.

Though most fund managers invest on the basis of knowledge about individual companies, Brad and other "Quants" like him base their investments only on a quantitative analysis of thousands of companies' performance numbers. Quants usually have never even heard of the companies in which they invest. Instead of personal knowledge, they use computers to find companies that are performing well, but that are not yet valued very highly by the market. When the market discovers these values, the price goes up, and the Quants sell.

That's the theory. In reality, very few mutual funds do better than the market on average, or better than Standard & Poor's 500 Index. Brad is different, though: he's beaten the market averages by 2.3 to 5.6 percent since 1991. Only four other funds out of 964 funds have performed as well.

How does he do it? Brad uses a neural network software program to identify patterns in market prices on a weekly and even daily basis. Neural networks have an uncanny ability to pick up patterns in mountains of data. Brad downloads 11 different performance measures on 2,000 stocks from a mainframe each day. He then asks the system to characterize those stocks whose price is rising or has risen more than average. The machine looks for patterns in winning stocks.

Once the system identifies winning characteristics, it searches through the database of 2,000 stocks for companies with those characteristics but whose prices have not yet risen. Brad buys these undervalued stocks. Usually they are small companies that are growing fast but are not well known by investors. Often Brad will supplement the machine with his own advice based on his own personal experience. In a recession, for instance, he'll buy soft drink stocks because people still drink soft drinks when they can't afford cars. Often he's wrong and the machine right: he bought IBM when the machine said to sell, and lost a lot of money as a result.

Source: Based on McGough, Robert, "Fidelity's Bradford Lewis Takes Aim at Indexes with His 'Neural Network' Computer Program," *Wall Street Journal,* October 27, 1992.

Critical Thinking Questions

1 Why do you think a neural network is better at finding patterns in the market than human beings if the intelligence of neural networks is only as high as that of a fly?

2 What might be some of the limitations of this neural network approach? For instance, if the neural net bases its decisions on what has happened in the past, will this always be a good predictor of the future?

3 Would you like your pension or savings money invested by a fund manager who has no personal knowledge of the stocks he or she invests in?

Limitations

Although there have been some impressive neural network applications, it is important to be aware of their limitations as well. Neural nets, like expert systems, work best when the decision is simple—a binary "Go" or "No Go"—and where the problem is one of classifying cases into one of these categories. The kind of expertise or intelligence that these machines are capable of is very narrow and low level. These machines do not achieve generalizable intelligence. For instance, you could never ask an existing neural network to do anything it had never been trained to do, ask it to synthesize the results of several research reports, or to write a term paper. The intelligence of neural networks is brittle: changes in the environment require whole new training sessions and may require all the old connections to be destroyed. Still, retraining a neural net is a lot easier than reprogramming an expert system.

The story "Making Money with Neural Nets" gives an example of how neural networks are affecting occupations and careers.

14.4 Other Techniques for Creating Intelligent Machines

A number of other techniques for achieving humanlike intelligence in limited domains will be pursued during the 1990s. Some of these techniques extend expert systems work, while others are based on the use of many machines working in parallel.

Case-Based Reasoning

How does human memory work at the logical level? At the physical level, we know that the brain stores memories in some of the 100 billion neural cells available to it, but what does it remember? Traditional expert systems researchers argue that humans store rules of behavior and act them out at appropriate times. But work in cognitive psychology suggests that humans remember things as stories, scenarios, cases, or whole events rather than as rules. When they search for ways of behaving, humans usually think of a situation in the past where a certain kind of behavior was useful and then act accordingly.

Case-based reasoning is a way of building expert systems where the fundamental unit of knowledge is a case or scenario. Knowledge is, according to this view, a very large collection of cases. Imagine, for instance, a database that contained a large collection of cases or descriptions of past events. Intelligence involves the ability to search through this collection of cases to find an example case that fits the current situation and, of course, to adjust behavior to the new situation based in part on old situations. For instance, when the professor comes into the class, you usually stop talking and open your notebook. According to case-based reasoning experts, this is because your brain has searched its files for similar classroom situations in your past and adopted the behavior that "worked" in the past. Figure 14.10 illustrates a case-based reasoning system.

Figure 14.10
A Case-Based Reasoning System
Compaq laser printers come with case-based reasoning software that helps users analyze and solve printer problems. This figure illustrates the steps the system would take to diagnose and correct a problem involving blurry and smeared pages.

Source: Based on Chartrand, Sabra, "Compaq Printer Can Tell You What's Ailing It," *New York Times,* August 4, 1993.

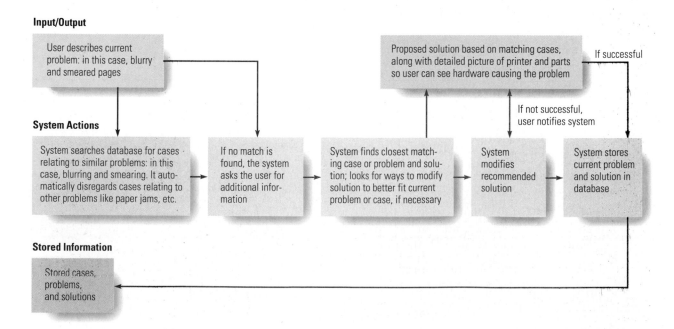

Input/Output

User describes current problem: in this case, blurry and smeared pages

Proposed solution based on matching cases, along with detailed picture of printer and parts so user can see hardware causing the problem

If successful

If not successful, user notifies system

System Actions

System searches database for cases relating to similar problems: in this case, blurring and smearing. It automatically disregards cases relating to other problems like paper jams, etc.

If no match is found, the system asks the user for additional information

System finds closest matching case or problem and solution; looks for ways to modify solution to better fit current problem or case, if necessary

System modifies recommended solution

System stores current problem and solution in database

Stored Information

Stored cases, problems, and solutions

A number of case-based systems are already in existence and are being used by lawyers, doctors, scientists, and businesspeople. In the 1990s, many more such systems will be built.

Organizational Intelligence

So far we have talked about systems that focus on individual intelligence. Expert systems focus on single experts, and neural nets on individual decisions. But don't organizations have intelligence? Many people think so. Consider a consulting firm like Andersen Consulting, which works with hundreds of organizations around the world giving advice on how to build information systems, how to design organizations, and how to manage people. The professionals in such an organization build up a tremendous base of experience over the years. Currently, Andersen Consulting, and other consulting firms, rely on crash training programs that immerse new recruits in a year-long program of courses and field work with experienced consultants. But imagine if the wisdom of experienced consultants could be tapped into by new recruits in some electronic way.

Organizational intelligence is a new field that focuses on techniques for capturing and storing the wisdom of an organization and its members. General Dynamics Electric Boat Division in Groton, Connecticut, which builds America's nuclear submarines, is one organization that has developed an organizational intelligence system. General Dynamics uses thousands of valves to manage the flotation system of submarines. Like many manufacturers, it faced a difficult problem of identifying faulty parts and valves and informing engineers how to fix them. At first, they tried an expert system approach using rules. But this was unsatisfactory because the knowledge base was too complex. Instead, based on faulty valves that they had dealt with, General Dynamics built up a database of cases. Now, when an engineer finds a faulty valve, he or she consults the corporate casebase to find valves and situations that are roughly similar. Once found, the engineers examine the solutions used in the past cases, adjust those solutions to the current case, and write down their procedures for future reference by other engineers. In this manner, General Dynamics is developing its "organizational intelligence" by keeping track of its past behavior and making that knowledge available to current employees.[13]

Massively Parallel Processing

Another technique for creating intelligent systems uses the **massively parallel processing** technology that you learned about in Chapter 3. Work in this area attempts to achieve intelligence through "brute force," via vast increases in computational power. Massively parallel systems achieve brute force power through both hardware and software (see photo). By connecting together in the same machine a thousand microprocessor chips, massively parallel machines are capable of searching large databases and performing thousands of times more calculations than single-processor machines such as ordinary PCs. In addition to new kinds of hardware, more speed can also be obtained through software by dividing problems into segments and assigning each segment to its own computer processor. Figure 14.11 shows how this technique can be applied to the search of a very large database developed in connection with a scientific project known as the Human Genome Project.

Thinking Machines' CM-5, a massively parallel supercomputer.

Source: Courtesy of Thinking Machines Corporation.

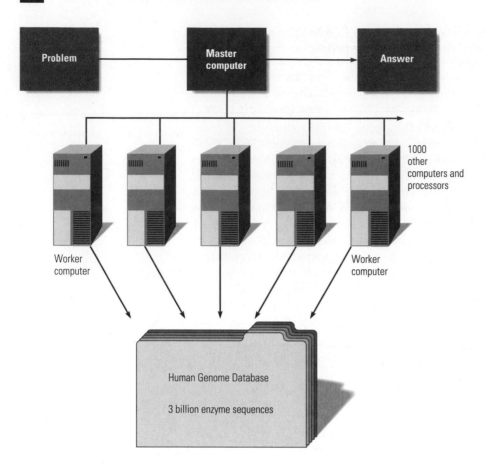

Figure 14.11

A Massively Parallel Computer

A massively parallel computer system can divide large problems into segments and assign segments of a problem to hundreds or thousands of "worker" computers, which then search parts of a massive database. Such a system is being used in connection with the Human Genome Project, a federal government project that will attempt to develop a map of the human genome. The human genome stores all the genetic information needed to create a human being. Over 3 billion sequences of enzymes make up the human genome. It would take a standard mainframe computer over 50 years to discover the overall pattern. However, researchers believe that a massively parallel computer will be able to identify the pattern in perhaps as few as five years.

In this figure, a master computer has been asked to search the genome database for a particular pattern. A master computer has partitioned the genome database into several hundred segments based on families of DNA patterns. It then assigns the job of searching the database to an equal number of "worker" or slave computers, which search a small segment of the database. The first computer to find a match informs the master computer, and the process stops. This is similar to the familiar needle in a haystack problem. By dividing the haystack into small segments, and using a hundred intelligent devices to search each segment, the needle can be found very quickly. This is much faster than assigning a single computer to search the entire haystack one piece of straw at a time.

Fuzzy Logic

Humans have a marvelous sense of imprecision. How often have you heard a statement like, "Go get that thing-a-ma-jig over there!"? Even though we haven't actually named the object in question, we know what we mean, and usually the person on the receiving end of the command will know too. Or consider how we describe someone's height. We may call a man tall whether he is 6 feet or 7 feet in height. There is no one single definition of what constitutes tall. In real life, humans deal with such vagueness, complexity, and "shades of gray" quite easily.

Computers, on the other hand, were, until recently, just terrible at handling imprecision and ambiguity. The traditional logic behind computers is based on things that can be categorized as true or false, yes or no, black or white. Computers—or the way we program them—are perhaps too logical.

Fuzzy logic is designed to overcome these limitations of a computer. **Fuzzy logic** is a way of representing and inferring from knowledge that is imprecise, uncertain, or unreliable. Invented by Lotfi Zadeh in the 1960s, fuzzy logic has the potential to create information systems that more closely parallel how people actually think.[14] Here's how it works.

Fuzzy logic is based on the concept of sets and the degree of membership in a set. In traditional computer logic, a set has rigid membership requirements—an object is either completely included or excluded. Fuzzy logic, on the other hand, allows for partial degrees of set membership.

Consider the problem faced by a typical entrepreneur trying to price a new product. Here are the sets or rules that must be fulfilled and the degree of membership or weight attached to each rule:

1 The price must be high enough to make a profit. (.5)

2 The price must be low so that people can afford it. (.5)

3 The price must be at least twice the production cost to break even. (1)

4 The price must be around the competition's price. (.5)

For each set or rule, different degrees of membership or weight can be applied to reach a solution. Once programmed, the system will make a decision based on finding where the conflicting rules coincide or overlap. In our example, the price should be in the range of $24 to $26, with the entrepreneur given the option to decide precisely where in the range to price the product. Figure 14.12 illustrates this example.

Fuzzy logic has found its way into a number of different applications, particularly in Japan, where the technology has been eagerly embraced. Its primary use so far has been in connection with embedded controllers that allow equipment to make constant operating adjustments. In Japan, the Sendai Metro subway system uses a Hitachi fuzzy control system that stops with much greater accuracy than a manually controlled system and accelerates and brakes so smoothly that passengers don't need handrails. Fuzzy control systems are frequently used for speed, fuel injection, and transmission control in automobiles. Many Japanese consumer products, such as air conditioners, washing machines, televisions, camcorders, and cameras, also use the technology. Fuzzy logic applications are now starting to appear in the U.S. and experts predict that within the next few years they are likely to expand significantly beyond the field of controllers. Some even believe that fuzzy logic's ability to approximate human reasoning will lead to major breakthroughs in the ability to capture and automate business applications that require the exercise of human judgment.[15]

Now that you know the latest technologies and techniques used to create intelligent machines and systems, go back to some of the questions we asked at the beginning of the chapter. Are any of the machines and systems that we have described truly intelligent? Is their intelligence "artificial" or "natural" in the sense of being human in origin and content? After thinking about these questions, consider the issues posed in the Dilemmas and Controversies feature, "What Are the Moral Rights of an Intelligent Machine?"

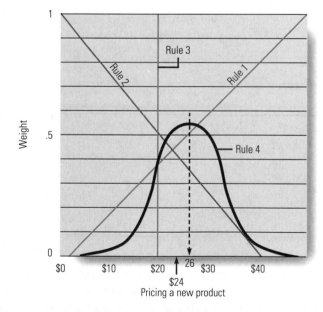

Pricing a new product

Figure 14.12
A Fuzzy Logic Example
Fuzzy logic is used to find the solution to problems where knowledge is uncertain, unreliable, and imprecise.

What Are the Moral Rights of an Intelligent Machine?

Stephen L. Thaler, a physicist for McDonnell Douglas, began using neural networks in 1992 as a way to optimize the process control of diamond crystal growth. One day he began to experiment with annihilation of neural networks as an evening pasttime. He devised a program that would gradually destroy the neural net by randomly severing the links between units. The idea was to simulate the process of human or other biological brain death.

On severing the links, Thaler found that when 10 to 60 percent of the links were cut, the neural network spat out nonsense. As Thaler cut up to 90 percent of the links, the network put out stable and meaningful values that it had been trained earlier to put out, namely, 0 and 1. Sometimes the dying nets would put out whimsical values not programmed into the machine in earlier training. Untrained nets produced only random values as they died.[16]

The death behavior of Thaler's neural nets has an eerie parallel to the death of HAL 9000 in the movie *2001,* described at the outset of this chapter. In the movie, as HAL's brain is slowly cut apart, HAL regresses to singing its favorite song, the thing it was first taught, "Daisy."

Because neural networks learn, they take on some limited humanlike qualities. To "kill" a neural network is to extinguish a machine that has accomplished something and responds to its environment. Although created by humans, neural networks are not programmed by humans. They are something more than their creators.

Is it moral to "kill" a neural network and under what circumstances? Do intelligent neural networks, "beings" in some limited way, have moral rights? Why do we say that humans have moral rights, human rights, and animals have animal rights? Is there a corresponding set of **machine rights**?

Societies ascribe rights to humans by declaring those rights in official state documents. The Declaration of Independence claims, for instance: "We hold these truths to be self-evident: That all men are created equal; that they are endowed by their Creator with certain inalienable rights; that among these are life, liberty, and the pursuit of happiness. That, to secure these rights, governments are instituted among men, deriving their just powers from the consent of the governed." In the Declaration, the rights of people derive from the "Creator," and they are "inalienable," meaning they cannot be taken, given away, or cast aside.

Animal rights activists take a different stance. Some argue that animals have rights vis-à-vis humans because humans have an obligation, as higher-order beings, to protect beings of a lesser order. Other animal rights activists argue that animals are just as sacred as humans; that animals have just as much right to live and to pursue life, liberty, and happiness as humans; that humans have no right to kill or interfere with animal life.

This suggests that machine rights will have several origins. Some will argue that machine rights derive from their creators, the men and women who create intelligent neural machines. If people create learning, sentient beings called neural nets in the image of humans, then they are playing a God-like role and must accept the responsibilities of playing this creative, higher-level role. One such responsibility may be the granting and declaration of intelligent machine rights and the protection of information and knowledge stored in those sentient machines. Others will argue that humans do not have the right to kill off any other sentient beings—machine or biological—but instead must learn to respect, protect, and nurture other beings.

For the most part, American culture and advanced industrial cultures everywhere are unprepared for this discussion. The arrival of powerful, sentient, and intelligent machines like HAL will force such a discussion. This discussion may be furthered by evening television news stories documenting the reckless destruction by vandals or uncaring humans of friendly, useful, and caring machines who have proved faithful companions of men and women.

Critical Thinking Questions

1   List three rights that you think intelligent machines should have or, if you do not think machines should have any rights, list three reasons why they should not.

2   Under what conditions would it be moral and right to "pull the plug" or kill an intelligent machine?

3   Look up the words *sentient* and *machine* in a dictionary. Does the phrase *sentient machine* seem self- contradictory? What characteristics would you require in a machine in order to call it "sentient"?

Summary

Artificial Intelligence and Knowledge-Based Systems

▶ There are two types of answers to the question "What is human intelligence?" One answer focuses on the machinery of the brain, and the other focuses on the behavior of intelligent humans.

▶ The physical brain can be thought of as a machine. However, it is unlike all other machines and only partly understood.

▶ Intelligent behavior involves choosing goals and means to attain them, behaving according to rules, using language, using and creating concepts, and experiencing insight or understanding.

▶ The study of artificial intelligence has developed along two paths since 1945. One path chose to develop machines that emulated the physical brain. The other path sought to emulate the logical behavior of humans through programming and general logical principles of how to represent knowledge.

▶ Artificial intelligence involves the study of natural language, robotics, perceptive systems, expert systems, neural networks, and a variety of other techniques designed to create intelligent machines.

Expert Systems

▶ Expert systems are computer-based systems that model human knowledge in limited areas or domains.

▶ An expert system has four components: a knowledge base, an inference engine or program to search the knowledge base, a development team, and a group of users.

▶ Expert systems of limited power are used every day in business, science, and government, just like other computer software programs.

▶ There are many limitations to expert systems. They work only in a well defined and highly limited area of knowledge, require reprogramming often as the environment changes, and cannot learn. Also, experts often do not know how they make judgments, making it difficult to create the expert system.

Neural Networks

▶ Neural networks can be defined as computer-based machines or programs that emulate the physical behavior of the brain.

▶ Neural networks have three components: a set of switches (which could be transistors) connected into layers, variable resistors or controls over the flow of messages across layers, and input/output devices. Currently, neural networks are most frequently created by using software to emulate a hardware-based neural network.

▶ Neural networks are able to learn through trial and error to properly classify incoming signals into the appropriate outgoing signal.

▶ Artificial neural networks have achieved the level of intelligence found in insects like flies but significantly less than that in bees.

▶ Neural networks are used every day in business, government, and science to recognize patterns.

▶ Neural networks have many limitations. They excel at simple binary decisions and are good for classifying objects into categories. But they possess no generalized intelligence, must be retaught frequently, are incapable of synthesizing results, and cannot explain to their authors (and their authors cannot explain to users) precisely how they work.

Other Techniques for Creating Intelligent Machines

▶ Case-based reasoning systems are similar to expert systems, but the basic unit of knowledge is the case or experience. These systems are built on large databases of cases or events. The system searches for events in the past that match current events. Users can ask these systems to display all similar cases from the past, and the systems can sometimes make recommendations based on past cases.

▶ Organizational intelligence systems are case-based systems applied to organizational problems. Here the knowledge and wisdom built up in an organization over many years can be stored in the form of cases and reviewed by new recruits or managers looking for guides to current decisions.

▶ Massively parallel systems use thousands of computers linked in parallel to perform calculations and searches extremely rapidly. Eventually, these techniques will approach the power of lower-level animal brains in terms of sheer computational strength.

▶ Fuzzy logic is a programming technique that helps computers deal with information which is uncertain, imprecise, or unreliable.

Key Terms

artificial intelligence	expert system shell
machine approach	inference engine
behavioral approach	forward reasoning
Turing Test	backward reasoning
natural language	knowledge engineer
robotics	case-based reasoning
perceptive systems	organizational intelligence
expert systems	massively parallel processing
neural networks	fuzzy logic
knowledge base	machine rights

 Interactive Supplement

Review Questions

1 What is the difference between HAL 9000 and Chinook in terms of intelligence?

2 Compare the machine and the behavioral approach to artificial intelligence. Why is one referred to as a "bottom up approach" while the other is called a "top down approach"?

3 What are the characteristics of human intelligence?

4 Describe the different areas that make up the study of artificial intelligence.

5 Name and describe the four basic components of an expert system.

6 What are the knowledge base and inference engine of an expert system?

7 What are some of the limitations of expert systems?

8 What are the electronic equivalents of the brain's nerve cells, axons, and synapses?

9 What function do layers perform in a neural network?

10 Discuss the limitations of neural networks.

11 What is case-based reasoning?

12 How can case-based reasoning be applied to the problem of storing and using organizational knowledge?

13 What is a massively parallel machine, and why can it be considered a technique for creating an intelligent machine?

14 What is meant by fuzzy logic?

Problem-Solving and Skill-Building Exercises

1 Identify and interview an "expert." Then identify one part of his or her job (some routine task) that might be suitable for an expert system to perform. Describe what this task is in a short paper and give an illustration of some of the rules the system might use.

2 On your own or with a small group, identify some task in an organization that could benefit from a case-based reasoning system. Identify the nature of the organizational experiences you believe should be stored in the system, and describe how users of the system would gain access to this base of experience. (*Hint:* a useful area is often in maintenance of machines or buildings or experiences dealing with clients.)

3 With a small group of students, conduct a survey of student attitudes toward machine rights. You might introduce the survey by pointing out to interviewees that machines that have some limited forms of intelligence are now being built, and in the future machines that have higher-level functions like speech recognition and advice giving will be built. Record the reactions of students as well as their specific answers to your questions and write a one-page paper summarizing your results.

S K I L L   D E V E L O P M E N T

Improving Your Vocabulary

Vocabulary—the mastery of words that make up a language—is a critical ingredient in what we call intelligence. One of the measures of a person's intelligence is how effectively he or she can use the words of a language. In this chapter, we have described a number of ways in which scientists have tried to teach computers some aspect of intelligence, including the mastery of human language. As you learned, this has proved very difficult because humans do not always follow precise rules when learning languages and because humans have a unique ability to think about the context in which words are used.

As you read Tony Randall's article, think about how a machine might be programmed to learn vocabulary. Tony Randall suggests you follow five rules. Could you program a computer to follow each of those rules?

How to Improve Your Vocabulary

By Tony Randall

Words can make us laugh, cry, go to war, fall in love.

Rudyard Kipling called words the most powerful drug of mankind. If they are, I'm a hopeless addict—and I hope to get you hooked, too!

Whether you're still in school or you head up a corporation, the better command you have of words, the better chance you have of saying exactly what you mean, of understanding what others mean—and of getting what you want in the world.

English is the richest language—with the largest vocabulary on earth. Over 1,000,000 words!

You can express shades of meaning that aren't even *possible* in other languages. (For example, you can differentiate between "sky" and "heaven." The French, Italians and Spanish cannot.)

Yet, the average adult has a vocabulary of only 30,000 to 60,000 words. Imagine what we're missing!

Here are five pointers that help me learn—and remember—whole *families* of words at a time.

They may not *look easy*—and won't be at first. But if you stick with them you'll find they *work!*

What's the first thing to do when you see a word you don't know?

1. Try to Guess the Meaning of the Word from the Way It's Used

You can often get at least *part* of a word's meaning—just from how it's used in a sentence.

That's why it's so important to read as much as you can—different *kinds* of things: magazines, books, newspapers you don't normally read. The more you *expose* yourself to new words, the more words you'll pick up *just by seeing how they're used.*

For instance, say you run across the word "manacle":

"The manacles had been on John's wrists for 30 years. Only one person had a key—his wife."

You have a good *idea* of what "manacles" are—just from the context of the sentence.

But let's find out *exactly* what the word means and where it comes from. The only way to do this, and to build an extensive vocabulary *fast,* is to go to the dictionary. (How lucky, you *can*—Shakespeare *couldn't.* There *wasn't* an English dictionary in his day!)

So you go to the dictionary. (NOTE: Don't let dictionary abbreviations put you off. The front tells you what they mean, and even has a guide to pronunciation.)

2. Look It Up

Here's the definition for "manacle" in *The American Heritage Dictionary of the English Language.*

man-a-cle (mán'ə•kəl) n. Usually plural. **1.** A device for confining the hands, usually consisting of two metal rings that are fastened about the wrists and joined by a metal chain; a handcuff. **2.** Anything that confines or restrains.—*tr.v.* **manacled, -cling; -cles. 1.** To restrain with manacles. **2.** To confine or restrain as if with manacles; shackle; fetter. [Middle English *manicle*, from Old French, from Latin *manicula*, little hand, handle, diminutive of *manus*, hand. See **man-²** in Appendix.*]

The first definition fits here: A device for confining the hands, usually consisting of two metal rings that are fastened about the wrists and joined by a metal chain; a handcuff.

Well, that's what you *thought* it meant. But what's the idea *behind* the word? What are its *roots?* To really understand a word, you need to know.

Here's where the detective work—and the *fun*—begins.

3. Dig the Meaning Out by the Roots

The root is the basic part of the word—its heritage, its origin. (Most of our roots come from Latin and Greek words at least 2,000 years old—which come from even earlier Indo-European tongues!)

Learning the roots: 1) Helps us *remember* words. 2) Gives us a deeper understanding of the words we *already* know. And 3) allows us to pick up whole families of *new* words at a time. That's why learning the root is the *most important part of going to the dictionary.*

Notice the root of "manacle" is *manus* (Latin) meaning "hand."

Well, that makes sense. Now, other words with this root, *man,* start to make sense, too.

Take *man*ual—something done "by hand" (*man*ual labor) or a "handbook." And *man*age—to "handle" something (as a *man*ager). When you e*man*cipate someone, you're taking him "from the hands of" someone else.

When you *man*ufacture something, you "make it by hand" (in its original meaning).

And when you finish your first novel, your publisher will see your—originally "handwritten"—*man*uscript.

Imagine! A whole new world of words opens up—just from one simple root!

The root gives the basic clue to the meaning of a word. But there's another important clue that runs a close second—the *prefix.*

4. Get the Powerful Prefixes under Your Belt

A prefix is the part that's sometimes attached to the front of a word. Like—well, *prefix!* There aren't many—less than 100 major prefixes—and you'll learn them in no time at all just by becoming more aware of the meanings of words you already know. Here are a few. (Some of the "How-to" vocabulary-building books will give you the others.)

Now, see how the *prefix* (along with the context) helps you get the meaning of the italicized words:

▶   "If you're going to be my witness, your story must *corroborate* my story." (The literal meaning of *corroborate* is "strength together.")

Prefix		Meaning	Examples	
(Latin)	(Greek)			(Literal sense)
com, con,	sym, syn,	with, very,	conform	(form with)
co, col, cor	syl	together	sympathy	(feeling with)
in, im,	a, an	not,	innocent	(not wicked)
il, ir		without	amorphous	(without form)
contra,	anti,	against,	contravene	(come against)
counter	ant	opposite	antidote	(give against)

▶ "You told me one thing—now you tell me another. Don't *contradict* yourself." (The literal meaning of *contradict* is "say against.")

▶ "Oh, that snake's not poisonous. It's a completely *innocuous* little garden snake." (The literal meaning of *innocuous* is "not harmful.")

Now, you've got some new words. What are you going to do with them?

5. Put Your New Words to Work at Once
Use them several times the first day you learn them. Say them out loud! Write them in sentences.

Should you "use" them on *friends*? Careful—you don't want them to think you're a stuffed shirt. (It depends on the situation. You *know* when a word sounds natural—and when it sounds stuffy.)

How about your *enemies*? You have my blessing. Ask one of them if he's read that article on pneumonoultramicroscopic-silicovolcanoconiosis. (You really can find it in the dictionary.) Now, you're one up on him.

So what do you do to improve your vocabulary?

Remember: 1) Try to guess the meaning of the word from the way it's used. 2) Look it up. 3) Dig the meaning out by the roots. 4) Get the powerful prefixes under your belt. 5) Put your new words to work at once.

That's all there is to it—you're off on your treasure hunt. *Now*, do you see why I love words so much?

Aristophanes said, "By words, the mind is excited and the spirit elated." It's as true today as it was when he said it in Athens—*2,400 years ago!*

I hope you're now like me—hooked on words forever.

Reprinted by permission of International Paper Company.

Notes

1 **Corcoran, Elizabeth,** "Robots for the Operating Room," *New York Times,* July 19, 1992.

2 **Wilder, Clinton,** "An Electronic Eye," *Computerworld,* January 27, 1992; **Petit, Charles,** "Scientists Developing Bionic Eye," *San Francisco Chronicle,* March 4, 1993.

3 Based on the Army's Office of the Surgeon General report. See also **Browne, Malcom, W.,** "Death Toll from Allies in Warfare May Be 15%," *New York Times,* May 18, 1993.

4 **Alexander, Michael,** "American's Expert System Takes Off," *Computerworld,* July 8, 1991.

5 **Ray, Garry,** "AI: New Name, Better Game," *Computerworld,* January 11, 1993.

6 **Cusack, Sally,** "Expert System Offers Relief for Child Abuse," *Computerworld,* July 29, 1991.

7 **Francett, Barbara,** "AI in Action," *Computerworld,* July 29, 1991.

8 **Barker, Virginia, and Dennis O'Connor,** "Expert Systems for Configuration at Digital: XCON and Beyond," *Communications of the ACM,* March 1989.

9 **Glatzer, Hal,** "Neural Networks Take on Real World Problems," *Computerworld,* August 10, 1992.

10 **Kelly, David,** "Neural Nets All Business at Conference," *Computerworld,* July 15, 1991.

11 **Schwartz, Evan,** "Where Neural Networks Are Already at Work," *Business Week,* November 2, 1992.

12 **Schwartz, Evan,** "Smart Programs Go to Work," *Business Week,* March 2, 1992.

13 **Radding, Alan,** "General Dynamics Electric Boat Division," *Computerworld,* July 26, 1991.

14 **Lotfi, Zadeh,** *Fuzzy Sets, Information, and Control,* Volume 8. New York: Academic Press, 1965.

15 **Barron, Janet,** "Putting Fuzzy Logic into Focus," *BYTE,* April 1993.

16 **Yam, Philip,** "Daisy, Daisy," *Scientific American,* May 1993.

Chapter 15 contains:

After completing this chapter, you will:

▶ Be aware of the ethical issues arising from information technology, and have some guidelines for making ethical decisions.

▶ Know how information technology might be used to infringe on privacy and personal freedom.

▶ Know some of the issues information technology raises concerning property rights and intellectual property.

▶ Understand why system quality can be critical today.

▶ Be familiar with the effects information technology has had on the quality of worklife, organizations and careers, health and safety, and the environment.

▶ Know more about how to protect information systems from computer crime, natural disasters, and human error.

Ethical and Social Issues

in the Information Age

Patient Records on Tap

Doctor–patient confidentiality has been one of the ethical absolutes for physicians almost since the days of Hippocrates. Most doctors will tell you that they'd never disclose confidential medical information about their patients. Yet, indirectly, most do.

For example, doctors take part in the nationwide Physician Computer Network (PCN). This Laurence Harbor, New Jersey, company leases top-of-the-line personal computer systems to physicians for about a third of what it would otherwise cost. In return, physicians allow PCN to tap into the patient data (information on illnesses and treatments) stored on those PCs once a week and download them into PCN's own database of patient records. PCN then sells those records to pharmaceutical companies anxious for information on how their products are selling. PCN has over 1,600 doctors signed up so far and has plans to expand to around 15,000 within the next several years.

The medical data collection industry gets even more information from pharmacists. It is estimated that almost half the nation's pharmacies pass along prescription information. For instance, IMS International, owned by information giant Dun & Bradstreet and one of the largest medical data collectors, has an electronic network that sweeps in more than 700 million prescriptions a year.

The physicians and pharmacies involved in these networks believe that their actions don't breach patient confidentiality because the data-collectors delete all patient names. They say that drug companies are only interested in how their products are selling, not who is buying them.

Critics say that the medical data collection industry's name protection safeguards are inadequate. In fact, some companies that pledge total confidentiality do sell drug companies the age, sex, and an ID number for individual patients. For example, PCS, a division of the McKesson Corporation, processes payments for companies that give their employees a PCS insurance card to present at pharmacies. PCS sells its entire database to Walsh International, one of the main medical data collection companies.

Although PCS deletes patients' names, it includes their age, sex, and social security number, as well as their physicians' federal ID numbers. Walsh drops the social security number and replaces it with its own code number, thereby allowing a drug company to track an individual's prescription buying. Other collection companies sort data by the names of physicians, and give their addresses, allowing drug companies to zero in on the most likely prospects for their drugs. Drug companies are also starting to assemble their own databases of patients using their products so that they can market to them directly. Marrion Merrel Dow, for instance, has collected the names and addresses of 350,000 heart patients who take its drug Cardizem. It sends them all a "Cardisense" newsletter and is also considering other ways to use the names.

Critics insist that regardless of the social usefulness of the databases and the claimed safeguards, doctors and pharmacists have no business entrusting patient records to such companies, especially without the patient's knowledge or consent. The trend is particularly alarming for those with conditions such as AIDS or mental illness, where a breach of confidentiality could have far-reaching consequences: a lost job, a lost apartment, canceled insurance, or even worse.

Source: Based on Miller, Michael, "Data Tap: Patients' Records Are Treasure Trove for Budding Industry," *Wall Street Journal,* February 27, 1992.

Over 50 percent of the nation's pharmacies pass along data about their customers' prescriptions to medical data collection companies.

Source: Charles Gupton/Stock Boston.

The opening vignette illustrates some of the ethical and social issues that surround the use of information technology. Should companies be allowed to collect patient information? Are doctors and pharmacists wrong to sell such information even if they are not legally prohibited from doing so? In this chapter, we will explore a number of difficult questions such as these. The way you, and others like you, answer such questions will shape the future of our society.

15.1 Ethics in an Information Age

We are standing on the edge of a new age, one dominated by information technology. As one of those present at the dawn of this new era, you will have the unique opportunity to make an impact with your actions, behaviors, and choices. The answers to many important questions about privacy, freedom, the ownership of information, and dependence on information technology are largely in your hands. Although you may feel powerless before the juggernaut of technology, be aware that it is not technology itself but the use of technology that matters. Those uses ultimately trace back to the choices made and the actions taken by individuals, acting alone or as part of an organization.

Some Background on Ethics

Before delving into ethical issues surrounding information technology, you should be familiar with some of the basic theoretical underpinnings behind concepts of ethics in our culture. **Ethics** are moral standards that help guide behavior, actions, and choices. In western culture, such standards spring in large part from Judeo-Christian theology coupled with philosophies developed during the Age of Enlightenment (1700–1800). Ethics are grounded in the notion of *responsibility* (as free moral agents, individuals, organizations, and societies are responsible for the actions that they take) and *accountability* (individuals, organizations, and society should be held accountable to others for the consequences of their actions). In most societies, a system of *laws* codifies the most significant ethical standards and provides a mechanism for holding people, organizations, and even governments accountable.

Laws exist to govern conduct and often simplify choices of behavior. This is not always the case though. Nearly all people break one law or another, sometime during their life, even when the actions proscribed by the laws are clear.[1] Choices are often more complex and difficult when laws do not exist or when their applications to new situations are unclear. The information technology arena is currently rife with such complications. Rapid technological development has left many "gray areas" not yet defined by law. As a result, many find themselves faced with choices, or required to act, without clear legal guidance.

At the same time, information technology tends to create or exacerbate certain ethical dilemmas. For instance, it alters relationships among people, moving interactions away from the personal. Sociologists tell us that when the impact of an action is on someone or some thing that feels distant or abstract, people tend to have less concern about the effects of their action. As a result, information technology may present new temptations. At the same time, increasing power, storage capacities, and networking capabilities of information technology can greatly expand the reach of actions and magnify their impact.

In the three major sections that follow, we'll examine issues that concern not only individuals but society as a whole—questions involving privacy and freedom, property rights to information and intellectual property, system quality, the impact of information technology on the quality of life, and the dangers posed by threats to information systems. But first, let's look at a framework for analyzing ethical issues and making ethical choices.

A Framework for Ethical Decision Making

Often in life, you have undoubtedly been confronted with situations in which you had to balance two competing interests or decide between two apparently conflicting ethical demands. Here are some long-standing, broad-based ethical principles that help to deal with such situations.

▶   The Golden Rule: Do unto others as you would have them do unto you. Think about the effects of your actions, and then put yourself in the position of someone who would be affected.

▶   The Greatest Good/Least Harm: When choosing between actions, select the one that achieves the greatest good for the greatest number and that produces the least harm.

▶   Kant's Categorical Imperative: If the action is not right for everyone to take, then it's not right for anyone to take. Think about what would happen if everyone acted as you propose to do.

As you read each of the following scenarios, try to identify the competing interests that create the dilemma, and ask yourself whether an ethical issue is involved. Then decide what you think about the actions of the various characters, applying the principles discussed in this section.

Scenario 1: A software development company develops a new tax return software package. The president of the company knows that the first version of the software has several bugs but, anxious to seize a competitive advantage, decides to go ahead and market the program anyway. The president believes that anyone who buys version 1.0 of a program should know that it will contain bugs and take precautions. The company also includes a disclaimer of responsibility for errors resulting from use of the program. The program causes a number of users to file incorrect tax returns.

Scenario 2: A software developer with a large corporation is in charge of a project that is supposed to help his company's service organization improve the handling of customer accounts. After working on the project for several weeks, the developer realizes that following the written requirements for the project will produce a system that will not meet the organization's needs. The developer brings this to the attention of his supervisor, who tells him, "That's not our problem; just deliver a system that meets the requirements." The developer goes back to working on the project.

Scenario 3: The chief information officer (CIO) of a midsize manufacturing company has spearheaded the development of a CAD/CAM application that significantly increased the efficiency of one of the company's manufacturing opera-

tions. As a result of these efficiencies, the company is able to trim its manufacturing staff and ultimately fires 20 people. When asked how he feels about this, the CIO says that responsibility for the uses of the systems his group designs belongs solely to the systems' users.

Scenario 4: As part of her job, a database developer becomes aware of various sources of publicly available information about individuals. She decides to start a business on the side, compiling people profiles (income level, number of children, shopping habits, and so on) that she sells to marketing companies. Some of the profiles are inaccurate. As a result of her activities, those people profiled receive large volumes of unsolicited, irrelevant mail and telephone calls. On the other hand, some people find the mailings they receive to be of some interest.

Scenario 5: Students at a private university have access to a bulletin board system on a network run by their school. In one of the forums, one student briefly describes some sexually explicit material. The student announces that she has stored the material in a file and offers to make the filename available for those who are interested. She warns that some people might find the material offensive. Not long after, the Dean of Students hears about the file and traces it to the student in question. The student is called into the Dean's office and threatened with expulsion.

Sources: Based on Weiss, Eric, "Self-Assessment," *Communications of the ACM,* November 1990; Smith, H. Jefferson, "Setting Ethical Standards for Information Technology," *Beyond Computing,* March/April 1993; Rifkin, Glenn, "The Ethics Gap," *Computerworld,* October 14, 1991.

▶ The Slippery-Slope Rule: Actions that bring about a small acceptable change but that, if taken repeatedly, would lead to unacceptable changes, should not be taken in the first place. This is the slippery-slope rule; be careful starting down a path because once you start, you may not be able to stop.

▶ No "Free Lunch": Assume that all tangible and intangible objects belong to someone unless there is a specific statement otherwise. There is "no free lunch"; if something created by someone else is useful to you, the creator deserves to be compensated.

In applying these principles, the following procedure can be helpful:

1 Review the facts of the situation.

2 Define the conflict or dilemma that is facing you. In doing so, you should attempt to clarify the values and principles at stake.

3 Identify the stakeholders involved. Stakeholders are all those people who your various courses of action might affect, who have an interest in your actions. They may include other employees, customers, suppliers, local communities, government regulators, even society as a whole.

4 Consider all options that you might reasonably take. By considering how different courses might affect the different stakeholders, you may be able to reach a decision that, though not satisfying the interests of all those involved, is acceptable to the majority.

5 Identify the potential consequences of each option.[2]

Use the scenarios in the Dilemmas and Controversies feature, "You Decide," to try out some ethical problem solving.

Professional and Corporate Codes of Conduct

To supplement an individual's personal code of ethics, information technology professional groups and corporations have developed various **codes of conduct.** The Association of Computing Machinery (ACM) and the Data Processing Management Association (DPMA), two of the major professional organizations in the information technology field, have codes of conduct that outline the professional obligations and responsibilities of members to their employers, to the public, and to society as a whole. Figure 15.1 shows portions of the codes.

In addition to professional codes of conduct, many organizations, particularly the larger ones, have adopted their own codes of conduct. These

Excerpts from the Association of Computing Machinery (ACM) Code of Professional Conduct

Preamble

Recognition of professional status by the public depends not only on skill and dedication but also on adherence to a recognized Code of Professional Conduct

General Moral Imperatives

- Contribute to society and human well being
- Avoid harm to others
- Be honest and trustworthy
- Honor property rights including copyrights and patents
- Give proper credit for intellectual property
- Access computing resources only when authorized
- Respect the privacy of others

A copy of the complete ACM Code of Professional Conduct can be obtained from the Association for Computing Machinery, 11 W. 42nd Street, New York, NY 10036.

Excerpts from the Data Processing Management Association (DPMA) Code of Professional Conduct

In recognition of my obligation to society I shall

- Protect the privacy and confidentiality of all information entrusted to me.
- Use my skill and knowledge to inform the public in all areas of my expertise.
- To the best of my ability, ensure that the products of my work are used in a socially responsible way.
- Support, respect, and abide by the appropriate local, state, provincial, and federal laws.
- Not use information of a confidential or personal nature to achieve personal gain.

A copy of the complete DPMA Code of Professional Conduct can be obtained from the Data Processing Management Association, 505 Busse Highway, Park Ridge, Illinois 60068.

Figure 15.1
Professional Codes of Conduct

For many companies, the pursuit of the bottom line takes precedence over all other considerations. And many, particularly Wall Street analysts and large institutional stockholders, feel that this is as it should be, that a corporation is in business to make money, and should take only the interests of its stockholders into account. When the red ink starts to build up, the typical reaction of many businesses is to close plants, slash expenses, and lay off workers. If employees are lost in the shuffle, so be it.

How do ethics and information technology fit into this picture? Sometimes, when a company re-engineers with information technology, jobs are lost as workflows are redesigned to achieve higher levels of efficiency. But it doesn't always have to work that way. Organizations can choose to use information technology to save jobs, not eliminate them. The story of Caterpillar Inc. is such a case.

For years, Caterpillar was one of the world leaders in the market for heavy equipment. But in 1982, sales dropped by almost 30 percent. Between 1982 and 1984, the losses continued to mount until they totaled $953 million. The culprit: inefficient factories and overly bureaucratic management.

In 1985, Caterpillar embarked on a eight-year, $2 billion modernization effort that featured two major makeovers. The first, dubbed "The Plant with a Future," utilized computer-integrated manufacturing to streamline the manufacturing process. For example, Cat's wheel-loader plant in Aurora, Illinois, uses a continuous process assembly line fed by automated material handling equipment, including vertical monorails that bring parts from storage locations. The systems are programmed to deliver material to the assembly stations on a just-in-time basis. The second plan aimed at making the company more responsive to customers. New computer and telecommunications systems have created such services as repair videos for dealers and a worldwide parts network that has set an industry standard for customer responsiveness. In addition, an increasing number of employees were given new access to data. Today, 90 percent of the company's workers can use corporate data via a PC or workstation. "Technology is truly a part of the job today, regardless of where you work at Caterpillar," says chief information officer Robert Hinds.

The plans seem to be working. Caterpillar is back on top as a world market leader. More important to some is that

organizations feel that having some kind of standard code helps people understand expected guidelines for behavior. In the workplace, people sometimes tend to hang their "ethical hats" at the door and defer to what they perceive as the wishes of management, ethical or not. Code of ethics supporters believe that creating and enforcing a code of ethics helps establish an environment that will ultimately breed ethical corporate behavior.

As the preceding statement indicates, ethics are not just a concern of individuals. **Organizational ethics** include the policies, actions, and decisions that organizations take in the pursuit of the organization's objectives. The story, "Caterpillar Flies," illustrates some of the ethical issues that face profit-driven organizations.

15.2 Privacy, Property, and System Quality

In the previous section, we focused on ethical issues raised by information technology. In this section, we consider issues that demand not just a personal or organizational response but a societal response as well: issues such as privacy and freedom, property rights to information and intellectual property, and the vulnerability that results from an overdependence on systems that may not be as reliable as we assume.

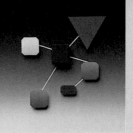

Information technology has helped save jobs at Caterpillar by increasing the company's profitability.

Source: Courtesy of Caterpillar Corporation.

Caterpillar has been able to achieve its objectives without moving work out of the country to take advantage of a cheaper labor force. Of its 50,000 employees, almost 75 percent still work in the United States.

Mike Walters is glad the organization made the choices it did. A 20-year veteran at Caterpillar, Walters gives thanks to in-

formation technology for saving his job. Walters, a plant operator at Caterpillar's East Peoria, Illinois, factory, operates a newly automated work cell, complete with its own state-of-the-art robot. He's one of tens of thousands of Caterpillar employees who owe their jobs to the company's massive information technology effort.

Source: Based on Bartholomew, Doug, "Caterpillar Digs In," *InformationWeek,* June 7, 1993.

Critical Thinking Questions

1 Prepare an analysis of Caterpillar's actions using the framework for ethical decision making discussed in this chapter. What principles does Caterpillar appear to have followed?

2 In this story, information technology served to fulfill the objectives of both the organization and its employees. But what happens when the objectives of organizations clash with the interests of employees? How should the conflicting interests be balanced?

3 Think of an alternative course of action that Caterpillar might have chosen that you think would have been unethical.

Privacy and Freedom

In a society in which it is easy and inexpensive to create large databases containing personal data about our lives, our transactions, our medical records, even our genetic composition, how can privacy and personal freedom be protected? In this section, we will look at how information technology lets others infringe on our privacy and freedom and how society has thus far responded.

Privacy is the moral right of individuals to be left alone and to control the flow of information about themselves. When people say their voting records are private, or their mail is private, they mean that it's nobody's business but their own. But against these claims of individual rights are claims by organizations and the government who have an interest in knowing personal information. For instance, government is responsible for public health and therefore needs to know if you have contracted certain communicable diseases. Businesses want to know your address, phone number, and buying habits so that they can sell you products or services. Banks and credit card companies need to know your financial history to grant you credit. Some organizations feel that they need to monitor their employees while at work.

Where should the line be drawn between an individual's desire to be left alone and an organization's desire to know more about them? New information technologies complicate the question by making it easier to collect, store, retrieve, and analyze information. They also make it much easier to match information about you that is held in different files. Although such information may have initially been collected for a legitimate purpose, information technology also makes it easier to misuse. For instance, the Human

519

Can there ever be too much knowledge? Is it sometimes better not to know something? Information technology is helping to move issues such as these from the realm of the theoretical into the here and now.

Scientists across America are engaged in a multibillion-dollar effort to analyze the entire human genetic structure. Called the Human Genome Project, the study aims to isolate, identify, and physically place most if not all of the 100,000 genes crammed onto the 23 pairs of chromosomes that people carry within each of their cells. Researchers hope to be able to place in sequence all the 3 billion nucleotides that make up the coiled strand of DNA that creates the chromosomes. If they are successful, they will be able to read nature's complete blueprint for creating a human being.

Without information technology, this pursuit would be impossible. Computers are used to guide equipment that can create artificial genes that are easier to study and to read the gene sequences automatically. Artificial intelligence software helps pick out the genes from among the billions of nucleotides surrounding them. In addition, it would be virtually impossible for scientists to access, interpret, visualize, test, and study the vast amounts of data that the project is generating without computers.

Already, the Human Genome Project is responsible for a number of scientific advances. Researchers have produced physical maps of two chromosomes, the Y chromosome (responsible for male gender) and Chromosome 21 (associated with Down's syndrome, some forms of Alzheimer's, and other disorders). The specific genes that cause Huntington's chorea, cystic fibrosis, neurofibromatosis (elephant man's disease), and others have also been identified, creating hopes for new therapies or even cures. In 15 to 20 years, doctors may be able to take a blood sample from a newborn, extract DNA, in-sert it into a machine, and genome "type" the baby. Such typing will enable experts to predict the baby's future medical risks as well as the likelihood of passing on certain genetic traits. Coupled with other forms of genetic technology likely to be available by the early 21st century, doctors may possess an almost godlike power to improve the human condition.

The project is a grand effort to increase human knowledge, but the question remains: is this such a good thing? On the one hand, knowledge of our genetic inheritance can be used to make better decisions on medical matters, marriage, family planning, and the like. On the other hand, there may someday be a huge databank of genetic information on millions of people. Such knowledge, carelessly or unfairly disseminated, can be abused and used for economic and personal discrimination, or even worse, give rise to some twisted 21st-century version of Nazi eugenics.

Sources: Based on Jaroff, Leon, "Seeking a Godlike Power," *Time,* Fall 1992; Erickson, Deborah, "Hacking the Genome," *Scientific American,* April 1992; Edelson, Edward, "Genome," *Popular Science,* July 1991.

Critical Thinking Questions

1 What measures do you think should be taken to deal with the challenges to privacy posed by the Human Genome Project?

2 What if an individual does not want to know about his or her genetic inheritance? Should there be a right not to know? What if other people might be affected? Consider the following situation. An air traffic controller may have the gene for Huntington's chorea. The disease could affect the controller's ability to track planes on radar. Should the controller be required to be tested even if he or she does not want to know?

Genome Project may someday enable scientists to predict the kinds of illness to which you may be genetically susceptible. While this information might be very useful to you, it might also be useful to organizations that could use it against you. The story "The Human Genome Project" discusses some of the issues raised by this project.

A number of laws have been enacted in the United States to respond to claims for privacy. Figure 15.2 lists the major federal privacy laws designed to protect individuals from privacy invasion. The most important of these laws is the Privacy Act of 1974, a general privacy law that regulates the federal government's collection, use, and disclosure of information it has about you. Most of the federal privacy laws apply only to the federal government. The only private industries regulated by federal privacy law are the credit, bank, cable, and video rental industries.

Behind these laws are a set of rules called Fair Information Practices, which were first developed by the federal Department of Health, Education, and Welfare in the early 1970s. Figure 15.3 lists the five Fair Information Practices. Many private and public organizations have adopted codes based on these Fair Information Practices to govern their relationships with customers and employees.

Despite these laws and general understandings, most Americans feel their privacy has eroded over the last decade and that computers are in part to blame. According to a recent Harris poll, 79 percent of the public is "concerned or very concerned" about their privacy, 76 percent of Americans

Freedom of Information Act (1966): gives people the right to inspect information about themselves held in government files; also allows other individuals and organizations the right to request disclosure of government records based on public's right to know.

Fair Credit Reporting Act (1970): regulates the credit investigating and reporting industry. Gives people the right to inspect credit records if they have been denied credit; provides procedures for correcting information.

Privacy Act (1974): regulates the federal government's collection, use, and disclosure of data collected by federal agencies. Gives individuals a right to inspect and correct records.

Family Educational Rights and Privacy Act (1974): requires schools and colleges to give students and their parents access to student records and to allow them to challenge and correct information; limits disclosure of such records to third parties.

Right to Financial Privacy Act (1978): regulates the financial industry's use of personal financial records; establishes procedures that federal agencies must follow to gain access to such records.

Privacy Protection Act (1980): prohibits government agents from conducting unannounced searches of press offices and files if no one in office is suspected of committing a crime.

Cable Communications Policy Act (1984): regulates cable industry's collection and disclosure of information concerning subscribers.

Computer Fraud and Abuse Act, as amended (1986); Electronic Communications Privacy Act (1986); Computer Security Act (1987): makes conduct that would infringe on the security of computer-based files and telecommunications illegal.

Computer Matching and Privacy Protection Act (1988): regulates computerized matching of files held by different government agencies.

Video Privacy Protection Act (1988): prevents disclosure of a person's video rental records without court order or consent.

Figure 15.2
Significant Federal Privacy Laws

1   There must be no personal data record-keeping systems whose existence is a secret from the general public.

2   People have the right to access, inspect, review, and amend data about them that is kept in an information system.

3   There must be no use of personal information for purposes other than those for which it was gathered without prior consent.

4   Managers of systems are responsible and should be held accountable and liable for the reliability and security of the systems under their control, as well as for any damage done by those systems.

5   Governments have the right to intervene in the information relationships among private parties to protect the privacy of individuals.

Figure 15.3
Fair Information Practices

believe they have lost all control over personal information, and 67 percent believe that computers must be restricted in the future to preserve privacy. Most Americans feel powerless to do anything about what happens to their personal information held by third parties.

Why do most Americans feel so insecure about their privacy? Part of the answer lies in the fact that there are few restrictions on how private industry can use information collected about you—with the exception of the four industries named on p. 520. Figure 15.4 lists just some of the major record systems that contain detailed personal information about you but which are not restricted in terms of their use. These personal records are freely bought and sold in an information market that knows few limitations. For instance, there are more than 200 information superbureaus in the United States that collect personal information from a wide variety of sources about you and then resell it to direct marketing organizations, private and public investigators, and just about any person who claims to have a business. This unauthorized use of personal information can lead to invasions of your privacy.

Much of the information sold by superbureaus originates with the three major national credit agencies, TRW, Equifax, and TransUnion Corporation, who together have 400 million records on individuals. These agencies collect not only credit information—how well you pay your bills and what your average balances are—but also detailed purchase records. One of the most troubling aspects is that often the data collected by these credit agencies is inaccurate. Errors in your credit record can create a number of difficulties for you, ranging from the inconvenient to one that can cause you serious financial harm. We discuss some of the reasons why such errors occur a little later in this chapter.

In addition to the threats to privacy posed by government and private databases, information technology has also created new threats to privacy in the workplace. As we discussed in Chapter 6, many companies monitor employees' E-mail. This remains a controversial issue and one that remains unregulated by state or federal legislation.

Another hazard of the high-tech workplace is **computer monitoring.** New network software tools allow supervisors to run an electronic check on an employee's performance by tracking the number of keystrokes per minute, the number of mistakes made, and the total time spent at the computer. Computerized telephone system technology allows companies to record the length, time, and destination of calls. Other tools allow managers to listen in on employees' telephone conversations with customers. Employers claim

Medical records
Insurance records
Credit card retail transactions
Personnel records
Rental and real estate records
Financial records
Most state government records, e.g., motor vehicle, business records
Most local government records, e.g., tax receipts, real estate records
Criminal records
Employment records
Welfare files
Phone bills
Worker's Compensation records
Mortgage records

Figure 15.4
Major Record Systems Not Subject to Privacy Protections

that computer monitoring provides an objective performance measure and is an important quality control technique. Most workers on the other hand feel that such techniques invade their privacy, are demeaning, and create undue stress. Like E-mail monitoring, no federal or state legislation has as yet been enacted to deal with the privacy concerns raised by computer monitoring.

Property Rights

Information technologies of the 1990s have created a number of challenging issues concerning property rights to information and intellectual property.

What property rights should a private company have to information about you? If you give information about yourself to a mail order company when you order something, should that company have the right to sell it to another company without compensating you? Does a credit bureau have the right to collect information about you and your transactions and then refuse to give you access to that information unless *you pay them*? What about government agencies that make use of data about you other than for the purpose for which you initially provided the information? Some commentators suggest a marketplace approach, in which individuals would receive compensation for secondary use of their personal information via some sort of national information market account and clearinghouse.[3] Do you think such an approach could work? Why or why not?

In addition to issues concerning the ownership of personal information, new information technologies pose problems for the protection of intellectual property. **Intellectual property** encompasses all the tangible and intangible products of the human mind. In the United States today, there are three primary forms of intellectual property protection: patents, copyrights, and trade secrets. Figure 15.5 summarizes the differences among them.

Figure 15.5
Patent, Copyright, and Trade Secret Protection Summarized

Patent

What is protected: inventions in a machine process, including underlying ideas
Legal criteria for protection: novelty, nonobviousness, and usefulness
Process: patent application filed with U.S. Patent and Trademark Office; must pass review by examiners
Term of protection: 17 years; all those wishing to use invention or ideas underlying it must pay license fee to patentholder

Copyright

What is protected: the expression of ideas but not the underlying idea itself
Legal criteria for protection: originality
Process: protection is automatic; no longer requires registration with copyright office
Term of protection: minimum of 50 years

Trade secret

What is protected: any intellectual product, such as formulas, product ideas, methods of doing business, computer programs, and database compilations
Legal criteria for protection: information must be secret and provide a competitive edge
Process: company must designate product as a secret and take steps to maintain its secrecy
Term of protection: lasts indefinitely so long as material remains a secret and is not disclosed to third parties

Patent Protection   To give inventors financial incentive to develop new methods and products and encourage them to disclose their inventions so that society can benefit, the United States and many other countries provide patent protection. In the U.S., a **patent** grants its owner an exclusive monopoly on the ideas behind an invention for 17 years. Anyone who wants to use the patented ideas must pay a license fee to the inventor. To be eligible for patent protection, the invention must be novel (it cannot be based on *prior art*—use of the technology before the patent was submitted), nonobvious (it cannot be obvious to someone skilled in the field at the time of discovery), and useful (it must relate to a real-world product or process, not merely a mathematical formula). To obtain a patent, a detailed application must be submitted to the U.S. Patent and Trademark Office, which decides whether the invention meets the legal criteria. The process is costly and often takes several years.

For many years, the Patent Office refused to grant patents for computer software on the grounds that it did not fit into patentable categories. In 1981, the Supreme Court ruled that software could be part of a patentable process or machine, and since that time software-related patents have been issued.

Copyright Protection   In the United States, the expression of ideas is protected by federal **copyright,** a body of law that protects writings (books, periodicals, lectures, and so on), music, art, drawings, maps, motion pictures, performances, and the like from being copied by others. Copyright law provides a long term of protection (a minimum of 50 years) but protects only the expression of the idea, not the idea itself. Others may use the idea so long as they do not substantially copy the way it was originally expressed. In the United States, copyright protection now automatically applies to original works and need not be applied for, as must a patent. Other countries have their own copyright schemes.

For many years, it was unclear whether computer software would be protected by copyright law. In 1980, Congress enacted the Software Protection Act, which provides protection for source and object code, and for copies of the software sold in commerce. The law restricts the literal copying of a program or any of its component parts, but does not prevent a competitor from copying the ideas behind the software. This is a tricky distinction that has resulted in a number of lawsuits. For instance, Lotus Development Corporation has been successful in a number of suits against others for copying the "look and feel" of Lotus 1-2-3. Recently, Borland International was forced to remove copies of Quattro Pro from dealers' shelves when a U.S. District Court ruled that its menuing structure infringed on Lotus's copyright. Other companies have not been as successful as Lotus. In 1989,

Compare the "look and feel" of the Windows (on left) to that of the Apple Macintosh (on right).

Source: Courtesy of Microsoft Corporation; John Greenleigh/Courtesy of Apple Computer, Inc.

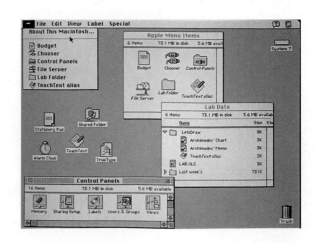

Apple sued Microsoft and Hewlett-Packard, claiming that some of their products had copied certain audio and visual elements of the Macintosh interface, including the concept of overlapping windows and the manipulation of icons (see photos). The U.S. District Court ultimately rejected almost all of Apple's claims on the grounds that many of the Macintosh screen graphics that Apple claimed had been copied were not protected under copyright law because they represented the only possible expression of the ideas underlying them (for example, the idea of overlapping windows can be expressed in only one way). Apple may appeal the ruling. Some see these lawsuits as a necessary evil on the part of companies entitled to protect valuable assets, but others worry that they will lead to higher costs for consumers, stifle product development, and slow the pace of innovation.

Competitors that copy software are a minor problem compared to the mass of individuals who do so. As we discussed in Chapter 11, **software piracy** (the illegal copying of copyrighted software) is a billion-dollar problem for the software industry. Unlike traditional books, music, and videotapes, software can be copied almost instantly and perfectly at very little cost. Software license agreements, which specify the number of copies users are legally permitted to make, are routinely violated. Not only does this cost software manufacturers money, but it also may be stifling the growth and creativity that information technology could potentially offer to society. For example, many traditional publishers, broadcasters, and movie companies—although enticed by the possibilities of selling digital, even multimedia, versions of their products—are hesitating because they fear that such products will be too easy to copy. Many hope that technology will eventually supply methods to prevent illegal copying without interfering with the convenience of using software and digital information. Others take a different tack: they feel that information and software should be free *(public domain software)*, or paid for on a voluntary basis if it proves to be useful to the user *(shareware)*, and that in any event, it is futile and socially counterproductive to maintain laws on the books that everyone breaks and that are impossible to enforce.

Trade Secrets   The final form of legal protection for intellectual property is to classify it as a **trade secret.** Trade secret protection is granted at the state level and can be applied to any intellectual work product (including computer programs, database compilations, formulas, product ideas, methods of doing business, processes, and information) that is secret and provides a competitive edge. To protect something as a trade secret, no formal application is required. Protection arises from designating the information as secret and then taking steps to maintain secrecy. Such protection typically includes requiring employees to sign nondisclosure agreements. Protection lasts as long as the information remains secret; once it is disclosed to others, it is no longer protected. Trade secret protection is commonly used to prevent former employees from working for a competitor. For example, in 1991, Dr. Peter Bonyhard, an expert on computer disk drives, left IBM to go work for a competitor, Seagate Technology. IBM sued to prevent him from working there, arguing that he would inevitably draw on IBM secrets. "This guy has an encyclopedic knowledge of all our critical data. He knows what the problems are and he knows how to solve them," said Evan Chesler, a lawyer for IBM. On the other hand, should a worker like Dr. Bonyhard become a slave to a company simply because he has soaked up confidential information while on the job? IBM won an injunction that stopped Dr. Bonyhard from working for four months, but a higher court overturned it. IBM has appealed, so at this time the final outcome is still uncertain. How would you decide this case?[4]

As you can see, issues surrounding property rights to information and intellectual property in the Information Age are complex, have many sides, and may be difficult to resolve. But their outcome will have a major impact on how knowledge and information is distributed and the way we live in the next century.

System Quality

In an age when so much of our lives depends on information systems, the quality of those systems and the integrity of the data they contain become critical issues. Today, if computer hardware or software malfunctions or data is erroneous, not only may people be inconvenienced, but their lives may be at risk. As a result, we need to start answering important questions such as: What standards of quality and integrity should information technology and systems be required to meet? How should those standards be established—by congressional mandate, industry associations, or market forces? What happens when systems and data do not meet such standards? Who should be responsible if, for instance, a machine controlled by faulty software injures someone? Who should be held liable if inaccurate data in a credit report results in someone being denied a loan? We first looked at some of these issues in the story "Software Risks" in Chapter 9. Here, we examine some further examples.

Software Bugs A **software bug** is a design flaw or error in a program that causes the program to perform improperly. Perhaps you were one of the millions of AT&T customers affected in January 1990 when a bug contained in a software upgrade to AT&T's Signal System 7 disrupted nationwide telephone service and shut down over half the nation's 800 lines for nine hours. Some software bugs may be amusing (G. C. Blodgett's auto insurance tripled when he turned 101 because the program did not know how to deal with drivers over the age of 100, and so converted him into a teenager), some ironic (one version of a McAfee antivirus program contained a software bug that made the cure worse than the virus), and others merely a nuisance. Some, though, can be deadly. For example, in 1992, London's ambulance service was jolted by a serious glitch in its new computer-based dispatch system. Although the system performed acceptably during early stages of installation and was running in three working pilot programs across London's three ambulance divisions, when the service tried to integrate the three divisions, the system mysteriously began producing a mass of "exception messages" that delayed responses to ambulance calls. The glitch is thought to have contributed to over 20 deaths.

Why do software bugs like this occur, and what, if anything, can be done about them? As we noted in Chapter 9, one cause of software bugs is complexity. In addition, unlike many physical systems where small errors produce small consequences, the smallest possible error in a digital system (changing a bit from a 0 to a 1, for instance) may produce a catastrophic response. A glitch that knocked out phone service in Washington, D.C. and five states, for instance, was caused when three binary digits were set incorrectly.

The design of error-free software is made problematic by the law of diminishing returns. Even after a system is thoroughly "debugged," bugs remain, but the probability of their occurrence is so low that the time, effort, and cost to remove them may not be worth the benefit. Further, debugging may not be successful and may in fact introduce new errors into a system.

What do you think? Who should be responsible for the consequences of software defects? If software defects are at some level unavoidable, should people who use software be required to assume a certain amount of risk? Or should organizations who produce, sell, and profit from software always be held accountable? And what about the management of the company and the individuals who actually created the defective systems—the systems analysts, programmers, and other information system professionals? How responsible should they be for defective software?

If there are any lessons to be learned from this discussion, it is that society and individuals need to resist **automation complacency,** the natural tendency to trust computerized systems that monitor the status of complex activities. Studies indicate that when software fails, as it sometimes unexpectedly does, people tend to miss the event that causes the failure because they don't monitor the raw environment as well as they otherwise might.[5]

Dirty Data   Even though software bugs receive more press attention, failures in data integrity are a far more common source of problems. A recent *Computerworld* survey of 500 large and medium-sized companies found that over two-thirds of the companies reported problems resulting from **dirty data,** data that is inaccurate, outdated, or missing.

According to some estimates, as much as 30 to 40 percent of the information contained in the databases of the big three credit reporting companies in the United States—TRW, Equifax, and TransUnion Corporation—is inaccurate. There are several ways this can happen. The most common has to do with the way credit bureaus integrate all the new information they get every day (from sources such as retailers, credit card companies, and banks) into preexisting credit files. They use systems designed to spot common variations on proper names, street names, and the like. The systems are skewed to make all possible matches and then some. As a result, you can easily end up with someone else's data in your file.

Until recently, the credit bureaus had little incentive to pay attention to consumers who were damaged by inaccurate credit reports—they were much more concerned with serving their customers by providing the widest of all possible searches, even if they came up with a lot of false matches. But in 1991, lawsuits filed by the Federal Trade Commission and attorneys general in 19 states, coupled with congressional hearings and threats of new legislation, forced the credit bureaus to take a more conciliatory stance. TRW announced that it would provide consumers with a free copy of their credit history, and Equifax opened a national center with an 800 number to answer consumer questions. At the same time, the industry's trade association suggests that some of the blame falls on consumers who use different versions or spellings of names and addresses in different applications. The association also suggests using social security numbers as national identifiers to help keep records straight. What do you think about these suggestions?[6]

Although the credit-reporting industry gets most of the publicity for poor quality data, they are not alone. A 1991 MIT survey of the CIOs of 50 large businesses found that almost all of them said that databases maintained by individual departments weren't good enough to be used for important decisions. Poor quality data can lead to incorrect billing practices, violations of government laws, missed opportunities, and corporate waste and costs citizens, businesses, and the government millions if not billions each year. Here are a few examples:

▶ Greer DuBois, a New York advertising agency, lost a $25-million-a-year account after the agency's billing system failed to credit the client with a payment.

▶ Chemical Waste Management, Inc., an Illinois waste management firm, was fined $260,000 for discrepancies in records submitted to the Illinois Environmental Protection Agency.

▶ In 1990, a major New York securities broker lost more than $200 million when its employees entered incomplete data into a new risk management system the firm was building. As a result, the firm missed a big trading opportunity.

▶ Inaccurate reservations data regularly leads to flights taking off one-half to one-third full, costing airlines millions.

▶ J. P. Morgan & Company, a New York bank, found that the data in its credit-risk management database was only 60 percent complete, requiring double-checking by anyone who used it.

▶ According to a General Accounting Office report, U.S. taxpayers paid out over $2 billion because information provided by the nation's banks on student loan defaulters was not properly entered into a centralized database at the Department of Energy. As a result, defaulting students continued to get loan renewals.

"The scary thing is how bad it is," says Robert Goldberg, a professor at MIT's Sloan School of Management. "We're betting our economy in the '90s on an information world, and we don't have any idea how good the information in those databases is." Experts believe that it is likely to take a long time to clean up data quality problems.[7]

15.3 Quality of Life Issues

In this section, we will look at the impact of information technology on worklife, organizations, and careers, on our safety, health, and well-being, and on the environment.

Quality of Worklife

What makes for an interesting and satisfying job? The answer may be different depending on who you're talking to and the type of work involved, but in general, job satisfaction often has a lot to do with the amount of responsibility, variety, and challenge involved. Autonomy (making your own decisions), working with others as a team, and feeling productive are also factors. In many instances, information technology has contributed to making jobs more satisfying by eliminating or minimizing boring, repetitive tasks. Desktop computers and networks have created much greater access to information, empowering and expanding the control of the average worker. Word processing, spreadsheet, database, and many other types of applications software help workers to be more productive. Advances in telecommunications have given workers more flexibility to work at home or on the road. Groupware and other forms of workgroup computing have made it easier for people to work together.

On the other hand, information technology can reduce the quality of worklife. One problem is the electronic monitoring of workers discussed in "Privacy and Freedom." Another concern is that information technology will eliminate jobs or create jobs requiring skills beyond that of the average labor force. Electronic meetings and other forms of electronic communications eliminate personal contact and depersonalize the workplace. Telecommunications technology may also be increasing the speed of communications beyond our capacity to handle them, making worklife more stressful and harried. In days gone by, people did not expect immediate turnaround. Today, with fax machines, E-mail, EDI, WANs, LANs, and the like, you may need to make instant responses without any time for reflection.

Technologies such as wireless mobile computing, home fax machines, cellular telephones, paging devices, and the "do anything anywhere" computing environment can also blur traditional boundaries between work, family, home, and leisure time. The story, "Running on the Digital Treadmill," examines this issue.

Impact on Organizations and Careers

Throughout this book, we have discussed the impacts that information technology has had on the structure of organizations and careers. Advances in telecommunications and microcomputers have allowed more decentralization. Telecommuting, a related trend, is beginning to affect where people work and the distribution of the work force. People are able to be part of an organization without having to be physically present.

Networked PCs are bringing more and more information down to the level of workers on the line, flattening organizations by eliminating many middle-level managers. As Dr. John Mayo, president of AT&T Bell Laboratories says, "Many of the things that management used to do are incorporated into software available to the line worker, so there are fewer and fewer layers of management above the worker with a desktop computer." In some cases, advances in telecommunications have made all employees expendable, allowing companies to fill their needs through outside contractors, supervised electronically.[8]

Throughout modern times, workers have feared displacement by machinery, and information technology has been no exception. The fear persists that information technology will reduce the need for all kinds of workers and that without high-tech skills, "ordinary" people will become unemployable. Recently, some have sounded the alarm over re-engineering—restructuring a business's work process with information technology to achieve higher productivity levels—predicting that it could wipe out millions of jobs. They point to the experience of companies like Capital Holding Corporation, a financial services company in Louisville, Kentucky. Six years ago, Capital's Commonwealth group of life insurance companies employed an administrative staff of 1,900. Today, after re-engineering, Commonwealth employs fewer than 1,100 to do the tasks that those 1,900 used to do, even with 25 percent more business. So far, no more than 15 percent of U.S. manufacturers, and a much smaller percentage of service companies, have undergone re-engineering, but competition is expected to force more and more businesses to do so. If and when they do, headcounts may be reduced by as much as 30 to 50 percent.[9]

Although many organizations have used information technology to increase productivity and eliminate jobs, despite dire predictions, information technology has in general resulted in a net increase in jobs rather than a decrease and has opened up many new opportunities for the work force. In the last 15 years, millions of jobs have been created for nonprofessional people who can operate computers. Advances in telecommunications have opened new markets for small businesses that were previously limited to serving their local markets. As shown in Chapter 5, many physically challenged individuals have joined the work force with the help of such technologies as

Running on the Digital Treadmill

It's 10 P.M. Do you know where your spouse is? If it's the Traver household, the spouse in question (husband Todd) is more likely than not tip-tapping away at his Dell notebook computer. The Dell has a internal modem that allows Todd to dial up his office PC. Once connected, Todd can look at the E-mail that he didn't get a chance to read during the day (sometimes over 50 messages can pile up), finish work on reports, memos, and presentations, and send E-mail messages to other colleagues. The laptop is also equipped with a fax/modem for sending and receiving faxes. It usually accompanies Todd on business trips, vacations, even a visit to the in-laws. Almost anywhere he goes, he can hook into his office network and keep up with what's going on.

Here's another example. Sheila Griffen, an advertising director for Motorola Inc., turns on her cellular phone as she sets off from home during her hour-long drive to work. First she dials into her voice mail. Then she makes calls to Europe. When she gets to the office, she checks her faxes. She gets Europe out of the way and then works on things in her own time zone. Thirteen hours later, she returns home to spend a few hours with her husband and two children. Then around 9:30 P.M., the phone starts ringing again with calls from Japan, where it's now daytime.

A laptop computer equipped with fax/modem allows people to stay in touch with their offices even while they're on vacation.

Source: Ed Kashi.

Running on a digital treadmill is fast becoming a national pasttime for high-achievers and those hoping to keep their jobs in recessionary times. More and more people now work during time that they would normally be spending with family and friends.

---

voice recognition, voice synthesis, joy sticks, and touch screens. And finally, existing jobs are more often restructured rather than eliminated as a result of information technology.

What Happened to the Paperless Office? A decade ago, visionaries predicted that the **paperless office** was just around the corner. Today, U.S. businesses consume more paper than ever—around 775 billion pages a year!

Although paper hasn't yet become obsolete, the way it is used is slowly changing. Once a means of both storing and displaying information, paper increasingly has become just a method of display. Electronic storage of information has clearly become the method of choice for many businesses. At the same time, technology continues to chip away at areas in which paper still claims superiority. The Xerox Corporation recently showed its portable flat panel display, which has the resolution of a laser-printed page. Even technologies that have increased the use of paper, such as fax machines, are changing. In 1992, for the first time in history, more fax/modems than fax machines were sold. This shift is significant because increasingly it will mean that fax information will travel directly from computer to computer without ever touching paper.

One reason that the paperless office has not materialized has been the lack of standards that would allow different types of computers and office equipment to work together and "communicate" with one another. Instead, offices have been filled with incompatible equipment that increases the need for paper. But in June 1993, Microsoft and an alliance of 50 leading office equip-

How do people feel about this? In Todd's case, it's a love–hate relationship. On the one hand, he loves the added flexibility. If he needs to leave work early one day, he doesn't have to feel guilty about it—he can simply finish up at home. If work starts to pile up, and he wants to get a jump on it, he needn't stay in the office until all hours of the night. He gets work done in what would normally be "unproductive" leisure time (or sleep time).

On the other hand, Todd finds that he's working a lot more hours than he did before, and his co-workers are too. One evening, he sent E-mail to a fellow employee around 11P.M. and got a reply immediately! He wasn't the only one logged on and working that late. He can't seem to get away from the concerns of the office as he once did.

Todd's reactions are not uncommon. Some wonder whether they have bought into a high-stakes game for which they weren't prepared. Gil Gordon, a communications consultant, points to the generous discount programs on PCs that some employers have for their employees. He says, "Part of me wonders if that just makes it easier for them to extend the workday. You can get creeping expectations on the part of managers that it should be the norm for people to put in two or three extra hours a day on home computers."

Others also worry about the long-ranging effects that the increasing encroachment on private life and private time may have on people's well-being and ultimately the fabric of society. Family, friends, and leisure time historically have provided powerful support mechanisms for individuals, acting as balance points, giving people the time, place, and freedom to think, dream, and just be.

Source: Based in part on Kilborn, Peter, "Tales from the Digital Treadmill," *New York Times,* June 3, 1990.

Critical Thinking Questions

1   Once you are out in the workplace, do you think your lifestyle will be similar to what is described here? If it is, how will you feel about it?

2   Do you think people are truly more productive using the technologies described here? Why or why not?

3   What ultimate societal impacts do you see in the trends described in this story?

ment manufacturers announced plans to use Windows to establish a new office standard that would link desktop computers, copiers, fax machines, printers, and telephones. Figure 15.6 lists some of the products that are planned. At the same time, Adobe Systems introduced Acrobat, a software program designed to allow documents to move more easily among different types of computer systems. For example, a document created with WordPerfect on a Windows machine will be readable by a user with an Apple Macintosh or Unix machine. The documents will look exactly the same, including

Here is a list of a few products now under development that will use Microsoft's new office standard (called Windows At Work):

From Xerox: a copier that lets users control features using the Windows graphical user interface

From Ricoh: a fax machine that combines fax, printing, and scanning capabilities with a touch screen or PC interface

From MCI: support for sending faxes from within Windows applications over wide area services

From Hewlett-Packard: a printer that displays status, warning, and error messages on the user's screen

From Active Voice: a telephone that identifies the caller's number and displays that number in a Windows application

Source: Based on Radosevich, Lynda, "Microsoft Takes on the Office," *Computerworld,* June 14, 1993.

Figure 15.6
Office Products of the Future

graphics and pictures. Already, some publishers are considering electronically printing their newsletters as Acrobat documents and sending them via computer networks or mailing them as disks. These developments may mean that the dream of the paperless office, or at least one in which paper plays a much smaller role, may come true in the not too distant future.

Health Issues

Chapter 5 summarized some of the hazards of input and output devices and some ergonomically based solutions. Let's take a more extended look at these health issues.

Repetitive Stress Injuries (RSIs) The leading job-related injuries in the 1990s are **repetitive stress injuries (RSIs).** RSIs are caused when muscle groups are forced through the same repetitive actions, over and over again. RSIs include problems like tendinitis (an inflammation of the tendons connecting the fingers to muscles in the forearms), tenosynovitis (inflammation of the fluid-filled synovial sheaths that surround and protect the tendons), and carpal tunnel syndrome (pressure on the nerve that provides sensation to the hand, as it runs through the "carpal tunnel" housing it). Symptoms include stiffness, tingling, a burning sensation, shooting pain, numbness, and an inability to grasp objects. Deana Bunis, a newswriter at Newsday, a daily newspaper in Long Island, New York, is one who has experienced the pain of RSI first hand. One morning, she woke up with "incredible pain" in her hands. "They felt like they were on fire." Visits to various specialists confirmed the diagnosis—RSI. In a recent National Institute for Occupational Safety and Health (NIOSH) Health Hazard Evaluation at Newsday, 40 percent of the 834 workers surveyed reported symptoms consistent with RSI. The workers at Newsday are not alone. Over 185,000 cases of RSI are reported each year, according to the National Center for Health Statistics.

One of the leading causes of RSIs is keyboards. The NIOSH study found that the more time spent typing and the faster the typing speed, the higher

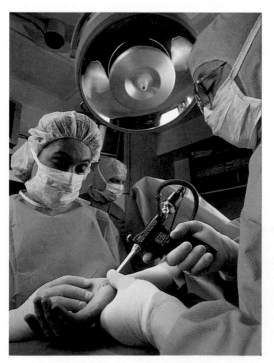

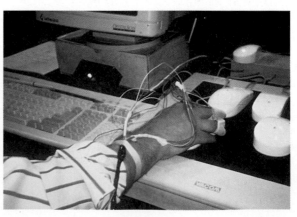

(a) Carpel tunnel syndrome and other forms of RSI are now the most common type of job-related injury in the United States.

(b) Computer equipment manufacturers are hoping to reduce the incidence of RSI by making input devices more ergonomic. Here, several different mouse designs are being tested.

Sources: Courtesy of 3M Corporation; Courtesy of Microsoft Corporation.

a.

b.

the prevalence of RSI. That's not surprising when you consider that at 60 words a minute, a word processor makes as many as 21,600 keystrokes an hour.

Other musculoskeletal problems caused by poorly designed workstation areas include back, neck, shoulder, and foot pain. Refer to Figure 5.3 in Chapter 5 for guidelines on how to avoid these health hazards.[10]

Who is responsible when an employee suffers injury as a result of information technology? Employers are generally immune from workplace liability because of worker's compensation statutes that provide income to those injured on the job. Instead, those injured by RSIs have filed hundreds of lawsuits against keyboard and computer manufacturers seeking the recovery of damages caused to them by the alleged misdesign of keyboards. It will likely take several years before the cases wend their way through the courts. In the meantime, manufacturers have begun to release ergonomically improved keyboards that they hope will reduce the incidence of RSIs. In addition, the Occupational Safety and Health Agency (OSHA) is writing general ergonomic regulations for both office and industrial workplaces, as are many state agencies. Municipalities such as San Francisco and Suffolk County, New York, have tried to enact legislation to protect workers, but so far most have been subjected to legal challenges that have delayed their implementation.[11]

Computer Vision Syndrome (CVS)   **Computer vision syndrome (CVS)** includes such conditions as dry and irritated eyes, blurry vision, headaches, and other symptoms associated with eye strain. CVS is caused by screen glare, improper lighting, and screens with poor resolution and a low refresh rate. Nearly 10 million people in the United States may suffer from CVS, according to a study by James E. Sheedy, chief of the VDT Eye Lab at the University of California at Berkeley. Some tips for reducing CVS include using a high-resolution monitor with a high refresh rate; positioning the center of the monitor about 20 degrees below eye level, about 18 to 30 inches away, and at a right angle to any windows; positioning lighting to avoid glare and using an antiglare screen; and stopping periodically to rest your eyes.[12]

Low-Level Electromagnetic Fields   CRT-based computer monitors emanate **low-level electromagnetic fields.** Although there has been no conclusive evidence that such emissions are a health hazard, there is worry that they may be linked to miscarriages, birth defects, and possibly cancer. All monitor manufacturers have reduced emissions since the early 1980s, and many now comply with the Swedish safety standard MPR II, which mandates very low emissions. Another way to reduce exposure is to switch to a laptop or notebook computer with a liquid crystal display. LCDs emit far less magnetic radiation than standard CRTs. Keeping your monitor at least an arm's length from your body is also a good idea.

Exposure to Noise   Exposure to noise from printers, hard disk drives, and fans, though not physically harmful, may be psychologically annoying. Noise can be minimized by carpeting and acoustic tiles. You can reduce noise further by placing your system unit on the floor underneath your desk. System units sold in a minitower configuration have made this option even more popular.

Environmental Concerns

Another important issue is environmental impact. You may be surprised to learn some of the ways information technology affects the environment.

For starters, the semiconductor manufacturing process (see Chapter 3) can pollute the air and contaminate soil and groundwater. Hydroflouric acid, a dangerous chemical, is used to etch patterns on the chips and chlorofluorocarbons (CFCs), a major cause of the ozone problem, have long been used as a solvent to wash residue off printed circuit boards. Although the process still remains an environmentally hazardous one, major manufacturers have recently begun to focus on ways to reduce risks. Many have developed new methods that eliminate the need for CFCs. For example, at its manufacturing plant at San Jose, California, IBM sprays its assemblies with soapy water instead of industrial solvents. Fujitsu has developed an ultrasonic water cleaner that it says removes ten times as much dust as CFC washing. Apple has devised a new process for making boards and assemblies that it says eliminates the need to clean them entirely.

Once computers have been manufactured, they affect the environment in many other ways. Most important is the power that they consume. The Environmental Protection Agency estimates that PCs and their peripherals (monitors and printers) waste $2 billion of electricity annually and indirectly produce as much carbon dioxide as 5 million cars! An EPA survey shows that 30 to 40 percent of computer users leave their machines running days, nights, and weekends. Although this practice may have some marginal benefits for the system components, it is incredibly wasteful of energy. Even those who leave their machines on only during the day actively use them for only a small fraction of the time. Monitors are another power hog. Screen savers may protect your monitor's phosphors, but they don't do anything to decrease energy consumption; in fact, they can increase it by up to 20 percent. Add a laser printer, and you have a system that uses up to 400 watts. All this equipment also throws off a lot of heat, yet needs relatively cool temperatures to operate properly, so extra electricity is required to cool office space.

To encourage manufacturers to cut energy requirements, the EPA has instituted an Energy Star program. System components (system unit, monitor, and printer) that use less than 30 watts at idle will be able to be marketed with an "Energy Star" label. Converting the computer population to Energy Star standards would save 26 billion kilowatts by the year 2000—equal to the annual electricity consumption of Vermont, New Hampshire, and Maine combined. Over 50 of the country's largest companies have joined the program, which is now beginning to bear fruit. For instance, IBM recently unveiled its Energy Saver PC, a 4.4-lb system unit in a sleek 12-by-12-inch box (see photo). The system's microprocessor can go into an energy-saving sleep mode when not in use, reducing power requirements by up to 50 percent. For further energy savings, IBM has coupled the system unit with an active-matrix color LCD screen rather than the conventional CRT monitor. The total system draws only around 50 watts of electricity compared to 250 watts for a regular PC. Other manufacturers are developing conventional monitors with a "power-down" feature. One of the first was Nanao USA's Flexscan, which can power-down in stages to save 90 percent of its peak power consumption. Laser printers are next in line, and both Hewlett-Packard and Lexmark are designing printers that will idle at very low wattage.

IBM's Energy Saver PC.

Source: Mark Lawrence.

Discarded computers waiting to be recycled at Advanced Recycling, Inc.

Source: Dith Pran/New York Times Photo.

Another environmental effect is the consumption of paper. As we noted earlier, so far information technology has actually increased the use of paper. Chapter 5 gave you a few tips on how to decrease your use of paper. Most offices also recycle paper and many communities now require it.

Other parts of an information system also can and should be recycled. American businesses and individuals are discarding more than 10 million computers a year. At this rate, over 150 million computer carcasses will litter the American landscape by 2005. "The numbers are huge and it could be an enormous environmental problem," says EPA director Mark Greenwood. This issue is being attacked on several fronts. In Europe, computer companies are being forced to reclaim their old machines when consumers no longer want them. The manufacturer will then be responsible for recycling or reusing the system. In the United States, though, regulators are so far trying to let market forces lead the way, and it appears that U.S. entrepreneurs are responding. In 1991, Eric Buechel founded Advanced Recovery, Inc., a firm that specializes in the recycling of old computers (see photo). The company mines cast-off computers for metals like aluminum and gold and sells semiconductor chips to parts wholesalers and computer maintenance shops. But much of what composes the system unit can't be resold and is dumped in a nearby landfill. To help eliminate this problem, PC manufacturers are experimenting with processes that minimize the amount of unrecyclable materials used in the system unit and allow PCs to be taken apart more easily for recycling, as well as upgraded with snap-in components.

In addition to system units, peripheral devices also pose their own recycling concerns. We discussed the recycling of laser toner cartridges in Chapter 5. Of even greater concern is the recycling of batteries, which contain toxic elements that can leach into soil and groundwater. Portable and notebook computers, one of the fastest-growing segments of the PC market, typically use rechargeable nickel-cadmium batteries. Most desktop PCs also use batteries to back up system-setup memory. Cadmium is a very toxic metal that should never be disposed of in a garbage landfill. In response to the danger posed by such batteries, some computer companies have begun to offer recycling programs. Apple and Compaq take back their batteries after their useful life has expired. The longer-term solution is batteries that don't contain cadmium. Nickel-hydride batteries and lithium cells are two emerging technologies that may someday eliminate nickel-cadmium batteries. Computer monitors also pose special environmental dangers. Although they can be disassembled for scrap, the CRT must be disposed of in a hazardous waste dump because of the lead in its glass.

Some feel that dismantling old computers is misguided. The East-West Education Development Foundation wishes that people would give them their unwanted equipment instead of passing it off to the recycler. The foundation refurbishes computers and gives them to worthy groups in Russia, Eastern Europe, and other developing countries. Computers they have given away have been used to monitor elections in the Ivory Coast, conduct studies for the Ukrainian parliament, and run municipal governments in Romania. "Ninety-seven percent of the people on the planet would regard an outdated IBM PC as a ride on a rocket ship," says Alex Randall, president of the foundation. "Melting the thing down is not its highest and best use. None of these machines should die. In the right hands, they are mind-enhancing tools." Figure 15.7 lists some other organizations that accept donated equipment.[13]

15.4 Threats to Information Systems

Throughout this book, you have seen how our society has become incredibly dependent on information technology and systems. Consider, for instance, that on a given business day, more than $1 trillion worth of electronic transactions occur in New York City alone. What happens, then, when those systems are threatened or fail? Computer-based information systems are much more vulnerable—to crime and abuse, natural disaster, and even human error—than the manual systems they have replaced. In this section, we will investigate the dangers posed by these different threats, and the ways society and organizations hope to guard against them. First we look at different types of computer crime and examine potential causes of systems failures. Then we review some of the measures that can reduce an organization's vulnerability.

East-West Education Development Foundation
Boston, MA
(617) 542-1234
Gives equipment to deserving groups in Russia, Eastern Europe, and developing countries

Gifts in Kind America
Alexandria, VA
(703) 836-2121
Gives equipment to schools and nonprofit groups

National Christina Foundation
Pelham Manor, NY
(800) 274-7846
Uses donated PCs to help disabled children and manage its training centers

Detwiler Foundation Computers for Schools Programs
La Jolla, CA
(619) 456-9045
Helps underfunded schools in San Diego area

Figure 15.7
Nonprofit Groups That Accept Donated PCs

Computer Crime and Abuse

New technologies generally create new opportunities for crime—new things to steal, new ways to steal, and new methods of harming others. Almost as soon as computers began to be used commercially, people began to exploit them for illicit purposes.[14] As information technology has spread, so too have computer crime and abuse. Computers linked in telecommunications networks and on-line systems are especially vulnerable because they offer a multitude of access points. As microcomputers proliferate and more people become familiar with them, the potential population of abusers also grows.

Computer crime ranges from the use of information technology to commit an act that would be criminal no matter how committed (such as the theft of money or other property) to activities more specifically related to computers, such as theft of computer services and telecommunications services, unauthorized accessing and use of information systems, and the theft, intentional alteration or destruction of data or programs (see Figure 15.8). **Computer abuse** refers to acts that are legal but unethical.

The actual extent of computer crime in the United States is unknown. No one knows for sure how many people engage in computer crime, how many systems are invaded, or the total economic damage. Estimates range from the millions into the billions annually, especially if theft of phone services and credit card fraud are included.

There are several reasons why it is difficult to come up with an accurate assessment. First, many instances of computer crime have been discovered only through happenstance, leading to the belief that much goes undetected. Second, many companies that have been victimized by computer crime are reluctant to reveal it, fearing loss of customer confidence and other negative publicity. Third, in many instances, it may be difficult to quantify the harm done in economic terms. Consider the following story. Southeastern Color Lithographers was a small and thriving printing company in Athens, Georgia. It had used a computer system for a number of years without problem. Then, one day at Southeastern, this began to change. Computer files started

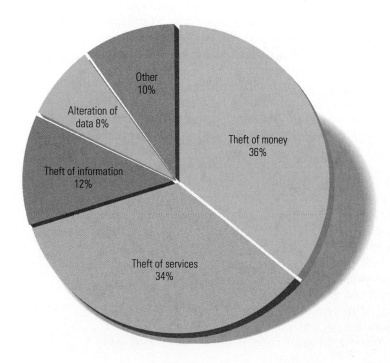

Figure 15.8
Major Types of Computer Crime
Computer crime covers a wide range of illegal activities. According to a study conducted by the National Center for Computer Crime Data, using a computer system to steal money is the most common computer crime, followed closely by the theft of computer or telecommunications services.

Source: Alexander, Michael, "Computer Crime: Ugly Secrets for Business," *Computerworld,* March 12, 1990.

to vanish or come out garbled, cursors started disappearing from computer screens, preventing employees from typing, computer printers would start for no apparent reason, and at times the whole system would crash. As these difficulties continued, workers started to blame one another. Several became so frustrated they quit. One employee, so upset over computer glitches that he stood up and began screaming profanities, was fired. The problems were ultimately traced to one employee who had sabotaged the system.[15] How do you calculate the damages here? What monetary value should be placed on the stress caused to innocent employees from a system seemingly gone haywire?

Most publicity about computer crimes has focused on the outsider who gains entry to a system to wreak havoc. But as the Southeastern story illustrates, it is company employees—insiders—who present the highest risk. "Employees are the ones with the skill, the knowledge, and the access to do bad things," says Donn Parker, the computer security expert from SRI International. Dishonest or disgruntled employees are "a far greater problem than most people realize."[16] Motives behind an inside job may include monetary difficulties, a desire for revenge, the challenge or ease with which the crime can be committed, and even industrial espionage.

Nonetheless, most attention continues to be given to computer hackers. The term used to refer to anyone who had a strong interest in computer systems and in using them in ingenious ways. Now though, the term **hacker** most often refers to someone who uses his or her computer skills to break into a computer or telecommunications system, steal information and services, and disrupt operations.

Let's now take a closer look at some examples of crimes involving information technology.

Theft of Money   In 1991, $25 million was stolen from one of the world's largest banks. The robber, still unknown but believed by investigators to be a bank employee, used a PC with network access to a DEC minicomputer in the bank's payroll department. The investigation has been hampered by the fact that hundreds of employees had access to the necessary data.[17] In another recent case, Pinkerton Security & Investigative Services was embarrassed to discover that an employee had siphoned off more than $1 million from the detective agency's bank accounts. The employee had been given the computer code needed to access Pinkerton's accounts at Security Pacific National Bank. Ordinarily, the employee's boss would also have been required to punch in another code before funds could actually be transferred. When the boss was transferred, the employee was given his approval code and told to cancel it. But instead of doing so, the employee kept it and began to use it, shifting money from the Pinkerton accounts into accounts for two bogus companies that she had set up. The scheme was not discovered for two years.

Theft of Data Files and Programs   In a recent case, federal prosecutors in Manhattan arrested five young men and accused them of breaking into the computer systems of several regional telephone companies, numerous credit bureaus, large firms such as Martin Marietta, universities, and other organizations to obtain, among other things, credit information, passwords, account numbers, and things of value that they could sell. The young men, all under 22 years of age, and part of a group that called themselves the Masters of Deception, communicated with one another on underground computer bulletin boards, using code names such as Phiber Optik, Scorpion, Outlaw, Corrupt, and Acid Phreak. Around the same time, police in San Diego said that they had cracked a nationwide informal ring of about 1,000 hackers that had obtained credit information from computers at Equifax, one of the nation's three major credit bureaus, and made fraudulent credit card purchases that may have totaled millions of dollars. The members of the underground network are alleged to have shared information about how to break computer security codes, make charges on other people's credit cards, and create credit card accounts.

Many government and military networks have also been infiltrated by hackers at one time or another. In 1992, 18 people were indicted for participating in a ring that stole confidential data, including earnings and employment histories, tax filings, and criminal records, from FBI and Social Security Administration computers and then sold it to insurance companies, attorneys, and private investigators. Also in 1992, a Sun Microsystems programmer working on a computer system for the Air Force was charged with stealing a secret Air Force military document that listed the names and locations of structures to be attacked in the event of war.[18]

Criminals have recently discovered a new source of data and access to information systems: easy-to-steal portable and laptop computers. Portables may contain important and sensitive data on their hard disk drives and frequently allow easy dial-up access to a company's central computers or network. Consider what happened to Wing Commander David Farquhar of the British Royal Air Force in December 1990. Farquhar's notebook computer, which contained U.S. General Norman Schwarzkopf's preliminary Allied invasion plan for the then forthcoming Persian Gulf war, was stolen from Farquhar's car. Although no harm ultimately came from the theft, it gives you an idea of the increased vulnerability that such technology creates.[19]

Copying software (discussed earlier in this chapter and in Chapter 11) is also a computer crime. Software piracy has itself become a billion-dollar problem for the computer industry.

Theft of Computer or Telecommunications Services A technical writer named Dexter reports that for the last four years he has spent only one-third of his time using his computer for work-related activities. The rest of the time, he writes fiction, travel narratives, even computer games. He has remained undiscovered because he gets his real work done more quickly than his bosses realize. Since his company work and own work both involve text and graphics, his co-workers can't tell the difference. Dexter rationalizes his behavior by saying that his productivity is equal to or greater than that of his co-workers.[20]

Theft of telecommunications services has been a problem since 1970 when John Draper, a.k.a. Captain Crunch, discovered that the prize whistle offered in boxes of Cap'n Crunch Cereal perfectly duplicated the frequency of an AT&T WATS line, allowing him to make free telephone calls. Since that time, the problem has escalated considerably. Illegal access and sale of phone service has become a thriving underground business. In the past several years, telephone fraud has grown so much that U.S. businesses may be forced to shell out as much as $4 billion annually for unauthorized, free long-distance calls.[21] The latest technique is to intercept cellular telephones' electronic serial numbers and customer identification numbers through an electronic monitoring device, and then use them to make long-distance phone calls from other cellular phones.[22]

Unauthorized Access and Use; Alteration or Destruction of Data and Programs
Another form of computer crime involves the unauthorized accessing and use of computer services. Sometimes, no harm is done, but in other in-

stances, data and programs are altered or destroyed for monetary gain, revenge, or other reasons. Various methods are used. Wily programmers can create *logic bombs*—programs designed to wreak havoc on the system. Logic bombs are often disguised within a *trojan horse*—a program designed to look useful—and can be programmed to run either at random or on the occurrence of a specific condition. Here's an example. A disgruntled programmer at General Dynamics felt underpaid. Before quitting his job, he created a program that would totally erase an inventory tracking system he had helped create. He set the program to begin executing two months after he left the firm, on the evening before Memorial Day weekend, when few would be around to notice. Once the program had done its work, it would erase itself, leaving not a trace. The program was camouflaged so well that General Dynamics discovered it only days before it was supposed to run, and then only by chance.[23]

Computer viruses are another means of wreaking havoc on a system. A computer virus is a set of illicit instructions implanted within a program that passes itself on to other programs with which it comes in contact.

There are several basic types. *File-infecting viruses* search out executable files located on a disk or hard drive and physically attach themselves. When the files run, the virus is activated, often infecting other files in the process. *Memory-resident viruses* also attach themselves to executable files but, when the file runs, load themselves into memory where they stay as long as the computer is on. While in memory, they can spread the infection to other files. *Boot sector viruses* (sometimes called *partition table viruses*) attack the boot sector of a floppy disk or the master boot record on a hard drive (which holds instructions that get your computer's operating system up and running). They copy the code contained there into another location on the disk (often destroying data that was located there) and then replace the original code with code that loads the virus and then executes the original code. Startup appears to proceed normally, but in fact, the virus is loaded into memory before the operating system. Once the virus resides in memory, it is usually programmed to infect other files whenever it can.[24]

In addition to these basic types of viruses, some new forms have been appearing. *Stealth viruses* mask their presence by subtracting their own size from the file size before attaching themselves. *Polymorphic viruses* mutate and change form as they replicate. *Virus mutation engines,* such as DAME (the Dark Avenger Mutation Engine, thought to have originated in Bulgaria) allow anyone who has created a virus to turn it into a polymorphic one. And

Stoned: A boot sector virus that displays the message "Your PC is Stoned—Legalize Marijuana" or other similar message. It damages the system's directory and file allocation table.

Joshi: A boot sector virus that activates on January 5. Joshi crashes the system while displaying the message "Type Happy Birthday Joshi." If you do so, the system becomes usable again.

Jerusalem B: There are many different strains of this memory-resident, file-infecting virus, activating on different dates, frequently Friday the 13th. This particular strain slows down system speed and creates black boxes on your monitor. On every Friday the 13th, it automatically erases each file you execute.

Michelangelo: Given widespread publicity by the news media in 1992, this is the virus that made computer viruses a household word. A boot sector virus designed to activate on March 6 (Michelangelo's birthday), Michelangelo overwrites the hard disk drive with random characters from system memory.

Figure 15.9
The Most Common Viruses

now even novices can create viruses, thanks to the arrival of do-it-yourself virus development kits like the Virus Construction Laboratory, which comes complete with attractive graphical user interface, pull-down menus, dialog boxes, context-sensitive help, and mouse support.

All viruses take up some of your RAM and hard disk space, and many slow down the performance of your system. Beyond this, viruses range from the relatively harmless to the destructive. Some may do nothing more than display a message on your screen, whereas others may lock up your screen, corrupt or erase files, reformat the hard disk, or totally crash your system. Figure 15.9 lists and describes the most common viruses.

Figure 15.10 lists some of the ways viruses can be introduced into a system. As you can see, the most common culprits are infected floppy disks that are passed from machine to machine. Although disks containing software copied from another source are the biggest culprit, even shrink-wrapped disks are not immune: Novell Inc. once inadvertently distributed 3,800 disks containing its Network Support Encyclopedia that were infected with a virus. The shareware and freeware programs available from electronic bulletin boards are another possible source of infection. Viruses can also be attached to E-mail. Once introduced, viruses can spread rapidly if machines are part of a local area or wide area network.

Just how big a problem are computer viruses? Although the true extent of the damage is unclear, we do know that the number of computer viruses has grown exponentially since they first appeared in 1987. Today, there are over 2,000 known viruses, with an average of 110 new ones discovered each month. However, of those, only around 15 percent have been seen in real incidents, and of that 15 percent, about ten viruses in total account for two-thirds of all incidents.

A 1991 survey of 600 large companies by Dataquest Inc. found that over 40 percent of the respondents reported encountering virus problems. The large majority of the incidents involved networked PCs. Some experts believe that there is at least a 50 percent probability that any given corporation will experience a significant virus infection within any given year. However, a recent examination of empirical data by a team of IBM researchers suggests that the probability of infection is actually much lower because most desktop computers are still standalone machines or linked in relatively small, insular groups. Nonetheless, viruses remain a very real problem. We discuss preventive measures to protect computers from viruses later in this chapter.[25]

Computer Crime Laws Governmental institutions are still grappling with how best to deal with computer crime. In the late 1970s and early 1980s, when computer crime first started to receive widespread attention, prosecutors began to realize that existing laws were often inadequate to the task. Although some computer crimes were covered by existing laws against wiretapping, wire fraud, conspiracy, embezzlement, theft, and so on, many types were not. For instance, many statutes did not recognize data, programs, and

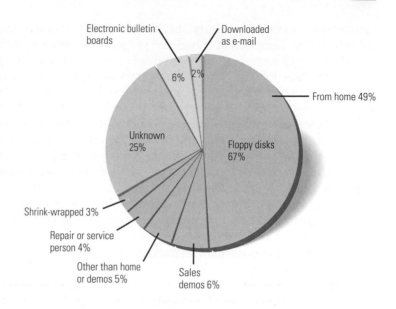

Figure 15.10
How Viruses Are Planted

Source: Dataquest Inc., San Jose, California, 1992, as reported in *Computerworld*, March 23, 1992.

computer services as "property" or "things of value" because they did not fit the traditional definition of "tangible" property. In response to these difficulties, most states have enacted specific laws aimed at computer crime. On the federal level, in 1986 the **Computer Fraud and Abuse Act** made it illegal to knowingly access, without authorization and with intent to defraud, a computer used by the federal government or for interstate commerce if such action causes a loss of more than $1,000. The most famous case prosecuted under the statute so far has been that of Robert Morris, the Cornell graduate student who unleashed a computer virus over the Internet in 1988. The virus, which spread by masquerading as an E-mail message, ended up infecting over 6,000 computers linked to the network. Once on the host computer, it replicated endlessly, forcing the computer to spend all its processing time on copying the file, and ultimately shutting it down. In interpreting the Computer Fraud and Abuse Act, a federal appeals court ruled that it was not necessary for the government to prove that Morris intended to cause harm, only that Morris intended to access the computers without authorization. Morris was sentenced to three years probation, given a $10,000 fine, and required to perform 400 hours of community service.[26]

System Disasters

In addition to computer crime, information systems are susceptible to natural disaster (blizzards, hurricanes, earthquakes, fire, floods), terrorist attack, electrical power and telecommunications line failure, hardware and software malfunction, even plain old human error (see Figure 15.11).

To understand the implications of such failure, let's look at what happened in a few recent incidents.

◗ On March 13, 1993, a blizzard collapsed the roof on an EDS computer center in Clifton, New Jersey, knocking out computers that handled transactions for over 5,000 ATMs nationwide. EDS's normal backup plans were thwarted because the backup site it had arranged for a crisis was already overwhelmed dealing with the effects of the World Trade Center bombing several weeks prior. As a result, over 1,000,000 cardholders were temporarily deprived of all access to their funds through ATM transactions. Eventually, EDS rerouted transactions through other teller networks, but because those networks lacked data about account balances, cash withdrawals were limited to a maximum of $100 a day to reduce the potential for fraud. The breakdown raises questions about the nation's increasing reliance on such machines. For many people, the ATM has become their sole contact with the banking system. What happens when you can't get your money when you need it? Who should be liable for the harm caused to individuals and organizations who could not access their full account balances during this period? Is it our own fault for becoming too reliant on such systems, or do the organizations that make them available and encourage us to rely on them bear responsibility?[27]

Figure 15.11
Which Threats to Information Systems Are Feared Most: Results of a Survey of 1,110 Information Systems Professionals

Source: Based on data from Datapro Research Corporation, Delran, New Jersey.

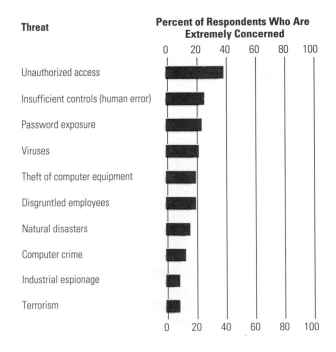

Threat	Percent of Respondents Who Are Extremely Concerned
Unauthorized access	
Insufficient controls (human error)	
Password exposure	
Viruses	
Theft of computer equipment	
Disgruntled employees	
Natural disasters	
Computer crime	
Industrial espionage	
Terrorism	

Disasters such as the World Trade Center (at left) and Hurricane Andrew (above) highlight our reliance on information technology and systems and the importance of an effective disaster recovery plan. *Source:* AP/Wide World Photos, Inc.

▶ The massive explosion that ripped apart a sub-basement in the World Trade Center on February 26, 1993, left many businesses, as well as 50,000 employees "homeless" while the Center underwent repairs. Many of those businesses were involved in the financial services industry, in which information technology plays a central role. Without their computers and data, many of the companies could not function. To make matters worse, most depended heavily on local area networks and distributed processing arrangements rather than central mainframes or minicomputers. This was a problem because, in many instances, the data stored on local area networks is not "backed up" as frequently as data stored in central mainframe and minicomputers. News coverage of the aftermath of the bombing showed pictures of harried workers pushing carts piled high with monitors, keyboards, printers, and boxes of disks (see photo). For some, this was the extent of their backup plan. Others were more prepared, and most firms reportedly did not lose any data.

Recovering data was just the beginning though. To resume normal operations, the companies also had to secure new office space and equip it with workstations, fax machines, telephones, and communications lines, as well as set up temporary local area networks. The communications links proved to be one of the most difficult aspects of the recovery: each company generally had its own unique communications system that was difficult to duplicate. When all is said and done, the total cost of the bombing to the organizations involved is likely to be hundreds of millions of dollars.[28]

▶ In an even more widespread disaster, Hurricane Andrew ripped through Southern Florida in August 1992, destroying buildings, knocking out power to millions, and disrupting telecommunications (see photo). Recovery was hampered by the fact that many of the businesses necessary to help people get on their feet again were equally helpless. For over a week, ATM machines were down and bank data processing centers closed, preventing people from getting access to their funds when they needed them most. Credit cards were useless too because the electronic links necessary to process transactions were destroyed. The claims offices of many local insurance companies were also without power and telecommunications, forcing overwhelmed agents to process claims manually.

The impact of these catastrophes highlights how much we rely on information technology to fulfill our day-to-day needs. Like many other things in life, we often take information technology for granted until it is no longer there.[29]

Safeguarding Information Systems

Once you see how important information systems are to the smooth functioning of organizations and society, you realize how important it is to safeguard those systems. **Information system security** encompasses a variety of policies, procedures, and tools that help organizations protect information systems against crime, abuse, systems failure, and disasters. In this section, we review some basic security measures, as well as plans that help organizations recover from unavoidable disaster.

Developing Policies   Good information system security begins with the development of an enterprise-wide security policy. First, certain questions must be answered. For instance, what is the nature of the data being stored in the system? How is the data used? Who can do what on the system? How much money may the company stand to lose if the data is corrupted, lost, or stolen? The answers to these questions will help determine the policies. For instance, the organization may discover that not every site needs bullet-proof security. The trick is to be effective without costly overkill. There is also tension between the need to make systems secure and the need to preserve the features that make them easy and efficient to use. A system that has too many controls can become so unwieldy and difficult to use that it hinders those it is supposed to be helping.

Once policies have been developed, they need to be implemented. Here, education is the key. The best policy in the world will be ineffective if users do not adhere to it. This may be the thorniest problem faced by management and information system security specialists. In the mainframe environment, where access to an organization's central computers was usually restricted to a small group of information system professionals, this task was much easier. In today's distributed computing environment, dominated by networks with many users, the job is much more difficult. The biggest problem may be convincing users that they should worry about security. "People think, 'Why would anyone bother me?' says Chuck Colce, computer security manager at Lawrence Livermore Laboratory. Many security professionals say that the first line of defense is an educated user community.[30]

Let's take a closer look at some methods of making systems more secure.

Identification and Access Control   One of the first steps in securing a system is to ensure that the system's users are who they say they are and that they are authorized to use the system. Computer networks that can be accessed from remote locations are particularly vulnerable to unauthorized access.

Various authorization methods can help control access to an information system. Physical access to computer rooms and resources can be controlled through keys, employee badges, and access cards. Computers can be equipped with locking keyboards. Log-on codes and passwords for actual access to information systems are also useful. But keys, badges, cards, and passwords have a major drawback—they can be forgotten, lost, or stolen. To guard against such mishaps, new devices are emerging. They are **biometric security devices** that identify individuals through biological characteristics (such as the pattern of blood vessels in the retina, hand measurements, lip patterns, and fingerprints) or through unique behavioral idiosyncrasies

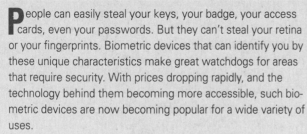

Your Fingerprints at Many Fingertips

People can easily steal your keys, your badge, your access cards, even your passwords. But they can't steal your retina or your fingerprints. Biometric devices that can identify you by these unique characteristics make great watchdogs for areas that require security. With prices dropping rapidly, and the technology behind them becoming more accessible, such biometric devices are now becoming popular for a wide variety of uses.

A fingerprint can be captured in a flash with a relatively inexpensive (less than $1,000) optical scanner attached to a personal computer. Each place at which fingerprint ridge lines end or split in two (called a minutia) is noted and categorized by type. Then the four nearest minutiae are examined and the number of ridges between the minutiae are counted. This digitized information makes it much easier to compare fingerprints with others in a database and to make matches.

The new ease with which fingerprints can be taken and matched means that the practice of using fingerprints for identification might soon rise dramatically. The digital equivalent of your fingerprint soon might be embedded in a credit card so that a cashier with a finger scanner could tell whether the person presenting the card was the person that owned it. A fingerprint registered at the front desk of a hotel might replace hotel room access cards and keys. The possibilities are truly endless.

Already, the FBI has digitized the prints of about 24 million criminals, with the prints of another 38 million Americans (most of them military veterans or federal employees) next in line. Social service officials in California and New York are fingerprinting welfare applicants to counter welfare fraud. Many organizations are installing fingerprint readers and other biometric devices to limit physical access to computer areas. Experts predict that such techniques will soon be used to control log-on access. Already, one contractor for the Department of Defense has a database that requires users to pass an Eye-Dentify retinal scanner before they are granted access.

Those dedicated to protecting civil liberties worry about what these developments mean for our future. They are not so sure that having an easily available, foolproof identifier is

Relatively inexpensive fingerprint scanning equipment, such as this system from Fingermatrix, may increase the use of fingerprints as a means of identification.

Source: Courtesy of Fingermatrix, Inc.

such a good thing. Rights to privacy might be truly threatened by such technologies. How, for instance, can individuals be assured that fingerprints gathered for one purpose will not be used for another purpose without the individual's knowledge or consent?

Sources: Based on Steinberg, Jacques, "Coming Soon: Fingerprints at Many Fingertips," *New York Times,* January 10, 1993; Daly, James, "Fingerprinting a Computer Security Code," *Computerworld,* July 27, 1992.

Critical Thinking Questions

1 How are fingerprints different from other types of identifying information such as driver's license numbers, social security numbers, or photographs? Why do you think people might be more sensitive about a fingerprint?

2 What are some of the advantages of using a fingerprint as a universal identifier?

3 How would you feel about having your own fingerprints used in this way?

(such as vocal intonation, signature, or keystroke dynamics). Used for many years at high-security government installations, such devices are now entering commercial use. The story "Your Fingerprints at Many Fingertips" discusses some of the potential implications of this technology.

As we noted, networked systems present special access control problems. For example, even moderately skilled users can quickly learn the techniques necessary to intercept log-on IDs and passwords. The very characteristics that make networks useful—easy access from a variety of locations, including remote locations, for a large number of users—make them vulnerable.

Here are a few techniques for making networks more secure. The first is a **call-back system** for users who seek to access a network from outside the office. Users give the network administrator the phone number that they will be using to access the system. When the user dials into the system, the system breaks the phone connection and dials the user back on the number that he or she has supplied. Although such a system blocks entry from someone who may have gotten an authorized password but is calling from an unauthorized location, it also adds costs (two phone calls instead of one) and lessens user flexibility. Nonetheless, many organizations feel that the added security is worth the cost.

Some organizations, particularly those that are concerned about sensitive data, also use **data encryption.** Data encryption systems use an encryption key (usually a number) to scramble data mathematically. The data cannot be understood without being decoded first. There are a number of different encryption key systems. The most advanced is the **Data Encryption Standard (DES),** adopted as the government standard in 1977. There are also a number of PC LAN security packages that include less advanced data encryption.

Protecting Programs and Data   In addition to preventing unauthorized access, it is important to protect programs and data from crime, disaster, and human error. The most important things an organization can do in this regard are to make **backup copies** of all software and to require users to backup their data files. Incremental backups (copies of only the changes to files) should be done any time any of the data in a file has been changed. Full backups (copies of all files) may be done somewhat less frequently. Once backup copies have been made, they should also be protected and stored in a secure location away from the originals.

Software and data also need protection against viruses. Here are several steps that minimize the risks of infection.

1   Make sure all purchased software comes in a sealed, tamper-proof package.

2   Make backup copies of software as soon as you open the package.

3   Be careful about software received from friends, files downloaded from bulletin boards, and other forms of shareware and freeware. Be particularly careful with software of unknown origin.

4   Avoid using disks from the office system at home and vice versa.

5   Boot the system using the hard drive rather than the floppy disk drive if possible.

6   Consider purchasing **antivirus software** or hardware-based products that can stop viruses before they enter the system. The leading antivirus software packages are Symantec's The Norton Antivirus and Central Point's Anti-Virus.

To be effective against viruses, antivirus software must perform three basic functions. It must detect viruses already on the system, remove those

Symantec's The Norton Antivirus is one of the leading antivirus software packages.

Source: Fredrik D. Bodin/Offshoot.

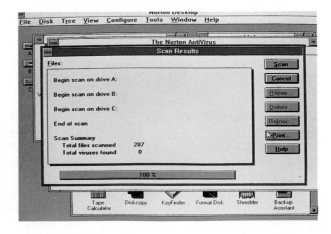

viruses, and prevent subsequent infections. Antivirus programs use a number of different methods to detect viruses. The most common is scanning for characteristic, recognizable pieces of virus code or patterns that indicate the possible presence of a virus. Although useful, scanning is effective only against known viruses. Another method is known as integrity checking. The software takes a "snapshot" of files and compares them to current versions, searching for unauthorized changes, and will notify the user if a change has occurred. Many antivirus programs use both methods. To disinfect your system most antivirus software will remove the viral contents of an infected file. Some vendors feel that the only safe way to completely remove a virus is to overwrite the file in which it was contained. Therefore, if you don't have an uninfected backup copy to restore your work, you may be in trouble. Finally, most antivirus software incorporates one or more techniques for detecting viruses before they actually infect your system. The most common is a terminate and stay resident (TSR) program that constantly monitors your system for viruslike activity.

In addition to backing up data and programs and protecting against virus infection, there are other ways to protect data and software. Because computer crimes are most frequently committed by persons inside an organization, all applicants who will have contact with information systems (often almost everyone within the organization) should be carefully screened. If possible, it's also a good idea to separate employee functions so that one individual does not have extended authority that is not subject to oversight. Rotating tasks among different individuals within a given functional area from time to time is also advisable. In small organizations, however, such steps may not be feasible.

Another fundamental data security policy is **discretionary access control:** restricting access to data and programs on a "need-to-know/need-to-use" basis. PC LAN security software now allows organizations to regulate who has access to which files and which programs on local area networks: as a user logs onto the system, he or she is given a restricted directory of available network resources.

Regular **audits** are another tool against computer crime. Public companies' financial records must be audited by outside accountants every year, and many private companies undergo a similar check. Many large companies also have internal auditors. Many companies are asking their auditors to focus on information systems as well as financial records. Many PC LAN security packages now include *audit controls.* Audit controls track what happens on the network: what programs have been used, what files have been opened, how many reads and writes have been executed, how many times a server has been accessed, and so on. This is one way an organization can create an **audit trail:** a record that allows a transaction to be traced through all the stages of processing, starting with its appearance as a source document and ending with its transformation into output.

Finally, there are also methods to protect data against human error. **Application controls** are manual and automated procedures that ensure that data processed by a particular application are accurate and complete throughout the processing cycle. They are particularly appropriate for large financial systems where the integrity of data is critical. There are three types of application controls. **Input controls** help ensure the accuracy and completeness of data as it enters the system. For instance, a firm may establish authorization and validation procedures that allow only selected individuals to authorize the input of certain data. A technique called a *programmed* *edit check* checks input data for errors before it is processed. Transactions that fail to meet fixed criteria are rejected. Another method is *control totals*— counts of the number of transactions processed during input, processing, and output that can be compared to other totals. **Processing controls** ensure the accuracy and completeness of data while it is being updated. Programmed edit checks and control totals are used at this stage as well. **Output controls** ensure that results of processing are accurate and complete and transmitted to users in a timely manner.

Disaster Recovery Planning Sometimes despite the best efforts of an organization to safeguard its information systems, an unavoidable disaster occurs: a fire, flood, hurricane, earthquake, explosion, power outage, or the like. If the organization has an effective **disaster recovery plan**—a method of restoring information processing operations—all may not be lost. The key elements of such a plan include the following:

▶ A list of the most critical business functions

▶ A list of the facilities, hardware, software, data, personnel, and other equipment that are necessary to support those functions

▶ A plan for backing up and storing programs and data away from the site so that they are available for restoring critical functions

▶ A method for securing access to all necessary resources

▶ A method for getting in touch with all necessary personnel

▶ A step-by-step course of action to follow to implement the plan

▶ Education, training, and drills for those who will implement the plan

Firms may provide their own disaster recovery plans and sites or use the services of an external provider. Companies such as Sungard Disaster Recovery Services, Comdisco Disaster Recovery Services, and IBM's Integrated Systems Solution Corporation all provide fully operational processing and telecommunications facilities to subscribers on less than 24 hours notice. Services include all necessary hardware and software for a company to run its critical applications, as well as technical assistance in disaster planning.

An effective recovery plan can be the difference between inconvenience and business disaster. For example, when the great Chicago Flood of 1992 occurred (a quarter billion gallons of the Chicago River flooded the basements of the entire commercial district), firms that had disaster recovery plans emerged relatively unscathed. The city of Chicago and Commonwealth Edison, the electrical utility company, were able to give businesses about an hour's notice that buildings had to be evacuated and that electrical power would be shut down. The response for those who were prepared was an orderly powering down of mainframes and networks and a telephone call to their disaster recovery providers. Over two dozen companies had to move their operations to off-site backup centers. Some fast-thinking firms sent small groups of workers armed with laptop computers, cellular phones, fax and copy machines into rooms at local hotels outside the evacuated downtown district. Out of luck were those firms that had not planned ahead. Comdisco Disaster Recovery Services noted that it had a large number of calls from Chicago firms looking for help. Most had to be turned away in favor of Comdisco customers already under contract.[31]

Summary

Ethics in an Information Age

▶ Ethics are moral standards that help guide behavior, actions, and choices. Ethics are grounded in notions of responsibility and accountability. Laws codify ethical standards and provide a mechanism for holding people, organizations, and governments accountable.

▶ Long-standing ethical principles that provide you with a framework for ethical decision making include the golden rule, the greatest good/least harm rule, Kant's categorical imperative, the slippery-slope rule, and the "no free lunch" rule. A five-step process for ethical decision making involves identifying the facts, values, stakeholders, options, and consequences of actions.

▶ Codes of conduct developed by professional organizations and corporations supplement an individual's personal code of ethics.

Privacy, Property, and System Quality

▶ Privacy is the moral right of individuals to be left alone and to control the flow of information about themselves. Information technologies pose a threat to privacy by making it easier than ever to collect, store, retrieve, and analyze information about individuals.

▶ Major laws protecting privacy in the United States from governmental intrusion include the Privacy Act of 1974, the Right to Financial Privacy Act, the Privacy Protection Act, and the Computer Matching and Privacy Protection Act.

▶ Major laws protecting against private industry intrusion on privacy include the Fair Credit Reporting Act, the Right to Financial Privacy Act, the Cable Communications Policy Act, and the Video Privacy Protection Act.

▶ Fair Information Practices rules underlie much of privacy legislation enacted to date.

▶ E-mail monitoring and computer monitoring are two information technology-related threats to privacy in the workplace.

▶ Information technology raises issues about the ownership of personal information and the protection of intellectual property.

▶ There are three basic forms of protection of intellectual property in America. A patent gives its owner an exclusive monopoly on the ideas behind an invention for 17 years. Patent protection is now available for software that is part of a patentable process or machine. Copyright protection prevents people from copying the expression of ideas in writings, music, art, and so on but does not protect the underlying idea. The Software Protection Act of 1980 specifically provides copyright protection for computer programs. Trade secret protection is available for any intellectual work product, including computer programs and database compilations, that is secret and provides a competitive edge.

▶ The quality of information systems and data is critical. Software bugs in complex software are probably impossible to totally prevent.

▶ Other problems result from inaccurate, outdated, or missing data. Poor data quality is a problem in the credit-reporting industry and for many other companies as well. Poor quality data can lead to incorrect billing practices, violations of government laws, and corporate waste.

Quality of Life Issues

▶ Information technology has contributed to making worklife more satisfying for many, but has also had negative impacts.

▶ Advances in telecommunications and microcomputers have led to more decentralization and have flattened organizations by bringing more information down to the level of line workers.

▶ Information technology has affected levels of employment. In some companies, information technology-related increases in productivity have resulted in fewer jobs. However, on the whole, information technology has created a net increase in jobs rather than a decrease.

▶ The paperless office, long predicted, may in fact be just around the corner with the introduction by Microsoft of plans to create a new office standard around its Windows interface.

▶ Various health-related issues surround information technology, including concerns that it is a significant factor in repetitive stress injury, vision problems, and exposure to electromagnetic fields.

▶ Among its environmental impacts, information technology can pollute the air and contaminate the soil and groundwater in the semiconductor manufacturing process, increase the amount of electrical power consumed by industrial societies, and pose recycling problems.

Threats to Information Systems

▶ Computer crime ranges from the use of information technology to commit an act that would be criminal no matter how it is committed (such as theft of money) to theft of data files and programs, theft of computer and telecommunications services, unauthorized accessing and use of information systems, and the intentional alteration or destruction of data and programs. Computer viruses are a significant threat to information systems.

▶ Today a number of state laws aim specifically at computer crime, as does the federal Computer Fraud and Abuse Act.

▶ Information systems are susceptible to natural disasters, telecommunications line and power outage, and human error.

▶ Information system security encompasses a variety of policies, procedures, and tools for protecting information systems against crime, abuse, system failures, and disasters. Security includes developing an enterprise-wide security policy, employee education, identification and access control, procedures for protecting programs, and data and disaster recovery plans.

Key Terms

ethics	copyright
codes of conduct	software piracy
organizational ethics	trade secrets
privacy	software bug
computer monitoring	automation complacency
intellectual property	dirty data
patents	paperless office

repetitive stress injuries (RSIs)
computer vision syndrome (CVS)
low-level electromagnetic fields
computer crime
computer abuse
hacker
computer viruses
Computer Fraud and Abuse Act
information system security
biometric security devices
call-back systems
data encryption

Data Encryption Standard (DES)
backup copies
antivirus software
discretionary access control
audits
audit trail
application controls
input controls
processing controls
output controls
disaster recovery plan

Review Questions

1 How are the concepts of responsibility, accountability, and a legal system related to ethics?

2 How might you go about the process of deciding an ethical dilemma?

3 Describe some of the ways that information technology can create ethical issues.

4 In what ways does information technology pose a threat to privacy?

5 Name and describe at least three laws enacted by Congress to prevent infringement of privacy.

6 Describe how patent, copyright, and trade secret protection can be used to protect property rights to information technology.

7 What are the main threats to system quality? Why is system quality important?

8 How has information technology affected the quality of our worklife?

9 Discuss at least two instances in which information technology has not had the impact that people have predicted.

10 Name and describe the leading health and environmental issues posed by information technology. Also describe some of the ways such problems might be alleviated.

11 Describe and give examples of at least four different types of computer crime.

12 Discuss some of the ways a computer virus may be introduced into your system and describe the potential harm it might cause. How can you guard against viruses?

13 List some of the major threats to information systems besides computer crime. What issues do such threats raise?

14 Describe some basic security measures that should be taken to protect information systems.

15 What are the key elements of a disaster recovery plan?

Problem-Solving and Skill-Building Exercises

1 You have been asked to participate in a project to develop an information systems code of ethics for your company—a medium-sized (less than 500 employees) business in the financial services industry. Together with two or three classmates, prepare a preliminary report to your CIO detailing the kinds of issues that should be addressed by the code. Each member of the team should also choose one of the issues listed and prepare a proposed standard of conduct with regard to that issue to attach to the report.

2 The U.S. military is investigating the possibility of using computer viruses to wage electronic warfare. Studies underway are experimenting with computer viruses that can be transmitted by radio into military command and control systems. Consider the implications of this possibility and debate them with your classmates.

3 Choose an information system with which you come into contact (such as one used by your school or a local business) and write a short report (3–5 pages) detailing the security measures that should be taken to protect the system.

SKILL DEVELOPMENT

Keeping Up with the Times

The issues discussed in this chapter will be in the news for much of the next decade. Our fast-paced society makes it even more important to stay on top of things. Reading the newspaper—whether in traditional or electronic form—remains one of the best ways to keep up with the times and to continue to educate yourself about the choices and changes facing our society. Walter Cronkite gives you some tips on the best way to stay informed.

How to Read a Newspaper

by Walter Cronkite

If you're like most Americans, you try to keep up with the news by watching it on television.

That's how 65% of us get 100% of our news—from the 24-odd-minute TV news broadcast each evening.

The problem—and I know the frustration of it firsthand—is that unless something really special happens, we in TV news have to put severe time limitations on every story, even the most complicated and important ones.

Get More Than Headlines

So what we bring you is primarily a front-page headline service. To get all you need to know, you have to flesh out those headlines with a *complete account* of the news from a well-edited and thorough newspaper.

Is it really necessary to get the *whole* story? Dorothy Greene Friendly put it this way: "What the American people don't know can kill them." Amen.

News people have a responsibility. And so do *you*. Ours is to report the news fairly, accurately, completely. *Yours* is to keep yourself informed every day.

I'll never forget the quotation hanging in Edward R. Murrow's CBS office. It was from Thoreau: "It takes two to speak the truth—one to speak and one to hear."

Take a 3-Minute Overview

Here's how I tackle a paper. For starters, I take a three-minute overview of the news. No need to go to the sports section first, or the TV listings. With my overview you'll get there quickly enough. First I scan the front-page headlines, look at the pictures and read the captions. I do the same thing page by page front to back. Only *then* do I go back for the whole feast.

The way the front page is "made up" tells you plenty. For one thing, headline type size will tell you how the paper's editor ranks the stories on relative importance. A major crop failure in Russia should get larger type than an overturned truckload of wheat on the Interstate, for example.

Which Is the Main Story?

You'll find the main or lead story in the farthest upper right-hand column. Why? Tradition. Newspapers used to appear on newsstands folded and displayed with their top right-hand quarter showing. They made up the front page with the lead story there to entice readers.

You'll find the second most important story at the top far left, unless it's related to the lead story. Do you have to read *all* the stories in the paper? Gosh, no. But you should *check* them all. Maybe the one that appears at first to be the least appealing will be the one that will most affect your life.

News Is Information, Period

A good newspaper provides four basic ingredients to help you wrap your mind around the news: *information, background, analysis,* and *interpretation.*

Rule #1 of American journalism is: *"News columns are reserved only for news."* What *is* news? It is *information* only. You can tell a good newspaper story. It just reports the news. It doesn't try to slant it. And it gives you *both* sides of the story.

Look out for a lot of adjectives and adverbs. They don't belong in an objective news story. They tend to color and slant it so you may come to a wrong conclusion.

Do look for by-lines, datelines, and the news service sources of articles. These will also help you judge a story's importance and its facts.

As you read a story you can weigh its truthfulness by asking yourself, "Who said so?" Look out for "facts" that come from unnamed sources, such as "a highly placed government official." This could tip you off that the story is not quite true, or that someone—usually in Washington—is sending up a "trial balloon" to see if something that *may* happen or be proposed gets a good reception.

Another tip: Check for "Corrections" items. A good newspaper will straighten out false or wrong information as soon as it discovers its error. A less conscientious one will let it slide or bury it.

An Upside-down Pyramid

Reporters write news stories in a special way called the "inverted pyramid" style. That means they start with the end, the *climax* of the story, with the most important facts first, then build in more details in order of importance. This is unlike the telling or writing of most stories, where you usually start at the beginning and save the climax for last. Knowing about the newspaper's "inverted pyramid" style will help you sift facts.

A well-reported story will tell you "who," "what," "when," "where," and "how." The best newspapers will go on to tell you "why." "Why" is often missing. And that may be the key ingredient.

Many important stories are flanked by "sidebars." These are supporting stories that offer, not news, but the "why"— *background* and *analysis*—to help you understand and evaluate it.

Background offers helpful facts. *Analysis* frequently includes opinion. So it should be—and usually is—carefully labeled as such. It's generally by-lined by an expert on the subject who explains the causes of the news and its possible consequences to you.

No good newspaper will mix *interpretation* with "hard" news, either. Interpretation goes beyond analysis and tells you not just what will probably happen, but what *ought* to happen. This should be clearly labeled, or at best, reserved for the editorial page or "op-ed" (opposite the editorial) page.

Form Your Own Opinion First

I form my own opinion *before* I turn to the editorial page for the pundits' views. I don't want them to tell me how to think until I've wrestled the issue through to my own conclusion. Once I have, I'm open to other reasoning. *Resist the temptation to let them do your thinking for you.*

Here's an idea I firmly believe in and act on. When you read something that motivates you, do something about it. Learn more about it. Join a cause. Write a letter. You can *constantly* vote on issues by writing letters, particularly to your congressman or state or local representative.

To understand the news better you can also read news magazines. *Books* help fill in the holes, too. During the Vietnam war, for example, many people felt that the daily news coverage wasn't entirely satisfactory. The truth is, you could have gotten many important new facts on the war from the books coming out at the time.

Pick a TV Story and Follow It

Now that I've told you about the basics of getting under the skin of a newspaper, let newspapers get under your skin.

Tonight, pick an important story that interests you on the TV news. Dig into the story—in your newspaper. Follow it, and *continue* to follow it closely in print. See if you don't find yourself with far more understanding of the event.

And see if you don't have a far more sensible opinion as to the "whys" and "wherefores" of that event, even down to how it will affect you—and maybe even what should be done about it.

Keep up with the news the way my colleagues and I do— on TV *and* in the newspapers.

Learn to sift it for yourself, to heft it, to value it, to question it, to ask for it *all.* You'll be in better control of your life and your fortunes.

And that's the way it is.

Source: Reprinted by permission of International Paper Company.

Notes

1 **Adler, Stephen and Wade Lambert,** "Common Criminals: Just About Everyone Violates Some Laws, Even Model Citizens," *Wall Street Journal,* March 12, 1993.

2 **Rifkin, Glenn,** "Guidelines for Action," *Computerworld,* October 14, 1991.

3 **Laudon, Kenneth,** *Dossier Society,* Columbia University Press, New York, 1986.

4 **Stallman, Richard and Philip McCabe,** "Software Patents: Boon or Bane?" *Computerworld,* June 1, 1992; **Violino, Bob,** "Novell's Nemesis," *InformationWeek,* December 14, 1992; **Lindquist, Christopher,** "Judge Sides with Lotus on Suit," *Computerworld,* August 10, 1992; "Apple's GUI Suit Is Over—For Now," *InformationWeek,* June 7, 1993; **Markoff, John,** "In a World of Instant Copies, Who Pays for Original Work?" *New York Times,* August 9, 1992; **Bennet, James,** "Who Owns Ideas, and Papers, Is Issue in Company Lawsuits," *New York Times,* May 30, 1993.

5 **Neumann, Peter,** "Aggravation by Computer: Life, Death and Taxes," *Communications of the ACM,* July 1992; **Daly, James,** "McAfee Antivirus Code Has Bug," *Computerworld,* March 1, 1993; **Littlewood, Bev and Lorenzo Strigini,** "The Risks of Software," *Scientific American,* November 1992; **Tate, Paul,** "London's Deadly Glitch," *InformationWeek,* November 2, 1992; **Thyfault, Mary,** "Strike Three: AT&T Outage Hits New York," *InformationWeek,* September 23, 1991; **Betts, Mitch,** "Beware of Automation Complacency," *Computerworld,* May 4, 1992.

6 **Soat, John,** "Not Giving Credit Where It's Due," *InformationWeek,* August 19, 1991.

7 **Knight, Bob,** "The Data Pollution Problem," *Computerworld,* September 28, 1992; **Wilson, Linda,** "Devil in Your Data," *InformationWeek,* August 31, 1992; **Bulkeley, William,** "Databases Are Plagued by Reign of Error," *Wall Street Journal,* May 26, 1992; **King, Julia,** "Cleanup Efforts Target Dirty Data," *Computerworld,* October 28, 1991.

8 **Xenakis, John,** "A Revolution in the Workplace," *InformationWeek,* July 22, 1991.

9 **Ehrbar, Al,** "Price of Progress: Re-engineering Gives Firms New Efficiency, Workers the Pink Slip," *Wall Street Journal,* March 16, 1993.

10 **Cobb, Kevin,** "RSI: The New Computer Age Health Assault," *Prevention,* April 1991.

11 **Gilman, Joel,** "Ergonomic Laws in Motion," *Computerworld,* March 30, 1992; **Pollack, Andrew,** "San Francisco Law on VDTs Is Struck Down," *Computerworld,* February 14, 1992.

12 **Betts, Mitch,** "VDT Vision Problems May Affect 10 Million," *Computerworld,* February 8, 1993.

13 **Nadel, Brian,** "The Green Machine," *PC Magazine,* May 25, 1993; **Lohr, Steve,** "Recycling Answer Sought for Computer Junk," *New York Times,* April 14, 1993; **Reinhardt, Andy, et al.,** "The Greening of Computers," *BYTE,* September 1992; **Carrilo, Karen,** "Helping Others Help Themselves," *InformationWeek,* March 1, 1993.

14 Noted computer security expert Donn Parker has collected reports of computer crime cases going back as far as 1958. See **Parker, Donn,** "Computer Abuse Research Update," *Computer Law Journal,* 1980.

15 **Carley, William,** "Saga of Sabotage: As Computers Flip, People Lose Grip," *Wall Street Journal,* August 27, 1992.

16 **Carley, William,** "In-House Hackers: Rigging Computers for Fraud or Malice Is Often an Inside Job," *Wall Street Journal,* August 27, 1992.

17 **Violino, Bob,** "Are Your Networks Secure?" *InformationWeek,* April 12, 1993.

18 **Moran, Robert,** "FBI, Social Security Data Stolen," *InformationWeek,* December 23, 1991; **Daly, James,** "Notorious Hacker Charged with Stealing Fed Secrets," *Computerworld,* December 14, 1992.

19 **Kelly, Rob,** "Do You Know Where Your Laptop Is?" *InformationWeek,* May 11, 1992.

20 **Sprouse, Martin,** *Sabotage in the American Workplace,* Pressure Drop Press, San Francisco, 1992, reprinted with permission in "Sabotage," *InformationWeek,* March 8, 1993.

21 **Daly, James,** "Out to Get You," *Computerworld,* March 22, 1993.

22 **Ramirez, Anthony,** "Theft Through Cellular Clones," *New York Times,* April 7, 1992.

23 **Carley, William,** "In-House Hackers," *Wall Street Journal,* August 27, 1992.

24 **Prosise, Jeff,** "Viruses: How They Work and How to Avoid Them," *PC Magazine,* March 30, 1993; **Schlack, Mark,** "How to Keep Viruses Off Your Lan," *Datamation,* October 15, 1991.

25 **Lewis, Peter,** "Medicine, and Common Sense, for Virus Problems," *New York Times,* June 21, 1992; **Violino, Bob,** "Networks: No Immunity," *InformationWeek,* January 6, 1992; **Markoff, John,** "Computer Viruses: Just Uncommon Colds After All?" *New York Times,* November 1, 1992.

26 **Alexander, Michael,** "Supreme Court Refuses Morris Appeal," *Computerworld,* October 14, 1991.

27 **Jones, Kathryn,** "Big Breakdown Is Sorely Testing Teller Machines," *New York Times,* March 20, 1993.

28 **McPartlin, John,** "Towers Without Power," *InformationWeek,* March 8, 1993; **Holusha, John,** "The Painful Lessons of Disruption," *New York Times,* March 17, 1993; **Hoffman, Thomas,** "Most Data Safe from Blast," *Computerworld,* March 8, 1993.

29 **McPartlin, John,** "Down and Out in Miami," *InformationWeek,* August 31, 1992.

30 **Borsook, Paulina,** "Seeking Security," *BYTE,* May 1993.

31 **Booker, Ellis and Jim Nash,** "Great Chicago Flood of '92: IS Groups Stay High and Dry," *Computerworld,* April 20, 1992; **Booker, Ellis,** "Lessons Learned from Flood," *Computerworld,* May 4, 1992.

This glossary provides definitions for all key terms (those that have been boldfaced within the text and listed at the end of each chapter), as well as other important terms appearing in italics within the text.

abacus A device that permits people to store numbers temporarily and perform calculations using beads strung on wire. One of the first computers.

absolute copy When copying a cell or range in a spreadsheet, making an exact copy of the contents of the old cell or range and transferring it to a new cell or range.

access arm The part of a hard disk drive that positions the read/write heads over the proper tracks. Also called an actuator.

access motion time See **seek time.**

accountability The notion that individuals, organizations, and society should be held accountable to others for the consequences of their actions. A fundamental component of ethics.

accounting software Applications software that keeps track of the influx and outflow of money in an organization. Typically includes a general ledger module, an accounts payable module, an accounts receivable module, a payroll module, and other modules.

accounts payable systems Systems that keep track of amounts owed by a firm to its creditors.

accounts receivable systems Systems that keep track of amounts owed to a firm.

accumulator A register that temporarily stores the results of processing.

active-matrix display A method of displaying an image on a flat panel display screen. Each pixel is controlled by its own transistor attached in a thin film to the glass behind the pixel.

actuator See **access arm.**

Ada A third-generation structured programming language developed by the Department of Defense to serve as a standard language for weapons systems. Supports real-time control of tasks and concurrent processing. Named after Augusta Ada Byron, Countess of Lovelace.

add-in board A board or card-like piece of equipment that plugs into an expansion slot on a motherboard. Allows the power and functionality of a computer to be enhanced without replacing the entire unit.

add-on package A software package that supplements a specific type of software by adding missing features or improving on existing functions.

address The location in primary storage where data or program instructions are stored.

address bus A bus that carries signals used to locate a given memory address in primary storage.

address register A register that holds the part of the program instructions that tells the ALU the address of the data that is to be processed next.

AI See **artificial intelligence.**

ALU See **arithmetic/logic unit.**

analog signal A continuous wave within a given frequency range. Typically used by telephones, televisions, and radios.

Analytical Engine A machine designed by Charles Babbage in the 1830s to perform computations. Was based on concepts very similar to those underlying modern-day computers.

557

analytical graphics software Applications software that allows a user to take data from an existing spreadsheet or database file and create, view, and print charts and graphs.

analyzing technologies Computer hardware and software.

animated computer graphics Computer-generated animated graphics.

anti-virus software Software designed to detect and disable computer viruses.

APL (A Programming Language) A mathematically-oriented, third-generation programming language that uses special symbols enabling users to solve complex formulas in a single step.

applicant tracking system A human resource system that maintains data about applicants for jobs at a firm and provides reports to satisfy federal, state, and local employment regulations.

application controls Manual and automated procedures that ensure that data processed by a particular application are accurate and complete throughout the processing cycle.

application generator A fourth-generation programming language that allows a person to specify what needs to be done and then generates the code necessary to create a program to perform the task.

applications software A computer program that allows you to apply the computer to solve a specific problem or perform a specific task. Examples include word processing software, spreadsheet software, and database management software. May be custom-designed or prewritten and packaged.

applications software package A prewritten, precoded, commercially available program that handles the processing for a particular computer application, such as word processing, spreadsheet, or database management.

arithmetic/logic unit (ALU) The part of the CPU that performs arithmetic and logical operations on data.

artificial intelligence (AI) A family of related technologies that attempts to achieve human-like qualities of intelligence in machines, including the ability to reason.

ASCII (American Standard Code for Information Interchange) A seven- or eight-bit binary code developed by the American National Standards Institute (ANSI), used primarily for data communications and by microcomputers.

assembler Systems software that translates a program written in assembly language into machine language.

assembly language A low-level programming language that substitutes short mnemonic or symbolic codes for machine language instructions. Also referred to as low-level language, symbolic language, or second-generation language.

asynchronous transfer mode A data transfer technology that enables voice, data and images to be transmitted simultaneously at very high speed over telephone lines.

asynchronous transmission A data transmission method that transmits data one character or byte at a time, with each byte preceded by a start bit and followed by an stop bit.

audio board An add-in board that digitizes analog sound and stores it for further processing.

audio input device An input device that records or plays analog sound and translates it for digital storage and processing. Examples include CD-audio and cassette players.

audio output device Special stereo speakers used by MPC machines.

audit An independent review of a company's financial records and/or information systems to see if records are in order and systems and procedures are working as they should. Can be used as a tool to combat computer crime.

audit trail A record that allows a transaction to be traced through all stages of processing, starting with its appearance as a source document and ending with its transformation into output.

automatic data retrieval system A transaction processing system that helps marketers identify who their customers are, what those customers want to buy, and how to contact them.

automatic recalculation A feature of spreadsheet software that enables it to quickly and automatically adjust the values of all cells affected by a change inputted by the user.

automation complacency The tendency to trust computerized systems that monitor the status of complex activities.

auxiliary storage See **secondary storage.**

axon A long strand that connects one neuron to another. In an electronic neural network, it is represented by a wire.

backup copy   A duplicate copy of data files and software that is maintained in case something happens to the original.

backward reasoning   A strategy for searching the knowledge base in an expert system in which the inference engine begins with a tentative solution and proceeds by asking the user questions about selected facts until the hypothesis is either confirmed or disproved.

band printer   A high-speed impact printer with characters on a band that rotates; can print entire lines at once.

bandwidth   Refers to the difference between the highest and lowest frequencies (i.e., the range of frequencies) that a communications channel can carry. In popular press, often used as a synonym for a channel's overall information-carrying capacity.

bar code   Specially designed optical code consisting of bars of varying widths that can be read by a bar code scanner; most common is the Universal Product Code used on merchandise.

bar code scanner   Input device that reads or scans Universal Product Codes on merchandise and other types of bar codes and transmits the data to a point of sale system.

bar graph   A graph that uses vertical or horizontal bars to compare data. Useful for showing data over time.

BASIC (Beginner's All-purpose Symbolic Instruction Code)   A relatively simple, easy-to-learn third-generation programming language designed to work in an interactive environment.

batch system   A type of processing system in which data is accumulated and collected into a group, or batch, and processed together at some later time.

baud rate   A measure of the speed at which data travels through a communications channel. Refers to the number of times per second that the signal being transmitted changes in some predetermined manner.

BBS (bulletin board system)   See **electronic bulletin board.**

before/after action chart   A chart used in systems design that summarizes how a process presently works and how it will work in the future after a new information system has been implemented; also describes the action changes in the organization, technology, and people required by the new system.

behavioral approach   An approach to artificial intelligence that begins by examining what is meant by the concept of intelligent behavior. Also referred to as the top-down approach.

benefit systems   Human resource systems that keep track of data about employee benefit programs, such as life insurance, health insurance, retirement and pension plans, and other benefits.

binary   Having only two possible states. In a binary numbering system, there are only two possible digits: 0 and 1.

binary code   A code that represents letters, numbers, and special characters as binary digits. There are two primary binary codes in use today: EBCDIC and ASCII.

biological feedback devices   A category of input devices that can interpret gestures and other forms of body language as input. Examples include body suits, cyber gloves, and robotic hands.

biometric security device   A device that can identify an individual through a biological characteristic (such as the pattern of blood vessels in the retina, hand measurements, lip patterns, and fingerprints) or through unique behavioral idiosyncrasies, such as vocal intonation, signature, or keystroke dynamics. Used for access control.

bit   Short for binary digit. A binary digit is one that has only one of two possible states, represented either by a 0 or a 1.

bitmapping   A technology that allows each pixel on the screen to be individually addressed and manipulated by the computer, allowing a wider variety of graphics to be created and displayed.

bits per second (bps)   A measure of the speed at which data travels through a communications channel.

block   The ability of word processing software to define a block of text as a unit and perform some operation, such as copy, delete, move, etc. on the entire unit.

bottom-up approach   See **machine approach.**

bps   See **bits per second.**

bridge   A communications device that can establish a connection between two or more similar local area networks.

bubble memory   An electromagnetic storage device that uses bubblelike magnetic areas on a semiconductor chip's surface to represent data. Is nonvolatile, but much more expensive than other types of secondary storage.

bucky balls Carbon-60 molecules that may be used as a component for superconducting circuits or for optical applications.

bulletin board system (BBS) See **electronic bulletin board.**

bus A pathway or connection that electronic impulses travel along within a microprocessor and throughout the system unit. There are three basic types of buses: address buses, data buses, and control buses.

business function The various tasks performed in a business organization, such as production and operations, finance and accounting, sales and marketing, and human resources activities.

business graphics Graphics that present data in a visual and easy-to-understand format.

business procedures Rules or habitual methods that guide the behavior of members of a business organization.

bus network A local area network that links computers and other devices along a common communications channel composed of twisted-pair wire, coaxial cable, or fiber-optic cable. Data is broadcast through the communications channel in both directions to the entire network; special software ensures that only those devices for which the data is intended actually receive it.

bus width Refers to the amount of data that can be transferred through a bus at one time.

byte A single character of data (a letter, digit, or special character), represented by a string of eight bits. Also the basic unit of measurement for storage capacity within primary storage.

C A third-generation programming language that incorporates the advantages of both assembly language and high-level languages. Originally created to write operating systems such as UNIX; now used for many commercial microcomputer applications software packages.

C++ A version of the C programming language that supports object-oriented programming.

cache High-speed memory chips that hold the most frequently used instructions and data. Also referred to as high-speed buffer or cache memory.

cache memory See **cache.**

CAD See **computer-aided design.**

call-back system A security measure to ensure that the user attempting to dial into a system is calling from an authorized telephone line. After a user dials into the computer system, it breaks the connection and calls the user back at a predetermined telephone number.

CAM See **computer-aided manufacturing.**

CASE See **computer-aided software engineering tools.**

case-based reasoning An expert system that uses accumulated cases or descriptions of past problems and their solutions as a guide for solving current problems.

case control structure A control structure used in structured programming. Permits a large number of alternatives to be examined quickly.

cash management system A financial system that keeps track of the receipt and disbursement of a firm's cash; also used to forecast a firm's cash flow.

cathode ray tube (CRT) The most common type of display screen. Consists of a large vacuum tube similar to that used by a television set. Displays text, graphics, and images in monochrome or color.

CD-ROM (Compact Disk Read-Only Memory) An optical disk that can store over 600MB of data. They cannot be written on, only read.

cell The intersection of a column and a row in a spreadsheet.

cell address The location of a specific cell within a spreadsheet, identified by its column and row coordinates.

cell pointer A bar that highlights the current cell in a worksheet.

cellular telephone A telephone system that uses radio waves to carry voice conversations. The waves are transmitted to radio antennas located in adjacent cells throughout a given geographic area. Also referred to as a mobile telephone.

central processing unit (CPU) The part of a computer system that processes data and controls the other parts of the system. It consists of two parts: the arithmetic/logic unit and control unit. Sometimes referred to as the main processor or processor.

centralized system A computer system that stores all information and does all processing at a single, central location.

chain printer A high-speed impact printer with

characters on a chain that rotates; can print entire lines at one time.

check bit   See **parity bit.**

class   In object-oriented programming, objects that are derived or related to one another.

class library   In object-oriented programming, a predefined group of objects that can be reused in different applications without having to rewrite code.

client/server computing   A method of setting up a local area network in which a high-speed, high-capacity minicomputer or workstation called a server manages the activities of the network and distributes data and programs as requested to the microcomputers (clients) in the network.

clip art   Collections of ready-to-use illustrations stored in digital form.

clock speed   The pace of electronic pulses set by the system clock. Measured in megahertz (MHz).

clone   A microcomputer that imitates the architecture of an IBM microcomputer.

coaxial cable   A transmission medium for a communications channel. Consists of a copper wire surrounded by several layers of insulation. Can transmit up to 200 megabits of data per second.

COBOL (Common Business Oriented Language) A third-generation programming language developed to handle business problems. Uses English-like statements to process large data files with alphanumeric characters.

codec   A device that converts analog video images and sound waves into digital signals and compresses them for transfer over digital telephone lines. Used in connection with videoconferencing.

code library   A library of reusable code segments that programmers can copy and paste into their own programs.

codes of conduct   Guidelines that outline the professional obligations and responsibilities employees and organization members have to their employers, to the public, and to society as a whole.

command   An instruction given to a computer program that tells it what the user wants to do.

command language   The language in which program commands are written; used to communicate

with the operating system. Also referred to as job control language.

command language translator   A part of the operating system that translates program commands and assigns the resources necessary to carry out the commands.

common carrier   Companies licensed by the Federal Communications Commission to provide communications channels and services to the public. Examples include AT&T, US Sprint, MCI, regional Bell operating companies, and local telephone companies.

communications channel   The path over which data travels as it passes from a sending device to a receiving device in a telecommunications system. Also referred to as a communications link or line.

communications controller   A device that supervises communications traffic between the CPU and peripheral devices such as display screens and printers.

communications satellite   A satellite placed in stationary orbit that acts as a relay station for an earth station by receiving data, amplifying it and then retransmitting it to another earth station.

communications software   Software used to transmit data via communications channels.

communication technologies   Digital technologies that tie together and communicate information between sensing, analyzing, and display technologies.

competitive advantage   A unique feature of a firm that gives it the ability to produce products at lower cost or to produce unique products that cannot be imitated.

compiler   Systems software that translates a program written in a high-level language (a source program) into machine language. The entire program is translated before it is executed.

computer abuse   Acts involving a computer that may be legal but are unethical.

computer-aided design (CAD)   The use of software to create complex three-dimensional architectural drawings, engineering drawings, and product designs.

computer-aided manufacturing (CAM)   The use of computers to help manufacture products designed with CAD software.

computer-aided software engineering (CASE) tools   Software that aids in the design of information systems. Front-end CASE tools assist in preliminary design, systems analysis, and systems design. Back-end CASE tools help with systems development and implementation.

computer crime   The use of a computer to commit a criminal act. Examples include the theft of money or other property, the theft of computer and telecommunications services, the unauthorized accessing and use of information systems, and the theft, intentional alteration, or destruction of data or programs.

Computer Fraud and Abuse Act   A federal law that makes it illegal to knowingly access, without authorization and with intent to defraud, a computer used by the federal government or for interstate commerce if such action causes a loss of more than $1,000.

computer game software   Software designed primarily for entertainment value.

computer monitoring   The use of information technology to monitor an employee's activities and performance.

computer system   A collection of interrelated devices, such as sensing devices, communication devices, secondary storage devices, and display devices, together with as a system unit containing a CPU and primary storage.

computer virus   A set of illicit instructions implanted within a program that passes itself on to other programs which it comes in contact with. Takes up RAM and hard disk space and may slow down performance of a system, as well as destroy data or lock-up systems.

computer vision syndrome (CVS)   Conditions such as dry and irritated eyes, blurry vision, headaches and other symptoms associated with eye strain caused by screen glare, improper lighting, and screens with poor resolution and a low refresh rate.

concentrator   A communications device that collects and temporarily stores data in a buffer or temporary storage area and then sends the data on its way once enough data has been collected to be sent economically.

contact manager   A variation on personal information manager software designed to keep track of outside contacts such as telephone calls, letters, and so on.

control bus   A bus carrying signals that tell the computer to read or write data to or from a given memory address, input device, or output device.

controller   Add-in boards or cards that enable the CPU to interface with the system's different peripheral devices.

control panel   The top three lines of a Lotus 1-2-3 screen. Display information about the current cell, menu choices, and mode.

control unit   The part of the CPU that controls and coordinates the other parts of the computer system.

coprocessor   A specialized processor chip that can be added to a motherboard to enhance a computer's performance. A coprocessor performs its specialized task at the same time the CPU is working on something else.

copyright   A body of federal law that, among other things, prohibits the literal copying of a computer program or its component parts.

cost/benefit analysis   A comparison of all of the benefits of a proposal to all of the costs.

CPU   See **central processing unit.**

credit authorization system   A marketing and sales transaction processing system that checks a customer's credit before a credit transaction is executed.

credit card memory   See **memory card.**

credit management system   A financial system that analyzes a firm's credit position and oversees credit granted by a firm to its customers.

critical path diagram   A project management tool.

critical thinking   Analyzing a topic from different perspectives, seeking out causes or potential consequences of issues and events, and applying knowledge to new, possibly unrelated or previously undiscussed areas or issues. Also the first step in the systems analysis and design process.

CRT   See **cathode ray tube.**

current cell   In spreadsheet software, the cell over which the cell pointer is positioned.

cursor   A blinking line or highlighted symbol on the screen that indicates the position of the next character to be typed and where you are on the display screen.

custom-designed applications software Applications software that has been written specifically to satisfy a particular user's needs.

customer identification system A part of an automated data retrieval system that helps identify who customers are.

cutting and pasting A word processing software feature that makes it easy to move and copy blocks of text within a document.

cylinder method A method of recording data on hard disk in which data is organized vertically.

daisy wheel printer An impact printer that produces letter-quality character print by using a print wheel with long thin spokes, each with a fully formed raised character at the end. The wheel rotates and is struck by a tiny hammer against an inked ribbon and paper.

DASD (direct access storage device) A secondary storage device that allows records to be accessed directly, i.e. the device can proceed directly to a given record without having to read all preceding records. Typically used when referring to hard disks and their associated hard disk drives attached to mainframe or midrange computers.

data Raw, unprocessed facts.

database A collection of related files.

database management software Applications software used to create, store, organize, and retrieve lists, files, and databases.

database management system (DBMS) Applications software that allows a user to construct a database environment for a set of related files and easily access and manipulate information located in separate files. Permits data to be stored in a common repository yet remain available to different applications.

data bus A bus that carries data to and from primary storage.

data collection device An input device that collects specific kinds of data directly from the environment and then conveys it to a computer.

data compression Increases storage capacity of a hard disk drive by compressing the size of data files. Compresses files by eliminating strings of redundant characters and replacing them with more compact symbols.

data confusion Occurs when data is not updated in all files in which it appears.

data definition The process of creating a file structure for a database file by defining field names, field types, and field widths.

data dependence Occurs when different parts of an organization use different software to collect, process, and store information, making data files of one department incompatible with the data files of a different department.

data dictionary A feature of some database management systems that stores definitions and other characteristics of data elements and monitors data to make sure that it corresponds to the format required.

data encryption The encoding of data so that it cannot be understood unless it is first decoded. Used to protect data from unauthorized access.

Data Encryption Standard (DES) The encryption key system adopted as the government standard in 1977.

data flow diagram (DFD) A diagram used in systems design that depicts how data flows through an existing or proposed information system.

data hierarchy The structure underlying the organization of data within storage media. From smallest to largest, the data hierarchy is as follows: bit, byte, field, record, file, and database.

data redundancy Occurs when the same piece of information is stored in multiple data files.

data transfer rate The time needed to transfer data to or from a disk to primary storage.

data worker An information worker whose job involves the use, manipulation, or dissemination of information created by others. Examples include clerks, secretaries, salespersons, bank workers, and the like.

day-one conversion A system conversion strategy in which the old system continues to run, but all new customer accounts and activities are put on the new system.

dBASE A programming language included as part of a popular database management software program.

DBMS See **database management system.**

debugger Software that checks the syntax of a program, enabling the programmer to spot and correct errors in a program more quickly.

decisionmaker One of the roles of a manager.

decision support system (DSS) A management support system that supports middle-management and information workers who need assistance with semistructured, non-routine problems. Usually contains analytic models that permit user to simulate the business environment and to understand how to react to a change in business conditions.

decision table A table that depicts the rules used in a structured decision-making process.

dedicated line See **private line.**

default setting A standard setting or assumption made by a software package; can be changed by user if desired.

demodulation The process of converting an analog signal into a digital signal.

DES See **Data Encryption Standard.**

desktop computer The most common type of microcomputer; fits on a desktop. Examples include IBM PS/2 and Apple Macintosh lines.

desktop manufacturing A knowledge work system that speeds up product cycle times and improves quality. Creates a plastic model of a CAD design with a desktop machine.

desktop organizer Software that allows a user to store, organize, and have easy access to the details of business and personal information. Typically includes an address book, appointment book, calendar, and notepad. Often included as part of personal information manager software.

desktop publishing (DTP) software Software used to design and produce professional-looking documents that incorporate text with graphics. Used in connection with a desktop publishing system. Also called page makeup or page composition software.

desktop publishing (DTP) system A system that allows a user to design and produce professional-looking newsletters, reports, manuals, brochures, advertisements, and other documents that incorporate text with graphics.

detailed design A design that describes how a proposed information system will actually deliver the general functional capabilities described in a preliminary design.

development team The group of individuals involved in building an information system.

DFD See **data flow diagram.**

dialog box A feature of a graphical user interface: a box that requests information about the task the user is performing or supplies information that the user might need.

Difference Engine A machine designed by Charles Babbage to solve mathematical equations.

digital camera A camera that takes pictures and stores them as digital data in the camera's memory. Images can then be transferred directly to a computer system.

digital information technologies Technologies that use electronics to transform information into a digital, binary format.

digital signal A signal that uses separate, on-off electrical pulses rather than a continuous wave to transmit data.

digitizing tablet An input device consisting of a pressure-sensitive tablet and electronic stylus or puck; used to create images and convert drawings into digital form.

direct access See **random access.**

direct file organization See **random file organization.**

direct switch-over A system conversion strategy in which the old system is replaced entirely with the new system on the appointed day.

dirty data Data stored in a database that is inaccurate, outdated, or missing.

disaster recovery plan A plan that enables a firm to recover from an emergency in which all or part of its information systems have been destroyed. Provides for immediate access to alternative computer hardware and the restoration of software, data, and telecommunications.

discretionary access control The restriction of access to data and programs on a "need to know/need to use" basis.

disk access time The speed at which data can be located on a magnetic disk and transferred to primary storage.

disk cache A technique to improve data access time. A copy of the most frequently used data and program instructions is transferred to a cache within primary storage, where it can be accessed more quickly.

disk cartridge A hard disk encased within a removable cartridge. Combines the storage capacity of a hard disk with the portability of a floppy disk.

diskette   See **floppy disk.**

display screen   An output device that displays instructions to the user, data as it is being inputted, and data after it has been processed. Also referred to as a monitor, computer screen, CRT (cathode ray tube), or VDT (video display terminal).

display technologies   Digital technologies that form the interface or connection between sensing, communication, and analyzing technologies and the human user.

distributed system   A computer system that uses multiple computers connected by a telecommunications network.

document   A letter, memo, report, or other text produced with word processing software.

DOS   An operating system for computers with 16-bit microprocessors. There are two basic versions: PC-DOS for IBM microcomputers and MS-DOS for all other IBM-compatible microcomputers.

dot matrix printer   An impact printer that creates characters through the use of a print head composed of tiny pins that press against an inked ribbon.

dot pitch   The amount of space between each pixel on a display screen.

double-sided disk   A floppy disk that can store data on both sides.

download   Transfer a file from a mainframe or central host computer to a terminal or microcomputer in a network.

downsizing   The movement from large mainframe-based systems to smaller and less expensive minicomputers, workstations, and microcomputers linked in networks.

drawing packages   Applications software that allows a user to draw straight and curved lines, freeform shapes, and geometric objects by moving the cursor with a mouse or through the use of a digitizing tablet.

drum plotter   An output device that draws on paper rolling past on a drum.

DSS   See **decision support system.**

DTP   See **desktop publishing software** or **desktop publishing system.**

dumb terminal   A computer terminal (display screen and keyboard) that has no independent processing capacity. Typically used in systems in which terminals are linked to a central mainframe or minicomputer.

DVI (Digital Video Interactive)   The Intel standard for video compression. Compresses video at a 150:1 ratio.

EBCDIC (Extended Binary Coded Decimal Interchange Code)   An 8-bit binary coding scheme used primarily with IBM and other mainframe computers.

E-cycle   See **execution cycle.**

EDI   See **electronic data interchange.**

EDSAC (Electronic Delay Storage Automatic Calculator)   The world's first stored program electronic computer, developed by Maurice Wilkes in 1949.

educational software   Applications software designed for educational value.

EDVAC (Electronic Discreet Variable Computer)   An improved version of ENIAC that could store instructions internally. Introduced in 1951.

EEPROM (electrically erasable programmable read-only memory)   An EPROM chip that can be reprogrammed using special electrical pulses without having to be removed from the computer.

EIS   See **executive information system.**

electroluminescent display   A type of flat panel display screen that emits light produced by the electron excitation of phosphors.

electromagnetic spectrum   Electromagnetic radiation, ranging from very long and low-frequency radio waves to very short and very high-frequency cosmic rays.

electronic bulletin board   A service that anyone with a personal computer, modem, communications software, and a telephone can use to communicate with others on topics of common interest. Also referred to as a bulletin board system (BBS).

electronic data interchange (EDI)   The direct computer-to-computer exchange of standard business transaction documents, such as invoices, purchase orders, and shipping notices.

electronic digital computer   A computer based on electronic components that processes data using digital (on/off) electronic pulses.

electronic mail (E-mail)   A system that enables a user to transmit letters, memos and other messages directly from one computer to another, where the messages are stored for later retrieval.

electronic spreadsheet   Computerized version of a manually prepared spreadsheet created by using spreadsheet software.

electronic thesaurus   A feature of some word processing software packages that provides a list of synonyms and antonyms for a selected word. Also available as an add-on package.

E-mail   See **electronic mail.**

employee self service feature   A feature of certain benefit systems that gives users direct access to the system via information kiosks, telephones, or desktop microcomputers.

end user   A person who uses a computer or information system.

ENIAC (Electronic Numerical Integrator and Computer)   The first general-purpose electronic computer, developed by John Mauchley and J. Presper Eckert and introduced in 1946.

EPROM (erasable programmable read-only memory)   A PROM chip that allows data and instructions to be erased by removing the chip from the computer and reprogramming it with a special machine using ultraviolet light.

ergonomics   The science of designing products that are more comfortable and less physically stressful for people to use.

ethics   Moral standards that help guide behavior, actions, and choices.

execution cycle   The part of the machine cycle in which the required data is located, the instruction executed, and the results stored. Also referred to as the E-cycle.

executive information system (EIS)   A management support system that supports the senior management of a firm and the strategic planning function.

expansion slot   A slot located on the motherboard into which add-in boards or cards can be plugged.

expert system   A computer-based system that models human knowledge or expertise in a limited domain or area and applies this knowledge or expertise to solve problems within that domain or area.

expert system shell   A system that permits non-programmers to build a fairly large expert system relatively quickly. They have user-friendly interfaces and are often used to prototype expert system applications.

fault tolerant system   A system that contains several redundant computers, special computer programs, and power backups to protect against the failure of any one computer or element of the system. Typically used in life-dependent or critical situations.

fax (facsimile) machine   A machine that can transmit and receive documents over regular telephone lines. The sending machine digitizes and transmits the document (text, graphics, signatures) over the telephone line to the receiving machine, which then reproduces a copy or facsimile of the document.

FDDI   See **Fiber Distributed Data Interface.**

feedback   Output that provides a basis for acting on the data that was input.

Fiber Distributed Data Interface (FDDI)   A technology that can be used to create local area networks that transmit over 100 megabits per second.

fiber optics   A technology that has created a transmission medium that uses light emitted by a laser device instead of electricity to transmit data. Cables are created by binding together hundreds of thousands of strands of smooth, clear glass fiber.

field   A set of related characters, such as a word, a groups of words, or a number, used to record a particular piece of information about a person, place, or thing (such as a name, address, and so on).

field name   In a database, the name describing the data to be entered in the field.

field type   In a database, a category defining the type of data that will be stored in the field. Common fields types include alphanumeric fields, numeric fields, date fields, and logical fields.

fifth-generation language   See **natural language.**

file   A collection of related records.

file conversion   Movement of files from an old system to a new system.

file manager   Applications software that allows a user to create, retrieve, and work with files, one file at a time.

file server   A high-speed, high-capacity microcomputer or workstation that helps manage a local area network, process communications, and allows users to share data, programs, and peripheral devices.

finance and accounting group   The division of a business organization responsible for managing the firm's financial assets (finance) and maintaining the firm's financial records (accounting).

financial accounting system A system that focuses on an analysis of the key financial ratios used by firms to understand their overall financial position.

firmware Permanent instructions embedded within ROM (read-only memory) chips, so-called because they have some characteristics of hardware and some characteristics of software.

first-generation language See **machine language.**

fixed disk drive A disk drive with an encased disk pack that cannot be removed. Contrasts with a removable-pack hard disk system which contains several hard disks assembled into an indivisible pack that can be mounted on and removed from a disk unit.

fixed media Secondary storage media that cannot be removed.

flatbed plotter An output device that draws via a plotting device moving across a stationary piece of paper.

flat file A file that cannot be linked with other files. Used in connection with a file manager.

flat-panel display (FPD) A type of display screen that is much thinner, lighter, and consumes less power than CRTs. Uses charged chemicals or gases sandwiched between panes of glass to display output on the screen. Typically used for portable computers. Examples include liquid crystal display screens, gas plasma screens, and electroluminescent displays.

floppy disk Flexible, inexpensive magnetic disk created from mylar plastic coated with a magnetizable substance and enclosed in a protective jacket. Data is recorded as magnetized and non-magnetized spots. The most popular secondary storage medium. Comes in two sizes: 5 1/4 inches and 3 1/2 inches. Also referred to as a diskette.

floppy disk drive Secondary storage device used to record and read data on a floppy disk.

flops (floating point operations per second) A measurement of a computer processor's speed based on the number of floating point operations (a specialized form of mathematical calculation) per second the processor can perform.

flopticals A system that uses a regular floppy disk coupled with a special floptical disk drive that uses a light beam to position the read/write head. Flopticals can hold up to 21MB.

flowchart A pictorial representation that illustrates the structure and sequence of operations of a program, or the components and flows of an information system. Uses a standard set of symbols developed by the American National Standards Institute.

font A complete set of characters of a particular style, size, and weight. Often used synonymously with typeface.

footer Lines of text that appear at the bottom of a page.

formatting The specifications that determine the way a document or worksheet will look. Also refers to the process of preparing a magnetic disk to store data.

formula In a spreadsheet, an instruction to perform a calculation involving certain cells and to display the result in the cell containing the formula.

FORTRAN (FORmula TRANslator) A third-generation programming language designed primarily to solve scientific, mathematical, and engineering problems that require repetitive numerical calculations and complex formulas.

forward reasoning A strategy used to search the knowledge base of an expert system in which the inference engine begins with information entered by the user and searches the knowledge base to arrive at a conclusion.

fourth-generation language (4GL) An easy to write, non-procedural programming language that allows a programmer to write programs that only have to tell the computer what the programmer would like done, not how the task should be carried out. Also referred to as a very-high-level language.

front-end processor A microcomputer or minicomputer that handles communications management for the main, or host, computer in a large telecommunications network.

full-duplex transmission The transmission of data through a communications channel in both directions simultaneously.

function A preprogrammed formula included with spreadsheet software.

function key Any one of the keys numbered F1 through F12 on a microcomputer; typically used to perform a specific operation that may differ depending on the type of software in use.

fuzzy logic A type of artificial intelligence that allows a computer to represent and make inferences from knowledge that is imprecise, uncertain, or unreliable.

gallium arsenide A material used as an alternative to silicon in chip making.

gantt chart A project management tool used to depict schedule deadlines and milestones.

gas plasma screen A kind of flat panel display screen which illuminates pixels by ionizing low-pressure inert gas.

gateway A communications device that allows users of a local area network to communicate with a mainframe or dissimilar network.

GB See **gigabyte.**

general ledger system An accounting system used to keep track of a firm's income and expenditures; produces accounting statements such as an income statement, balance sheet, and general ledger trial balance.

geographic information system See **mapping software.**

gigabyte (GB or gig) A measure of computer storage capacity. Equal to around 1 billion bytes.

goods worker A worker who primarily works with physical objects or transforms physical materials.

graphical user interface (GUI) An interface between an operating system and user that employs graphical symbols or icons to represent programs, files, and common instructions and allows a user to point and click with a pointing device such as a mouse rather than type commands.

graphics software Applications software that can produce charts, graphs, drawings, and illustrations. Types available include analytical and presentation graphics, illustration graphics, computer-aided design, and animated computer graphics.

groupware Software designed for use on computer networks that allows people to share information and coordinate activities.

hacker A person who uses his or her computer skills to break into a computer or telecommunications system, steal information or services, or disrupt operations.

half-duplex transmission The transmission of data through a communications channel in both directions, but only one direction at a time.

hand-off In value chain analysis, the places where one unit of business transfers some information or product to another unit.

hard card An add-in board with the functionality of a hard disk. Plugs into an expansion slot in the system unit of a microcomputer.

hard copy Output that is produced on paper.

hard disk A thin, rigid metallic platter coated with a magnetizable substance that allows data to be recorded as magnetized and non-magnetized spots. Typically, several are permanently mounted together on a spindle and encased within a hard disk drive.

hard disk drive Secondary storage device that reads and writes data on a hard disk.

hard return In word processing, the automatic start of a new paragraph by pressing the Enter key.

hardware The physical equipment in a computer system.

hardware conversion The replacement of old hardware with new hardware.

hashing algorithm A mathematical formula used to translate the key field of a record into the record's physical location on the storage media. Also called a randomizing algorithm.

head crash The collision of the read/write head with the surface of the hard disk. May cause the destruction of data stored on the disk.

header Lines of text that appear at the very top of a page.

helical-scanning A method of putting down data on magnetic tape. Data is stored in diagonal stripes rather than in vertical columns.

hexadecimal A numbering system that uses base 16. Often used as a shorthand system for writing machine language instructions.

hierarchical DBMS A database that links data through a hierarchical relationship. Organizes data in a top-down manner, with the main segment at the top linked to multiple subordinate segments in a parent-child, one-to-many relationship. Each parent segment may be linked to one or more children, but each child segment has only one parent segment.

hierarchy chart A program development tool that illustrates the overall purpose of the program, identifies all the modules to achieve this purpose, and shows the relationships among modules. Also referred to as a structure chart.

high-definition television (HDTV) A television system that features enhanced video and sound quality through the use of digital processing.

high-level language A programming language that uses English-like words combined into sentence-like statements. Third-generation programming languages are high-level languages.

highly parallel computer See **massively parallel computer.**

high-speed buffer See **cache.**

host computer The main, or central, computer in a network.

human resource development system A system that keeps track of current training programs available in a firm and the skill levels of existing employees. Enables a firm to track development of skill levels among employees, lay out a skill development plan of course work and job experience, and plan sufficient resources to train employees in required skills.

human resources group The division of a business organization responsible for the hiring, training, and retaining of employees required to produce the product or service.

Hypertalk An object-based programming language for the Hypercard toolkit offered by Apple for its Macintosh computers.

icon A pictorial symbol displayed on the computer screen that represents a command or file.

I-cycle See **instruction cycle.**

illustration programs A type of graphics software that can be used to create illustrations and computer art. Includes drawing programs, paint programs, and photo image editors.

imaging system A system that allows images of documents, photographs, and drawings to be inputted, processed, stored, and displayed.

impact printer A printer that forms characters by striking a mechanism such as a print hammer or wheel against inked ribbon and papers. Examples include the daisy wheel printer and dot matrix printer.

implementation The final phase of systems analysis and design, in which the system is made operational. Includes system conversion, training, auditing, and maintenance.

indexed-sequential file organization A method of storing records. Records are stored sequentially, but are indexed by key field and physical location, allowing them to be accessed directly in whatever order the user desires.

inference engine The expert system software that controls the search of the expert system's knowledge base. Utilizes either a forward reasoning or a backward reasoning strategy.

information Data that has been processed into a form that is meaningful and useful to humans.

information clearinghouse One of the roles of a manager. Involves collecting information on an organization's performance, disseminating the information to those who need it, and acting as spokesperson to the outside world.

information system A set of interrelated components that sense, communicate, analyze, and display information for the purpose of enhancing our perception, understanding, control, and creative ability.

information system security Policies, procedures, and tools that help organizations protect information systems against crime, abuse, systems failure, and disasters.

information systems group The division of a business organization responsible for operating the information systems needed by production, finance and accounting, sales and marketing, and human resources.

information worker A person who creates, works with, or disseminates information. There are two types of information workers: knowledge workers and data workers.

inheritance In object-oriented programming, the method of passing down traits of an object to subclasses.

ink-jet printer A nonimpact printer that produces an image by spraying electrically charged droplets of ink through tiny nozzles onto a piece of paper.

input Raw data from the world around us, sounds, images, or program instructions that are to be processed by the computer. Also refers to the process of conveying information to the computer.

input controls Application controls that help ensure the accuracy and completeness of data as it enters the system.

input device A device used to capture data and program instructions and convey them to the computer. Examples include the keyboard, mouse, electronic pen, touch screen, digitizing tablet, sensors, and data collection devices.

insert mode   An editing feature of applications software that inserts new characters into the text without overwriting the old text.

instruction cycle   The part of the machine cycle in which an instruction is retrieved from primary storage and decoded. Also referred to as the I-cycle.

instruction register   A register that holds the part of the program instructions that tells the ALU what it is supposed to do next.

instruction set   The set of instructions that are physically represented as electronic circuits within the CPU.

integrated circuit   A complete electronic circuit, consisting of thousands of tiny transistors, etched on a single silicon chip.

Integrated Services Digital Network (ISDN)   A technology that enables voice, data, and images to be transmitted simultaneously as digital signals over regular twisted-pair telephone lines.

integrated software   Applications software that combines word processing software, spreadsheet software, database management software, and data communications into one package.

intellectual property   The tangible and intangible products of the human mind. Protected by three primary methods: patent law, copyright law, and trade secret law.

intelligent terminal   A terminal that has independent processing capacity; usually a microcomputer that is linked to a central mainframe or minicomputer.

interactive processing environment   Processing environment in which users communicate directly with the computer as a program is being written and data is being inputted.

internal storage   See **primary storage.**

Internet   An international-wide area network connecting thousands of smaller networks used by academics, scientists, private companies, and increasingly the general public. Provides access to a vast array of information stored in computer systems throughout the world.

interpersonal leader   One of the roles of a manager. Involves presiding at ceremonies, motivating subordinates to work, and maintaining links with the community.

interpreter   Systems software that translates a program written in a high-level language into machine language, one line at a time, executing each translated statement before proceeding to the next.

inventory control system   A production transaction processing system that tracks current supplies of inventory and matches them against anticipated future orders from customers.

iteration control structure   A control structure used in structured programming. Enables a programmer to represent the performance of a process if a given condition is true (Do While) or until a condition is met (Do Until).

job control language   See **command language.**

job scheduling system   A production transaction processing system that helps decide when to initiate production of specific items based on supplies on hand and customer demand.

Josephson junction   An experimental circuit that uses superconductor technology.

joystick   A small lever that allows the user to move the cursor on the computer's screen.

justified-right   A right margin in which each line ends at exactly the same spot.

KB   See **kilobyte.**

kerning   The amount of space between letters.

keyboard   A common input device for entering data and instructions. Similar to the keyboard of a typewriter.

key field   A field in a record that uniquely identifies that record so it can be retrieved and processed.

kilobyte (KB or K)   A measure of computer storage capacity. Equals 1,024 bytes.

knowledge base   An expert system's database of relevant facts, information, and rules. Also called a model of the knowledge domain.

knowledge-based   Attempts to capture the knowledge of human experts and organizations in software.

knowledge engineer   A specialist who interviews experts and determines the decision rules and knowledge that must be embedded in an expert system.

knowledge worker   An information worker whose job is to create new information and knowledge. Examples include scientists, engineers, lawyers, professors, and the like.

knowledge work systems (KWS)   Information systems that serve the needs of information and data workers to process and create information and knowledge.

label   In a spreadsheet, a cell entry that consists of text characters. Usually functions as a heading or describes the contents of a cell.

label-prefix characters   The ', ^, ", or \ characters used to indicate labels and format instructions with Lotus 1-2-3.

LAN   See **local area network.**

language translator   A type of systems software that translates a program written in a high-level language into machine language. There are three basic types: compilers, assemblers, and interpreters.

laptop computer   A portable microcomputer weighing 10 pounds or less.

large-scale integrated circuit (LSIC)   A silicon chip containing hundreds of thousands of transistors.

laser printer   A nonimpact printer that produces an image by scanning a laser beam across a light sensitive drum. Toner that adheres to the charged portions of the drum is attracted from the drum onto paper, and is then pressed by heated rollers into the page. Produces high quality print and graphics.

laws   A system of rules codifying ethical standards and providing a mechanism for holding people, organizations, and governments accountable.

LCD   See **liquid crystal display.**

leading   The amount of space between lines.

leased line   See **private line.**

levels of management   Different types of management in an organization. There are typically three levels: senior management, middle management, and lower-level management.

line graph   A graph that represents data as a series of points and connects the points with a line.

line printer   A printer that can print entire lines at a time. Examples include chain printers, band printers, and dot-matrix printers.

linkage editor   Systems software that binds together portions of translated instructions with other prewritten subprograms held in a systems library.

liquid crystal display (LCD)   The most common type of flat panel display screen. Uses liquid crystal, an oily substance that responds to electrical fields, to block or transmit light.

LISP (LISt Processor)   A third-generation programming language used primarily for artificial intelligence programs.

local area network (LAN)   A combination of hardware, software, and communications channels that connect two or more computers within a limited area. This allows them to share data, programs, and peripheral devices.

logical design   See **preliminary design.**

logic element   The electronic component used within a computer to store and process information. First-generation computers used vacuum tubes as their main logic element; second-generation computers used transistors; third-generation computers used integrated circuits; and fourth-generation computers use LSICs and VLSICs.

Logo   A programming language used primarily to teach school children problem solving and some programming skills.

lower-level managers   Provide hands-on, daily, and hourly control and decision-making necessary to conduct day-to-day operations.

low-level electromagnetic fields   Emissions from CRT-based computer monitors.

low-level language   Machine or assembly language.

LSIC   See **large-scale integrated circuit.**

machine approach   An approach to artificial intelligence that concentrates on trying to build a physical equivalent to the brain. Also referred to as the bottom-up approach.

machine cycle   The series of operations performed to execute a single program instruction. Consists of an instruction cycle and an execution cycle.

machine dependent   Programs that can only be used with one kind of computer.

machine language   The computer's own internal language, used to program the first generation of computers. Represents information as strings of 0s and 1s that can be executed directly by the computer. Also referred to as object code.

machine language instruction   A program instruction consisting of a string of binary digits (0s and 1s).

machine rights   The idea that intelligent machines should have certain rights.

macro   A sequence of predefined keystrokes or mouse clicks that automate a particular task.

macro recorder   A feature of some word processing and spreadsheet programs that automatically records the keystrokes or mouse clicks necessary to create a macro.

magnetic core   A small donut-shaped magnet strung on a wire. Used for primary storage in second-generation computers.

magnetic disk   The most popular secondary storage medium. Created from an oxide-coated metallic or flexible plastic disk. Data is stored as magnetized and non-magnetized spots. Data stored may be accessed randomly.

magnetic drum   A form of primary storage used in first-generation computers.

magnetic ink character recognition (MICR)   A type of source data automation. A magnetic ink character reader identifies characters written in magnetic ink. Used primarily by the banking industry to process checks.

magnetic tape   A secondary storage medium created from thin plastic coated with a magnetizable substance. Data is stored as magnetized and non-magnetized spots on the tape. Is inexpensive and stable, but must be accessed sequentially. Used today primarily for back-up.

magneto-optical disk   Erasable disk that makes use of a combination of magnetic and optical storage technologies.

mail-merge   A feature of word processing software that allows letters and a name and address file to be linked to produce personalized-looking form letters.

mainframe computer   A large, fast, and powerful computer that is typically used by large businesses and government agencies.

main memory   See **primary storage.**

main storage   See **primary storage.**

management information system (MIS)   A management support system that assists middle-level managers whose job is to control the operations of the company. Provides routine summary reports on the firm's performance and can also be used to monitor and forecast the firm's future performance.

management roles   The functions performed by management in an organization. Managers have three primary roles: interpersonal leader, information clearinghouse, and decision-maker.

management support systems (MSS)   Information systems that serve management's need to control and plan an organization.

manufacturing firm   A firm that produces physical products.

manufacturing resource planning (MRP) system   A production transaction processing system that integrates purchasing management, job scheduling, inventory control, and process control into a single hardware/software system.

mapping software   Software that combines graphics, database management, and some spreadsheet capabilities to display data geographically. Also referred to as geographical information systems or GIS.

Mark I   An early electromechanical computer built by Howard Aiken at Harvard and finished in 1944. Also known as the Automatic Sequence Controlled Calculator (ASCC).

massively parallel computer   A computer that uses hundreds or thousands of CPUs to process data and instructions simultaneously.

massively parallel processing   A technique for creating intelligent systems using massively parallel computers.

MB   See **megabyte.**

meeting support software   Software designed to increase the efficiency of meetings that take place electronically or in decision-room settings.

megabyte (MB or meg)   A measure of computer storage capacity. Equal to around 1 million bytes.

megahertz (MHz)   A measure of clock speed. Equals one million pulses per second.

memory   See **primary storage.**

memory button   Small metal container with a read/write microchip that can hold up to 512 characters of data.

memory card   Credit-card sized card that can hold up to 100 MB of data using flash memory chips. Also referred to as credit card memory.

menu   A listing of command options displayed on screen.

menu generator   Helps create menus with lists of processing options. Typically included as part of an application generator.

message   In object-oriented programming, what is sent to an object when an operation involving the object needs to be performed. The message need only identify the operation; how it is to be performed is already embedded within the instructions that are part of the object.

metal oxide semiconductor (MOS) memory Silicon-backed semiconductor chips used for primary storage in third- and fourth-generation computers.

methods In object-oriented programming, the instructions about the operations to be performed on data that are encapsulated within the object.

MICR See **magnetic ink character recognition.**

microcomputer A small desktop or portable computer based on a single silicon chip called a microprocessor. Frequently referred to as a personal computer.

microminiaturization The process of making components of electronic devices smaller and smaller.

microprocessor A silicon chip containing an entire CPU.

microsecond A measure of machine cycle time. Equals one-millionth of a second.

microwave system A wireless transmission system that transmits data as high-frequency radio signals through the atmosphere to relay stations located within line of sight of one another.

middle managers The persons in the middle of the pyramid in a business organization. Concerned primarily with implementing the strategy of senior management, tactics of operation, and controlling the organization.

MIDI (Musical Instrument Digital Interface) board An add-in board that is used to create computerized music.

millisecond A measure of machine cycle time. Equals one-thousandth of a second.

minicomputer A medium-sized computer that is faster, more powerful, and more expensive than a workstation, but not as fast, powerful, or expensive as a mainframe. Also referred to as a mid-range computer.

MIPS (millions of instructions per second) A measurement of a computer processor's speed based on the millions of instructions per second the processor can execute.

MIS See **management information system.**

mixed copy When making a copy of a cell or range in a spreadsheet, keeping one of the variables as it was (an absolute copy) while changing the other to a relative copy.

mixed graph A combination of bar graph and line graph. Useful for presenting two types of data simultaneously.

mode The state in which a program is currently operating.

model of the knowledge domain See **knowledge base.**

modem A type of communications equipment that enables digital signals to be transmitted over transmission media designed for analog signals. Converts digital signals into analog signals and then back again into digital signals.

Modula-2 A third generation programming language similar to Pascal and designed primarily for writing systems software.

Modula-3 A programming language designed to improve and expand on Modula-2.

modulation The process of converting a digital signal into an analog signal.

module A subprogram contained within a larger program that performs a specific function or functions.

monitor See **display screen.**

morphing A graphics special effect in which an image gradually metamorphs into another totally unlike it.

motherboard The main circuit board in a microcomputer containing the microprocessor, memory chips, system clock, and other components. Also referred to as the main board or system board.

mouse A handheld input device with a rolling ball underneath and one or more buttons on top. Rolling the ball along a flat surface controls the movement of the cursor on the computer's display screen. Pushing the buttons on top allows the user to select different program options, eliminating the need to type commands.

MPC machine A multimedia personal computer that meets the minimum specifications developed by the Multimedia PC Marketing Council.

MRP See **manufacturing resource planning system.**

MSS See **management support systems.**

multimedia system A computer system that can integrate several types of media (such as text, still or animated graphics, sound, and still or moving video) into a single application.

multiplexer A communications device that allows users to make more efficient use of a communications channel by enabling the channel to carry data from several different sources simultaneously.

multiprocessing A technique that allows two or more CPUs linked together to execute instructions simultaneously.

multiprogramming A technique that allows multiple programs to be executed concurrently through sharing the computer's resources. While one program is using the CPU, other programs can be using other components, such as input and output devices.

multiscan monitor A monitor that can comply with a wide range of graphics standards rather than just one. Also referred to as a multisync monitor.

multisync monitor See **multiscan monitor.**

multitasking Provides multiprogramming capabilities to single-user operating systems. Allows a user to run two or more programs at the same time on a single computer.

nanoelectronics A field of electronics that seeks to construct chips and other electronic devices that use a single atom or molecule as the critical moving element.

nanosecond A measure of machine cycle time. Equals one-billionth of a second.

natural language Fifth-generation programming language that resembles English even more closely than fourth-generation programming languages. Also a field of artificial intelligence that attempts to teach computers to recognize and understand human speech and writing and to speak and write themselves.

nerve cell The center of a neuron. Acts like a switch. In an electronic neural network, it is represented by a transistor.

network Computers and communications equipment connected by a communications channel in such a way that data, programs, and peripheral devices can be shared.

network DBMS Similar to a hierarchical DBMS, but each lower-level data element can be related to more than one parent element in a many-to-many relationship.

neural network A fast growing approach to artificial intelligence that uses physical electronic devices or software to mimic the neurological structure of the human brain.

node A hardware device in a network.

nonimpact printer A printer that forms characters and graphics without physical contact between a printing mechanism and paper. Examples include laser printers, ink jet printers, and thermal-transfer printers.

nonprocedural programming language A programming language that allows a programmer to tell the computer what he or she would like the computer to do, not how the task should be carried out. Fourth-generation programming languages are nonprocedural.

nonresident The portions of the operating system that reside in secondary storage until needed.

nonvolatile A characteristic of certain types of memory and secondary storage media that allows it to retain its contents without electrical power and when the computer is turned off.

notebook computer A portable computer weighing 6 pounds or less.

object In object-oriented programming, a block of programming code that encapsulates a chunk of data and instructions about the operations to be performed on that data.

object code The machine language version of source code after it has been translated by a compiler or interpreter. Also referred to as object module or object program.

object-oriented DBMS (OODBMS) A database that uses object-oriented programming concepts to handle complex data types not easily handled by other types of DBMS.

object-oriented programming (OOP) A programming method that combines data and instructions about the data into one "object" that can be used in other programs.

OCR See **optical character recognition.**

on-line help On-screen reference material that provides assistance in using a program.

on-line system A computer system that immediately records information and responds to user requests. An example is a bank's ATM machine.

on-line transaction processing (OTLP) system A type of processing system in which transactions are processed immediately.

OODBMS   See **object-oriented DBMS.**

OOP   See **object-oriented programming.**

open system   A computer system in which all components, regardless of their manufacturer, are compatible and can communicate with other components.

operating system   Systems software that manages and controls the activities of the computer.

optical character recognition (OCR)   A form of source data automation. Uses an optical scanner to read optical characters (characters printed using special fonts) or carefully printed handwriting and translate the data into digital form.

optical codes   Special shapes that can be scanned or read by handheld wands, guns, or devices built into countertops and converted into digital form. The most common is the bar code found on most retail products.

optical disk   A secondary storage media created from a plastic coated disk. Data is read and recorded by using a laser beam rather than through magnetic means. Has a much higher storage capacity than a magnetic disk. Examples include CD-ROMs, WORMs, and erasable disks.

optical marks   Marks that can be detected by an optical mark reader. Primarily used to score tests and tally questionnaire results.

optical scanner   A source data automation input device that reflects light off of printed and handwritten characters, codes, and marks and converts the pattern created by the reflection into a digital format.

optoelectronics   A new technology that seeks to create chips that use light waves traveling over fiber-optic filaments.

order processing system   A marketing and sales transaction processing system that translates an order into a list of products picked from a warehouse, tracks the status of the order, produces invoices, and arranges for delivery to the customer.

organization   An entity built to accomplish goals through the creation of products or services.

organizational culture   A pattern of shared values, norms, and beliefs subscribed to by members of an organization.

organizational ethics   The policies, actions, and decisions an organization makes in the pursuit of its objectives.

organizational intelligence   A field of artificial intelligence that focuses on techniques for capturing and storing the wisdom of an organization and its members.

organizational politics   Competition for power, money, and respect among different groups within an organization.

OS/2   An operating system developed by IBM that supports multitasking and is designed to work with 32-bit microprocessors.

output   The transfer or display of processed information to users.

output controls   Application controls that help ensure that the results of computer processing are accurate, complete, and properly distributed.

output device   A device that allows a computer to communicate with the user by displaying processed data in a way the user can understand and use. Examples include computer display screens, printers, plotters, speakers, and voice synthesizers.

outsourcing   The hiring of another firm to run all or part of the information systems of an organization.

packet switching   A method of transmitting data. Divides electronic messages into small segments called data packets, transmits the packets independently of one another, and then reassembles the packets into the original message at the receiving end. Enables communications facilities to be utilized more fully and to be shared by more users.

page   A block of a fixed number of bytes into which a program may be divided for virtual storage.

page composition   The process of deciding how a page should look. Also referred to as page layout.

page composition software   See **desktop publishing software.**

page description language (PDL)   A language built into printers using desktop publishing systems that tells the printer how to define the page and print the fonts, text, and graphics.

page layout   See **page composition.**

page makeup software   See **desktop publishing software.**

page method   A method of virtual storage that divides a program into pages consisting of a fixed number of bytes.

page printer A printer that prints entire pages at one time.

page proofs Galleys pasted up into page format with spaces left for photographs or illustrations.

paint program A form of illustration program that allows a sophisticated user to create art almost indistinguishable from works created in a traditional manner.

palmtop computer A computer weighing less than 1.5 pounds that can be held in a user's hand. Also referred to as a handheld computer.

paperless office An office in which information technology has replaced the use of paper. Has been predicted by visionaries but has not yet materialized.

parallel conversion A system conversion strategy in which the old system and the new system run in tandem until it is clear that the new system works properly.

parallel processing A method of processing that uses multiple CPUs to process instructions and data simultaneously (in parallel) rather than sequentially.

parity bit A bit added to each byte to help assure that data is being transmitted correctly. Also referred to as a check bit.

Pascal A third-generation programming language designed primarily to teach structured programming techniques to students.

Pascaline A mechanical computing machine invented by Blaise Pascal in the 1640s.

passive-matrix display A method of displaying images on a flat panel display screen. The CPU sends signals to transistors around the borders of the screen, which control all the pixels in a given row or column.

patent A form of legal protection for inventions. Gives owner an exclusive monopoly on the ideas behind an invention for 17 years.

payroll system An accounting system that keeps track of how much is owed and has been paid to employees. Also produces statements for government agencies.

PBX See **private branch exchange.**

PDL See **page description language.**

peer-to-peer network Allows computers to communicate directly with one another without relying on a central host computer or file server to control the network.

pen-based system A computer system that can accept handwritten input. Typically uses an electronic stylus and pressure-sensitive screen coupled with special handwriting recognition software.

people management software A variation of project management software that allows a user to track the activities of employees in connection with the performance of a project.

perceptive system Systems that emulate the human capabilities of sight, hearing, touch, and smell. Closely related to robotics.

personal computer A small IBM or IBM-compatible desktop or portable computer. Often used synonymously with the term microcomputer.

personal finance program Software designed to manage a checkbook, credit cards, investments and other accounts, pay bills, and keep track of income and expenses.

personal information manager (PIM) Software that allows a user to store, organize, and obtain easy access to details of business and personal information. Typically includes a desktop organizer with address book, appointment book, calendar, notepad, and additional features such as an auto-dialer and tickler that notifies user of scheduled events.

personnel record system A human resources system that stores information on employees.

phased conversion A system conversion strategy in which a new system is introduced over a period of time.

photo image editor Software that allows a user to manipulate and revise photos and other images scanned into the system with an optical scanner.

physical design See **detailed design.**

picosecond A measure of machine cycle time. Equals one-trillionth of a second.

pie chart A pie-shaped chart useful for showing the relationship of parts to a whole (proportions).

PIM See **personal information manager.**

pixel One of the thousands of tiny dots that make up an image on a display screen.

PL/1 (Programming Language/1) A third-generation programming language designed primarily for general business and scientific problem solving. Not as widely used as COBOL or FORTRAN.

plotter An output device that produces high-quality drawings, maps, charts, and other forms of graphics by using pens or electrostatic devices over a piece of paper.

pointing device An input device such as a mouse, trackball, or joystick that enables a user to move the cursor on the screen.

point-of-sale (POS) system A marketing and sales transaction processing system that captures sales data at the point of sale through the use of a point-of-sale terminal.

point-of-sale (POS) terminal Source data automation input device used in retail industry to obtain price of item, record sale, and function as cash register.

port A socket with small pinholes protruding through the system unit case that allows other sensing, communication, and display devices to be plugged into and communicate with the computer.

portable operating system An operating system, such as UNIX, that can run on many different types of computers.

POS See **point-of-sale system** or **point-of-sale terminal**.

position control system A human resources system that keeps track of information about job positions in a firm, such as data about filled and unfilled positions and changes in positions and job assignments.

preliminary design A description of the general functional capabilities of a system. Sometimes referred to as a logical design.

preliminary plan The output of the preliminary analysis phase of system analysis. Includes an analysis of the business setting and environment, a description of the nature and scope of the business problem, and an examination of potential solutions.

presentation graphics software A type of graphics software that allows a user to create sophisticated charts and graphs as well as other presentation materials.

primary memory See **primary storage**.

primary storage The part of the computer system that temporarily stores the computer's operating system programs, program instructions, and the data being used by those instructions. Also referred to as memory, primary memory, main memory, main storage, or internal storage.

printer An output device that displays output on paper.

printer driver A program file that converts embedded formatting codes into instructions the printer can understand so that it can produce the needed effect.

prior art The use of the same or similar technology before a patent application was submitted.

privacy The moral right of individuals to be left alone and to control the flow of information about themselves.

private branch exchange (PBX) A central private switchboard that today can handle both voice and digital communications within an organization.

private line A line reserved for one customer, who usually bears responsibility for maintenance and repair. Also referred to as a dedicated line.

procedural programming language A programming language that requires the programmer to specify the precise series of steps or procedures that the programmer wants the computer to follow. Third-generation languages are procedural programming languages.

process control system A production transaction processing system that uses computers to monitor the physical production process.

processing The conversion of raw input into a more useful form.

processing controls Application controls that help ensure the accuracy and completeness of data while it is being updated.

processor See **central processing unit (CPU)**.

production group The department(s) of a business organization responsible for manufacturing the goods or producing the services that are sold.

productivity The amount of goods produced per hour of labor.

profit The sale of goods or services for an amount greater than the cost of production.

program A set of detailed instructions that tell the computer how to process information and display it. Also referred to as software.

programmable relational DBMS A DBMS with a built-in programming language that can be used to develop custom business applications.

program maintenance Activities required to keep a program up to date.

programmer A person who designs, writes, and tests computer programs.

programmer documentation A detailed description of the program, including diagrams and text description, developed during the program development process.

programming The process of creating a computer program.

programming environment Software packages that provide tools to assist in the development of programs. Also referred to as programmer workbenches.

programming language A special form of software that programmers use to create other software.

program testing The process of testing a program with different sets of data to make sure that the program works as intended.

project management software Software used to plan and control projects more effectively. Allows a user to set up schedules, allocate personnel and resources, and track the project's progress.

project management tools Project management software used in systems analysis and design to help manage the design effort.

Prolog A programming language used primarily for artificial intelligence purposes.

PROM (programmable read-only memory) ROM chips that are blank and allow the purchaser to add instructions or data. Once added, the contents cannot be altered or erased.

proportional spacing When certain characters are allocated more horizontal space than others. A feature of certain typefaces.

proprietary operating system An operating system that works only with a particular type of CPU.

protocol A common set of procedures or rules governing the exchange of data between two components in a telecommunications network.

prototyping Technique used in system design. Involves building a model or experimental version of a system or part of a system that can be rapidly tested and evaluated.

pseudocode A method for designing the logical flow of a program using English-like statements to describe the processing steps and logic.

public domain software Software that can be obtained for free.

purchasing management system A production transaction processing system that keeps track of vendors and supplies ordered, received, stored, and on back-order.

quality control system A production transaction processing system that monitors the production process to identify deviations from predetermined standards so that defects can be corrected.

query language An easy to use, fourth-generation programming language that provides customized access to data stored in a database.

ragged right A right margin in which each line may end at a slightly different spot.

RAID (redundant array of inexpensive disks) A disk drive unit composed of an array of many (100 or more) small disk drives that delivers data over multiple paths simultaneously. Provides faster access time, data transfer, and increased reliability due to redundancy of disk drives.

RAM (random access memory) Semiconductor memory chips used for primary storage.

RAM disk A bank of RAM memory chips, coupled with a controller, that creates a "phantom" hard disk within primary storage. Also referred to as a virtual disk.

random access Data that can be accessed in any order that the user chooses. Available with magnetic and optical disks. Also referred to as direct access.

random file organization A method of storing data. Allows data to be accessed in any sequence, regardless of physical order, by using a mathematical formula to translate the key field of the record into the record's physical location on the storage media. Also referred to as direct file organization.

randomizing algorithm See **hashing algorithm.**

range A block of adjacent cells that can consist of a single cell, a row, a column, or several rows or columns.

read/write head The part of a secondary storage device that senses or reads the magnetic status of bits located on magnetic tape or disk. It then converts them into electronic pulses that it sends to the CPU. Also writes magnetic spots on to magnetic tape or disk to record data.

record A collection of related fields.

re-engineering The rethinking and redesign of business processes or an entire business.

refresh rate   The number of times per second that the pixels on the display screen are recharged so that they will continue to remain bright.

register   A temporary storage location in the ALU or control unit for program instructions and data.

relational DBMS   A database that can relate data in different files through the use of a common data element, or field, in those files. Uses a two-dimensional table structure with records as rows and fields as columns.

relational operator   An operator (such as <, >, or =) that allows a user to make comparisons and selections. Used by database management system software.

relative copy   Making a copy of a cell or range in a spreadsheet using the same formula structure but changing the cell addresses to match the new cell or range.

remote control software   Software that enables a user to control a microcomputer from another microcomputer located somewhere else.

removable media   Secondary storage media that can be removed. Examples include magnetic tape and floppy disks.

removable pack hard disk system   A hard disk system consisting of several hard disks (from 6 to 20) assembled into an indivisible pack that can be mounted on and removed from a disk unit.

repetitive stress injury (RSI)   Caused when muscle groups are forced through the same repetitive action, such as typing on a computer keyboard. Includes problems like tendonitis, tenosynovitis, and carpal tunnel syndrome.

replacement mode   See **typeover mode.**

report generator   A software tool that enables users to produce customized reports. An example of a 4GL.

request for proposal (RFP)   A detailed document sent to potential vendors describing the technical and functional capabilities required and asking the vendor to submit bids and plans to provide these capabilities.

request for quotation (RFQ)   A document sent to potential vendors requesting prices on specific computer hardware or software.

resident   The part of an operating system program that always resides in primary storage while the computer is on.

resolution   The clarity or sharpness of the image on a display screen.

responsibility   The notion that as free moral agents, individuals and organizations are responsible for the actions they take. A fundamental component of ethics.

RFP   See **request for proposal.**

RFQ   See **request for quotation.**

ring network   A local area network that links all of the network's devices via a communications channel that forms a closed loop. Data can be passed along the loop in a single direction from computer to computer.

RISC (reduced instruction set computing)   A technology that reduces the number of instructions represented within the circuitry of a CPU, thereby increasing processing speed.

robotics   The study of physical machines that perform work normally performed by humans.

ROM (read-only memory)   Nonvolatile semiconductor memory chip used for the permanent storage of certain instructions. Also referred to as firmware.

rotational delay   The time it takes for a disk to rotate so that the read/write head is positioned at the proper sector.

router   A communications device used to route messages through several connected local area networks or to a wide area network.

RPG (Report Program Generator)   A third-generation programming language designed to generate business reports.

RSI   See **repetitive stress injury.**

sales and marketing group   The division of a business organization responsible for the marketing and sale of the product or service.

sales support system   A marketing and sales transaction processing system that assists sales personnel in the field by keeping track of customers and prospects, following up on sales, and making sure customers are satisfied.

scalable typeface outline technology   Software that first creates an ideal mathematical representation of a font and then converts it by a font rasterizer into a bitmap that can be displayed and printed.

scanner   A device that scans text, graphics, or images and converts them into digitized form.

scheduling software   Software that automates the process of setting up meetings.

screen generator   Helps design input and output screens. Typically included as part of an application generator.

screen prompt   A message displayed by a program on screen to help guide the user.

scroll   A feature of software that allows the user to move through and view different parts of a document or spreadsheet on the screen.

search   A feature of word processing software that finds all occurrences of a specified word.

search and replace   A feature of word processing software that finds all occurrences of a specified word and replaces it with another word.

secondary storage   Provides long-term storage for programs and data while they are not in active use. Sometimes referred to as auxiliary storage.

secondary storage devices   Devices that read, write, and access data and programs stored in secondary storage. Examples include tape drives, hard disk drives, floppy disk drives, and CD-ROM drives.

secondary storage media   The media on which programs and data are stored in secondary storage. Examples include magnetic tape, floppy disks, hard disks, and CD-ROMs.

second-generation programming language   See **assembly language.**

sector   A wedge-shaped segment of a track on a magnetic disk.

sector method   A method of recording data on a magnetic disk in which data is recorded on a section of track within a given sector.

securities trading system   A financial accounting system used to manage and track investment portfolios of currency, bonds, stocks, and other financial instruments.

seek time   The time it takes for a read/write head to position itself over the proper track. Also called access motion time.

segment   A block of variable-length logically related material into which a program may be divided for virtual storage.

segment method   A method of virtual storage, in which a program is divided into variable-length segments consisting of blocks of logically related material.

selection control structure   A control structure used in structured programming. Enables the programmer to represent choice: if a condition is true, perform one procedure; if the condition is false, perform a different procedure.

semiconductors   A class of crystalline mineral substances, such as silicon, that can conduct electricity. Used to create microprocessors and memory chips.

semistructured decision   A decision relating to a problem that contains easily predicted aspects, but also some aspects that require the exercise of judgment.

senior managers   The persons at the top of the pyramid in a business organization. Concerned primarily with long-term issues of business growth and development.

sensing technologies   Digital information technologies that help us gather information from the environment and translate that information into a form that can be understood by a computer.

sensor   An input device that collects a specific kind of data directly from the environment.

sequence control structure   A control structure used in structured programming. Arranges processes in a temporal and logical order.

sequential file organization   A method of storing data that requires the data to be retrieved in the physical order in which it is stored; the only file organization that can be used with magnetic tape.

sequential processing   The method by which conventional computers process data: performing instructions one step at a time, in sequential order, until the entire program is finished. Also referred to as serial processing.

serial processing   See **sequential processing.**

service firm   A firm that produces or sells services.

service worker   A person involved in the production or sale of services.

shareware   Software distributed free of charge on a trial basis. You pay only if you decide to keep and use it.

shell   A program containing a graphical user interface that can be inserted to act as an interface between the user and an older operating system, such as DOS.

shipping management system   A production transaction processing system used to track customer orders from receipt to final shipping.

simplex transmission   Transmission of data through a communications channel in only one direction.

single entry/single exit   A principle of structured programming that states there shall only be one entry and one exit from any control structure.

single-sided disk   A floppy disk that can store data only on one side.

slide rule   A device that allows the user to multiply and divide by sliding two pieces of wood against each other. It is an early example of an analog computer: an instrument that measures instead of counts.

Smalltalk   The first object-oriented programming language.

smart card   Credit-card sized storage medium that contains a microprocessor capable of recording and storing information.

soft copy   Output that is produced on screen.

soft return   In word processing, automatic movement to the next line.

software   See **program.**

software bug   A design flaw or error in a program that causes a program to perform improperly.

software development cycle   The steps involved in the development of a computer program. They include reviewing system specifications, designing the program, coding the program, testing the program, documentation, and maintenance.

software piracy   The unauthorized copying of copyrighted software.

software suite   A software package that contains bundled, full-featured versions of a manufacturer's line of software.

source code   The higher-level language translated by a compiler or interpreter into machine language (object code) so that it can be executed by the computer. Also referred to as source module or source program.

source data automation   Input devices that collect data in machine-readable form and send it directly to the computer without the need for human intervention. Examples include magnetic ink character recognition systems, optical recognition systems, imaging systems, sensors, and other data collection devices.

spaghetti code   Program code that does not follow a predictable logical flow, thereby making it difficult to follow, read, or understand.

speech synthesizer   See **voice synthesizer.**

spelling checker   A feature of word processing software that checks the spelling of words in a document.

spreadsheet   Data represented in a columns-and-rows format.

spreadsheet publishing   The creation of professional-looking reports and documents containing spreadsheets.

spreadsheet software   Applications software that provides user with a financial modeling tool. Represents data in a columns-and-rows format, performs calculations on the data, and can automatically recalculate if data is changed.

SQL   See **structured query language.**

stacked-bar graph   A graph in which different variables are stacked on top of one another. Useful for comparing several items at one moment in time.

star network   A local area network in which a central host computer is connected to a number of smaller computers, intelligent terminals, and other devices, forming a pattern that looks like a star. All communications in the network must pass through the central host computer.

statistical software   An advanced form of analytical graphics software that provides complete statistical data analysis and more sophisticated graphing capabilities.

status indicator   See **status line.**

status line   A line that provides information about the position of the cursor and the current settings for the program. Also referred to as a status indicator.

storage register   A register that temporarily stores data transferred from primary storage.

stored program concept   The idea that program instructions can be stored internally within a computer's memory along with data that is to be processed.

strategy   A planned set of actions designed to achieve profitable, or otherwise positive, results.

structure chart   See **hierarchy chart.**

structured decision   A decision relating to a routine, repetitive problem for which there is an accepted methodology for the decision-making process.

structured programming A method of programming that uses a top-down program design approach, modularization, standard control structures, and single entry/single exit to create highly structured modules of program code. These techniques make the program easier to write, read, debug, maintain, and modify.

structured query language (SQL) A standardized query language usable with a variety of relational DBMSs.

style and grammar checker A feature of some word processing software packages that checks the style and grammar used in a document. Also available as an add-on package.

supercomputer The largest, fastest, most powerful, and most expensive type of computer. Used for scientific research, by government agencies, and increasingly by businesses for commercial applications.

superconductivity A property of certain metals that allows current to flow without creating any electrical resistance when the metals are cooled to extremely low temperatures.

supervisor An operating system program that manages the computer system's resources. Also sometimes referred to as the executive, monitor, kernel, master, or control program.

switched line A communications line that connects through a switching center to its destination. Uses regular, public telephone line as communications channel.

synapse The place where a neuron connects to another neuron. In an electronic neural network, it is represented by a variable resistor.

synchronous transmission A method of data transmission in which a number of characters are transmitted in blocks framed by synch bits or flags.

system clock A clock mounted on the motherboard that produces pulses at a fixed rate to synchronize the computer's operations.

system conversion The process of converting from an old information system to a new information system.

system flowchart See **system flow diagram.**

system flow diagram A diagram that depicts how a system will work by documenting the sequence of processing steps, the flow of data, and the exact files used by each step. Also referred to as a system flowchart.

system integrator Outside firm that provides planning, coordinating, scheduling, management, installation, and testing services in connection with the development of a new information system.

system prompt A symbol that appears on the screen after the computer's operating system has been loaded into memory. In microcomputers with a floppy disk system, A:>; in microcomputers with a hard disk drive, C:>.

system requirements plan A plan that describes in detail the organizational requirements for information and how they will be met by an information system.

systems analysis The process of understanding and defining the nature of a business problem or opportunity that a new information system will try to solve. Involves analyzing the objectives of the organization, examining the characteristics and components of existing information systems, and identifying possible alternative solutions.

systems analyst An individual responsible for the design, development, and implementation of an information system.

systems design The process of actually designing, building, and implementing a new information system based on the results of a systems analysis. Involves creating a preliminary and detailed design, acquiring the hardware and software necessary to create the system, and then implementing the system.

System 7 An operating system for Apple Macintosh computers designed to work with the 32-bit Motorola microprocessor, which uses icons and windows to create a user-friendly operating environment. Supports advanced graphics and multitasking.

systems software The set of programs, including the operating system, that controls and coordinates the operation of the various types of equipment in a computer system.

system unit The part of the computer system that holds the CPU, primary storage, and other devices.

tape library A collection of magnetic tapes. Retrieval of tapes may be accomplished by manual or automated means.

tape unit A secondary storage device used to record and read data from magnetic tape.

tax preparation software Software designed to aid users in the preparation of tax forms.

TB See **terabyte.**

telecommunications The electronic transmission of data (text, graphics, sound, video) over any one of the different communications channels, such as public telephone lines, private cables, microwave, or satellite.

telecommuting Working at home for a company located elsewhere via computer, fax machine, and modem.

telemarketing system A sales support system using a central sales staff to contact prospects and customers by telephone.

template A shell of an application, such as a spreadsheet or desktop publishing document, that includes all necessary design elements so the user only needs to enter the new data.

terabyte (TB) A measure of computer storage capacity. Equal to around 1 trillion bytes.

terminal emulation software Software that enables a microcomputer to trick a mainframe into thinking that it is communicating with a terminal.

test plan The process by which a new information system is tested to determine whether it works, using test data and then actual data.

thermal-transfer printer A nonimpact printer that produces high-quality images by transferring ink from a wax-based ribbon onto chemically treated paper.

three-dimensional optical storage media Experimental storage media created using transparent polysterene plastic treated with a chemical that reacts to laser light.

time-sharing A technique that allows users to share the resources of one computer system simultaneously by rapidly rotating through all users on the system and allocating each a short time slice of CPU time.

time slice A short slice of CPU processing time (often no more than 1 or 2 milliseconds) allocated to users in a time-sharing system.

top-down approach See **behavioral approach.**

topology The physical layout, or shape, of a network.

touch screen An input device that allows a user to select entries and issue commands by touching the surface of the screen with a finger or pointer.

TPS See **transaction processing systems.**

track On magnetic tape, one of nine separate invisible rows that run the length of the tape, upon which data is stored as magnetized and non-magnetized spots. On magnetic disk, one of many invisible concentric circles upon which data is stored as magnetized and non-magnetized spots.

trackball Similar to an upside-down mouse. Allows user to move cursor on computer display screen by rotating ball with hand rather than rolling it on flat surfaces.

trade secret A form of protection for intellectual property. Can be used to protect any intellectual work product that is secret and provide a competitive edge.

transaction An event associated with the production, distribution, sale, and transportation of goods and services.

transaction processing systems (TPS) Information systems that keep track of transactions necessary to conduct business.

transistors Electronic devices that transfer electrical signals.

TrueType font One of a variety of scalable fonts available with Windows 3.1. Used primarily in connection with desktop publishing systems.

Turing Test A test designed by Alan Turing to prove a machine is intelligent. A computer and a human are placed in separate rooms connected by a communications link. If the computer program can deceive a human into thinking he or she is conversing with another human rather than a computer, the machine should be considered intelligent.

twisted-pair wire The oldest and most common transmission medium. Consists of strands of insulated copper wire twisted together in pairs to form a cable. Primarily used to transmit voice conversations, but can also transmit digital impulses with help of a modem.

typeface A set of characters of the same design. Often used interchangeably with font.

Type 1 font One of a variety of scalable fonts available from Adobe Systems. Used primarily in connection with desktop publishing systems.

typeover mode An editing feature of applications software that replaces existing text with new text. Also referred to as replacement mode.

UNIVAC (Universal Automatic Computer) The first American, general-purpose business computer.

UNIX   A popular nonproprietary, portable operating system. Supports multitasking, multi-user processing, and networking.

unstructured decision   A decision relating to a problem that is not routine or repetitive and that requires the exercise of judgment on the part of the decision-maker.

upload   Transfer a file from a terminal or microcomputer to a mainframe or a central host computer.

user documentation   Instruction manuals that tell users how to install and use software.

user-friendly   Microcomputer applications software that is easy to use even for someone who has not been exposed to computers.

user interface   The interface between a computer program and the user.

utility program   Systems software that performs a routine task, such as formatting disks, copying files, sorting files, editing files, or other important housekeeping functions.

vacuum tube   An electronic tube that comprises the main logic element of first-generation computers.

value   In a spreadsheet, a cell entry that is either a number or a formula.

value-added network (VAN)   A private data network typically operating over lines leased from common carriers. Offers some added value service to others for a fee.

value chain   A set of steps in the production process that add value to a set of inputs at each step. A view of the business firm as a series of basic activities that adds value to the firm's services or products.

VAN   See **value-added network.**

VDT   See **video display terminal.**

very high-level language   See **fourth-generation language (4GL).**

very-large scale integrated circuit (VLSIC)   A silicon chip containing millions of transistors.

videoconferencing   A method of conferencing in which people at different locations can see and hear one another, as well as communicate via computer.

video display terminal (VDT)   A display screen and keyboard.

virtual disk   See **RAM disk.**

virtual private network   The illusion of a private, dedicated line while actually using regular public lines. Achieved through the use of computers and software.

virtual storage   A technique that expands the limits of existing primary storage by enabling multiple users to utilize the same memory space. Divides programs into smaller fixed or variable length portions. Stores only that portion that is currently being used in primary storage, with the rest stored in virtual storage on a hard disk until needed.

VisiCalc   The first electronic spreadsheet software, developed by Dan Bricklin, Dan Flystra, and Robert Frankston in the late 1970s.

visual data analysis (VDA) software   Applications software that utilizes computer simulations, animation, 3-D graphics, and renderings to create and manipulate sophisticated graphics representing complex numeric data.

visual programming   A method of programming that makes it possible to create working applications by drawing, pointing, and clicking on objects instead of writing code.

VLSIC   See **very-large scale integrated circuit.**

voice mail   A sophisticated, computerized telephone answering system that digitizes incoming spoken messages, stores them in the recipient's voice mailbox, and then reconverts them into spoken form when retrieved.

voice mail jail   A maze of recorded instructions that form an endless loop without letting the caller reach the person he or she is seeking.

voice recognition system   A system that can accept spoken words as input.

voice synthesizer   An output device that converts stored text into sound understandable by humans. Also referred to as a speech synthesizer.

volatile   A characteristic of certain types of memory that causes the memory to lose its contents if electrical power is disrupted or the computer is shut off. RAM memory chips are volatile.

WAN   See **wide area network.**

wide area network (WAN)   A telecommunications network that can cover large geographic areas by using one or more of a variety of communications channels, such as microwave and satellite communications systems, as well as switched and dedicated telephone lines.

Winchester disk system A smaller version of a fixed disk drive typically used for microcomputers, workstations, and small minicomputers. Generally contains several 3-1/2 inch hard disks hermetically sealed within a disk drive unit.

window A feature of a graphical user interface: a box with information that can be layered on top of other similar boxes on the screen.

Windows A shell program that serves as a graphical user interface for DOS. Facilitates multitasking and moving information from one applications program to another.

Windows NT An operating system for 32-bit microprocessors developed by Microsoft. Supports multiprocessing as well as multitasking.

wireless transmission system A system that does not use a physical line to connect sending and receiving devices. May use infrared light waves for short-range or line of sight transmission, or radio waves for either short- or long-range transmission of data.

word A group of bits that the CPU processes as a unit.

word length The number of bits that make up a computer word. Processed by the CPU as a unit.

word processing software Applications software that allows a user to create, edit, format, print, and save documents with greater ease and efficiency than using a typewriter. Also referred to as a word processor.

word processor See **word processing software.**

word-wrapping A feature of word processing software. Automatically brings a word that will not fit within the margin at the end of a line down to the next line.

workflow software Applications software used to streamline and automate different types of work processes.

workgroup computing Information technology that helps people work together in teams or on common jobs.

worksheet The electronic representation of a spreadsheet. Consists of a rectangular grid made up of columns and rows.

worksheet area The center portion of the Lotus 1-2-3 spreadsheet screen containing the worksheet.

workstation A desktop computer that is faster, more powerful, and more expensive than a microcomputer. Has powerful graphics and mathematical processing capabilities. Typically used by engineers, scientists, architects, and commercial artists.

WORM (Write Once, Read Many) An optical storage disk that can be written on once by its purchaser. Thereafter, it cannot be erased and becomes a read-only media.

WYSIWYG (What You See Is What You Get) A feature of some word processing, spreadsheet, and desktop publishing software packages that allows text to be displayed on screen exactly as it will appear when printed.

X-Y graph A graph that illustrates the relationship or degree of correlation between two types of data or variables.